ANNA MARIA ORTESE

Celestial Geographies

Anna Maria Ortese: Celestial Geographies

Edited by Gian Maria Annovi
and Flora Ghezzo

*With an interview with the author
by Dacia Maraini*

UNIVERSITY OF TORONTO PRESS
Toronto Buffalo London

© University of Toronto Press 2015
Toronto Buffalo London
www.utppublishing.com

ISBN 978-1-4426-4900-2

Toronto Italian Studies

Library and Archives Canada Cataloguing in Publication

Anna Maria Ortese : celestial geographies / edited by Gian Maria Annovi and Flora Ghezzo ; with an interview with the author by Dacia Maraini.

(Toronto Italian studies)
Includes bibliographical references and index.
ISBN 978-1-4426-4900-2 (bound)

1. Ortese, Anna Maria – Criticism and interpretation. I. Annovi, Gian Maria, editor II. Ghezzo, Flora, 1965-, editor III. Series: Toronto Italian studies

PQ4875.R8Z53 2015 853'.914 C2015-900734-8

This book has been published with the support of University of Southern California, Dana and David Dornsife College of Letters, Arts and Sciences.

University of Toronto Press acknowledges the financial assistance to its publishing program of the Canada Council for the Arts and the Ontario Arts Council, an agency of the Government of Ontario.

University of Toronto Press acknowledges the financial support of the Government of Canada through the Canada Book Fund for its publishing activities.

Contents

Acknowledgments

First and foremost, we are thankful to the contributors to this volume, for their forbearance and incredible dedication. This project has taken shape in the hallways and classes of Columbia University. It was inspired by the many bright insights and novel ideas of both undergraduate and graduate students of modern Italian literature. We are immeasurably grateful to Ramsey McGlazer, Samuel Fleck, and Savannah Cooper-Ramsey for the translation of the original Italian essays and the editorial assistance. And, for the same reasons, to Steve Baker, who has been a constant source of positive energy and intellectual inputs, with his passion for life, books, and translations. Our gratitude goes also to Sean Pessin for preparing the index of the volume. We would like to thank the colleagues and friends without whose example and encouragement this project would never have seen the light: Andrea Baldi, Teodolinda Barolini, Gabriella Bellorio, Monica Farnetti, Joseph Keckler, Lucia Re, Margaret Rosenthal, Sara Teardo, and Paolo Valesio. Our grateful acknowledgment goes to Adelphi and to the Paul Getty Foundation for providing kind permission to publish Ortese's letters. We also thank Dacia Maraini and Rizzoli for permission to translate and print her interview with Anna Maria Ortese, originally published in *E tu chi eri?* (Milan: Rizzoli, 1998). Working with Richard Ratzlaff at University of Toronto Press has been a great pleasure from start to finish, and we thank him and the staff at the press for their wonderful assistance, including Gretchen Albers for her graceful copyediting. This book is dedicated to the memory of Ron Schoeffel, editor for the University of Toronto Press, who first enthusiastically embraced this project.

Abbreviations

AD	*Angelici dolori*
AG	*L'alone grigio*
AV	*Alonso e i visionari*
BN	*The Bay Is Not Naples*
CA	*Il cardillo addolorato*
CC	*Corpo celeste*
CJ	*La carrozza di Jane*
CT	*Il cappello piumato*
ET	*Estivi terrori*
GC	*I giorni del cielo*
IG	*L'Iguana*
IS	*L'infanta sepolta*
LL	*The Lament of the Linnet*
LM	*La luna sul muro*
LS	*La lente scura*
LT	*La luna che trascorre*
MF	*La morte del folletto*
MOB	*Da Moby Dick all'Orsa Bianca*
MON	*Il monaciello di Napoli*
MN	*Il mare non bagna Napoli*
MW1	*A Music Behind the Wall.* Vol. 1
MW2	*A Music Behind the Wall.* Vol. 2
PN	*Il mio paese è la notte*
PS	*Poveri e semplici*
PT	*Il porto di Toledo*
R1	*Romanzi.* Vol. 1
R2	*Romanzi.* Vol. 2

SM	*Silenzio a Milano*
SV	*In sonno e in veglia*
TIG	*The Iguana*
TR	*Il treno russo*

ANNA MARIA ORTESE

Celestial Geographies

Introduction: Anna Maria Ortese and the Red-Footed Angel

FLORA GHEZZO

Finora abbiamo parlato solo – mi perdoni – di cose astratte. Posso sapere se in lei c'è un'idea concreta della Terra, e della sua situazione nello Spazio? Là, mi sembra che anche a guardare con infiniti binocoli non si scorga nessun piede rosso di Angelo (suppongo che gli Angeli, come i piccioni, abbiano piedi rossi…). E allora?

Sì, anch'io penso che gli Angeli abbiano i piedi rossi.

(So far we have only talked – and I apologize – about abstract things. Might I ask if you have a concrete idea of the Earth, and its place in Space? There, it seems to me that even looking with infinite binoculars no Angel's little red foot can be seen (I imagine Angels' feet are red like pigeons'…). What do you think?

Yes, I too think that Angels have red feet.)

Anna Maria Ortese, *In sonno e in veglia*

Diffident and timid, a young woman in her early twenties opens the door of her modest little apartment near the port in Naples to give her first interview, in 1938, for the literary review *Gli oratori del giorno.* Her hair is dishevelled and her eyes "attraversati dal lampo" ("crossed by a flash of lightning").[1] Anna Maria Ortese is her name. She had just burst onto the Italian cultural scene in 1937, becoming a literary prodigy with the publication of critically acclaimed surreal and visionary short stories: with them, the debutante had delicately explored the emotional turmoil and amorous affairs of her adolescence and, at the same time, had perceptively investigated the "stranezza e […] meraviglia" (CC 47; "strangeness and […] marvel") of a world that seemed unfathomable through her innocent eyes. The sudden notoriety she received after the publication of *Angelici dolori* (1937) cast her into the spotlight, revoking her anonymity and creating what was truly a literary phenomenon, heightened not only by the intrigue of her eccentric and visionary writing but also by the mystery surrounding her identity. What lurked behind the obscure name of this young woman who declared herself "ignorante" ("ignorant"), who claimed to know "né i greci né i latini; poco dei moderni; nulla o quasi dei modernissimi" ("neither the Greeks nor the Latins; little of the moderns; nothing if anything at all of her contemporaries") and who unabashedly confessed that the most influential and charismatic literary figure of her time, Gabriele D'Annunzio, was "con reverenza, un Ignoto?" ("in all reverence, an Unknown")?[2] Was she truly a literary *enfant prodige* or a consummate artist masquerading behind a complex set of diversionary tactics?

The young woman responds concisely to the interviewer, and her words are still striking to us, almost a century later, for their fierce intensity. On the one hand, her literary naiveté comes as a surprise, as she confesses to only having read Manzoni's masterpiece *I promessi sposi* and all of Leopardi poetical and philosophical writings, because reading "è come una doccia d'acqua fredda" ("is like taking a cold shower") and had always repulsed her.[3] On the other, she is already confident that she will resolve for herself two irreconcilable roles, as a woman and as a writer: since art had become her life, she admits – matter of factly – that she will never marry, nor will she ever be "una donna come tutte le altre" ("a woman like all the others").[4] From the outset, then, with the kind of foresight that will persist into her adult life, Ortese precociously adopts an authorial *persona* in which the cultural constructs of gender and the biological dictates of the body are radically negated in the name of writing. The confidence that shines forth from this portrait is, nevertheless, undermined and complicated by a profound sense of uncertainty, which envelops the core of her very identity and her being in the world: "Non mi conosco" – she confesses in her interview – "non so che cosa sono; di nulla sono sicura" ("I do not know myself, I don't know what I am: I am certain of nothing").[5]

In these terse responses – from her first precious 1938 interview – Ortese's personality is already fully formed, *in nuce*, and so is a good deal of her future poetics (the inscrutability of the self, the unknowability of the world). Candour and artifice, humility and arrogance, self-awareness and self-denial: very little in the rest of the Italian literary *Novecento* compares to this paradoxical authorial self-fashioning, coherently and consistently performed, which constitutes Ortese's characteristic signature.

On these very same tones, fifty years later, disheartened by long neglect and failure, the writer will artfully craft her "ombra lunga di autrice" ("long authorial shadow"), as critic Carla Benedetti would say, assembling her authorial persona by means of complex strategies of disguise and authorial disavowal: "Anna Maria Ortese" – she writes of herself in the 1990s – "ritiene in verità impossibile esprimere un'opinione sul proprio lavoro, del quale ha un'idea molto confusa e anche irrilevante [...] Un lavoro [...] affidato al caso. Spesso, eseguito male. [...] Anna Maria Ortese non sa che cosa ha voluto, né chi è" ("Anna Maria Ortese thinks it truly impossible for her to express an opinion about her own work, of which she has a only very confused and even irrelevant idea. [...] Work [...] entrusted to chance. Often, executed poorly. [...] Anna Maria Ortese doesn't know what she wanted, or who she is").[6] A striking instance of authorial self-denial, this highly self-conscious portrait of herself as a writer, only apparently fraught with naiveté, defines Ortese's mode of writing as an unintentional, "entrusted to chance" gesture, an "adespota" creative expression, without an agent. I shall term this most uncommon creative modality as Ortese's *antygrafe.*[7]

Do Ortese's unusual rhetorical and psychological strategies that I have outlined thus far allow us to sketch out, even with broad brushstrokes, a likeness of the author? Do they provide a point of entry for "mapping" the geography of her work? One could hypothesize, indeed, that her strategies of denial actually reveal the very real symptoms of an "anxiety of authorship," or rather, according to a more recent distinction, a condition of "anxious power"[8] stemming from her psychology as a woman, as well as from her role as a writer and the hybrid, hard-to-categorize, explosive nature of her writing. In other words, Ortese's "anxious power" is the conflictual feeling of a woman writer of humble origins with no formal education, from an often "marginalized" part of the country (Naples and the south),[9] who in the 1930s – as her biographer, Luca Clerici, points out[10] – gained access to literary language in an entirely autonomous and independent way, as an autodidact, thus transgressing age-old gender-based cultural norms and social boundaries. It is the anxious power of a woman writer who crossed in tangential ways the entire Italian literary *Novecento,* entering into the orbit of several literary movements and great authors (Massimo Bontempelli, who ascribed her 1937 collection *Angelici dolori* to the domain of his "realismo magico"; Italo Calvino and Elio Vittorini, who launched her again in 1953 in the name of neorealism by promoting the success of *Il mare non bagna Napoli*) without ever being absorbed or fully contained by any of them.[11] Lastly, it is the anxious power of a woman writer who – endowed with a haphazard and idiosyncratic exposure to American and European literature, though taking very little from the Italian tradition – managed to blend, in original and unprecedented ways, the real and the visionary, the visible and the invisible, dream and reason, pain and utopia, reverie and ethical engagement, reshuffling, remixing, and reconfiguring every literary, linguistic, and cultural category she encountered along the way. "Passioni e incantesimi mi trasportano da tutte le parti: vedo aloni e sento voci ovunque. Come niente scivolo sul ghiaccio dell'invenzione" ("Passions and enchantments transport me every which way: I see halos of light and I hear voices everywhere. Effortlessly, I slip on the ice of invention"),[12] she writes. And these very sentiments of "passions and enchantments" crystallize her entire poetics, which we can summarize in the following way: finding herself in a real as well as a metaphorical position of exile, loss, displacement, and melancholy, Ortese develops her original literary poetics with the gaze at its centre and roots it in a profound ethical stance, excavating "the real" with visionary eyes, laying bear its various invisible strata. This peculiar enchanted optics, situated at the threshold of the visionary and the realistic, characterizes every aspect of her work. On the one hand, the writer's imaginative power springs forth from zones of transition and fluctuations of consciousness, on the brink between light and dark, sleeping and waking (and this is true of many of her vaguely dreamy and surreal stories, from the youthful pieces in *Angelici dolori* and *L'infanta sepolta* to the more mature tales of *In sonno e in veglia*). On the other hand, Ortese's visionary "poetica dello sguardo" (poetics of the gaze) emerges from a fully awake consciousness. Therefore, her enchanted eyes are able to *perceive* and represent – without any sort of bewilderment – fantastic invisible creatures, red-footed angels as well as iguanas, sprites, and linnets, transforming them into allegories of pain and suffering, into emblems of a sophisticated discourse on alterity and its abuse (as in the great visionary novels of her mature years: *L'Iguana, Il cardillo addolorato, Alonso e i visionari*). Just as naturally, the writer realistically explores with an incisive and penetrating gaze that which remains invisible or goes unnoticed in society and in history: namely, the human and urban degradation brought about by industrial and capitalistic modernity in post-war Italy. She also denounces the violation of the sacredness of nature and its creatures, thus taking sides in ecological and humanitarian battles, defending in the same way "tartarughine del levante" (little tortoises of the east), imaginary dragons, and actual individuals who have been sentenced to death (which is where the short stories and journalistic pieces of *Il mare non bagna Napoli* and *Silenzio a Milano,* as well as the meditative prose of *Corpo celeste,* fit). Finally, the author's estranged and enchanted optics often produces narcissistic doublings and projections, mirrors and masks of the self, staging vertiginous autobiographical forms of writing and magisterial reflections on time, memory, ephemerality, and the disintegration of forms (*Il porto di Toledo, Il cappello piumato,* and *Poveri e semplici*).

Placing herself decisively outside the great *logos* of Western civilization, but also outside the *phaos* – the principle of a clarity of sight that corresponds to and enables a clarity of reason – Ortese thus deconstructs the ontological categories of the physical and the metaphysical, of identity and alterity, as well as those literary "laws" that set mimetic representation up against fantastic and visionary imagination: rendering extremely difficult the task of the literary critic, who for several decades now has undertaken to define her indefinable writing. Thus, for Ortese, occupying a marginal space in both the cultural tradition and social fabric paradoxically turns out to be quite an empowering and liberating position: from this margin, which certainly cost her both psychological suffering as well as material poverty and cultural discrimination, she is able to challenge and question the centre of normative discourse, compelling us – readers, critics, editors, reviewers – to jump from one epistemological system into another.[13] It is precisely this ambiguous displacement that lies at the heart of Ortese's anxious power and her antygrafe.

With a conspicuous legacy of six novels – which seem to form of their own accord two distinct cycles that span the autobiographical, the allegorical, and the visionary – travel memoirs, self-interviews, creative essays, poetry, dozens of short stories, and other prose works strewn through the pages of magazines, newspapers, and collections, this "creatura notturna fatta per l'ombra dove meglio si irradia il suo nebuloso splendore"[14] ("nocturnal creature made for the shadows where its nebulous splendor shines brightest") has left an indelible mark on the literary culture of the European *Novecento.* Bridging the gap between modernism and postmodernity, she helped shape the history of twentieth-century novelistic and essayistic prose. Since her death in 1998 (she was born in 1914 in Rome), at the height of a brief, belated burst of success that had arrived just in time to redeem a life of hardship and marginalization, Ortese has become a cult figure in Italy, a legendary name that has only just begun to emerge – alongside those of Elsa Morante, Italo Calvino, Pier Paolo Pasolini, Carlo Emilio Gadda, and very few others – as one of the most significant authors of the second half of the last century. The cultural horizon that contains her (provided that Ortese allows herself to be contained) seems, however, to be far vaster.

Ortese comes of age as a literary voice in the 1930s under the sign of literary modernism and of the "ruin of representation" that accompanies its advent in the arts. The writer finds her niche in that variegated and contradictory constellation of Italian authors and artists who, at the beginning of the century, relate and react to the social, technological, and cultural transformations engendered by modernity by developing new aesthetic and formal solutions:[15] D'Annunzio's decadent and sensual aestheticism; Marinetti's avant-gardistic, hypermasculine celebration of wars, machines, and linguistic dissolutions; Svevo's excavation of human consciousness; Pirandello's disintegration of identity; and Savinio's and De Chirico's metaphysical imagination. In this lively frame, the "eccentric" and ingenuous little novellas of our *enfant prodige*, full of magic and mystery, seem to have been made to wear the label of "magic realism." The label was coined in the 1920s by the writer Massimo Bontempelli, after his encounter in Paris with the surrealism of Breton, in the pages of his *L'Avventura novecentista* and put to use in his own work of those years, from *La vita operosa* (1921) to *Gente nel tempo* (1937). Bontempelli's magic realism is an investigation on the mysterious and magical quality of reality, an ethereal and essential art that, distancing itself both from the mimetic realism of the nineteenth-century novel as well as from the enervating decadence of D'Annunzio and the avant-garde experimentation of Marinetti, recreates an absolute mythic dimension and a "primitive" atmosphere full of "lucid stupor." "Raccontare il sogno come fosse realtà e la realtà come fosse sogno" ("To recount a dream as though it were reality and reality as though it were a dream")[16]: for Bontempelli, opening new mythical and magical perspectives on reality represents the core of a true revolutionary *novecentista* magic-realist aesthetics for the twentieth century.

The young writer, nevertheless, seems to have already taken in the 1930s an original and personal path that distances her from both Surrealism and the *novecentista* poetics of her mentor, as well as the metaphysical tragic-noir style of her friend (and Bontempelli's partner) Paola Masino.[17] In opposition to the abstract intellectualism of Bontempelli's magic though ascetic art, to his static and immobile narrative frames, to his notion of an art detached from the binds of emotions and history, Ortese opposes an intuition of extraordinary force: at the core of her visionary, magic reality lies a true "passion for reality" ("*la passione della realtà*," to put it in Giulio Ferroni's words) and the "experience of the pain that one undergoes from reality itself" ("l'esperienza del dolore che si subisce dalla realtà stessa").[18] Her enchanted figures and dreamy forms, then, arise from an infinite, sorrowful *planctus* over an unredeemable loss. If, in other words, Bontempelli's magic realism recalls the frigid and mysterious atmosphere of De Chirico's metaphysical paintings (and behind that, the realistic precision and the magic atmosphere of the fifteenth-century paintings of Masaccio, Mantegna, and Piero della Francesca, who are the true precursors of Bontempelli's *novecentismo*),[19] Ortese's multiform writing, far more restless and tragic, dreamlike and visionary, melancholic and baroque, instead recalls by affinity the hallucinatory and delirious realism of Goya, the architectural dematerializations of Turner and Monet, the unreal atmospheres of Spanish baroque painting, the play of mirrors, reflections, and perspectives of Velasquez and Watteau (as seen, for instance, in *Las Meninas* and *L'Enseigne de Gersaint*).[20]

Thus, in a strictly Bontempellian sense, magic realism turns out to be a restrictive category that is historically inadequate to "explain" Ortese. Equally unsatisfactory in defining her poetics are, at least in large part, the various theories of the fantastic and the *Unheimliche* (along with its related notions of transgression, paradigm ruptures, epistemic uncertainties, and hesitations), despite the fact that these theories have been updated and reworked over the last decades of the twentieth century (also in a feminist key).[21] There is an inescapable binarism (Self / Other) inherent in the Freudian category of the *Unheimliche* (Uncanny) on which the literary Fantastic is founded: the unsettling extraneousness of the Other is found in the very heart of the subject itself, in its domestic intimacy, as Freud explains; or, as Julia Kristeva would put it, "the stranger is within us," it is a figuration of the incontrollable pulsions of our subconscious. Yet the subtle interdependence between Self / Other seems to me profoundly inadequate to explain the work of a woman writer who, to the contrary, wants to affirm through her fictional fantastic creatures the ontological *irreducibility* of the Other. Abandoning all philosophical binarisms and logocentric metaphysics, Ortese's Other, whether in the form of a beast or an angel, of a baby turtle or a Caribbean servant girl, wants to assert her or his absoluteness and irreducibility as a subject, independently of "our" definition and perception. The foreigner is thus outside of us.

Having staked a claim on this theoretical framework, we can provisionally hypothesize a different constellation of authors and texts as coordinates to approach Ortese's "ordinary enchantments," her irreducible magical fairy-tale and visionary elements "glowing alluringly from within the realistic matrix of reality."[22] We have to come to terms, yet again, with the term "magic realism," understood now as an inclusive category that supersedes the boundaries of national cultures and that evokes both different geographical latitudes (not merely Eurocentric) and an extended temporal arc (from modernism to postmodernism): from Jorge Luis Borges to Gabriel García Márquez, from Salman Rushdie to Günter Grass, from Milan Kundera to Isabelle Allende, from Franz Kafka to Isaac Singer, and including postcolonial Maghreb, Canadian, Indian, and Caribbean authors.[23] Can we hypothesize an entirely involuntary form of affinity between Ortese's work and that of these authors? Does the Italian "zingara assorta in sogno" ("gypsy ensconced in dream"),[24] as Elio Vittorini described her, figure in this group portrait? The conceptual and textual framework of *this* magic realism could in fact prove useful, at least as a point of departure.[25] It allows us above all to measure the diachronic development of Ortese's poetics and her problematic position between modernity and postmodernity. It also allows us to assess some elements of her poetics that are present, according to critics, also in the work of many magical realists. These elements include: a critique of the disenchantment of the world that occurred with the advent of post-enlightenment modernity and the desire for its "re-enchantment"; the assertion of the rights "del molteplice, del particolare, del diverso, del difforme, dell'incommensurabile" ("of the multiple, the particular, the different, the deformed, the incommensurable");[26] the many textual palimpsests and master narratives, Eurocentric and otherwise, that constitute the subtext of her work and that the author rewrites and reorients in various ways; an incongruous passion for a heightened visionary experience and an equally passionate critique of the real and of history. Subversive and always in-between, a "corrosion within the engine of system,"[27] magic realism, it has been written, may resemble Shakespeare's Caliban who learns the master's language then uses it to curse. Like Caliban (and the parallel is particularly suited for an author who, in her *Iguana*, stages the crisis of Eurocentric colonial representation), magic realism has mastered the empirically based discourse of European modernity and now uses it to undermine some of the master's assumptions.

Studying Ortese's work through the lens of international magic realism could then reveal itself to be productive and intriguing: I propose it as a "working model" that still needs to be put to the test, without, however, wanting to constrain the writer's style in any way. This dreaming thinker, lest we forget, defies easy definition, imposing herself in the power of her originality and in the fascinating elusiveness of her writing.

A wandering nomad (as much between the cities of the Italian peninsula as between forms of writing), the writer transcends that which she touches, always positioning herself on the slippery slope of the liminal and the in-between. Ultimately, it is precisely this ambiguous image of in-betweenness that best captures the sense of Ortese's poetics. In a certain way, the writer's symbolic positioning vis-à-vis normative literary categories recalls that of the Spanish painter Velasquez in his acclaimed canvas *Las Meninas* (1656). Raising questions about reality, illusion, and visibility, this painting seems to visually crystallize several aspects that are to be found in Ortese's ultra-realist and meta-visionary writing. The painter, representing himself in the canvas, is able to simultaneously dominate two different visual planes: on the one hand, his gaze is focused on an indefinable beyond – namely, a space beyond that of the actual representation, which remains invisible to us as viewers; on the other, his gaze can wander in a real space, occupied by luxurious *infantas*, grotesque buffoons, gracious *meninas*, bizarre animals, and figures reflected in a mirror. This is, of course, the actual space of the representation visible to us as viewers of the painting. On the very verge of a similar imaginary threshold, at the intersection of two different epistemic and visual domains, the ultra-realist Ortese poises herself: in contrast to the baroque painter, however, who "rules at the threshold of [...] two *incompatible* visibilities,"[28] as Michel Foucault states in his well-known interpretation of the painting, the (post)modern Ortese is able to make them congruent and conciliable, rendering ambiguously fluid those apparently (in)compatible visions and spaces, epistemes and modes of discourse.

The essays collected here take into account some of the lines of inquiry described above. The title of the volume, *Anna Maria Ortese: Celestial Geographies*, encapsulates multiple meanings and interpretive strategies.

The foremost aim of this volume is to offer to an anglophone audience an initial map of the critical geography of Ortese scholarship and of its developments over the last two decades, synthesizing the scholarly debate but also opening the discourse to new interpretations and perspectives. The map that this volume intends to sketch out, nevertheless, is not only metaphorical, but also literal and aims to demonstrate the richness of Ortese's transnational legacy. The Ortese scholars who have contributed to this volume in fact come from a variety of cultural geographies: from Italy to the United States, from Belgium to Switzerland. The names are not limited to those already known in the field, like Monica Farnetti and Andrea Baldi, who have edited the important Adelphi edition of Ortese's novels, but also include "new" critical voices that have been developing fresh, often interdisciplinary, approaches to the study of this author's work. The broad critical horizon is a fitting counterpart to the transnational and trans-Atlantic geography evoked in Ortese's writing: not only did a mythical America inspire one of her earliest literary experiments – the short story "Pellerossa" – but it also figures at the centre of her last novel, *Alonso e i visionari*; and while her writing projects an imaginary Mediterranean – primarily Naples and the Libya of her childhood – it charts ulterior geographic coordinates: from the Portuguese and the Caribbean islands of the *Iguana* to the magical and fantastical northern European landscape evoked in *Il cardillo addolorato*, the novel that more than any other has contributed to her success.

The mapping of Ortese's work that this volume intends to carry out, far from being definitive and complete, is limited almost exclusively to the author's novels, short stories, and travel writing, including a few exploratory forays into her letters and literary criticism: insofar as the other typologies of her writing are important and demand further study – among which her poetry stands out in particular[29] – we have chosen to follow a strict selective criterion in the interest of a theoretical-critical coherence.

The adjectival qualifier in the title – "celestial" – could seem rather unusual for a collection of scholarly essays. It actually encapsulates a dual reference to Ortese: *intra-textually*, it refers to *Corpo celeste* (Celestial Body, 1997), a little hybrid gem in the writer's variegated narrative output, a cross between creative essay and self-interview, critical fable and diaristic moral reflection. This slender volume not only emblematizes Ortese's ability to reconfigure literary forms and canons according to her own personal literary geography, but also situates her at the centre of an illustrious international tradition that, from Montaigne to Leopardi, from Joseph Brodsky to Simone Weil, from Voltaire and Emerson to Pier Paolo Pasolini and Cristina Campo, confirms the "essayistic" proclivity of modernity. *Metatextually* (and perhaps by synecdoche), the adjective "celestial" seems in the end to be the most opportune to crystallize, in a word, Ortese's ethics as well as her poetics: for, literally, many epiphanic apparitions and either angelic, magic, or bestial creatures populate her universe – perhaps limping or suffering, or else hidden in a cardboard box or underneath a subterranean trapdoor – thus evoking a deep creatural pietas. These celestial epiphanies, moreover, decree a profound disarticulation of the Western philosophical categories that divide the physical and empirical from the metaphysical world. *Metaphorically*, then, the adjective "celestial" conjures the deep sense of estrangement and displacement – of boundaries and borders, of structures and thresholds, of languages and meanings, of literary genres and levels of fiction – that constitutes the heart and soul of Ortese's "pensiero sognante" ("dreamy thought"). This very same sense of alienation and profound stupor, as she herself wrote in *Corpo celeste,* enraptures those of us who, all of a sudden, realize our planet Earth is not a "palla scura, terrosa, niente affatto aerea" (CC 10; "dark earthy ball, anything but light and airy"), but rather a *celestial body,* a brilliant blue object located in space:

> Quando ho compreso questo, non subito, a poco a poco, nel continuo terremoto del crescere, nell'amarezza di scoperte inattese (della infelicità, del passare delle cose), sono stata presa da un senso di meraviglia, di emozione indicibile. [...] Mi trovavo anche io sulla terra, nello spazio, e il mio destino non era molto dissimile da quello degli oggetti e corpi celesti tanto seguiti e ammirati. [...] Una cosa era certa, era nozione ormai incancellabile: tutto il mondo era quel sovramondo. Anche la terra e il paese dove abitavo; e la collocazione, o vera patria di tutti, era quel sovramondo! (CC 10)

> [When I came to this realization, not all of sudden, but little by little, in the perpetual earthquake of growing, in the bitterness of unexpected discoveries (of unhappiness, of the passing of things), I was taken by a sense of marvel, of unspeakable emotion. [...] I too found myself on the Earth, in space, and my destiny was not so unlike that of the objects and celestial bodies so sought after and admired. [...] One thing was certain, it was an indelible notion: the whole world was that overworld. Even the land and country where I lived; and our allocated place, or everyone's true motherland, was that overworld!]

Celestial Geographies sets out, therefore, to restore the sense of a profoundly destabilizing writing that – in the heart of a secular and rational *Novecento,* which had lost every metaphysical buttress and had been rocked by the fury of human violence and devastation – wants to recover both the metaphysical matrix and the ethical root of existence, by promoting an emphatic bond with the undifferentiated creatural substance of the universe.

All together, the essays collected in this volume trace the creative trajectory of Ortese's career: they pinpoint rhetorical and narrative strategies that cross in pervasive ways the different forms of writing adopted. Engaging in a dialogue with each other, the studies present new perspectives – thanks largely to the contribution of careful archival research and an interdisciplinary and intertextual approach – illuminating various facets of the writer's style. The essays have been grouped in sections that are organized neither chronologically nor exclusively according to genre. We decided rather to adopt a "logic of resonance" – similar themes and issues are analysed from different angles, in heterogeneous textual genres and forms. This logic, creating a sort of hermeneutical short circuit, sheds light on the extraordinary compactness and cohesion of Ortese's metamorphic writing and, at the same time, on its unexpected mobility.

A cohesive group of essays opens the volume, under the rubric *From Naples to Paris (via Jerusalem): Modern Alienation and Utopian Reality*. They investigate Ortese's shorter writings – tales, journalistic reportages, travelogues, autobiographical accounts – a textual corpus that spans an extensive arc of time, from the haunted realism of *Il mare non bagna Napoli* (1953) and *Silenzio a Milano* (1958) to the travel writing of *Il mormorio di Parigi* (1986). As heterogeneous as this textual corpus is, the essays highlight a subtle orchestration of intertwining themes and motifs: a trenchant indictment of modern urban alienation under late capitalism and, at the same time, of the atavistic existential decay of the Southern Italian condition; the perceptual, scopic experience and the importance of Ortese's visionary poetics; the sense of displacement, exile, and estrangement; the ethical engagement and the emphatic gesture of intimacy and inclusion towards the disenfranchised.

Ortese's most famous and controversial book, *Il mare non bagna Napoli* – a hybrid text that earned her both the recognition of the 1953 Premio Viareggio and the harsh resentment from the Neapolitan intellectual élite depicted in the stories – is the subject of Lucia Re's analysis that opens the volume. Situating for the first time the stories of *Il mare non bagna Napoli* in the historical context of a post-war Naples dominated by both the disastrous politics of the magnate-mayor Achille Lauro and the "intractably tragic" urban decay of the city, Re focuses on the unifying theme of vision and addresses the author's use of optical metaphors: from the narrator-reporter's empathic yet probing look into the unspeakable horror of the Granili tenements or the wretched squalor of Forcella and San Biagio, to the myopia of Eugenia, the spectacled protagonist of the gem-like story "Un paio di occhiali." What emerges from Re's keen observations – building on theoretical notions developed by Berger and Mulvey on the male gaze, Irigaray and Cixous on Western ocular-centrism – is an authorial gaze entirely free from the burden of the reification, envy, and exploitation that characterizes the dominating and powerful gaze of the male Western subject. Eugenia's blurred, imprecise vision, like Ortese's, Re argues, becomes metatextual, a metaphoric key to the writer's non-realistic visionary poetics, a deliberate act of an alternative vision that seeks to bring authenticity, intimacy, and physical proximity back to the centre of human relations: nearsightedness, thus, becomes a cognitive force (*voir-savoir*, as Cixous would put it) that, by de-familiarizing the readers from the usual order of things, forces them to deflect the gaze and to reflect *critically* on the real. If the spectacle of human abjection in the urban, premodern city of the south is the object of Re's critical investigation, Andrea Baldi turns his attention to Ortese's incisive look at the devastating effect of urban industrial and capitalistic modernity, as epitomized by Milan, the city Ortese adopted in 1948. Scrutinizing reportages, narratives, letters, and newspaper articles from the 1950s and 1960s – some of which have been brought to light here – Baldi interweaves the chronicle of a personal and professional journey with the development of an ambiguous ideological standpoint: the writer's initial optimism for the economic miracle and the promise of national well-being as well as for personal professional opportunities (as a writer-journalist) subsequently shifts to a poignant indictment of the moral breakdown and disintegration of the urban social fabric brought about by modernity, Americanization, and the culture of mass consumption. As a nomadic woman intellectual endowed with an inquisitive eye and a magnifying glass, the reporter-storyteller of *Silenzio a Milano* is able to establish a sympathetic bond with the marginalized figures and pariahs who inhabit the transitional spaces and the back-alleys of modernity, thus eluding the discriminating logic of late capitalism. As for *Il mare non bagna Napoli*, to jar the readers out of their moral lethargy is, ultimately, the task of Ortese's writing in *Silenzio a Milano*. The theme of the pariah, combined with a focus on the writer's peculiar urban gaze, is taken up again by Cristina Della Coletta from an original theoretical and comparative perspective. At first investigating a series of autobiographical and essayistic meditations collected in *Corpo celeste*, Della Coletta builds on Hannah Arendt's notion of the "conscious pariah" – intellectual outcasts who, refusing the deception of mere material possessions, turn themselves into the forebears of an inclusive idea of humanity – as a springboard to explore Ortese's ideation of the "non consenzienti" ("non-consenting ones") and her meditations on collective memory and belonging, past and community, freedom and intellectual independence. As a conscious pariah who has experienced loss, displacement, and exile, Ortese, in Della Coletta's view, is then able to craft a liberating, utopian projection in the form of an urban encounter with Paris. In her most famous travelogue, *Il mormorio di Parigi*, Ortese self-consciously exploits Eurocentric technologies of vision – the panoptic and panoramic views that organize the representation (and spectacularization) of Paris in modernity – voiding those technologies of the euphoric *telos* of progress and universal well-being associated with them. Proposing an alternate vision, the writer refashions the city as a utopian, fluid, totalizing, aerial, and exhilarating urban space, open to the infinite possibilities of the (female) desiring subject.

Under the rubric *Life of a Celestial Body: Making and Unmaking the Self*, a group of four essays investigates Ortese's innate propensity for self-fashioning and the creation of alter egos and fictional masks, focusing on a variety of textual forms, short stories, letters, and novels. Taken together, these pieces demonstrate not only the profound coherence of Ortese's "autobiographical" project and of her techniques of self-representation and dissimulation, but also her keen awareness of the fictitious and performative nature of any self-representational act. Ortese's "I" is an ever-changing stage of conflictual representations and performances of the Self. In an essay on Ortese's twenty-four letters to her mentor Bontempelli, written between 1936 and 1952, Amelia Moser turns her attention to the overlooked relationship between the young, formally uneducated *enfant prodige* from the port of Naples and the great writer who was already at the height of his influence and fame. Despite the candour and innocence that Bontempelli seems to detect in the young writer as a guarantee of a truly authentic art, Ortese the epistolographer already exhibits a consummate and skillful toolbox of rhetorical and self-representational strategies that will carry over into her mature autobiographical writing: a complex dialectic between sincerity and falsehood, a strategic use of the pseudonym and other fantastical self-creations, thus paving the way for the alter egos of her mature novels; a tendency to resist any fixed identity, and a self-deprecating tone mixed with a strong drive to succeed and prevail. To be true to her contradictory, ever-changing, inconsistent self, Moser argues, is Ortese's only way to be authentic and "sincere" in her epistolary rapport with Bontempelli. Three of these precious letters have been published and translated for the first time at the end the essay, thus enriching our understanding of the author through an epistolary rubric that is becoming increasingly more important among scholars in Italy and abroad. The letters' value as documentary evidence is remarkable: in addition to the psychological insights they give us into the young writer, they shed light on the earliest stages of a still-obscure process of literary formation and allow us to reconstruct the cultural *milieu* in which Ortese-the-apprentice began to assume her authorial shape.

The relationship between Ortese and Bontempelli is also the subject of Luigi Fontanella's study of Ortese's turbulent literary debut. Carefully tracing threads through the tapestry of historical memory, Fontanella highlights Bontempelli's relationship to the cultural and political landscape of the time (Pirandello and D'Annunzio, in particular) and his increasing tendency to dissent from the fascist regime. Like Moser, the critic notices a striking coincidence between Bontempelli's poetics of candour, echoing the Pirandellian idea of *nudità*, and the anti-D'Annunzian stance of Ortese's own personal and stylistic naiveté. Fontanella's reading draws on documentary evidence in support of the observation well known to critics that, behind the brutal attack of a few of the reviewers of Ortese's first work, there really lurked a desire to strike her mentor. Offering a close (re)reading of the thirteen short stories of *Angelici dolori,* Fontanella delves into the structure, *topoi,* and representational strategies of the text, capturing above all Ortese's intense expressive delicacy, the fragile weave of emotions and suspended fantastical atmospheres, and, most importantly, the intimate connection between the imaginative autobiographical impulse and those visionary and fantastic elements so present in her work.

In the third essay of this section, Beatrice Manetti meticulously reconstructs the tortuous compositional path and the intricate editorial history of two interlaced autobiographical manuscripts – aided also by the support of some previously unpublished letters Italo Calvino addressed to Ortese, recently uncovered at the Archivio Einaudi in Turin. Manetti compellingly argues that the two twin-texts *Poveri e semplici* (1968) and *Il cappello piumato* (1979), far from being mere "peripheral incidents" in Ortese's corpus, as critics are accustomed to say, rather represent two essential moments in the development of her self-representational strategies: the invention of alter egos (like Bettina) who appropriate for themselves the narrator's authorial agency, a constant pattern of un-becoming and disillusionment that characterize the textual "I," and a metatextual dimension superimposed onto the autobiographical one. While, predictably, these discursive patterns converge in her mature autobiographical work *Il Porto di Toledo,* Manetti also identifies a subtle connection between two apparently unrelated texts: in other words, the fragmentary and meditative structure of *Il cappello piumato* – the self-portrait of an intellectual – proleptically anticipates the meditative and self-referential tone of the creative essays of *Corpo celeste*, thus demonstrating that a deep sub-textual, intra-textual, and intra-generic thread runs through Ortese's narrative fabric.

Along the lines of self-representational strategies, my own essay addresses the pseudo-autobiographical work of her maturity, *Il porto di Toledo* (1975, 1998), re-reading it in light of the narrator's psychological, metaphorical, and metaphysical obsessions: transience, loss, and the tension between transcendence and permanence. As theorists of the genre underscore, gazing at oneself in the mirror of an autobiographical act is always a risky and ambivalent gesture, perennially hanging in the balance between (re)-birth and the crystallization (i.e., the death) of the self. Thus, as I argue, a paradoxical project lies at the heart of *Il porto di Toledo*, rendering its narrative fabric and tropological texture extremely complex and elusive. The paradox of wanting to fix and / or crystallize the self and the past (to counteract the passage of time) and fearing of actually doing so (because it freezes the self in a *rigor mortis*); the paradox of wanting to transcend transience and flux and of actually doing so by means of a writing style saturated with "water": a fluid form of writing, rich in marine metaphors that is nothing more than the visual and metaphorical translation of her obsession with impermanence. The autobiographical representation in Il *porto di Toledo*, I argue, is caught in the crosscurrents of these paradoxes.

In contrast to the different orchestration of themes and forms analysed in other sections of the volume, Part 3 ("On Becoming Beast: Iguanas, Linnets, Lions, and the Geography of Otherness") focuses on a thematically compact group of novels – *L'Iguana* (1965), *Il Cardillo addolorato* (1993), and *Alonso e i visionari* (1996) – that marks a definitive stage in the development of Ortese's ethical thought, secular "ecological spirituality," and highly allegorical aesthetics. Deconstructing forms and structures, multiplying narrative planes and perspectives, mixing, in a very idiosyncratic way, elements of fantasy, magic, and realism, these novels resist every distinction of genre. Inge Lanslot opens the section with an intra-textual analysis featuring analytical charts and graphs. Taking as its focal point the character of the "iguana," the study explores the hybrid morphological, ethical, and ontological status of Ortese's metamorphic creatures (the goblin Käppchen, the Cardillo, and the puma Alonso), thus demonstrating not only their intricate genealogy and profound affinity but also Ortese's cohesive, progressive, and teleological metamorphic "design." Always oscillating between opposite categories – human and animal, good and evil, objectivity and subjectivity – but also striving to transcend all binaries (and here Lanslot resorts to the notion of the "monad" as conceived by the seventeenth-century philosopher Gottfried Leibniz), these creatures seem to originate from an ontological place of multiplicity, from an uncanny, chaotic site of undifferentiated indistinctness that profoundly destabilizes the Cartesian dualism that has served as the foundation of modern philosophical thought in the West. If the creatures' chameleonic shape shifting mirrors the dizzying and polymorphous textual tapestry of the novels, ultimately, Ortese's aesthetics of "multiplicity" (in terms of genre, style, meaning, textual layers, and intertextual references) represents her own epistemological quest, her own unique way of textualizing the profound inconsistency and mystery of our reality.

A striking image of a mummified iguana (found in Ortese's unpublished textual variants) provides the entry point for Gian Maria Annovi's reflection on the "animalization of the Other." Transporting us to the island of *L'Iguana*, Annovi draws on a variety of heterogeneous sources and discourses, ranging from the syntax of postcolonial discourse to fifteenth-century theological disputations on witchcraft and the "bestial nature" of the Natives; from Italian philosopher Luciano Parinetto's insights into the link between rising capitalism, colonialism, and witch hunts to the diaries of the first conquistadors and the early modern iconographies of the New World. The breadth of this theoretical frame allows Annovi to argue that the epistemic violence and the "shaping power" of colonial discourse are inscribed on the slight body of an indigenous little servant girl, whose subjectivity is located in the gaze of the Imperial Other: thus, the servant undergoes at first a process of "iguanization" (she is turned into a monster, an animal, a green reptile), and then she is "*streghizzata*" (turned into a witch, associated with the Devil), in a striking parallel with the fate of Native peoples after the "conquest" of America. Have the old European witches crossed the ocean and become iguanas? To the violent imposition of colonial and inquisitorial master narratives, the "unrepresentable" iguana can only respond and resist with an obstinate silence and an equally obstinate refusal to be defined either by a name or a fixed identity of any kind.

The next piece marks the transition from a colonial Caribbean geography to that of northern Europe. Opportunely situating the novel *Il cardillo addolorato* in its historical context, between the French Revolution and the Declaration of the Rights of Man, Gala Rebane explores the dark underbelly of the project of modernity and the defeat of the political utopia of Enlightenment, uncovering ideological clues, overlooked by critics, that turn out to be fundamental for an understanding of the novel's historical facets. What emerges, then, from Rebane's analysis is a subtle thread that connects everything that has been excluded, marginalized, or suppressed by the totalizing rational categories and proscriptive discourses of modernity: society's outcasts, like Kappchen-Lillot, the mysterious sprite doomed to death; marginalized subjects, like the elusive figure of Elmina, who through her obstinate silence is able to resist her inscription into male-centred narratives and erotic desires; or, on another level, the invisible, the unreal, the irrational, the imponderable that, escaping the constrains of rational categories, are accessible only to children and visionary artists, like Sasà-Palummella and the artist Duprè. Finally, Rebane delves into the novel's dense "melancholic palimpsest" of intertextual references to high European culture – a culture that the advent of modernity had turned into a dormant repository of collective memories. Rising up over this modern world dominated by the "rational" and the "real" is the mysterious song of the linnet "to announce the invisible in grand projects and the silenced in master narratives, to lend his voice and to give hope to all the desperate *piccerilli* and their faithful sisters."

Focusing on the same novel, Margherita Pieracci Harwell analyses the mysterious and elusive character of Elmina and her obstinate muteness. She investigates similarities between this enigmatic woman and other characters in the novel by tracing her gestation through other novels and the previous draft of *Il cardillo addolorato*, entitled *Mistero doloroso*. What emerges from her research is a vertiginous web that connects different texts and themes that span the entirety of the Ortese corpus, a web of prefigurations and variations of sprites, *monacielli*, soulless animals, godless churches, passionate children, and heartless mothers. And if, in her minutely detailed textual and thematic analysis, Pieracci reveals and interprets some of the enigmas regarding the plot and its characters (the surprises this essay has in store for the impassioned readers of the novel I will not spoil here), what remains inviolate and unexposed is the impalpable sense of mystery that constitutes the intimate substance of the novel. As Pieracci writes, taking her cue from Cristina Campo, the mystery is "encircled and questioned, with a love suffused with reverence."

The theme of the critique of rational enlightenment, modernity and its philosophical discourse, already addressed by Lanslot and Rebane, is also taken up in the last essay by Tatiana Crivelli Speciale who, from what is at once a Derridean and an eco-logical perspective, addresses the encounter between the "visionary human being" and the animal in Ortese's last novel *Alonso e i visionari.* The critic juxtaposes the perspective of poetry and poets with some of Derrida's notions (the "*animot*" and the "*animal-séance*") and his deconstruction of the Hegelian philosophical discourse that differentiates humans and animals only on the basis of rational and linguistic faculties: only visionaries, as well as poets (like the novel's protagonist Jimmy Op), can empathize with the suffering of society's outcasts and feel a profound affinity with all of nature's living creatures. While this exclusion is rooted in the Enlightenment's rational philosophical system of thought (and here Ortese shows her Leopardian vocation in her condemnation of "le magnifiche sorti e progressive"), Crivelli identifies in the span of time between the post-war period and the age of terrorism (the novel's historical-political backdrop) a crucial and decisive turning point in Western culture and ideology: under the impetus of reconstruction, normative culture leads to the celebration of human supremacy, to the triumph of progress and economic utility, to the exaltation of the visible and phenomenal world, eradicating and erasing every trace of the "imponderable" and non-rational in its various forms: nature, memory, desire, faith, magic, poetry. The piercing void that is produced in this act of uprooting is occupied by the mysterious, uncanny apparitions of a puma: like Derrida's famous cat, the cub challenges our own identity by showing the disturbing contiguity and proximity between animals and humans.

Monica Farnetti, in the final section *An Uncommon Reader*, looks at an usual aspect of the author's output for the first time: her literary criticism. Ortese proved to be an attentive and discerning reader, despite her lack of formal education, starting as early as her undaunted discussion of her impressions of Bontempelli's works, as Moser has highlighted in her essay in Part 2. Through the analysis of a series of fourteen articles that are admittedly incoherent, scattered, and a-systematic (published between 1939 and 1977) and a couple of passages excerpted from *Corpo celeste*, Farnetti outlines Ortese's literary predilections as well as her protocol of literary critical reading, in search of a coherent pattern and a criteria for literary value. The creative and penetrating gaze of this "uncommon reader" – her "double vision" – transcends the level of the literary signifier, delving into the human and ethical depth of literature. From Chekhov to Kafka, from Hemingway ("a piece of sea and wind") to Anne Frank (with whom she emphatically establishes a sort of elective sisterhood): her literary reviews emphasize an ethical and "ecological" reading, a method reminiscent of Simone Weil's "desire to read with justice." What matters for Ortese, Farnetti argues, is the writer's ability to render, without altering it, the totality of life – its "tremendous and minuscule variations" (as philosopher Maria Zambrano would say) – and the freedom of its becoming. Among the documents upon which Farnetti draws, one letter in particular stands out. Previously unpublished, it is a letter that Ortese addressed to the critic Pietro Citati in which she comments on the work of Elsa Morante ("a mountain, a genius"). The letter is a priceless document and it takes our breath away: not only because it shows, yet again, the extraordinary refinement and profundity of Ortese's prowess as literary critic, but also because it lays bare the literary sensibility, as well as the human wisdom, of a marginalized writer measuring herself up to a far more accomplished and famous one. Ortese and Morante: two great novelists united by their shared "complicity with the celestial order" of things.

Along the same lines of intellectual exchange and dialogue between women writers, this volume concludes. Appearing in the Appendix, in English for the first time, is "E tu chi eri?," an interview with Ortese conducted by Dacia Maraini, one of the most influential and internationally translated Italian writers, who was awarded the 2012 Campiello Prize for her career of artistic and intellectual achievement. Recorded in the early 1970s – when discussing the personal was a political act – the interview is a priceless document: it reveals moments, gestures, and faces of the writer's childhood that, in other texts, Ortese transforms and disguises, making them cryptic and indecipherable. The interview originally appeared in Italian in a volume that featured other interviews of luminaries from the pantheon of Italian intellectuals and artists: Bellocchio and De Chirico, Callas and Rossellini, Pasolini and Strehler, Gadda and Ginzburg. Anthologizing Ortese in that way turned out to be prophetic as these are the figures to whom she continues to be compared to this day. The interview, though, conveys also other symbolic meanings. For the young and as of then relatively unknown Maraini, the dialogue with a great but almost forgotten artist of the past generation represents a metaphoric gesture of creation and self-creation. Searching for a female literary family, as an entire generation of intellectual women was doing in the 1970s, Maraini configures Ortese as a precursor and a literary mother. At the same time, though, by creating a matrilineal bond, Maraini is legitimizing her own role as a writer, her own authorship and creative activity. The interview, then, marks a pivotal point in the making of an Italian female literary genealogy.

With this volume Anna Maria Ortese disembarks on the North American continent. A circle is closed and a destiny is fulfilled. America, so dearly beloved by Ortese "di un amore antico, senza barriere" (CC 26; "with an ancient love, without barriers"), repeatedly appears in fact in her reflections and subtly runs through her imaginary, in contradictory ways. For a writer who felt she was an American born in Boston a century or two ago, as she confesses in *Corpo celeste*, the United States represented, above all, a mythic and utopic ideal and a source of literary inspiration – as it did for a whole generation of 1930s intellectuals weaned on the pages of the American literature translated by Vittorini and Pavese. Ortese's literary models were, among others, the authors of American Transcendentalism (veritable "*figli della luce*"), Emerson, Whitman, Thoreau, Melville, Dickinson, but her greatest admiration went also to Poe, Lee Masters, Crane, James, Wilder, and Hemingway.[30] Though a mythic and inspirational land, America is equally a source of ideological disappointment. In the post-war period of the capitalistic Americanization of Italy, Ortese reassessed her political stance, giving rise to a scathing critique against American politics in her essayistic prose as well as in her fiction: from *Il porto di Toledo*, where the "American utopia" collapses under the Allied bombardments to *Alonso*, where the United States is, at the same time, an emblem of an original purity and the symbol of a Western world unequivocally devoted to destruction in the name of reason, supremacy, and economic interest.[31] Beyond this personal mythography of the United States, the American continent figures into Ortese's life also as a land of emigration: Toronto was, in fact, the coveted destination of Ortese's family of sailors when times were tough in Italy, and it is precisely from Toronto that her "Canadian" brother Francesco returns in the 1990s to look after the aging writer at the time of her brief and belated success.

One of the protagonists featured in her last novel, *Alonso e i visionari*, is the American Jimmy Op: a poet, a mystic, but also an "italianista appassionato" (R2 634; "passionate Italianist"), professor at the "University of H." in Boston. Creating a *mise en abyme* and a mirroring effect that would certainly tickle Ortese's fancy, this volume is dedicated to all of the *italianisti appassionati* of the North American continent who, in the footsteps of Jimmy Op and an uncanny puma from Arizona, will want to investigate the enchantments and the ethical passions of the last great visionary of the Italian *Novecento.*

NOTES

1 Di Prisco, 36–37.

2 Anna Maria Ortese, *Angelici dolori* (Milan: Bompiani, 1937), jacket flap, repr. in Luca Clerici, *Apparizione e visione*, 77. This is Ortese's first self-portrayal. See also Giancarlo Vigorelli, 175–76.

3 Di Prisco, 36–37. It is no surprise that Ortese contradicts herself the following year, in her second interview, when she gives us the first glimpse of her literary background: "*Quali libri avete letto finora?* Tanti, tanti! ... Chi se li ricorda più [...] *Quali dei moderni scrittori preferite?* È moderno Collodi? *Tra i modernissimi?* Ungaretti mi piace. *Tra gli stranieri?* Dickens, Poe, Mansfield, Wilde, Hoffmann, Shakespeare" ("*Which books have you read so far?* Many, many! ... Who remembers them anymore [...] *Which modern writers do you like?* Is Collodi modern? *Among contemporary writers?* I like Ungaretti. *Among foreign writers?* Dickens, Poe, Mansfield, Wilde, Hoffman, Shakespeare"; Greco, "Anna Maria Ortese, littrice," in Clerici, *Per Anna Maria Ortese,* 44).

4 Di Prisco, 36–37.

5 Ibid., 37.

6 Ortese, "Anna Maria Ortese," 247–48.

7 The notion of "*antygrafe,*" defined as "writing-without-having-written," is discussed in relation to Christine de Pizan's ambivalent rhetorical strategies and disclaiming of her own authorial agency by Christine Moneera Laennec in her essay, "Christine's Antygrafe: Authorial Ambivalence in the Works of Christine de Pizan," 35–36.

8 In the formulation of Carol J. Singley and Susan Elisabeth Sweeney, the term "*anxious power,*" which builds from Harold Bloom's "*anxiety of influence*" and Gilbert's and Gubar's "*anxiety of authorship,*" refers to both women's ambivalent perceptions of themselves in relation to male authorship and to various formal strategies adopted to cope with the uneasy "empowerment" inscribed in the act of reading and writing. Anxious power, in other words, at the same time negates and reinforces authorial legitimacy (Singley and Sweeney, *Anxious Power,* 3–15). For related concepts see also: Bloom, *The Anxiety of Influence*; Gilbert and Gubar, *The Madwoman in the Attic,* 48–49.

9 Although Naples is the cultural "capital" of the South of Italy, the city has often been misrepresented in popular culture. See Nelson Moe, *The View from Vesuvius: Italian Culture and the Southern Question* (Berkeley / Los Angeles: University of California Press, 2002) and Mario Niola, "The Invention of the Mediterranean," in *Sites of Exchange: European Crossroads and Faultlines*, ed. Maurizio Ascari and Adriana Corrado (Amsterdam-New York: Rodopi, 2006), 75–85.

10 For the first monumental and richly detailed biography of Ortese, reference must be made to Clerici, *Apparizione e visione.*

11 Ortese's extraordinary confidence and determination to achieve poetic independence emerges as early as the 1939 interview, when the writer affirms: "molti giornali, tutti quelli che potrebbero pagarmi, hanno già pronto il titolo delle novelle, come dire, il cappello di moda bell'e fatto per la mia

testa. Ora, sfortunatamente, non mi è ancora accaduto che la mia testa entrasse in uno di quei cappellini" ("many newspapers, all those that could pay me, have already prepared the titles of my stories, that is, the fashionable hat all ready for my head. Now, unfortunately, I still haven't placed one of those little hats on my head"; Greco, "Anna Maria Ortese, littrice," in Clerici, *Per Anna Maria Ortese*, 44).

12 Ortese, letter to Franz Haas (3 July 1990), quoted in Clerici, *Apparizione e visione*, 584.

13 Although in her seminal study *Feminist Theory: From Margin to Center*, bell hooks writes that "to be in the margin is to be part of the whole but outside the main body" (xvi), other critics have deconstructed our understanding of the margin-center binary, proposing a more nuanced relation. For critic Gayatri Spivak, in fact, the relation between margin and center is always "intricate and interanimating," always shifting and precarious (Spivak, "Explanation and Culture: Marginalia," 383). For the somewhat related concept of "eccentricità" and its relation with "il doppio fuoco dell'ellisse," see Rimondi, "Il cerchio e l'ellisse: Contributo a una topologia dell'eccentrico," 51–60. For her part, Ortese conceptualizes her position vis-à-vis the cultural establishment through Mana, the autobiographical alter ego featured in the recently uncovered *Diario*: "Sempre di qua e di là, di sopra e di sotto; mai al centro: ecco dove mi trovo" ("Always here and there, up and down; never at the center: that's where I am"; Ortese, *Diario*, in R1, 1098).

14 La Capria, "Creatura notturna e senza pace: Concepiva la vita come male assoluto," 31.

15 In one of the first studies on modernism and Italian culture available in English, Luca Somigli writes: "If we interpret modernity as the ground of formation of epistemes, of knowledge centered on the Enlightenment categories of reason, social emancipation, and scientific progress [...] modernism can then be considered as the network of cultural responses – at times openly antagonistic, at others characterized by a much greater ambiguity – which reflect upon, react to, and seek to articulate alternatives to the triumph of the institutions of modernity" (Somigli and Moroni, *Modernism in Italy: An Introduction*, 12).

16 Bontempelli, *L'avventura novecentista*, 251. Other benchmarks of Bontempelli's poetics are summarized in the following well-known formulations: "La vita più quotidiana e normale, vogliamo vederla come avventuroso miracolo"; "il mondo immaginario si verserà in perpetuo a fecondare e arricchire il reale" ("The most ordinary daily life, we want to see it as an adventurous miracle"; "the imaginary world will perpetually spill over to fertilize and

enrich the real"; Bontempelli, *Opere scelte,* 750–51). On Bontempelli and *Novecentismo,* see Saccone, *Il mito del '900.*

17 Without ever entering into the merit of a deeper analysis, critics agree on this point. Reflecting a posteriori on the relationship with her master Bontempelli and his companion, the writer Paola Masino, Ortese seems, in the novel *Il porto di Toledo,* to distance herself from the famous literary couple, paying due literary homage to them in the form of an intertextual nod: before the couple (in the fictional guise of Maestro D'Orgaz and Robin) arrive for the first time at the girl's poor home where they are to finally meet the mysterious author of the stories published in D'Orgaz literary review, Toledana takes a bath. In my interpretation, the ritual with water and soap marks the birth of Toledana's new independent identity as a woman writer and her "washing" away of any literary influences. Interestingly, Toledana's ritual washing echoes another bath that, in Masino's *Nascita e morte di una massaia* (1945), marks the passage of the protagonist from a world of infantile pre-Oedipal closure to a Lacanian adult world. On Masino, see Blelloch, "From Trunk to Grave: The Hallucinated Story of a Housewife," 89–103.

18 Ferroni, *Passioni del Novecento,* 156.

19 Bontempelli, *L'avventura novecentista,* 37.

20 For an interesting comparison between Watteau's masterpiece and Ortese's *Il cardillo addolorato,* see, in this volume, Rebane, "The Flickering Light of Reason: Anna Maria Ortese's *Il cardillero addolorato* and a Critique of European Modernity."

21 Of differing opinion, Danielle E. Hipkins, in her study of the fantastic as a way to encounter and counter anxieties arising from the female subject position vis-à-vis a male-dominated literary canon, writes that Ortese, along with Morante, "have begun to shine more brightly for critics as authors of the fantastic" (Hipkins, *Contemporary Italian Women Writers and Traces of the Fantastic: The Creation of Literary Space,* 30). In her pioneering work, Monica Farnetti, on the other hand, puts forth a different hypothesis, positing a female use of the fantastic that is "anxiety-free": "in place of the dilemma-like, conflictual and, more precisely, anxious power that we normally associate with the paradigm of the uncanny, I was in fact struck by an attitude of openness, kindness, compassion, even affection and love. This opened up a dramatic new perspective on the perturbing, dislocating, alienating element [...] that is taken to be characteristic of fantastic literature" (Farnetti, "Anxiety-Free: Re-readings of the Freudian Uncanny," 46–47). Of this peculiar "feminine fantastic" that recognizes the perturbing extraneousness as a part of itself, without trauma and without restlessness, Ortese would be,

according to Farnetti, "il campione esemplare." See also Farnetti, "Fantastico (La Perturbante)," *Anna Maria Ortese*, 53–59.

22 Faris, *Ordinary Enchantments*, 9.

23 The umbrella term "magic realism" encompasses a great variety of authors and texts. The term itself has generated much discussion and disagreement. For a history of magic realism and its many ambiguities, see Roh, "Magic Realism: Post-Expressionism" (originally published in German in 1925), 15–30, and Carpentier, "On the Marvelous Real in America" (originally published in 1947 as a prologue to the novel *El Reino de Este Mundo*), 75–88.

24 Clerici, *Apparizione e visione*, 240.

25 I have based this hypothesis of affiliation on the several magic realism's paradigms and the broad historical and geographical literary horizon outlined by Lois Parkinson Zamora and Wendy B. Faris in their *Magic Realism: Theory, History, Community*. "Magic realism," the editors write, "is a mode suited to exploring – and transgressing – boundaries, whether the boundaries are ontological, political, geographical, or generic. Magic realism often facilitates the fusion, or coexistence, of possible worlds, spaces, systems that would be irreconcilable in other modes of fiction [...]. So magic realism may be considered an extension of realism in its concern with the nature of reality and its representation, at the same time that it resists the basic assumption of post-enlightenment rationalism and literary realism. Mind and body, spirit and matter, life and death, real and imaginary, self and other, male and female: these are boundaries to be erased, transgressed, blurred, brought together, or otherwise fundamentally refashioned in magic realist texts" (5–6).

26 Tassinari and Fornero, "Il postmoderno e le sue filosofie," 1187. Regarding Ortese, the horizon of magic realism – which originates in modernism and surrealism, continues to develop over the course of the whole century, and, thus, collides with the problematics of postmodernism (with which it coincides in part) – has the advantage of better framing the diachronic development of Ortese's narrative and its collocation between modernism and postmodernism (a crucial aspect critics have yet to address). Therefore, Ortese's loose affiliation with magic realism turns out to be more effective with respect to that "foto di gruppo con signora" described by Farnetti that instead links Ortese to the modernists of the first part of the century, such as Woolf, Joyce, Proust, Kafka, Stein, etc.: a group photo, it seems, not entirely appropriate for Ortese, although the influence of some of these authors on Ortese herself is undeniable (Farnetti, "Introduzione," R1, xii–xiv). On the relation between magic realism and postmodernity, see D'Haen, "Magical Realism and Postmodernism: Decentering Privilege

Centers," 191–208. "Magic realism is truly postmodern in its rejection of the binarism, rationalism and reductive materialism of Western modernity" (Zamora, "Magical Romance / Magical Realism: Ghosts in U.S and Latin American Fiction," 498).

27 Zamora and Faris, 6.

28 Foucault, *The Order of Things*, 4.

29 Although neglected by critics and considered a minor episode in her career, Ortese's experience with poetry, which she began to write in 1933 with a triptych of free verses on the occasion of the death of her brother Emanuele Carlo, has always played a prominent role. Beyond the two collections *Il mio paese è la notte* (Rome: Empiria, 1996) and *La luna che trascorre* (edited by Giacinto Spagnoletti, Rome: Empiria, 1998), it is worth noting also the romantic ballad *La carrozza di Jane* (Lugano: Laghi di Plitvice, 1988), inspired by her beloved Jane Brontë, not to mention numerous other poetic texts – affectionately called "rhyming lines" – that break up the prose of *Il porto di Toledo.* Even the novel *Il cappello piumato* features poetic compositions. For an initial assessment of Ortese's poetic activity and several important observations (namely, the influence of Paul Valery's *Cimitière marin* on the novel *Toledo*), see Giovannetti, "Poesia in cerca di libro: Sulla scrittura in versi di Anna Maria Ortese," 165–81, and Fontanella, "Sulla poesia giovanile di Anna Maria Ortese," 115–32. On the influence of Spanish poetry, particularly that of Jorge Manrique and Luis De Góngora, see Mazzocchi, "Anna Maria Ortese e l'ispanità," 90–114.

30 On the importance of literature in English, Ortese writes: "In questa loro lingua familiare e insieme strana, tutta azione e visione – sono nati, hanno le loro radici, quegli uomini e donne che hanno dato vita a una straordinaria letteratura. Una letteratura appunto, di azione e visione, di insegnamento, gioia, profezia insieme" (CC 26–27; "In this language of theirs that is at once both familiar and strange, all action and vision – those men and women who gave life to extraordinary literature were born, have their roots. A literature of action and vision, of instruction, joy, prophecy all together"). The gallery of often-cited authors in English, important to her literary formation, include Shakespeare, Keats, Coleridge, Shelley, Tennyson, Stevenson, Defoe, Conrad, not to mention her much-beloved fellow woman writers: Woolf, Austen, Brontë, and Mansfield (cfr. SV 117–18, 176–77, and CC 72, 100–101, 123). For a study, instead, on the influence of American Transcendentalism (Emerson, Hawthorne, and Whitman), see Loreto, "*Alonso e i visionari*: La vocazione americana di Anna Maria Ortese," 245–64. See also Fofi, "Alonso e la luce," 3, and Monica Farnetti, "Introduzione," R1, xvii.

31 "Esistono diverse Americhe, e non è detto che la più vicina all'età moderna sia la più vera" ("There are many Americas, and the most recent is not necessarily the true America"; Ortese, letter to Roberto Calasso, 18 January 1996, quoted in R2 1131).

WORKS CITED

Blelloch, Paola. "From Trunk to Grave: The Hallucinated Story of a Housewife." *NEMLA Italian Studies* 13–14 (1989–1990): 89–103.

Bloom, Harold. *The Anxiety of Influence: A Theory of Poetry.* New York: Oxford University Press, 1973.

Bontempelli, Massimo. *L'Avventura novecentista.* Florence: Vallecchi, 1938.

– *Opere scelte.* Ed. Luigi Baldacci. Milan: Mondadori, 1978.

Carpentier, Alejo. "On the Marvelous Real in America." In *Magic Realism: Theory, History, Community,* ed. Lois Parkinson Zamora and Wendy B. Faris, 75–88. Durham and London: Duke University Press, 1995. First published 1947 as a prologue to the novel *El Reino de Este Mundo.*

Clerici, Luca. *Apparizione e visione: Vita e opere di Anna Maria Ortese.* Milan: Mondadori, 2002.

– ed. "Per Anna Maria Ortese." *Il Giannone* 4, no. 7–8 (January–December 2006).

D'Haen, Theo L. "Magical Realism and Postmodernism: Decentering Privilege Centers." In *Magic Realism: Theory, History, Community,* ed. Lois Parkinson Zamora and Wendy B. Faris, 191–208. Durham and London: Duke University Press, 1995.

Di Prisco, Massimo. "Anna Maria Ortese: A tu per tu." *Gli oratori del giorno: Rassegna mensile d'eloquenza* 12, no. 1 (1938). Repr. in *Per Anna Maria Ortese,* ed. Luca Clerici, 41.

Faris, Wendy B. *Ordinary Enchantments: Magical Realism and the Remystification of Narrative.* Nashville, TN: Vanderbilt University Press, 2004.

Farkas, Alessandra. "Dal Texas alle Cinque Terre: l'ultimo viaggio del condannato a morte." *Corriere della sera* 28 (October 1999): 21.

Farnetti, Monica. *Anna Maria Ortese.* Milan: Bruno Mondadori, 1998.

– "Anxiety-Free: Re-readings of the Freudian Uncanny." In *The Italian Gothic and Fantastic: Encounters and Rewritings of Narrative Traditions,* ed. Francesca Billiani and Gigliola Sulis, 46–58. New Jersey: Fairleigh Dikinson, 2007.

Ferroni, Giulio. *Passioni del Novecento.* Rome: Donzelli Editore, 1999.

Fofi, Goffredo. "Alonso e la luce." *L'unità,* 10 June 1996, 3.

Fontanella, Luigi. "Sulla poesia giovanile di Anna Maria Ortese." *Narrativa* 24 (January 2003): 115–32.

Foucault, Michel. *The Order of Things: An Archaeology of the Human Science.* New York: Routledge, 2002.

Gilbert, Sandra, and Susan Gubar. *The Madwoman in the Attic: The Women Writer and the Nineteenth-Century Literary Imagination.* New Haven, CT: Yale University Press, 1979.

Giovannetti, Paolo. "Poesia in cerca di libro: Sulla scrittura in versi di Anna Maria Ortese." In *Per Anna Maria Ortese,* ed. Luca Clerici. *Il Giannone* 4, no. 7–8 (January–December 2006): 165–81.

Greco, Ludovico. "Anna Maria Ortese, littrice." *Belvedere* 1, no. 4 (1939). Repr. in *Per Anna Maria Ortese,* ed. Luca Clerici, 44.

Hipkins, Danielle E. *Contemporary Italian Women Writers and Traces of the Fantastic: The Creation of Literary Space.* London: Modern Research Association and Maney Publishing, 2007.

hooks, bell. *Feminist Theory: From Margin to Center.* London: Pluto Press, 2000.

La Capria, Raffaele. "Creatura notturna e senza pace: Concepiva la vita come male assoluto." *Corriere della sera,* 10 March 1998, 31.

Loreto, Paola. "*Alonso e i visionari*: La vocazione americana di Anna Maria Ortese." In *Per Anna Maria Ortese,* ed. Luca Clerici, 245–64.

Mazzocchi, Giuseppe. "Anna Maria Ortese e l'ispanità." *Modern Language Notes* 1, no. 112 (1997): 90–114.

Moneera Laennec, Christine. "Christine Antygrafe: Autorial Ambivalence in the Works of Christine de Pizan." In *Anxious Power: Reading, Writing, and Ambivalence in Narrative by Women,* ed. Carol J. Singley and Susan Elisabeth Sweeney. Albany: State University of New York Press, 1993.

Ortese, Anna Maria. "Anna Maria Ortese." In *Autodizionario degli scrittori italiani,* ed. Felice Piemontese. Milan: Leonardo, 1990.

Ortese, Anna Maria, and Alessandra Farkas. "Ortese: lettere per il piccolo indiano condannato a morte." *Corriere della sera,* 5 June 1999, 33.

Rimondi, Giorgio. "Il cerchio e l'ellisse: Contributo a una topologia dell'eccentrico." In *Le Eccentriche: Scrittrici del Novecento,* ed. Anna Botta, Monica Farnetti, and Giorgio Rimondi, 51–60. Mantova: Tre Lune Edizioni, 2003.

Roh, Franz. "Magic Realism: Post-Expressionism." In *Magic Realism: Theory, History, Community,* ed. Lois Parkinson Zamora and Wendy B. Faris, 15–30. Durham and London: Duke University Press, 1995.

Saccone, Antonio. *Il mito del '900.* Naples: Liguori Editore, 1979.

Somigli, Luca, and Mario Moroni. "Modernism in Italy: An Introduction." In *Italian Modernism: Italian Culture between Decadentism and Avant-Garde,* ed. Luca Somigli and Mario Moroni, 3–31. Toronto: University of Toronto Press, 2004.

Spivak, Gayatri Chakravorty. "Explanation and Culture: Marginalia." In *In Other Worlds: Essays in Cultural Politics.* New York and London: Routledge, 1988.

Tassinari, Salvatore, and Giovanni Fornero. "Il postmoderno e le sue filosofie." In *Le filosofie del Novecento.* Milan: Bruno Mondadori, 2002.

Vigorelli, Giancarlo. "Anna Maria Ortese – *Angelici dolori.*" *Letteratura* 1, no. 4 (1937). Repr. in *Per Anna Maria Ortese,* ed. Luca Clerici.

Zamora, Lois Parkinson. "Magical Romance / Magical Realism: Ghosts in U.S. and Latin American Fiction." In *Magic Realism: Theory, History, Community,* ed. Lois Parkinson Zamora and Wendy B. Faris, 497–548. Durham and London: Duke University Press, 1995.

PART ONE

From Naples to Paris (via Jerusalem): Modern Alienation and Utopian Reality

1 "Clouds in Front of My Eyes": Ortese's Poetics of the Gaze in "Un paio di occhiali" and *Il mare non bagna Napoli*

LUCIA RE

"Un paio di occhiali" ("A Pair of Glasses") is one of Anna Maria Ortese's most famous stories.[1] Written in Naples in May 1949, it was first published in the journal *Omnibus* under the title "Ottomila lire per gli occhi di Eugenia" ("Eight Thousand Liras for Eugenia's Eyes").[2] With the new title, "Un paio di occhiali" appeared as the opening story of the 1953 volume *Il mare non bagna Napoli* (literally *The Sea Does Not Bathe Naples*), a collection composed of five chapters. The story is more than just a beginning, constituting rather a kind of musical overture through which some of the major recurrent themes of the book and of Ortese's poetics are introduced. Although each chapter is self-standing, in fact, each is also connected to the other in an artful orchestration of recurring images and themes that make the volume an organic and unified whole. The overall meaning and aesthetic significance of the book can only be grasped, as we shall see, in light of this inaugural story. A second fictional short story entitled "Interno familiare" ("Family Scene") follows immediately after "Un paio di occhiali," and is followed in turn by three "racconti-inchiesta" (a hybrid of the genres of the short story, the autobiographical essay, and the reportage): "Oro a Forcella" ("The Gold of the Via Forcella"), "La città involontaria" ("A City in Spite of Itself"), and "Il silenzio della ragione" ("The Silence of Reason").[3] Oddly, this hybridization of different genres continues to be considered scandalous (even in the postmodern era) by Ortese's detractors, who invoke standards of purity and factuality that Ortese is accused of having transgressed. Alternately, Ortese's "monstrous" hybridity in *Il mare non bagna Napoli* is condoned by those who see her book as just another work of fiction, mere literary invention that has little to do with documentary "reality."[4] Ortese's book may thus be included in the list of her literary monsters, strange and "marvellous" creations that have become in turn the object of wonder and bewilderment, admiration and reprobation. Yet, as Ortese herself insisted in 1994, "Erano molto veri il dolore e il male di Napoli, uscita in pezzi dalla guerra" ("They were all too real, the pain and suffering of Naples, which emerged from the war a broken city").[5] Together, the book's chapters provide both a sympathetic documentation of the dark and disintegrating reality of post-war Naples and something like a vast, novelistic fresco of the city that embraces all its social classes, from the poorest and most marginal to the petty bourgeois and middle class, the "nobility," the clergy, and the intellectuals. The persistence of inhuman conditions of life, of everyday practices of abuse and exploitation, and, indeed, the lingering (in post-Reconstruction, economic-miracle Italy) of a colonialist and paternalistic attitude towards the populace of Naples are forcefully exposed by Ortese.

Il mare non bagna Napoli was published in Einaudi's distinguished series "I Gettoni," whose editor in chief was the writer Elio Vittorini. Italo Calvino, who at the time worked for Einaudi, after reading the second chapter ("Interno familiare") and seeing a plan for the fifth ("Il silenzio della ragione") warmly recommended that Vittorini publish the book; both were actively involved as editors in finalizing the order of the chapters.[6] Calvino especially encouraged Ortese to opt for "Il mare non bagna Napoli" (among various options she and Vittorini proposed) as the definitive title. In his view, this paradoxical, yet memorable and pithy phrase from the chapter "Oro a Forcella"[7] encapsulated the sad reality of the port city, where the once-flourishing harbour was now in deep economic crisis. Urban decay was such that the proverbial, beneficial presence of the Mediterranean could virtually no longer be felt. The city, entirely cut off from the sea, seemed to be suffocating.[8] The neo-monarchist (and previously fascist) millionaire shipping magnate Achille Lauro was mayor, undisputed populist ruler, and "boss" of Naples. He owned the Naples soccer team and the influential newspaper *Roma*. He ruthlessly manipulated the populace through demagogic "gifts" and organized highly popular folk festivals promoting the solar myth of Naples even while contributing to the further ruin of the once-thriving city port, which was turned largely into a NATO and US Navy base, and a venue for emigration.[9]

Ortese assembled *Il mare non bagna Napoli* at the very moment when the consequences of Lauro's irrational and predatory leadership and the lack of any real opposition to it (from either inside or outside Naples) were becoming clear; the city's situation, painstakingly documented in the book through its impact on people's daily lives, seemed uglier and sadder than ever.[10] Yet Calvino, although his own taste and sensibility were surely rather different from Ortese's, told her that she should "feel happy" because she had written "un libro bellissimo" ("a very beautiful book").[11] Ortese's volume grew out of an extended period of intense research undertaken, as Ortese herself explained, in order to "see the reality of Naples" in the post-war era "senza paraocchi" ("without blinders").[12] But the eye and the gaze for Ortese are not so much a means to gather images of the real, as ways of grasping and establishing relationships.[13] In recent years, critics have begun to see the book as a masterpiece, and it is now widely considered one of Ortese's most original achievements as well as an outstanding – albeit idiosyncratic – example of the Neapolitan narrative tradition, and of the Italian neorealist season.[14] Although it earned one of the coveted Viareggio awards for narrative in 1953, the book was initially very controversial. According to a polemical review letter by the Neapolitan journalist Nino Sansone published in the Communist journal *Rinascita* (then directed by its founder, Palmiro Togliatti), the book was far from wonderful. Rather, it was malicious because it gave a negative, degraded image of Naples and its inhabitants. It was unworthy of a leftist publishing house like Einaudi, especially the Gettoni series. Publishing it was, in Sansone's words, "un atto di miopia" ("an act of nearsightedness").[15] In the pages that follow, I will discuss briefly the book's role in relation to the Neapolitan narrative tradition, give a sense of its various parts (and how they are assembled), and explain its ambivalent reception. I will subsequently focus on "Un paio di occhiali" and on the theme or image of nearsightedness: not the purported publishing nearsightedness of Elio Vittorini and Italo Calvino, but the nearsightedness of Eugenia, the young girl who is the protagonist of "Un paio di occhiali," as a metaphoric key to Ortese's tragic poetics.

As a truthful representation of the inhuman conditions of life that persisted in early 1950s Naples despite the post-war reconstruction efforts, Ortese's *Il mare non bagna Napoli* may be associated with the diverse and abundant (and still-thriving) production of Neapolitan prose writers. Their works, up to and including Roberto Saviano's (perhaps equally controversial) *Gomorra* (2006), focus on Naples, seeking not only to portray its dismal reality but attempting at the same time to grasp the seemingly perennial, intractably tragic condition that afflicts the city (despite the solar myths of *napoletanità* or *Neapolitanness*).[16] Even though she was born in Rome, Ortese adopted Naples as one of her "native cities" from

1928, when she settled there with her family in an old run-down neighbourhood near the harbour, where she continued to live off and on until the time of *Il mare non bagna Napoli.* The book, however, became in many ways her sad farewell to the city.[17] In 1945–46, Ortese and her family experienced first-hand the poverty, hunger, and desperation of the city devastated by war. They lived for a time with refugees in a dilapidated shelter similar to those described in the penultimate chapter of the book. Between 1950 and 1952 (the very years in which she was working on the book), both her parents died. Ortese had by then lost all but one of her siblings: two of her brothers were sailors who died at sea in faraway places; two others were lost to emigration to America and Australia. Of the decimated family, only one sister remained, the inseparable Maria who followed Ortese in her move north where, in a perennially restless existence from the mid-1950s to the mid-1970s, she gravitated towards her two other "native cities," Rome and Milan. Even when transfigured into the imaginary Toledo of *Il porto di Toledo* (*The Port of Toledo,* 1975) and into the fantastic city of *Il cardillo addolorato* (*The Lament of the Linnet,* 1993), Naples remained a kind of central city of the soul for Ortese. While Ortese's contribution to the literature of Naples is unquestionable, her literary vision is that of someone who is at once inside and outside the city and its people. It thus tends to transcend the specificity of Naples (even while remaining largely faithful to it). Through the devices of poetry and tragedy, Ortese is able to transform il vicolo della Cupa (in Chiaia), Monte di Dio, San Biagio dei Librai, and I Granili, and their inhabitants, into the scene of a drama that encapsulates some of the most painful paradoxes of what it means to be alive in the modern world of the mid-twentieth century.

The book connects and weaves together the life of the streets and the life of the home, interiors and exteriors, private and public, in a cinematic way worthy of masterpieces of cinematic and narrative realism such as Vittorio De Sica's *Ladri di biciclette,* Francesco Rosi's *Le mani sulla città,* Balzac's *Le Pére Goriot,* and Matilde Serao's *Il romanzo della fanciulla.* Serao's book in particular, which is structured as a series of interconnected short stories with a strong autobiographical element, is one of Ortese's models for *Il mare non bagna Napoli.* Yet Ortese's technique is paradoxically uncanny, in the double sense of the Freudian *Unheimlich,* which turns the most familiar and reassuring places and spaces into the most disquieting and deadly (and yet as a consequence also profoundly revelatory), and in the sense of sheer "spaesamento" – the effect of disorientation, defamiliarization, and estrangement that Ortese herself attributes both to Naples as a city and, retrospectively in the 1994 foreword to her own book. In formal terms, *Il mare non bagna Napoli* is also "estranging" in the Brechtian sense of *Verfremdungseffekt*; by using the devices of the reportage and the critical essay in conjunction with fictional, dramatic, and realist narrative, Ortese encourages the reader to reflect critically on the stories she tells rather than merely be caught up in them emotionally.[18] However, the emotional dimension is also very important to her, and she leads the reader to empathize with her characters like she does. One of the most painful consequences of the book's perturbing effect on its Neapolitan readers was unfortunately that of making her feel unwelcome in a city where she once was – however uneasily – at home.[19]

In "Interno familiare," the heart-warming interior of a Neapolitan home, familiar from a long literary, cinematic, and theatrical tradition, turns into its uncanny, estranging opposite. Ortese does not invent this strategy; rather, she brilliantly refashions in her own way an ironic mode whose antecedents in Neapolitan literary culture include Serao (at her best) and Eduardo De Filippo. "Interno familiare" portrays the tragic disillusionment of a middle-aged unmarried woman in a petty-bourgeois environment, a home in the Neapolitan neighbourhood of Monte di Dio. Anastasia Finizio, the daughter of a hairstylist, works hard, owns a successful clothing store, and enjoys dressing elegantly. Since her father's death she has lived what she thinks of as "una vita da uomo" (MN 35, "a man's life") in terms of work, responsibility, and supporting her entire family, composed of her mother and her older spinster aunt, a pampered younger sister, and two ineffectual, parasitic brothers. The sister and one of her brothers, who is sickly and only precariously employed, are both engaged to be married, but along with their spouses they plan to go on living under the same roof with the rest of the family, relying on Anastasia's financial protection. To accommodate the new brother-in-law (Giovannino – a mere sales clerk), Anastasia will give up her place in the room she shares with her sister and move into the master bedroom, with their mother. The mother is a petty woman who resents her daughter's difference from her, her "masculine" independence, and lack of subservience, losing no opportunity to humiliate her and make her suffer by reminding her that she is still single. Yet, hypocritically, the possibility that Anastasia may one day marry is dreadful to the mother, for she thinks it would irreparably undermine the family's financial stability and her own position. She untiringly drives home to her daughter the notion that she is ugly and undeserving of a man's love

(MN 48). Her gaze is both envious and entrapping. Ortese thus subverts the wisdom of the Neapolitan proverb according to which "Ogni scarrafone è bello a mamma soja" ("Even an ugly child is beautiful to his mother"). Yet, as we shall see, Ortese does not embrace the notion that the human gaze, in its ocular relationships, is fundamentally envious, jealous, vindictive, and entrapping.[20] Anastasia, whose hidden weakness is seeing herself through her mother's eyes, seems to accept her verdict along with the idea that "una vera donna serve un uomo" (MN 41; "a real woman waits upon her man," BN 59). She is thus a prisoner on the one hand of the negative self-image that transforms her into a "non-woman," and on the other hand of her duty as a breadwinner and moneymaker for the family. Ortese implies that the chronic obsession with material things, financial matters, and money poisons human relations among the middle classes and dehumanizes even the natural bond between mother and daughter. A similar vision informs Balzac's masterpiece, *Le Pére Goriot*, in which the relationship between the father and his three daughters is tainted by gold and the worship of wealth. Yet the relationship between the two Neapolitan women in Ortese's story is also specific to the predicament of women in petty-bourgeois families in Italy after the Second World War and well into the 1950s, when a new sterile materialism was grafted onto the misogynous legacy of fascist and Catholic images of woman's femininity, defined as naturally subservient and sacrificial. The mother is ultimately responsible for crushing Anastasia's love dream and for keeping her subservient and enslaved to the family as she thinks she ought to be, in order to preserve the mother's own sense of identity and self-image.

"Interno familiare" is tightly and dramatically structured. It takes place in less than twenty-four hours on Christmas day within the walls of the Finizio apartment, with Murolo's folksy, proverbially sentimental Neapolitan songs as a musical background. This setting is mercilessly described (with an exact style worthy of Flaubert) in all its banal petty-bourgeois squalor, kitschy furnishings, and revolting bric-a-brac. At the centre of the house, an elaborate, horrid *presepio* made by one of the brothers with cork and cardboard and innumerable figurines in traditional little Neapolitan "scenes," stands as an emblem of the vacuous sentimentality and superficial religiosity of this representative Neapolitan petty-bourgeois family (and, implicitly, of Naples itself). Ortese's unsympathetic rendering of this kind of Neapolitan religiosity (usually looked upon with condescending indulgence even by non-believers), and her pointed critique of the Catholic Church and the clergy (evident especially in the third chapter, "Oro a Forcella"), may have contributed to fostering the enduring resentment against her by those who, many years later, still considered her book a cruel betrayal.[21] There is an uncanny analogy between Anastasia and the plaster infant Jesus, described as "larger than his parents" and "like a man," yet also as expressionless and dead-like, "passive and congealed" – or a mere lifeless simulacrum (BN 74). Anastasia too is like a man and has a larger role than her parents, for it is her work that redeems and saves the family; at the same time, however, she is lifeless and mechanical, just like the plaster Jesus. Yet the dream to marry the man she once loved, who has now returned to Naples after a long absence, suddenly resurfaces on Christmas morning and interrupts Anastasia's dull routine, moving her profoundly, humanizing her and making her forget her dismal destiny for a few hours. In a stupefied reverie, she hopes for a kind of resurrection, or redemption. It is the ability to feel moved by love for another human being (rather than heeding the dubious ideal of a subservient "femininity") that humanizes Anastasia. By the end of the Christmas day, that glimmer of life and hope is all but extinguished as Anastasia obediently answers her mother's call back to the reality of her "duty." However, the kernel of hope that Ortese places at the centre of this story, and indeed of all the stories of *Il mare non bagna Napoli*, is a sparkle of light that, however illusory, dazzles the reader and persists in her memory long after the book is closed.

In "Interno familiare," Ortese entirely subverts the traditional myth of the "warm," affectionate Neapolitan family and of the earthy, nurturing, and loving or wise mother.[22] Not only does this particular mother not love her oldest daughter: she has no liking or love for her ("non aveva nessuna simpatia per Anastasia," MN 54).[23] Surely this must be the story (and not "Un paio di occhiali") that was inspired by Matilde Serao's powerful "O Giovannino o la morte!" (the name Giovannino points clearly to the connection between the two tales), where there is a similar but even more blatant subversion of the maternal myth and a biting critique of the petty-bourgeois obsession with money. Its emblem for Serao is the stepmother's practice of usury and her theft of the daughter's fiancé, whom she corrupts and turns into another usurer. Usury contaminates the family and leads to the daughter's suicide.[24] A liberating suicide, interpreted by Ortese as an act of real protest of which only some working-class people are still capable, is committed by a young maid later in "Il silenzio della ragione." Yet the shocking spectacle of her corpse on the pavement leaves a journalist standing next to the narrator entirely cold and indifferent (MN 152–56). In "Interno familiare," Anastasia's youngest brother insinuates that Anastasia too is cold and indifferent, and has no feelings about anything except for money. Serao's theme of usury and the cold deadliness of money also appears, amplified and expanded, in the story "Oro a Forcella."

Anastasia lives to support her family yet she is portrayed as joyless and uncannily dead-like, dazed and inert, like an automaton or a sleepwalker. This particular aspect of her character recalls the figure of Olympia, the automaton in the story that inspired Freud's essay on the uncanny: "The Sandman" by E.T.A. Hoffmann, an author Ortese also admired. "The Sandman" is clearly another source for "Interno familiare." Hoffmann's protagonist, Nathanael, suffers from a paralysing childhood trauma related to his fear of being blinded by the evil Sandman; incapable of love, he becomes fixated on Olympia, ironically the daughter of a man – Coppelieus, a peddler of spectacles, lenses, and telescopes – who may be the very same who was trying to take away his power to see. Freud interprets this man as symbolizing Nathanael's own Oedipal, castrating father.[25] Anastasia, like Olympia, cannot become the object of authentic love because she is not human but, instead, mechanical. But Anastasia's predicament is doubly complex and ironic: she is, like Nathanael, incapable of loving because she cannot see; she cannot recognize who among those closest to her in her own home is stifling her and blinding her. The text's final description of Anastasia looking at and fetishistically caressing her elegant blue coat hanging in the wardrobe "come una persona abbandonata" (MN 61; "like someone abandoned," BN 81) suggests that material things and the need to keep making money like a man in order to satisfy her mother (and the rest of her parasitical family) have in fact taken a toll on Anastasia's ability to feel love and to be loved and thus, in Ortese's eyes, to see and live authentically. In contrast to Serao's story, where the daughter finally sees the truth about her stepmother and finds release in death, here, once Anastasia's reverie and short-lived fantasy of reconnecting with her youthful lover have dissipated, there is no further breakthrough, no revelation. Similarly, Hoffmann's Nathanael recovers neither his humanity nor his lucidity. Overtaken by a blinding vertigo, he dies insane. It is important to note, however, that for Ortese, as for the poet Giacomo Leopardi (one of her principal literary inspirations), dreams, fantasies, and reveries – in this case Anastasia's reverie – are not merely symptoms or deceptive visible signs of a deeper truth to be uncovered; they are, however illusory and obscurely or dimly lit, the truth itself, or at least the only truth that can provide us with the warm joy of self-recognition. And, as we shall see, Ortese's understanding of blindness or impaired vision and their symbolic implications finally differ substantially from Freud's.

The themes of vision – childhood vision and the maternal gaze– and the dehumanizing effect of money and greed in a capitalist world are taken up again and woven into the next story. "Oro a Forcella" plunges us into one of the most crowded and poorest sections of Naples, Via San Biagio dei Librai and Via Forcella. Here what is defamiliarized is not a family home, but the street itself, stripped of its usual picturesque aura: "non vedevo le lenzuola di cui è piena la tradizione napoletana" (MN 66; "I saw no sheets hung up to dry, according to the time-honoured Neapolitan tradition," BN 86). This "picturesque" tradition was alive and well when *Il mare non bagna Napoli* was published in 1953. De Sica's comedy *L'oro di Napoli* (*The Gold of Naples*) was made that same year, based on Giuseppe Marotta's 1947 bestselling collection by the same title, and the operetta-like musical directed by Ettore Giannini, *Carosello Napoletano*, came out in 1954.[26] In Marotta and in De Sica, "gold" stands as a nostalgic metaphor for the proverbial treasure trove of compassionate and comic humanity that lies at the heart of the Neapolitan people's way of life, a common resilience, resourcefulness, and theatricality that invariably help Neapolitans to survive poverty as well as tragic historical and natural events and to retain their warm humanness. Even Roberto Rossellini's *Paisà* (1946), which in its second episode revealed the ruins of war-torn Naples to the world through the encounter of a Neapolitan street urchin with an African American GI, is not immune from stereotypes.[27] Ortese reverses this stereotyped metaphoric meaning of Neapolitan gold almost entirely, reverting instead to Balzac's dark depiction of gold and silver in *Le Pére Goriot* as metaphors for the estrangement and dehumanization of family affections and relations through greed and commodification. Ortese's narrator's gaze in traversing the crowded streets is entirely unlike either De Sica's or Giannini's celebratory, populist, and folkloric camera eye. Her attitude also differs remarkably from that of the dandified flâneur and nonchalant aesthete typical of decadent Romanticism and male modernism, from Baudelaire to Poe, d'Annunzio, and T.S. Eliot. Nor does the city street become in Ortese a vehicle for sensual awakening and feminine fantasy, as it does in Rossellini's 1954 film *Viaggio in Italia*, which records the uncanny flâneuse experiences in Naples of an English woman, Katherine (Ingrid Bergman).[28] Instead, Ortese's account is that of a sympathetic observer and narrator "plagued by a burning sense of compassion" and "the passionate intensity of a sorrowful participant in grief."[29] The traditional modernist representation of the crowd as "other," animalistic, monstrous, and threatening that emerges on the first page ("si gonfiava, come una serpe, tanta folla" ["the swelling throng writhed like a snake"]) is interrupted by an exchange with an old woman, who, in answer to the narrator's question, clarifies that what looks so strange and nightmarish to her is just normal everyday life. The narrator realizes that the hallucinatory spectacle of the crowd seen confusedly from afar as an amorphous, monstrous, and revolting mass will give way, once she moves up close, to recognizable human figures and faces, much as in the observation of a tapestry or fresco. Nonetheless, the spectacle is dreadful and heart-rending, comparable in fact to the vestibule of hell in Dante's *Inferno* (3.55–57) and in *The Waste Land*, when in the "Unreal City" section the poet exclaims: "I had not thought death had undone so many."

> Non avevo visto ancora tante anime insieme, camminare o stare ferme, scontrarsi e sfuggirsi, salutarsi dalle finestre e chiamarsi dalle botteghe, insinuare il prezzo di una merce o gridare una preghiera, con la stessa voce dolce, spezzata, cantante, ma più sul filo del lamento che della decantata allegria napoletana. Veramente era cosa che meravigliava, e oscurava tutti i vostri pensieri. (MN 65)
>
> (I had never seen so many persons together, walking or standing still, bumping or avoiding one another, calling out from windows and shop doors, hinting at the price of something to be sold or shouting a prayer, all in a broken, singsong voice which seemed more a lament than an expression of the celebrated Neapolitan joy of living. This tone of voice was so surprising as to overshadow all other impressions. [BN 86])

A similarly hellish effect will reappear, amplified, in "La città involontaria." Here, as also in "Un paio di occhiali" (as we shall see), the sound of human voices carries particular significance and is more intimately revealing than visual perception. The use of the word "meravigliava" is typical of Ortese's poetic vocabulary, and more than merely "surprising" it indicates, in accordance to the Neapolitan meaning of the word (which first appears in "Un paio di occhiali"), something that is real, yet so powerfully astonishing and stunning that it threatens to obscure the mind and interfere with one's sanity.[30] In the midst of unspeakable squalor and refuse, the porous street offers an extraordinary exhibition of human misery exposed for everyone to see: grotesquely deformed beggars, dwarfs, stray dogs, and swarms of emaciated, semi-naked children with their heads shaved.[31] In uncanny contrast, San Biagio dei Librai is lined with gold shops where, through semi-opaque windows, one can observe, endlessly repeated, the same surreal scene of poor women with tears in their eyes pawning or selling their tiny, beloved gold objects to indifferent bespectacled dealers who, with scales in their hands, look coldly at their customers' possessions. The sound of church bells is the incongruous musical background to this scene, and delicate images of the Virgin Mary leaning sweetly over the baby Jesus in his gilded cradle and looking lovingly at him may be seen in all the gold dealers' shops. This loving maternal gaze for Ortese is the emblem of another kind of vision; a vision that is free from the burdens of isolation, deception, envy, reification, and loss that characterize capitalist exploitation. Such burdens weigh heavily on the profoundly negative Western way of understanding the gaze's relationship to human knowledge (and hence the desiring subject) as essentially alienated.[32] Ortese takes the opportunity to comment bitterly on the degradation of a culture such as the Neapolitan one that had once made a cult not of gold, but of family affections. Merciless exploitation, poverty, and greed have irreparably estranged a city where mothers no longer have feelings for their offspring, who are left to their own resources in the streets, while the population grows out of control in what Ortese calls the "fire of sex," or dehumanized copulation. Naples in the post-war era, under Achille Lauro's rule as mayor, had the highest infant and child mortality in Italy. Ortese minces no words here in denouncing both the city government's ineffectualness and the Catholic Church's misguided pride and false promises of redemption for the souls of those innumerable unloved children thrown indifferently into a world of misery and suffering due to the lack (and indeed, the prohibition) of birth control.

In the closing scene of the story, the action moves to the nearby enormous building, once a hospice for the poor, now the *Monte dei Pegni*, the great official pawnshop belonging to the Bank of Naples (an institution that was controlled by the Catholic Church and the Christian Democrats). In the cold bureaucratic hall at the top of the majestic staircase that she climbs along with innumerable women who are lined up holding their miserable parcels in their hands, Ortese's narrator witnesses the commotion caused first by the announcement that there has been an official order by the bank to lower the loans to the minimum and then by the dramatic appearance of a desperate mother with her two young children who pushes her way in shortly before closing time. She must pawn her gold chain in order to send money with her husband to take care of a son who lies in a sickbed in faraway Turin. The crowd is moved by this exhibition of motherly love and immediately makes room for her in a touching display of communal and Christian solidarity and selfless compassion, then mumbles in protest at the stinginess of the loan. Yet the narrator makes us wonder if what she sees is real or not. This might be a Neapolitan *sceneggiata* or farce, for the children have cynical little smiles on their faces, and a guard insinuates that this woman, who rushes away clutching her money, has nobody in Turin, and no husband, though she puts on this act regularly at the pawnshop. For Ortese, women and mothers as such do not have privileged access to a more authentic vision. Their gaze may be as caught up in the cold mechanism of deception, envy, reification, and loss as men's. But the probable mendacity of this mother, who exploits her children as props, and the theatrical situation, do not undermine the narrator's admiration for the crowd's ability to feel compassion, however misguided in this case. That this compassion still can exist in a place like modern Naples (and indeed in the modern world that has seen the Second World War, the Nazi concentration camps and the destruction of Hiroshima and Nagasaki, and the displacement of millions of refugees) is a kind of miracle. The poetic symbol of this miracle and kernel of hope is a brown butterfly with tiny specks of gold on its wings that inexplicably appears on the last page, seemingly careless and happy, having made its way fluttering up the stairs, inside the cold and cavernous hall, and causing the crowd to be distracted and awed for a brief, magical moment. Those tiny specks, Ortese seems to suggest, are the only trace of the gold left in Naples from the old treasure trove. This butterfly is a progenitor of a lineage of magical animals, symbols of hope, that will increasingly come to inhabit the world of Ortese's fiction (the iguana, the goldfinch of *Il cardillo addolorato*, and the puma of her last novel, *Alonso e i visionari*).

Ortese's narrator in *Il mare non bagna Napoli* is able to observe from the outside and yet also feel from the inside how "una miseria senza più forma, silenziosa come un ragno, disfaceva e rinnovava a modo suo quei miseri tessuti, invischiando sempre di più gli strati minimi della plebe, che qui è regina" (MN 67, "Shapeless poverty, working as silently as a spider, had destroyed this wretched human fabric and then rewoven it in a pattern of its own, entangling the lowest of the lower classes, which in this region holds undisputed sway," BN 87). Yet, unlike fellow writers Domenico Rea and Pier Paolo Pasolini, Ortese does not idealize Naples' "plebeian soul" as more authentic.[33] Ortese's narrator has neither the neutral, purportedly objective point of view of the traditional reporter (and this was in fact a flaw in the book, according to Vittorini), nor, despite her allusions to Dante and Eliot, does she have the detached, superiorly comprehending attitude of the believer, or (as we have seen) the aesthetic detachment and nihilism of the modernist flâneur. She also lacks, in her descriptions of Naples' decay, the morbid and nihilistic complacency of Curzio Malaparte, author of the graphic *La pelle* (1949) (though his work also caused among Neapolitan intellectuals a negative, resentful reaction). Ortese's narrator allows herself to become touched, even contaminated by what she calls the body of "una razza svuotata di ogni logica e raziocinio" where "l'uomo era adesso ombra, debolezza e nevrastenia, rassegnata paura e impudente allegrezza" (MN 67; "a race devoid of logic and reason [...] man was reduced to a shadow, a bundle of weakness and neurasthenia, alternately a prey to resigned fear and uninhibited gayety," BN 87). For this "weakness" of her narrator, which has been criticized by some as an excessive sensitivity,[34] Ortese paid a high price, first of all that of being mistaken for a neurotic, even a hysteric. Even her retrospective explanation in the 1994 "Foreword" to *Il mare non bagna Napoli* about the real origins of her so-called neurosis (the same condition indeed that she found afflicting the Neapolitan *plebe*) has been consistently mistaken for an apologetic acknowledgment of a real mental illness, or psychic condition, while it was instead a metaphor for a philosophical, lucid *prîse de position*:

> Quella "nevrosi" era la mia. E da dove avesse origine, sarebbe troppo lungo e impossibile dire; ma poiché una origine, seppure confusa, è giusto indicarla, indicherò la più incredibile e meno atta all'indulgenza dei "politici" (che furono, direi, i miei soli critici e contestatori): quella origine, e perfino ascendendenza della mia nevrosi, aveva solo un nome: metafisica. Da molto, da moltissimo tempo, io detestavo con tutte le mie forze, senza quasi saperlo, la cosidetta *realtà*: il meccanismo delle cose che sorgono nel tempo, e dal tempo sono distrutte. Questa realtà era per me incomprensibile e allucinante [...] Aggiungo che l'esperienza personale della Guerra (terrore dovunque e fuga per quattro anni) aveva portato al colmo la mia irritazione contro il reale; e lo spaesamento di cui soffrivo era ormai così vero, e anche poco dicibile – perché senza riscontro nell'esperienza comune – da aver bisogno di una straordinaria occasione per manifestarsi. Questa occasione fu il mio incontro con la Napoli uscita dalla guerra. Rivederla e compiangerla

> non bastava. Qualcuno aveva scritto che questa Napoli rifletteva una lacera condizione universale. Ero d'accordo, ma non sull'accettazione (implicita) di questo male. (MN 10)
>
> [That "neurosis" was mine. And it would take too long, in fact it would be impossible, to pinpoint its origin. But since it is fair to point to an origin, even if confused, I will pick the most incredible, the least forgivable by "the politically minded" (for they, I would say, were my only critics and objectors). That origin, and are even ancestry of my neurosis, had a name: metaphysics. For a long, very long time, I had been hating, with all my strength, almost unwittingly, the so-called reality: the mechanism of things that arise in time, and are destroyed by time. This reality was for me incomprehensible and are hallucinatory [...] I must add that my personal experience of the War (pervasive fear and four years on the run) exacerbated my intolerance for the real; and the disorientation that plagued me had become so complete, and also so unspeakable – for it was beyond any common experience – that it needed an extraordinary occasion to manifest itself. That occasion was my encounter with Naples just after the war. To see Naples once again and feel pity for it was not enough. Someone had written that this Naples expressed a universal human condition of painful laceration. I agreed, but disagreed with the (implicit) acceptance of this condition.]

The "metaphysical" origin of Ortese's "neurotic" writing, then, is her desire to look and think beyond the seemingly unobjectable evidence of the universal horror of human existence epitomized by Naples.

Nowhere is Ortese's philosophical, deliberate neurosis, chosen as an act of opposition to the "modern condition" revealed by the war, clearer than in the second chapter of *Il mare non bagna Napoli.* "La città involontaria" is a shocked and shocking, profoundly sympathetic account and denunciation of the horrors of daily life in the ruined Granili, an enormous Neapolitan tenement where a legion of poor squatters occupies the abysmal lower floors. Ironically, this building was originally a grandiose eighteenth-century masterpiece of Enlightenment rationalism by the great architect Ferdinando Fuga. Situated by the sea in Portici, at the foot of Vesuvius, it was meant to function as both an immense arsenal for the storage of weapons and as a warehouse for wheat, ropes, and other merchandise essential to the defence, life, and well-being of the city of Naples. However, the huge building later became a prison, and later yet was turned into military barracks. It was heavily bombed by the Allies in 1943. Of this porous, dystopian historical palimpsest, bearing the visible traces of Enlightenment reason's ruins, today only a single long wall is left standing by the harbour along the Via Regia di Portici. "La città involontaria" evokes Ortese's journey as a reporter through the hallucinatory, infernal reality of I Granili, dismantling even further the proverbial idyllic image of Naples as the city of song, of the sun and the sea. Surreal, often grotesque notations make Ortese's Granili a visionary mid-twentieth century equivalent of Dante's Inferno crossed with T.S. Eliot's waste land, and an anticipation of Calvino's Cottolengo in *La giornata di uno scrutatore* (*The Watcher*, a short novel written between 1953 and 1963). Yet this is a text that even in its most horrific evocations (and with its utter lack of either stereotypical "local colour" or of the populist moralizing that is found in some neorealist and even later Neapolitan prose) is able to create not so much "beauty" but a kind of compelling poetic effect which both stuns and moves the reader. This is surely the beauty Calvino was alluding to in his letter when he called *Il mare non bagna Napoli* "un libro bellissimo" ("a beautiful book"). As observed by theorists such as Theodor Adorno and Ernst Bloch, poetry, including the poetry of prose writing, has in its own aesthetic form the uncanny power to denounce and undermine the unbearable negativity of the real: of subverting this negativity by pointing in the direction of hope and of another, more authentic possible reality.[35] In fact, Ortese's 1994 "Foreword" asserts: "Mi domando se il *Mare* è stato davvero un libro 'contro' Napoli, e dove ho sbagliato, se ho sbagliato, nello scriverlo, e in che modo, oggi, andrebbe letto. La prima considerazione che mi si presenta è sulla scrittura del libro. Pochi riescono a comprendere come nella *scrittura* si trovi la sola chiave di lettura di un testo, e la traccia di una sua eventuale verità" [MN 9; "I ask myself whether the *Bay* was really a book 'against' Naples, and where was my mistake (if any) in writing it, and how one should read it today. My first consideration is the writing itself. Only a few people realize that one must look at how a text is written in order to find its real meaning, and the trace of its possible truth"]. The truth that Ortese ultimately discloses through her poetic writing is the specular opposite of the horrific Neapolitan real. This does not mean that for Ortese writing merely has a consolatory or sublimating function. Through writing, Ortese denounces the real as unacceptable so that we may hope and work towards a different, more humane life. One of the key predecessor texts for Ortese's novel in this regard is certainly "La ginestra" ("The Broom") by Leopardi. The poet's grave, as Ortese reminds us in "Il silenzio della ragione," is in Naples' Mergellina. It was his encounter with Naples at the end of his life that triggered the inspiration for his testamentary poem of unprecedented epic and tragic dimensions. In "La ginestra," Leopardi builds on his own rigorous and radical philosophical pessimism and continues his merciless indictment of the presumptuous idealism of Enlightenment rationality, yet he comes to see his own nihilism as sterile and insufficient. He embraces instead a new positive view of humanity itself as a community, and of the life-giving force and heroic value of merciful solidarity, of generous dreams and compassionate efforts. Of this life-giving force and heroic value, art (and poetry in particular) is the privileged vehicle and principal source.

Ortese's description of the Granili complex, as the narrator first approaches it, recalls the gloomy, devastated landscape of Vesuvius in "La ginestra" and the equivocal, deformed remnants of the ghostly city of Pompei that Leopardi evokes as an emblem of the perennial subjection of humanity to natural and historical catastrophes. The image of the dark, cave-like dwellings also amplifies the theme of darkness that is first introduced in "Un paio di occhiali," as does the character of the near-blind child, Luigino, whose tragic figure recalls Eugenia, the protagonist of the first story. The question of the gaze, also introduced in the first story and engaged throughout the volume, is here elaborated further and reflected on explicitly as the author-narrator-reporter highlights the paradox of the compulsion to look and see, and at the same time the revulsion and horror caused by doing so. "Guardavo [ma] ritraevo continuamente gli occhi. Non sapevo, d'altra parte, dove posarli" (MN 80; "I looked [but] but had to keep averting my eyes, without knowing where to direct them," BN 100). Here as in the other stories, Ortese inserts a line of light, a kernel of hope that discloses the prospect of a different world beyond the horror of the present one. Antonia Lo Savio, a grotesquely disfigured and deformed woman with incongruously beautiful long hair who works in the tenement's clinic and whom we see in the merciful act of giving bread with mother-like kindness to the starving orphan, Luigino, acts as the narrator's guide, her uncanny Virgil and Beatrice in this dark Inferno. Humble, yet filled with courage, dignity, and kindness, she is one of Ortese's beneficial "monsters" or wonders: "Alla luce di poche lampade, la vedevo meglio: regina nella casa dei morti, schiacciata nella figura, rigonfia, orrenda, parto, a sua volta, di creature profondamente tarate, rimaneva però in lei qualcosa di regale [...] Dietro quella deplorevole fronte esistevano delle speranze" (MN 80; "In the dim light of the corridor I could see her better, this queen of the house of the dead, with her horrendous body, dwarfish and swollen. She must have been the offspring of hideously diseased parents, and yet there was something regal in her [...] Yes, beneath that lamentable forehead there were hopes and dreams," BN 100). Not unlike Calvino's Cottolengo in *The Watcher*, I Granili is a place that, despite or perhaps in light of its horror and the spectacle of human abjection, with the seeming collapse of any order or reason, enables the reader to reflect on the question of what is "human," and what ethical and biopolitical perspectives may emerge from the nightmarish experiences of the twentieth century. In addition to its documentary and literary qualities and its utopian / dystopian force, the book had an impact that was immediately real.[36] The piece on I Granili in particular caught the attention of, among others, the president of the Italian Republic, Luigi Einaudi, who helped Ortese to obtain some much-needed financial support that enabled her to put together the book. President Einaudi was instrumental, as well, in dismantling the tenement.[37] Few works of literature have left a comparably powerful trace and had a comparable real, positive effect on the city.

Ironically, *Il mare non bagna Napoli* was most controversial especially among those very same writers and intellectuals in Naples gravitating around the journal *Sud* (*South*) to whom Ortese was very close, and who had originally inspired her to undertake the project. The journal founded by Pasquale Prunas and published over two years (1945–47) was typical of the idealism and enthusiasm of enlightened liberal and left-wing "committed" intellectuals in the immediate post-war period and during the Reconstruction, an idealism and enthusiasm that Ortese in her own way shared. The book's extended last chapter, "Il silenzio della ragione," based on conversations and interviews conducted by Ortese in 1952 with, among others, Luigi Compagnone, Domenico Rea, and Pasquale Prunas, turned into a sorrowful indictment of what Ortese saw effectively as the group's "selling out": the ways it had dissolved and abandoned its original generous cultural project and reformist zeal in exchange for the shallow satisfactions of safe jobs for the State Radio and Television (RAI), new homes and material goods, literary prestige and a more secure bourgeois life, self-absorbed and far removed from the painful reality of the city and its poor. The chapter's title alludes to the Italian phrase traditionally used to translate the title of Goya's famous 1797 etching, "El sueño de la razón produce monstruos" ("Il sonno della ragione genera mostri" [The Sleep of Reason Produces Monsters]) and is thus one of several allusions to painting in the book.[38] It is significant that Ortese should have changed "sonno" or "sogno" into "silenzio": sleep and dream always have positive connotations for her and, as for Dante, they are conduits to a more truthful vision. What the last chapter ultimately deprecates, however, is not the inevitable loss of youthful ideals that she finds among these particular "intellectuals," but rather their callous and cowardly indifference. She regrets their inability, as bourgeois men, to feel and express outrage and pity and to become aware of their increasing blindness to the reality of the human condition that Naples so clearly reveals to those capable of looking at it without fear: "Tutti erano indifferenti, qui, quelli che desideravano salvarsi. Commuoversi, era come addormentarsi sulla neve" (MN 156; "Here, all those who wished only to survive were indifferent. To feel moved to compassion was like falling asleep in the snow"). In "Il silenzio della ragione," the narrator is dismayed to discover that her own sense of sorrowful pity for the Neapolitan poor is dismissed by her intellectual interlocutors as a form of feminine emotional weakness. If embraced, such "emotionality" would emasculate them, and threaten their very existence and ability to survive.

The book's release in fact triggered bitter, resentful accusations of "betrayal" by some and claims that it was defamatory, even fascist. Some of the men and women featured in the last chapter took it, to Ortese's dismay, as an attack ad hominem. Each new printing caused new protestations. Even its re-release in 1994, despite the new "Introduction" and "Afterword" by the author that reaffirmed Ortese's affection for and indebtedness to the *Sud* group (and its original idealism) while spelling out more clearly than ever her real motives for writing the book, seemed to reopen an emotional wound that had never really healed.[39] The publication prompted, once again, polemical comments by La Capria and Compagnone – an indication perhaps that the book had in fact hit the mark and continued to trouble them in a profound way. Among the *Sud* writers portrayed in "Il silenzio della ragione," only novelist Michele Prisco wrote a positive review when the book first came out. Yet Ortese had depicted him as a man isolated in his new house on Naples' aristocratic Via Crispi, busy creating abstract literary characters entirely removed from Neapolitan reality. To Compagnone's outrage upon reading the review (another betrayal!), Prisco replied: "la differenza di giudizio sul libro di Anna Maria è data dal fatto che tu hai letto solo l'ultimo capitolo, e ti sei infuriato. Io l'ho letto tutto, e in certi momenti mi sono anche commosso" ("my different judgment of Anna Maria's book is due to the fact that you have only read the last chapter, and became infuriated. I on the other hand read the whole book, and at times I really felt profoundly moved").[40] Prisco's acknowledgment of the book's tragic power to move is a tribute to Ortese's real intentions as well as to the effectiveness of her work as a literary creation. A work is indeed tragic, as Aristotle stated, only if through its poetic narration it moves the spectator to feel fear and pity. Making a reader feel these emotions through narrative involves, as Martha Nussbaum and others have since recognized, not just the production of an aesthetic and cathartic, healing experience, but the fostering, through an awakening of the narrative imagination, of an active sense of empathy and human solidarity. This may help the reader to see others not as undifferentiated and faceless, or as animalistic brutes who are doomed and whose suffering does not concern us, but as uniquely human, and deserving to share in a life of dignity and justice.[41]

Among the other early readers and reviewers who were impressed and deeply appreciative of Ortese's achievement were Eugenio Montale and the Neapolitan film director Francesco Rosi, who had been one of the original collaborators of *Sud.* The latter declared to have long pursued the dream of "fare un film su Napoli pescando nell'atmosfera meravigliosa di due racconti inseriti in quel libro stupendo che è *Il mare non bagna Napoli*" ("making a film about Naples based on the amazing atmosphere of two stories included in that wonderful book, *Il mare non bagna Napoli*").[42] One of those two stories was "Un paio di occhiali," the other was "La città involontaria." The former was turned into a film only much later, in 2001. It was a sixteen-minute short, shot not by Francesco Rosi but by the young Carlo Damasco, who presented it at the Venice Film Festival. Nevertheless, there is no doubt that Ortese's book helped shape the vision that ten years later led Rosi to create his own Neapolitan masterpiece and impassioned *J'accuse,* the film *Mani sulla città.*

* * *

Let us now examine the characters, setting, plot, and development of "Un paio di occhiali," as well as some of its subtexts and literary implications. It takes place in post-war Naples in "un quartiere di poveri" (a "poor neighbourhood"), that of Santa Maria in Portico, a little after "l'anno che il re era andato via" (MN 22; "the year that the king had gone away," BN 17). This is the only fairly explicit historical marker in the story, clearly a reference to 1946, the year of the referendum that abolished the monarchy in Italy.[43] It is also a political marker, as the poorest people of Naples were notoriously still attached to the monarchy and resented the post-war republican government. 1946 is also the year of Teresina's birth; she is the youngest child of Peppino and Rosa Quaglia, and the little sister of the ten-year-old protagonist, Eugenia. The Quaglia family, including Peppino's spinster sister Nunziata, lives on the aptly named "vicolo della Cupa" (based on Via Palasciano, the street where Ortese resided in 1946 with her family in conditions of dramatic poverty),[44] in the humid and cold basement of a building that belongs to the Marquise D'Avanzo, whose spacious apartment is instead located on a sunny upper floor. Through the marquise's intercession, the two eldest Quaglia daughters have been sent away to a convent, where they are about to "prendere il velo" ("take the veil"). Rich and avaricious, the marquise extorts a substantial rent of three thousand lire from the Quaglia family for their cave-like basement dwelling. Its dampness is the cause of Rosa's nearly paralysing rheumatoid pain, as well as of health problems for her children, including Eugenia's extreme nearsightedness. Her condition literally places a veil over her eyes, although different from the one that will soon be drawn over her two sisters in the convent. The building's doors and windows open onto the courtyard, which at its centre has a well, the family's only source of water. Ortese organizes our vision of the spectacle of her characters' world in and around this courtyard, as if it were a stage. In the different floors and corresponding social levels of the building, she portrays a microcosm, a stratified cross-section of the vast reality of Naples' infimous *vicoli* or alleyways, focusing on the life of the exploited poor and on those who are, literally and figuratively, above them. With mere pocket change as compensation, the marquise keeps Peppino Quaglia and his wife at her service. They, along with a grotesque dwarfish doorwoman, Mariuccia, who has incongruently feminine, beautiful long hair (she is in fact a prefiguration of Antonia Lo Savio), occupy the lowest social and physical levels of this world, and are in constant contact with the mud, junk, and general filth of the courtyard. Cavalier Amodio and the Greborio sisters reside on the middle level with their maidservants, one of whom, Lina Tarallo, every day as she sweeps carelessly lets the dust and refuse that she has collected fall into the courtyard. "La polvere scendeva a poco a poco, mista a vera immondizia, come una nuvola, su quella povera gente, ma nessuno ci faceva caso" (MN 22; "Dust mingled with garbage, floated down like a cloud, on those poor people, but no one paid attention," BN 17). This daily shower of dust and trash is, it seems, the least of the Quaglias' problems, and they hardly even notice it. The cloud from the sky in fact ironically evokes a benign, almost beatific image, as in a faded old fresco on the walls of a country church showing humble saints being called up to heaven. But for Ortese the abused and meek protagonists of "Un paio di occhiali," "quella povera gente" (a phrase that pointedly echoes a key predecessor text, Matilde Serao's *Il ventre di Napoli*),[45] are more than saintly; she compels us to see them, to "farci caso," to look at them directly through that cloud of dust, and to see them in a light that is essentially not so much saintly as heroic.

The story begins at sunrise and, like a classical tragedy, takes place in less than twenty-four hours. The drama that the story tells has a precise unity of action, time, and place, in accordance with the classical criteria of Aristotle's *Poetics.* In structural terms, the tale has a calculated, truly dramatic, and tragic dignity, in striking contrast to its humble lower-class protagonists: not noble heroes, but rather wretched, poor souls. This is not unusual in neorealism of course. A classic example of this technique is De Sica's film *Ladri di biciclette* (*Bicycle Thieves*). Like De Sica, Ortese is able, using a spare, unemphatic narrative style and a carefully constructed Aristotelian structure, to imbue the story of simple, apparently insignificant and common people with the moving intensity and pathos of an ancient tragedy about noble heroes and heroines. Not coincidentally, the central theme of "Un paio di occhiali" is, as in the quintessential tragedy of *Oedipus,* the inability and at the same time the need, the imperative to see: blindness in its relation to truth and knowledge. In contrast to the "plebe dall'informe faccia" ("Il silenzio della ragione"), the faceless, anonymous yet despicable and threatening mob – a kind of unspeakable monster – that many still "see" when they look at Naples (even as the rest of Italy is experiencing the optimism of the post-war Reconstruction), Ortese wishes us to look directly at these specific individuals, on whom she throws the spotlight of her powerful narrative eye, so that we may see them up close and recognize their faces and tragic humanity. The sympathetic gaze of the implicit narrator, who sees and shows us what others cannot or would not look at, is a constant focalizing presence throughout the story.

Edgar Allan Poe's story "The Spectacles" (1844) has been recognized as one of the literary sources for "Un paio di occhiali," and Poe was acknowledged as a beloved master by Ortese herself.[46] The analogy between the two tales, however, is only partial. Like some of the greatest modernist writers (Borges and Kafka are major examples), Ortese in fact has a critical, parodic relationship with many of her models. In Poe's comic and highly ironic tale, based on a case of mistaken identity in the tradition of Greek and Latin comedy, an unreliable narrator affected by severe nearsightedness tells the story of how, when he was only twenty-two, he fell in love "at first sight" with a seemingly beautiful young French woman (Eugenie) and came close to marrying her. Only when Eugenie, who mistakenly believes he is actually in love with her young and beautiful friend, makes him a gift of her opera glasses to be turned into spectacles, does he perceive through his new glasses that she is in reality a very old woman; in point of fact, she is none other than his own great-grandmother! Poe is parodying here the incestuous tale of Oedipus, and Eugenie is a comic composite of the Sphinx and the Medusa, the monster whose task it is to reveal to "man" his true identity and finally lead him to take on his proper masculine role of "watcher" and "knower." The narrator, in the end, marries the young woman. The unreliable narrator's blindness is subtly mocked throughout the story and, through a series of clues and puns, nearsightedness is equated metaphorically with effeminate narcissism, childish fantasies, intellectual impotence, and a lack of virility. Poe's divertissement, in spite of its comic tone, is thus firmly entrenched in the Western patriarchal tradition of visual power (and at the same time suspicious fear of the eye's unreliability), and in the misogynous system of sexuality rooted in the primacy of the male scopic drive.[47] Ortese's Eugenia is in many ways the opposite of Poe's Eugenie. For example, Eugenia is very young but looks like an old woman, while Eugenie is very old but looks young. In addition Ortese, as we shall see, also reverses Poe's visual metaphor, foregrounding the uncanny advantages rather than the disadvantages of nearsightedness. The basic events of Ortese's story (its narratological *fabula*) are easily summarized. Eugenia, the acutely nearsighted girl, joyously awaits the arrival of her first pair of glasses, generously paid for from her spinster aunt's meagre savings. A series of mishaps, however, dispels Eugenia's initial enthusiasm. When the glasses finally arrive at the end of the day, Eugenia puts them on, but they cause her to feel a sense of vertigo; a wave of nausea overtakes her and makes her throw up. Curtain. There are a number of nodal points and key episodes in the narrative and in the characterization of its protagonists. In the introductory episode, upon waking in the morning Eugenia reminds her mother that today is the day when her glasses will be ready; she will be able to wear them for the first time and thus put an end to her severe nearsightedness: "Mammà, oggi mi metto gli occhiali" (MN 15; "[Mum], To-day I'm getting my glasses!" BN 15). The Italian original, with its poetically alliterative sound, subtly emphasizes the auditory dimension in implicit opposition to the visual, thus foreshadowing one of the key themes of the story and of the book. Ortese consistently invites us to listen to the sound of language and of writing itself, the play of the signifier in her text. Eugenia eagerly anticipates finally seeing the world after living for so long in a fog, and the joy that this revelation will provoke. The cost of the glasses intensifies and complicates her emotional investment and desire for them. With her modest and mysterious savings, Aunt Nunziata has offered to "fare gli occhiali a Eugenia" (MN 16; "pay for Eugenia's glasses," BN 16 – literally "make glasses for Eugenia"). Here Ortese's lexicon, which retains throughout a subtle literary elegance reminiscent of her earlier highly poetic style (in the Novecento and "magic-realist" modernist vein associated with Massimo Bontempelli and his followers) typically adopts and adapts a colloquial expression that allows her lovingly to evoke the very voices, inflections, and linguistic world (and mental landscape) of her characters even when she is not reporting their speech directly. Ortese's gaze is never (unlike the *école du regard*) remote and cold, and her visuality is synesthetic, seeking to evoke the sounds, voices, and smells of the real along with its appearance. Nunziata "aveva qualcosa da parte" ("had put some aside"), the text states, though she herself depends on the charity of her sister-in-law and brother. She reminds the child that the glasses are very expensive: "Ottomila lire vive vive!" (MN 15; "Eight thousand lire, hard cash!" BN 10; literally "Eight thousand living lire!"), as if to say that money is the poor's own sweat and blood. With its alliterative sound pattern and powerful metaphoric connotations meshing money with life and with the body, this line, which reoccurs several times through the text, becomes a kind of unifying musical leitmotif. In the story, Nunziata is a fragile, all-too-human Neapolitan spinster (the heir to many such characters portrayed in the work of Matilde Serao) who seems almost cut off from life and yet is a mysteriously powerful and knowledgeable figure. She seems to play, among others, the archetypical role of the benefactor or "donor," somewhat similar to the benevolent fairy in fairytales or at least, as we shall see, this is Eugenia's naïve perception of her.[48] As she emerges uttering some of her habitual bitter pronouncements from the cave-like little *sgabuzzino* where she usually hides, Nunziata uncannily resembles the prophetic Cumaean Sibyl (whose ancient cavern was thought to be near Naples). In Virgil's *Aeneid*, the Sibyl warns the hero about the darkness of the underworld that he is about to enter and the difficulty of ever finding a path back to the light.

After this introduction to the story's main theme, a brief analepsis in the narrative relates events of the previous week, providing the reader with the necessary background to the current day and the reasons for Eugenia's feeling of uneasy anticipation. Nunziata, we are told, had taken Eugenia to an optometrist on Via Roma, the main street of an elegant neighbourhood in the city centre, and there, before proceeding with the order, the child with the help of the doctor had tried on a pair of glasses for the first time. Eugenia's joy in being able to look out through the glasses into the street from the entrance of the shop, finally seeing the world clearly for the first time in her life, seemed boundless, making the anticipatory desire for her own pair of lenses all the more powerful, almost intoxicating and exhilarating. As the French feminist Hélène Cixous observes in her autobiographical "Savoir," suddenly being able to see creates the joyful illusion of being born, "the laughter of childbirth" and of the apparition into a world that seems to say "yes." The supreme happiness is not so much in what one sees, or in seeing itself, but in the "no-longer-not-seeing."[49] This is why the world appears beautiful to Eugenia. As Cixous' title implies, the promise that seeing (*Voir*) holds is a promise of revelatory knowledge (*Savoir*). However, this analeptic preamble contains another obscure premonition of the tragic catastrophe and of the reversal of fortune typical of classical tragedy, for just before she removes the glasses to leave the elegant shop Eugenia's joy turns suddenly into sorrow. As her aunt complains about their poverty and how it renders the price of the glasses so burdensome, Eugenia catches the salesgirl looking at her. Eugenia suddenly feels ashamed because that pitiless gaze clearly establishes a distance, identifying her as poor and inferior, and she immediately takes off the glasses. This is the first occurrence of Eugenia's instinctive refusal to see and to be seen. Seeing, looking, the gaze and its power are crucial themes that inform the entire story and reoccur as a leitmotif throughout the book. As she leaves the store, in a symbolic harbinger of her imminent fall from a condition of elevation and supreme exaltation to one of total prostration, Eugenia stumbles on the doorstep. It is at this point that she hears the sibylline pronouncement of her aunt, who obscurely yet poetically declares, "Il mondo è meglio non vederlo che vederlo" (MN 18; "As far as this world's concerned, you're better off without seeing it," BN 13). It is a dictum that uncannily echoes the dark, despairing words of the blind Oedipus at Colonus, but also recalls Leopardi, an important influence, as we have seen, on this book and all of Ortese's work.[50] In Leopardi's "L'infinito" ("The Infinite"), the only sea that can give one joy is a sea not seen, but imagined, dreamed as a kind of immense nowhere.[51] Yet Leopardi, like Ortese, ironically never tires of making his reader look directly at the real, no matter how painful, without blinders.

Before the final catastrophe, the story unfolds through a series of narrative sequences and brief episodes, each of which is structurally necessary to the plot and the understanding of the characters' psychology and motivation. The marquise descends upon the Quaglias to ask Peppino to come up and repair her mattress. Eugenia is struck by the majestic glow of beauty that, to her myopic eyes, emanates from the radiant figure of the marquise, and by her apparent benevolence, for she seems to treat her father with great courtesy, as if he were a "gentleman." In engaging Peppino, however, the marquise introduces an obstacle in the path towards the fulfilment of Eugenia's wish. Rosa, Eugenia's mother, in fact that day is ill and Nunziata unavailable: Eugenia's father is the only one who can conceivably go and collect the glasses. Only the invisible narrator can see and make us see her pain: "Senza che nessuno li vedesse, i grandi occhi quasi ciechi di Eugenia si riempirono di lacrime" (MN 21; "Without anyone's taking notice, tears welled up in Eugenia's nearly blind eyes," BN 16). The narrator's role is that of making us see and feel what nobody else sees and can feel. The problem is apparently resolved when Rosa promises to go despite her illness and gets ready to leave for the Via Roma. This leaves the children under the care of Nunziata, who, however, does not feel up to the task and is exasperated by this unexpected burden.

In the subsequent episode, Nunziata sends Eugenia on a mission to purchase two sweets to soothe a tantrum of little Pasqualino. The errand turns into an epic journey of sorts through a world that to Eugenia is as dark and ominous as the underworld was for Aeneas. For nearsighted Eugenia, the alley is bristling not only with dangerous obstacles (she dodges an oncoming handcart and narrowly avoids turning over a neighbour's basket), but also encounters that threaten, even undermine, the prefigured fulfilment of her desire. In fact, upon discovering that Eugenia will receive her glasses today, one of the neighbour's housemaids, whom the child recognizes by her voice, reveals a secret that leaves Eugenia perplexed. She says, "Io pure me li dovrei mettere, ma il mio fidanzato non vuole" (MN 24; "I need glasses myself, but my fiancé won't hear of my wearing them," BN 20). Thus fundamental notions pertaining to human sexuality and gender difference are introduced to Eugenia along with the indispensable connection between vision and sexuality, all of which cast an ominous shadow on Eugenia's sunny state of mind. On a basic level, the exchange with the maid first suggests to Eugenia the idea that not wearing glasses – therefore remaining nearsighted – can be preferable for a female-gendered being. The text says, however, that "Eugenia non afferrò il senso di quella proibizione" (MN 24; "Eugenia did not grasp the significance of that prohibition," BN 20), therefore implicitly inviting the reader to decipher it. In part, it is obviously a reference to the cliché that glasses, traditionally thought to be not very feminine, spoil the appearance of women and must therefore be minimized or eliminated. Beyond this cliché, however, the reader is led to trace the ideology and power structure of the gaze in patriarchal societies and its dichotomous organization. It is a cultural structure, not innate, but unquestionably learned precisely through the gaze by observing and being observed in a social context. According to this structure, as the critic John Berger stated in his classic 1972 essay, men are the ones who have the monopoly of looking, the control of the "active" gaze. "Men act and women appear. Men look at women. Women watch themselves being looked at. This determines not only most relations between men and women but also the relation of women to themselves. The surveyor [or watcher] of woman in herself is male: the surveyed [or watched] female. Thus she turns herself into an object – and most particularly an object of vision."[52] The duty of woman, insofar as she is traditionally an object and not the active subject of vision, is to "enjoy" being observed, not to observe or see (unless as a function of pleasure for the male gaze). Through Eugenia's suffering, Ortese, long before the post-1968 critique of ocularcentrism, thus questions the patriarchal structure of the gaze and its cold objectification of woman as a prerequisite for her entrance into "femininity" and sexuality.

The episode following the encounter with the nearsighted maidservant suggests that Eugenia will remain outside the Western patriarchal order of the gaze for only a short time. She feels her hand taken by a boy, Luigino, who proposes that they go for a walk and looks at her with a gaze that she does not see or know, and with which she has never looked at herself. Eugenia remains indifferent to the proposition and explains that she is awaiting her glasses. Luigino becomes irritated and maliciously acts as a mirror, substituting his male gaze for, or superimposing it on, her impotent female gaze by scornfully revealing that she is unkempt and thus in reality undesirable to him. Raising a hand to her hair she responds ingenuously, "Io non ci vedo buono, e mammà non tiene tempo" (MN 26; "I can't see well, and mother doesn't have time," BN 21), revealing that until now her only mirror has been the loving eyes of her mother, just the person who will soon bring her the glasses. Still, Luigino insists, indirectly confirming the maid's initial insinuation to Eugenia, that only old, ugly women wear glasses, and the only permissible ones for women are sunglasses for going to the beach.

Eugenia barely succeeds in escaping this dangerous encounter with her faith in her precious glasses still intact. She imagines these glasses with gold rims, or even all gold, and gold thus becomes established as the ironic, ambivalent sign of both illusion and despair that it will be throughout the book. Upon her return to the courtyard, however, instead of her mother and the coveted package, Eugenia encounters her aunt who is infuriated by her lateness. Her violent slaps and insults reveal – at least to the reader – her resentful and malicious disposition, undermining even more deeply the seemingly positive value of her initial gift. Nunziata, who thus prefigures Anastasia's mother, wants Eugenia to see the horror of the real and to suffer (like she did) from this devastating experience, which is in fact what will happen.

Turning to the wretched yet compassionate Mariuccia, the building's doorwoman with the uncannily beautiful hair who lives in another miserable *basso* on the courtyard, Nunziata laments time's havoc on her face: her old woman's sunken cheeks, which fill her with rage (MN 28). Often compared to an old woman, pallid and frail Eugenia is, in fact, already physically similar to her aunt but still oblivious to this reality, for she has yet to suffer the full humiliation of the gaze of others. Nearsightedness therefore begins to emerge in the story as a kind of salvation, the forestalling of a tragic destiny. Mariuccia, in her mercifulness, finds the strength to denounce this destiny. "Avranno tempo per piangere" ("They will have plenty of time to cry"), she says referring to "le povere creature" ("the poor children") and to Eugenia. "Io quando li vedo, e penso che devono diventare tale e quale a noi ... mi domando che cosa fa Dio" (MN 28; "When I stop to think that some day they'll be the way we are now ... I wonder what God's really up to," BN 24–25).

The last episode before the tragic culmination and conclusion of the story is when Eugenia ascends to the "noble floor" to fetch a dress that the marquise wants to donate to Nunziata. Like the glasses, this gift is hardly disinterested. Even though Eugenia cannot see it, the dress is "vecchissimo e pieno di rammendi" (MN 29; "very old, mended and patched all over," BN 25) and the Marquise D'Avanzo uses it both to bind Nunziata in a debt of gratitude and to underline – as her name ironically suggests – that women like Nunziata and her family only deserve the leftovers (*avanzi*) of the wealthy, that is, the remnants, crumbs, rubbish, that which would otherwise be thrown away. "Ognuno nel suo rango ... tutti ci dobbiamo limitare" (MN 29; "Each of us in our own rank ... we all need to limit ourselves," BN 25). Once again, Eugenia hears the marquise repeat this phrase, an epigrammatic summary of the fundamental reason for class difference, a theme interwoven with that of gender difference throughout the story.

When she hears that the child is about to receive a pair of glasses that cost eight thousand lire, the marquise is appalled and asserts that for two thousand lire they could have found a pair perfectly suitable for Eugenia's needs. When the child innocently replies that her condition requires the highest quality of glasses, the marquise asks her, with a look that Eugenia luckily does not see, "Che ti serve veder bene? Per quello che tieni intorno!" (MN 29; "I don't know what good it will do you to see ... in those surroundings!" BN 27). The unnoticed condescending look of the marquise is another version of the gaze of the salesclerk in Via Roma: both define, discriminate, and immobilize according to class and wealth criteria. The marquise increases the dosage by insinuating that a poor child like Eugenia needs neither to see well nor to read. Having noticed that Eugenia does in fact know how to read, though with difficulty, the marquise offers her a "regaluccio," a gift in the same vein as the others. It is a book on the lives of the saints, which the marquise hopes will help Eugenia to find the path to the convent, like her two older sisters. If the veil of Eugenia's nearsightedness is to be removed, the marquise hopes that it will be replaced by the veil of the convent. In her sally to the expensive optician, Eugenia has glimpsed too much of a view of the world forbidden to her by the marquise and by those like her.

At the entrance of the shop on Via Roma, Eugenia glimpsed a desirable world of well-dressed passers-by, elegant women, beauty, affluence, colours, and joy. This world is denied to her; she should not be able to see or desire it. Gender difference, presented twice in the scenes with the nearsighted housemaid first and then with Luigino, superimposes itself on class and rank difference. In fact the marquise says, "Non sei bella, tutt'altro, e sembri già una vecchia. Iddio ti ha voluto prediligere, perché così non avrai occasioni di male. Ti vuole santa, come le tue sorelle!" (MN 30–31; "You are not much to look at, and you look old already. It's a sign of God's favor that he should preserve you from temptation. He wants you to be a saint like your two sisters!" BN 27).[53] Thus Eugenia is denied, by a malevolent and falsely maternal female figure, not only the rights to see and read freely, but also, like later in the book Anastasia will be, those of eros and pleasure, and any claim to beauty. True to form and rather like a female Perceval, Eugenia does not completely understand the meaning of this declaration, even though it disturbs her: "Le parve, per un attimo, che il sole non brillasse più come prima, e anche il pensiero degli occhiali cessò di rallegrarla" (MN 31; "For a second, it seemed as if the sun were shining less brightly, and even the prospect of the glasses failed to please her now," BN 28). And yet, before the concluding catastrophe, this scene ends with an illumination, a sublime epiphany with a Leopardian subtext. From the marquise's elevated terrace, Eugenia imagines that her weak eyes can see the sea of Posillipo. "Guardava vagamente, coi suoi occhi quasi spenti, un punto del mare, dove si stendeva come una lucertola, di un colore verde smorto, la terra di Posillipo [...] 'Io pure, una volta, ci sono stata ...' cominciava Eugenia, rianimandosi a quel nome e guardando, incantata, da quella parte" (MN 31; "She stared vaguely, with all the light gone out of her eyes, at a point across the distant water, where the outline of Posillipo lay, like a dull green lizard, against the sky [...] 'I went there once ...' Eugenia said hesitatingly, roused by this familiar name, and staring spellbound in its direction," BN 28). Through this Leopardian manner of looking into an imagined space beyond the horizon, memory, desire, and imagination become intertwined for a brief moment. The mind's eye reaches that sea whose infinite beauty and comfort are completely foreign to the poor inhabitants of Naples, as the title of the book, *Il mare non bagna Napoli,* controversially implies. The shape of the green lizard in the distance uncannily foreshadows for the reader the tiny woman who is both young and old, like Eugenia, and lives beyond the sea on an imaginary island – "una bestiola verdissima e alta quanto un bambino, dall'apparente aspetto di una lucertola" (R2 23, "a bright green beast, about the height of a child – an enormous lizard from the look of her," TIG 17) – in Ortese's utopian 1965 masterpiece, the novel *L'Iguana.* Preparing to descend to the muddy courtyard, Eugenia turns one last time towards "quel punto luminoso" (MN 31; "that vision of light," BN 28).

In the final scene in the courtyard Eugenia recognizes the familiar silhouette of her mother and runs to her joyously finally to receive her glasses. Everyone watches the seemingly blessed scene of the glasses' unveiling and the affectionate motion with which Rosa puts them on her daughter's face. They all congratulate Eugenia; however, her reaction is not the one they anticipated and desired, but rather its exact opposite. It is as if the bewitched glasses, like the maddening multitude of eye-like spectacles, lenses, and lorgnettes that the peddler offers to Nathanael in Hoffmann's tale, made her the victim of an evil spell. Eugenia feels sick and stammers a little, saying in a stifled voice that everything appears very small. Her father Peppino immediately provides the rationale for her reaction: it is normal to feel discomfort and nausea when wearing a pair of glasses for the first time. However, Eugenia's discomfort is not caused by the glasses, it is caused by what she sees now, and by what she has glimpsed during that long day. Repeating her behaviour in the shop scene, Eugenia goes to the threshold and looks out, but instead of being carried away by a sense of joy or swept up in contemplation of the external world, she is overcome by a painful, vile vertigo. In fact, what she sees are not the lights, beauty, and colours of Via Roma, but a vision that presses upon her and pushes her back into the filthy courtyard:

> l'imbuto viscido del cortile, con la punta verso il cielo e i muri lebbrosi fitti di miserabili balconi; gli archi dei terranei neri, coi lumi brillanti a cerchio attorno all'Addolorata; il selciato bianco di acqua saponata, le foglie di cavolo, i pezzi di carta, i rifiuti, e, in mezzo al cortile, quel gruppo di cristiani cenciosi e deformi, coi visi butterati dalla miseria e dalla rassegnazione, che la guardavano amorosamente. Cominciarono a torcersi, a confondersi, a ingigantire. Le venivano tutti addosso, gridando, nei due cerchetti stregati degli occhiali. Fu Mariuccia la prima ad accorgersi che la bambina stava male, e a strapparle in fretta gli occhiali, perché Eugenia era piegata in due e, lamentandosi, vomitava. (MN 33)

> (The courtyard was like a sticky funnel, pointed toward the sky, with peeling walls and thickly clustered balconies around it. On the ground, there was a circle of low arches and at one point a statue of the Madonna surrounded by votive lights. The paving stones were marked with streaks of soapy water and littered with scraps of paper, cabbage leaves and other bits of garbage. And in the middle of the scene there stood a little group of sickly, ragged individuals, with the pockmarks of poverty and despair on their faces, staring at her with adoring expectation. Mariuccia was the first one to realize that the child was unwell and to snatch the glasses away. For Eugenia was bent over double, moaning and vomiting upon the ground. [BN 31])

In the noise and chorus of voices that follow as everyone comments on Eugenia's illness and tries to tend to her as "il suo viso di vecchia inondato di lacrime" (MN 34; "her little old face [was] flooded with tears," BN 31), the voice of compassionate Mariuccia is heard with epigrammatic concision: "Lasciatela stare, povera creatura, è meravigliata" (MN 34; "Let her be, the poor child, she's astonished"). The use of the Neapolitan dialect version of the word "meravigliata" here to indicate anxious bewilderment (and the uncanny opposite of the "meraviglia" first glimpsed through the glasses on the elegant and prosperous Via Roma),[54] foreshadows its occurrence in the chapter "Oro a Forcella," when the narrator is awed and horrified by the spectacle of the miserable crowd and especially by the children among them, and again in "La città involontaria," when the crippled infant-like toddler girl named Nunzia Faiella sees a light that reminds her of the sun she has seen only once.[55] Eugenia's experience in beholding the horror of her world is similar to that of the narrator of the chapter on I Granili, and Eugenia is in fact a figure for the narrator herself as a child, but also as an old woman. Nearly eighty, Ortese wrote about her book in the 1994 "Afterword": "dunque, fu visione dell'*intollerabile*" (MN 175; "so, it was a vision of the *intolerable*"). Eugenia's astonishment, we must conclude, is an expression of extreme disenchantment not only because her glasses nauseate her, but also because the reality that she finally sees is the complete opposite of what she had glimpsed and desired on the threshold of the optician's shop. As a result, a fundamental point emerges from the very structure of the story, without being didactically superimposed. It is not a matter of a generic, absolute Leopardian discovery of the pain of human existence; nor is it a discovery of Sartrean nausea caused by the phenomenon of living itself.[56] It is first of all a precise, circumstantial condemnation of the nauseating Neapolitan reality, the condition of oppression and exploitation of the impoverished in that city where all good and beauty are denied to them, in sharp contrast with the prosperity of the rich neighbourhoods and upper stories, and of the Italy of the "economic miracle" in the north. Eugenia, upon whom the curtain of the story closes, is certainly not a "positive hero" and has no "class consciousness," which partially explains the contemporary left's unpleasant reception of the story. The condemnation, however, is evident in all of its human and political resonance. Still, the literary richness and profundity of the text does not end here, although many rather nearsighted readers were incapable of discerning its depth of vision, a depth that ironically has to do with Eugenia's very nearsightedness.

Of the stories in *Il mare non bagna Napoli*, this was the one that Elio Vittorini liked the least because he found it both excessively naturalistic and overly influenced by autobiographical elements.[57] As a matter of fact, in a 1993 interview, Ortese revealed one of her own experiences to be at the base of the story:

> Non ci vedevo bene, forse già da piccola, ma non me ne accorgevo. Poi l'oculista mi disse di mettermi gli occhiali: erano lenti leggere, se mi vedesse

> adesso che ho le nuvole davanti agli occhi ... Dunque, misi questi occhiali e subito fui presa da una nausea violenta: era la disperazione di vedere tutte le crepe dei muri, tutto il lercio, quel che mai avrei voluto guardare: tutto il vecchiume stava lì, nel mio quartiere. Era insopportabile. Poi mi passò, ma fu un impatto grave con la verità delle cose; per questo l'ho ricordato nel racconto. (MN 246)

> (I could not see well, perhaps since childhood, and did not realize it. Then the optician told me to wear glasses: they were thin lenses, if he could see me now that I have these clouds in front of my eyes ... Well, I put on these glasses and was suddenly seized by a violent nausea: it was the despair of seeing all the cracks in the walls, all the filth, all that I never would have wanted to see: all the old rubbish was there, in my neighborhood. It was unbearable. Then the feeling subsided, but it was a serious impact on the truth of things; that is why I put it in the story. [BN 246])

I would like to call attention to two expressions in this passage: "now that I have these clouds in front of my eyes," and "the truth of things was unbearable." "Clouds in front of my eyes" will help us read and understand the profound meaning of Eugenia's nearsightedness, the whole metaphoric field of vision in the story, and Ortese's poetics. For most critics, even the well-intentioned and paternalistic ones like Vittorini, the story does nothing beyond "naturalistically" recording an episode in reality – however squalid and painful; and the glasses that allow Eugenia to emerge from her nearsightedness, simultaneously provoking in her an attack of nausea, are merely a mechanical expedient, a simple device to highlight the squalor of the reality that she finally sees with clarity. Everyone presumes that this clarity, however painful and nauseating, is necessary and binding. The realist, naturalistic, and neorealist tenets state that it is in fact necessary to look and see reality as it is, in a concrete and objective way. Eugenia's nearsightedness, however, performs a more complex metaphoric function with a wider and deeper reach. Ortese's 1993 statement "now that I have these clouds in front of my eyes" certainly makes us reflect and look away from the direction of naturalism, realism, or indeed neorealism. In other words, it points towards a new interpretation of nearsightedness as metaphor. Nearsightedness, near-blindness, does not represent merely the impairment of an obfuscated or weakened vision but, as Ortese helps us understand, it is a metaphor for an alternative vision that is a deliberate choice. From one perspective, Eugenia's vague, Leopardian vision is in itself poetic; but from another perspective in several moments of pictorial inspiration, Eugenia's imprecise and blurred vision, which is based more on colour spots and light than on form, assumes all of the aesthetic aspects of an Impressionist painting. In her nearsightedness, Eugenia is capable of an aesthetic view of reality; she imagines beauty that others are unable to see, beauty that exists because her eyes and imagination create it. Certainly this does not redeem, purify, nor transform the objective horror of the real, but it serves rather to estrange it and defamiliarize it, to let us glimpse at and desire another reality, just as Eugenia does. But there is also a cognitive reality that supplements the aesthetic one. Uncertainty, doubt, the way Eugenia hesitates when she crosses a threshold and never presumes to recognize or to know: these characteristics make her live in a perpetual state of attention that has a positive value in contrast to an arrogant or hackneyed vision that may consider itself absolute, all-knowing, and complete, or simply normal. Paradoxically, nearsightedness is therefore a cognitive force, as Hélène Cixous wrote in "Savoir," a text that is her nostalgic reflection on the value of her own nearsightedness, a poor fairy's "gift," which she discovered only after forever losing her condition to laser eye surgery.[58] Not seeing and especially not being able "to see herself seen" give the myopic woman a lightness, a strength, and a "liberty of self-effacement" that she would not have otherwise: "elle vivait dans l'au-dessus sans images où coursent les grands nuages indistincts" ("She lived in the above without images where big indistinct clouds roll").[59] One of the positive consequences of Eugenia's – and implicitly Ortese's – nearsightedness is that it widens her desire and capacity to listen, to recognize, and to know through voices instead of through the eyes. In fact, the sounds and the voices that identify the characters may be heard through the whole story. Moreover, the way nearsightedness softens edges, merging bodies and shapes normally perceived as distinct, disparate, and different, suggests that everything is or could be joined into a continuum, a single whole. It therefore harkens back to a dimension of non-separation from the mother, to the joy of still being one with her, unable to distinguish between the two bodies; but it also has potentially political and social connotations that are diametrically opposed to Marquise D'Avanzo's rigid vision of class and social distinction.

A positive implication also emerges from the strictly optic definition of nearsightedness. The nearsighted person usually sees up close clearly. The word *nearsighted* itself denotes the capacity to see details that are very close, even the smallest blemishes on the face of another or one's own body, instead of a wider perspective from afar that is by definition more remote, colder, and abstract. One of the many pictorial scenes in the story uses an image of faces and bodies dimly illuminated by a lantern or candle to evoke the warm, precisely detailed paintings for which Georges de la Tour and his school were famous, thus allowing the veil over the eyes of Eugenia to dissipate: "il viso dei familiari, la mamma specialmente e i fratelli, [li] conosceva bene, perché spesso ci dormiva insieme, e qualche volta si svegliava di notte e, al lume della lampada a olio, li guardava" (MN 19; "the faces of the family, especially those of her mother and the younger children, were familiar to her, because often they slept in the same bed and when she woke up in the middle of the night, she would examine them by the glare of the kerosene lamp," BN 13). Paradoxically, this close contemplation of the dirty faces of her suffering family inspires Eugenia to think that the world must indeed be beautiful. The nearsighted gaze stands for a vision that, unlike the traumatized gaze of the alienated subject (which is par excellence *the* one and only subject for both Freud and Lacan) establishes a relationship of intimate proximity and togetherness with the loved one.[60] Nearsighted vision comes closer to the texture of paintings and the warmth of faces and bodies, becoming almost tactile.

Ortese's nearsightedness or, with increased age, perhaps cataracts ("now that I have these clouds in front of my eyes") is not an endured disability, an incurable condition that causes pain and embarrassment and is only worsened by time; it is instead a choice, a deliberate "act" of nearsightedness. Nor is it a refusal to see reality, an attempt to evade it by seeking out dream and illusion and keeping one's head among the clouds. Unlike blindness, traditionally cultivated by male poets and writers from Homer and Milton to d'Annunzio and Borges as a privileged condition and metaphor that generates a visionary or prophetic power to see "inside" or "beyond" into a transcendent, metaphysical, absolute or, alternately, exclusively aesthetic-literary dimension, Ortese wants to look at the world and make us see it up close. Only this renewed, humble act of looking up close can restore authenticity and humanness to vision. Eugenia and Ortese's nearsightedness generates the impulse, arising from the spectacle and intolerability of the real (with all of its painful elements of squalor and exploitation), to seek, imagine, and see another world, a different reality. In her afterword to the 1994 edition of *Il mare non bagna Napoli*, Ortese concludes, "Insomma, io non amavo il *reale*, esso era per me quasi intollerabile ... Quella [realtà di Napoli] non l'accettavo" (MN 174; "I did not love the real, it was for me ... almost intolerable ... I did not accept [that reality of Naples]," BN 174). Ortese therefore refuses to be a "realist," not in the sense of refusing to see, but refusing passively to accept reality as it is defined and represented by power.

Ortese's text becomes ultimately itself like a human face, reminding us that the act of reading is inherently "nearsighted."[61] It brings the reader's eyes to look closely at the pages of the book, the lines on the page and the words in a line. Reading restores to the act of vision the closeness, intimacy, and uncertainty or tentativeness of which the powerful mastering or jealous gaze deprive it. Ultimately, "voluntary nearsightedness" corresponds to the utopian charge of literature, or rather, of poetry itself.

NOTES

1 This chapter is a shorter, updated version of Lucia Re, "Invisible Sea: Anna Maria Ortese's *Il mare non bagna Napoli*," *California Italian Studies* 3, 1 (2012), 1–34.

2 It was subsequently republished under the new title in *Il Mondo* (7 July 1951) and *Noi donne* (20 September 1953). See Clerici, *Apparizione e visione*, 233.

3 All Italian quotes will be from the revised edition, Anna Maria Ortese, *Il mare non bagna Napoli* (Milano: Adelphi, 1994, henceforth cited as MN), which includes a new introduction ("Il mare come spaesamento") and afterword ("Le giacchette grigie di Monte di Dio"). As observed by Monica Farnetti in her bibliographical note to Ortese, *L'infanta sepolta* (Milan: Adelphi, 2000), 173–74, MN is the only one among Ortese's collections of short texts to have retained its original contents unchanged through its various Italian editions (Vallecchi, 1967; Rizzoli, 1975; La Nuova Italia, 1979), while others, including the stories of *L'infanta sepolta* (first edition 1950), have been subject to various reshufflings. Most quotes in translation are from Ortese, *The Bay Is Not Naples: Short Stories by Anna Maria Ortese*, trans. Frances Frenaye (London: Collins, 1955, henceforth cited as BN). All other translations are mine. I have on occasion slightly altered the Frenaye translation to stay closer to the quoted original. This edition includes only a partial translation of the last chapter ("The Silence of Reason"). About twenty pages of the last section are not included, without explanation. However, this edition includes three additional texts that were never part of any Italian edition of *Il mare non bagna Napoli*: "The Sea and Naples" ("Il mare e Napoli"), first published in *Sud* in June 1946 and January 1947 under the title "Dolente spirito del vicolo" and republished in *L'infanta sepolta* (1950 and 2000); "Traveler's Return" ("Ritorno fra la mia gente"), originally published in *L'Unità*, Milano (28 March 1954), now included in *Angelici dolori e*

altri racconti, ed. Luca Clerici (Milan: Adelphi, 2006); "A Strange Apparition" ("Un personaggio singolare"), originally published in two parts as "Due pariglie alla carozza di passione" and "Sulle case nere splendeva l'arcobaleno," in *Milano Sera*, 8 September 1950 and 6 February 1951, and subsequently under the new title in *L'infanta sepolta* (1950 and 2000).

4 Contarini, "Tra cecità e visione," 1–13.

5 "Il *Mare* come spaesamento," MN 10.

6 It was Vittorini who insisted that "Il mare e Napoli" (cfr. note 2 above) not be included in the volume, on the grounds that it was not "objective" enough, that it was excessively "personal," and that it referred to an episode of the immediate post-war period that was no longer relevant to a chronicle of "today's Naples" (which was his understanding of what the book was meant to be about).

7 "Qui il mare non bagnava Napoli. Ero sicura che nessuno lo avesse visto, e lo ricordava" (MN 67; "Here, indeed, Naples is not cleansed by the sea; for that matter few of these people have seen it or can even remember it," BN 88).

8 Calvino, *I libri degli altri*, 93, letter to Elio Vittorini and Anna Maria Ortese, 16 June 1953.

9 See Ghirelli, *Achille Lauro*, 119.

10 On the irrationality of Lauro's system, which only fostered chaos and uncontrolled growth, see Allum, *Potere e società a Napoli nel dopoguerra*.

11 Letter to Anna Maria Ortese, 21 May 1953, in Calvino, *Lettere 1940–1985*, 370. Traces of her influence on his own writing may be detected in the tale "Storia di un miope" and in *La giornata di uno scrutatore* (*The Watcher*), while the optic metaphor of "Un paio di occhiali" still resonates even in the later *Mr. Palomar.* See Lucia Re, "Invisible Sea: Anna Maria Ortese's *Il mare non bagna Napoli.*"

12 Ortese, *La lente scura: Scritti di viaggio*, ed. Luca Clerici (Milano: Marcos y Marcos, 1991). See also Clerici, 252.

13 On this way of understanding the eye and the gaze, it is still helpful to read Jean Starobinski, *L'Oeil vivant.*

14 Ortese, like Calvino and others, did not like the label "neorealism," which never came together as a real movement per se, but rather represented a mood and a moment, and a compulsion to narrate in a certain way the tragic experiences shared by Italians during and after the Second World War. See my "Neorealist Narrative: Experience and Experiment," 104–24.

15 Clerici, 260. Ironically, Christian Democrat politician Giulio Andreotti, in an article published in *Il Popolo* on 26 February 1952 and elsewhere, launched a similar attack against De Sica's neorealist films, with particular

reference to *Umberto D*, accused of being an embarrassment and a disservice to Italy.

16 In the post-war era, they range from Domenico and Ermanno Rea to Raffaele La Capria, Michele Prisco, Luigi Compagnone, Fabrizia Ramondino, and Erri de Luca (among others). Ramondino is especially critical of the idea of Neapolitanness in her *Dadapolis: Caleidoscopio napoletano* (written with Andreas Friedrich Müller). On the stereotypes surrounding Naples and especially the Neapolitan lower classes, see the essays in Signorelli, ed., *Cultura popolare a Napoli e in Campania nel Novecento.* On the fate of the romantic myth of Napoletanità after the Second World War, see Gatt-Rutter, 245–72. See also Bruno, *Atlas of Emotion: Journeys in Art, Architecture, and Film*, chapter 11, and the essays in Caspar, ed., *Napoli e dintorni: De Filippo, De Luca, La Capria, Marotta, Orsini Natale, Ortese, Prisco, Rea.*

17 See the 1994 "Foreword" to MN 9: "Questa condanna mi costò un addio, che si fece del tutto definitivo negli anni che seguirono, alla mia città" ("This sentence forced me to an exile, which became permanent in the following years, from my city").

18 On the Brechtian notion of estrangement, see Ernst Bloch, "*Entfremdung, Verfremdung*: Alienation, Estrangement," 3–11.

19 Although some Neapolitans still see Ortese as treacherous and shortsighted, her book is increasingly enticing new and younger audiences and interpreters. For example, the Teatro Stabile di Napoli commissioned five directors to stage for the Teatro Ridotto's 2013 season a cycle of five separate short plays, each based on one of the chapters from *Il mare non bagna Napoli.*

20 On the notion of "sguardo invidioso" or "jealous gaze," see Petrosino, *Visione e desiderio.*

21 De Luca, "Cara Ortese, questa non è Napoli," *Il Corriere della sera*, 21 May 1994.

22 This undoing of the maternal myth by Ortese has earned her some criticism by Italian feminists who stand by Luisa Muraro's mother-based thought. See for example Torriglia, *Broken Time, Fragmentes Spaces*, 133–36.

23 The translation skips this sentence, rendering it indirectly as "Her love was all for Anna" (BN 67).

24 See Clerici, 233, who claims that Ortese told him "Un paio di occhiali" was inspired by Serao's story.

25 Freud, "The Uncanny," 219–52.

26 The abundant production in the 1950s of films based on Neapolitan folklore, music, and stereotyped images of the city included works such as Camillo Mastrocinque's *Tarantella napoletana* (1953) and *Napoli terra d'amore* (1954) and Armando Grottini's *E Napoli canta* (1953). See the essays in Aprà, ed., *Napoletana: Images of a City.*

27 The stereotypical way in which the black GI is portrayed has been noticed by several critics, but the ethnic cliché represented by the thieving Neapolitan "scugnizzo," a figure that dates back to the nineteenth century, has received less attention. See Ranisio, "L'immagine delle classi 'pericolose' al volgere del secolo: scugnizzi, prostitute e 'mariouli,'" 85–96.
28 See Bruno, *Atlas,* 377–99.
29 Baldi, "Ortese's Naples: Urban Malaise through a Visionary Gaze," 218. See also Baldi, "Infelicità senza desideri: *Il mare non bagna Napoli* di Anna Maria Ortese," 81–104 and *La meraviglia e il disincanto: studi sulla narrativa breve di Anna Maria Ortese.*
30 Ortese's writing, here and elsewhere, represents a modernist version of the uncanny as described by Todorov, *The Fantastic*; in other words, "events are related which may be readily accounted for by the laws of reason, but which are, in one way or another, incredible, extraordinary, shocking, singular, disturbing or unexpected, and which thereby provoke in the character and in the reader a reaction similar to that which works of the fantastic have made familiar" (46). Todorov's definition of the uncanny is applied to nineteenth-century stories in which the character or narrator realizes that he or she is mad or has just awakened from a dream. In Ortese's modernist uncanny, instead it is reality itself that has become uncanny, defying the limits of reason.
31 I borrow the notion of a "porous street" and of Naples as a porous city from the 1925 essay by Walter Benjamin and Asja Lacis, "Naples," in *Reflections,* 171. See also Ernst Bloch, "Italy and Porosity" (1925) in *Literary Essays,* 450–57.
32 This tradition, which arguably starts with Plato, is particularly strong in French thought from Decartes to Bataille and Sartre and culminates in the work of Freud and Lacan. See for example Jacques Lacan's *The Four Fundamental Concepts of Psychoanalysis,* 103: "When I love, I solicit a look. What is profoundly unsatisfying and always missing that – *You never look at me from the place from which I see you.* Conversely, *What I look at is never what I wish to see.*" For a thorough unpacking of this tradition, see Jay, *Downcast Eyes: The Denigration of Vision in Twentieth-Century French Thought.*
33 See for example Pasolini, "Gennariello" (1975), in *Lettere Luterane.*
34 Baldi, "Ortese's Naples," 223.
35 Adorno, "On Lyric Poetry and Society" (1957) in *Notes to Literature*; Bloch, *The Utopian Function of Art and Literature: Selected Essays.* Ortese's fascination with the mode of utopia is spelled out in *La lente oscura,* iii–iv. For an interesting and innovative feminist-utopian reading of Ortese, with particular reference to her travel writing, see Della Coletta, "Scrittura come utopia: *La lente scura* di Anna Maria Ortese," 371–88.

36 For the third and fourth chapter, originally published as articles in the journal *Il Mondo* between October 1951 and January 1952, Ortese received the 1952 Saint Vincent journalism award.

37 Clerici, 230–32.

38 On Ortese's interest in painting and Goya's possible influence, see Ghezzo, "Chiaroscuro napoletano: Trasfigurazioni fantastiche di una città," 85–104.

39 The Introduction is entitled "Il *Mare* come spaesamento"; the Afterword "Le Giacchette Grigie di Monte di Dio" (MN 9–11; 173–76).

40 Prisco, "Ortese, la lettera del felice dolore," *Corriere del Mezzoggiorno*, 8 April 1998, quoted in Clerici, 241.

41 See Nussbaum, *Poetic Justice.*

42 Franco, "Quando sognavo un film dal *Mare*," *Corriere del Mezzogiorno*, 12 March 1998, cited in Clerici, 259.

43 For other more indirect historical references, see Vilma De Gasperin, *Loss and the Other in the Visionary Work of Anna Maria Ortese* (Oxford: Oxford University Press, 2014), pp. 108–109. The discussion of *Il mare non bagna Napoli* in this monograph, which expands on several points made in my "Invisible Sea: Anna Maria Ortese's *Il mare non bagna Napoli*," offers a useful, documented reading of the chapter "Il silenzio della ragione."

44 See the interview with Dacia Maraini in *E tu chi eri? Ventisei interviste sull'infanzia*, 30. Now included in this volume.

45 Serao, *Il ventre di Napoli* (1884), 105: "Per distruggere la corruzione materiale e quella morale, per rifare la salute e la coscienza a *quella povera gente*, per insegnare loro come si vive – essi sanno morire, come avete visto! – per dir loro che essi sono fratelli nostri, che noi li amiamo efficacemente, che vogliamo salvarli, non basta sventrare Napoli: bisogna quasi tutta rifarla" (emphasis mine).

46 Wood, *Italian Women's Writing, 1860–1944*, 169–70; Farnetti, *Anna Maria Ortese*, 45. Farnetti also draws an interesting analogy between the Ortese story and a story by Ingeborg Bachmann, "Ihhr glücklichen Augen" ("Eyes of Wonder" or "Happy Eyes") from the 1972 collection *Simultan.*

47 The most lucid critic of the mutual implications of ocularcentrism and patriarchal phallologocentricism is Luce Irigaray. See for example this well-known passage from her interview in *Les Femmes, la Pornographie et l'Erotisme*, 50: "Investment in the look is not as privileged in women as in men. More than any other sense, the eye objectifies and masters. It sets at a distance, and maintains a distance. In our culture the predominance of the look over smell, taste, touch and hearing has brought about an impoverishment of bodily relations."

48 The classic definition of the narrative function of the donor is in Propp, *Morphology of the Folktale.*
49 Cixous, "Savoir," in the volume *Voiles* (which also includes a text by Jacques Derrida and drawings by Ernest Pignon-Ernest), 16, originally in *Contretemps* 2/3 (1997).
50 *Oedipus at Colonus* (trans. Eamon Grennan and Rachel Kitzinger), 1225–28: "Never to be born is the best story. / But one has come to the light of day / second best is to leave and go back / quick as you can back where you came from." Cfr. Giacomo Leopardi, *Zibaldone,* 4100: "E però, secondo tutti i principi della ragione ed esperienza nostra, è meglio assoluto ai viventi il non essere che l'essere" ("And yet, according to all principles of our reason and experience, not being is absolutely preferable for the living than being.")
51 Cfr. this famous passage from Leopardi's *Zibaldone,* 4418: "All'uomo sensibile e immaginoso, che viva, come io sono vissuto gran tempo, sentendo di continuo ed immaginando, il mondo e gli oggetti sono in certo modo doppi. Egli vedrà cogli occhi una torre, una campagna; udrà cogli orecchi un suono d'una campana; e nel tempo stesso coll'immaginazione vedrà un'altra torre, un'altra campagna, udrà un altro suono. In questo secondo genere di obbiettivi sta tutto il bello e il piacevole delle cose. Trista quella vita (ed è pur tale la vita comunemente) che non vede, non ode, non sente se non che oggetti semplici, quelli soli di cui gli occhi, gli orecchi e gli altri sentimenti ricevono la sensazione" ("To a sensitive, imaginative man who lives – as I have for a long time – a life of constant feeling and imagining, the world and its objects in a sense have doubles. He sees with his eyes a tower, a landscape, with his ears he hears a bell ringing, and at the same time his imagination sees another tower, another landscape, hears another ringing. All the beauty and pleasure of things live in this second world. Sad is the life (and it's like this for most) that simply sees, hears, and feels objects that only the eyes, ears, and other senses register.")
52 Berger, *Ways of Seeing,* 49. The classic feminist critical essay on the patriarchal gaze is Mulvey, "Visual Pleasure and Narrative Cinema."
53 Translation slightly altered to correct an omission and reflect the original more closely.
54 On this use of *meravigliata,* and for a sensitive albeit dark reading of the whole story, see Baldi, "Infelicità senza desideri."
55 In this passage we find a dialect variation of the word, "stupetiata": "*guardava l'aria … 'o sole … era stupetiata.*' Anche adesso, Nunzia Faiella era meravigliata." (MN 95; BN 116)

56 Readings that argue that Ortese's is an utterly desolate, dark, pessimistic vision that rejects the real and the body altogether and privileges fantasy instead include Seno Reed, "Anna Maria Ortese: 'Un paio di occhiali' e 'Interno familiare': Due diversi tipi di estraniamento," 131–42 and Baldi, "Infelicità senza desideri."

57 Clerici, 234, 237.

58 In *Savoir*, 19: "Ent'en allant, ma pauvre fée, ma myopie, tu me retires les dons ambigus qui m'angoissaient et m'accordaient des états que les voyantes ne conaissent pas, murmurait-elle. – Ne m'oublie pas. Garde a jamais le monde suspendu, désirable, refuse, cet enchanté que je t'avais donné, murmurait la myopie" ("By going, my poor fairy, my myopia, you are withdrawing from me the ambiguous gifts that filled me with anguish and granted me states that those who see do not know, she murmured. – Do not forget me. Keep forever the world suspended, desirable, refused, that enchanted thing I had given you, murmured myopia").

59 *Savoir*, 18.

60 Elsa Morante uses Ortese's trope of myopia in this way and greatly expands on it in the novel *Aracoeli* (1982).

61 Lyotard, *Discours, figure*, 213.

WORKS CITED

Adorno, T.W. "On Lyric Poetry and Society" (1957). In *Notes to Literature*, ed. Rolf Tiedemann. Vol. 1. New York: Columbia University Press, 1991.

Allum, P.A. *Potere e società a Napoli nel dopoguerra.* Turin: Einaudi, 1975.

Aprà, Adriano, ed. *Napoletana: Images of a City.* New York / Milan: Fabbri Editore, 1993.

Baldi, Andrea. "Infelicità senza desideri: *Il mare non bagna Napoli* di Anna Maria Ortese." *Italica* 77, no. 1 (2000): 81–104.

– *La meraviglia e il disincanto: studi sulla narrativa breve di Anna Maria Ortese.* Naples: Loffredo Editore, 2010.

– "Ortese's Naples: Urban Malaise through a Visionary Gaze." In *Italian Women and the City: Essays*, ed. Janet Levarie Smarr and Daria Valentini, 215–38. Madison: Farleigh Dickinson University Press, 2003.

Benjamin, Walter, and Asja Lacis. "Naples." In *Reflections*, ed. Peter Demetz. Trans. Edmund Jephcott. New York: Harcourt Brace Jovanovich, 1978.

Berger, John. *Ways of Seeing.* New York: Penguin, 1972.

Bloch, Ernst. "*Entfremdung, Verfremdung*: Alienation, Estrangement." In *Brecht*, ed. Erika Munk. New York: Bantam, 1972.

– "Italy and Porosity" (1925). In *Literary Essays*, trans. Andrew Joron and others, 450–57. Palo Alto, CA: Stanford University Press, 1998.

– *The Utopian Function of Art and Literature: Selected Essays*. Cambridge, MA: MIT, 1988.

Bruno, Giuliana. *Atlas of Emotion: Journeys in Art, Architecture, and Film*. New York: Verso, 2002.

Calvino, Italo. *I libri degli altri: Lettere 1947–1981*. Ed. Giovanni Tesio. Turin: Einaudi, 1991.

– *Lettere 1940–1985*. Ed. Luca Baranelli. Milan: Mondadori, 2000.

Caspar, Marie Hélène, ed. *Napoli e dintorni: De Filippo, De Luca, La Capria, Marotta, Orsini Natale, Ortese, Prisco, Rea*. *Narrativa* 24 (2003).

Cixous, Hélène. *Voiles*. Paris: Galilées, 1998.

Clerici, Luca. *Apparizione e visione: Vita e opere di Anna Maria Ortese*. Milan: Mondadori, 2002.

Contarini, Silvia. "Tra cecità e visione. Come leggere *Il mare non bagna Napoli* di Anna Maria Ortese." *Chroniques Italiennes* 5 (2004): 1–13.

De Gasperin, Vilma. *Loss and the Other in the Visionary Work of Anna Maria Ortese*. Oxford: Oxford University Press, 2014.

Della Coletta, Cristina. "Scrittura come utopia: La lente scura di Anna Maria Ortese." *Italica* 76, no. 3 (1999): 371–88.

De Luca, Erri. "Cara Ortese, questa non è Napoli." *Il Corriere della sera*, 21 May 1994.

Farnetti, Monica. *Anna Maria Ortese*. Milan: Bruno Mondadori, 1998.

Franco, Carlo. "Quando sognavo un film dal *Mare*." *Corriere del Mezzogiorno*, 12 March 1998.

Freud, Sigmund. "The Uncanny." In *The Standard Edition of the Complete Psychological Works of Sigmund Freud*, ed. and trans. James Strachey, 219–52. Vol. 17. London: Hogarth, 1953.

Gatt-Rutter, John. "Liberation and Literature: Naples 1944." *Journal of Modern Italian Studies* 1, no. 2 (1996): 245–272.

Ghezzo, Flora. "Chiaroscuro napoletano: Trasfigurazioni fantastiche di una città." *Narrativa* 24 (2003): 85–104.

Ghirelli, Antonio. *Achille Lauro*. Naples: Gaetano Macchiaroli, 1992.

Irigaray, Luce. *Les Femmes, la pornographie et l'erotisme*. Ed. Marie Françoise Hans and Gilles Lapouge. Paris: Éditions du Seuil, 1978.

Jay, Martin. *Downcast Eyes: The Denigration of Vision in Twentieth-Century French Thought*. Berkeley / Los Angeles: University of California Press, 1993.

Lacan, Jacques. *The Four Fundamental Concepts of Psychoanalysis*. Ed. Jacques-Alain Moller. Trans. Alan Sheridan. New York: Norton & Co., 1981.

Leopardi, Giacomo. *Zibaldone*. 3 vols. Milan: Mondadori, 1996.

Lyotard, Jean-François. *Discours, figure.* Paris: Klincksieck, 1971.

Mulvey, Laura. "Visual Pleasure and Narrative Cinema" (1975). *Visual and Other Pleasures.* Bloomington: Indiana University Press, 1989.

Nussbaum, Martha. *Poetic Justice: The Literary Imagination and Public Life.* Boston, MA: Beacon Press, 1995.

Ortese, Anna Maria. *La lente oscura: Scritti di viaggio.* Ed. Luca Clerici. Milan: Marcos y Marcos, 1991.

Pasolini, Pier Paolo. "Gennariello" (1975). In *Lettere Luterane.* Turin: Einaudi, 2003.

Petrosino, Silvano. *Visione e desiderio: Il tempo dell'assenso.* Milan: Jaca Book, 1992.

Prisco, Michele. "Ortese, la lettera del felice dolore." *Corriere del Mezzoggiorno,* 8 April 1998.

Propp, Vladimir. *Morphology of the Folktale.* Trans. Laurence Scott; second edition revised and edited with a preface by Louis A. Wagner, introduction by Alan Dundes. Austin, Texas: University of Texas Press, 1968.

Ramondino, Fabrizia. *Dadapolis: Caleidoscopio napoletano.* Written with Andreas Friedrich Müller. Turin: Einaudi, 1989.

Ranisio, Gianfranca. "L'immagine delle classi 'pericolose' al volgere del secolo: scugnizzi, prostitute e 'mariouli.'" In *Cultura popolare a Napoli,* ed. Amalia Signorelli, 85–96. Naples: Guida, 2003.

Re, Lucia. "Invisible Sea: Anna Maria Ortese's Il mare non bagna Napoli." *California Italian Studies* 3, 1 (2012): 1–34.

– "Neorealist Narrative: Experience and Experiment." In *The Cambridge Companion to the Italian Novel,* ed. Peter Bondanella and Andrea Ciccarelli, 104–24. Cambridge: Cambridge University Press, 2003.

Seno Reed, Cosetta. "Anna Maria Ortese: 'Un paio di occhiali' e 'Interno familiare': Due diversi tipi di estraniamento." *Rassegna Europea di Letteratura italiana* 20 (2002): 131–42.

Serao, Matilde. *Il ventre di Napoli* (1884). Naples: Avagliano, 2003.

Signorelli, Amalia, ed. *Cultura popolare a Napoli e in Campania nel Novecento.* Naples: Guida, 2003.

Sophocles, *Oedipus at Colonus.* Trans. Eamon Grennan and Rachel Kitzinger. New York: Oxford University Press, 2005.

Starobinski, Jean. *L'Oeil vivant: La Relation critique.* Paris: Gallimard, 1970.

Todorov, Tzvetan. *The Fantastic.* Ithaca, NY: Cornell University Press, 1975.

Torriglia, Anna Maria. *Broken Time, Fragmented Spaces: A Cultural Map of Postwar Italy.* Toronto: University of Toronto Press, 2002.

Wood, Sharon. *Italian Women's Writing, 1860–1944.* London: Athlone, 1995.

2 Cities "Paved with Casualties": Ortese's Journeys through Urban Modernity

ANDREA BALDI

la rue, seul champ d'expérience valuable

(the street, the only valid field of experience)

André Breton, *Nadja*

This essay addresses some aspects of the relationship between Ortese and modernity that have been overlooked by critics, focusing on her travel writings and, in particular, a few of her reportages centred around Milan, which appeared in *Silenzio a Milano* (*Silence in Milan*, 1958) or were issued in periodicals and not subsequently republished. Having moved to the Lombard metropolis in 1948,[1] in these works Ortese takes a probing look at the devastating effects of industrialization and unbridled urbanization, which distinguish the development of northern Italy during the "reconstruction" following the Second World War.

In mapping the peninsula, the author situates Naples, the "capital" of the south and the city of her upbringing, in polar contrast with Milan, capital of labour, the epicentre of mechanized production and rapidly changing urban configurations.[2] Ortese's response to the industrial metropolis is highly ambivalent, as it embodies and magnifies the excitements as well as the dangers of this phase of modernity, marked by the "reorganization of capitalism around consumption."[3] On the one hand, Milan represents a promised land for the disenfranchised who aspire to attain economic stability; on the other, the city is saturated with the evils of a contemporary life geared towards assimilation, rejection, and dehumanization.

This dynamic underscores a dichotomy in post-war Italy between the south, underdeveloped and still agrarian in large part, and the "northern triangle," where a burgeoning market economy is taking hold, establishing groundbreaking social and cultural models. Attracted by these phenomena, Ortese at the same time recognizes the disastrous consequences of consumerism, which engenders the commodification and alienation of individuals.

Her indictment of the disintegration of social connections coalesces with the censure of the "Americanization" she detects throughout the country, albeit in a more subtle fashion. In her view, the dominant influence of the United States, dissociated from any redeeming cultural and literary traditions of that country, leads necessarily to a loss of national identity. Exposing the threats of late capitalism, Ortese unknowingly echoes Benjamin's and Adorno's theories, while supplementing their claims with the insight of a woman's perspective (thus also demystifying some tenets of patriarchal ideology implicit in their critique).

The allure of the modern city assumes a special significance for a writer who, after the critical clamour created by her *Angelici dolori* (1937), finds herself at a creative impasse by the late 1940s, despite her occasional collaborations with newspapers. Ortese is compelled to leave Naples, searching for means to support herself and aspiring to establish her professional profile, freed from her constricting family environment. While Milan offers her vital opportunities to break social barriers, to work as a journalist, and to participate in a vibrant intellectual life, the mechanisms of its cultural industry ultimately prove inhospitable. A woman who lacks strong allegiances and connections, Ortese feels estranged from the Milanese intelligentsia and the publishing industry, and ultimately rejects the inducements of the metropolis. During these years, she suffers from a pervasive sense of foreignness and existential displacement, and she cannot relinquish the cherished memories of her youth. Her commitment to writing as a moral mission does not allow her to compromise her beliefs and vocation.

Wanderings

Anna Maria Ortese's narratives and newspaper articles dating from the 1950s and 1960s constitute a sustained analysis and repudiation of the culture of mass consumption. Her reportages, often fashioned as travelogues, share a profound ethical commitment with her storytelling. They articulate the writer's distrust of contemporary myths of progress and success and indict the dominant ideology, which thrives on denying the past and fostering the "horror of memory." By effacing historical awareness, culture surrenders to the manipulations of mass production and sanctions the immutability of the present.

Her move north from the south of her youth, undertaken to sustain her professional status as writer-journalist, charts the social and moral breakdown of modernity and strives to establish contact with its victims. In so doing, she also tests dimensions of her own subjectivity, as her prose arises from a first-hand, emotional investment in the very circumstances she is observing. These peregrinations do not permit her narrator to embark on imaginative adventures: on the contrary, they are urgent confrontations with the brutality of the ordinary. Ortese's nomadic practice is a "search for the invisible,"[4] for what defies conventional expectations and is therefore banned from common perception (and by the same token, from canonical narrative codes). Feverishly moving from one place to another, she rejects the tedium of habit in favour of cognitive dynamism,[5] thus textualizing "the position of the nomadic intellectual in modernity."[6] In her case, as in the most significant travel writing, changing locations sets the stage for an experience favoured by "un double déplacement: déplacement dans l'espace [...] et déplacement en soi-même" ("a double displacement: displacement in space [...] and displacement within one's own self").[7] Ortese's chronicles and accounts of her wandering are idiosyncratic, as she avoids traditional features of these genres and devotes selective attention to physical descriptions. Her prose eschews picturesque landscapes and escapist fantasies. Ortese does not envision her journeys as a leisurely immersion in a seductive elsewhere, promising a release from everyday dreariness and disillusions. Instead of tracing the cartography of exterior spaces, she draws maps of intimacy: even her approach to unknown urban settings requires a gesture of identification, as she believes in the "necessità d'identificarsi con una città, per conoscerla" (LS 399; "need to identify with a city, to come to know it").[8] When venturing into an unfamiliar environment, her observer-narrator struggles to break down barriers that force her into the role of stranger or inattentive visitor. She perceives this foreignness as a prohibition and a punishment: "Provavo, d'un tratto, una specie di smarrimento, la sensazione penosa di chi non vede piú niente, di chi è costretto a passare correndo davanti a una sfilata di meravigliose porte chiuse. Non avrei visto Genova [...]. In una città [...] bisogna identificarsi, per vedere realmente" (LS 369; "All of a sudden, I felt a sense of bewilderment, the anguished sensation of someone who no longer sees anything and who is compelled to run past a long series of marvelous closed doors. I would not have seen Genoa [...]. In a city [...] it is necessary to identify oneself to truly see.")

These explorations celebrate the primacy of her gaze, which gathers material that the observer-author submits to her intellectual and ethical scrutiny. Her eyes are wide open on the outside world. The magnifying glass of her outlook retrieves images that arouse wonder, an act that resembles the call of philosophical inquiry: "L'atto di 'accogliere' o 'riconoscere' equivale a quello di aprire bene gli occhi, lasciando che la conoscenza di ciò che si rivela 'prenda piede' in noi. Anche là dove questo è particolarmente doloroso, quando il fatto cui bisogna aprire gli occhi è il male, e la sua efficacia in terra" ("The act of 'receiving' or 'recognizing' is akin to opening one's eyes wide, allowing that the knowledge of that which is revealed 'takes a foothold' in us. Even where this is particularly painful, when the fact on which one has to open one's eyes is evil, and its effectiveness on earth.")[9] Italian critic Pietro Citati has emphasized Ortese's ability to capture details easily overlooked, which elicit harrowing, often desperate revelations: "una specie di proprietà del suo sguardo, che la porta a vedere grande quanto grande non è (la stessa proprietà di ingrandimento che ha fatto dell'Iguana un simbolo)" ["a certain quality of her glance, which brings her to magnify things beyond their proportion (the same quality of enlargement that made the Iguana a symbol)"].[10]

In *Il porto di Toledo* (1975), Ortese retraced the first steps of these inspections, recalling the days of her Neapolitan adolescence as a combination of angst and emotional discoveries. In this peculiar *Bildung*, her reminiscences enforce Walter Benjamin's claim that "childhood is the divining rod of melancholy, and that to know the mourning of [...] radiant, glorious cities one must have been a child in them."[11] In the novel, Ortese's early excursions in the city and environs are fashioned as exercises in forgetting herself, attempts to dull her pain and apathy, or journeys into her memories:

> La mattina, io riordino le mie carte ritmiche. Per tre o quattro giorni della settimana faccio questo lavoro; gli altri, vago per la città e i colli intorno, tornandomene la sera grandemente stanca e stordita. La domenica è il mio pane dorato dei ricordi, la consumo silenziosa tra le vie del barrio, la Plaza del Quiosco; talora il molo. (R1 455)

(In the morning, I revise my rhythmic papers. Three or four days out of the week I do this work; on the other days, I wander about the city and the surrounding hills, returning in the evening exhausted and dazed. Sunday is the gilded cake of my memories, I savour it silently through the streets of the barrio, the Plaza del Quiosco; occasionally the wharf.)[12]

As it happens with the writer's travelogues, Damasa's peregrinations refuse "the superficial inducement, the exotic, the picturesque," searching instead for an existential connection with the surrounding environment, one deeply rooted in her past. Once again, her perambulations confirm Benjamin's assertion that, to "portray a city, a native must have [...] deeper motives – motives of one who travels into the past instead of into the distance. A native's book about his city will always be related to memoirs; the writer has not spent his childhood there in vain."[13] The author-protagonist seeks asylum in the streets, which become the locus of a form of rootedness ("they were our home" the author writes to Pasquale Prunas),[14] replacing the claustrophobic household and insular family dynamics that would condemn her to a destiny of neglect.[15] Her urge to roam through the city is of a unique kind. While Benjamin, commenting on the Baudelairian flâneur, remarks that the "street becomes a dwelling" for him ("he is as much at home among the façades of houses as the citizen is in his four walls. To him the shiny, enameled signs of business are at least as good a wall ornament as an oil painting is to a bourgeois in his salon"),[16] in Ortese's case we find a more troubling approach and emotional investment. Her tireless explorations testify to an anxious *quête*, which cannot be accomplished through the self-centred enjoyment of the modern urban aestethics. Her narrator is searching for existential repose, for significant encounters with the "other," hoping to recover communal bonds and to restore a harmonious measure of life, but often unearthing visions of affliction. Gazing at the southern city in *Il mare non bagna Napoli* (1953), Ortese uncovers a premodern culture, an archaic world founded on a misguided attachment to elementary instincts; in fact, a deadly surrender to primal forces.

In a break from the circumstances recounted in her fictional autobiography, Ortese cannot confine her wandering to Naples, which she soon finds suffocating, as it stalls her intellectual growth and thwarts her ambitions as a writer. The author entertains deeply contradictory feelings towards this city, which, in the immediate aftermath of the Second World War, she perceives as a phantasmagoric yet bewitching spectacle, filled with the promises of a luxuriant nature while showing the ruins of a decaying civilization.[17] While fascinated by its sky and coastline, she describes it as a cemeterial landscape, which enchains and annihilates whomever falls under its spell: "A casa, in questa Napoli, sento che finirei per impazzire, col perdermi come in una palude. L'aria è dolce e bella, ma – per la mia giovinezza – asfissiante" ("At home, here in Naples, I feel I'd end up going mad, losing myself as though in a swamp. The air is sweet and pleasant, but – for my youth – asphyxiating").[18]

In "Dodici ore straordinarie prima di salutare Napoli" ("Twelve Extraordinary Hours Before Leaving Naples"), an autobiographical piece Ortese published in *Milano-sera* in 1951, she contends that for an impoverished native of the south, the possibility of having money at her disposal and aspiring to a successful profession comes at a very high price. To grant their miracles, the merciless idols of modernity – goods, wealth, and professional success – require the symbolic death of the convert, who must proffer her neck for the slaughter, submitting herself to the torment of leaving the beloved city: "Vi sembra di essere morta da lungo tempo, e di tornare solo per una concessione di Dio, solo per un attimo, nella vostra terra" ("You feel like you have been dead for a long time and have returned only by the grace of God, only for a brief moment, to your land").[19] Having heeded the call of the sirens of the north, launched towards economic prosperity,[20] the narrator breaches the forbidden threshold. She is attracted by the allures of modernity, which could rescue her from the immobility of a backwards south, frozen in time. She has now obtained the ticket allowing her to purchase those goods to which, in her wanderings within the city of her youth, she had never been granted access ("quelle piccole affascinanti spese che avete sempre sognato di fare, ma inutilmente, finché vi aggiravate per le vie [di Napoli]"; "those charming small purchases that you always dreamed of making, albeit fruitlessly, until you roamed the streets of [Naples]")[21]:

> Intanto, fatto che ha del miracoloso, sapete di avere in un angolo della vostra valigia [...] una busta con cinque o diecimila lire, che a Napoli non avete posseduto mai e che una misteriosa potenza vi concede solo a condizione che lasciate Napoli.
>
> (Meanwhile, by some sort of miracle, you know that you have stashed in a corner of your suitcase [...] an envelope containing five or ten thousand lira, which in Naples you never had and which a mysterious power bestows upon you only under the condition that you leave Naples.)[22]

The transformation from premodern to modern metropolitan subject entails renouncing one's personal past, engaging in a separation rite of rebirth. In order to partake in the feast of commodities, instead of merely contemplating it as an outsider, the heroine must renounce her former self and, with it, family bonds, as well as the comfort of living in a close-knit community.

Only thanks to the "mysterious power" of modernity, perhaps a treacherous force, can she venture into forbidden spaces, beyond the shop windows, previously admired only from without: to assume a new identity, she must obtain the talismans that sanction her passage into the sphere of consumerism ("il golf, i guanti, i giornali, tutto ciò che avete desiderato lungamente" ["the jumper, the gloves, the newspapers, all the things that you have long desired"]).[23] In order to be received into the world of possessions, she is compelled to renounce her former self. By venturing forth into the bewitching domain of commodities and accepting them as signs of identity, the writer surrendered to a temptation and perpetrated a betrayal. The items she purchased will transform her, rendering her unrecognizable to her peers, relegating her to the anonymity of the metropolis and moulding her into a compliant subject. Ortese writes:

> Entrate e v'impadronite di queste cose che contribuiranno a mutarvi, a fare di voi l'estranea, l'amica che vive lontano. Sfogliate dei giornali: ecco il mondo, le voci enormi che v'invitano, vi lusingano, vi persuadono col miraggio di mille doveri, di soddisfazioni infinite. Tutto bene. Avete già obbedito.
>
> (You enter and take possession of these things that will help in transforming you, in making you the stranger, the friend who lives far away. You leaf through newspapers: here is the world, the great voices that beckon you, that flatter you, that lure you with the illusion of a thousand duties, of endless satisfaction. Everything is fine. You have already complied.)[24]

In the fictional setting of the article, a shining yet ominously deserted bus ferries the narrator towards the shadow realm of modernity from which there is no return ("Non rimetterete piú piede nella casa di vostro padre" ["You will never again set foot in your father's house"]).[25] In the absence of any recourse, protection, or safeguard, she is exiled from her "beloved city" and so condemned: "È ora. Non c'è piú nessuna speranza, nessuna possibilità di dubbio, di errore. Su uno di quei sedili è segnato il vostro numero" ("It's time. There is no longer any hope, any chance of doubt, of mistake. One of these seats bears your number").[26]

Driven by her literary vocation and ambitions, Ortese faces the uncertainties of the unknown. Her relocation opens more prestigious professional opportunities, allowing her to be accepted into intellectual circles and to strengthen her reputation as a writer-journalist. She transcribes this sense of wanderlust to the page, tracing a dense web of movements and travel notes.

Behind her itinerant writing we find an ambivalent strategy: while denying the consolation of safe havens, at times this practice appears to be a therapeutic exercise to lessen the pain of "knowing too much," to unmask the deceptions of modernity, and to perceive the suffering of the disenfranchised: "I viaggi, in questo lavoro, possono essere un grande aiuto per ritrovare della calma" ("In this line of work [journalism], travels can be of great help in finding some peace of mind"), Ortese confesses to Prunas.[27] Being affected by economic need and personal neuroses – a victim of what she defines a "confino di classe," a confinement inflicted on her because of her low social standing – she searches for temporary relief in these escapes from captivity. Reflecting on a visit to Nice, where she would be the guest of a Canadian friend, her spirits are lifted ("questo viaggio mi è necessario come l'ossigeno. Da due giorni mi sembra di essere un'altra" ["I need this trip like I need oxygen. In the last two days I have been feeling like a different person"])[28] and she worries about the "caso disgraziato che non *le* riuscisse per qualche ragione di partire"[29] ("unfortunate situation that by some twist of fate *I* should not manage to leave"). The thought of setting out and crossing borders fills her with enthusiasm: "Prepararsi a partire, prendere, a Milano, *il treno* per Parigi!" ("Getting ready to leave, taking the Paris *train* from Milan!").[30]

In the aftermath of the Second World War, though, these journeys often heighten her sense of displacement and withhold the consolation of human encounters:

> vado su e giú come un commesso viaggiatore. I treni sono sporchi e squallidi, la gente avidissima e diffidente. Ho cercato l'Italia e non l'ho trovata piú. Tutta l'Italia dev'essere a Napoli: forse, dove siete voi, amici miei. Non tornerò piú a Milano. Ma dove debbo andare?
>
> (I am moving all over the place like a travelling salesman. The trains are dirty and seamy, the people so greedy and mistrustful. I looked out for Italy yet did not see it anymore. All of Italy must be in Naples: maybe, where you are, my friends. I will never go back to Milan. But where am I supposed to go?)[31]

More than forty years later she described her rides on uncomfortable trains while working on assignment as a journalist, often without having planned her accommodations, as exhausting, yet exhilarating adventures. The chaos and insecurity of the post-war era were filled with vague expectations:

> Nel periodo compreso tra gli anni '48 e '62, ma anche un po' prima e anche un po' dopo, mi accadde di prendere una quantità di treni, scendere in molte stazioni all'alba, e ripartire ancora di notte, barcollando per la stanchezza, senza sapere precisamente dove avrei riposato il giorno successivo. Qualche volta viaggiavo per un giornale, qualche volta no. [...] L'Italia era ancora molto povera, non offriva una vita facile. Tuttavia questa vita era simile a un campo pieno di confuse, grandiose possibilità; e la speranza – e il rischio – bastavano. (LS 1)
>
> (In the years between 1948 and 1962, but even a little earlier and a little later, I happened to take many trains, to get off in many stations at dawn and leave at night, staggering from fatigue, without knowing for sure where I would rest the following day. Sometimes, I ventured out for a newspaper, sometimes I did not. [...] Italy was still very poor, it did not offer an easy life. However, that life was akin to a field full of confused, yet great possibilities; and the hope – and the risk – were enough for me.)

This frenetic journeying partakes in the excitement and the optimism of the "reconstruction" and the "economic miracle," as a war-torn country resurged from its ashes and embraced the prospect of gaining prosperity, along with social and political renewal. Before "the inflationary crisis of 1962," Italy underwent sweeping changes, which involved its entire way of life.[32] Initially, this array of opportunities allowed Ortese to overcome obscurity and her sense of failure, and to achieve her potential as a reporter and storyteller. However, her faith in a bright professional future had to face numerous setbacks and disillusions,[33] and was to be short-lived: "Conobbi un solo periodo di speranza, a Milano, nel '53. Subito finí e cominciarono le terribili ansie per vivere (affitto, pane) che non sono mai piú finite" ("I experienced only one period of hope, in Milan, in 1953. It soon ended and there started my terrible anxieties about making a living (rent, food), which have never come to an end").[34]

Despite the newly found, if fluctuating, confidence, Ortese's Milan years were accompanied by a disturbing leitmotif: the perception of a threat against a sustainable, humane existence. From the writer's perspective, the modern city is a site of abuses, a theatre of cruelty whose dwellers are subjected to the violence of the everyday, leading to their reification or extinction at the hands of technology or of more insidious mechanisms of domination.

In the "Capital of Italian Labour": The Train Station, the Prostitute, and the Reporter

Ortese charts the spreading threat of commodification while travelling to the north of the peninsula, under the seductive spell of prosperity and success. In the short stories and reportages that she collected in *Silenzio a Milano,* the Lombard metropolis stands opposite to Naples as a site hostile to communal bonds. Issued by the prominent publisher Laterza, the volume offered an indictment of predatory industrialization, with hints of a socialist sensitivity in its strenuous defence of the victims of industrial production: the labour forces and the underprivileged.

Despite its lure of economic plenitude, Milan harbours a dynamic of historical progress that does not eliminate suffering:

> Con la guerra e il dopoguerra vennero i racconti "realistici" – ma neppure tanto – del *Mare non bagna Napoli* e di *Silenzio a Milano.* Qui c'era il *mondo,* c'erano i fatti della storia e della società, ma c'era ugualmente incredulità e malinconia: come se il dolore del mondo non fosse *tutto spiegabile.*
>
> (With the war and its aftermath came the allegedly realistic stories – well, not quite – of *The Bay Is Not Naples* and *Silence in Milan.* Here there was the *world,* there were historical and social facts, yet at the same time there was incredulity and melancholy, as if it were not *entirely possible to explain* the suffering of the world.)[35]

While Naples lies in a state of torpor, virtually anaesthetized by emphatic sentimentality (in popular culture the city was traditionally associated with such displays),[36] Milan celebrates the triumph of riches with ruthless abandon, emboldened by economic fervour. The images of promiscuity and unbearable destitution of the Neapolitan streets are replaced, in the Milanese narratives, with the portrayal of an advanced "civilization" that appears to be merciless in isolating and degrading individuals. In the "città dura, austriaca, crudele" ("harsh, cruel, Austrian city"), the writer traverses locations that are paradigms of existential drift. She crosses the boundaries between affluent neighbourhoods and destitute districts, grieving over the persistence of injustice and the despair of the downtrodden.

Milan has abdicated its putative protective vocation and reneged on its maternal calling as nurturer of the fresh energies of the nation. In fact, it has developed into a rapacious, tentacular apparatus. Looking over the sprawling city at night-time, the narrator senses the "slargamento, fino all'inverosimile, di un corpo muto, un corpo meccanico, gigantesco, pieno di luci […] ma assolutamente muto. Milano, dal centro, che fu nobile e umano, e ora è appassito, gonfiandosi e palpitando […] come una cosa stregata, supera continuamente il segno che la limitava ieri, stamattina" ("broadening, beyond recognition, of a silent, gigantic, mechanical body, filled with lights […] but absolutely mute. From its centre, which was once noble and humane, and now has withered, Milan, swelling and quivering […], as something bewitched, constantly trespasses the limit that circumscribed it yesterday, even this morning […]").[37] Initially laid out in response to human needs and aspirations, the city has discarded any plan of organic, sustainable development, instead absorbing and destroying its surroundings.

In the article "La città senza paura" ("The City Without Fear"), published in the first years of Ortese's stay in Milan,[38] she takes an ambivalent position towards the capital of labour, a stance that reflects her recurrent changes of mind,[39] but also her wavering moods regarding her status as a writer. In this text the critique of the metropolis is attributed to an anonymous "ingenua signora di provincia" ("simple-minded country woman"), oblivious to the "povertà" ("poverty"), "dolore" ("suffering") and the "lotte che sono necessarie a certuni per sopravvivere" ("struggles that some people must sustain to survive").[40] She had warned the author's mother about the risks of moving to Milan: "'È una città terribile,' scriveva quella intatta mente, 'è come un ingranaggio enorme che afferri continuamente cose e creature, se ne serva per la sua fame turbinosa, e quando le abbia succhiate, ne getti via i rifiuti'" ("'It's a terrible city,' wrote the naïve soul, 'it's like an enormous gear that continuously seizes creatures and things, using them as fuel to propel its turbine, and when it has bled them dry, it spits out the refuse'").[41] This notion is countered by the author's claim that the Lombard capital, cradle of work ethic and entrepreneurial spirit, provides an antidote to idleness and indigence, embracing those who are struggling to improve their condition ("Evidentemente la signora […] non era mai stata a Milano, […] comunque non vi era giunta da lontano, senza pane, né casa, né speranza, per chiedere, e ottenere, tutto questo" ["Apparently the lady […] had never been to Milan, […] at least she had not arrived here from afar without bread, home, hope, in order to ask, and obtain, all this"]).[42]

If the narrator seems to fall prey to the illusions of the industrial city, with its promises of opulence and professional success,[43] she also engages in difficult negotiations with this wealth of prospects and reveals a residue of distrust. This land of opportunity requires its dwellers to renounce contact with nature as the price of financial security (a benefit nonetheless denied to Ortese, as most of her writings set in Milan demonstrate):

> Qui, il sole non c'è, o ben poco, per solo una metà dell'anno; non vi sono colline né boschi, né fiumi, né mari; non vi sono nuvole, ma solo il fumo delle ciminiere, né vento, ma solo il rumore delle macchine.
>
> (Here, there is no sun, or little of it, for only half of the year; there are no hills, nor forests, nor rivers, nor seas; there are no clouds, only the smoke from the factory chimneys, nor is there wind, only the sound of the machines.)[44]

The gratitude Ortese expresses in this article towards the generosity of the Milanese who are willing to assist anyone on the verge of destitution[45] is contrasted in other writings by her bitterness on account of being exiled from her "homeland" and estranged from her friends. No suitable living spaces are made available to those excluded from "economic power."[46]

On 10 August 1948, the writer, having just settled in Milan, takes up the paradigm of the "homo homini lupus" to stigmatize the struggle for survival that she observes around her: "Io, dopo i primi giorni di grande fiducia, sono un po' triste, e proprio nei confronti del mio lavoro. [...] Qui è come tra i lupi. Tutti si guardano con occhi avari, fremendo dal desiderio di divorarsi e leccarsi poi le ossa del compagno" ("After the first days with a lot of confidence, I am a little sad, and especially about my own job. [...] It's like being among wolves here. Everyone looks at one another with greedy eyes, quivering with desire to devour each other and lick the bones dry").[47] With this image of competitive fierceness Ortese reverses, on the ground of the concern for one's fellow human beings, the mythical construction according to which northern modernity defines itself by erasing the traces of primitivism embedded in southern customs.[48]

In the candid confessions she made to her friend Pasquale Prunas, however, metropolitan life, though dominated by anonymity and bewilderment, seems to compensate in part for the chagrin of her Neapolitan youth:

> Qui la vita è dura, in un certo senso. Non c'è nessuno che ti venga incontro con una lode, tutti, o quasi, aspettano che tu cada. Non credere che io mi affidi a compiacenze tristi [...]. Si è soli. *Molto* piú soli che a Napoli, e uno può morire. Ti coprono col mantello dell'ironia, non altro. Almeno, questo è tutto quanto vedo per oggi di questa grossa Milano, eppure resisto: perché infine non ho che ombre alle spalle; meglio quelle davanti e intorno, almeno sono nuove. [...] Occorre che faccia appello a tutto il mio poco istinto di vivere, alle cose lontane, ai ricordi, alle speranze buone. [...] Importanti, qui, non sono che la cattiveria, una cattiveria elegante, fine a se stessa. Bisogna essere cattivissimi, per riuscire.
>
> (Here life is hard, in a manner of speaking. There's no one who comes to greet you with praise, everyone, or almost everyone, waits for you to slip up. Don't think that I am giving in to a pathetic state of self-indulgence [...]. It's lonely here. *Much* more lonely than in Naples, and you can die. They just cover you with a cloak of irony, nothing more. At least this is all I see today of this gritty Milan, yet I am still holding up because at the end of the day I only have shadows behind me; better those in front and around, at least they are new. [...] I am forced to appeal to what little instinct I have to stay alive, to far off things, to memories, to good hopes. [...] What's important here is nothing more than wickedness, an elegant wickedness, an end in itself. You have to be extremely mean to succeed.)[49]

In this brutal battleground, even a helping hand extended to the destitute turns out to be a paternalistic gesture. By the end of the 1950s Milan was the vanguard of a country thrown into a self-defeating process of blind, imported modernization: "l'Italia viveva di valori che non erano piú attualissimi. Cercava i mercati, si americanizzava violentemente e rapidamente. Moriva come entità spirituale – che è sempre la critica e il rinnovamento" ("Italy was living by values of the past that were no longer valid. It sought out markets, rapidly and violently becoming Americanized. It was dying as a spiritual entity – which always means critique and renewal").[50]

To stigmatize this contamination, the representation of city life cannot be limited to the mere record of everyday occurrences, taken at face value as a "cronaca di fatti che accadono" ("chronicle of things that happen"). It needs to be enveloped by "un alone [...] di immagini" ("a halo [...] of figures") and by *humour*, "un lievito interiore" ("an internal additive"), or else risk becoming a monotonous documentary, a "cosa semplicemente atroce e [...] viziosa, inutile come un vizio" ("purely vile and […] depraved thing as useless as a vice.") Writing to Prunas, Ortese concludes:

> In sostanza, i pezzi che vorrei fare per *Omnibus* dovrebbero essere una cronaca disintossicata della vita milanese, del mondo borghese di qui, ma non contro gli uomini veri e propri (com'è possibile odiare?) solo contro quanto di fatuo e di mortale c'è nel loro costume. […] Ho scoperto, stando qui, il cancro, un cancro tanto necessario e pur malinconico, di questa forte città, e direi la sua debolezza e vergogna, ignote a lei stessa: la passione, l'avidità del guadagno; passione e avidità quasi fine a se stesse, morbose, eccitate, fatali, come da noi l'ozio e le canzonette.

> (Basically, the texts that I would like to write for *Omnibus* should provide an unadulterated chronicle of Milanese life, of the bourgeois world here, but not against the people themselves (how is it possible to hate anyone?), only against how vain and deadly their behaviour is. […] Living here, I have discovered the cancer of this strong city (a cancer so necessary and yet melancholic), and her weakness and shame, I would say, which she herself ignores: the passion, the hunger for wages; a passion and a form of greed that appear to be almost self-sustaining, morbid, frantic, lethal like the idleness and the popular tunes for us in Naples.)[51]

A few years later, when the professional opportunities that had filled her with hope were dashed by the inexorable laws of the culture industry, Ortese became disenchanted yet again. Furthermore, in time she would suffer the consequences of her overt criticism of Milan, her eccentricities, and her idiosyncrasies in dealing with publishers (not to mention being anguished by the painful ending of a love relationship),[52] thus facing increasing isolation. Enduring these hardships, while trying to make ends meet and pursuing her writing projects, she went through phases of "disperazione" ("desperation") and "abbrutimento" ("dejection").[53]

If the literary marketplace was creating new spaces for women writers, their work continued to be subject to restrictions and patriarchal control. In the 1960s, to cite one example, Ortese was asked to comply with the dominant cultural codes and compromise her literary integrity. Antonio Alberti, then director of the magazine *Amica*, rejected one of her stories,[54] judging it inappropriate for the readers of the women's publication. He suggested that she submit lighter, more upbeat narratives:

> Purtroppo glielo debbo rinviare [i.e., il Suo racconto], perché mi sembra che la storia non sia adatta a un pubblico come il nostro. Non vorrei che questo mio "rifiuto" bloccasse i nostri successivi rapporti. Io ci terrei ad avere la Sua firma, e con una certa ritmicità, su "Amica." Vorrei però farLe, se mi permette, una raccomandazione: invitarLa a raccontare delle storie ottimistiche. Per storie ottimistiche non intendo racconti rosa, ma racconti che concilino la lettrice con la vita e con il piacere di vivere. Il nostro giornale cerca di essere utile e pratico in tutte le sue parti. Solo nella narrativa noi concediamo alle lettrici una specie di evasione. Lei sa come la donna oggi abbia le stesse preoccupazioni, gli stessi affanni e le stesse ansie dell'uomo. Per questo vogliamo che il nostro settore della narrativa sia un invito, non diciamo al sogno banale, ma al respiro dopo tanti fastidi quotidiani.
>
> (Unfortunately, I must send it [i.e., your short story] back to you, because I don't think that the story is suitable to a readership such as ours. I would not like my "rejection" to hinder our future relations. It would be very valuable for me to have your contribution [literally: your signature], with a certain regularity, in "Amica." However, I would like, if you don't mind, to make you a recommendation: to invite you to tell optimistic stories. By optimistic stories I do not mean fairy tales but stories that acquaint the reader with life and the joy of living. Our publication tries to be useful and practical throughout all its sections. Only with the narrative section do we allow the readers a sort of escape. You know how a woman today has the same worries, the same concerns and the same anxieties as does a man. For this reason we would like for our narrative section to invite our readers, if not to trivial daydreaming, at least to take a deep breath after so many everyday troubles.)[55]

According to this condescending ideological stance, women readers should be given only fictionalized, sugar-coated stories, pieces that can be enjoyed as escapist forms, detached from the disappointments of daily experience. Indeed, the act of reading should induce forgetfulness and disengagement from the present. The writer's contribution must be divested of any hints of cultural critique (or of melancholy reflection): she is merely valorized as a "signature," an emblem that conveys an aura of intellectual sophistication.

Ortese cannot subscribe to these escapist fantasies, nor will she settle for merely offering a documentary account of what she sees. In light of the absurd growth of the city bent on disrupting social cohesion, a rational, poised account of what the observer perceives would not do justice to the harshness of her impressions and meditations. In order to reproduce her disorientation, she has to renounce well-ordered, uplifting, or facile storytelling. To bear testimony to the deprivation and malaise caused by modernity, her reportages on Milan must convey a bewildered wandering through the metropolis. To capture the exemplary site of displacement, she realizes that a language foreign to conventional codes must be crafted, a language that partakes in the "unreality" of her uncanny perceptions. Her narratives must evoke fragmentation and dismay.

With an attitude somewhat akin to Benjamin's critical posture in *The Arcades Project*, Ortese acts as an "urban physiognomist" in search of locations and figures that the collective memory would prefer to erase. Shedding the ambiguities that she recorded in some of the texts previously discussed, in *Silenzio a Milano* she investigates the backstage of modernity, chronicling transitional spaces, the city's outskirts and sites of marginality: the train station, the dancing halls, the "Case albergo" (housing facilities for lower middle-class people in need), and the reformatory.

The author has gained first-hand experience of the metropolis's dynamics of subordination, failure, and exclusion, living in close quarters with the marginalized people who fail to conform to the economic credo. In "Le piramidi di Milano" ("Milan's Pyramids"), a short piece on the "Case albergo" included in the collection, Ortese calls attention to the strategies of control that the "industrial culture" enforces upon its noncompliant, but powerless subjects:

> Invisibile, su ciascuna porta [degli ospiti delle Case], c'è un cartellino che invita il personale a tenere d'occhio quel professionista o artista o insegnante: la ragazza col golfino e la signora coi capelli quasi bianchi, il giornalista e l'impiegato, lo studente negro e il vecchio pensionato. Tutti probabili contravventori della legge della grande città industriale e medioevale insieme [...], che dovunque sospetta un'infrazione alla regola, all'ordine stabilito; e consiglia continuamente il silenzio, predica incessantemente il silenzio; dispone senza stancarsi la condizione prima del silenzio: la solitudine. (SM 78)

> (On each door [of the guests in residence], there is a little invisible tag that encourages the staff to keep an eye on that professional man, artist or teacher; the girl in the jumper and the lady with nearly white hair, the journalist and the office employee, the black student and the old pensioner. All these

> probably transgressors of the law of the great city that is at once industrial and medieval [...], which ubiquitously suspects an infraction of the rules, of the established order; and constantly recommends silence, incessantly preaches silence; it tirelessly lays down the first condition of silence: solitude.)

As in a panopticon designed to inspect everyone's movements, here these marginalized figures, who appear to resist conformity, are subject to constant scrutiny and sanitization ("come pesci rossi in una boccia di vetro, nuotano nella pulita e disperata atmosfera di quelle stanze," SM 78; "like goldfish in a glass bowl, they swim in the clean and desperate atmosphere of those rooms"). Compartimentalized in separate, identical cells, they undergo constant inspection and intrusion. As Foucault has demonstrated, a disciplinary mechanism ensures "the penetration of regulation into even the smallest details of everyday life," through "rituals of exclusion."[56] Segmentation and separation are implemented in the routine of these dispossessed "citizens," in order to avoid the spreading of critical judgment, which is feared as an insinuating, contagious malaise. These residents are subjected therefore to a system of surveillance that cannot tolerate their faith in a now-obsolete value system: "La vita, cioè i rapporti umani, l'amicizia, il conversare, il discutere, l'intelligenza di uno sguardo, la gioia" (SM 77–78; "Life, that is, human relationships, friendship, having a talk, having a discussion, the intelligence of a glance, joy"). Thought and dialogue, scrutinized and prosecuted by the ruling economic power, become dangerous distractions and potential forms of rebellion that must be stifled; they stand in the way of the acritical surrender to market forces on which the new economy is built.

These buildings appear as metaphor and synecdoche of the oppressive order of the modern cityscape. The urbanistic grid and its institutions shape and regulate the relations between individuals: the confined space confirms the dysphoric quality of life in Milan, characterized by way of negation, overturning current stereotypes. Contributing to this process of surveillance and control, the architecture of the "Case albergo" feeds the nightmares of depersonalization: "Nata per proteggere, opprime; per rassicurare, spaventa; per confortare, incupisce. Dice tutto il nostro tempo: l'intenzione di assistere l'uomo, e il disprezzo misterioso dell'uomo" (SM 76; "Born to protect, it oppresses; to reassure, it frightens; to comfort, it traumatizes. It succeeds in expressing our time: the intent to help man, and the mysterious contempt for man"). With its false escape routes, its places of contention, and the gloomy monuments erected "in memoria dell'uomo moderno" (SM 79; "in memory of the modern man"), the "capital of labour" forecasts the nightmares of modernity.

"Una notte nella stazione" ("A Night at the Station"), the reportage that opens the collection, is one of its most powerful chapters. It investigates the underworld hidden behind the smokescreens of progress. In Ortese's inquisitive eyes, the cityscape becomes a portrait bearing the scars of violated existence:

> Le rughe [...] si vedevano sulla città. Quella parte della città di Milano, quelle cinque tettoie nere, quella collina di cinque semicerchi neri, formanti una specie di corpo di ragno appiattito al suolo con le zampe aperte; quel suolo, quel piazzale vastissimo ricoperto da una fitta rete di binari, di piccoli pali e di caselli d'acciaio; quei vagoni immobili come strisce d'ombra [...] erano veramente un volto, particolari di un volto aggrondato, duro, stranamente invecchiato e perduto. (SM 7)

> (Wrinkles were displayed [...] by the city. That part of Milan, those five black roofing sheds, that hill of five black semi-circles, forming what looked like the body of a spider which had dropped to the earth on tense and extended legs; that flooring, that vast roadbed covered by a dense, intricate web of railway tracks, of upright poles and steel boxes; those immobile railway carriages like strips of shadow [...]; all of it formed a face, the lineaments of a scowling, hard, strangely aged and hopeless face. [MW2 123])

Here the outline of the train station turns into a repulsive, threatening creature, with a mesmerizing power. Paradoxically, this architectural wonder emblematizes a frozen life, with no emergency exits, on the brink of dissolution. Instead of encouraging human encounters, the building serves as the backdrop of the comings and goings of anonymous commuters, whose mechanical steps and gestures are dictated by their routine and work schedule. Its animation is purely artificial, confined to the time and rhythms of production, as a result of social engineering. Once the travelling crowds have receded, the large halls become the bleak setting of solitude and despair, offering refuge to vagabonds, "cittadini che non si decidono a rientrare a casa, o che non ne hanno alcuna" (SM 18; "citizens who can't make up their minds to return home, who have no homes to return to," MW2 133). As Augé reminds us, in modernity "les espaces du vide sont étroitement mêlés à ceux du trop-plein. Ce sont les mêmes parfois, mais à d'autres heures" ("empty spaces are closely associated to those that are overfilled. They are sometimes the same, but at different times").[57]

Belying its early promises of progress and sustained growth, the city's monstrosity mirrors the mercilessness of the present: "Ed ecco, come in viaggio, a una svolta, questa città non c'era piú; o meglio, il suo buon volto onesto aveva preso una espressione selvaggia, sotto la quale le care linee erano cancellate, perdute" (SM 15; "But now, as though after a bend in a traveler's road, the city was no longer there. Or, better, its fine, honest face had assumed an expression of savagery, which had totally undone and canceled out its dear, familiar features," MW2 130).[58] The intimidating, oppressive structure of the station symbolizes a metropolis that has degenerated and become utterly alien to its dwellers who are now stranded.

The documentary tone of the first pages of the reportage gives way to the weight of Ortese's anti-industrial stance: her testimony tells the story of automatization and alienation through the language of allegory and revelation. The text condemns the devastating powers of modernity, responsible for the demise of subjectivity and social bonds. Forced to conform to the dominant ethos and embrace the goals of industrial society, individuals have lost any trace of identity, surrendering to their roles as cogs in the machine, either as members of the workforce or consumers. Their agency has collapsed into a passive response to market injunctions, and they are degraded into inert matter. In accord with the social critique of Adorno, Ortese stresses how, in "its fight against the particular and the individual, mass society marginalizes or represses what might emerge as a voice of resistance to the all-embracing unity of its system."[59]

In front of the vast flux of commuters and newcomers, whose movements are regulated by predetermined laws and ordinary duties, the narrator's attention is drawn to the desperate "dwellers" of the train station: marginalized figures, ejected from the boundaries of economic security and social recognition. Lacking professional obligations or reasonable purposes, these dispersed individuals are summoned here by the aura of the place or in search of an escape. They have fallen prey to the illusions of the transformative power of the metropolis, but have finally recognized its machinations, and they anxiously seek out brief encounters with others and words of compassion. Here they witness and confront their own marginality. These outcasts, wounded and betrayed by Milan, search for solace in the station, which is the gateway to the city and its outpost. They temporarily occupy this transitional space, as both the historic centre and the urban perimeter have denied them citizenship.

Looking for the company of these pariahs, also discussed in light of Hannah Arendt's thought in the following essay by Cristina Della Coletta, the narrator encounters a destitute family of migrants from the south now returning to their birthplace, without having benefited from the promises of the economic miracle. Those excluded from the rituals of mass consumption can only brush the dark margins of the forbidden metropolis, never enjoying its lustre. The centre of manufacturing industry lures and captures the downtrodden in order to exploit and then expel them as waste products. Caught in the "girone della civiltà industriale" ("hellish circle of industrial civilization"), the nameless urban subject will be ultimately reduced to "un automa o un rottame" (SM 11; "a robot or a scrap of junk," MW2 126).

With this perverse mechanism, the "capital of labour" eradicates logic and crushes the practices of social cohesion. The alleged triumph of reason – degraded in fact to commercial cunning and shrewd "economic ideology"[60] – regards the fate of the weak with indifference. The victims will be quickly forgotten as the accidental, albeit massive, casualties of a shipwreck. Left without any safety net, they can only mourn the disappearance of empathy and brotherhood, resorting to allusive, fragmented utterances, interspersed with voids and disseminated with prophetic warnings. A literature professor, "smarrito come una bestiola, leggero" (SM 24; "as lost and weightless as a little beast," MW2 138), who paces aimlessly through the station, alternates from "un mormorio indecifrabile" (SM 25; "an indecipherable mutter," MW2 139), to "[n]essuna risposta" (SM 27; "[n]o reply," MW2 141), to fulminating verdicts: "'[Prima della guerra] C'era speranza. Cosí era'" (SM 27; "'[Before the war] There was hope. That's how it was,'" MW2 141); "'[...] il solo vero diritto sta nella potenza economica'" (SM 29; "'[...] the only true rights are the ones conferred by economic power,'" MW2 143).

Reacting against the use of language as a means of domination, which hides the collateral damages of industrial expansion, "silence" is at the same time the result of a prohibition and a sign of resistance (significantly, the term opens the title of the collection, forming a pair with the toponym). In fact, "the *telos* of instrumental rationality" is predicated upon the "silencing of reflection."[61] On the other hand, disjointed speech voices the rejection of the professed logic behind inhuman labour practices and their rationalization, enforced in the name of progress and conspicuous consumption. Therefore, the outsiders' reticence and elliptical utterings function as forms of resistance and subversion, opposing the status quo and displaying the mutilations that have been inflicted upon thought and language.

Among the victims of the urban wasteland, streetwalkers stand out as emblems of the commodification of the female body, showcased for male pleasure and consumption. In "Una notte nella stazione" the initial description of a prostitute enforces the notion that she has taken "the concept of marketability itself for a stroll."[62] Through the representation of this archetype – prominently featured in cinematic and literary texts of the time – Ortese not only articulates her critique from a woman's perspective, but (perhaps unwittingly) calls into question the assessments of the male interpreters of modernity, thus challenging the assumptions of patriarchal discourse.

The prostitute's stiff physiognomy exhibits rigor mortis, "the petrifying and fantastic workings of commodity fetishism and reification."[63] In her portrayal, however, emerge symptoms of ambivalence, details that fracture it. The woman's recognition of herself as an object of desire coexists with her intimate sense of unease:

> La donna che si guardava nello specchio del bar, alle undici di sera, in mezzo a una folla di viaggiatori, di curiosi, di inoccupati [...], non era una bellezza. Come smemorata, si passava una mano corta e pesante, dalle unghie rosse, sui capelli, intorno al viso volgare e timido insieme, sfrontato e tetro. [...] Il suo corpo [...] non aveva piú età: come il viso, era impercettibilmente appesantito e disfatto. Una dura capellatura color rame, dove brillavano dei fili argentati, le ricadeva rigida e artificiosa sulle spalle rosa dell'abito. (SM 32)

> (The woman who regarded herself in the mirror of the bar, at eleven o'clock in the evening, in the midst of a crowd of travelers, as well as of the idle and curious [...] was surely no beauty. There was something quite slack in the way she passed a short, heavy hand, the fingernails red, over her hair and around her face, which at once was vulgar and timid, arrogant and grim. [...] Her torso [...] no longer had any age at all. Like her face, it had an indistinct air of heaviness and decay. A hard, copper-colored hairdo, streaked with strands of silver, hung down stiffly and artificially on the pink shoulders of her dress. [MW2 145])

Looking at herself in the mirror, the woman assesses her viability as merchandise and spectacle, and it is not a pretty sight. Her gaze is that of the alienated subject who has had a harsh awakening but needs desperately to cling to a false image of herself in order to sustain her value on the sexual market. The mirror reflects the traits of an aging body, whose deterioration cannot be dissimulated by her heavy make-up. Her elaborate coiffure, which Ortese pictures as a metal shield, points to her transformation into an automaton, to her capitulation to the inorganic. It also emblematizes her subjection to the metal of exchange.

The prostitute has given in to the phallocentric notion of woman as commodity, without foreseeing the dangers of her reification. Her ambiguous appearance reveals the "hidden workings of desire and fear."[64] Despite her accoutrements, her body is outmoded, worn out merchandise, no longer capable of eliciting arousal, thus revealing "the consumption of mortal energy."[65] Under her impassive face (she had the "aria stupida e assorta di un volatile" (SM 32; "the stupid, single-minded air of a bird," MW2 146)[66] there are the marks of a "persona spaventata" (SM 32; "person who's scared," MW2 145), aware of her demise. The alluring façade of youthful vitality has been replaced by a disillusioned, hardened skin, covered by lines of worry and age. As Esther Leslie remarks, commenting on Benjamin's diagnosis of modernity, "the whore – the commodified woman – plays out the logic of the capitalist system, which is immanently destructive."[67]

Unlike Ortese's description, however, Benjamin's portrayal of the prostitute betrays a fascination with this embodiment of the reified woman that falls prey to the trappings of patriarchal culture. His archetype combines "carnal lust and corpse," denying the streetwalker any consciousness of her condition, as though in her gaze "the magic of distance" were "extinguished."[68] Benjamin's account fails to acknowledge the woman's identity and objectifies her as a shadowy and muted presence, much as Baudelaire had done. Notwithstanding her censure of a livelihood based on utilitarian relations ([un'] "attività [...] esclusiva quanto cieca," SM 39; an "activity, equally exclusive and blind," MW2 152), Ortese, instead, is sympathetic: she recognizes in this figure the casualty of systemic exploitation, and she tries to probe under her character's skin. In surveying this broken life, the author's feminine gaze makes, as I have already suggested, a crucial difference.

In "Una notte nella stazione," the narrator does not succumb to the outer shell of this mannequin and restores an image of debased innocence: she reads beyond the surface of this "viso dipinto" (SM 32; "painted face," MW2 146) and looks "sotto l'attacco dei capelli, sotto quell'orribile metallo rosa e bianco" ("below her head of hair, below that horrid skein of pink and white metal"), until she can "scorgere la fronte fresca e pulita che certo aveva avuto da giovane" (SM 40; "glimpse the fresh, clear forehead which she surely had as a girl," MW2 152).

Underneath a body constructed as a fetish – fashioned also as armour against life's trials – the reporter detects the disillusionment and the wounds of a lacerated existence. This woman is the victim of a miscalculation, of a self-defeating surrender to the market economy ("immersa in un equivoco ch'era quello di generazioni niente affatto educate, in un modo o in un altro dedite esclusivamente al denaro," SM 39; "caught up in the ancient confusions of the legions of unschooled minds which, in this way or that, are dedicated only to money," MW2 152). She has likely been crushed by the loss of a male companion and by her own naïveté and inability to make provisions for her future ("Forse l'ultimo uomo era morto, o si era sposato troncando ogni aiuto. Forse lei non lo aveva previsto, questo, aveva perduto tempo," SM 39–40; "Perhaps her last man had died, or had gotten married and had cut off all assistance. Perhaps she hadn't foreseen a thing like that, and had wasted time," MW2 152). The sexual politics is highly involved in her fall from an affluent lifestyle.

In fact, this prostitute is living proof of the failure of a worthless modus vivendi, predicated upon exteriority and the accumulation of material possessions, leading to the decay of the self. No longer in her prime, she cannot find solace in her glamorous past ("Doveva aver vissuto benissimo, perché la roba che indossava era bella, ma adesso era finita," SM 39; "She must once have been accustomed to living quite well, since the clothes she wore were indeed quite fine, but now it was over," MW2 152).[69] Her body is displayed as an easily available good, offered to men's advances, in a closed circle of unemotional exchanges: in the café, a man who "le fece scorrere una mano sulla schiena [...] dové mormorarle qualcosa, essa non rispose assolutamente, come se solo una zanzara si fosse posata sul suo orecchio" (SM 32–33; "ran a hand down her back [...] must have murmured something to her, but she gave absolutely no response, as though only a mosquito had settled onto her ear," MW2 146). She is a weak subject, probably a newcomer to the train station, who is brutally barred from the third-class waiting room by its custodian, the surrogate representative of the law.

After an unprofitable night, when the streetwalker's fading cosmetics are revealed by the unforgiving light of daybreak, Ortese offers a close-up of the woman that shows the disfigurements left by her defeats:

> Il suo viso era calmo e opaco, gli occhi senza gioia cercavano vagamente qualcosa in quelle volte, al di là di quelle volte, la prima luce grigia che

nasceva. Guardava e piangeva silenziosamente. Le vedevamo adesso, cosí da vicino, le mani vecchie, piene di vene; il corpo appariva pesante, il trucco se n'era andato, tra i capelli rosati saltavano i fili bianchi. (SM 39)

(Her face was calm and opaque, her joyless eyes vaguely searched for something in those vaulted roofings, beyond those vaults, the first gray light which was newly returning. She absorbed the sight and cried. From so close up, we now saw her hands, which were old and veined. Her body seemed heavy, her make-up was gone, the strands of white stood out in her reddish hair. [MW2 152])

Her ornate hairstyle, a camouflage prescribed by the market, has lost its glittering hues, revealing the signs of her aging. Despite her reliance on these embellishments, she has not lost her capacity for reflection and feeling.[70] Ortese's streetwalker speaks for scores of "citizens" consumed by their "ansietà, il mancare continuo di qualche cosa, lo sforzo di tornare a galla" (SM 34; "anxieties, the constant lack of something, the effort of rising back to the surface," MW2 147). Along with her own denatured femininity and demise, the woman mourns the disappearance of vital spaces, invaded by concrete, and the loss of human connections: "'Dovunque vi sono case alte [...] Gli alberi si vedono sempre meno [...] Non si respira [...] I muri crescono sempre [...][non c'è] nessun uomo e nessuna donna'" (SM 40–41; "'These great tall buildings are everywhere [...] It gets harder and harder to see a tree [...] You can't breathe [...] More and more walls, nothing but walls [...][There are] no men, no women,'" MW2 153). The prostitute's complicity with the industrial order is redeemed by her suffering and, more significantly, by her outcry against commodification. With a clear intuition of modernization's poisonous by-products, she acknowledges "the brutality to which she is subjected and which lays waste to her."[71] Only madmen and outlaws are capable of grieving at the devastation of nature[72] and the collapse of sensitivity, sacrifices at the altar of progress.

As a storyteller and fellow woman, the reporter is especially committed to give voice to these characters, who are banned from meaningful social interactions and crushed by market forces. Having crossed into a nightmarish world, Ortese and the photographer accompanying her are initiated into a form of sleepwalking, marred by terrifying visions ("[...] non sapevamo piú se dormivamo o eravamo svegli," SM 38; "We could not tell [...] if we were sleeping or awake," MW2 151), inspired by the station's essential nature of "cosa allucinante, sognata" (SM 37; "a latent dream or hallucination," MW2 150). They, too, have become aware of the denaturalization caused by industrialism, as they awaken to a crude reality of mechanization and dispossession. They now stare at the catastrophe of modern life. It is only from this vantage point – a memorial to the industrial city – in a suspended, empty time, that one can break the spell of artificial life and restore a dialogue with other survivors-seers, even at the risk of being ostracized:

> uno spavento c'invase. Dov'eravamo? Perché parlavamo senza conoscerci? Lei era fuori della Legge, e in certo senso anche noi, intrattenendoci con lei cosí familiarmente, ci mettevamo fuori della Legge, eppure proseguivamo. Avevamo la sensazione di non aver parlato da secoli, fino a questa notte. (SM 41)

> ("a fear flooded over us. Where were we? And why were we talking with one another? We were strangers. This woman lived ouside the law; and we too, in a certain way, placed ourselves outside the law by standing here and talking so freely with her. Yet we didn't break it off. We had the impression of not having talked for centuries, up until tonight." [MW2 154])

Inhabiting the extra-territoriality of the train station at night, the narrator can elude the discriminating, ferocious pseudo-logic of capitalism, at least temporarily. She can disregard the new social codes and re-establish primal, sympathetic bonds with defenceless creatures, whose humanity, albeit mutilated, is still alive.

Awakenings

The texts of *Silenzio a Milano* coalesce into a chronicle of the times and a passionate memoir. The result of this combination is a subjective and prescient look at the contradictions and wounds of modernity, articulated as a poignant cultural critique. Complying with a writer's intellectual duty, Ortese's storytelling refrains from a fictional account of the present and forces readers to face its paradoxes, eliciting their emotional and cognitive response.

The exploration of the settings of a widespread alienation provokes a cry of alarm in the reporter, who wishes to reawaken readers from apathy. Her restless wandering cannot be separated from the moral demands of writing and the ethics of witness. Her meanderings are designed to survey zones of resistance, the fringes that remain estranged from the discourse of order. This quest for redemption propels Ortese to level her accusation against our literary tradition, guilty of being "in genere un soliloquio, uno sfogo [...] curioso" ("usually a soliloquy, a curious [...] rant") that never recorded "un'autentica voce, un richiamo, un grido che turbi, una parola che rompa la nebbia in cui dormono le coscienze" ("an authentic voice, a cry out, a troubling screech, a word that breaks through the fog where consciences lay dormant"). Whoever is devoted to true writing cannot cultivate, Ortese claims, a solitary project but must contribute to the collective quest for sensitivity: "per farsi uomo, uomo che esprime gli altri, che rivela in sé gli altri, che sia un'aggiunta al patrimonio degli altri" ("to become a real person, one who represents the others, who reflects the others in himself, who is an addition to the legacy of the others").[73] The author's commitment goes far beyond mere social criticism and righteousness: it demands nothing short of a "reawakening":

> Era, il compito della cultura, risvegliare di nuovo, nell'uomo, amore per l'uomo, ritrovare la sua misura piú profonda, partendo dall'unico dato indiscutibile: l'incognita che lo circonda. Era tener conto di questo segreto. Era compito della cultura ergersi contro scienza, tecnica, mercati, in quanto avevano di estraneo all'uomo, di mortale al suo spirito. Mai servirli! Tentare di possederli, piegarli. Era amare l'uomo, disarmando in ciascuno, per quanto possibile, l'uomo guerriero, l'uomo foresta, l'uomo caverna [...].
>
> (Culture's duty was to reawaken, in man, love for his fellow man, to rediscover his deepest nature starting from the only indisputable fact: the unknown that surrounds him. It was to acknowledge this secret. It was culture's duty to stand up to science, technology, the markets, insofar as they alienated man and were lethal to his spirit. Never to serve them! [It was culture's duty] To try to possess them, to subdue them. It was to love mankind, disarming in everyone, as much as possible, the warrior man, the forest man, the cave man [...].)[74]

In her Milanese prose, Ortese wanted to jar the readers out of their moral lethargy, much as she had done, with respect to the city of her upbringing, in her earlier pieces in *Il mare non bagna Napoli*:

> Quando tornai a Napoli nel dopoguerra, ero ridiventata una sconosciuta. Ma "vidi" la città per la prima volta. Da ragazzina non avevo avuto alcun

> contatto con la realtà. Le cose terribili cui assistetti mi sconvolsero. C'era un gruppo di intellettuali – di cui facevo parte anch'io – che riusciva a vivere, anche con pochi soldi, a divertirsi. E accanto a noi c'era l'inferno. Con il mio secondo libro, *Il mare non bagna Napoli*, che [...] mi procurò poi tante amarezze, io volevo svegliare questi amici, svegliare la città ... il compito dello scrittore è questo, stimolare, portare luce ...
>
> (When I went back to Naples after the war, I had again become an unknown. But I "saw" the city for the first time. As a young girl I had had no contact with reality. The terrible things I witnessed upon my return astounded me. There was a group of intellectuals – of which I myself was a member – that managed to live, even with little money, and enjoy itself. And all around us there was hell. With my second book, *Il mare non bagna Napoli*, which [...] later brought me so many bitter feelings, I wanted to awaken those friends, awaken the city ... the duty of the writer is this, to stimulate, to bring light...)[75]

Ortese's intention to denounce the devastation around her turns out to be equally detrimental in the capital of industry:

> Avevo lasciato la Milano delle grandi speranze [...], "gettata via," veramente, quasi "sputata" (espressione troppo colorita?) dalla grande Milano, comunque la Milano-bene. Nessuna di quelle loro case mi conosceva piú: perché *non avevo vinto*, perché avevo raccontato, dopo Napoli, e il suo urlo continuo, il "silenzio" di Milano.
>
> (I had left the Milan of great hopes [...], "thrown out," really, almost "spewed" (too vivid an expression?) out of the great Milan, the Milan of the well-off, anyway. Not one among their houses knew me any longer: because *I had not won*, because I had recounted, after Naples, and its continuous cry, the "silence" of Milan.)[76]

Fueled by great expectations, Ortese's experience of the metropolis ends up unearthing and exposing its pitfalls and the trials and tribulations of its victims. In keeping with her solidarity with the oppressed and her ethical commitment as a writer, she cannot but chronicle this fall from grace, at the risk of being ejected from the realm of privilege. Ultimately, Ortese espouses her mission as a wandering intellectual through the ruins of modernity.

NOTES

1 Ortese stayed in Milan until 1950 and lived there again between 1952 and 1958. After a sojourn in Rome, in December 1959 she returned to Lombardy, where she remained until July 1961. She subsequently moved to Rome and Genoa, then went back to Milan in October 1965, for four years. See Farnetti, *Anna Maria Ortese*, 4–5; 94–95 and Clerici, *Apparizione e visione*, 181 and 349.

2 On the complexity of this model, see Petrillo, *La capitale del miracolo* and Foot, *Milan since the Miracle*, 19–59.

3 Restivo, *The Cinema of Economic Miracles*, 5.

4 Maffesoli, *Del nomadismo*, 164.

5 Ibid., 9–10. On Ortese's itinerant writings, see Wood, "Strange Euphorias and Promised Lands," 181–92, and Gramone, "Travelling through the 'I'," 95–108.

6 Hanssen, "Introduction," 2.

7 Augé, *Le temps en ruines*, 61.

8 Ortese, "Viaggio in Liguria," LS 399. On these travelogues, see Della Coletta, "Scrittura come utopia," 371–88.

9 De Monticelli, *L'ordine del cuore*, 280. Ortese's stance is akin to Edith Stein's assessment that the philospher must "guardare il mondo con occhi spalancati" ("watch the world with wide-open eyes," Ibid., 33).

10 See Pietro Citati's letter to Ortese, dated Paris, 23 February 1979 (Archivio di Stato di Napoli, Archivio Ortese, 181).

11 Benjamin, "Marseilles" (1979), 211.

12 On Ortese's "flânerie," see Ghezzo, "Chiaroscuro napoletano," 94–99 and Baldi, *La meraviglia e il disincanto*, 45–61.

13 Quoted in Szondi, *Walter Benjamin's City Portraits* (1962), 20. On urban representations in Benjamin's writings, see Gilloch, *Myth and the Metropolis*.

14 "Erano la nostra casa," Ortese, *Alla luce del Sud*, 129.

15 On Ortese's years in Naples, see Clerici, passim.

16 Benjamin, *Charles Baudelaire*, 37.

17 In "Dove il tempo è un altro" ("Where Time is Another") Ortese recounts the trauma of her return to Naples in 1945, after a period she spent in Mestre to avoid the dangers of the war: see Ortese, CC 75–77. On the city's decay in the post-war era, see Ghirelli, *Napoli italiana*, 255–73.

18 The passage belongs to a letter written to Paola Masino on 15 June 1937 (quoted in Serri, "Ortese: Ti scrivo le mie ossessioni").

19 Ortese, "Dodici ore straordinarie prima di lasciare Napoli," 3.

20 On the "dualism of the Italian economy," created by the imbalance between the north and the south of the country, see Castronuovo, "La storia economica," 45–54.
21 Ortese, "Dodici ore," 3.
22 Ibid.
23 Ibid.
24 Ibid.
25 Ibid.
26 Ibid.
27 Ortese, *Alla luce del Sud*, 91. The editors date the letter "(Milan), 17 August, (1948)."
28 Ibid., 65. The letter is dated Rome, 21 March 1947.
29 Ibid., 66. The letter is dated Rome, 26 March 1947.
30 Ibid., 73. The letter is dated Pesaro, 7 May 1947.
31 Ibid., 46. The letter is dated Genoa, 9 August 1946.
32 Dainotto, "The Gubbio Papers," 67–83; 67. On Italy's "economic boom" see Ginsborg, *A History of Contemporary Italy*, 210–53; Crainz, *Storia del miracolo italiano*; Mafai, *Il sorpasso.*
33 See, for instance, what Ortese writes in a letter to Prunas, dated Milan, 3 June 1949, under the pressure of her numerous commitments as a journalist: "Passo giorni vuoti-tristi-cosí disperati. Non puoi immaginare quanto mi sembri *inutile* tutto e terribile e oscura la vita. Qui sono cadute tutte le illusioni e le protezioni. Qui, dove la natura non ti parla, tu sei solo di fronte alla comunità umana – ch'è nemica o comunque estranea. Senza piú illusioni né tenerezze, come perduti" ("I spend empty-sad-so desperate days. You can't imagine how everything seems to me *useless* and life terrible and obscure. Here all the illusions and protections have fallen down. Here, where nature does not talk to you, you are alone in front of the human community – who is hostile or at least alien. One feels without illusions or affections, as if she were lost"), Ortese, *Alla luce del Sud*, 99.
34 Ortese, "Il mare non bagna la Liguria," interview given to Giuga, 8.
35 Ortese, "…Tutti i grandi romanzi non sono che storie di labirinti…," 41.
36 On the myth of the south of Italy (of which Naples was considered the "capital") as the locus of primitivism and naïveté, see Niola, "The Invention of the Mediterranean," 75–85.
37 Ortese, "Pubblicità e indifferenza," 7.
38 Ortese, "La città senza paura," 3.
39 "Siamo qui, ma a me personalmente Roma non va piú, e desidero con tutta l'anima ritornare a Milano […] oggi, come ieri, Milano è ritornata per me, per mia sorella, equilibrio, serenità, pace (com'era prima). Non ne posso

più di conoscere città che non sono quella della Madonnina – una città che bisogna allontanarsene per capire che valore ha" ("We are here, but personally I do not like Rome any longer, and I wish with all my soul that I could go back to Milan [...] today, as in the past, Milan has become for me, for my sister, emotional balance, serenity, peace (as it was before). I can't stand any longer to know cities other than that of *Madonnina* – a city from which you have to depart in order to understand what it is worth"). The passage belongs to a letter that Ortese wrote to Maria Cumani, dated 16 October 1962; quoted in Clerici, 376.

40 Ortese, "La città senza paura," 3.

41 Ibid. While here Ortese treats with irony "queste paurosissime parole" ("these frightening words"), in the following years she will use similar terms in defining her Milanese experience: see note 46.

42 Ibid.

43 "Chi, a un certo punto, si è trovato solo nella vita, e ha scoperto soprattutto la sua condizione di non privilegiato, non può avere che un amore, una patria: Milano" (Ibid.; "Whoever at some point has found himself alone in life, and, especially, has discovered his condition of being underprivileged, cannot have but one love, one homeland: Milan").

44 Ibid.

45 Ortese repeatedly acknowledged the "genuine hospitality" she found in Milan: see, for instance, Polese, "La signora è ricomparsa," 3.

46 See, for instance, Ortese, "La città è venduta," SM 81–88.

47 Ortese, *Alla luce del Sud*, 84. A similar imagery occurs in *Silenzio a Milano*: see "Lo sgombero" ("The Move"), 136–37.

48 See Niola, "The Invention of the Mediterranean," 76.

49 Ortese, *Alla luce del Sud*, 89–90. This correspondence illustrates Ortese's determination to pursue a career as a writer, despite the family troubles that would call her back home: "Ero piuttosto eccitata da queste novità, divertita anche, se aggiungi che oggi non dovevo tornare in ufficio. Ma, svegliandomi, trovo una lettera di mia sorella, con cose poco liete. Niente soldi, la salute di mia madre che si aggrava. Ed eccomi nella vecchia prigione dei miei pensieri. Sta' tranquillo, però, per le mie intenzioni. Non lascio Milano" (Ibid., 95; "I was quite excited because of these novelties, entertained, too, if you add that today I did not have to go back to the office. But, waking up, I found a letter from my sister, with sad news. No money, my mother's health is deteriorating. And here I am, back in the old prison of my thoughts. Do not worry, however, regarding my intentions. I am not leaving Milan").

50 This passage appears in an unpublished text that Ortese wrote on 4 March 1981 (see Archivio di Stato di Napoli, Archivio Ortese, 1150, f. 7). The

process of Americanization that Ortese detects here was propelled by the economic measures implemented during the "reconstruction": see Castronuovo, *La storia economica*, 357–60.

51 Ortese, *Alla luce del Sud*, 94.

52 See Clerici, 313–36.

53 Ibid., 332.

54 I have been unable to identify this text.

55 The letter is dated 30 June 1964 (see Archivio di Stato di Napoli, Archivio Ortese, 110).

56 Foucault, *Discipline and Punish*, 198.

57 See Augé, *Le temps en ruines*, 87.

58 Significantly, here travelling is textualized as a movement correlated to a mobility of the gaze, which discloses unsuspected perspectives.

59 Bernstein, Introduction to *The Culture Industry*, 7.

60 See Iacono, *Autonomia, potere, minorità*, 74.

61 Bernstein, 11.

62 As Benjamin remarks about the flâneur: see Benjamin, *The Arcades Project*, 448.

63 Leslie, "Ruin and Rubble in the Arcades," 95.

64 Pile, "Sleepwalking in the Modern City," 76.

65 Leslie, "Ruin and Rubble in the Arcades," 104.

66 Modified translation.

67 Ibid., 105. See also Buck-Morss, *The Dialectics of Seeing*, 190–93, and "The Flâneur," 99–140; Chisholm, "Benjamin's Gender, Sex, and Eros," 259–60.

68 Leslie, "Ruin and Rubble in the Arcades," 105.

69 Modified translation.

70 In "Locali notturni" ("Night-Clubs") the author portrays a more conventional version of the prostitute: "Beve, sorride, perché nella sua testa non c'è niente" (SM 71; "She drinks, smiles, because her head is empty" [Ortese, "Locali notturni"]). Listening to a sorrowful melody, though, even this figure has a sudden shudder of recognition: "Il suo viso è scomparso sotto grandi macchie che si moltiplicano, come nebbia. La mano artigliata nei capelli, senza smettere di sorridere, pensa" (Ibid., 73; "Her face has disappeared under large spots that spread like fog. With her hand clasping her hair, without stopping smiling, she is thinking").

71 Leslie, "Ruin and Rubble in the Arcades," 106.

72 In "Locali notturni," the vulgarity of the streetwalker is softened during "certi lunghi silenzi" ("certain prolonged silences"), by a "grazia malinconica, come un ricordo di fiumi e d'erba" (SM 68; "melancholy grace, like a memory of rivers and grass").

73 Ortese, "Il piacere di scrivere," 3.
74 Ortese, "È tempo di capire," 3.
75 Ortese, "È cosí difficile trovare a Milano il silenzio," 9. In a letter to Arnold Ruge, written in September 1843, Karl Marx warned, "The reform of consciousness consists *entirely* in making the world aware of its own consciousness, in arousing it from its dream of itself, in *explaining* its own actions to it."
76 The passage appears in a letter that Ortese wrote to Franz Haas on 12 June 1990 (quoted in Clerici, 383).

WORKS CITED

Augé, Marc. *Le temps en ruines.* Paris: Galilée, 2003.
Baldi, Andrea. *La meraviglia e il disincanto: Studi sulla narrativa breve di Anna Maria Ortese.* Napoli: Loffredo Editore, 2010.
Benjamin, Walter. *The Arcades Project* [1927–1940]. Trans. Howard Eiland and Kevin McLaughlin. Cambridge and London: Belknap Press of Harvard University Press, 1999.
– *Charles Baudelaire: A Lyric Poet in the Era of High Capitalism.* London: New Left Books, 1978.
– "Marseilles." In *One-Way Street and Other Writings.* Trans. Edmund Jephcott and Kinsley Shorter. London: New Left Books, 1979.
Bernstein, Jay M. Introduction to *The Culture Industry: Essays on Mass Culture,* by Theodor W. Adorno, ed. Jay M. Bernstein, 1–26. London-New York: Routledge, 2001.
Buck-Morss, Susan. *The Dialectics of Seeing: Walter Benjamin and "The Arcades Project."* Cambridge-London: MIT Press, 1989.
– "The Flâneur, the Sandwichman and the Whore: The Politics of Loitering." *New German Critique* 39 (1986): 99–140.
Castronuovo, Valerio. "La storia economica." In *Storia d'Italia,* 5–506. Vol. 4. Turin: Einaudi, 1975.
Chisholm, Dianne. "Benjamin's Gender, Sex, and Eros." In *A Companion to the Works of Walter Benjamin,* ed. Rolf J. Goebel, 247–72. Rochester: Camden House, 2009.
Clerici, Luca. *Apparizione e visione: Vita e opere di Anna Maria Ortese.* Milan: Mondadori, 2002.
Crainz, Guido. *Storia del miracolo italiano: Culture, identità, trasformazioni fra anni cinquanta e sessanta.* Roma: Donzelli, 1996.
Dainotto, Roberto M. "The Gubbio Papers: Historic Centers in the Age of the Economic Miracle." *Journal of Modern Italian Studies* 8, no. 1 (2003): 67–83.

Della Coletta, Cristina. "Scrittura come utopia: *La lente scura* di Anna Maria Ortese." *Italica* 76, no. 3 (1999): 371–88.

De Monticelli, Roberta. *L'ordine del cuore: Etica e teoria del sentire.* Milan: Garzanti, 2003.

Farnetti, Monica. *Anna Maria Ortese.* Milan: Bruno Mondadori, 1998.

Foot, John. *Milan since the Miracle: City, Culture and Identity.* Oxford-New York: Berg, 2001.

Foucault, Michel. *Discipline and Punish: The Birth of the Prison.* Trans. Alan Sheridan. New York: Vintage Books, 1995.

Ghezzo, Flora. "Chiaroscuro napoletano: Trasfigurazioni fantastiche di una città." *Narrativa* 24 (2003): 85–104.

Ghirelli, Antonio. *Napoli italiana: La storia della città dopo il 1860.* Turin: Einaudi, 1977.

Gilloch, Graeme. *Myth and the Metropolis: Walter Benjamin and the City.* Cambridge, MA: Polity Press, 1996.

Ginsborg, Paul. *A History of Contemporary Italy: Society and Politics, 1943–1988.* London: Penguin, 1990.

Gramone, Antonella. "Travelling through the 'I': Anna Maria Ortese's Melancholic Cities." *Romance Studies* 19, no. 1 (2001): 95–108.

Hanssen, Beatrice. "Introduction: Physiognomy of a Flâneur: Walter Benjamin's Peregrinations through Paris in Search of a New Imaginary." In *Walter Benjamin and "The Arcades Project"*, ed. Beatrice Hanssen, 1–11. London-New York: Continuum, 2006.

Iacono, Alfonso M. *Autonomia, potere, minorità: Del sospetto, della paura, della meraviglia, del guardare con altri occhi.* Milan: Feltrinelli, 2000.

Leslie, Esther. "Ruin and Rubble in the Arcades." In *Walter Benjamin and "The Arcades Project,"* ed. Beatrice Hanssen, 87–112. London-New York: Continuum, 2006.

Mafai, Miriam. *Il sorpasso: gli straordinari anni del miracolo economico, 1958–1963.* Trezzano sul Naviglio: Euroclub, 1998.

Maffesoli, Michel. *Del nomadismo: Per una sociologia dell'erranza.* Preface by Lella Mazzoli. Milan: Franco Angeli, 2000.

Niola, Marino. "The Invention of the Mediterranean." In *Sites of Exchange: European Crossroads and Faultlines,* ed. Maurizio Ascari and Adriana Corrado, 75–85. Amsterdam-New York: Rodopi, 2006.

Ortese, Anna Maria. *Alla luce del Sud: Lettere a Pasquale Prunas.* Ed. Renata Prunas and Giuseppe di Costanzo. Milan: Archinto, 2006.

– "Dodici ore straordinarie prima di lasciare Napoli." *Milano-sera,* 4–5 June 1951, 3.

– "È cosí difficile trovare a Milano il silenzio." *Il Giorno,* 6 April 1966, 9.

– "È tempo di capire." *La Nazione*, 1 October 1961, 3.
– "Il mare non bagna la Liguria." Interview given to Giovanni Giuga. *Fiera letteraria* 53, no. 107 (13 February 1977): 8–9.
– "Il piacere di scrivere." *l'Unità*, 13 November 1957, 3.
– "La città senza paura." *Risorgimento*, 7 April 1950, 3.
– "Pubblicità e indifferenza." *Il Mondo*, 5 January 1960, 7.
– "...Tutti i grandi romanzi non sono che storie di labirinti ... La loro forza è che rispecchiano la condizione umana..." *Uomini e libri* 15, no. 75 (September-October 1979): 41–42.
Petrillo, Gianfranco. *La capitale del miracolo: Sviluppo lavoro potere a Milano, 1953–1962*. Milan: Franco Angeli, 1992.
Pile, Steve. "Sleepwalking in the Modern City: Walter Benjamin and Sigmund Freud in the World of Dreams." In *A Companion to the City*, ed. Gary Bridge and Sophie Watson, 75–86. Oxford: Blackwell, 2000.
Polese, Ranieri. "La signora è ricomparsa." *Leggere* 83 (September 1996): 3.
Restivo, Angelo. *The Cinema of Economic Miracles: Visuality and Modernization in the Italian Art Film*. Durham and London: Duke University Press, 2002.
Serri, Mirella. "Ortese: Ti scrivo le mie ossessioni." *La Stampa*, 19 June 1998.
Szondi, Peter. *Walter Benjamin's City Portraits* (1962). In *On Walter Benjamin: Critical Essays and Recollections*, ed. Gary Smith, 18–32. Cambridge, MA: MIT Press, 1988.
Wood, Sharon. "Strange Euphorias and Promised Lands: The Travel Writing of Anna Maria Ortese." In *Literature and Travel*, ed. Michael Hanne, 181–92. Amsterdam-Atlanta: Rodopi, 1993.

3 Biographies of Displacement and the Utopian Imagination: Anna Maria Ortese, Hannah Arendt, and the Artist as "Conscious Pariah"

CRISTINA DELLA COLLETTA

At a first glance, the only commonality between the German-Jewish political theorist Hannah Arendt and the Italian novelist Anna Maria Ortese is that both were women who lived and wrote during the "dark times" of the twentieth century.[1] However, from different social and ethnic backgrounds and in separate areas of human expression, these two women addressed analogous concerns and explored remarkably similar issues. Their common experiences of displacement, albeit prompted by different causes – political in Arendt's case and socio-economic in Ortese's – inspired parallel lifelong meditations on notions of belonging and independence, political involvement and intellectual freedom, the preservation of collective memories and the overcoming of an inherited past. Neither Arendt nor Ortese offered simple answers and straightforward solutions, because both refrained from construing these notions as binary opposites – the positive and negative poles of unambiguous existential choices. By highlighting the hybrid complexity of these notions, and by exploring their shared and liminal domains, Arendt and Ortese drafted strategies for intellectual emancipation, hermeneutical insight, and utopian projection out of daunting and destructive experiences of displacement.

At great personal cost, Arendt and Ortese provided insightful examinations of what Arendt defined as the condition of the "conscious pariahs" and Ortese that of the "non consenzienti" ("those who do not consent"), the intellectuals as social outcasts who, by being both committed to and critical of their heritage, envision a more hospitable and inclusive future for minorities and pariahs of all kinds. In comparing Ortese's and Arendt's reflections on the notion of displacement, this essay addresses how these two intellectuals' self-conscious construction of a complex sense of Self required their simultaneous revisions of conventional concepts of one's home, community, and country. This theoretical framework provides the platform for a discussion of Ortese's *Il mormorio di Parigi* (*Paris' Murmur*, 1986) as the conscious pariah's effort to overcome historical and existential constraints through the liberating practice of utopian writing.

Defining the Conscious Pariah: a "Hidden Tradition" in the Vanguard of History

Ortese's biography traces a meandering itinerary of recurring displacements – a story of internal migrations, the starting point of which, Rome, is just a casual stop that blurs all sense of individual selfhood as belonging to a sanctioned national community, however imagined.[2] Ortese's fond assertion of the Catalan origins of her last name, Ortez, and her claim to feeling Neapolitan, Milanese, and "Toledana," was a statement of fantasized otherness and fragmented plurality rather than a concrete effort to establish historical and geographical ties to a specific urban polity or Spanish ancestry.[3] "Sono figlia di nessuno" ("I am nobody's daughter"), writes the first-person narrator of the semi-autobiographical *Il porto di Toledo*, and the author of "Memoria e conversazione" similarly states that she is "uno 'scrittore' che viene dal nulla" (CC 12; "a 'writer' who comes from nowhere"). The double void marking Ortese's social and literary genealogies underscores both the subject's claim of individual freedom and independence and the pariah's awareness of her exclusion from an unwelcoming socio-professional elite.[4] It also identifies the oxymoronic "empty origin" of Ortese's changeable and often contradictory lifelong project of self-determination and aesthetic self-construction.

The many autobiographical references scattered in Ortese's writings construct a narrative in which the family's rootlessness is both willed by temperament and imposed by social and historical occurrences. Anna Maria described her father, a petty government employee, who was regularly dispatched across the peninsula on sundry job assignments, as "irrequieto, sognatore" ("restless, a dreamer") and unable to "stare mai fermo in un posto" ("ever stay still in one place") and provide for his numerous children.[5] Between 1915 and 1928, the Ortese family, "miserrima" and "priva di rilievo sociale" (CC 55; "utterly destitute and without any social relevance") moved from Puglia to Portici (Naples), and from Potenza to Tripoli, Libya, then an Italian colony. Strident counterpart to the expansive rhetoric of contemporary imperialist propaganda, Ortese condensed her memories of her family's African adventure in the uncanny image of an unfinished home – a hollow parable of permanence in stone – built upon the sand of a ghostly settlement abutting the Libyan Desert:

> La [casa] era grande, tutta di pietra. Mio padre la volle costruire con le pietre di una cava che aveva comperato assieme con il terreno. Ma non poté mai finirla [...] È rimasta a metà. Sembrava la casa dei fantasmi. Senza porte, senza finestre, col tetto metà coperto e metà no, il pavimento mezzo di pietra e mezzo di terra.
>
> (The [house] was large and all made of stone. My father decided to build it with the rocks of a quarry that he had bought with the land. But he could never finish it [...]. The house remained half-finished. It looked like a ghost house. Without doors or windows, with the roof half-covered and half-uncovered, the floor half-stone and half-dirt.)[6]

The uncanny hearth of Anna Maria's *paradis enfantin* hollows out the Edenic unity of the African landscape[7] and symbolically evokes one of the emotional clusters that mark much of Ortese's writing: the paradox of a reminisced original fullness of Being coexisting with the awareness that a void fissures this phantasmal totality at its very core.

In numerous memories inspired by autobiographical events, Ortese presented her family's map of migration as drawn by the inflexible laws of poverty: a tragic diaspora causing the estrangement of family members from one another, and saddened by hunger, death, and the devastation of war.[8] The precarious domain of the Orteses' sense of home (viz., their rented *casupola* or *catapecchia* in the transient neighbourhood of the harbour of Naples, rendered uninhabitable by Allied bombings in 1944) was, simultaneously, the creative nest of the budding writer's "stanza d'Angolo" (PT 25; "corner room") and the gloomy dungeon that the harbour's gates separated from the sunny world beyond. The experience of *sfollamento* that many other Italian families lived as a unique and traumatic event of the war was for the Orteses yet another chapter in the family's ongoing biography of displacement.[9]

After the death of her parents in the early 1950s, Anna Maria, a self-taught writer with barely an elementary school education and no ties to the literary, publishing, and academic institutions, pursued her literary vocation from a position of marginality marked by repeated resettlements across Italy. While reminiscing about her sundry job assignments and precarious employment in numerous Italian cities (Venice, Trieste, Florence, Naples, Milan, Rome), Ortese summarized her lifelong literary vocation as ruled by two opposite drives. One, euphoric and liberating, was the power to "esprimersi" seen as the "libertà assoluta della mente umana" (CC 78; "expression as absolute freedom of the human mind"). The other, dysphoric, included all the cultural, material, and financial restrictions imprisoning the artist who "comes from nowhere" in a "tempo di naufragio" (CC 84; "a shipwreck's time") – a chronotope of exile and separation from the free domain of expression, that is, from the artist's utopian home: "Scrivere [è] tornare a casa. Chi scrive [...] rientra a casa" (CC 104; "To write means to return home. She who writes [...] goes back home").[10]

There are very few biographical analogies between Hannah Arendt and Anna Maria Ortese. The only daughter of a well-to-do Jewish engineer, Arendt studied philosophy under Martin Heidegger and Karl Jaspers at Marburg and Heidelberg universities, respectively. In the best tradition of German humanism, Arendt received a rigorous training in Classics and German philosophy, obtaining a PhD at the age of twenty-two. Though the rise of Nazism forced her to escape to France and then settle in the United States, she remained politically involved in the Jewish community, working as an active Zionist in Paris (1933–40) and holding important posts in several Jewish organizations in the United States. While publishing extensively on Jewish topics, she taught at numerous universities, including Princeton (where she was the first woman to receive a full professorship), the New School for Social Research, and the University of Chicago.[11]

From different sociocultural backgrounds and historical experiences, Arendt and Ortese cherished a similar ideological nonconformism and fierce intellectual independence. The ostracizing reactions of the Neapolitan intelligentsia to "Il silenzio della ragione" ("The Silence of Reason") – Ortese's blunt *j'accuse* against her fellow intellectuals' indifference towards Naples' rampant corruption and squalor, as insightfully discussed in the previous essay by Lucia Re – can be paired with the Jewish community's response to *Eichmann in Jerusalem* (1963), Arendt's controversial criticism of Jewish leadership during the Holocaust and of Israel's handling of Adolf Eichmann's trial in 1961. Ortese's reportages from the Soviet Union, where she travelled with the first delegation of the Unione Donne Italiane (Union of Italian Women), fomented harsh criticism among the most rigorous representatives of Communist doctrine, such as Rossana Rossanda. Ortese's terse response, "Sono uscita dal partito perché volevano che io non ragionassi con la mia testa ma con la loro. [...] Io scrivevo in un modo non ortodosso" ("I left the party because they didn't want me to think with my own head but with theirs. [...] I wrote in an unorthodox way"),[12] echoes Arendt's sentiments in a different context, as she expressed them in a letter to Gershom Scholem:

> What confuses you is that my argument and my approach are different from what you are used to; in other words, the trouble is that I am independent. By this I mean, on the one hand, that I do not belong to any organisation and always speak only for myself, and on the other hand, that I have great confidence in Lessing's *selbstdenken* [self-thinking] for which, I think, no ideology, no public opinion, and no "conviction" can ever be a substitute.[13]

Similarly, in "Dialogo sull'appartenenza" ("Dialogue on Belonging") Ortese stated, "La non-appartenenza [...] mi pare condizione inevitabile per una certa libertà. Tutti infatti *appartengono*, o desiderano follemente di appartenere" ("The inevitable condition to achieve a certain amount of freedom is one of not belonging. Everybody, in fact, *belongs*, or frantically wishes to belong").[14] The courage of *selbstdenken* and the pursuit of a "certain amount of freedom" allowed Ortese to transform a disheartening biographical experience of social marginalization and cultural exclusion into a "visionary" literature that gave aesthetic expression to Arendt's notion of the "conscious pariah."

Arendt theorized the notion of the "conscious pariah" in two seminal essays: "We Refugees" (1943) and "The Jew as Pariah: a Hidden Tradition" (1944). Focusing primarily if not exclusively on the Jewish experience following the tragedy of genocide and trauma of dislocation during the Nazi era, Arendt poignantly summarized her people's encounter with unspeakable loss with these words:

> We lost our home, which means the familiarity of daily life. We lost our occupation, which means the confidence that we are of some use in this world. We lost our language, which means the naturalness of reactions, the simplicity of gestures, the unaffected expression of feelings. We left our relatives in the Polish ghettos and our best friends have been killed in concentration camps, and that means the rupture of our private lives.[15]

The nostalgia for a collective past and a place of belonging ("once we were somebodies about whom people cared, we were loved by friends")[16] begets a present in which the natural desire to *be* and to *belong* risks turning the Self into a masquerade and the individual into what Arendt defines a "social parvenu." Arendt expresses a chillingly Pirandellian sense of humour, when she recounts the anecdote of a Mr Cohn from Berlin who had always been "a 150% German, a German super-patriot."[17] Mr Cohn shaped himself as a Czech nationalist after finding refuge in Prague in 1933, an Austrian loyalist after escaping to Vienna in 1937, and a child of "Vercingetorix" when he fled to France after Hitler's invasion of Austria. Mr Cohn is the apt representative of all the "loyal Hottentots" – the "social parvenus" who according to Arendt "change identity so frequently that nobody can find out who we actually are."[18] Unlike social parvenus, conscious pariahs, to whom Arendt devotes the "Bernard Lazare" section of "The Jew as Pariah: A Hidden Tradition," are rebels who, being aware of their marginalized and ostracized status, become champions of the oppressed. Their "fight for freedom is part and parcel of that which all the down-trodden of Europe must needs wage to achieve national and social liberation."[19]

While at times Arendt sees the social parvenu and the conscious pariah as antithetical,[20] in other cases the borders between these opposing positions are more porous than one may expect, and therefore deserve careful examination. Arendt denounces the "hopeless sadness" and self-mystification of the parvenus who renounce their individual and collective identities and memories in order to belong to and be accepted by society: "The confusion in which we live," Arendt claims, "is partly our own work."[21] This sadness and confusion corresponds to the very "sensazione di nebbia" ("sensation of fog") that Ortese describes when discussing her generation's ignorance of the reasons why "siamo cosí cambiati, il [nostro] non ricordare" (CC 18; "we have changed so much, and why [we] fail to remember") in a piece significantly titled "Attraversando un paese sconosciuto" ("Crossing an Unknown Country").[22] Ortese's denunciation of the "orrore della memoria" and "solitudine dell'intelligenza" (CC 38; "horror for memory and solitude of the mind") that marks Italian post-war society stems from her belief that all forms of political tyranny and social oppression begin precisely with such an erosion of collective identity:

> per condurre un paese alla *perfetta tristezza,* o non identità, che assicura il dominio di qualcuno bisogna prima avvezzare la gente a non vivere se stessa, la propria terra, memoria, civiltà [...] memoria di lingua e linguaggio del passato; e degli affetti, i pensieri, i dolori delle passate generazioni [che] altro non sono, lo sappiamo che identità di nazione. Dunque libertà

> nazionale. [...] Comincia con questa aratura imponente del suolo umano qualsiasi seria operazione di colonizzazione o dominio. (CC 24, emphasis added)
>
> ("In order to bring a country into a state of *absolute sadness*, or non-identity, which ensures domination by others, one first has to get people used to giving up their identities, land, memories, and civilization [...]. The identity of a nation is nothing other than the memories of its language and the language of its past, of the affections, thoughts, and suffering of bygone generations. This is national freedom. All serious operations of colonization and domination begin with this imposing plowing of the human soil.")

How this form of oppression may end up does not escape Ortese's own recent memories, as she identifies with people being locked up in a sealed train "e trasportati [in] un paese straniero, sconosciuto [senza] poter più tornare indietro" (CC 18; "and carried [into] a strange and unknown country [without] ever being able to come back").

The reiterated and emphatic first-person plural through which Arendt builds her critique of the social parvenus places her *within* the boundaries of the very experience she is analysing: "we were reminded that the new country would become a new home; and after four weeks in France or six weeks in America, we pretended to be Frenchmen or Americans."[23] Ortese follows a similar strategy in "Attraversando un paese sconosciuto," as she included herself among those who succumb to society's instructions to forget: "Ecco anch'io non ricordo. O ricordo a stento" (CC 18; "Here, I, too, don't remember. Or I have trouble remembering"). In Ortese's view, the post-war society's refusal of memory corresponds to the abjuration of history that has led to capitalistic assimilation and cultural homogenization: "senza più storia [...] fummo America" (CC 25–26; "without history any longer [...] we became America").[24] Instead of a polity based on bonding and dialogue, Ortese sees a country in a state of collective trauma and alienation: "L'estraneità a noi stessi non era il nostro scopo. [...] Non ci riconosciamo più, [...] non possiamo più intenderci, [...] siamo tristi" (CC 22; "Our goal was not the estrangement from ourselves. [...] We don't recognize one another any longer, [...] we can't understand one another any more, [...] and we are sad"). Both Arendt and Ortese make it clear that this estrangement results from acts of social discrimination, political persecution, and cultural "colonization." Though different in their causes and outcomes, these acts are similar in the responses they cause: "The less *we* are free to decide who *we* are or to live as *we* like, the more *we* try to put up a front, to hide the facts, and to play roles."[25]

The presupposition of self-inclusion marking both Arendt's and Ortese's use of the first-person plural is deliberately deceptive, as the very logic of their arguments partially dislocates the speaking voice from the intellectual domain of this communal "We." Arendt's dispassionate yet sympathetic analysis in "We Refugees" both connects her to, and separates her from, the unreflective naïveté and self-imposed optimism with which she claims the Jewish people have reinvented themselves and found new homes in order to survive: "The more optimistic among us would even add that their whole former life had been passed in a kind of unconscious exile and only their new country now taught them what a home really looks like."[26] If the grammatical logic of Arendt's discourse includes her in the object of her critique, the rhetorical movement of her text and the logical construction of her argument place her firmly within the intellectual and ethical domains of those few whom, following Bernard Lazare, one may call "conscious pariahs."[27] This is the tradition of people such as Salomon Maimon, Heinrich Heine, Rahel Varnhagen, Frank Kafka, Sholom Aleichem, and even Charlie Chaplin – the conscious pariahs who "did not think it worth while to change their humane attitude and their natural insight into reality for the narrowness of caste spirit or the essential unreality of financial transactions."[28] As such, they were able to gain a discerning perspective on both Jewish and European matters, one that allowed the distinctively Jewish and broadly European experiences to inform and enlighten one another.

Similarly, Ortese defends the slim group of intellectuals who remained faithful to their collective pasts by refusing to wear profitable and changeable masks. Ortese includes herself among those writers who succeeded in combining their "memorie fiorentine o romane o napoletane o venete [con] le memorie d'Europa e della classica America" (CC 29; "memories of Florence, Rome, Naples and the Veneto [with] the memories of Europe and classical America"). Like Arendt, Ortese promotes an inclusive ideal of humanity – one that does not sacrifice authenticity to either sectarian labels or convenient acts of collective forgetting (CC 28). The artist "who comes from nowhere" thus readjusts her self-definition. While rejecting any form of narrow and prejudiced belonging, Ortese defends the value of personal and communal memories in a pliable, expandable, and inclusive cultural framework.

Like Ortese's, Arendt's conscious pariah inhabits a hybrid place that ideally transcends the Manichean grammar of inclusion ("We") and exclusion ("They"). Inviting Jews and non-Jews alike, it is a space that from inside the ruins of unspeakable horror and away from sectarian strife and grotesque masquerades looks with hope to a capacious world that encompasses cultural specificity while transcending it. Conscious pariahs are indeed "refugees who represent the vanguard of their peoples – if they keep their identity."[29] However, Arendt does not conceal the fact that historically these vanguards have been the most exposed and vulnerable positions. Their inclusive and unfettered ideals do not translate easily into the world of praxis, a world built upon fixed rules of belonging and exclusion. "The very few among *us* who have tried to get along without all these tricks and jokes of adjustment and assimilation," Arendt writes, "have paid a much higher price than *they* could afford; *they* jeopardized the few chances even outlaws are given in a topsy-turvy world."[30]

Paradoxically, as bearers of a message of inclusiveness and authenticity, conscious pariahs remain marginal in relation to their own communities, whose parochialism they overcome; marginal in relation to the assimilated peers whose "disguises" they reject; and marginal in relation to a society whose insidious and ambiguous offers of assimilation they decline. Arendt's "conscious pariahs" can be paired to what Ortese defines "i non consenzienti" and "i diversi" (CC 30; "those who do not consent; the different ones"). Voluntarily refusing the deceptions of false belonging, the "non consenzienti" are cast "fuori dalla [loro] terra" (CC 30; "out of [their] own land"), away, that is, from the fullness of life that a non-oppressed existence should guarantee to all people alike:

> I veri diversi, per mia esperienza sono [...] i cercatori d'identità, propria e collettiva, e nazionale, e d'anima. Coloro [...] che non credono, o credono poco, ai partiti, le classi, i confini, le barriere, le fazioni, le armi, le guerre. Che nel denaro non hanno posto alcuna parte dell'anima, e quindi sono incomprabili. Quelli che vedono il dolore, l'abuso; vedono la bontà o l'iniquità, dovunque siano, e sentono come dovere il parlarne. (CC 30)

> (In my experience, the real different ones are [...] the seekers of identity, their own as well as collective, and national, and of the soul. Those [...] who do not believe, or hold scarce belief in parties, classes, boundaries, barriers, factions, arms and wars. Those who have not given any part of their souls away to money, and therefore cannot be bought. Those who see suffering and abuse; who see goodness and iniquity wherever they are and feel it is their duty to speak about them.)

Visionaries and seekers who have been separated from their own people by the events of history as well as by their own nonconformism, these men and women constitute what Arendt calls a "tacit," "latent," or "hidden" tradition.[31] The oxymoronic value of this concept defines the sociopolitical conundrum of the conscious pariahs – great but *isolated* individuals who, by affirming their pariah status have severed all ties of convenience with their own assimilated communities, and, yet, constitute a tradition nevertheless, because for centuries "the same basic conditions have obtained and evoked the same basic reaction."[32]

Ortese describes herself in terms that evoke Arendt's notion of the conscious pariah when she defines the hidden tradition from which she emerged with these apparently sarcastic words: "Uno scrittore-donna, proveniente da quella parte del paese che nel 1861 si aggiunse, come dote in un contratto di matrimonio, alla decorosa storia del Piemonte [...] è una bestia che parla" (CC 50–51; "A woman-writer, coming from that part of the country that in 1861 was added like a dowry in a marriage contract to the proper history of Piedmont, [is] a talking animal.") Undoubtedly, the *bestia* from *Il Mezzogiorno* reflects the double yoke of the sexual and geographical "naturalness" of the southern woman – she is a mere body, a synecdoche of the cultural "nowhere" that is cheaply sold in order to be integrated into the higher realm of reason, decorum, and northern male history. And yet, this *bestia* does, indeed, *speak*. As such she is a *monstrum*, an outlandish wonder, a *lusus naturae* that pays for her challenge to a silent "normality" with isolation from other dissident and equally segregated voices such as those of Anna Banti and Elsa Morante, just to cite the most obvious members of Ortese's own hidden tradition.

More broadly, the "besta che parla" also reflects the tradition that Arendt identifies with Heinrich Heine's "Princess Sabbath" (*Hebrew Melodies*). In "Princess Sabbath," the poet presents the Jewish people as a fairy prince turned by witchcraft into a dog. As the "voice" of his people, the poet is a pariah "excluded from formal society and with no desire to be embraced within it" who eagerly turns to celebrate "the open and unrestricted bounty of the earth."[33] As "Lord of Dreams" (*Traumweltherrscher*), the people's poet shifts the accent to a "higher reality," and his displacement from the social order becomes the core of aesthetic and creative freedom.[34]

The pariah is always remote and unreal; as "lord of dreams" he stands outside the real world and attacks it from without. Indeed the Jewish tendency towards utopianism – a propensity most clearly in evidence in the very countries of emancipation – stems, in the last analysis, from just this lack of social roots. The only thing that saved Heine from succumbing to it, and that made him transform the political non-existence and unreality of the pariah into the effective basis of a world of art, was his creativity.[35]

In a context unrelated to Jewish history yet remarkably attuned to Arendt's own analysis, Ortese admired the "visionary" creators of revolutionary – because of its morality – literature: "una letteratura [...] di azione e visione, insegnamento, gioia, profezia insieme. Potrei chiamarla, anche, letteratura del coraggio" (CC 26; "a literature [...] uniting action and vision, teaching, joy, and prophecy. I could also call it the literature of courage").[36] If, with these words, Ortese appears to believe in the concrete potential of the written word to create a bridge between aesthetic "vision" and sociopolitical "action," Arendt was more soberly aware of the price the conscious pariahs often paid for their prophetic stance. As social outcasts, often the only liberty they could achieve was the liberty allowed "by the sheer force of imagination."[37]

As individuals they started an emancipation of their own, of their own hearts and brains. Such a conception was, of course, a gross misconstruction of what emancipation had been intended to be; but it was also a *vision* and out of the impassioned intensity with which is was evinced and expressed it provided the fostering soil in which Jewish creative genius could grow and contribute its products to the general spiritual life of the Western world.[38]

The ability of truly "visionary" literature to achieve positive and concrete changes in the world of political praxis and social engagement was indeed a question that haunted Ortese during her entire life, and one that did not yield easy and univocal answers. Undoubtedly, as Ortese retreated further and further away from social interaction, her outlook became more and more disheartened, and her historical pessimism turned into a tragic view of the human condition as a whole.[39] However, even from a perspective that, borrowing Leopardi's terminology, reflected cosmic pessimism, Ortese savours the *concretely* revolutionary potential of Utopia:

> Nel vivere umano, mentre i decenni e i mezzi secoli rotolano via sempre più in fretta, con un effetto di turbine e di rovina – non visibile e quindi non rimediabile io vedo da tempo una macchia, come vedo una macchia nella natura dell'uomo anche buono, e forse una macchia nel sole stesso. E a questa percezione – devo dire – è forse dovuta la mia propensione per il

poco – o il nulla – e la mia reverenza per l'Utopia – sempre alta e presente come una luce bianca tra le nuvole basse, nello sconfortato vivere; la vita si muove, viaggia; e alta [...] sui paesi come sulle campagne perse – mentre i convogli del tempo continuano a inseguirsi – alta sui paesi deserti e campagne mute, resta la mirabile, cara, fedele Utopia. (LS iii–iv)

("In human life, while decades and half-centuries roll away faster and faster, with an effect of whirlwind and ruin – invisible and therefore irreparable, for some time I have seen a spot, as I see a spot even in a good man's nature, and perhaps a spot in the sun itself. I must say that this perception of mine might justify my inclination for the little things – or for plain nothingness – and my reverence for Utopia – always high and present in our discouraged living, like a white light among low clouds. Life moves on and travels; and high upon the villages and lost countryside – while the trains of time keep chasing one another – high on deserted villages and silent countryside, endures Utopia: admirable, cherished, and faithful.")

In the domain of a fleeting present careening towards its own ruin, human existence displays itself in dysphoric terms, as a space of dejection ("sconfortato vivere") and moral error (the blemish or "macchia," recalling the Judeo-Christian tradition of the human condition marked by sin, imperfection, and death). Missing from this dystopian world, presence, permanence, and communal bonding belong to the metaphysical plane of Utopia. The utopian Logos, however, has an uncanny epistemological status: to assert itself as enduring *presence,* Utopia must affirm its absolute *absence* – its otherness and separation – from the *hic et nunc* of human existence. Or, to put it differently, to posit and theorize Utopia, one must be in a situation of *self-conscious displacement* – the condition of the "conscious pariah" who is removed from the metaphysics of presence and the dream of fullness that marks the utopian domain – thence Ortese's intellectual inclination for *il poco,* or *il nulla.* Utopia, *ou-topos,* is conceivable only from the outside, from a position of loss, *manque,* and exile. To think utopically, then, does not mean to build and inhabit alternative worlds, but, rather, to sharpen the tools that allow us to "see" the limitations of the world in which we live. Whether inherent to the human condition subjected to finitude and the passing of time or imposed upon the individual by socio-economic oppression and political persecution, these very limitations become for conscious pariahs like Ortese and Arendt the springboard for diverse forms of intellectual engagement, ranging from imaginative creation to political theory and social practice.

Il mormorio di Parigi: The Conscious Pariah's Search for a Utopian Home and the Role of Literature between Displacement and Self-Definition

In Ortese's *Il mormorio di Parigi* (*Paris' Murmer*, 1986), the narrative "I" defines herself in opposition to her casual travel companion, a young Italian student who is moving, via Paris and Marseille, to New York City, where he has found a job.[40] Resentful about having to reject his European past and longing to fit in his new American home, the young student voices his "amaro risentimento" and "eloquente diffidenza" (MP 223; "bitter resentment and eloquent distrust") towards Paris, France, and Europe in general. The young man's act of unreflective rejection (the rejection, Arendt would claim, of the parvenu), inspires by contrast Ortese's hermeneutical journey across Paris.[41] Both unknown and familiar to the narrator, who feels mad with fear but also full of happiness, and both lost and at home in the peace and silence of the core of Europe, Paris is a quintessentially uncanny space:[42]

> Sono in un punto di questa città, non so se est o ovest, nord o sud, in una strada sconosciuta, anche se vagamente familiare [...]. Premo debolmente il bottone di legno di un campanello che non suona. Qui, a questo numero [...] dovrebbe esserci un avvocato italiano per il quale lo studente mi ha lasciato un biglietto (è un vecchio amico di famiglia) pregandolo di volermi essere di qualche aiuto. [...]
>
> Una volta rinchiuso il portoncino, mi trovo in un pozzo, in un antro.
>
> Non un pozzo né un antro per dire, un vero pozzo, un vero antro. Il suolo, sotto i miei piedi è sparito, ci sono buche e acqua. Il buio è perfetto, un buio da prima della creazione, o, più modestamente, da inverno di periferia. Mi accorgo in tempo di avere in tasca dei fiammiferi, e comincio ad accenderli uno per volta, cautamente. E appaiono dei muri corrosi, e una scaletta a chiocciola, rapidissima, che si perde verso l'alto. I fiammiferi si spengono e ritorna il buio. Comincio a salire, pian piano, trattendendo il fiato, sicura che mi imbatterò, da qui a un istante, in qualche mostro, o inciamperò in qualche cadavere. (MP 236)

> ("I am in a spot of this city, I don't know whether it's east or west, north or south, in an unknown street, albeit vaguely familiar [...]. Faintly, I press the wooden knob of a doorbell that does not ring. Here, at this number [...] should live an Italian lawyer for whom the student left a note with me. He is a friend of his family and the student is pleading him to be of some help to me.

> Once I close the door, I find myself in a pit, a cave.
>
> Not a figurative pit or a cave, but a real pit, a real cave. The ground below my feet has disappeared and there are holes and water. Darkness is perfect, a darkness like that before the Creation, or more modestly, like that of a suburban winter. Just in time, I realize that I have some matches in my pocket and I begin to light them cautiously, one at a time. Corroded walls appear, and a very steep spiral staircase that fades away up high. The matches burn out and darkness returns. I begin to ascend the stairs, slowly, holding my breath, sure that in a few seconds, I will run into a monster or step on a corpse.")

The mixture of fairy tale and *banlieue-noir* elements, and the strident contrast between the tenor of the connotations (the Biblical darkness turning into a pedestrian wintery gloom), invests the writer's quasi-mythical ascent through this symbolic birth canal with anticipatory irony. Reversing the trauma of birth, the narrator's tentative climb towards the prenatal *chōra* is both familiar and strange – *heimlich* and *unheimlich* at once. This maternal receptacle – matrix of creation and origin of the Self as well as core of the polis at the centre of Europe – is indeed an ambiguous domain.[43] Doubly in the *middle* and yet un-positioned (the subject is disoriented), real ("un vero antro") and evocatively symbolic, it is a centred non-place. While suggesting the amniotic sphere of pre-Oedipal unity between the Self and its surroundings, this *chōra*, like the belly of Pinocchio's "gigantesco Pesce-cane" ("terrible shark"),[44] turns out to be the dwelling of the Father – the Logocentric home of the Law:

> La porta si apre, e vedo l'avvocato Gaetani. Gaetani perchè un nome bisogna averlo, s'intende, ma il realtà è Mazzini giovane, col volto olivastro, i lisci capelli grigio-ferro, gli occhi pieni di luce che non possono sorridere e neppure chiudersi. Mi fa entrare. (MP 236)
>
> ("The door opens, and I see the lawyer Gaetani. Gaetani because one must have a proper name, of course, but in truth he is young Mazzini, with his olive complexion, straight iron-gray hair, and eyes full of light that cannot either smile or close. He lets me in.")

Surprisingly, the centre of Europe is home to the father of the Italian Risorgimento, an incongruous and anachronistic figure in contemporary Paris. This Mazzini is a choric *inventio*: as Ortese states, his name is Gaetani only in the merely referential world. As brought to life via the writer's imaginative and discursive strategies, he *is* young Mazzini. However, as soon as it is originated in discursive form, Ortese's locus of beginning and creation undergoes a process of ironic displacement:

> La casa, esternamente di fango e pietra, all'interno è solo di legno e carta, legno e libri, legno e candelieri dimenticati, legno e carte geografiche, mappe di isole e mari lontani, cornici d'oro e d'argento, tagliacarte, tra i tagliacarte e in qualche cornice ritratti ovali di morti, fotografie di dame e fanciulli e soldati già dentro il fiume del tempo, ma qui ancora riuniti sotto un albero, sorridenti. Ma lo spazio maggiore è riservato ai libri: immensi o piccolissimi, di tutti i generi, le dimensioni, i colori, le epoche, i tipi. E una cosa li accomuna: sono libri italiani, c'è la vita, la storia, il colore dell'Italia quando nasceva, appena un secolo fa. 1860.
>
> [...] Qui scende la sera. (MP 236–37)

> ("The exterior of the house is made of mud and stone, but the inside is mere wood and paper, wood and books, wood and forgotten candlesticks, wood and geographical maps, maps of island and remote seas, gold and silver frames, and letter openers. Among the letter openers, there are frames with oval portraits of now dead people, photographs of ladies, young men, and soldiers already lost in the flow of time, but here still together, smiling under a tree. The bulk of the space however is reserved to the books: very large or very small, of all genres and dimensions, colors, eras, and types. One thing groups them together: they are Italian books – containing the life, history, and color of Italy when it was born, just a century ago. 1860.
>
> [...] Here, evening approaches.")

Insulated from the outside piazza full of sunshine and noise, this *chōra* is a space of birth and death, simultaneously. The place of origin is already a space of memory, not the matrix from which the Self can "take an initiative, begin [...], set something into motion,"[45] and move forward, as Arendt argued in defining the notion of human *action* as the ability *to begin* in *The Human Condition.* Here, the locus of origin is an invention that ironically subverts its own generative implications by mimicking the cadences of Guido Gozzano's crepuscular and melancholy prose. This is also a domain where "wood" remains inanimate, and "paper" – the written word, the record of a country's collective memories – does not have the power to act upon life and is no longer, as Ortese claims elsewhere, "diaframma tra l'essere e il fare" (CC 19–20; "a diaphragm between being and doing").[46] Gaetani / Mazzini's eyes have the fixity of a daguerreotype, and the compendium of the history of Italy contained in his library is unrelated to the present, a present symbolized by Gaetani's ancient telephone that fails to establish any communication with the outside world, and his doorbell, which does not ring.

Contrary to Arendt's social parvenu, ready to cast his past aside with every change of home, Ortese's émigré appears eager to superimpose the familiar onto the foreign, the safety of a lost home upon a land of exile. If the former is frantically reinventing himself in order to belong to the present, the latter reverses the generative potential of the domain of origins as described by Ortese. This sterile crucible of melancholia and nostalgia displays the Logos as a simulacrum – a frozen likeness of Mazzini, and its dwelling as a "vecchia madre" ("old mother") who has exhausted her generative power (MP 238). The *artifex* of Italy's collective identity reincarnated and displaced in this ambiguous *chōra* under the name of a lonely Italian émigré is hopelessly isolated from the here and now of social life. Gaetani / Mazzini's vacuum-sealed existence among the cherished mementos of a dead past is of no use to the southern woman-writer who cannot translate this sterile archaeological collection into useful memories or practical directives to orient her current quest for identity.

Ortese signs a different experiential and creative contract with the surroundings in her encounter with the foreign city, rather than in the retreat into the museum-like interior. As she is neither a professional journalist nor a leisurely tourist, the narrator's immediate experience of Paris depends upon the rules of *need* (need to find directions, a phone, a cheap hotel, food, and acquaintances who can offer lodging and provide connections). However, the stranger's gaze transforms the alien metropolis, and all that it contains, into a treasured *gift*, and the writer-pariah thus becomes the beneficiary of an entire world. The sense of total dispossession morphs into a state of full spiritual ownership that exceeds the boundaries of selfhood and that the writer shares with her sympathetic readers. A novel and eccentric definition of collective memory thus emerges:

> Per molto tempo ricorderò questo pezzetto di marciapiede sul boulevard de Clichy e questa fioca luce d'estate, come di una estate ricordata o dipinta, non vera, e i colori, il traffico, le vetrine dei caffè […] e la processione verde degli alberi, la banda delle nuvole, da cui piove su tutto, insieme ai raggi del sole, una musica di gioia, di malessere, di confusa, ostinata speranza. Colori, colori, colori. Folla, folla, folla. Movimento, sole, musica. Tutti i palloncini delle vostre pasque, colmi di puro colore, sono stati

spremuti su muri; tutte le automobiline verdi e gialle, e le diligenze rosse delle vostre epifanie – chiuse in un sacco per trenta, quaranta anni – sono state sparpagliate stamane per la città; tutte le vetrinette e le tazzine e le bilance dorate della casa di bambola, custodite gelosamente da un'antica ragazzina, hanno fatto su questo marciapiede la loro apparizione. [...] è un paradiso perduto. (MP 228–29)

("I will long remember this slice of pavement on the Boulevard de Clichy, together with this dim summer light, like a remembered or painted summer, not a real one; and the colors, the traffic, the windows of the cafes [...], and the green pageant of trees with the musical band of the clouds pouring, together with the sun's rays, a music of joy and malaise, of confused and obdurate hope upon everything. Colors and colors and colors. Crowds and crowds and crowds. Movement, sunshine, music. All the balloons of all your Easter Sundays, filled with sheer color have been squeezed onto the walls. All the green and yellow toy cars, and the red stage coaches of your Epiphanies – closed up in a sack for thirty or forty years – have been scattered today around the city; all the little shop windows, and tiny cups and golden scales of doll houses, jealously saved by a little girl of long ago, have appeared on this pavement. *It is a lost paradise.*")

In a clever *mise en abyme*, the narrator anticipates her future memory of the Boulevard de Clichy ("ricorderò") not as her mnemonic rendition of the objective world of the present ("*questa* fioca luce") but as her recollection of another mnemonic and aesthetic construct ("ricordata o dipinta"). Twice removed from the referential space, this double memory becomes the realm of a collective utopia that merges past, present, and future into a chronotope of unity (see the reiterated "tutte") – a tribute to the fullness of human existence via the remembered recurrence of life-celebrating festivities, which overcomes the tyranny of chronology, isolation, and death: "tutto è festa, incantesimo, vita" (MP 229; "all is merriment, enchantment and life").

The woman-writer who "comes from nowhere" sees Paris as the very opposite of the sociocultural void that both haunted and nurtured her efforts of self-definition. The diverse specificity of the Parisian crowd epitomizes the utopian totality, ranging from the ordinary and mundane to the bizarre and eerie, characterizing the centre of Europe:

Passano popolani dalle maglie rosse e i berretti neri, passano cittadini di colore in completi blu o verde, passano esili e cinguettanti marinai stranieri, con pipe e bianchi berretti; passano donnette vistose e umane; soldati stanchi; passa un uomo d'età, dall'aspetto bonario, conducendo per mano un cane vestito alla marinara, in blu rosso e bianco, che poi si rivela un giovanetto cieco. [...]

Passano prostitute [...], portinaie autorevoli, con la spesa. Preti protestanti. Facce di giustiziati. Vecchie coppie americane. Un *blouson noir.*

Si potrebbe raccontare per ore della gente che passa, senza sosta, incantevole e orrida, per le vie di Montmartre; e sarebbe, per ogni volto, una storia e un linguaggio diverso. La infinita libertà di Parigi ha creato questo miracolo della diversità, delle differenze, delle dissonanze, che tutte insieme fanno l'uguaglianza, l'unità, l'armonia del volto di Parigi. Vi è di tutto: e tutto è esattamente come avrebbe dovuto essere. [...] E perció vi sono brutture e bellezze infinite, salute e morte, allegria e noia, il disfacimento e la fioritura, tutte le grazie su tutti i vizi possibili [...]. Ecco coltelli e nuvole, le fogne e la Place de l'Étoile, il mercato erotico e Chagall, la soavità del diavolo e la durezza di Dio. (MP 231)

("Common people in red shirts and black berets pass by; black townspeople in blue or green suits; slender and chirping foreign sailors, with pipes and white hats; flashy and humane little women; tired soldiers; an elderly man, his demeanour kindly, holding the hand of a dog dressed in a blue, red, and white sailor suit, who turns out to be a blind young man. [...]

Prostitutes pass by, [...] and commanding doorkeepers, carrying their groceries. Protestant pastors. Faces of executed men. Elderly American couples. A *blouson noir.*

One could talk for hours about the enchanting and horrible people that go by without pause, along the streets of Montmartre; and for every face it would be a different story in a different language. The infinite freedom of Paris has created this miracle of diversity, differences, and dissonances, which, combined, make the equality, the unity and harmony of the face of Paris. There is a bit of everything, and everything is exactly how it should be [...]. Therefore, there is infinite beauty and infinite ugliness, health and death, cheerfulness and boredom, decay and flourishing, all the graces upon all the possible vices [...]. Here are knives and clouds, the sewers and the Place de l'Étoile, the erotic market of Chagall, the suavity of the Devil and the harshness of God.")

Crucible of the world and cornucopia of diversity, Paris is a spectacle for the eyes, a catalogue of dissonances, an unabridged encyclopedia of humanity, and a heterogeneous domain where the similar and the discordant, the real and the ideal converge and coexist. Paris is the utopian paradise where the possible has indeed become practicable. Yet, this utopian existence is a déjà vu – a cultural memory: "Ma è una vita di ieri o di oggi?" (MP 229; "But, is this a life of yesterday or one of today?"), rhetorically asks Ortese, not without implied regret, only to reply: "è un profondo ieri" (MP 244; "it's a profound yesterday").

In *Il mormorio di Parigi*, Ortese self-consciously "sees" Paris as the capital of the nineteenth century, a spectacle organized according to the same representational criteria that the universal expositions popularized during their European golden age (1860– 1914), namely, the panoramic and panoptic views, and the phantasmagoria. The world's fairs displayed themselves and their host cities as perspectivist and totalizing domains, the function of which was to deploy and survey the world's spectacular multiplicities and differences. The perspectivist space is, by definition, "open to virtually infinite expansion," just like the slice of the Boulevard de Clichy that Ortese describes as a compendium of the entire city.[47] The crowd parading down the boulevard is not an amorphous, threatening, and engulfing mass, but a moving panorama – a procession of discrete individuals that the narrator classifies and defines from careful hermeneutical distance – from the perspective, that is, which allows her to organize her view according to a "panoramic gaze" that permits accurate understanding.[48] The same all-encompassing understanding occurs with the panoptic view.[49] From hills, towers, raised platforms, elevators, and Ferris wheels, spectators could enjoy that bird's-eye perspective that presented the urban space as a totality that their eyes could encompass and control. "[D]alla piazza dove c'è la chiesa del Sacro Cuore," Ortese writes with an obvious nod to Victor Hugo of *Notre Dame de Paris*, "si vede Parigi, si abbraccia Parigi con i suoi tetti celesti, il suo cappello di nuvole bianche, l'ineffabile ampiezza del suo orizzonte" (MP 232; "From the square where there is the Church of the Sacre Cœur, one sees Paris, one embraces Paris, with its blue roofs, its cover of white clouds, the ineffable breadth of its horizon").

The world's fairs' utopian vision consisted in the statement of the unstoppable progress of the Western world. The idea of progress expressed itself in the fairgrounds' crafted topography, and in the many sophisticated operations of mass make-believe that collapsed reality and illusion into what Walter Benjamin dubbed as the world's fairs' "phantasmagoria in which each person enters to be distracted."[50] In *Il mormorio di Parigi*, Ortese evokes the phantasmagoria effect with both technical savvy and a wink to referential accuracy:

> A due passi dal falso e incredibile Moulin Rouge [...] c'è un muro completamente nero. [...] Ha qualcosa di allarmante e insieme inerte: "Cabaret du Néant," c'è scritto a lettere bianche, cubitali.
>
> Pochi centimentri più su di quel divertimento funereo si aprono piccole finestre che sembrano inventate: hanno tendine di trina, piante fiorite, sedie di paglia, gabbiette con uccelli. E rivelano tranquilli interni familiari. Ma non si ode una voce, un grido.
>
> Una donna, sopra la parola "Néant" appoggiata a una bassa graziosa inferriata [...] guarda nella strada senza guardare. (MP 233–34)

> ("Two steps away from the fake and unbelievable Moulin Rouge [...] there is a wall, completely black. [...] There is something simultaneously alarming and inert in this wall that displays in white enormous letters the writing: 'Cabaret du Néant.'
>
> Just a few centimetres over that funeral joke there are little windows that appear made up: they have embroidered little curtains, flowering plants, straw chairs, and tiny cages with birds inside. They reveal peaceful family interiors, but you cannot hear a single voice or shout.
>
> A woman, leaning over a low pretty railing just above the word 'Néant,' looks at the street, without seeing it.")

Historically one of the first venues where phantasmagoria shows were created and projected in Paris, the Cabaret du Néant was founded in 1892. Ortese resuscitates it in her anachronistic Paris in order to blur the lines between reality and its representations, truth and fiction, and being and nothingness (*le néant*). However, unlike in the phantasmagorias (either as pre-cinematic illusionist tricks or, *lato sensu*, in Benjamin's definition of the term), Ortese does not conceal either herself or her craft, but rather displays agency, intent, and technique. "Non consiglierei a nessuno," Ortese writes, "di attraversare Parigi senza ironia" (MP 238; "I would never recommend that anybody goes through Paris without irony").

Ortese creates a brilliant objective correlative of the filter of irony when she highlights the double screen of a window reflected into a mirror through which she observes the panorama of the metropolis and its parading crowd: "Dalla pasticceria, dietro la vetrinetta – riflessa la vetrinetta nei lunghi specchi orizzontali – cominciavo a distinguere i volti di [...] Parigi" (MP 231; "from the pastry shop, behind the little window that reflected itself into the long horizontal mirrors, I began to make out the faces of [...] Paris"). This mediated position is both perceptual and hermeneutical. Like the prisoners in the allegory of the great cave in Plato's *Republic*, the observer does not see the things themselves, but their reflections. However, if Plato's chained men mistook mere shadows for reality, as they were ignorant of their perceptive location and of the fire that caused the shadows, Ortese's highly framed perception self-consciously emphasizes that what she sees is not the city in itself but the city as it displays itself through specific cultural, semiotic, and interpretive codes. These codes too are double, as they are those of the world's fairs as appropriated by the belated and ironic observer in the summer of 1960. Irony is precisely what transforms the definition of reality as phantasmagoria from its negative connotations (a false reality, a fiction deceptively presented as true in order to reduce gawking viewers into a state of passive wonder) to new, positive ones (a liberating, because critical and self-conscious, "expression," an aesthetic "idea" – in sum, a utopia).

In *Il mormorio di Parigi*, irony indeed separates the parvenu from the conscious pariah, and the mere antiquarian display of the world's fairs' systems of representation (and their implicit ideology) from their disruptive mimicry. As conscious pariah, Ortese is bitterly aware of the failure of the gospel of communal progress and universal well-being that the world's fairs touted. Her ironic re-appropriation of the semiotic systems that displayed this progress demystifies its outcomes and proposes alternative visions. Upon abandoning the view of the city as reflected in the pastry shop's mirrors, the woman-artist enters the urban stage with what Judith Butler would call a "performative gesture" and Arendt an "action" that turns "power against itself to produce alternative modalities of power, to establish a kind of political contestation that is not a 'pure' opposition, a 'transcendence' of contemporary relations of power, but a difficult labour of forging a future from resources inevitably impure."[51]

In *Il mormorio di Parigi*, the "impure resources" are the technologies of vision that defined Paris as the capital of modernity. In the conscious pariah's hands, these resources are estranged and re-functioned to generate a fluid, open, and aerial urban design according to an aesthetic of lightness similar to that of Calvino's *Invisible Cities*:

> La macchina su cui ero salita [...] non correva, ma volava, e non produceva alcun rumore, solo un debole fruscio di seta strappata. [...] Io cercavo con gli occhi una città come quelle che noi tutti conosciamo, fatte di pietra, di cemento armato e semafori, e vedevo soltanto un'aria grigio-azzurra sui cui [...] pietra grigia e semafori erano solo disegnate od ombreggiate, ma molto leggermente.

> Case, piazze, strade, boschi, castelli, tetti, tende, vertrine, fanali, uccelli, semafori, non esistevano, ma erano suggeriti, sognati. [...]
>
> I quartieri si susseguivano ai quartieri, le strade alle strade, le piazze alle piazze, i boschi ai parchi, ai castelli, ai giardini, alle fontane [...]. Tutto questo non finiva mai. [...]
>
> Quest'aria interminabile [...] diveniva sempre più trasparente e sensibile, e tenue, finché [...] io vidi la fonte di tutti questi prodigi, questa tenerezza, questa immaginazione [...], vidi l'anima stessa di Parigi, cioè la Senna, la sua bell'acqua verde-mattina. (MP 239–40)

> ("The car I jumped into [...] did not just run, but took flight without making a sound beyond a faint rustle of torn silk. [...] My eyes were looking for a city like those that we all know, made of stone, reinforced concrete, and traffic lights, and all I saw instead was the grey-blue air [...] on which grey stone and traffic lights were simply pencilled in and shadowed, but very lightly.
>
> Houses, squares, woods, castles, roofs, curtains, shop-windows, street-lights, birds, and traffic lights did not exist but were only suggested, dreamed. [...]
>
> Neighbourhoods followed neighbourhoods, boulevards followed boulevards and squares followed squares. Woods gave way to parks, and castles, and gardens, and fountains. All of this never ended. [...]
>
> This infinite atmosphere [...] was becoming more and more transparent and sentient and tenuous, until [...] I saw the source of all these prodigies, tenderness and imagination. [...] I saw Paris' very soul, the Seine, its beautiful sunrise-green water.")

The woman-writer feels "at home" in a metropolitan phantasmagoria that anticipates Calvino's 1973 definition of utopia as "less solid than gaseous: [...] a utopia of fine dust, corpuscular, and in suspension."[52] Liminal space between air and water, the finished and the unfinished, and day and night, Ortese's utopian topography exists in a state of flux that disrupts the world's fairs' meticulously designed structures. Replete with undefined potential, Ortese's urban utopia is not a "form to be fleshed out," but, rather, a form in need of being estranged, "pulverized," and dissolved from within. In this sense, Ortese's utopian writing can be defined as post-representational, inasmuch as it exploits Eurocentric and patriarchal representational forms (forms that, as we have seen, the woman writer uncomfortably and conflictingly inhabits), while altering and re-functioning them. By doing so, Ortese does not fall prey to the sense of vertigo and disintegration that Baudrillard saw as the apocalyptic corollary to the collapse of all coherent systems of representation "not only at the level of objective culture, the level of public discourse, but also in the daily experience of people, inside 'the subject.'"[53] On the contrary, from a position of marginality and exile, Ortese creates a counter-text that fissures the Eurocentric and patriarchal domain at its very core.

Ortese's revolutionary "action" consists in introducing elements of novelty and unpredictability into the inherited paradigms of modernity. As Hannah Arendt theorized in *The Human Condition*, this action, placed outside the domain of necessity and causality, ushers in the principle of freedom.[54] Freedom, so evocatively rendered by the woman writer's exhilarating flight over a city that "a poco a poco si sollevava, lasciava la terra, si perdeva nel cielo" (MP 241; "little by little, lifted itself, left the ground, and lost itself into the sky"), is the "miracle"[55] that counters the subjection to mechanization, isolation, and routine that Ortese saw as the dehumanizing result of technological progress.[56]

In *Il mormorio di Parigi*, Ortese projects a utopian mode of inhabiting the centre of Europe by re-painting the topography of Paris with an aerial and meandering brush. Undoubtedly, this mode expresses a dream of autonomy, lightness, and joy that hardly mirrors the experience of an ill-paid journalist charged with writing a short piece on the French capital in the summer of 1960. However, by altering and reorienting conventional modes of perception, interpretation, and imaginative creation, Ortese's Parisian narrative surpasses the realm of mere contingency. As "movement beyond set limits," Ortese's utopian writing abandons "the logic of ideology and of teleological progress" and shapes a free-flowing domain of "open potentiality and [...] desire"[57] that redefines the difficult relationship between a nomadic subject and her environment according to what Ernst Bloch famously defined as the "principle of hope." In spite of intermittent disillusionment, this principle sustained Ortese's search for "expressivity" as the "absolute freedom" of the mind, Arendt's analysis of political praxis as the springboard for freedom and agency, and the many other practical and theoretical efforts of generations of conscious pariahs during the many "dark times" of humanity's troubled existence.

NOTES

1 I use "dark times" to refer to Arendt's own designation in *Men in Dark Times*.

2 "[Sono nata] a Roma, ma casualmente. Mio padre aveva un lavoro che lo portava in giro per l'Italia"; "Non frequentavamo nessuno"; "Appena ci

eravamo stabiliti da qualche parte dovevamo traslocare" ("[I was born] in Rome. But by chance. My father had a job that took him all over Italy"; "We didn't really have many friends"; "As soon as we got settled somewhere, we would have to move"), Ortese, *E tu chi eri?*, 24 [460 in this volume].

3 The reference to Toledo is not related to the Castilian city, but to an imagined locale inspired by Naples's Spanish Quarter and the Via Toledo that crosses it. On the mythical resonances of Ortese's fantastic "Toledo," see Clerici, *Apparizione e visione*, 472–73 and Ghezzo, "Chiroscuro napoletano," 88.

4 The complete sentence reads: "Sono figlia di nessuno. Nel senso che la società quando io nacqui non c'era, o non c'era per tutti i figli dell'uomo" (PT 23; "I am nobody's daughter in the sense than when I was born society did not exist, or, rather, it existed only for some of the children of Man").

5 Ortese, *E tu chi eri?*, 24–25: "Aveva il senso dell'avventura. Credeva in mille cose impossibili. Si entusiasmava per delle astrazioni. Perdeva la testa dietro grandi progetti irrealizzabili" ("He had a sense of adventure. He believed in countless impossibilities. He was excited by abstractions. He lost his head over grandiose, unfeasible projects").

6 Ortese, *E tu chi eri?*, 25 [462].

7 On this Edenic unity, see Farnetti, *Anna Maria Ortese*, 154–55.

8 Some of Anna Maria's siblings left for America and Australia, while misfortune and loss tragically marked places like Martinique and Albania, where two of Anna Maria's brothers, both sailors, died at a young age. The lack of basic human necessities, such as food and shelter, marks Ortese's description of the post-war period: "Ho avuto proprio fame. Una fame angosciosa, da mangiarsi le scarpe bollite. Come ho fatto a sopravvivere, non lo so. […] Non avevo neppure casa: con i miei andavamo come zingari da un posto all'altro." "I experienced real hunger. A hunger so full of anguish that I could have eaten a boiled shoe. How I managed to survive I don't know [...] I didn't even have a house: with my parents, we wandered like gypsies from one place to the next"), Ortese, *E tu chi eri?*, 31 [466].

9 See Ortese, *E tu chi eri?*, 28 [465].

10 See also *Il porto di Toledo*: "Ogni volta che la mente umana entrava nel mondo dell'Espressività, lavorava a nient'altro che la costruzione di un nuovo continente, o terra, dove, finché sul mondo vi fosse stata la caducità, i naufraghi avrebbero trovato salvezza, sebbena temporanea" (PT 112; "Every time that the human mind entered into the world of Expression it worked toward creating a new continent, or land, where, as long as finitude ruled the world, shipwrecks would find safety, however temporary").

11 Feldman, "Introduction," 16.

12 Ortese, *E tu chi eri?*, 34 [468, 469].

13 Arendt, "Eichmann in Jerusalem," 250.

14 Ortese, "Dialogo sull'appartenenza," 1.
15 Arendt, "We Refugees," 55–56. In Ron H. Feldman's poignant words, Arendt was "one of the most remarkable – as well as one of the last – offspring of a German-Jewish milieu which produced more than its share of great literary, scientific, and artistic figures" (15).
16 Ibid., 60.
17 Ibid., 62.
18 Ibid., 62.
19 Arendt, "The Jew as Pariah," 76.
20 "[Bernard Lazare] saw that what was necessary was to rouse the Jewish pariah to a fight against the Jewish parvenu" ("The Jew as Pariah," 76).
21 Arendt, "We Refugees," 62.
22 On Ortese own reading of post-war "confusione," see CC 33.
23 Arendt, "We Refugees," 56.
24 Ortese juxtaposes classical against contemporary America. The former is the America that nurtured the imagination of many anti-fascist intellectuals such as Vittorini and Pavese during the war. The latter betrayed these intellectuals' very ideals of individual freedom and self-definition for a new imperialism "without history" (see CC 25–28).
25 Arendt, "We Refugees," 61 [emphasis added].
26 Ibid., 56.
27 Ibid., 65.
28 Ibid., 66.
29 Ibid., 66.
30 Ibid., 65.
31 Arendt, "The Jew as Pariah," 68.
32 Ibid., 68.
33 Ibid., 71.
34 Ibid., 72.
35 Ibid., 73.
36 See also Ortese, "Attraversando," CC 44.
37 Arendt, "The Jew as Pariah," 68.
38 Arendt, "We Refugees," 68.
39 Arendt was always intensely aware of the seduction of self-isolation, a condition in which pariahs could enjoy "the freedom and untouchability of outcasts. Excluded from the world of political realities, they could [...] retreat into their quiet corners there to preserve the illusion of liberty." The Nazi persecution made such isolation no longer possible: "there is no protection in heaven or earth against bare murder. You cannot stay aloof from society" (Arendt, "The Jew as Pariah," 90). In this sense, Ortese's progressive

detachment from social communion differs from Arendt's sustained engagement: "Only when a people lives and functions in consort with other peoples can it contribute to the establishment of a commonly conditioned and commonly controlled humanity" (Arendt, "The Jew as Pariah," 90).

40 The first of five sections of an account of Ortese's trip to Paris was originally published in the *Corriere d'informazione* in 1960 with the title "Vacanza col batticuore di una donna a Parigi: 13–14 agosto 1960"). Ortese revised the narrative and published it as *Il mormorio di Parigi* in 1986. See LS 472.

41 "Lo studente [...] sembrava ancora più inasprito [come se Parigi] preferisse non vederla affatto" (MP 227; "the student seemed to have gotten even more sour, [as if he] preferred not to see Paris at all").

42 "Che silenzio di centro Europa!" (MP 233, "What a silence in Central Europe.") On the definition of the "uncanny" as an ambivalent concept evoking both the "familiar" and the "strange," see Freud's seminal essay "The Uncanny." On the paradox of the "uncanny" as theorized by Freud see, especially, Weber, Cixous, and Bernstein.

43 On the use of the term "chōra" to mean land or city when used in the context of the polis in the *Timaeus*, see Rickert, 255, and Sallis, 116. For a seminal discussion on the "chōra," see also Kristeva, *Revolution in Poetic Language.*

44 Collodi, *Le avventure di Pinocchio*, 141.

45 Arendt, *The Human Condition*, 157.

46 In a more direct sociopolitical context, Ortese underscored the sterile, nostalgic power of these memories in "Memoria e conversazione": "C'era la memoria dell'Italia passata, e non altro. C'era una pace inerte, senza più speranza" (CC 11; "There was the memory of the Italy of the past, nothing else. There was an inert peace, without any hope").

47 See Baudrillard, "La fin de la modernité," 32.

48 On the techniques of the panorama and the moving panorama, see de Cauter, "The Panoramic Ecstasy."

49 On panopticism, see Foucault. For an analysis of the panoptic view in universal exhibitions, see my *World's Fairs Italian Style.*

50 Benjamin, *The Arcades Project*, 7.

51 Butler, *Bodies that Matter*, 241.

52 Calvino, "On Fourier, III," 255.

53 De Cauter, "The Panoramic Ecstasy," 21.

54 Arendt, *The Human Condition*, 222.

55 Ibid., 222.

56 See, for example, Ortese's description of the subway's commuters "i cui occhi non si staccavano mai dal giornale [...] come la gente vecchia, a cui tutto dà noia" (MP 227; "who never averted their gaze from their newspapers

[...] like old people, bored by everything"), or of the passengers at the Gare de Lyon: "viaggiatori in attesa di chissaché, freddi, indifferenti,con gli occhi al marciapiede" (MP 225–26; "travelers waiting for who knows what, cold, indifferent, staring at the pavement").

57 Braidotti, *Nomadic Subjects*, 103.

WORKS CITED

Arendt, Hannah. "Eichmann in Jerusalem: An Exchange of Letters between Gershom Scholem and Hannah Arendt." In *The Jew as Pariah: Jewish Identity and Politics in the Modern Age*, ed. Ron H. Feldman, 240–79. New York: Grove, 1978.

– *The Human Condition*. Garden City, NY: Doubleday, 1959.

– "The Jew as Pariah: A Hidden Tradition." In *The Jew as Pariah: Jewish Identity and Politics in the Modern Age*, ed. Ron H. Feldman, 67–90. New York: Grove, 1978.

– *Men in Dark Times*. New York: Harcourt, 1986.

– "We Refugees." In *The Jew as Pariah: Jewish Identity and Politics in the Modern Age*, ed. Ron H. Feldman, 55–66. New York: Grove, 1978.

Baudrillard, Jean. "La fin de la modernité ou l'ère de la simulation." In *La modernité ou l'esprit du temps*. Biénnale de Paris. Section d'architecture, 32–33. Paris: L'Equerre, 1982.

Benjamin, Walter. *The Arcades Project*. Trans. Howard Eiland and Kevin McLaughlin. Cambridge, MA: Belknap Press, 1999.

Bernstein, Susan. "It Walks: The Ambulatory Uncanny." *MLN* 118 (2004): 111–39.

Bloch, Ernst. *The Principle of Hope*. Trans. Neville Plaice, Stephen Plaice, and Paul Knight. Oxford: Blackwell, 1986.

Braidotti, Rosi. *Nomadic Subjects*. New York: Columbia University Press, 1994.

Butler, Judith. *Bodies That Matter: On the Discursive Limits of "Sex."* New York: Routledge, 1993.

Calvino, Italo. "On Fourier, III: Envoi: A Utopia of Fine Dust." In *The Uses of Literature*, 245–55. San Diego: Harvest / HBJ, 1982.

Cixous, Hélène. "Fiction and Its Phantoms: A Reading of Freud's *Das Unheimliche* (The 'Uncanny')." *New Literary History* 7 (Spring 1976): 525–48.

Clerici, Luca. *Apparizione e visione: Vita e opere di Anna Maria Ortese*. Milan: Mondadori, 2002.

Collodi, Carlo. *Le avventure di Pinocchio*. Ed. Ornella Castellani Pollidori. Pescia: Fondazione Nazionale Carlo Collodi, 1983.

De Cauter, Lieven. "The Panoramic Ecstasy: On World Exhibitions and the Disintegration of Experience." *Theory, Culture and Society* 10 (1993): 1–23.

Della Coletta, Cristina. *World's Fairs Italian Style: The Great Expositions in Turin and Their Narratives, 1860–1915*. Toronto: University of Toronto Press, 2006.

Farnetti, Monica. *Anna Maria Ortese*. Milan: Bruno Mondadori, 1998.

Feldman, Ron H. Introduction to *The Jew as Pariah: Jewish Identity and Politics in the Modern Age*, by Hannah Arendt, 15–52. New York: Grove, 1978.

Foucault, Michel. "Panopticism." In *Discipline and Punish: The Birth of the Prison*, 195–228. Trans. Alan Sheridan. New York: Vintage, 1955.

Freud, Sigmund. "The Uncanny." In *The Standard Edition of the Complete Psychological Works of Sigmund Freud*, 217–52. Ed. James Strachey. Vol 17. London: Hogarth, 1955.

Ghezzo, Flora Maria. "Chiaroscuro napoletano: trasfigurazioni fantastiche di una città." *Narrativa* 24 (2003): 85–104.

Hugo, Victor. *Notre Dame de Paris*. Paris: Garnier Frères, 1976.

Kristeva, Julia. *Revolution in Poetic Language*. New York: Columbia University Press, 1984.

Ortese, Anna Maria. "Attraversando un paese sconosciuto." *Corpo celeste*. Milan: Adelphi, 1997.

– "Dialogo sull'appartenenza." *Lo straniero* 1 (1997): 7.

– *E tu chi eri? Interviste sull'infanzia*. Interview with Dacia Maraini, 23–35. Milan: Bompiani, 1973.

Plato. *The Republic*. Ed. Robin Waterfield. Oxford: Oxford University Press, 2008.

Rickert, Thomas. "Toward the *Chōra*: Kristeva, Derrida, and Ulmer on Emplaced Invention." *Philosophy and Rhetoric* 40 (2007): 251–73.

Sallis, John. *On Beginning in Plato's Timaeus*. Bloomington: Indiana University Press, 1999.

Weber, Samuel. "The Sideshow, or: Remarks on a Canny Moment." *MLN* 88 (December 1973): 1102–1133.

– "Uncanny Thinking." In *The Legend of Freud*, 1–31. Stanford: Stanford University Press, 2000.

PART TWO

Life of a Celestial Body: Making and Unmaking the Self

4 Epistolary Self-Storytelling: Anna Maria Ortese's Letters to Massimo Bontempelli

AMELIA MOSER

Dear Bontempelli, I am thus happy to write to you because, following my habit, I will do nothing but talk and perhaps talk only nonsense about myself, an obscure subject, always loaded with emotion. But no, no, that's not true, it's the saddest topic I know.

Anna Maria Ortese, Letter to Massimo Bontempelli dated 4 July 1940*

The immediate effect of candour is sincerity. The candid spirit does not make concessions [...]. The candid spirit is divinely headstrong.

Massimo Bontempelli, *Pirandello o del candore* **

In May 1983, and during the following four months, Anna Maria Ortese engaged in a series of interviews with Sandra Petrignani, initially by telephone and later – in a very indirect manner – through mail correspondence. Of her general unwillingness to grant interviews in person and of her reclusive lifestyle, Ortese would write to Petrignani: "Come vede, sono una persona scomodissima, e questo spiega ampiamente la mia

* (Caro Bontempelli, io dunque sono felice di scriverLe perché, secondo le mie abitudini, non farò che parlare e forse straparlare di me, argomento sconosciuto e sempre carico di emozione. Ma no, no, non è vero, il più triste argomento ch'io conosca.) In Amelia Moser, "*Il futuro è tutto nella notte*": *Anna Maria Ortese, Massimo Bontempelli and Magic Realism*, PhD diss., Harvard University, 117 (Letter 17). Translations are mine unless otherwise indicated.

** "L'effetto immediato del candore è la sincerità. L'anima candida non fa concessioni [...]. L'anima candida è divinamente incauta," Massimo Bontempelli, *Opere scelte*, 812–13.

scarsa fortuna" ("As you see, I am a very troublesome person, and this explains my lack of success").[1] Believing in these words, a reader might indeed suppose that Ortese's self-imposed exile made her a de facto outsider to the Italian literary scene, completely removed from intellectual discussions of the moment. However, a deeper look into her letter-writing activity would quickly prove this assumption to be utterly inaccurate since, while it is true that Ortese rarely made public appearances to promote her work, she nonetheless maintained active epistolary exchanges with major Italian literary figures of the time, including Italo Calvino, Natalia Ginzburg, Alfonso Gatto,[2] Raffaele La Capria,[3] Gianna Manzini,[4] Paola Masino, Pasquale Prunas, and critics and philosophers such as Giorgio Agamben, Pietro Citati, and Roland Barthes, to name a few.[5] A complete cataloguing of Ortese's scores of letters (which have been noted to be in the thousands) is almost impossible since, while some individual missives have been published in assorted reviews, many more have not been presented to the public. Indeed, to my knowledge, the only collections of correspondence that have been published to date are Ortese's letters to Pasquale Prunas and those to Dario Bellezza.[6] Her corpus of letters to the writer Paola Masino, which has for several years been announced as forthcoming, is still awaiting release.[7] In short, while this immense documentation is testimony to the central role that letter writing played in Ortese's life, it nonetheless has been little studied by scholars.[8] In the present article, I examine Ortese's letters to another important literary figure of her time: prominent intellectual and writer Massimo Bontempelli – her mentor and the founder of magic realism in Italy. This particular collection is currently held at the Getty Research Institute in Los Angeles, California, within the Massimo Bontempelli papers.[9] In addition to presenting said unique group of letters, my intent is to consider how these particular writings express a distinctive telling of Ortese's life story. The value of such documents is twofold: they afford us a singular glimpse of the constant battles that the young Ortese waged during the course of her early days (viz., her struggle to defend the purity of her creative inspiration throughout this initial stage of her poetic formation, and her desperate desire to establish a literary career in the face of a life mired in poverty and isolation). They also reveal the sway that Bontempelli (and – indirectly – his *realismo magico*) had on the young writer's creative sensibilities, an influence not previously studied by critics.

While my interest in this topic stems from the critical edition of Ortese's letters to Bontempelli, which I have prepared for separate publication, my aim on a more general level is to investigate personal letter writing as a form of life writing, or more precisely as a form of self-storytelling, a term I coin to convey the willful creation of self-image engaged in by a letter writer over the course of a correspondence. In the specific case of Ortese, I address this potential quality of her letters by analysing the narratological value that her missives offer a reader.

For a writer whose prose is defined by fantastic motifs such as hallucinatory dreams, animal and human hybrid characters, magical spells, and communication with the dead, and whose expressed disdain for the mimetic led her to shun direct discussions of her personal life story, the opportunity to read in these letters about her struggles is a rare and important event for scholars studying her work. In addition, Ortese is a writer whose veiled use of autobiographical information has a way of seeping into many of her fictional works, but such information always appears transformed, serving merely as the basis for fantastical elements, rendering the task of separating the true biographical facts from fantasy almost impossible for the reader. Interestingly, it is precisely in these early letters that Ortese inaugurates her propensity to assume new and various personas, a premise which will become central to such works as *Poveri e semplici* (1967) (through the character of Bettina) and in the book to which Ortese, in her last days, gave perhaps the most importance, *Il porto di Toledo* (1975).[10] In this latter novel, self-storytelling mixed with a fantastical representation of self comes to the fore, since by Ortese's own definition, the volume was meant to be her "false memorie" (R1 355; "false memoir"), a fantastical revisiting of her life during the 1930s, when her career was first launched, and not coincidentally, the same years during which the bulk of her letters to Bontempelli were written, years she would describe as "i giorni della fede nel mondo" ("days of faith in the world").[11] While admittedly a *memoir* dedicated to the retelling (and reliving) of her past, what is new for Ortese is that the character representing herself (her professed alter ego, Damasa) was utterly unknown to her before she came alive in the book. Fourteen years after having composed the volume, indeed, in an Endnote to the 1985 edition, Ortese tellingly reveals the following of her project:

> M'impegnai dunque a scrivere un libro di memoria. E come lo pensai, venne fuori questa Damasa, a me sconosciuta. Tutto il resto, di Toledo, lo conoscevo: ma questa Damasa non l'avevo mai veduta. (R1 998)

> (I thus worked hard to write a book of memory. And as I imagined it, out came this Damasa, unknown to me. Everything else, about Toledo, I was familiar with: but this Damasa I had never seen.)

The potentiality of one's inner self, the inability to truly "know" one's own character, and the willingness to accept (and even foster) contradictory desires within oneself are a few of the struggles that we will see come to light in Ortese's letters to Bontempelli, struggles which undoubtedly inform the direction of her future literary work.

Correspondence from Ortese to Bontempelli

Ortese's correspondence to Bontempelli includes twenty-four unpublished letters written from 1936 to 1952, which clearly record the former's respect for and devotion to her mentor as well as the latter's efforts to foster and promote the younger writer's career, including references to the books he recommended that she read.[12] This extraordinary correspondence also includes a very poignant twenty-fifth letter of condolence, which Ortese wrote to Bontempelli's long-time companion, Paola Masino, after Bontempelli's death in 1960.[13] The letters initially possess a formal tone and gradually become more informal as the years pass. However, the confidential and revelatory approach set out in the earliest letters is maintained throughout, as Ortese maintains her confessional voice from the very first to the last letter. Initially written from Via Piliero 29, Naples (Ortese's humble family residence), the letters will later reflect the peripatetic movements of her career, with the final missives originating from Milan. The first eight letters were written between August and November 1936, the next six in 1937, only two are recorded in 1938, four are dated in 1940, and two respectively in the years 1950 and 1952.[14] The bulk is written by hand, with frequent notes added vertically in the margins. Letters 22–24, all dated in the early 1950s, are typewritten, as she explains, "per farsi leggere meglio" ("to make them easier to read"). Even the typewritten correspondence, nonetheless, has handwritten notes added to them, including most often afterthoughts. In one letter (no. 23; 12 December 1952), Bontempelli annotates his response at the bottom, proving indeed that he replied to her in earnest.[15]

Ortese's earliest letters detail the extraordinary efforts that Bontempelli took to launch his protégé's first work, *Angelici dolori* (*Angelic Sorrows*), including his labours in helping her win an important literary prize with the Accademia d'Italia in 1937.[16] Bontempelli was most certainly intrigued by this unknown writer's work since her writing (and what she represented) ascribed to the criteria he had outlined, a decade earlier, in his review *900*.[17] In this short-lived journal, published from 1926 to 1929,

Bontempelli espoused his views on what he hoped would be the new literature of the century, defining in the theoretical sections of each issue thorny terms like *novecentismo* as well as *realismo magico*, for which he was considered the main proponent.[18] In 1943, Bontempelli somewhat unwillingly revisited his definitions of these expressions in an article for *Tempo*, explaining that his hope was that each writer of the twentieth century would strive to "risolvere, o scrutare, o rappresentare ciascuno il proprio mistero" ("resolve, or probe into, or represent each his own mystery") and that *realismo magico* was simply a means through which writers could work to portray the "avventuroso miracolo" (adventurous miracle) of life within art. In other words, *realismo magico* meant that

> ciò che è realtà, natura, deve, per acquistare un valore d'arte, essere dominato dalla immaginazione. L'arte di dominare la natura, appunto s'è chiamata un tempo "magia."
>
> (That which is reality, nature, in order to acquire an artistic value, must be dominated by imagination. The art of dominating nature, in the past, was fittingly called "magic").[19]

Suffice it to say that Bontempelli most probably saw Ortese as representative of his *novecentismo* because he believed her writing – at its core – revealed the elementary or originally pure dilemmas of life. Indeed, in his theoretical discussions of what he felt writers should do to renew Italian literature in the new century, Bontempelli recommended: "che l'artista riporti ogni sua situazione ai suoi aspetti più originarii, semplificati, immutevoli; perciò, in una parola comprensiva, 'elementari'" ("that the artist should restore every situation to its most primary, simplified, unchangeable state; therefore, simply put, 'elementary'").[20] Not surprisingly, in a review he wrote of *Angelici dolori*, republished in *l'Avventura Novecentista* (1938), Bontempelli lauds the "semplificazione spietata degli argomenti e degli atti" ("merciless simplification of the ideas and events") with which Ortese illuminates "le persone e cose più comuni della vita" ("the most common people and things of life").[21] He is also struck by the "miraculous" quality of her writing, as he sees her work overcoming the division between prose and poetry, noting indeed that her essential and simple plotlines maintain a poetic effect. He, additionally, admires how her prose transcends any distinction between ability and inspiration: in other words, her best writing – he writes – is born not from artifice, but from a state of innocence.[22]

In Ortese's letters to Bontempelli, two constant themes are Anna Maria's gratefulness to him for his help and support and yet also her need to recount the numerous doubts and setbacks that she faced in her early career. In a letter dated 13 April 1937, Ortese expresses her gratitude to Bontempelli for having helped her win her first literary prize:

> Tutto questo che ho avuto è opera della Sua bontà, perché se anche un po' di merito io ce l'ho, da sola nessuno me lo avrebbe riconosciuto.
>
> (All of this which I have received is the work of your kindness, because, even if I have some talent, alone, no one would have acknowledged it.)

An example of one of her numerous moments of self-criticism can be seen a few years later (4 July 1940), when she would write:

> Non so creare nulla. E c'è un'altra cosa. Un tempo, io credevo di potere cogli scritti guadagnare la vita: ora sento ch'è impossibile; che solo una rara e forse non vera fortuna potrebbe conciliare interessi così contrastanti.
>
> (I don't know how to create anything. And there is one more thing. In the past, I believed I could make a living with my writing: now I feel it is impossible; that only rare and perhaps unreal luck could reconcile interests which are so contradictory.)

These contrasts in humour will become a unique feature of Ortese's expressivity within the letters. Noteworthy is also her propensity to communicate her ideas and opinions, even when they could be deemed critical of Bontempelli's work. While always placing herself in a position of deference towards her mentor, Ortese nonetheless proves herself to be an attentive – and even discerning – reader of her mentor's work, commenting on many of the books that he authored, such as *Donna nel sole* (1928), *Vita e morte di Adria e dei suoi figli* (1930), *Galleria degli schiavi* (1934), *Gente nel Tempo* (1937), *Giro del sole* (1941), and his *Discorsi* on Leopardi and Pirandello (1938). Ortese's observant readings of Bontempelli's works, as expressed in the Getty letters, would merit an entire article. Here let me note, in brief, that what is most striking is that – despite her young age at the time, and her lack of formal education – she was able to dialogue openly with an eminent scholar such as Bontempelli, and she was undaunted in discussing her impressions of his work. One particular example of this forthcoming attitude, and of her interest in literary critique, occurs in a lengthy discussion she gives of *Gente nel tempo.* In a letter dated 3 April 1937, she begins quite frankly with the following sincere analysis:

> Ho letto *Gente nel Tempo.* Dapprima mi ha sconcertata, perché è un'arte che penetra e scompiglia le cose più ragguardevoli, che smonta le figure più serie, scopre quasi un "meccanismo" della vita, quella "costruzione" ch'è la vita umana acutamente guardata. Ma poi, man mano procedevo nella lettura, tutto mi piaceva e divertiva (se questa parola non è volgare) sempre più: giacché tutto è vita nuova, senza orpelli, immediatamente resa, anche se nella fantasia abbia già trovato quel "riposo" necessario alla chiarezza dell'arte.

> [I read *Gente nel Tempo.* At first it disconcerted me, because it is an art which penetrates and unravels the most substantial things and which takes apart the more complex characters, almost discovering a secret "mechanism" of life, in other words a "construction" of what human life is, when examined keenly. But then, little by little as I continued in my reading, everything began more and more to please and entertain me (if this word is not too unrefined): after all, everything in it reflects new life, with no frills, instantly rendered, even if in the imagination this new life had already found the "rest" that is necessary for clarity in art.]

Ortese's observations thereafter in regard to the novel centre on character development, especially in the case of Nora, her expressed favourite. While revealing her enjoyment of many of the novel's scenes precisely because they struck her as "quadri magici" ("magical pictures"), she also admits that she found the ending "desolata, troppo" ("too bleak"). But, above all else, what haunts and compels her is the mysterious sacrificial nature of Nora, which displays a purity that strikes Ortese as the real poetry of the work. She praises Bontempelli for his restrained treatment of this character by stating:

> Lei fa molto bene a non investigare il suo animo, a non tentare di spiegarla, a lasciarla *sola* correre e morire: perché essa è anzi tutto uno spettacolo di purezza e di gioia e questo occorre al libro per ridargli valore umano; questo arcano *più vero* occorre alla Poesia per scendere nelle pagine di uno scrittore.

> (You are right not to investigate her spirit, not to attempt to explain her, but to leave her *alone* to run and to die: because she is, above all, a beautiful

show of purity and joy and this is essential in restoring a sense of humanity to the book; this *truer* mystery must be present for Poetry to descend into a writer's pages.)

It is noteworthy that even in her early assessments of her mentor's works, what first strikes Ortese are those characters who are victimized by a destiny utterly beyond their control. This is the type of character – not surprisingly – who will become the beacon of her own works, as for example Estrellita in *L'Iguana*, Hieronymus Käppchen in *Il cardillo addolorato*, and Alonso in *Alonso e i visionari*. From these honest remarks regarding Nora, it is clear that Ortese's sensibility towards the victim character is awake and aware early on. It seems a telling coincidence, then, that *Gente* is considered by critics as emblematic of Bontempelli's *novecentismo* and that it was one of the texts to which Ortese allocates the most analysis in her letters.[23]

In addition to the central tie to Bontempelli, on a secondary level, the letters reveal the complex web of people with whom Ortese indirectly interacted. Indeed, through her mention of various literary critics, editors, and fellow writers, like Valentino Bompiani, Arnaldo Frateili,[24] and Franco Ciliberti,[25] the letters weave a picture of the growing framework of influences on her early literary experiences, adding a new understanding of her beginnings as a writer.[26]

Towards a Theorizing of Epistolary Self-Storytelling

A letter, it can be said, is a form of personal writing that rests in the liminal space between the private and public spheres. While it is true that a letter is an expression of only the voice of the person who writes it, it is nonetheless addressed and sent to someone other than its author, therefore making it, as Mikhail Bakhtin notes, "half someone else's."[27] A letter, thus, belongs both to its author and also to its receiver, creating a shared context of the story it recounts. Mary Favret, in her 1993 study entitled *Romantic Correspondence: Women, Politics and the Fiction of Letters*, reminds us, rightly so, how the epistolary form urges us "to read the envelope of contingency that surrounds" it.[28]

But what are some of the factors that play a part in an epistolary storytelling? First, we must recognize the individual nature of each letter, since in order to create a continued narrative, we must consider each separate letter as it is woven within the larger correspondence. In the case of Ortese, we must also regard the peculiar literary entity that is born when a correspondence takes into account only letters sent by one party, ignoring – if you will – the response that these letters might have elicited from their intended receiver (this is, of course, because the responses have gone missing). On this last note, we must assume that Bontempelli's replies to her letters no longer exist if we are to believe Ortese's assertion that she destroyed all correspondence that she received, an act which she herself described as a "discutibile quanto radicata abitudine" ("questionable as much as ingrained habit").[29] Such a one-sided representation – of only Ortese's point of view – undoubtedly limits our knowledge about the written conversation that took place between the two. Nevertheless, the clear unity of voice certainly creates a more cohesive work, in which each missive calls out into the dark to the friendly – albeit, physically absent – ear of an ally, who is initially Bontempelli, but who later becomes the reader when the letters are gathered into a collection.[30] Janet Altman, in her work *Epistolarity: Approaches to a Form,* distinguishes between the internal reader, described as "a specific character represented within the world of the narrative whose reading of the letters can influence the writing of the letters" and also the external reader, explained as "we, the general public who read the work as a finished product and have no effect on the writing of individual letters."[31] Ortese is of course most interested in creating a rapport with Bontempelli – our internal reader – but an external reader would be hard-pressed not to feel that the letters somehow are addressed also to him or her. And it is precisely this effect of blurring between the internal and external reader which Meredith Ray, in her recent book *Writing Gender in Women's Letter Collections of the Italian Renaissance,* rightly asserts "serves to draw the reader into a relationship of complicity through identification with the epistolary 'I.'"[32]

Yet, even if the external reader feels drawn into Ortese's story, he cannot help but wonder if the author was truly aware that, by writing her thoughts and feelings and sending them in a letter, she was effectively creating a narrative of her own life, presented to the world. I would argue that in Ortese's case, she was highly conscious of her own self-representation given the many instances of metadiscourse and commentary that she adds in the margins of her letters, and in which she indicates how she hopes Bontempelli will interpret what she has written. One interesting example of this can be found in letter 22, dated 2 September 1950 in which, when describing her desire for Bontempelli to help secure her a job at the Einaudi bookstore in Rome, she writes in a note on the left margin that her exaggerated tone was meant to "fare indignare un po' Paola, per scherzare, s'intende" ("to make Paola become a little indignant, as a joke, of course").[33] This self-commentary, this gesture of granting her reader instructions on how she hopes he would or would not interpret her thoughts, reveals her keen awareness of the risks of being misinterpreted, while also exposing her perhaps tenuous confidence in the rhetorical control she held over her writing. Such a form of intervention carries over into her fictional writing, as seen in the many authorial intrusions, or *appelli al lettore*, scattered throughout her novels. Indeed, the narrator's use of metadiscourse becomes a defining characteristic of Ortese's novelistic writing.

Furthermore, to create a frank relationship (at times rife with urgency) with her mentor, Ortese consistently engages his attention through the use of questions, whether rhetorical or direct, to maintain contact, as seen in examples like: "Lei sa che sono molto libera, non è vero?" ("You know that I am very free, don't you?"), "Collaboro a Roma, lo sa?" ("I am collaborating with Roma, did you know?"),[34] and also "Sa che cosa penso, Bontempelli?" ("Do you know what I think, Bontempelli?").[35] As an extension of this concern with establishing a connection with her reader, Ortese also at times even creates an imaginary, yet plausible dialogue with her addressee, replete with words that Bontempelli himself might very well have thought while reading her missive. For example, in the same letter of 4 July 1940, she asks him "Lei s'interessa sempre a me?" ("Do you still care about me?") to which she assumes he responds "yes," prompting her to continue with the following candid admission: "e allora voglio dirLe che un certo periodo iniziatosi da moltissimo tempo di svogliatezza e scontento, a me sembra adesso entrato nella sua fase maggiore" ("well then I want to tell you that a spell of inertia and dissatisfaction, which began quite some time ago, has now, it seems to me, entered into a more acute stage").[36] This moment is quite revealing of Ortese's rhetoric since it shows how, before confessing a private shortcoming, she makes a clear appeal to Bontempelli's emotions, in a bid to reassure herself of the established pathos with which she hopes he will receive her story.[37]

One other theoretical aspect central to the reading of Ortese's letters regards the reader's tendency to create an overarching story from one letter to the next, even when the author might not have initially intended there to be one. In other words, the composer of the thoughts has no vision of what her longer story will be, nor a sense of what the compilation of her letters over the years will look like in collected form. Only the recipient or, in a more distant moment, the person editing her correspondence – the external reader – can have that complete vision. Thus, a potential "literary" or "storytelling" value in texts, such as letters, hinges not on the writer's, but precisely on the reader's ability or interest in ascertaining whether he or she views a narrative within the text. In this sense, the writer is effectively ceding a part of her authorial agency to the reader since only the reader has the supreme vision to tie the various individual letters together and thus to create a cohesive work.[38]

A final factor to consider is the role of sincerity within personal letters, and to this end, one might ask: How much truth or authenticity can be attributed to the feelings and emotions expressed in these types of personal writings? Philippe Lejeune, in his discussion of autobiography, recognizes this very dilemma as it pertains to life writing when he proposes the requirement of a pact between writer and reader as a necessity in creating true autobiography. In Lejeune's view, only when there is complete synonymity among the protagonist, the writer, and the person whose name appears on the title page can an autobiographical pact be secured and can the reader believe that he or she is truly reading someone's life story, as told by that person.[39] In a similar way, one could argue, letter writing is an act that also presupposes an analogous pact between addresser and addressee. But this is perhaps where similarities between the two genres end since, while an autobiography is generally intended to be read by an audience of more than one – and therefore is a public presentation of the self – a written correspondence between two people is usually meant to be read in the private sphere only. In addition, a personal correspondence is composed of self-reflections that the author, motivated by the desire to communicate with his addressee, fixes over a certain span of time through writing.[40] Because the epistolary pact is based on the private relationship between two people (sender and receiver), authenticity and sincerity on a personal level assume a much more central role than occurs in the traditional autobiography. In other words, the intimate human rapport between two people, and the potential confessional characteristic of an epistolary exchange with a known recipient – with whom the letter writer most usually has (or would like to have) a relationship – makes the role of sincerity and honesty paramount, a characteristic of writing which Montaigne, who was much revered by Ortese,[41] espoused in his *Essays*.[42] Sincerity, in modern terms, of course, does not mean veracity, but has come to be defined (by critics like Lionel Trilling) as "staying true to oneself."[43] Such a stance, which does not pretend to encompass a representation of the truth, would permit the expression of contradictory desires and natures within the same person, as long as said person believed sincerely that his or her personality possessed this potentiality. As we comb through the letters, we begin to see Ortese much like the "I" of Walt Whitman's "Song of Myself," who represents a being that resists conventional limits of personhood:

> Do I contradict myself?
> Very well then I contradict myself,
> (I am large, I contain multitudes.)[44]

The notion of inconsistency when portraying one's own personality plays a central role in Ortese's characterization of herself since, as we will see, she does not shy away from expressing conflicting desires, but rather fully accepts and fosters her contradictory nature (through dissimulation of her identity, revelations of self-deprecating personal information, and yet all amidst determined requests for help in promoting her work). What becomes evident during our reading of these documents is that, already in these early letters, Ortese the person and Ortese the character of her letters both resist a fixed identity, much like her beloved Montaigne who, in his chapter in his *Essays* on "Of Repentance," acknowledges that a central fact of the human condition is the instability of character. Ortese most certainly admired the French thinker's admission of his own attempts to write about his ever-changing self, explained as such:

> My history needs to be adapted to the moment. I may presently change, not only by chance, but also by intention. This is a record of various and changeable occurrences, and of irresolute and, when it so befalls, contradictory ideas: whether I am different myself, or whether I take hold of my subjects in different circumstances and aspects. So, all in all, I may indeed contradict myself now and then: but truth, as Demades said, I do not contradict.[45]

As we will see, Ortese will take even further the notion of her own shifting character (replete with multiple identities) that she expresses in her letters by mirroring this trait in many of the strangely fantastical protagonists of her future novels.

Ortese la Candida: Sincerity and Fictionality in Letter Writing

Ortese begins a correspondence with Bontempelli because, in 1936, he becomes director of the journal *L'Italia letteraria*, where two of her short stories and three poems had previously been published[46] while the review was under the direction of Corrado Pavolini.[47] Ortese describes her life up until that point as rather dismal:

> Ma io non ho mai studiato, né letto molto, né vissuto fra persone che sapessero parlar bene. E intanto, avendo ora 22 anni, e trovandomi a scrivere da sei, e in condizioni pressoché malinconiche, comincio a provare un certo desiderio di conseguire qualche scopo, farmi avanti anche io.[48]
>
> (But I have never studied, nor read much, nor lived among people who know how to speak correctly. And so, now that I am 22 years old, and I find myself writing for the past six years, and in almost melancholic conditions, I am beginning to feel a certain desire to achieve some purpose, to come forward.)

She also laments her frail physical health: "non sto mica bene in salute come una volta" ("I am not at all healthy like I once was," Letter 10, 13 April 1937), while also revealing frustrations with the progress of her writing: "sono stanca, come in questo momento, o perplessa o addirittura scoraggiata da tante cose volgari" ("I am tired, as in this moment, or confused or even discouraged by many vulgar things," Letter 13, 6 June 1937). In short, she is not afraid to divulge her shortcomings, although she is fully aware that her sincerity might be counterproductive ("Certe domande dovrei tenerle per me. Pure è naturale che le rivolga anche agli altri," Letter 13, 6 June 1937; "I should keep certain questions to myself and yet it is natural to address them to other people"). These revelations of weakness and self-doubt, however, mix with an undying desire to prevail: "Mi aiuti, e Le assicuro che non se ne pentirà, e sarà invece molto molto soddisfatto del mio lavoro e di me" (Letter 2, 12 August 1936; "Help me, and I assure you that you will not regret it, and that you will instead be very, very satisfied with my work and with me"); "E ancora più spero potermi fare avanti e, con un nome che veramente vale" (Letter 3, 19 August, 1936; "And now even more I hope to move ahead and, with a name that truly has value"); "Io voglio diventare bravissima (anche se a volte temo di morire 'spiritualmente,' lasciare tutto)" [Letter 12, 27 April 1937; "I want to become very good (even if at times I fear of dying 'spiritually' and leaving everything)"].

One telling case in point of this exculpatory nature regards her use of a pseudonym in her initial letter to Bontempelli, as well as in her first short stories. While the use of a false name by Ortese is well known among scholars,[49] her treatment of the issue in her correspondence to Bontempelli reveals new details about her mental state and her rapport with her mentor, as well as about her uncertainty in finding her precise role as a writer. The *nom de plume* is certainly a noted characteristic of women's writing in general, especially in the nineteenth century with writers such as Neera, Marchesa Colombi, Contessa Lara, Bruno Sperani, but also into the twentieth century with Sibilla Aleramo and Anna Banti, to name a few. While the reasons for the use of a pseudonym are manifold, they generally originate from the desire to protect one's true identity in a society that may not condone intellectual activity among women. A pseudonym permitted a splitting of one's personality, effectively protecting the socially acceptable side of one's self from the writing voice. The other force driving some writers to adopt a false name is the desire to recreate oneself through writing, to be reborn. This last case most certainly describes Aleramo's situation. Through her unusual experimentation with the pseudonym, however, Ortese sets herself outside the margins and appears to forge her own path.

In her first letter dated 3 August 1936, Ortese writes to Bontempelli using the signature Franca Nicosi and requests that her short story "Avventura" be published under that name. Then, in a second letter written nine days later, she recants her request to be published under the pseudonym, revealing her true identity with the following:

> Non so resistere al sentimento di angoscia che l'attesa e il dubbio mi danno. Ho paura, malgrado mi sforzi a sperare, che la prosa firmata "Franca Nicosi," e che deve essere giunta in Direzione (senza di che non varrebbe la pena che Lei seguitasse a leggere), Le sia parsa puerile, disprezzabile, e sia stata gettata. In questo spavento che mi fa veramente male, sento il bisogno di essere sincera, quasi che la poca lealtà abbia costituito finora l'oscuro e veramente unico ostacolo alla riuscita. Dunque, non sono Franca Nicosi, ma soltanto A. M. Ortese, di cui Lei ha pubblicato tempo fa una prosa.

> (I don't know how to stand up to the feeling of anguish that the wait and doubting has instilled in me. I am fearful, regardless of my attempts at hoping, that the prose work signed "Franca Nicosi," and which must have arrived in the main office (if this is not the case, it is not necessary for you to continue reading this letter), appeared to you puerile, worthless, and was thrown out. In this fear that is really tormenting me, I feel the need to be

> sincere, as if my limited honesty until this point has been the obscure and truly sole obstacle to my success. Well then, I am not *Franca Nicosi*, but only A.M. Ortese, of whom you have published a prose work some time ago.)[50]

In the same letter, she justifies her use of the false identification by stating that she feared being derided by her family and because, as she confesses, "Uno, quando scrive, lo fa al *solo* e perfetto scopo della *sua* momentanea gioia, mica per essere compatito" ("When one writes, he does so *only* for the perfect purpose of *his own* immediate delight, not to be pitied by others").[51] In this assertion, Ortese intimates that protecting her identity is akin to defending the sanctity of her writing, conceived as a private endeavour during these early years of her career.

Although in the third letter, dated 19 August, Ortese assures Bontempelli that she approves of his intent to publish "Avventura" under her real name, in her next correspondence – written the following day – she desperately disavows her previous statements by retracting approval to use her true identity, all the while apologizing profusely and admitting that her morbid attachment to the pseudonym is rooted in her unstable mental status. In this regard, she writes: "io me ne potrei *infischiare* se fossi sana di nervi e di cervello, ma io *là* sono malata" ("I would be able to care less about this if my nerves and brain were healthy, but it is *there* that I am sick").[52] Luca Clerici, in his comprehensive biography of Ortese, notes that the use of the pseudonym was most probably due to the fact that the four short stories that bear the false name in *L'Italia letteraria* ("Angelici dolori," "Il sogno," "L'avventura," "La penna dell'angelo") are all writings that reflect a more intimate side of Ortese's sentimental life and, in particular, centre around the male character Enrico, whom Clerici believes had a direct tie to Ortese's own life. As he states: "Enrico non è solo un personaggio di carta. Enrico è un ragazzo che esiste per davvero" ("Enrico is not only a character on the page. Enrico is a young man who exists in real life").[53] Through the testimony of Alda Croce, a friend of Ortese's in the 1930s, Clerici shows that the youthful love of Ortese was, in reality, Aldo Romano, a person whose name surfaces in two of her writings.[54] This very real characterization of "Enrico" in her short stories, states Clerici, would have openly revealed Ortese's secret infatuation to her family, a fact that Ortese must have wanted to conceal.

In the end, Bontempelli consents to publishing the short stories "Angelici dolori," "L'avventura," "Il sogno," and "La penna dell'angelo" in *L'Italia letteraria* under the false name, Franca Nicosi, and thus, I would argue, becomes complicit in her lie. And yet it is precisely this immediate falsehood and subsequent confession from letter writer (Ortese) to recipient (Bontempelli) that lead the reader to believe even more in Ortese's sincerity. By requesting Bontempelli to conceal her secret and to make her false persona a reality – or at least a truth for the reading public of *L'Italia letteraria* – Ortese effectively has her mentor enable her fantastical self-creation. Interestingly, this joint effort of dissimulation works not to show Ortese's false intentions, but – quite the opposite – to bolster the faith that readers of her correspondence have in her honesty as letter writer.

Perhaps contributing to the reader's willingness to trust Ortese is the faith that she demonstrates in Bontempelli, seen ultimately when she places the final decision regarding the pseudonym in her mentor's hands: "Ma Lei, occorrendo, risolva come più Le sembra…" ("But you should feel free to resolve the issue as you see fit…") she tells him in Letter 7, dated 10 November 1936.[55] In other words, just as Ortese trusts in Bontempelli (a person she had not yet met in person),[56] so the reader can believe in the sincerity of the thoughts expressed in her letters. While initially this gesture of assuming a false name would appear to be a desire to protect her own identity by creating a sort of alter ego, the attempt to carry through with the new invention of self could not be upheld, unlike other women writers – such as Aleramo and Banti – who successfully (and for entire careers) adopted pseudonyms. Perhaps it was her understanding of the ever-changing, complex nature of herself (a self that could include multitudes, in the Whitmanian sense) that made Ortese realize that veiling her true name would contradict the premise of her writing. In other words, she did not need to look outside herself for alter egos since she encompassed them already within herself.

This combined gesture of confession and, yet, confidence in Bontempelli's understanding, seen through the episode of the false name, is a theme which recurs a few years later in a letter written on 19 September 1940 when Ortese reveals another dissimulation committed against her mentor:[57]

> Ma Lei anzitutto mi dovrà perdonare una cosa: dal 1937, anno in cui Lei regalò a mia sorella i tre *Discorsi*, io avevo appena qualche volta aperto quel libro. Questa cosa è enorme e assurda come parecchie cose della

mia anima (che così spesso sembra non esistere), ma se glielo dico è per un'altrettanto vasta fiducia che Lei sappia perdonare questo torto fatto a un amico così puro.

(But, above all, you must forgive me for something: since 1937, the year in which you gave my sister the three *Discorsi,* I have hardly, if at all, opened that book. This action is tremendous and absurd like many things in my spirit (which so often seems not even to exist), but if I tell this you now it is because of the equal amount of deep faith I have that you will find it in your heart to forgive me this wrong done upon such a pure friend.)

The act of letter writing seems to take on, for Ortese, the gesture of an *excusatio,*[58] through the disclosure of her literary "sins" to her mentor and confessor: she did not read Bontempelli's *Discorsi,* a collection of celebratory speeches on important figures of the Italian literary scene, when she said that she would.[59] While *I discorsi* were not published until 1938, two years after Ortese's initial letters to him, Bontempelli nonetheless appears to have seen in Ortese an ever-so-rare example of an "anima candida" ("candid spirit"). And so it is quite an interesting fact that Ortese makes reference to the very text in which Bontempelli, during his discussion of Pirandello, espouses his definition of an "anima candida" and his views on "candore":[60] The speech, "Pirandello o del candor," was read on 17 January 1937 in commemoration of Pirandello's death, a very close friend of Bontempelli's. While describing Pirandello, Bontempelli also seems to be echoing Ortese's behaviour when he states:

L'anima candida affacciandosi al mondo lo vede subito a suo modo: la impressione e il giudizio degli altri, anche di tutti gli altri, di tutto il mondo, che si affretta ad andarle incontro e cerca insegnarle tante cose, tanti giudizi fatti, questo non la scuote, ella può tutt'al più maravigliarsene. [...] E l'effetto immediato del candore è la sincerità. L'anima candida non fa concessioni.

(The candid spirit, looking out onto the world, immediately perceives it in her own way: the impression and judgment of other people, of everyone else, including the entire world, who hasten to target her and try to teach her many things, many opinions; all of this does not shake her. At most she might be amazed. [...] And the immediate effect of candour is sincerity. The candid spirit does not make concessions.)[61]

The "anima candida," which he further describes as an "elemental force" (recalling his observations of Ortese's *Angelici dolori*), is sincerity at its core since it goes to the roots of the issues and can immediately, "con instinto maraviglioso," understand the difference between what is elemental from what is simply decoration. This instinct requires a propensity for risk and therefore, Bontempelli states, prudence cannot be a part of the candid spirit. Hypocrisy, even the type of hypocrisy that might lead to morally good results, is foreign to the candid spirit, for whom,

> il bene e la verità sono la stessa cosa; appunto perché il candore ha dimora in quella zona elementare e radicale della vita nella quale non sono ancora avvenute le distinzioni.
>
> (Good and truth are the same thing; precisely because candour dwells in that elementary and radical zone of life in which distinctions have not yet come about.)[62]

Ortese – even before reading these words – was certainly aware of Bontempelli's affinity for "candid spirits," a concept he put into play most notably through the eponymous character in *Minnie la Candida* (1929). In this last case, the purity and honesty of Minnie ultimately leads to her demise as she becomes overwhelmed by the possibility that what is reality is perhaps just human invention. Once again, Ortese's confessions to her mentor make her an ever more believable character within the story she aims to paint of herself, resulting in her reader being able to accept as feasible even her most outlandish requests, as for example when she expresses her desire to embark on a career as an actress, a vocation most unsuited to her reticent personality. And yet, in her explanations to Bontempelli, she clarifies that the appeal of acting lies in how it could "realize" as she says in Letter 17, 4 July 1940: "a desire within my spirit to exist in various forms, intensely and to 'strut' around, in an unaffected manner" (see original below). What is key here is that Ortese closes this unexpected revelation with a request to Bontempelli for information, once again in hopes that he will empathize with her situation. The entire passage reads:

> Giorni fa (veramente ce l'avevo da molto e molto, ma dormiva) m'è venuta un'idea: recitare, imparare a recitare e lavorare per il teatro.

Ho l'impressione (può darsi che sia una semplice impressione) che saprei rivestire con acuta passione, con compiacimento, panni non miei ed essere oggi una e domani un'altra. Infine, questo realizzerebbe un desiderio del mio spirito, ch'è di esistere variamente, intensamente e di "pavoneggiarsi," inteso con semplicità.

Ora, mi dica: è molto difficile imparare? ci sono delle scuole? come si può entrare in teatro?

[A few days ago an idea struck me (in truth, it has been in my mind for a long while, but dormant): act, learn to act and work for the theatre.

I have the impression (and it could just simply be an impression) that I would know, with acute passion, with satisfaction, how to wear clothing that is not mine and to be someone today and tomorrow someone else. In short, this would fulfil a desire within my spirit to exist in various forms, intensely, and to "strut" around, intended in an unaffected manner.

Now, please tell me: is it difficult to learn? Are there any schools? How does someone go into theatre acting?][63]

And – on a second look – this behaviour might not be so out-of-character if we consider that in many of her written works she aimed to do just that – create fantastically various personas of herself. In a letter written a few months later, on 15 October 1940, she makes reference to this discussion by stating boldly, "Se dovessi recitare mi piacerebbe fare parti da uomo, per esempio un giovanetto di sentire straordinario, sempre commosso ..." ("If I acted, I would like to play the part of a man, for example a young man with extraordinary emotional abilities, always moved ...").[64] Taking on new identities and, in this case, a new gender, as expressed in her desire to pursue acting, is clearly for Ortese not a way to falsify her self-image, but rather a means to allow diverse sides of herself to come to life. It is in this very way we should contextualize her choice of becoming a giovanetto (in her letters and later even in her fantastical autobiography of those years in *Toledo*): not so much as a desire to become a man, but rather as a yearning to set free a part of herself existing beyond or before gender. In much the same way, she describes the character of Damasa in *Il porto di Toledo* as representing the potential force in the development of many other characters:

Nella mia natura stava in agguato, sempre, una forza che mi soffocava, stavano degli smarrimenti, delle assenze, sorgevano degli ottundimenti che mi annullavano. Da un momento all'altro ero la miseria e l'idiozia medesima. E poi altre miserie, come luci negli occhi, mali di capo. Aggiungi una mutevolezza eterna. Io, insomma, ero a tanti strati, ora ragazzo serio e attivo, ora fanciullina piangente, ora animale strambo, ora adulto freddo ed esperto; e ora di questi strati prevaleva l'uno, ora l'altro. (R1 478)

(Lying in ambush within my personality has always been a suffocating energy; mental confusion and emptiness, numbing feelings have always cropped up and overcome me. From one moment to the next I would embody misery and idiocy. And then more miseries, like lights blinding the eyes, headaches. Then add to this an eternal fickleness. In short, I was existing on many layers, at first a serious and active young man, then a crying little girl, afterwards a strange animal, subsequently a cold and experienced adult; and sometimes one layer prevailed, sometimes another.)[65]

Her imperative to embrace the contradictory sides of her nature, but to do so with sincerity, brings us back to the episode regarding the pseudonym and, precisely, to the moment in her second letter, dated 12 August 1936, right before she reveals her true identity to Bontempelli, when she writes: "sento il bisogno di essere sincera, quasi che la poca lealtà abbia costituito finora l'oscuro e veramente unico ostacolo alla riuscita" ("I feel the need to be sincere, as if my limited honesty until this point has been the obscure and truly sole obstacle to my success"). Here, in this noteworthy revelation, Ortese recognizes sincerity as a requisite for successful writing; sincerity on a personal and emotional level and not in the sense of an absolute truth, much like Bontempelli championed in the "candid spirit," for whom "expression and feeling" – he felt – were born from the same place: "e in questo senso si può dire che il candore coincide con lo spirito poetico" ("and in this sense it is possible to assert that candour coincides with the poetic spirit").[66] In other words, her subsequent request of Bontempelli to reinstate her false name proves that, at the moment of revealing her true identity, she was not driven by concern for tricking her reading public with a false identity, but rather by the fear of being dishonest on a personal level towards her addressee Bontempelli. Effective writing, in Ortese's own personal rhetoric, is contingent on the very Aristotelian concept of ethos, or credibility of the author. In other words, insincerity through use of a pseudonym while addressing Bontempelli weakened the persuasive force of her writing and thus needed to be rectified through a confession. And it is precisely by way of this confession that she ironically shows herself to be truly sincere.

Tied directly to the tendency to confess her literary uncertainties and contradictions is the underlying loneliness expressed even when she conveys gratefulness to her mentor. Out of feelings of isolation, letter writing becomes her form of self-expression, an extension of her attempt to dialogue, and a creation of a fantastic or imaginary conversation to which one person (in this case Bontempelli) is invited to listen: "Le scrivo – e come parlerei a me stessa, senza pensare che Lei debba per questo rispondermi" ("I am writing to you, and as if I were speaking to myself, without expecting that you have to respond to me") she discloses in Letter 19, dated 3 October 1940.[67] Indeed, this could explain the roots of her extreme gesture of destroying all letters that she received, as it would be an act that breaks the initial dialogue between her and Bontempelli, creating in its place (for those who may read her letters published as a collection in the future) a dialogue she establishes only with herself.

Echoing in many ways the *dissidio interno* of a writer like Petrarca, Ortese's profound psychological division is marked by continuously mixing assertions of clear self-loathing with forceful aspirations for excellence. She admits her failings on 19 August 1936 with: "Io ho tanti difetti ancora (e sospetto cresceranno) e debbo farmi perdonare moltissime cose, da chiunque..." ["I still have so many faults (and I suspect they will grow in number) and I should seek forgiveness for many things, from everybody ..."].[68] And later, on 4 July 1940, she goes as far to say that speaking of herself is "il più triste argomento ch'io conosca" ("the saddest topic I know").[69] Three months after, on 15 October 1940, she even arrives to the point of revealing serious doubts about her work: "Quel che mi manca, quando mi metto a scrivere una novella, ora come in un prossimo ieri, è la fede nelle cose che racconto" ("What I'm missing, when I sit down to write a story, now just as in the past, is the faith in the stories I tell").[70] And yet, these moments of despair do not, in the end, dim her hopes of moving ahead "con un nome che veramente vale" ("with a name that truly has value"), as she writes on 19 August 1936,[71] nor to stop her from asking the key question, as she elucidates when beseeching Bontempelli in her second letter, dated 12 August 1936: "Ma veniamo all'importante: me la vuole pubblicare, questa prosa? Poi gliene manderò altre, e saranno sempre migliori, creda. Tutto sta ad incoraggiarmi, a credermi" ("But let's get to what's important: do you want to publish this piece? After, I will send you others, and they will continue to improve, believe me").[72]

Yet her inner *dissidio* cannot help but seep out even when she expresses hope for the future, a hope overshadowed by a melancholic acceptance of sadness. "Il futuro è tutto nella notte" ("The future is all in the night"), she writes in Letter 19 (September 1940), recalling an earlier discussion in Letter 16 (20 September 1938), when she confided:

> Non credo che Roma Milano o altre città potrebbero darmi una più grande pace, serbarmi sensazioni migliori. Credo che tutto il meglio sia nel peggio. Sa, il meglio delle cose umane è la speranza, e questa non si trova ai banchetti, ma forse sulle pietre della strada, dove cadono i suoni e la luce. In questo buio, vedo tante belle cose.
>
> (I do not believe that Rome, Milan or any other city could give me a greater sense of peace, or preserve in me better sensations. I believe that all that is good rests in what is the worst. You know, the best of human things is hope, and this is not found at banquets, but rather on the stones of the street, where sounds and light fall. In this darkness, I can see many beautiful things.)[73]

The centrality of night-time in Ortese's letters and in her works in general[74] is without doubt an element that ties her closely to Leopardi, a writer whom she much revered as "l'unica voce reale della letteratura italiana dopo Dante" (CC 98–99; "the only real voice in Italian literature after Dante").[75] Describing, indeed, Bontempelli's *Discorso* on Leopardi as "uno spirituale, leggerissimo, meraviglioso conforto" (Letter 18, September 1940; "a spiritual, ever gentle, marvellous comfort"), Ortese most certainly was aware of how night-time was the preferred moment of discussion for the majority of the *Operette morali*.[76]

And yet her doubts never halt her undying drive to communicate through writing. Writing for her is an ontological gesture not dependent on her motivation or desire for recognition, but rather stemming from her need to live through words. At one point, on 4 July 1940, revealing her tendency to exist through her writing, she even describes a piece, which seems to be the emblem of her entire opus, by saying: "Io non ho attualmente che un solo scritto su cui mi faccia qualche illusione: una favola, un mito, che so io, una storia che è me e non è più me" ("at this moment I only have one piece that I am holding out hope for: a fable, a myth – I don't know – a story which is me and is not me").[77]

The identification of self with one's writing leads us back to her "false memorie" ("false memoirs"), *Il porto di Toledo*. An intriguing discussion could certainly be made about how, in her visionary "autobiographical" novel, she creates not only a fantastical self – a wholly literary version of her youth – but also perhaps a somewhat transformed Bontempelli, replete with multiple and changing names and identities.[78] But more to the point of this article is precisely the weight that the act of letter writing has in the storytelling process. To be sure, most of the major events recounted by the main character Damasa (a stand-in for Ortese herself as a young woman, as I said) are perceived and, thereafter, experienced by her precisely through the reading of a letter. And therefore it is not by chance that while reading a letter our protagonist becomes enlightened to the possibility of a double reality, of a fantastical space in which life is re-lived and can even be transformed. In this regard, Damasa explains that after combing through an important missive, she realized that the letter "era *doppia*: era due volte una lettera, e *due volte era una lettera bianca*" (R1 520; "it was *double*: it was a letter two times, and *twice it was a blank letter*"), making reference perhaps to the fact that the fantastical letters of Ortese's false autobiography are (but not exactly) the same letters sent to her in real life, letters which, as I discussed before, she herself had professed to have physically destroyed in the original, only to have made come to life again, under a form of her own making, in her fictional, fantastical world. After this realization of the double letter, an understanding of the possibility of the "unreal" or of a double reality strikes her "come di notte si sente il grido del vento" ("much like at night when you hear the wind screaming"). Yet, it is a double-edged revelation, since, she explains, she felt both "rischiarata e oscurata a un tempo" ("illuminated and clouded over at the same time").[79] This double reality of the unreal is precisely where Ortese perceives that literature can flourish, beyond the constraints of time and space, but not, of course, without maintaining a direct connection to her reader whose participation in the text (as we have seen in her experience as letter writer to Bontempelli) is predicated on how authentic he or she deems Ortese's writing. This recognition of the reader's importance is, perhaps, why, in *Il porto di Toledo*, after recreating Damasa's final letter to her mentor, the narrator precedes the presentation of the last *rendiconto* (or short story) with another *excusatio*, this one directed, not to an internal reader, but rather to an "eternal" external reader. "Here is an old story which I present to you," the narrating voice says, "chiedendo, più forte che in altri momenti, scusa all'eventuale Eterno di un Lettore" (R1 913; "begging pardon, more profoundly than I have in the past, to the potential Eternity of a Reader").

Four Letters of Anna Maria Ortese to Massimo Bontempelli and a Condolence Letter to Paola Masino*

1.

3.8.36. XIV

Signor Direttore,
mi scusi se busso alla porta dell'*Italia.* Vuole leggere questa novella e, se le piace, pubblicarla? Io credo che vi si riscontri scarsissima conoscenza della lingua (improprietà, errori, punteggiatura pazzesca) e forse, chissà, anche povertà di fantasia. Ma io non ho mai studiato, né letto molto, né vissuto fra persone che sapessero parlar bene. E in tanto, avendo ora 22 anni, e trovandomi a scrivere da sei, e in condizioni pressoché malinconiche, comincio a provare un certo desiderio di conseguire qualche scopo, farmi avanti anche io. È possibile? glielo domando umilmente, perché so Lei come potrebbe, s'io non valgo, ridere.

Io non mi diressi mai ad altri giornali, appunto temendo che, oltre alla ... bocciatura aggiungessero la beffa. Ma questa vecchia *Italia* non credo ne sia capace, anche perché c'è Lei, ch'è un Accademico, e non si mette certo a ridere per questi sbagli "da scolaro."

Grazie dunque della lettura. Comprerò il *Giornale* tutte le settimane, per vedere se Lei ha o no accettato.

Con ossequi

---

* The five letters that I am publishing below are held, together with the entire correspondence of Anna Maria Ortese to Massimo Bontempelli (and one letter to Paola Masino, Bontempelli's heir), at the Research Library, the Getty Research Institute, Los Angeles (910147). The complete edition of the letters to Bontempelli is published in my dissertation, *Il futuro è tutto nella notte* (see Works Cited). The collection contains twenty-four letters sent from Anna Maria Ortese to Massimo Bontempelli (between 1936 and 1952). In addition, there is a letter of condolence (Letter 25; dated 16 August 1960) sent by Ortese to Paola Masino. All letters are handwritten, except numbers 22, 23, 24, which are typed. Paola Masino organized the papers and, after her death in 1989, the collection was purchased by the Getty Institute. In my transcriptions I faithfully reproduced Ortese's punctuation. In addition, I maintained all underlinings as they appear in the original except for the titles of journals, reviews, and books, which I transcribed in italics even when in the original they were written in quotation marks. The few corrections I made to the text are noted in the footnotes. Any additions are added between block parentheses. I thank the Research Library of the Getty Research Institute for granting me permission to publish these letters here. The numbers of the letters correspond to the position of the letters within the entire collection.

Franca Nicosi
(fare indirizzare, nel caso di una risposta, alle mie sole iniziali; cioè:
F.N. presso: Signor Francesco Ortese Via Piliero 29 – Napoli –)

1.

August 3, 1936, [Fascist] Year XIV

Dear Editor,
Pardon me if I am so bold as to knock directly on the door of the *Italia.* Would you kindly read this short story and, if it pleases you, publish it? I believe it contains a meagre understanding of the language (inaccuracies, errors, and crazy punctuation) and, perhaps, who knows, even lack of imagination. But I have never studied, nor read much, nor lived among people who know how to speak correctly. And so, now that I am 22 years old, and I find myself writing for the past six years, and in almost melancholic conditions, I am beginning to feel a certain desire to achieve some purpose, to come forward. Is it possible? I ask you with humility, because I know how you could laugh if I have no merit.

I would never approach other reviews, precisely because I fear that, in addition to the … rejection, they could mock me. But I do not believe this good old *Italia* is capable of such a thing, mostly because you are there, an Academic; and certainly you wouldn't laugh at these errors "of a student."

Thank you, then, for reading my work. I will buy the *Giornale* every week to see if you accepted my piece (or not).

Respectfully,

Franca Nicosi

2.

12.8.36. XIV Napoli

Signor Direttore,
non so resistere al sentimento di angoscia che l'attesa e il dubbio mi danno. Ho paura, malgrado mi sforzi a sperare, che la prosa firmata "Franca Nicosi," e che deve essere giunta in Direzione (senza di che non varrebbe la pena che Lei seguitasse a leggere), Le sia parsa puerile, disprezzabile, e sia stata gettata. In questo spavento che mi fa veramente male, sento il bisogno di essere sincera, quasi che la poca lealtà abbia costituito finora l'oscuro e veramente unico ostacolo alla riuscita. Dunque, non sono *Franca Nicosi,* ma soltanto A.M. Ortese, di cui Lei ha pubblicato tempo fa una prosa.

Si ricorda *Quartiere*? Le fu portato, se non sbaglio, dal Signor Alberto Consiglio, che lo ebbe dal Prof. Aldo Romano. Io non provai in seguito volontà alcuna di farmi viva: e perché la prosa mi fu criticata ironicamente e ferocemente da varie persone, e perché avevo giurato, dopo che il Signor Pavolini andò via dal Giornale, di non riconoscere più nessun direttore dell'*Italia*.

Poi miseria, ansie, solitudine ed altro, mi hanno fatto mutar parere: cosicché non debbo che chiederLe francamente scusa.

Dice Lei: "Va bene, ma perché ha preso adesso un altro nome?" – Ecco perché: non solo tutti della famiglia mi burlano lungamente ogni qualvolta rintracciano miei scritti; ma vi sono poi dei sentimenti che uno morirebbe prima che persone interessate avessero modo di scoprirli e compatirli. Uno, quando scrive, lo fa al *solo* e perfetto scopo della *sua* momentanea gioia, mica per essere compatito.

Per carità, non faccia quindi sapere a nessuno, e particolarmente ai due signori Consiglio e Romano (escludo il Signor Pavolini, a cui lo direi anch'io, coraggiosamente) ch'io son tornata qui, con quella prosa, sotto altro nome. Adesso che *nessuno* più s'incarica di me, non voglio che nessunissima persona si ricordi più di Ortese e del suo indirizzo.

Ma veniamo all'importante: me la vuole pubblicare, questa prosa? Poi gliene manderò altre, e saranno sempre migliori, creda. Tutto sta ad incoraggiarmi, a credermi. Se io fossi stata presentata da quei due Signori, forse Lei mi avrebbe considerata con più indulgenza. Ma non è forse più degno uno che va avanti con le sue sole forze? Dunque, mi aiuti, abbia della leggera compassione; consideri che se *ci ride* Lei, *ci ridono* tutti su me, e posso buttarmi a mare. Mi aiuti, e Le assicuro che non se ne pentirà, e sarà invece molto molto soddisfatto del mio lavoro e di me. Io non chiedo che l'onore di un "piccolo spazio" nell'*Italia*. Mi contenti.

Grazie. Mi creda, coi più rispettosi saluti, Anna Maria Ortese

F.N. presso: Francesco Ortese –Via Piliero 29 – Napoli

2.

August 12, 1936 / [Fascist Year] XIV / Naples

Dear Editor,

I don't know how to stand up to the feeling of anguish that the wait and doubting has instilled in me. I am fearful, regardless of my attempts at hoping, that the prose work signed "Franca Nicosi," and which must have arrived in the main office (if this is not the case, it is not necessary for you to continue reading this letter), appeared to you puerile, worthless, and was thrown out. In this fear that is really tormenting me, I feel the need to be sincere, as if my limited honesty until this point has been the obscure and truly sole obstacle to my success. Well then, I am not *Franca Nicosi*, but only A.M. Ortese, of whom you have published a prose work some time ago.

Do you remember *Quartiere*? It was presented to you, if I am not mistaken, by Mr. Alberto Consiglio, who received it from Prof. Aldo Romano. I did not feel any desire, after that, to write: both because my work was criticized ironically and ferociously by various people, and because I had sworn that after the departure of Mr. Pavolini from the Review, I would not acknowledge any other editor of *Italia*.

Then poverty, anxiety, loneliness and more made me change my mind: and I frankly must say to you that I am sorry.

You might say: "All right, but why has she taken on another name?" – Here is why: not only does my entire family laugh at me without end whenever they discover my writings, but there are also certain feelings that one would die before interested people had the opportunity to discover and pity. When one writes, he does so *only* for the perfect purpose of *his own* immediate delight, not to be pitied by others.

For goodness sake, please do not make known to anyone, and above all to the two gentlemen Consiglio and Romano (I've not mentioned Mr. Pavolini, to whom I will tell him myself when I work up the courage) that I have returned here, with that writing, under another name. Now that *no one* is fostering my career any longer, I don't want any person at all to remember Ortese and her address.

But let's get to what's important: do you want to publish this piece? After, I will send you others, and they will continue to improve, believe me. Everything rests in encouraging me, in believing in me. If I had been presented to you by those two gentlemen, perhaps you would have considered me with more lenience. But is it not more worthy a person who moves ahead, alone, on her own effort? Therefore, please help me and have a little compassion; please consider that if you are laughing at me, everyone laughs at me, and I might as well just throw myself into the sea. Help me, and I assure you that you will not regret it, and that you will instead be very, very satisfied with my work and with me. I am not asking but for the honour of a "small space" in the *Italia*. Please fulfill my wish.

Thank you. Sincerely, with the most respectful regards,

Anna Maria Ortese

F.N. c/o: Francesco Ortese –Via Piliero 29 – Naples

3.

Napoli 19.8.36 XIV

Signor Direttore,

Le rispondo commossa, e per l'aiuto quasi insperato, e pel particolare Suo interessamento, che è forse fin oggi il più incredibile fra gli onori sognati. Grazie.

Acconsento subito, naturalmente, a firmare l'*Avventura* col mio vero nome di A.M. Ortese: e questo per seguire il Suo avviso e perché mi convinco anch'io della sciocchezza di distruggere il già conquistato. Certo se a casa mia scopriranno questa prosa, io soffrirò molto, non so fino a che punto: perché vi sono alcune, pur nobili e care figure della mia famiglia *borghese,* le quali non ammettono, e chiamano anzi delitto, l'esposizione sincera di sentimenti e moti che esse pure provarono e ricordano anzi con dolcezza. Io sono assolutamente soggetta alla mia famiglia, e mi figuro, nel breve spazio di poche stanze, e nella continuata intimità, quale e quanto patimento. Inoltre perderò – credo – alcuni carissimi amici che finora avevo, i quali saranno presi da paura o scrupolo innanzi alla mia prosa malinconica.

Ma a tanto mi preparo con gioia, perché ora che la Sua stima è là, ferma (e questo mi faceva soffocare, in attesa, il pensiero della Sua opinione carica di conseguenze), ogni altra preoccupazione cade al confronto, si rivela inferiore.

Grazie ancora per non essersi offeso del mio mutismo dopo *Quartiere.* So che – a parte quest'ultimo fatto – la Sua di oggi è veramente un'azione generosa: e valutandoLa come posso, cercherò ricambiarLa con un lavoro sempre migliore e, mi auguro, costante.

Io ho tanti difetti ancora (e sospetto cresceranno) e debbo farmi perdonare moltissime cose, da chiunque: cosicché oltre di Lei, ringrazio fin d'ora anche quelli "che mi lasceranno passare, saranno contenti di me": primissimo con lei quel Signore che La aiuta nella direzione dell'*Italia.*

La Sua lettera – incoraggiamento, gioia e orgoglio altissimo – la farò vedere soltanto se "si accorgeranno," oppure quando *quel* numero sarà esaurito.

Signor Direttore, io ho parlato tanto: ma Le avrò fatto intanto capire il mio animo pieno di gratitudine e devozione infinita? Lo spero. E ancora più spero potermi fare avanti e, con un nome che veramente vale, ripeterLe *allora* quanto oggi è simile a frase povera.

Grazie ancora, Signor Direttore, mille volte, e mi creda, con più rispettosi saluti

devotissima
Anna Maria Ortese

3.

Naples August 19, 1936 [Fascist] Year XIV

Dear Editor,

I am responding to you with great emotion, and for the almost unexpected help, and your particular interest, which is perhaps until today the most incredible among all the honours I could have dreamt. Thank you.

I agree right away, naturally, to sign *Avventura* with my true name A.M. Ortese: and this in order to follow your advice and because I have convinced myself of the absurdity of destroying what I've already achieved. Of course if at my home they discover this prose writing, I will suffer greatly, and I don't know to what point: because there are some characters, albeit noble and dear, of my bourgeois family who do not admit, and who even believe to be criminal, the sincere expression of feelings and impulses which they themselves feel and remember even with sweetness. I am completely dependent on my family, and since we live in the small space of a few rooms, and in continual closeness, I am able to imagine what type and how much suffering I would have to endure. In addition, I will lose – I believe – some very dear friends who up till now were mine, who will be seized with fear and apprehension when confronted with my melancholic prose writing.

But for all of these situations I am preparing myself with joy, because now that your approval of my work is here to stay (and this is what was stifling me, as I awaited: the thought of your opinion loaded with consequences for me), every other worry has fallen in comparison and has revealed itself as inferior.

Thank you again for not having been offended by my silence after *Quartiere*. I know that – notwithstanding this last fact – your letter from today is truly a generous act: and valuing it to the best of my abilities, I will try to return you the favor through always working better and, I hope, with consistency.

I still have so many faults (and I suspect they will grow in number) and I should seek forgiveness for many things, from everybody: so that in addition to you, up till now I must thank also those "who will allow me to pass, and will be happy with my work": first of whom, with you, is the gentleman who helps you in the editorial board of *Italia.*

Your letter – encouragement, joy and highest pride – I will show it only if "they realize it's me," or when that issue has gone out of print.

Mr. Editor, I have spoken so much: but have I in the meanwhile allowed you to understand my spirit filled with gratefulness and infinite devotion? I hope so. And now even more I hope to move ahead and, with a name that truly has value, repeat for you in the future what today seems still a weak sentence.

Thank you again, Mr. Editor, a thousand times over, and sincerely, with the most respectful regards,

yours truly

Anna Maria Ortese

4.

20.8.36 XIV Napoli

Signor Direttore,

so bene che Lei mi chiamerà pazza, se non stupidissima persona, ma non importa, è proprio necessario che Le scriva una seconda volta.

Ieri, nella gran gioia, "non pensavo" più, e diedi il consenso a mettere la mia firma. Veramente non pensavo più a nulla, e questo è stato il mio torto. Ma stamattina una infinità di considerazioni mi hanno assalita, fortissime, che non posso non ascoltare.

Senta, Signor Direttore, e mi scusi: s'io pubblico l'*Avventura* col mio nome vero, se in casa mia entra quella novella con quel nome, io sono finita. Non si meravigli, non si annoi, La prego. Le ho già detto com'è la mia famiglia, e come io vi sono soggetta. A una scoperta simile (che avverrebbe sicuramente) io non sarò meno di un comunista in un convento di frati. Mi mangeranno.

Signor Direttore, senta: io me ne potrei *infischiare* se fossi sana di nervi e di cervello, ma io *là* sono malata; anzi Le dico che in questa casa proprio, così innocente e benevola nell'apparenza, e cupa nell'intimo, io mi son fatta strana. Qui non ammettono la vita vera di *alcuni* figli: tutto è falso, sbagliato, è carta dipinta. Ma vi sono dei congegni che schiacciano, sotto questo cartame. Cominceranno con late epressioni di orrore, con tali atteggiamenti di disgusto, con tali altre prove di disprezzo, di quasi tutti contro una sola, ch'io finirò al manicomio, o getterò la penna per sempre. Non è più la perdita di amici, non è più alcun sentimento malinconico: è la paura, la *paura* maiuscola dei miei, della desolazione da lebbrosario in cui mi getteranno, che mi fa pregarLa vivamente di *non considerare* quella semplice lettera di ieri, di non tener conto del mio facile consenso, di non mettere, per favore, la mia firma.

Mi scusi, se può! Davvero son matta, e forse irriverente, facendoLa partecipe delle mie tumultuose variazioni: ma non è colpa mia. *Tutti,* infine, sì, tutti, possono sapere che sotto quel nome di Nicosi c'è Ortese, meno che i miei. Le piace il mio modo di scrivere? Se lei ci tiene un poco (per me ragione di orgoglio e conforto) non deve far sì che mi avvelenino l'aria che respiro, perché qua è il mio posto, e se mi avvelenano l'aria niente mi salva.

Mi scusi, Signor Direttore, non so come dirLe "mi scusi"; e non strappi quell'*Avventura,* che per me è tutto, e sia compiacente, e voglia comprendermi, perché se adesso Lei s'infastidisce ed irrita, e chiude le porte dell'*Italia,* io finirò soffocata in questa casa. Non strappi quel racconto, La prego ancora, e mi scusi.

Ad ogni modo, sempre ugualmente grata per l'alto onore di ieri, La prego di credermi devotissima

Anna Maria Ortese

4.

Naples August 20, 1936 [Fascist] Year XIV

Dear Editor,

I know well that you will call me crazy, if not the stupidest person, but it makes no difference, for it is really necessary that I write to you a second time.

Yesterday, in my great joy, "I wasn't thinking" any longer, and I gave you permission to put my signature. I was truly not thinking of anything and this was my mistake. But this morning an infinite amount of considerations assailed me, and they are so strong that I am not able to ignore them.

Please listen, Mr. Editor, and excuse me: if I publish *Avventura* with my true name, if in my home that short story ends up with my name, I am finished. Please don't be surprised, don't be irritated, I beg you. I told you how my family is, and how I am dependent on them. To a discovery like that (which I am sure would happen) I will be nothing less than a communist in a convent of friars. They will eat me alive.

Mr. Editor, please listen: I would be able to care less about this if my nerves and brain were healthy, but it is *there* that I am sick; and in fact I tell you that right in this house, so innocent and benevolent in appearance, and yet dark deep inside, I have become strange. Here they don't admit the true life of some of the children: everything is false, wrong, it's painted paper. But there are mechanisms that crush, under all this paper. They will begin with broad expressions of horror, with such airs of disgust, with so many other demonstrations of scorn, with almost everyone against just one, that I will end up in the insane asylum, and I will throw away my pen forever. It is no longer the loss of friends, nor any melancholic feeling: it's the fear, the *Fear* with a capital F of my family, of the anguish in which they will throw me, similar to what a leper must feel. This fear makes me beg you intensely *not to consider* that naive letter from yesterday, not to take into consideration my easy consent, and please not to use my real name.

Forgive me if you can! I am truly insane, and perhaps irreverent, making you take part in my tumultuous changes: it's not my fault. *Everyone,* in the end, yes, everyone, will know that under that name of Nicosi is really Ortese, except for my family. Do you like my way of writing? If you like it (which for me would be a reason for feeling pride and comfort) you shouldn't do anything that would poison the air that I breathe, because here is my place, and if they poison the air, nothing could save me.

Please forgive me, Mr. Editor, I really do not know how to say "forgive me" enough; and please do not rip up that *Avventura,* which for me is everything, and please be willing to help, and want to understand me, because if now you become annoyed and irritated, and close the doors of the *Italia* on me, I will end up suffocated in this house. Do not rip up that short story, I beg you again, and forgive me.

No matter what, always equally grateful for the high honour of yesterday, please believe me yours sincerely

Anna Maria Ortese

25.

Anna Maria Ortese to Paola Masino[80]

Milano, 16 agosto 60

Carissima Paola,

ho saputo di Massimo, e non sono riuscita finora a scriverLe niente: mi perdoni.

Non riesco ad accettare l'idea di questo allontanamento di Lui dalla Sua vita e dalla vita di tutti noi, che bene o male, a seconda delle nostre forze, lo abbiamo amato. Del resto, non credo che Egli si sia veramente allontanato, se non dal meccanismo piuttosto limitato dei nostri sensi.

È ancora presente, ma nascosto. Questo io credo. E non è più infelice, come non può esserlo, uscito dalle leggi naturali che ci governano, il Suo vero essere, sempre risplendente, sempre giovane e pieno di gioia.

Ora io rivolgo a Lui, presente e nascosto, il mio saluto familiare, il grazie felice per tutta la vita, gli insegnamenti, l'intelligenza e la felicità che ha dato anche a me, così splendidamente. E gli ripeto che gli voglio bene, (e gliene volevo, anche se stavo lontana), e gli prometto che cercherò, per quanto è possibile, di essere degna della Sua amicizia, del Suo aiuto. E che sono sicura ci rivedremo. Bacio il Suo caro meraviglioso viso, e abbraccio anche Lei, coraggiosa e bella Paola, tanto, tanto affettuosamente.

Sua Anna

***

Anna Maria Ortese to Paola Masino

Milan, August 16, 1960

Dearest Paola,

I found out about Massimo, and until now I was not able to write anything to you: please forgive me. I cannot accept the idea of this distance between him and his life and the life of all of us, who, one way or another, loved him. In fact, I do not believe that he has gone away, if but, perhaps, only from the rather limited mechanism of our senses.

He is still present, only hidden. This is what I believe. And his true being, always shining brightly, always young and filled with joy, is no longer unhappy, as it cannot be since he has escaped from the natural laws that govern us.

Now to him, present and hidden, I direct my devoted goodbye, a happy "thank you" for the entire life, teachings, intelligence and happiness that he gave even to me, so splendidly. And I am repeating to him that I love him, (and that I loved him, even though I was far away), and I am promising him that I will try, as much as possible, to be worthy of his friendship and of his help. And I am sure we will see each other again. I give a kiss to his dear and wonderful face, and I also hug you, Paola, courageous and beautiful, with the deepest affection.

Your Anna

NOTES

1 Ortese, "La meraviglia e l'innocenza," 67. This interview would later be altered by Ortese herself and included as "La libertà è un respiro," CC 107–33.
2 In the four letters to him, Ortese laments of feeling "isolata e come sopravvissuta" ("isolated, a survivor") and that Italian literary critics had passed her by "con viso arcigno" ("with grim faces"), Lavezzi et al., eds., *Catalogo delle lettere ad Alfonso Gatto (1942–1970)*, 170.
3 Motta, ed., "Caro, molto caro La Capria," 85–87.
4 A letter written by Ortese to Gianna Manzini dated 9 September 1967 (in which Ortese thanks Manzini for her letter of congratulations on winning the Strega prize in 1967 for *I poveri e i semplici*) is included in Trevisan, "Da scrittrice a scrittrice," 263–91. The letter is also printed in the catalogue edited by Bernardini Napoletano and Yehya, *Gianna Manzini*, 95.
5 For an extensive bibliography of the many individual letters to various authors (including open letters printed in newspapers) that have been published in reviews up until 1998, see Clerici, *Apparizione e visione*, 658–720 (here Clerici also extensively quotes from more than 300 letters to various authors). For letters published after 1998, see a brief cataloguing in my dissertation: Moser, "*Il futuro è tutto nella notte*," 260–61. For a succinct overview in paragraph form of the numerous people with whom Ortese corresponded, see Clerici's comments in "Sotto il segno di Giannone," the introduction to the volume edited by Clerici and dedicated to Ortese: *Il Giannone* 4, no. 7–8 (2006): 7–11. Exceptionally useful is *L'Archivio di Anna Mario Ortese: Inventario*, "Epistolario," 15–73; "Corrispondenza con case editrici e agenzie letterarie," 75–92; "Lettere aperte," 149–52. Also, Clerici, "*Sono lieto di questo tu fraterno*," 61–70, and Urettini, "L'irrequieto vagabondaggio di Anna Maria Ortese in due lettere a Giovanni Comisso," 103–16. For a detailed presentation and discussion of the correspondences between Ortese and Natalia Ginzburg and Ortese and Pietro Citati see De Caprio, "Gli amici di Anna Maria," 273–91. Adelia Battista edited the collected correspondence between Ortese and Dario Bellezza, *Bellezza, addio*. See also her recent work *Ortese segreta: Ritratto intimo di Anna Maria Ortese*. It would certainly be interesting to read the following volume, which, unfortunately, was privately printed and is not for public sale: Nicodemo and Spadaccini, eds., *Anna Maria Ortese: Le carte*.
6 Pasquale Prunas (1924–85) was founder and editor of the review *Sud*, with which Ortese collaborated. He was also a noted film director of the documentaries *Benito Mussolini* (1962) and *Italiani come noi* (1964). Ortese's

letters to him were published in Ortese, *Alla luce del Sud: Lettere a Pasquale Prunas.* See also Ortese, *Bellezza, addio: Lettere a Dario Bellezza.*

7 Paola Masino (1908–89) authored such novels as *Monte ignoso* (1931), *Periferia* (1933; second prize winner at the Premio Viareggio), *Nascita e morte della massaia* (1945) and was Massimo Bontempelli's longtime companion. The publication of Ortese's letters to Masino, held at the *Archivi del Novecento* (Università degli studi di Roma "La Sapienza") has long been announced forthcoming as: Ortese, *Toccare l'impalpabile vita,* edited by Marinella Mascia Galateria. For a discussion of this correspondence and of the friendship between the two writers, see Vittori, "Storia di un'amicizia," 10–11. For a photographic reproducion of only the front side of one of Ortese's letters to Masino (dated 25 June 1937), see Bernardini Napoletano and Mascia Galateria, eds., *Scrittrici e intellettuali del Novecento,* 49.

8 Very few critical contributions are dedicated to Ortese as letter writer, except: Mascia Galateria, "Anna Maria Ortese epistolografa," 49–66.

9 I published a critical edition of this entire collection of letters to Bontempelli in my disseration: "*Il futuro,*" 96–128. All the letters quoted in the text of this present article derive from this edition. A volume edition of the correspondence is prepared for separate publication.

10 Ortese's return to the re-editing of the 1998 edition of *Toledo* during her last days and of the writing of the preface attest to this work's central importance to her poetics.

11 Ortese, *Il Porto di Toledo* (Milan: Rizzoli, 1975), inside flap.

12 Among the texts that Bontempelli recommends: Shakespeare's *Hamlet,* Calderon de la Barca's *Vida es sueño.* Regarding the other, unmentioned, books, Ortese writes: "Leggerò tutti gli altri da Lei consigliati e, s'intende, anche l'*Amleto,* di cui poi Le parlerò" ("I will read all of the others that you recommended to me and, of course, also Hamlet, which I will discuss with you"; Letter 14, 28 June 1937), Moser, *Il futuro,* 114.

13 A collection of Ortese's letters to Paola Masino is held in the *Archivi del Novecento* (see above, note 7).

14 The place of origin and the dates of the letters are as follows: Letter 1 (Naples, 3 August 1936), Letter 2 (Naples, 12 August 1936), Letter 3 (Naples, 19 August 1936), Letter 4 (Naples, 20 August 1936), Letter 5 (Naples, 27 August 1936), Letter 6 (Naples, 12 September 1936), Letter 7 (Naples, 10 November 1936), Letter 8 (Naples, 30 November 1936), Letter 9 (Naples, 3 April 1937), Letter 10 (Naples, 13 April 1937), Letter 11 (no place indicated, 19 April 1937), Letter 12 (Naples, 27 April 1937), Letter 13 (Naples, 20 June 1937), Letter 14 (Naples, 28 June 1937), Letter 15 (Naples, 4 September 1938), Letter 16 (Naples, 20 September

1938), Letter 17 (Sant'Agata sui Due Golfi [outside Sorrento], 4 July 1940), Letter 18 (no place indicated, 19? September 1940), Letter 19 (Naples, 3 October 1940), Letter 20 (no place indicated, 15 October 1940), Letter 21 (Milan, 22 March 1950), Letter 22 (Agnano, Naples, 2 September 1950), Letter 23 (Milan, 12 December 1952), Letter 24 (Milan, 27 December 1952), Letter 25 (Milan, 16 August 1960).

15 At the end of the letter, in blue pen on the bottom right, Bontempelli wrote a note to himself: "risposto il 15 / 16 che oggi poco gli editori stampano e niente ristampano, nemmeno a noi anziani. E che non ci danno + anticipi ma *solamente le percent. sopra le copie vendute.* – Che riscriveremo quando tornerà Paola" ("responded on the 15 / 16 that these days editors print little and reprint nothing, not even for us older writers. And that they no longer give us advances but *only a certain percentage above the number of copies sold.* – That we will write back again when Paola returns"), Moser, *Il futuro*, 126.

16 Regarding this episode of her life and Bontempelli's influence: "accolsi con grande sollievo – sebbene fossi sorpresa, e mi sembrasse di rubare – la proposta di uno scrittore italiano, Massimo Bontempelli, che era succeduto al primo direttore nella guida del giornale, di pubblicare tutti insieme, in volume, i miei primi racconti. La cosa si realizzò immediatamente, io non ci entrai affatto (non erano in molti a scrivere, allora), e mi fu anche assegnato un premio di denaro, di cinquemila lire, col quale potei aiutare mio padre e ricomporre un momento la dissestata economia della casa" [CC 73; "I welcomed with great relief – even if I was suprised, and I felt like I was stealing – the proposal of an Italian writer, Massimo Bontempelli, who took over as Chief Editor at the helm of the journal, to publish all my early short stories together, in a book. The project was carried out immediately, and I had nothing to do with it (not many people were writing at that time), and a literary prize was even awarded to me, worth five thousand lire, with which I was able to help my father and to reassemble, if even for a moment, the unravelled financial situation of my family"].

17 For a history of *900* and Bontempelli's definitions of *Novecentismo* and *realismo magico*, see Moser, *Il futuro*, 5–63.

18 During these occasions, Bontempelli created a list of writers he considered "*novecentieri*" including: Corrado Alvaro, Antonio Aniante, Giovanni Artieri, Francesco Cipriani, Marcello Gallian, Aldo Bizzari, Gian Gasparo Napolitano, Giulio Santangelo, Pietro Solari, and Alberto Spaini. To this original list, he would later add Paola Masino, Cesare Zavattini, Roberto Papi, and Anna Maria Ortese. See Bontempelli, *l'Avventura novecentista.* See also Falqui, ed., *Il Futurismo: Il Novecentismo*, 100.

19 Originally published in *Tempo* (Milan, 24 June 1943): 4. Reprinted in its entirety in Moser, *Il futuro,* 59–62 (Appendix A). Here I've cited from pp. 60–61. Bontempelli disliked having to define these terms, as proven in 1950 when, in response to the Belgian scholar Rik Lanckrock's request for a definition of the term *realismo magico,* Bontempelli writes (in a letter dated 6 May 1950) a brief definition and then reveals: "Comme je vous l'ai dit, cette formule je l'ai trouvée il y a peut-être trente ans; mais il y en a peut-être vingtneuf que j'ai cessé de m'en servir" ("As I told you, I came across that expression about thirty years ago, but it's been about twenty-nine years since I've ceased using it"). Lanckrock's letter and Bontempelli's response are both held within the Getty Collection and are reproduced and commented on in Moser, *Il futuro,* 42–44 and 63 (Appendix B).

20 Bontempelli, *l'Avventura Novecentista,* 499.

21 Ibid., 529.

22 "Distinzione tra abilità ed estro, ché in questa prosa sempre gli effetti che diresti più abili sono ottenuti da uno stato di innocenza" ("distinction between ability and fancy, so that in this prose the effect that you would deem successful is always obtained through a state of innocence"), Ibid., 529.

23 For an analysis of *Gente nel Tempo* as a *novecentista* work, see Cesaretti, "Outplaying Kronos' Hunger," 384–404. In his reading of this work, Cesaretti focuses on the childlike innocence and candour that characterize Nora, and even Dirce, and he concentrates especially on the role of play as a sign of the simplicity and unknowingness of these characters when faced with the forces of the outside world that determine their destinies. Although not stated in the same terms, Ortese was also drawn to this innocence of the characters.

24 Arnaldo Frateili (Piediluco, Terni 1888 – Roma 1965), a literary critic who collaborated with and edited *La Tribuna* and who also wrote film criticism, went on to direct the film *Cesare Birotteau* (1921). In collaboration with Giuseppe Bottai, he also directed the short-lived fascist-leaning review *Spettatore italiano* in 1924. Frateili began his career as a writer in 1932 with the novel *Capogiro,* which won the Viareggio Prize for that year. His harsh review of *Angelici dolori,* entitled "Un caso letterario?," which was originally published in *La Tribuna* (24 April 1937): 3, was reprinted in *Il Giannone,* 99–101.

25 Franco Ciliberti was editor of *Valori primordiali* (Roma-Milan: Edizioni Augustea, 1938). Only one number of the review was published. Collaborators included: Antonio Banfi, Massimo Bontempelli, Carlo Carrà, Tommaso Catalano, Enrico Prampolini, Berto Ricci, Ernesto Rogers, and Alberto Sartoris. See Cammarota, *Futurismo,* 250.

26 A thorough discussion of the context surrounding Ortese during her early career can be found in Moser, *Il futuro*, 64–93.

27 Bakhtin, "Discourse in the Novel," 293.

28 Favret, *Romantic Correspondence*, 56. I would be remiss not to mention that Ortese's correspondence falls within the long tradition of women letter writers. For an insightful analysis of women's contribution to this genre during an earlier time, see Daybell, *Women Letter Writers in Tudor England*. Daybell identifies underlying similarities among these texts (i.e., that for early modern women the letter "represents the dominant form by which [they] exerted power and influence" [26] and that "letters were reactive, written largely for practical reasons, and reflective of particular events, crises, and emotional states which occasioned the writing of a letter" [266]). Nonetheless, he also acknowledges that "in many ways women's correspondence differs very little from that of their male counterparts. The vast range of correspondence examined resists an over-simplified distinction between women's and men's letters based on content" (266). Also, for an excellent history of letter writing as female writings, see Ray, *Writing Gender in Women's Letter Collections*, 10–15. For a selected collection of letters exchanged among noted twentieth-century Italian women writers in which they discuss various aspects of their writing, see Trevisan, "Da scrittrice a scrittrice," 263–91.

29 Ortese admits to Valentino Bompiani (letter dated 3 October 1938) that "le poche lettere di uomini illustri o no, che avevo ricevute dopo la pubblicazione del mio libro, le ho distrutte tempo fa, seguendo in questo una mia discutibile quanto radicata abitudine" ("I destroyed long ago the few letters from famous men which I received after the publication of my book, following in this act one of my questionable as much as ingrained habits"), d'Ina and Zaccaria, eds., *Caro Bompiani*, 484. The destruction of letters received appears to be a habit that Ortese did not uphold in her later years, as attested to by the fact that certain letters (received after the mid-sixties, but mostly those dated in the 1980s and 1990s) were saved by Ortese. Of these are included letters from Giacinto Spagnoletti, Enzo Siciliano, Leonardo Sciascia, Gina Lagorio, Vivian Lamarque, Natalia Ginzburg, Pietro Citati, Italo Calvino, and Giorgio Agamben. See Spadaccini et al., eds., *L'Archivio di Anna Mario Ortese: Inventario*.

30 To my knowledge, it was Cicero who first referred to letters as the conversations of absent friends ("amicorum colloquia absentium") in *Phillipics* II, 7.

31 Altman, *Epistolarity*, 112, note 1. Altman bases her definitions here on Gérard Genette's discussion of intradiegetic narratee (internal reader) and extradiegetic narratee (external reader) as it pertains to all forms of narrative discourse. See "Discours du récit" in *Figures* 3, 265–66.

32 Ray, *Writing Gender in Women's Letter Collections*, 219.

33 Moser, *Il futuro*, 129.

34 Ibid., 116. (Letter 16, 20 September 1938).

35 Ibid., 117 (Letter 17, 4 July 1940).

36 Ibid. Also in Letter 2 dated 12 August 1936 (99), Ortese creates an imaginative, almost script-like dialogue between herself and Bontempelli when she begins a paragraph with: "Dice Lei: 'Va bene, ma perché ha preso adesso un altro nome?' – Ecco perché: non solo tutti della famiglia mi burlano lungamente ogni qualvota rintracciano miei scritti; ma vi sono poi dei sentimenti che uno morrirebbe prima che persone interessate avessero modo di scoprirli e compatirli" ("You might say: 'All right, but why has she taken on another name?' – Here is why: not only does my entire family laugh at me without end whenever they discover my writings, but there are also certain feelings that one would die before interested people had the opportunity to discover and pity"). This behaviour of inventing a dialogue with an imaginary speaker is a trademark of several of her interviews, as she reveals openly in *Corpo celeste*: "avevo già scritto, e continuai successivamente, alcune 'conversazioni'; erano, poi, interviste in parte immaginarie [...] Nelle prime due interviste, che ho chiamato 'conversazioni,' solo l'inizio, o una parte delle domande è condotto dall'intervistatore. Regolarmente, a un certo punto, proseguo, domande e risposte, per mio conto" (CC 13; "I had already written, and I continued subsequently to write, some 'conversations'; they were partly imaginary interviews [...]. In the first two interviews, which I called 'conversations,' only the beginning, or a part of the questions were conducted by the interviewer. Regularly, at a certain point, I would proceed on my own, through question and answer").

37 In Aristotelian terms, persuasion was achieved through three means: ethos (the credibility of speaker), pathos (an appeal to the listener's emotions), and logos (reasoning). See Aristotle, *The Art of Rhetoric*.

38 This participation of the reader required to give meaning to the text recalls Iser's discussion in *The Reading Process*, in which he reminds us that the creation of meaning within a text depends on collaboration between writer and reader insomuch as the writer artistically invents the text, while the reader aesthetically interprets it. A text can only take on life, Iser explains, when it is realized by a reader, not as a result of the simple exercise of subjective interpretation on his part, nor as the result of a biased reinvention of what the author intended, but rather as the manifestation of the reader's response to the text. Iser, "The Reading Process," 50–69.

39 See Lejeune, *On Autobiography*.

40 Ray uses the term "familial letter" to denote a very similar type of writing, defined as "letters in which the author appears as a protagonist and which were not written in an official capacity," Ray, 222, note 2.

41 "La Francia è grande per Pascal, ma prima ancora per Montaigne. Leggi il suo saggio sulla crudeltà! Come è l'orrore – sembra intramontabile – dell'uomo-*nature*! Dopo che lo hai letto, sai che *umanità* è una parola vaga, se non è ripensata" (CC 100; "France is great because of Pascal, but even before him because of Montaigne. Read his essay on cruelty! You will be shocked by the ever-timeless horror of the Natural man! After you've read it, you will know that *humanity* is a vague word, if in fact we don't decide to rethink its meaning").

42 In his "On the Education of Children," Montaigne specifies of raising a child: "Make him understand, that to acknowledge the error he shall discover in his own argument, though only found out by himself, is an effect of judgment and *sincerity*, which are the principal things he is to seek after" [italics mine], de Montaigne, *Essays of Michel de Montaigne*, 32–33. Ralph Waldo Emerson, in his essay "Montaigne; or, the Skeptic," would centre precisely on the sincerity of the French thinker's rhetoric, describing his words as so authentic that they became living entities: "The *sincerity* and marrow of the man reaches to his sentences. I know not anywhere the book that seems less written. It is the language of conversation transferred to a book. Cut these words, and they would bleed" [emphasis mine]. Emerson, *Representative Men: Seven Lectures*, 96.

43 Trilling, *Sincerity and Authenticity*.

44 Whitman, *The Complete Poems of Walt Whitman*, 84.

45 The full quotation reads: "Now the lines of my painting do not go astray, though they change and vary. The world is but a perennial movement. All things are in constant movement – the earth, the rocks of the Caucasus, the pyramids of Egypt – both with the common motion and with their own. Stability itself is nothing but a more languid motion. I cannot keep my subject still. It goes along befuddled and staggering, with a natural drunkenness. I take it in this condition, just at it is at the moment I give my attention to it. I do not portray being: I portray passing. Not the passing from one age to another, or as the people say, from seven years to seven years, but from day to day, from minute to minute. My history needs to be adapted to the moment. I may presently change, not only by chance, but also by intention. This is a record of various and changeable occurrences, and of irresolute and, when it so befalls, contradictory ideas: whether I am different myself, or whether I take hold of my subjects in different circumstances and aspects. So, all in all, I may indeed contradict myself now and then: but truth,

as Demades said, I do not contradict," de Montaigne, *Selections from the Essays*, 75 (Chapt. 2 "Of Repentance").

46 Before Bontempelli arrived at the review, Corrado Pavolini had already published the following works by Ortese: three poems: "Manuele," "Al mio faro che non c'è più," and "Sempre a una soglia," and two short stories: "Pellirossa" and "Quartiere." "Pellirossa" would later be included in *Angelici dolori* (1937) as "Pellerossa." For a discussion of these early poems by Ortese, see my article: Moser, "The Poetry of Prose," 443–68.

47 Brother of Alessandro Pavolini, Corrado (Florence 1897 – Cortona 1980) – also a declared fascist – was an influential intellectual and author of several poetic collections. In *Corpo celeste*, Ortese describes him as "uno spirito di qualità superiore; egli, in altri termini, apparteneva alla grande Chiesa dell'Estetica, e sapeva che solo qui si forma l'anima umana. Aveva simpatia, e grande, per l'anima umana, ma come i teologi e i santi non dissociano la sua formazione e salvezza dall'iscrizione a una Legge e regola religiosa, per lui, la fede e l'obbedienza alle grandi tavole della Legge estetica erano fondamentali. Solo così l'anima umana si salvava. Egli pubblicò questo lungo scritto (non mi soffermo sulla mia gioia, non conoscevo nessuna gioia uguale a questa), dandomi poi dei suggerimenti: ma sempre in modo così distaccato e marginale, da evitare sia mortificazione che esaltazione (si pensi che allora io non conoscevo l'apostrofo), così che sempre, per questa discrezione, lo considerai un autentico educatore di anime" [CC 67–68; "A spirit of superior quality; In other words, he was part of the great Church of Esthetics, and he knew that only there could the human spirit be formed. He had quite a fondness for the human spirit, but just as theologians and saints do not dissociate the spirit's formation and salvation from its adherence to a religious law or rule, also for him, faith and obedience at the great table of Esthetic Law was fundamental. Only in that way could the human spirit save itself. He published a long work of mine (I won't linger on the joy I felt but to say that I had never known any joy that was equal to it), he gave me some suggestions: but always in a detached and marginal way so as to avoid both mortification and exhaltation (and if you think that at that time I did not even know what an apostrophe was). For these reasons, for his tact, I considered him an authentic educator of spirits."] Ortese credits him with having encouraged her to write her first short stories: "mi chiese di provarmi a scrivere un racconto, cioè della prosa, per il settimanale. Furono i miei esami di ammissione a questa cara (e quanto male seguita!) scuola dello scrivere" [CC 69; "He asked me to try to write a short story, a piece of prose writing, for his weekly review. Those were my admissions exams to this dear (and so poorly followed!) writing school."] Pavolini

collaborated on the review *Tevere* from 1923 to 1932 and directed *L'Italia Letteraria* before Bontempelli. For a presentation of his life, see the biography by his wife: Pavolini Hannau, *Cinquantanove anni meno un giorno*. Also, for an interesting collection of letters written to Pavolini [by Cardarelli and Ungaretti], see Bernardini Napoletano and Mascia Galateria, eds., *Lettere a Corrado Pavolini. V. Cardarelli – G. Ungaretti*. See Clerici, *Apparizione e visione*, 71–72, for a description of how Pavolini supported Ortese in the beginning of her career. Pavolini's wife, Marcella Pavolini Hannau, writes of Ortese: "Mi ricordo che andammo una volta a casa di lei con i Da Napoli; una casa poverissima, dove viveva con i genitori. Nella soffitta, che lei aveva tappezzato con grandissimi disegni eseguiti da un suo fratello marinaio, morto in mare, che le era stato tanto caro, Anna Maria scriveva le sue fantasie. Per qualche anno abbiamo contiuato a vederci molto spesso: veniva a casa nostra [...]. Una volta, ricordo, quando il pranzo si faceva aspettare un poco, lei svenne per il lungo digiuno" ("I remember that we once went to her house with the Da Napolis; a very poor house, where she lived with her parents. In the loft, which she had covered with huge drawings made by her sailor brother who died at sea and who was very dear to her, Anna Maria wrote her fiction. For a few years we continued to see each other often: she used to come to our house [...]. Once, I recall, when lunch was taking longer to be served, she fainted from hunger"), M. Pavolini Hannau, *Cinquantanove anni meno un giorno*, 41. Strangely, after their close ties during the years 1935–37, it seems Ortese rarely contacted Pavolini. Marcella complains that Ortese ignored them: "Ma da tanti, tanti anni non ci ha più scritto e non ci è mai venuta a trovare nel nostro 'Bacchino'; questo mi rattrista moltissimo. Soprattutto avrei desiderato di ricevere una sua parola di ricordo quando Corrado, il suo primo 'scopritore,' ci ha lasciati. Ma forse lei non lo ha saputo" ("But for many, many years she did not write to us and she never came to see us in our 'Bacchino'; this saddens me a great deal. Above all, I would have appreciated receiving a word of remembrance from her when Corrado, her first 'discoverer,' left us. But perhaps she did not know of it"), *Cinquantanove anni meno un giorno*, 42.

48 Moser, *Il futuro*, 98 (Letter 1, 3 August 1936).

49 See Clerici, *Apparizione e visione*, 72.

50 Moser, *Il futuro*, 99 (Letter 2, 8 August 1936). The underlining is original in the text. The piece she makes reference to here is "Quartiere," published on 5 April 1936.

51 Ibid. A similar reaction occurs to Damasa in *Toledo* right after she reads the publication of her rendiconto "Tutte le case erano spente (Il mago)" [All the houses are dark (the magician)] – a slightly altered version of her short

story *Angelici dolori*. Bemoaning the publication of her intimate feelings, she laments: "Ah, perché lo avevo fatto! Ora, ben presto, Lemano saprebbe, i due studenti saprebbero, Samana saprebbe, tutta la Toledo borbonica sarebbe al corrente dell'animo mio. [...] Di me che sarebbe – pensavo – così improvvisamente impoverita, destituita della ma privatezza, perduta al mondo notturno per una infantile debolezza – ché altro non era, se non infantile debolezza, il sentimento che mi aveva permesso di separarmi dal mio rendiconto. Ecco, era finita!" (R1 642; "Oh, why did I do that! Now, very soon, Lemano might find out, the two students might find out, and Samana and the entire bourbonic Toledo will be wise to my feelings. [...] What would become of me, I thought, so suddenly impoverished and deprived of my privacy, lost into a world of darkness all for a childish weakness because it was just that, a childish weakness, the feeling that allowed me to separate myself from my written account. And there it was, everything was ruined!").

52 Moser, *Il futuro*, 101. (Letter 4, 20 August 1936).

53 Clerici, *Apparizione e visione*, 74.

54 Clerici notes those two references to Romano as being in the Getty letters (12 August 1936) and in an unpublished poem. For a reproduction of the poems, see Clerici, *Apparizione e vision*, 75. Ortese's friend, Alda Croce, states: "la Ortese amava Aldo, un gran bel ragazzo" ("Ortese loved Aldo, a fine-looking young man"). But Aldo was engaged to her friend, Adriana Capocci. Croce says that for Ortese: "i suoi angelici dolori erano loro" ("they were her angelic sorrows"), quoted in Clerici, *Apparizione e visione*, 75.

55 Moser, *Il futuro*, 104.

56 Luca Clerici discusses how Ortese first met Bontempelli at the Festa del Libro in Rome in 1937. Clerici, *Apparizione e visione*, 81.

57 Moser, *Il futuro*, 119 (Letter 18).

58 Ortese's revelations show the truth behind the Latin phrase: "*Excusatio non petita, accusatio manifesta*" ("He who excuses himself, accuses himself").

59 Ortese makes reference to the first edition of the *Discorsi*, entitled *Pirandello, Leopardi, D'Annunzio: Tre discorsi di Massimo Bontempelli* (Milan: Bompiani, 1938). Bontempelli read these papers publicly between 1937 to 1938, so this would explain Ortese's (mistaken) reference to 1937 in this letter. The second edition of the *Discorsi*, published in 1942, would include another four essays / conferences on Verga, Aretino, Scarlatti, and Verdi. The fifth and definitive edition (1945) would also include an essay on Galileo.

60 Monica Farnetti notes the various works by Ortese that seem to recall several novels by Pirandello. See Farnetti, "Appunti per una storia del bestiario femminile," 279. But she also acknowledges that he is an author whom

Ortese never openly cites. This letter is the only instance in which Ortese reveals her admiration for Pirandello.

61 Bontempelli, *Opere scelte,* 812.

62 Ibid., 813.

63 Moser, *Il futuro,* 118.

64 Ibid., 122 (Letter 20).

65 For a description of her "transformation" into a boy: "Con una forbicina furono dimezzati i capelli. Scarpe di tela bianca e un berretto verde completavano l'abbigliamento. Di me, insomma, nulla rimaneva; l'antica toledana sostituita meravigliosamente da un adolescente svelto e allegro" (R1 447; "With a small scissors my hair was cut off. White canvas shoes and a green beret completed my outfit. In short, nothing was left of me; the old Toledian girl had been marvelously subplanted by a svelte and happy adolescent boy").

66 Bontempelli, *Opere scelte,* 813–14.

67 Moser, *Il futuro,* 121.

68 Ibid., 100 (Letter 3).

69 Ibid., 117 (Letter 17).

70 Ibid., 122 (Letter 20).

71 Ibid., 100 (Letter 3).

72 Ibid., 99.

73 Ibid., 116.

74 See Ortese, *Il mio paese è la notte* (Empirìa: Roma, 1995).

75 A testament of her adoration of Leopardi during those years can be noted in the fact that she penned: "Pellegrinaggio alla tomba di Leopardi nell'imminenza della traslazione dei resti gloriosi," *Gazzetta di Venezia,* 14 February 1939, 3.

76 For an analysis of this point, see Anedda, "Il grido del vero," 268–69.

77 Moser, *Il futuro,* 117 (letter 17). Unfortunately, from the limited information given in the letter, it is difficult to know what writing this is.

78 The figure of Bontempelli, as he appears to be portrayed in *Il porto di Toledo,* is an interesting one. There is a clear correlation to the very minor figure of Bento, who never emerges in person, but who is named occasionally. It is interesting that Bento is an anagram of the first five letters of Bontempelli's name. Described simply as the "scrupoloso e amabile dirigente, di cui potevo fidarmi" ("scrupulous and lovable director, whom I could trust"), Bento, a friend of Damasa's true mentor, D'Orgaz, takes over the direction of the *Gazeta Literaria* from her mentor. According to the letter Damasa receives from her book editor, Bento is among those who had convinced him to publish her work in book format (see R1, 794). The question remains,

however, if the figure of D'Orgaz (who also goes by the name Conra or Maestro d'Armi) is perhaps, in part, reflective of Bontempelli, or if it encompasses only Corrado Pavolini, the first to publish her work when *La Fiera Letteraria* was under his direction. Of course, a "fantastical" autobiography does not lend itself well to the attempt of correlating true events and people to those within the story, so this exercise is destined to render only enigmas. Appropriately, Ortese admittedly described the text as a "nuovo evento fantastico" (CC 84; "new, fantastical event"). Nonetheless, the centrality of Conra for Damasa is clear: "Io devo a Conra, cioè D'Orgaz, come a Rassa, devo a Conra gran parte dell'anima mia. [...] la parte più acuminata mi fu data, come una spada, da Conra" (R1 398–99; "I owe Conra, that is D'Orgaz, much like with Rassa ... I owe Conra a great part of my spirit. [...] the sharpest part, like a sword, was given to me by Conra").

79 Ibid. Here, regarding writing as a creation of an alternative reality, see Moser, "The Poetry of Prose," 449. Monica Farnetti notes Ortese's indebtedness to Leopardi for this concept of the "doppia vista" ("double vision") in Farnetti, *Anna Maria Ortese,* 68.

80 Added in black pen and written by hand. This is the condolence letter that Ortese sent to Masino after Bontempelli's death. Although the letter is signed *Anna,* the handwriting matches Ortese's. In addition, Ortese resided in Milan from Dec. 1959 to July 1961 (see Clerici, *Apparizione e visione,* 349.)

WORKS CITED

Altman, Janet. *Epistolarity: Approaches to a Form.* Columbus: Ohio State University Press, 1982.

Anedda, Antonella. "Il grido del vero: Ortese e Leopardi." In *"Quel libro senza uguali": Le operette morali e il novecento,* ed. Novella Bellucci and Andrea Cortellessa. Rome: Bulzoni, 2000.

Aristotle. *The Art of Rhetoric.* Trans. by John Henry Freese. Cambridge, MA: Harvard University Press, 1926.

Bakhtin, Michael. "Discourse in the Novel." In *The Dialogic Imagination: Four Essays by M.M. Bakhtin.* Ed. Michael Holquist, trans. Carol Emerson and Michael Holquist, 259–422. Austin: University of Texas Press, 1996.

Battista, Adelia. *Ortese segreta: Ritratto intimo di Anna Maria Ortese.* Rome: Minimum Fax, 2008.

Bernardini Napoletano, Francesca, and Giamila Yehya, eds. *Gianna Manzini.* Milan: Fondazione Mondadori, 2005.

Bernardini Napoletano, Francesca, and Marinella Mascia Galateria, eds. *Lettere a Corrado Pavolini: V. Cardarelli – G. Ungaretti.* Rome: Bulzoni, 1989.

– eds. *Scrittrici e intellettuali del Novecento: Paola Masino.* Milan: Fondazione Arnaldo e Alberto Mondadori, 2001.

Bontempelli, Massimo. *Discorsi. Pirandello, Leopardi, D'Annunzio: Tre discorsi di Massimo Bontempelli.* Milan: Bompiani, 1938.

– *L'avventura novecentista.* Florence: Vallecchi, 1938.

– *Opere scelte.* Ed. Luigi Baldacci. Milan: Mondadori, 1978.

Cammarota, Domenico. *Futurismo: Bibliografia di 500 scrittori italiani.* Milan: Skira, 2006.

Cesaretti, Enrico. "Outplaying Kronos' Hunger: Massimo Bontempelli's *Gente nel tempo.*" *Forum Italicum* 2 (Fall 2009): 384–404.

Clerici, Luca. *Apparizione e visione: Vita e opere di Anna Maria Ortese.* Milan: Mondadori, 2002.

– "Sono lieto di questo tu fraterno: cinque lettere di Anna Maria Ortese a Lalla Romano." *Il Giannone* 4, no. 7–8 (January–December 2006): 61–70.

Daybell, James. *Women Letter Writers in Tudor England.* Oxford: Oxford University Press, 2006.

De Caprio, Caterina. "Gli amici di Anna Maria: Natalia Ginzburg e Pietro Citati." *Il Giannone* 4, no. 7–8 (January–December 2006).

de Montaigne, Michel. *Essays of Michel de Montaigne.* Trans. Charles Cotton. Garden City, NY: Doubleday & Comp., 1947.

– *Selections from the Essays.* Trans. and ed. Donald M. Frame. Northbrook, IL: AHM Pub. Corp., 1989.

d'Ina, G., and G. Zaccaria, eds. *Caro Bompiani: Lettere con l'editore.* Milan: Bompiani, 1988.

Emerson, Ralph Waldo. *Representative Men: Seven Lectures.* New York, NY: Modern Library, 1994.

Falqui, Enrico, ed. *Il futurismo: Il novecentismo.* Turin: Edizioni Radio Italiana, 1953.

Farnetti, Monica. *Anna Maria Ortese.* Milan: Mondadori, 1998.

– "Appunti per una storia del bestiario femminile: il caso di Anna Maria Ortese." In *Bestiari del Novecento,* ed. Enza Biagini and Anna Nozoli, 271–83. Rome: Bulzoni, 2001.

Favret, Mary A. *Romantic Correspondence: Women, Politics and the Fiction of Letters.* Cambridge, MA: Cambridge University Press, 1993.

Genette, Gérard. *Figures III.* Paris: Seuil, 1972.

Holquist, Michael, ed. *The Dialogic Imagination.* Trans. Caryl Emerson and Michael Holquist. Austin: University of Texas Press, 1990.

Iser, Wolfgang. "The Reading Process: A Phenomenological Approach." In *Reader Response Criticism from Formalism to Post-Structuralism,* ed. Jane P. Tompkins, 50–69. Baltimore, MD: Johns Hopkins University Press, 1980.

Lavezzi, Gianfranca, Clelia Martignoni, Anna Modena, and Nicoletta Trotta, eds. *Catalogo delle lettere ad Alfonso Gatto (1942–1970).* Pavia: Università degli Studi di Pavia, 2000.

Lejeune, Philippe. *On Autobiography.* Trans. John Paul Eakin. Minneapolis: University of Minnesota Press, 1989.

Mascia Galateria, Marinella. "Anna Maria Ortese epistolografa." In *Convegno di studi su Anna Maria Ortese: Rapallo, sabato 16 maggio 1998,* ed. Francesco De Nicola and Pier Antonio Zannoni, 49–66. Genova: Sagep, 1999.

Moser, Amelia. *"Il futuro è tutto nella notte": Anna Maria Ortese, Massimo Bontempelli and Magic Realism.* PhD diss., Harvard University, 2004.

– "The Poetry of Prose: Anna Maria Ortese's Early Writings." *Italian Poetry Review* 2 (2008).

Motta, Antonio, ed. "'Caro, molto caro La Capria': tre lettere a Raffaele La Capria." *Il Giannone* 4, no. 7–8 (January–December 2006).

Nicodemo, Raffaela, and Rossana Spadaccini, eds. *Anna Maria Ortese: Le carte.* Atti del Convegno di studi Archivio di Stato di Napoli, 7–8 novembre 2006. Naples, Istituto Italiano per gli Studi Filosofici e Archivio di Stato di Napoli, 2009 (Privately printed, not for public sale).

Ortese, Anna Maria. *Alla luce del Sud: Lettere a Pasquale Prunas.* Ed. Renata Prunas and Giuseppe Di Costanzo. Milan: Archinto Editore, 2006.

– *Bellezza, addio: Lettere a Dario Bellezza (1972–1992).* Ed. Adelia Battista. Milan: Archinto, 2011.

– *Il mio paese è la notte.* Rome: Edizioni Empirìa, 1995.

– "La meraviglia e l'innocenza." Interview. In *Le signore della scrittura: Interviste,* ed. Sandra Petrignani, 67–80. Milan: La Tartaruga edizioni, 1984.

Pavolini Hannau, Marcella. *Cinquantanove anni meno un giorno.* Cortona: Calosci, 1983.

Ray, Meredith. *Writing Gender in Women's Letter Collections of the Italian Renaissance.* Toronto: University of Toronto Press, 2009.

Russi, Valentina. "La 'Tigre nel Cielo': Il reale-reale della guerra ne *Il porto di Toledo.*" *Quaderni del '900* 5 (2005): 107–17.

Spadaccini, Rossana, Linda Iacuzio, and Claudia Marilyn Cuminale, eds. *L'Archivio di Anna Mario Ortese: Inventario.* Naples: Archivio di Stato di Napoli & Associazione, 2006.

Trevisan, Myriam. "Da scrittrice a scrittrice: Lettere sulla vita e sull'arte." *Bollettino di Italianistica* 2 (2006): 263–91.

Trilling, Lionel. *Sincerity and Authenticity.* Cambridge, MA: Harvard University Press, 1972.

Urettini, Luigi. "L'irrequieto vagabondaggio di Anna Maria Ortese in due lettere a Giovanni Comisso." *Terra d'Este* 13, no. 26 (2005): 103–16.

Vittori, Maria Vittoria. "Storia di un'amicizia." *Leggendaria* 9 (May–June 1998): 10–11.

Whitman, Walt. *The Complete Poems of Walt Whitman.* Hertfordshire, UK: Wordsworth Editions Limited, 1995.

5 Anna Maria Ortese's Early Short Fiction: A Re-reading of *Angelici dolori*

LUIGI FONTANELLA

Io avevo inoltre la malinconia dell'inattuabilità [...] e con questa lo sgomento vago e crescente ogni giorno più, del dilagare che faceva intorno a noi, gonfia di clamore la civiltà contemporanea ...

(Furthermore, I suffered the melancholy of impracticability [...] and along with it the indefinite fear, growing in me daily, of the flood that gathered around us, contemporary civilization swollen with clamour ...)

Anna Maria Ortese, "Pellirossa"

Some Preliminary Notes

Published 16 April 1937 by Bompiani, *Angelici dolori* (*Angelic Sorrows*) is Anna Maria Ortese's precocious first book of short stories. The author was little more than twenty-two years old at the time. Tommaso Landolfi also debuted that same year with *Dialogo dei massimi sistemi*, and Massimo Bontempelli, the prime sponsor of *Angelici dolori*, not to mention its first reviewer, published his most popular work (what today would be considered a bestseller), *Gente nel tempo*.[1] These three authors, beyond their obvious differences, shared a disposition for what we could very generically call the realm of fantasy. This is, of course, a simple observation that does not pretend to establish any literary relationship between them; but merely intends to diagnose a shared "symptom," apparent in their individual poetics. However, Ortese's readers will effectively encounter a few Landolfian influences in *L'Iguana*, which is one of the most atypical, visionary, and enigmatic novels of the Italian twentieth century.

I said the sponsor of Ortese's book was Massimo Bontempelli, the celebrated creator of magic realism, who had been *accademico d'Italia* since 1930 thanks to Luigi Pirandello's support, as well as an important intellectual leader of the fascist regime, from which he had received benefits and sinecures, though in those years he had already begun to distance himself. It is necessary at this point to contextualize Bontempelli's relationship to the cultural and political landscape of the time. To do so will shed some light on Ortese's turbulent debut. Her first book was, indeed, brutally attacked by two authoritative critics (Antonello Falqui and Giancarlo Vigorelli), whose violently harsh criticisms were dictated more than anything else by the profound ideological and literary differences in opinion they had with Bontempelli himself.

Yet, Bontempelli's writings provide a good deal of evidence for a slow, complex, but certain turn to the left, which is never fully highlighted by critics (with some exceptions), who have always preferred to classify Bontempelli as a mere follower of fascism. I am pressed to recall those instances in his work that have hardly been explored. As early as 1932 with *Decorazioni del "Rex"* (*Decorations of the "Rex"*), which came out in October of that year, and *Contro il decorativo* (*Against Decorative Style*), published in January 1934 (both of which are now available in *Avventura novecentista*, first published in 1938), Bontempelli begins to warn those who are still misled by the equivocation that the fascist regime's new architecture continued to respond to an avant-garde ideal. Between these two works he travelled to South America with Luigi Pirandello, Marta Abba, and Paola Masino (summer–fall 1933). This journey inspired him to write a fascinating little book that – even though it bears a title that is still "dangerous" and only partially mitigated by its subtitle (*Noi, gli Aria: Interpretazione sudamericane*) [*We, the Arias: South American Interpretations*] – already contains sure signs of a break with fascism. Indeed, a critical consciousness of the long duration of Western civilization, of its ethnocentric hegemony and its colonizing violence begins to emerge from his "prismatic" writing, entirely animated by the "marvellous."[2]

The very same year in which this unique book appeared (1934), Bontempelli's play *La fame* (*The Hunger*) was vetoed by fascist censorship officials and was banned from the stage, only two days before its premiere at the Teatro Valle in Rome, through the direct intervention of Mussolini. The writer himself documented the event, adding: "la rivista *Scenario*, che era pronta a pubblicarlo nel numero da uscire dopo la prima rappresentazione, dové scomporre le pagine" ("the journal *Scenario* that was ready to run the piece in the issue that was due to be released right after the first performance had to remove the pages").[3]

In 1936, two years later, Pirandello dies – the intellectual with whom, more than any other, Bontempelli had shared ideas, criticism, and innovation in *mutually fruitful* ways, especially in terms of their theatrical work. That same year, on 23 August, he published an article in the *Gazzetta del popolo*, entitled "I soliti spunti" (later collected in *Avventura novecentista* under a new title "Protezione"). When reread today, it reveals several concrete forms of dissent directed against the Caesarism of the "protectionist" regime, namely, fascism, which was extremely damaging to the free expression of art that then necessarily became "politicized art."

Six months after the publication of "Protezione," precisely 17 January 1937, Bontempelli was invited to give, at the Accademia d'Italia, a commemorative speech on Pirandello. It is an important speech that marks his further departure from the rhetoric of the regime in favour of a poetics of "candour" (the speech was, in fact, entitled "Pirandello o del candore"), to which he had always identified his own "interior atmospheres." In the speech, Pirandello's work is essentially regarded as an accusation, a "condanna implacabile" ("relentless condemnation"), of an era. The overall feeling of *nudità* that it yields coincides with that of *candore*: "Quel candore nudo, dal quale ha preso vita tutta la sua visione, coincide con la aspirazione alla povertà, su cui egli ha dato l'ultimo salute" ("That exposed candour, from which his whole vision took its life, coincides with the aspiration to poverty, on which he lavished his final farewell").[4] A "poverty" that screams, evidently, with the concept of power and well-being bandied about by the fascist system: an antinomian warning to its "fullness," to the bloated nature of fascism's decoration, its imperial pseudo-pomp, its glitter and feathers.

In July 1937, just three months after the publication of Anna Maria Ortese's *Angelici dolori*, Bontempelli will return to the concept of poverty as an equivalent of "nudity," simplicity, and candour in an essay on Leopardi ("Leopardi l' 'uomo solo'"), referring in particular to the "Canto notturno di un pastore errante dell'Asia" ("Night Song of a Wandering Asian Shepherd").

Bontempelli's detachment from fascism is especially evident in his commemorative speech on D'Annunzio ("D'Annunzio o del martirio"), given at Pescara the following year (27 November 1938). Here he articulates his critical stance in the form of a clear opposition even amidst a tangle of ambiguous tones and sophisticated insinuations. Bontempelli is, in fact, interested in the contemplative D'Annunzio (that of *Alcyone* and *Contemplazione della Morte*), not the worldly, indulgent, and sensual Nietzschean *Übermensch* behind his previous work (*Il piacere*, *L'innocente*,

Trionfo della morte, etc.). D'Annunzio, ultimately, "completed his task." His work "concludes an era that, in the name of action, violence and the will to power had come to reject meditation, thought, even poetry itself."[5] Hence Bontempelli's propensity for liquidation: the death of the great Poet (or *Vate*) is, in conclusion, a simple ending and not a "grand finale" as his "spectacular and complex" life could have demanded. A few years later, with a more serene retrospective eye, far from the conditioning urgency of this speech, reflecting yet again on D'Annunzio and the rhetoric of the regime, he declares unequivocally:

> D'Annunzio fu l'uomo più retorico e più vanitoso del nostro tempo. E Mussolini è stato l'attuazione politica della vanità retorica dannunziana, e ha potuto operare sopra una massa borghese imbevuta di dannunziana cafoneria.
>
> (D'Annunzio was the most rhetorical and vain man of our time. And Mussolini was the political implementation of D'Annunzio's rhetorical vanity, and he was able to operate on the middle-class masses imbued with D'Annunzio's boorishness.)[6]

An unambiguous assessment, he leaves no doubt and no longer clings to vague sophistry. Following this speech, Bontempelli was expelled from the Accademia d'Italia and he was suspended from every occupation. His P.N.F. (National Fascist Party) card was withdrawn, and he was sentenced to twelve years of confinement, despite the fact that he had the sympathy of Giuseppe Bottai, minister of education and a prominent member of the National Fascist Party. This could be considered the official, decisive moment of his departure from the fascist regime, which is underscored by yet another very significant episode from his biography that occurred a few months before his speech on D'Annunzio. In 1938, a year that was in many ways decisive for Bontempelli's new political, social, and literary agendas, the chair in Italian literature at the University of Florence – which up to that time had been held by Attilio Momigliano and was revoked from him for racial reasons – was offered to Bontempelli, who refused it: an important event that was reported in the weekly magazine *Centomila: Dizionario storico enciclopedico di molti italiani d'oggi.*[7]

Against this larger cultural and political backdrop, Bontempelli personally recommended that Bompiani publish Ortese's stories. Is it possible to assume that the author of *Minnie la candida* (*Candid Minnie*) saw in the young Neapolitan writer the consummate embodiment of the ideal he had in mind of a "poor" and "simple" writer (which are, after all, two fatally Ortesian adjectives)? A writer whose equation "poverty = candour" naturally placed her on an anti-D'Annunzian level? A writer, after all, who – as he himself wrote in his initial review of *Angelici dolori* – exceeds all methodological distinctions including that of genre, in particular that which he called the "distinzione tra abilità ed estro" ("distinction between ability and creative inspiration"), whose most convincing and fascinating effects derive precisely "da uno stato di innocenza" ("from a state of innocence")?

On the occasion of her debut, Ortese herself also confirms the reference to D'Annunzio, however, by denying his presence among the authors the young Anna Maria held dear. The back cover of the original 1937 edition presents the following disarming statement that is worth quoting:

> Sono nata a Roma nel Giugno del 1914. Per l'impiego statale che mio padre occupava, ebbi la fortuna di mutare spesso residenza, conoscendo così gran parte dell'Italia Meridionale, e, dal 1914 al 1927, anche la Libia. E a Tripoli terminai le elementari. Ora sono a Napoli da nove anni, sempre in questo quartiere del porto, dove conosco pochissima gente, e concerti letterati. Amicizie di coetanei nemmeno ne ho, perché non ho frequentato più le scuole. Un corso di avviamento professionale, iniziato nei primi mesi della mia vita napoletana, lo lasciai quasi subito, non resistendo alla reclusione, e allo studio imposto. E furono gli ultimi banchi. Vita solitaria, dunque, in una specie di isola, dove le notizie del mondo arrivano fioche e disperse. Però, mi piace.
>
> Sono ignorante. Non conosco né i greci né i latini; poco dei moderni; nulla o quasi dei modernissimi. *D'Annunzio è per me, con riverenza, un Ignoto.*
>
> (I was born in Rome in June of 1914. Due to my father's work for the State, I had the good fortune of moving around a lot, getting to know much of Southern Italy, and, from 1914 to 1927, Libya. And in Tripoli I finished elementary school. I've now been in Naples for nine years, always in this neighbourhood near the port, where I know very few people and literary concerts. I don't have any friends my own age either, because I stopped going to school. I left almost immediately a professional development course that I started in the first months of my life in Naples, resisting imprisonment and the studies imposed on me. And from the back of the classroom. A solitary life, then, on an island of sorts, where news of the world arrives muted and scattered. But, I like it.

I am ignorant. I know neither Greek nor Latin; little of the moderns; nothing or almost nothing of the very most recent writers. *D'Annunzio is for me, with reverence, an Unknown.*)[8]

The Adolescent Epic

Working "sulle scale di casa" ("on the steps of the house") or at her "tavolaccio" ("rough-hewn table") in the room known as the "stanza d'angolo" ("corner room") of the humble Neapolitan apartment on the top floor of the "misera casa gialla" ("poor yellow house") at Via del Piliero 29, Ortese mostly wrote the thirteen stories that make up *Angelici dolori* over the course of just a few short months.[9] The whole stretch of houses overlooking the harbour on Via del Piliero, which was destroyed in the bombings of December 1942 and the subsequent urban restructuring of the area near the port of Naples, are evocatively described not only in her autobiography, *Il porto di Toledo,* but also in the beautiful pages of "Via del mare," a story Ortese published in the journal *Meridiano di Roma*[10] that was recently recovered by Luca Clerici.[11]

Regarding the short period of time in which she wrote *Angelici dolori*: if you exclude the first three pieces that constitute a story of their own, starting from "Quartiere" (the fourth story of *Angelici dolori,* which appeared in *L'Italia Letteraria,* 5 April 1936), all the other stories had but a brief gestation period lasting from April to early December of that same year. Further testimony is found in a letter dated 4 January 1937, written by Anna Maria to the editor Valentino Bompiani, in which one infers not only the successful conclusion of the collection and consignment of the manuscript to the publisher, but also the polite request for a "definitive agreement" for its publication. The agreement would arrive from Bompiani just a few days later: "Sono molto lieto di aver trovato in Lei uno scrittore di tanta ricchezza e di così singolare potenza. E sarò lieto di pubblicare la Sua raccolta di novelle" ("I am very pleased to have found in you a writer of such wealth and of such rare power. I will be happy to publish your collection of short stories").[12]

Considering that Ortese composed the first two stories in the collection ("Isola" and "Pellerossa") in 1934, the exceptional precocity of her genius, nearly unequalled in Italian twentieth-century fiction, is self-evident. Such precocity is found in only a very few writers; the first that come to mind are the Tommaso Landolfi of "Maria Giuseppa," a short story he wrote when he was just twenty years old; Silvio D'Arzo, who, at little more than twenty, wrote *All'insegna del buon corsiero*; the Alberto

Moravia of *Gli indifferenti,* written at the same age; and Giose Rimanelli who wrote *Tiro al piccione* when he was only eighteen. We should also remember that Ortese's earliest creative writing dates back to 1932–33, at which time she turned to poetry in the wake of her brother Manuele's death, on 16 January 1933. This tragic event would forever mark the inner life of Anna Maria, who was only eighteen years old at the time.[13]

The title Ortese "chose" for her first volume of short fiction presents an interesting history. In Paolo Mauri's interview with Anna Maria, published in 1996 in *La Repubblica,*[14] the writer attributes the paternity of *Angelici dolori* to Massimo Bontempelli. But a quick glance at the titles of the stories reveals that one of them bears the same title of *Angelici dolori,* a story that Ortese had already published under the pseudonym Franca Nicosi in *L'Italia Letteraria,*[15] whose new series was in fact directed by Bontempelli himself. However, in his review of Ortese's volume, it was Giancarlo Vigorelli who mentions a line from a poem by the French poet Albert Samain, entitled "Nuit blanche," in which the original phrase appears ("Pour respirer tous nos bonheurs avec emphase, / Sur le piano triste, où trembleront des pleurs, / Tes mains feront chanter d'*angéliques douleurs* / Et je t'écouterai, silencieux d'extase").[16] Samain's poem is part of a collection entitled *Le jardin de l'infante* (*The Infant's Garden,* 1893). Curiously, "Infanta" is the name that Ortese will later give to a black Madonna, the protagonist of one of her most extraordinary stories found in the later collection that also bears the very same name: *L'Infanta sepolta* (*The Buried Infant*).

Let's take a closer look at the stories in *Angelici dolori.*

If "Isola" ("Island") is little more than a captivating narrative exercise between fairy tale and fantasy projection, entirely pervaded by a "somma amorosa angoscia" ("supreme amorous angst"), it nevertheless quickly allows the reader to become familiar with some of Ortese's narrative techniques, as well as with the truly "isolated" place, something like a small self-sufficient realm, in which the young author spent her adolescence. Apart from a certain general stylistic inconsistency and syntactic extravagance, such as the frequent use of double and triple adjectives, or the inclusion of obsolete terms and phrases (also found in Ortese's early poems "avida figgevo l'occhio avanti," "la luna non era apparita," etc.), what is most striking is her clearly defined ability to transfigure reality, which will become her stylistic signature. To put it in her words, Ortese mines the imagination's ability to transcend the sad straits of our private lives, its "squallore e la pena delle mortali vie" ("squalor and the suffering of mortal ways"). In this realm of complete fantasy conjured by the narrator's imagination, "the torments of mankind" vanish as if by enchantment, and there are no longer any "esigenze sociali, non rimproveri di religione" (AD 17; "social demands, no religious reprimands").[17]

More important and mature is "Pellerossa" ("Redskin"), the story that marks Ortese's true official debut.[18] As indeed happened to eight of the thirteen stories of *Angelici dolori*, even this story was absorbed later into the text of her autobiography *Il porto di Toledo* (1975) and "ne costituisce uno dei centri simbolici e tematici" ("constitutes one of its symbolic and thematic centres").[19]

And "Pellerossa" is truly as suggestive as it is poignant, born as an "absurd and plaintive" dream (AD 21), in the so-called "corner room" that looks out over the harbour. In this little room, devoid of furniture, Anna Maria imagined adventurous voyages with her beloved brother Manuele on an imaginary ship dubbed the "Maria Rosaria," "sopra i mari aperti del mondo, quali l'Atlantico e l'iridato (nella mente) Pacifico. Lui avrebbe capitanato la nave, io, provvista di colori tedeschi portati da casa, avrei dipinto i paesaggi e la gente colorata di quei posti" (AD 21; "out onto the open seas of the world, like the Atlantic or the mind's smiling Pacific. He was to captain the ship, and I, equipped with German paints from home, was to paint the landscapes and the colorful people of those places" [MW2 41]). The central theme of this story was born precisely of this passion of hers for drawing and painting: the young woman's idea is to paint a life-size portrait of a Native American to hang on an entire wall of the room. With an increasingly inventive frenzy Anna Maria sets herself to work and draws on a huge sheet of packing paper the Sioux warrior, to whom she gives the name Cavallo Bianco, or White Horse. The following excerpt is rife with Ortese's intense expressive delicacy.

> Trascorrevo avanti a lui ore intere di fremente analisi e poi, senza aver trovato rimedio alcuno, andavo via, sospirando, per non essere sopraffatta dalla tenerezza che lo sguardo dell'Eroe – grave sdegnoso dolorante – sapeva destarmi. Sentivo di amarlo con disperazione, ma più tale sentimento cresceva, più la coscienza come fuori di me stessa, mi rappresentava quell'idea di ridicolo, della grottesca inverosimiglianza di lui, dell'assurdità della sua presenza in una casa come la mia d'impiegati e studenti, borghese. (AD 24–25)

> (I spent whole hours of fervent analysis before him, and then, having found no possible remedy, would heave a sigh and leave the room, as so not to be wholly overwhelmed by the tenderness that my Hero's gaze – heavy, pained

and disdainful – was able to arouse within me. I loved him desperately, and couldn't have denied it. Yet the more this feeling grew, the more I my conscious mind, as though from somewhere outside of me, plagued me with a sense of the ridiculous, of his grotesque lack of verisimilitude, of the absurdity of his presence in a house like ours – that bourgeois home of white-collar workers and high school students. [MW2 46])

At this point she is already on the threshold of becoming a pure visionary: the young woman attributes human feelings and reactions to the Paper Hero. Next to him she then feels the need to draw "un gruppo di Rivoltosi Messicani, in un cortile illuminato da scialbe lanterne" (AD 26; "a group of Mexican Revolutionaries, in a courtyard lit by sooty lanterns" [MW2 47]). Her mind dreams up memorable deeds to the tune of a popular verse, *Libertad, haz que dulce resene,* as "lagrime di riverente estasi" ("tears of reverent ecstasy") run down her face.

These "amici più diletti" ("most beloved friends"), all of whom are products of her vivid adolescent imagination, will inevitably have to disappear just as that fabulous phase of life, so closely connected to it, is destined to disappear. After a while, in fact, her other brothers, "ragionevolmente fatti grandi e autoritari" ("having reasonably taken on an air of authoritative importance"), no longer tolerate the crazy posters hanging on the walls, which will dramatically have to be removed. Here the story reaches its most evocative and disturbing climax:

mi furono strappati tutti, portati via, chissà dove, che il cuore ne sanguinava segreto. Ed ecco che il Sioux, scendendo, forse per il curvarsi della carta, piegò la grande testa sul petto, particolare che non scordo e mi strinse d'irrefrenabile angoscia, quasi fosse stato un segno ultimo d'addio, fatto intendere solo a me che tanto gli avevo voluto bene, sempre. *Ciudadanos, morir es mejor,* pareva singhiozzassero ora tutti, mentre l'indiano aggiustatasi una penna in bocca scendeva adagio dal muro con la suprema pace ironica della gente sua. Caro Cavallo Bianco, non lo vidi mai più. (AD 29)

(all of them were stripped away from me, carried off who knows where, leaving my heart in bloody tatters. And the Sioux, as he descended, owing perhaps to the buckling of the paper, bent his mammoth head to his breast, which is a detail I always remember. It gripped me with uncontainable anguish, almost as though he had signalled a final gesture of farewell, intended only for me, who so greatly had loved him, always. *Ciudadanos, morir es mejor,* all of them now seemed to sob; whereas the Indian, having slipped a feather between his teeth, slowly descended from the wall with the supreme sardonic peace of his race. Dear White Horse. I was never to see again. [MW2 52])

A shocking sequence in the film *Fellini's Roma* comes immediately to mind. The sequence presents the underground discovery of a fresco that had languished in the dark for centuries, hidden from everyone. As soon as it is exposed to the brutal light of day the ancient wall painting fades and withers away in an instant, as if to confirm the definitive loss of a glorious era.

A densely metaphorical story, "Pellerossa" represents the height of Ortese's already mature and compelling mastery of storytelling. Among other things, blurring the dimensions of autobiography and fantasy, the story also underscores the author's inability to confront the practicalities of life in modern society, from which she will always seek refuge in the sailing ship "Maria Rosaria" ("Strano a dirsi, io non posso fare a meno di attenderla," AD 30; "It may seem strange, but I can't help awaiting her arrival" [MW2 53]).

Many years later, in his biography *Apparizione e visione*, Luca Clerici writes:

Quando la andavo a trovare a Rapallo, in Via Mameli, Anna Maria mi riceveva nella camera di fronte all'ingresso. Pochi i mobili: la poltrona su cui dormiva con accanto il posacenere a stelo, un tavolino ordinatissimo – sopra l'Olivetti *Lettera 22* e le cartelle dei dattiloscritti su cui stava lavorando. Davanti alla poltrona, il letto inutilizzato da chissà quanto tempo e una piccola libreria cubica, di legno, stipata di volumetti in edizione economica (soprattutto la vecchia "BUR"). Alle pareti, poche riproduzioni: fra queste, una stampa seppiata (o forse soltanto una vecchia fotografia ingiallita) raffigurava alcune tende indiane distanti fra loro. Sulla soglia, dei pellirossa che fumano, accucciati, qualche squaw e dei piccoli dal viso dipinto: l'immagine simbolica di una fanciullezza che Anna non ha mai rinnegato.

(When I went to visit her in Rapallo, in Via Mameli, Anna Maria received me in the room opposite the entryway. Sparsely furnished: the armchair in which she slept with an ashtray on a stand next to it, an extremely organized desk – with an Olivetti *Lettera 22* typewriter on it and a stack of typewritten pages on which she was working next to it. In front of the armchair, a bed that hadn't been used in who knows how long and a small cube-shaped bookshelf, made of wood, overflowing with cheap paperbacks (mostly old

> BUR editions). On the walls, a couple of prints: among them, a sepia-toned reproduction (or perhaps merely an old yellowing photograph) depicting a group of Indian tents each different from the other. At the threshold, a group of red-skinned Indians smoking, crouching, a couple of squaws and some children with painted faces: a symbolic image from the childhood that Anna never rejected.)[20]

The story perhaps most intensely steeped in Bontempelli's influence is "Solitario lume" ("Fehla and the Melancholy Light"), which is entirely enveloped in a mysterious atmosphere that is suspended, played out between that which is visual and visionary in the soul of the young female observer / narrator. Between the visionary and the fictional that are inextricably intertwined, the lights she observes in the distance constantly change like her thoughts; especially "him," the "Solitario lume," which in its / his uniqueness is the "emblema di ogni fede, di ogni idealità, di ogni amorosa trasfigurazione" ("emblem of every faith, every ideal, every loving transfiguration").[21]

I hinted at a vague Bontempellian influence thinking primarily of the stories collected in *La donna dei miei sogni* (*My Dream Woman*) and *Galleria degli schiavi* (*Slaves' Gallery*), two volumes that Bontempelli published in 1926 and 1934 respectively. In particular, as far as "Solitario lume" is concerned, I have in mind "Quasi d'amore," one of Bontempelli's mature narrative gems, which he himself called a "piccola avventura misteriosa e patetica" ("mysterious and pathetic little adventure"), in short, a "miracolo quotidiano," *based entirely on the gaze,* just as "Solitario lume." Critics have never recognized this evocative Bontempellian interference, nor indeed has Ortese ever mentioned it – regardless of whether or not she was familiar with Bontempelli's narrative. Yet it would not be too risky to assume that Anna Maria might have had a chance to read something by the writer from Como, whose books over the course of the twenties and thirties were widely disseminated throughout Italy.

More convincing, however, in the case of "Solitario lume," is the possible influence of Katherine Mansfield, whom Ortese had read thanks to Corrado Pavolini, the director of *L'Italia Letteraria.* In a letter to Antonio Franchini dated 18 March 1941, in which, declaring her sincere enthusiasm for the stories "Preludio" and "Alla baia ("furono vette illuminate dal sole quelle che io guardai. Non avevo mai visto una bellezza simile"; "they were peaks illuminated by the sun those that I gazed upon. I had never seen such beauty"),[22] Ortese ambiguously hints at the possibility of Mansfield's influence: "Non ricordo se Katherine Mansfield egli

[Pavolini] me la fece conoscere perché aveva già letto un mio lungo racconto, 'Solitario lume,' o se io scrissi 'Solitario lume' perché avevo letto questi racconti" ("I cannot remember whether he [Pavolini] brought Katherine Mansfield to my attention because he had already read my long story, 'Solitario lume,' or if I wrote 'Solitario lume' because I had read these stories").[23] The fact of the matter is that "Solitario lume," like the stories by Mansfield she explicitly mentioned, contains the same delicate hypnagogic, hallucinatory dimension characteristic of the New Zealand writer, a trembling, emotionally charged, and magical atmosphere that is completely absorbed in the tenuous plot.

"Quartiere" ("Neighbourhood"), the fourth story in *Angelici dolori* that had also already appeared in *L'Italia Letteraria*,[24] is a sort of gallery of characters inserted into a para-autobiographical description of the ("pezzente" ["ragamuffin"]) neighbourhood in which Ortese lived as a girl. She presents the popular worship of the neighbourhood's two Madonnas: one called "La Regina" (who "veniva posta in barca con azzurra vela," [AD 48; "would be placed on a boat with a blue sail"] in a lavish procession to the sea), and another, whose celebration was "più calma e come segreta" (AD 48; "more calm as if secret"), called "La Moreneta" (who anticipates the "Black Madonna" in the *Infanta sepolta*). She also presents a vivid and moving description of three extremely poor Tunisian children who live in the house across the street, especially Stefano, the proud yet sensitive little boy "dalla voce maschia e dolcissima" ("with a virile yet sugary sweet voice"). Delicately written with tip of her pen, the story also contains incisive wisdom: in it Ortese poignantly describes life in the poor neighbourhoods of Naples, a life "oscillante tra l'incanto e la tristezza, tra i cieli e la squallida gente" (AD 51; "oscillating between enchantment and sadness, between the heavens and the unwashed masses"). To these same neighbourhoods, from Forcella to Toledo, Anna Maria will return with much greater awareness and critical distance, and without her original genuine enthusiasm, in a bitter later story, the famous "Un paio di occhiali," which is certainly one of the masterpieces of her short fiction (see Lucia Re's essay in this volume).

By now the indissoluble link between autobiography and literary invention in the stories in *Angelici dolori* should be clear. Anna Maria often invokes members of her family as both real and imaginary characters in very direct ways, in particular her brother Manuele (who will remain forever in her heart and whom we saw as her "accomplice" in "Pellirossa") and her twin Antonio. Ortese specifically refers to the latter in the story "Il capitano" ("The Captain"), which also features their youngest brother

Franco. Antonio had in fact become an accredited naval captain. More than anyone else it was Anna Maria who had helped him with his schoolwork. As a child she loved to "make tents" with Antonio on the terrace of the house, with the help of little Franco ("sopra ogni cosa mi beava il ritrovarmi coi fratelli, accolta tra loro ch'erano giovinetti valorosi e domani entravano rispettati nella vita," AD 57; "more than anything else being with my brothers made me happy, being accepted by those young men who were valorous and would later enter into life respected"). It is especially in the company of her brothers (who, impelled by the same emotional force, tended to gravitate to her) that Anna Maria lives by dreaming and dreams by living her adolescence like a "warrior." The action and effects of the two verbs (to live, to dream) intersect one another continuously in her lively mind. Truly extraordinary, therefore, is the transfiguring power of this evocative story that concludes with the final assault of the other family members who are opposed to the "pioneering" dimension of the three siblings and their desire to camp on the terrace of the house. "Coloro" or "those guys" (as the hostile family members are called) will be metamorphosed into a gang of armed men who will chase the three down from their beloved terrace, the theatre of their imaginative projections.

The end of this adventure serves as the prelude to another adventure, the partnership between the two brothers, which marks the end of their fantastic epic adolescence as well as the conclusion of the story. Shortly thereafter, in fact, a ship (a real one this time) will come to take the "Captain" away to America ("Egli scendeva rapido verso il mondo, com'è destino dei fratelli, chino il cuore su affetti suoi, propri," AD 65; "He quickly descended back to the world, as is the fate of brothers, heart bowed on his own affections").

Imbued with an emotional and inventive intensity, but always kept under lucid control, "Il Capitano" seems to emblematize the "mythical" period of Ortese's adolescence as well as the general inspirational force that connects all the stories in *Angelici dolori*: namely, a Leopardian sense of detachment, perceived as irreparable, from a pubescent stage of life, studded with illusions, to the phase of maturity that not everyone manages to fully accept. And while for the majority of human beings it amounts to a brief moment that is quickly overcome, for others (in this case, for the young Anna Maria) this "overcoming" was somehow precluded, both by environmental conditions and, above all, by a sense of profound loneliness (or better, a feeling of "separateness") that began to grip the writer very early in her life, but of which she was the proud custodian. Precisely this "desperation" together with the "thrill" of adolescence would stir up the phantasms and projections that inevitably became the material of her early fiction as a sort of compensation.

In the next four stories, "Angelici dolori" ("Angelic Sorrows"), "L'avventura" ("The Escapade"), "Il sogno" ("The Dream"), and "La penna dell'Angelo" ("The Angel's Feather"), which had previously appeared in *L'Italia Letteraria*[25] under the pseudonym Franca Nicosi, the feeling of love makes its entrance, albeit hedged in with delirium, hope, anxiety, and emotional instability. It is exactly her "first love" as it is announced peremptorily in the incipit of the first of these four stories: the one that brings "angelici dolori" ("angelic sorrows") with it, fits of passion and trepidation, enthusiasm and hesitation, apprehension and the purest joys, tears, and happiness. The young man with whom the protagonist has fallen in love is considered a true "magician." She loves to converse with him in his "heavenly dwelling"; "e non tanto per sete della sua dottrina, quanto della sua voce e la luce dei suoi occhi" (AD 71; "and not so much out of a thirst for his learning, as for his voice and the light of his eyes").

He is an "arcane" character, difficult to identify, who in the stories in question goes by the name of Enrico. In his presence the young woman experiences a diffuse tremor, and yet, paradoxically, in that "trembling" she exhibits all the defiance of a girl in love, all of its disruptive power, delight, and wonder. In fact, the mere sight or sound of Enrico, her "impossible boyfriend," her "dear friend and true child," casts an ineffable spell on her:

> è un autentico fanciullo, come non ho forse dimostrato abbastanza. Vederlo, udirlo, è un incanto. Egli possiede certa grazia e purezza nel piegare il viso bianco sulla spalla, certa ironia e calore nel fissare ed esclamare, certa bontà e anzi misericordia gioconda nel venire accanto a una ragazzetta povera, che l'Anima s'è naturalmente ammalata. Non vi era forse, prima di lui, idea di Angelo, Celeste Giovane che sognare sarebbe delirio, e toccare sacrilegio. Egli non poteva essere il fidanzato di me: era ricco e, per suo carattere, naturalmente portato alla gloria e ai molteplici incontri con sublimi donne ... (AD 79)

> (he was a real boy, as I have perhaps not yet fully demonstrated. To see him, to hear him, is enchanting. He has a certain grace and purity in folding his white face into his shoulder, a certain irony and warmth in staring and exclaiming, a certain abundance and a rather joyous charity in approaching a poor little girl, whose Soul has naturally been taken ill. Perhaps there

> wasn't, before him, the idea of an Angel, Celestial Young Man whom to dream would be a delirium, to touch sacrilege. He could never be my boyfriend: he was rich and, for his character, naturally inclined to glory and to many encounters with sublime women ...)

Who is this young "magician" that the narrator now calls "Signore," now calls "autentico fanciullo," now calls "Enrico il Cattivo," now calls "Professore"? Most likely, "Enrico," a few years older than Anna Maria, is to be identified as Aldo Romano, a pupil of Gioacchino Volpe, member of the Italian Communist Party and an intellectual among the most active. Ortese's description of the young man in these four stories corresponds to the physiognomy of the future historian. She is secretly and madly in love with the young "professor." Anna loves taking walks with him on the promenade near the sea. But it is an impossible love: Romano is engaged to the beautiful Adriana Capocci, her closest friend. Luca Clerici, in his careful biographical research, informs us that Aldo Romano's name appears only twice in the Ortese archives (and I summarize from his book): the first in a letter dated 12 August 1936 addressed to Bontempelli on the subject of the story "Quartiere," delivered to him by Alberto Consiglio as a result of Romano's interest. The second reference is found in an unpublished poem, the opening lines of which read: "L'abbiamo visto insieme questo piccolo mare / in cui, la sera, si riflettono i lumi / delle case; insieme / l'abbiamo contemplato sfiorandoci le mani, / ma così non sarà più mai, / o mio amico, giovane Romano" ("We saw this little sea together / in which, come evening, reflect the lights / of the houses; together / we contemplated it, our hands touching, / but it won't be like this ever again, / O my friend, young Romano").[26] It is he who later, again in Ortese's writing, will be called "Lemano" for its assonance with his real name.[27] With this young man the girl has oneiric adventures that she experiences with a "bewildered soul." As if in a dream, she even imagines a life in which they live together in a "quieta e limpida casetta dai vetri gialli" ("quiet and crystal-clear house with yellow windows") in Brittany, facing the frothy ocean.

Rather than present organic plotlines, these "love" stories display an extremely fragile state of mind in a very disorderly and delicate way. They effectively express what the young woman ultimately calls "*l'impressione fantastica di una 'irrealtà'*" (AD 93; "*the fantastic impression of a 'non-reality'*"). It is the first time that Ortese uses this key word to describe her narrative imagination. Many years later, returning to the autobiographical vicissitudes described in the novel *Il porto di Toledo*, she eventually refers to them as "ricordi di una vita irreale" ("memories of an unreal life").

Love – still embodied by Enrico – even has the miraculous power to temporarily "save" one from death, as indeed happens in the fourth of these stories ("La penna dell'angelo," "The Angel's Feather"). In this tale of madness and death, the sick soul of the young woman, "divisa tra fierezza naturale e celeste docilità" (AD 97; "torn between natural arrogance and celestial docility") and as if "fatta straordinariamente acuta dall'aria e dall'ora" (AD 97; "made extraordinarily acute by the air and the hour"), will be miraculously rescued by her beloved Enrico, who appears at her bedside shortly after the arrival of nine beautiful young angels "vestiti di un mantello di foggia militare d'un azzurro intenso" ("dressed in military style robes of deep blue"). He, the tenth ("il Capo" or "Chief"), invites her for a long walk "on the soft shore" of the sea. Trembling, she gives him the blue feather that she had only just taken, "cieca di gioia e cauta" ("blinded by joy yet cautious"), from one of the young angels.

But the young woman's pleasant illusion will not last long. After boarding a boat headed to sea, Enrico cruelly declares that he is taking her back "to her dark house." And that's not all: he will soon have to leave her as he is about to marry ("'io me ne vado' egli terminò con certa ineffabile brutalità ... 'Ben presto, signorina. Ho da sposarmi io. Una grande mattina azzurra, lei potrà assistere, in un angolo della chiesa, alle liete nozze del suo amico'" AD 103; "'I'm leaving,' he concluded with a certain ineffable brutality ... 'Very soon, young lady. I will be married. One beautiful blue morning, you will witness, from a corner of the church, the joyous wedding of your friend'").

The story ends with the young woman lying on the bottom of the boat with her burden of dashed hopes. A disheartening ending, in which her pain all of a sudden becomes "il male della terra, del sangue, delle lagrime; il terribile e squisito male di che mai nessuna celeste quiete potrà compensare coloro che bene a fondo lo seppero" (AD 104; "the pain of the earth, of blood and tears; the terrible and exquisite pain for which no celestial peace will ever be able to compensate those who have thoroughly plunged its depths").

"We Were Poor Primitive Siblings"

Her love for an impossible boyfriend having failed, the young protagonist seems to seek ever more shelter in her brothers' love and in an unrelated world entirely constructed to scale in her imagination. The last few stories in *Angelici dolori* constitute a vertiginous psychic regression that gives rise, as if by enchantment, to fantastic and idyllic places, magical encounters, and even mystical apparitions. The reader is swept away – by the sheer force of fantasy – to New Zealand (in "La vita primitive," "The Primitive Life"), a remote corner of the world in which the brother Giovanni and the narrator build themselves a "marinaresca casetta" ("seaside cottage") facing the Pacific. Here, far from the deafening bombardment of civilization, the two siblings intend to live in communion with the beauty of creation, in a ceaseless phantasmagoria of colour. Alone and blessed, nourished solely by their immaculate familial love, they eventually feel the need to kneel and pray to "l'Autore e Signore di tali stupende cose" (AD 109; "the Author and Lord of such wonderful things"). It is a significant moment in Ortese's narrative psychology, which, as we will see, will expand in a transcendent key over the course of the whole next story.

This transcendent turn serves, among other things, to compensate for the weaknesses or inadequacies of human existence; to calm the "pain" that we thought we had averted by fleeing to distant, though imaginary, lands. This is an extremely important consideration that the narrator nonchalantly states over the course of the story.

Therefore also the "vita beata," as lived through the power of her imagination, is destined to fade away in precisely the moment in which rational awareness prevails in the face of a Leopardian notion of nature as an indifferent force that is ignorant of our suffering (Leopardi's "dolci illusioni" irresistibly come to mind). The author concludes bitterly:

> Sentivo per la prima volta, precisamente, irrimediabilmente, la superficialità infernale di questa situazione. E anche l'affetto per Enrico era, in me, una amata esasperazione; l'amore per il Primitivo un meditato tormento. Tutto in me – affetti, speranze, dolcezze, meravigliose sofferenze – era l'artificioso frutto di una fantasia perdutamente invaghita del bello, della mirabile Compostezza, sorgente, splendida come un fiore, dal gioco brutale dei moti e delle attività umane ...
>
> Fuori il Mare parlava sempre; il Mare che nulla sapeva. (AD 119)

(I felt for the first time, precisely, irreparably, the infernal superficiality of this situation. And my affection for Enrico was, in me, a beloved exasperation; my love for the Primitive an intentional torment. Everything in me – feelings, hopes, joys, marvellous sufferings – was the artificial fruit of an

> imagination hopelessly enamoured of the beautiful, of the wonderful Composure, surging, splendid like a flower, from the brutal game of the movements and activities of men ...
>
> Outside the Sea spoke continuously; the Sea that knew nothing.)

Hence seeking solace in a supernatural dimension as a possible remedy for or redemption of our earthbound ills is almost inevitable. Having just mentioned it in the analysis of "La vita primitiva," the transcendent dimension occupies an important place in the next story , "La villa" ("The Villa"), which is the third to last in the collection. This story demands a close reading. The narrator (Anna Maria herself) has become extremely wealthy thanks to her writing (we are fully ensconced, from the very beginning of the story, in its fantastic atmosphere), and she now lives in an immense and gorgeous mansion, far from the city and her family. The woman goes in her elegant carriage to visit her elderly mother, known as "la Principessa," or Princess, who lives alone in a modest apartment since all of her other children are either married or dead. Her only consolations are the kitten Anima that she habitually keeps on her lap and the memories of her children, including the indelible memory of Manuele, who died in his twenties. The daughter has come to bring the Principessa to live with her in the beautiful villa. Once they have arrived, after a journey "di tre giorni e tre notti, traverso città maravigliose e praterie immense" (AD 123; "of three days and three nights through marvelous cities and enormous meadows" [MW2 61]), the story shortly thereafter converges on a purely surreal atmosphere: the two women are greeted by none other than their beloved Manuele, who is alive and well! Or has he been brought back to life? There are still more surprises in store for the reader. Among the inhabitants of this idyllic place is "the Lord Jesus himself," who at one point appears to the Principessa bathed "in una gran luce ovale, tra candida e vermiglia [...], vestito di bianco, col suo mantello rosso di operaio" (AD 123–24; "in a great oval of light, between white and vermilion [...], dressed in white, his red worker's cape"). That's not all. In the garden of the villa, in "a red, Chinese-style pavilion," lives also the Lord's Mother, who goes by the name "Regina" and is described as being "so fine and elegant." She is in name and in deed the Queen of the Garden, as she is consummately devoted to the countless flowers that she lovingly cultivates and waters every day. The following excerpt captures the intense transfiguring effects of the subtly hyperreal, chromatic, transcendental atmosphere:

> Era uscita, sulla soglia, la Madre del Signore, così fine ed elegante come sempre è stata, col suo manto di seta celeste ombreggiante gli occhi neri e arguti, la bocca rosea, il volto sorridente. Con un piccolo innaffiatoio laccato di verde, andava innaffiando tra l'ombra cupa dei castagni, certi gerani scarlatti della sua aiuola. La corona d'argento, a tre punte, e il rosario, si confondevano con la pioggerellina dell'acqua. (AD 125)

> (The Mother of God had come out for a turn on the threshold. Quite an elegant little figure. Her veil of pale blue silk shadowed her narrow black eyes, her red mouth, her smiling face ... In the other hand a tiny watering can, painted green, and she was using it, among the heavy shadows of the chestnut trees, to water the pink geraniums in one of her flowerbeds. The shimmer of her silver, three-pointed crown and her rosary blended with the sparkling streams of water. [MW2 61])

In this story the author's innate ability to *transfigure* is indistinguishable from her desire to *transcend* the squalor of empirical reality (the two verbs are interchangeable). By virtue of an imagination so fertile, she is able to twist around and turn upside down life's adventitious misfortunes. This "intent" of hers seems even programmatic right from the very beginning of this story, which in itself provides conclusive evidence.

Hence the natural transposition – the fruit of a densely imaginative form of writing that is never merely an end in itself – from the sad reality of everyday existence to another far superior reality that is by design more comforting, joyful, serene, and rewarding. Significantly, after having spent a few days at the villa and after having forged a friendship with the Lord's Mother (she pays her a visit every day to talk about plants, flowers, and grafts), the Principessa feels "migliorata," that is "better" or "improved," and calmer than she had ever been before.

"La villa" could, in conclusion, be considered both a mystical and a fantastic story at the same time. While the fantastic permeates the whole story, it is, nevertheless, of a particular kind. It is always the offspring, so to speak, of a painful necessity, a sublime remedy for overcoming anxiety. In short, we are dealing with a consciously desired retreat into the fantastic, albeit never chosen in full expressive freedom. In the background there is always, extremely vigilant, the mind of the narrating "I" who is fully aware – as, for example, in the case of Manuele who was restored to life – that it's all based on a pure, transient desire, largely nurtured by the sheer force of imaginative writing. My point will be made even clearer with a specific example in which the painful awareness of the true nature of things is always lurking behind the fantastic.

> La villa era molto bella. Tutta una successione di stanzette tappezzate di carta a fiori, con finestrine pure adornate da fiori ... In una camera dormiva il mio caro fratello, sempre un po' stanco: e questa soltanto offriva nell'insieme qualcosa di bizzarro, a ricordare la dolce vita di lui prima della morte. Bandierine, vi erano, di segnalazione, per tutti i paesi. Poi la branda. La valigia consunta che ci era tornata indietro ... Ma non voglio, non voglio più insistere. (AD 126)

> (The villa was very beautiful. A whole succession of smallish rooms, tapestried with flowered wallpaper, and with smallish windows no more than three feet tall, adorned with flowers ... One of the rooms was where my brother slept; he was always a little tired. And this was the only place where the general impression was somewhat bizarre, a re-evocation of the forthright life he had led before his death: there were banners, little signal banners, from all different countries; then his cot; his dilapidated suitcase, which had been sent back from the Island ... But I really don't want to think about it, I don't want to remember. [MW2 63])

And so, this is how things really are: Jesus, the Madonna, and even her beloved brother inhabit the fantastic villa, where she enjoys a wonderful life with her mother. However, in her capacity as the conjurer of this marvellous creation, she knows that Manuele is dead, forever.

"La villa" is the story that explores the theme of religion more than any other in *Angelici dolori*, and it does so delicately that it seems to become a natural part of everyday life. The proof lies in the dialogue, entirely realistic, exchanged between the two mothers (one of whom, Principessa, is human through and through; the other, Regina, is divine though she embodies a happiness that is wholly of this world), as well as in the conversation between Anna Maria and Jesus at the end of story. At this juncture, the narrator is not afraid to call herself by her real name ("'Buon giorno, Anna.' 'Buon giorno, Signore,' risposi tremante..." AD 130; "'Good day, Anna.' 'Good day,' I replied trembling..." [MW2 69]).

On the presence of the divine in Ortese's life and fiction and more generally on Ortese's attitude towards religion, it may be useful to reread an old but interesting interview with Dacia Maraini, later collected in a volume entitled *E tu chi eri? Interviste sull'infanzia.* In the interview Ortese vividly recalls the terror and horror she experienced when, as a child, her devout mother Beatrice would take her to visit certain gloomy Neapolitan churches with grim and bloody paintings from the Counter-Reformation era. These visions certainly left an indelible mark on the mind of the precocious little girl. This religion neither attracted nor engaged Anna Maria. In the interview she irrefutably affirms: "Le chiese mi incantavano e mi incupivano [...] Mi pareva terribile la chiesa storica; incomprensibile l'infermo, incomprensibile l'Inquisizione, inaccettabile poi la sorveglianza sulle coscienze" ("Churches enchanted and depressed me [...] The historic Church seemed terrible to me; incomprehensible the inferno, incomprehensible the Inquisition, unacceptable therefore the surveillance of consciences"). Yet in the same interview she confesses: "Dio per me si identificava con la speranza di vivere eternamente e liberamente, era il nome, l'identità, la stabilità" ("I identified God with the desire to live eternal and free, He was the name, identity, and stability").[28] And this is precisely the God that we find in the story "La villa": a very human and compassionate God, an endearing presence who emanates sweetness, confidence, and happiness – not terror or dismay. Extremely significant, from this point of view, is the soothing, lullaby-like whisper of the story's ending.

The last two stories of *Angelici dolori* add little to what has been said so far. The first, "Valentino," is a synthesizing "summary" of her adolescence, of her first amorous trepidations (here the young woman's attention turns to Valentino, a "povero ragazzo impiegato come fattorino in un Ufficio-Spedizioni" ("poor young man who works as an errand boy in a shipping office"), of the "felici e incantevoli momenti della giovinezza" ("happy and enchanting moments of youth"), of time that passes inexorably cancelling out everything in its wake: not only neighbourhoods, houses, people, and things, but perhaps even the mental images themselves, like that of the young Valentino, who vanishes "simile al riflesso d'una nube bella sulle onde" (AD 140; "like the reflection of a beautiful cloud on the waves"). The fascinating lyrical allure of this story is so well executed that it can be classified as a long, tender, and accommodating *poème en prose.*

Angelici dolori concludes with "Sole di un sabato" ("A Saturday's Sun") in which, as in a dizzying synthesis, motifs and characters from the previous stories reappear. First and foremost, "Enrico": the professor and beloved friend whom the narrator visits at his home with her heart throbbing. In a scene as touching as it is imaginative, the girl engages in an internal dialogue with her heart (that she turns into a character she calls "il fanciullo" or "the boy"). The dense and heartbreaking dialogue they exchange functions as a sort of sentimental anamnesis in which she attempts to bring into focus the elusive, impossible "Enrico il Cattivo." These are the last visionary, fantastic flashes: a love by now long gone and out of reach once and for all, swallowed up forever in the anonymous night of time.

> Il cielo era nero. I palazzi neri e raggianti d'innumerevoli quadratini gialli. Donne e donne eleganti passavano; uomini allegri, con l'ala del cappello sugli occhi; ricchi fanciulli; serve. Ma nessuno mi conosceva, nessun cortese mi salutava. E io, sempre affettuosamente parlando con l'immagine di "Enrico il Cattivo," lasciavo che la Notte, autentico fiume brillante nelle cupe onde di lumi, mormorando, finalmente quietando, mi avvolgesse nella prediletta ombra del sogno. (AD 150)
>
> (The sky was black. The buildings were black with countless glowing yellow squares. Women and elegant women passed by; happy men, with the brim of their hat over their eyes; rich children; servants. But no one knew me, no one greeted me politely. And I, always talking affectionately with the image of "Enrico the Evil," I allowed the Night, authentic brilliant river in the dark waves of lights, murmuring, finally falling silent, to envelope me in my favourite shade of dream.)

Thus concludes the first collection of short stories by Anna Maria Ortese: a long, dark, uninterrupted introspective journey, illuminated by sudden eruptions of tenderness and absolute emotion. From this "unstable" yet extremely personal platform the "voice" of the writer will take flight along with her narrative adventure that certainly ranks among the most distinctive and exciting, though at times misunderstood, in the Italian tradition.

Translated by Steve Baker

NOTES

1 See Massimo Bontempelli's timely article published in the *Gazzetta del Popolo*, 22 April 1937.
2 Bontempelli, *Noi, gli Aria*, 10.
3 Bontempelli, *Teatro*, 201. Unless otherwise noted, all translations are by Steve Baker.

4 Bontempelli, *Introduzioni e discorsi*, 865.
5 Ibid., 885.
6 Bontempelli, *Il Bianco e il Nero*, 84.
7 Berti, ed., *Centomila*, 99.
8 From the back cover of the original 1937 edition of *Angelici dolori*. Emphasis mine.
9 Clerici, *Apparizione e visione*, 76.
10 *Meridiano di Roma*, no. 1 (2 January 1938).
11 I refer also to the author's own drawing of the topographic layout of this house. Clerici, *Apparizione e visione*, 296–304.
12 Clerici, *Apparizione e visione*, 78.
13 In this regard I refer the reader to my essay "La poesia di Anna Maria Ortese," 123–38.
14 Mauri, "Anna Maria Ortese," 27.
15 Franca Nicosi [Anna Maria Ortese], "Angelici dolori," *L'Italia Letteraria* 37 (4 October 1936).
16 Clerici, *Apparizione e visione*, 96.
17 Ortese, *Angelici dolori e altri racconti*, 17. Citations to this volume will henceforth appear as AD.
18 The story was published for the first time with a slightly different title, "Pellirossa," in the magazine *L'Italia Letteraria* 52 (29 December 1934).
19 Clerici, *Apparizione e visione*, 55.
20 Ibid., 56
21 Borri, *Invito alla lettura di Anna Maria Ortese*, 25.
22 Clerici, *Apparizione e visione*, 64.
23 Ibid.
24 Nicosi [Ortese], "Quartiere," *L'Italia Letteraria* 11 (5 April 1936), Nuova Serie, edited by Massimo Bontempelli.
25 Issue nos. 34, 37, 41, and 44 of 1936, respectively.
26 Clerici, *Apparizione e visione*, 75.
27 I refer the reader to my aforementioned essay on the poetry of Anna Maria Ortese. Lemano also appears in her autobiographical novel *Il porto di Toledo*.
28 Maraini, *E tu chi eri?*, 24–25. [464 in this volume.]

WORKS CITED

Berti, Giuseppe, ed. *Centomila: Dizionario storico enciclopedico di molti italiani d'oggi*. No. 1. Rome: 1949.

Bontempelli, Massimo. *Il Bianco e il Nero*. Ed. Simona Cigliana. Naples: Guida, 1987.

– *Introduzioni e discorsi.* Milan: Bompiani, 1945.
– *Noi, gli Aria: Interpretazioni sudamericane.* Ed. Sebastiano Martelli. Palermo: Sellerio, 1994.
– *Opere scelte.* Ed. Luigi Baldacci. Milan: Mondadori, 1978.
– *Teatro.* Milan: Mondatori, 1947.

Borri, Giancarlo. *Invito alla lettura di Anna Maria Ortese.* Milan: Mursia, 1988.

Clerici, Luca. *Apparizione e visione: Vita e opere di Anna Maria Ortese.* Milan: Mondadori, 2002.

Fontanella, Luigi. "La poesia di Anna Maria Ortese." In *Napoli e dintorni: De Filippo, De Luca, La Capria, Marotta, Orsini Natale, Ortese, Prisco, Rea,* 123–38. Paris: Università de Paris X – Nanterre, Centre de recherches italiennes, 2003.

Maraini, Dacia. *E tu chi eri? Interviste sull'infanzia.* Milan: Bompiani, 1973.

Mauri, Paolo. "Anna Maria Ortese: un puma, un drago e altri animali." *La Repubblica,* 26 May 1996.

Ortese, Anna Maria. *Angelici dolori e altri racconti.* Milan: Adelphi, 2006.
– "Pellirossa." *L'Italia Letteraria* 52 (29 December 1934).
– "Quartiere." *L'Italia Letteraria* 11 (5 April 1936).

6 The Three Lives of Bettina: From *Il cappello piumato* to *Poveri e semplici* (and Back)

BEATRICE MANETTI

In Ortese's literary domain, *Poveri e semplici* (Poor and Simple) and *Il cappello piumato* (The Feathered Hat) occupy a sort of no-man's-land. Overlooked by critics, with the exception of the reviews that accompanied their release in 1967 and 1979 respectively, the two novels were neglected, if not entirely forgotten, by Ortese herself, who always regarded her autobiographic Milanese diptych, retrospectively, with a combination of indulgence, shame, and denial.

There is no doubt that the two novels, when compared to the ambitions and complexity of the writer's other, more famous titles, cannot aim any higher than the rank of "minor" works. However, it is true that the first draft, subsequent versions, rewrites, and revisions of *Poveri e semplici* and *Il cappello piumato* kept Anna Maria Ortese busy from 1960 to 1967, and the editorial process, full of "betrayal," delays, and rejection, lasted until 1979. Twenty years in all: too long for a "vacation" or "uno scherzo dello scrivere" ("a joke of writing").[1] As a matter of fact the two "Milanese" novels cannot be dismissed as peripheral incidents that merely occurred along the way: they are too crucial in the author's overall development.

Between the end of the 1950s and the beginning of the 1960s, Ortese was in the midst of a delicate, painful process of transition. The resulting crisis – private, political, and creative – was the driving force behind the manuscript written in Milan in December 1960 that slowly evolved into both *Poveri e semplici* and *Il cappello piumato.* In the "autobiographical space" inaugurated by this earlier manuscript, Ortese completes, on the one hand, a "transition from the regime of the 'short story' to that of the novel,"[2] on the other, she identifies and clarifies the Janus-faced character of her autobiographical writing, at once novelistic (dropping anchor in *Il porto di Toledo*) and essayistic (extending from *In sonno e in veglia* to *Corpo celeste*).

In the pages that follow I propose to restore the Milanese diptych to its rightful place as a turning point in the author's development. I will first analyse the genesis and editorial history of the two novels (largely conjectural, since many documents have been lost). I will then, by means of a comparison of the two texts, delineate the characteristic constants and evolutionary variables of Ortese's autobiographic writing.

The Story of Two Books in One

"Prima di andar via da Milano [...] buttai giù, in un mese, un racconto che voleva essere divertente e sarcastico, invece fu abbastanza tenero. Era *Il cappello piumato.* [...] Riuscii a pubblicarlo solo dopo vent'anni" (CC 79; "Before leaving Milan [...] I jotted down, in a month, a story that wanted to be funny and sarcastic but became rather quite tender. It was *Il cappello piumato.* [...] I managed to publish it only twenty years later").[3] In the house on Corso Monforte, to which she had returned to live at the end of 1959 and where she remained until July two years later, Ortese quickly composed, between 7 December 1960 and 7 January 1961, "un racconto dedicato allo spavento del vivere" (R1 153; "a story dedicated to the fear of living").[4] Consisting of 240 pages, it recounts, through the narratorial voice of the protagonist Bettina (the transparent alter ego of the author), the hopes and disappointments of her long stay in Milan: including the rise and the decline of her relationship with Marcello Venturi (known as Gilliat in the fiction); the betrayal of the communist dream by Khrushchev and the Soviet tanks in Budapest; the precariousness – happy one moment, desperate the next – of the *vie de bohème* she lead with her Neapolitan friends.[5] The manuscript, however, was born with a peculiarity – one apparently marginal, yet destined to have decisive consequences in successive revisions of the text. It was divided in two, crossed by a fault line, as invisible as it was insurmountable, separating two different points of view and two distinct narrative strategies:

> C'era un personaggio più divertente degli altri, in quel racconto [...] Era una specie di donna [...]
>
> Questo personaggio era proprio colui che scrive, il fastidioso e ormai usualissimo "io narrante" [...] M'interessai e affezionai particolarmente a questa *Bettina* [...] e mi accorsi ben presto che mi prendeva la mano, se ne

andava per conto suo, povera figlia! [...] Poco alla volta, ripeto, mi ci affezionai, e [...] la lasciai dire quello che voleva, dimenticandomi del tutto delle prime quaranta cartelle, dove avevo scritto finora solo quello che volevo io. (R1 154–55)

(One character was more entertaining than any other in the story [...] She was a woman of sorts [...]

She was the one who did the writing, the irritating and by now entirely customary "narrating I" [...] Intrigued I grew particularly fond of this *Bettina* [...] and I realized very soon that she took me by the hand as she went about her business, poor little girl! [...] Little by little, I repeat, I grew fond of her, and [...] I allowed her to say whatever she wanted, forgetting entirely the first forty pages in which I had written only what I wanted.)

The two hundred pages in which Bettina takes charge of the narration will become, twenty years later, without any major changes, *Il cappello piumato,* whereas the path that leads from the first forty pages of the original manuscript to *Poveri e semplici* is more tortuous and rugged. In the introductory chapter of *Il cappello piumato,* Ortese clarifies the relationship between the two books and describes the genesis of *Poveri e semplici* as a rapid, linear process in two stages:

un altro giorno, in un'altra casa del solenne e deserto Sud [...] staccai dal fascicolo i ferretti, liberai le prime quaranta pagine. Su quelle, iniziando dal giorno stesso, mi misi a lavorare ... lisciandole, ornandole. Ed ecco un festoso libretto! Non mi andava, misteriosamente. Subito ne scrissi un altro, di tono dimesso [...] Questo mi parve decente. (R1 156)

(on another day, in another house in the solemn and deserted South [...] I took the clasps from the bound manuscript, I removed the first forty pages. On those, beginning that very day, I put myself to work ... polishing them, adorning them. And out came a festive little book! I strangely didn't like it. I immediately wrote another, modest in tone [...] This seemed appropriate to me.)

As a matter of fact, the process of enlargement, revision, and reworking of those forty pages will occupy the author for more than five years. The first draft of *Poveri e semplici* is only finished in June 1963, at which time the already difficult compositional process had only just begun to entrench itself in an equally intricate editorial knot. On 31 January 1961, in fact, Ortese signed an agreement with Rizzoli to publish the book, without mentioning the fact that she had been bound to the Florentine publisher Vallecchi since May 1958 by a twenty-year contract. Then breaking her agreement with Rizzoli, the editor in chief of the Florentine house, Geno Pampaloni, was next to receive the manuscript, and he enthusiastically embraced it, recommending it for publication with only a few minor modifications. That, at least, is what Ortese affirms in a letter written on 20 November 1963 to the publishing house Einaudi, with whom she was simultaneously negotiating the publication of another novel, *L'Iguana*:

> Vi unisco infine copia delle prime cinquanta pagine di un mio breve romanzo [...] intitolato "L'IGUANA." Tale romanzo si trova attualmente presso Vallecchi, che però non ha alcun interesse a pubblicarlo, e lo ha preso [...] unicamente a titolo di garanzia nei confronti dell'Amministrazione. Infatti, io avevo consegnato a Vallecchi, in giugno, un altro romanzo, che a lui piaceva molto [...] A questo romanzo, un mese fa, Geno Pampaloni mi consigliò di portare delle modificazioni, e io fui del suo avviso. Riebbi quindi il manoscritto e ci si mise d'accordo in quell'occasione che, non appena lo avessi consegnato tutto in ordine, avrei riavuto indietro "L'IGUANA."
>
> (I am finally including a copy of the first fifty pages of my short novel [...] entitled "THE IGUANA." The novel is currently at Vallecchi, but he has no interest in publishing it, and he took it [...] only as a guarantee against the Administration. In fact, I gave Vallecchi another novel in June that he liked very much [...] A month ago, Geno Pampaloni advised me to make some changes, and I agreed with him. I had the manuscript again and we made a pact on that occasion that, as soon as I could straighten it out for publication, he'd give "THE IGUANA" back to me.)[6]

A situation of gridlock begins to take shape. With Pampaloni at Vallecchi, on the one hand, uncertain about the publication of *L'Iguana* yet convinced that *Poveri e semplici* has a "qualità di commozione e di completezza narrativa che mi sembrano più adatte per un rilancio del Suo nome dopo tanti anni di silenzio" ("emotional quality and a cohesive narrative that seem more suited to reviving your name after so many years of silence");[7] and the author on the other, who, feeling betrayed, offered *L'Iguana* to other editors: in August to Rizzoli, from whom she received a clean rejection,[8] and in November, as we have seen, to Einaudi, who, in order to proceed with the publication, required Ortese to submit a corrected copy of *Poveri e semplici* to Vallecchi.

But the small changes to the manuscript that could have resolved the impasse eventually became an insurmountable obstacle over time: they were continuously postponed, multiplied, thickened. A year later, on 14 November 1964, Ortese wrote to Calvino at Einaudi that she had sent Pampaloni the same copy of *Poveri e semplici* "che, approvata da Vallecchi nel '63, stava per passare in tipografia, se io non l'avessi trattenuta" ("which, having been approved by Vallecchi in '63, was about to go to press, had I not delayed it"), and that "su una copia che ho con me, devo fare ancora qualche cambiamento, che porterò a termine nel giro di qualche settimana" ("on a copy I have with me, I still have to make some changes, which I will finish in a few weeks").[9] Instead, three months passed and on 12 February 1965, quite surprisingly, Ortese writes to Calvino again, begging him to return *The Iguana* manuscript to Vallecchi, who, having changed his mind, in fact published the novel in March of that very same year.

Ortese's unpredictable, contradictory, and ultimately self-destructive behaviour is propelled by a more serious motive than to arm-wrestle Pampaloni over the priority of publication of the two novels. It happened that "un lavoro abbastanza facile" – so Ortese continues in her letter to Calvino – "quale il rifacimento di alcuni capitoli del libro per Vallecchi, è diventato sempre più complesso, oscuro, impossibile" ("a fairly easy job as the rewriting of a couple chapters of the book for Vallecchi became increasingly more complicated, obscure, impossible").[10] So impossible that seven months later, while preparing for her latest move from Rome to Milan, she set aside the first version of *Poveri e semplici* once and for all. On 14 September 1965 Ortese informs Calvino of her new address and adds: "A Milano spero di finire l'altro libro [...]. *L'ho ricominciato da capo*" ("In Milan I hope to finish the other book [...]. *I started from scratch*").[11]

Ortese dedicated another year to the second and final draft of *Poveri e semplici.* "Lavoro molto, sette ore al giorno a quel libro (lo sto riscrivendo tutto), ma non so se lo finirò" ["I work a lot, seven hours a day on the book (I'm rewriting the whole thing), but I don't know if I'll finish it"], she writes again to Calvino on 22 November 1965.[12] And in April of the following year, in an interview with Alfredo Barberis, she declared that "adesso sto perdendo gli occhi su un nuovo romanzo. Dovrebbe essere in due parti. La prima è già quasi finita" ("now I'm losing my eyesight over a new novel. It should be in two parts. The first is already almost finished").[13] Eventually Pampaloni writes on 28 July 1966 to thank her for having allowed "[him] to read both versions of your new book."[14]

It is clear that one of the two versions is the new and final draft of *Poveri e semplici.* The second remains a mystery. Nothing excludes the possibility that Ortese had also sent the previous draft back to the publishing house, so that someone else might resolve the uncertainty that had plagued her during the hard-fought reworking of the book; but it is difficult to imagine that she would circulate a draft that only a year and a half earlier she had so resolutely set aside. More likely is that the second version in reality conceals the text from which it all started, that is, the one composed in Milan between December 1960 and January 1961.

In a letter dated 27 January 1967, in fact, when the choice between the two versions had presumably already been made by Vallecchi (*Poveri e semplici* was released in March of that year), Ortese offers Rizzoli the very 1960–61 manuscript, asking, however, that it only be published abroad.[15] That this is the version Vallecchi rejected, and which will see the light only in 1979, Pampaloni seems to confirm in two places. The first is in a review of *Il cappello piumato* in which he mentions "[la] lunga esitazione tra due testi paralleli che l'autrice aveva presentato alla casa editrice (che allora dirigevo)" ["the long indecision between two parallel texts that the author had submitted to the publishing house (that I directed at the time)"]. He does not comment, however, on the relationship "fra il testo allora accantonato e questo che ora leggiamo" ("between the text then sidelined and the one we now read").[16] The second, more explicitly, in 1988: "Poi, alla Vallecchi, le pubblicai tre o quattro libri, tra cui quello con cui vinse il premio Strega. Me ne aveva proposto due versioni; scelsi, non so ancora perché, la peggiore, e suggerii il titolo vergognosamente anti-ortesiano di *Poveri e semplici* (1967). L'altra stesura, *Il cappello piumato,* pubblicato nel 1979, è senz'altro più felice" ["Then, at Vallecchi, I published three or four of her books, including the one that won the Strega Prize. She had proposed two versions to me; I chose, I still do not know why, the worst, and suggested the shamefully anti-Ortesian title *Poor and Simple* (1967). The other version, *The Feathered Hat,* published in 1979, is without a doubt much happier"].[17]

To these elements, Ortese's own affirmation at the time of the release of *Il cappello piumato* should finally be added: "quel mio libro [...] fu rifiutato, in vent'anni, (quasi), da *tre* editori, da uno addirittura con assoluto disprezzo, tramite uno scrittore famoso" ("that book of mine [...] was rejected, over twenty years (almost), by three publishers, by one even with absolute contempt, through a famous writer").[18] Of two of these rejections, both dating from the mid-seventies, unambiguous documentary traces remain: the first rejection comes from Einaudi, in the person of Calvino, the "famous writer" to whom Ortese sent a typewritten manuscript on 5 September 1972,[19] the second from Rizzoli, to which the writer addressed a letter on 18 June 1977 demanding the return of "quel dattiloscritto (una prima versione incompleta di *Poveri e semplici* [...] che le feci avere a Roma, forse nel '74). Quella copia che credevo di avere è – a causa di carta o carattere della macchina o solo perché sciupata – difficilmente leggibile: ["that manuscript (an early incomplete version of *Poveri e semplici* [...] that I gave you in Rome, probably in '74). The one copy that I thought I had is – due to the nature of the paper or to the print of typewriter or just because it is damaged – barely legible"].[20] The third rejection, and in fact the first in chronological order, is therefore most likely that of Vallecchi.

Rizzoli's response was late in coming. When in September 1978 Sergio Pautasso announced to Ortese that "nel luglio '77 Le è stato restituito un Suo dattiloscritto [...] che si ricollegava chiaramente a *Poveri e semplici*" ("in July '77 one of your manuscripts was returned to you [...] which is clearly linked to *Poveri e semplici*"),[21] *Il cappello piumato* had already been taken up and revised by the author to be published by Mondadori.

From this compositional and editorial journey, as tangled and incomplete as it is, it seems to me that at least two facts emerge that demand to be taken into account when comparing the two novels beyond their obvious common origin, their differences in terms of the distribution of narrative material, and their generic differences in tone.[22] The first is that right up to the end, that is, until the publication of *Poveri e semplici* in 1967, Ortese cultivated the project of rewriting the entire manuscript of 1960–61 and not merely the first forty pages. In other words, she considered the narrative material from which the two books emerged as two parts of a single book. In letters written between 1961 and 1962 to Paolo Lecaldano at Rizzoli, her repeated hints at "a first part" most likely imply the existence of a second part, along with the intention to complete her revision.[23] Such an intention was still valid in 1966 as evidenced by the aforementioned interview with Barberis, and was basically never fully abandoned, if the repeated attempts she made in the seventies to publish the remaining two hundred pages of the original text are to be considered as dictated not only by economic necessity, but also by her awareness that, without its sequel, *Poveri e semplici* was a "mutilated" novel.

The texts themselves offer further and more concrete proof: from the disposition of narrative material, identical in both books (titled chapters internally subdivided into paragraphs uniform in length and in number – from a minimum of one to a maximum of four, but more often two or three), to those traces that the failure of the original project has left in either novel, which are particularly apparent where cuts were made. This happens in the first chapter of *Il cappello piumato*, where Ortese retrieves part of the forty pages of the old manuscript in order to situate Bettina's story in the context of events recounted at greater length in *Poveri e semplici*; it is also the case in the final chapter of *Poveri e semplici*, where events subsequent to the night of the party and the exchange of necklaces between Bettina and Gilliat, with which the first forty pages of the original manuscript presumably ended, are hastily summarized, with glaring chronological discrepancies. Perhaps hard-pressed by the need to finish the book and unable to add the revised second part, Ortese condensed in the last pages of the 1967 novel scenes and episodes contained in the following two hundred pages.[24]

Of this phantom book we only know, therefore, that it was supposed to be comprised of two parts. The two novels that have taken its place, however, help us to hypothesize its contents: in the first part, the story of Ortese's first year in Milan, punctuated by friendship, by her earliest success as a writer (she won the Viareggio prize for *Il mare non bagna Napoli* in 1953), and above all by her love for Gilliat; in the second the story of the slow, inexorable attrition of her creative energy, of her political faith, and of the life she shared with her companion. Two parts, or rather two pieces of a single movement: from adolescence to maturity, from the discovery of love to its abandonment, from having faith in the future to placing it in a barren present. In conclusion, the proto-text of 1960–61, considered in its entirety, acts as a sort of foundational model for Ortese's autobiographical writing – and it is no coincidence that it is faithfully reflected in the same bipartite division of *Il porto di Toledo*.[25]

If it is true that every autobiography has death as its implied horizon,[26] in the case of Ortese this is true in the sense not of biological death, but of the dissolution of an existential project in which the individual experiences her own annulment. In the traditional autobiography, "it is because the past self is *different* from the present 'I' that the latter can truly claim all its prerogatives. The 'I' will tell not only what happened to it in *another* time but even more how *another* person came to be itself."[27] Ortese's autobiography, by contrast, is founded on the belief that one's real life resides in that difference, in that lost alterity, through which the actual "I" can only produce representations of herself *ex negativo* – to speak no longer of how she became herself, but how she ceased to be anything at all.

External circumstances played an undeniable role in ensuring that the work originally conceived as a book in two parts was to become over time, and in large part very fortuitously, two separate books. But the fact remains that, in the parallel and intertwined story of the Milanese diptych, there is a vacillating star, *Poveri e semplici,* and a fixed star, *Il cappello piumato;* a book on which Ortese worked for years, as was her habit, and one that she could hardly bear to touch.

And so we come to the second element worthy of note in the history of these "two books in one": the imperceptible borderline that divides the first forty pages from the subsequent two hundred of the original manuscript and that determined the fate of either tranche. In the introduction to *Il cappello piumato,* Ortese identifies it with the moment in which the character Bettina replaces the author not only as the narratorial voice (which she had already co-opted for herself), but also as an organizing force and agent behind the narrative subject matter. Hers is a taking of authorial agency, the most glaring consequences of which are found both in terms of content – in the transition from the choral nature of *Poveri e semplici* to the centrality of the protagonist's story in *Il cappello piumato* – and on the level of tone, in the difference between the "rivisitazione elegiaca del tempo della giovinezza che in alcuni punti conduce a esiti visionari nel primo caso" ("elegiac re-examination of the time of her youth that in some places leads to visionary outcomes in the first case") and the "sguardo adulto e disilluso su un mondo raffigurato più aggettivamente nel secondo" ("disillusioned adult gaze on a world more objectively portrayed in the second").[28] But the suspicion remains that there is something else; that what really counts, in Bettina's gesture, is not so much her effect on the narration, but the act of storytelling in and of itself. However, I will return to this point later.

The Double Life of Bettina

The manuscript of 1960–61 did not materialize out of thin air. In the contract she signed with Vallecchi on 7 May 1958, Ortese undertook to publish an autobiographical book on the years she spent in Milan entitled *Diario d'inverno* (Winter Diary) and *Viaggio in Russia* (Russian Journey), which most likely would have constituted an expanded version of the correspondence that appeared in the magazine "L'Europeo" four years earlier.[29] The backdrop of the idea of a memoir – where autobiography, diary, and chronicle intersect – inevitably had an effect on *Il cappello piumato,* which is the direct descendant of that manuscript. From diaristic writing, the novel borrows above all its fragmented, cyclical, and open narrative form.[30] To the chronological linearity of the principal story (the birth and death of a love affair), recurrent reflections are superimposed that enrich the text with a variety of heterogeneous genres of narrative material: journalistic prose, wandering meditative excursions, poetic interjections.[31]

But dominating over the work as a whole is an essayistic element. Having reduced the facts to a minimum, the novel finds its driving force in Bettina's relentless reflections – in addition to her encounters and clashes with other characters – on the important issues of the time and on the recurring themes of Ortese's thought: the failure of ideology in the face of universal suffering, the need for a new order that is ethical and existential in nature rather than political, the commodification of humanity and nature, the withdrawal of reality when confronted with "una nebbia che avanza da tutte le parti: e questa nebbia [...] siamo noi tutti quanti, come viviamo, e le cose per cui viviamo" (R1 265; "a fog spreading in all directions: and we are this fog [...] all of us, in the way we live, and the things for which we live").

Under the rubric of the autobiographical novel, under which *Il cappello piumato* is generally catalogued, the most fragile and arbitrary term is the second: more than a novel, we are faced with a sort of public diary, an intellectual self-portrait. To these two types of writing about oneself *Il cappello piumato* owes its hybrid nature and a similar project of salvation: to neutralize a void of inspiration by opening a metanarrative dimension in which writing reflects back on itself.[32]

Reviewing *Il cappello piumato,* Giuliano Gramigna is among the first to note how the "'storia d'amore' [...] in tanto funziona come struttura del romanzo in quanto diventa il luogo in cui si incontrano, si intrecciano, risuonano il tema politico della caduta delle attese rivoluzionarie e il tema simmetrico degli sconvolgimenti naturali" ("'love story' [...] provides the structure of the novel inasmuch as it becomes the place where the political theme of the disappointment of revolutionary expectations and the symmetrical theme of natural upheavals meet, intertwine, resonate with each other").[33] But this triple crisis – sentimental, political, and "philosophical" – is further complicated by yet another crisis, which is both the cause and consequence of those: Ortese's creative crisis, tied to the exhaustion of a literary season in which the writer had found, even if in a rather eccentric way, the motives and justifications for her writing:

> Attraversavo poi, come tanti altri artisti o intellettuali di sinistra, una vera crisi, formale o sostanziale, non so, in quanto il neo-realismo [...] non aveva fatto in tempo a nascere che già, si sentiva, era morto. Non restavano, per esprimersi, che due strumenti: o una specie di neo-realismo tutto arzigogolato per le sinistre, o il piatto e insipido vecchio realismo per le destre. E mi dispiacevano tutti e due. (R1 194–96)
>
> (I was then passing through, like many other artists and intellectuals of the left, a real crisis, formal or substantial, I don't know, inasmuch as neo-realism [...] hadn't been born, one felt, that it had already died. Only two instruments of expression were left: either a kind of completely artificial neo-realism for the left, or the flat and insipid old realism for the right. And I didn't like either of them.)

Of this impasse, *Il cappello piumato* is a unique result and a temporary solution. Ortese expresses the "pena di non poter scrivere, di non aver più nulla da scrivere" (R1 290; "pain of not being able to write, not having anything left to write"), and at the same time, by speaking of it, she surpasses it. Only in this way can we explain the hybrid nature of the text and its special vocation, which is at once both specular and speculative: its vocation as a realistic book that verifies the inadequacy of realism; as a political book that challenges politics and upsets its language ("Bisognava svegliare quanta più compassione fosse possibile sulla terra, e amore degli altri [...] Questa era la Rivoluzione," R1 332; "We needed to stir up as much compassion as possible on earth, and love for each other [...]. This was the Revolution"); and as a novel that breaks the anecdotal pace of the narrative with pauses increasingly more dilated with meditation.

The creative crisis place the narrative "I" in conflict with itself. The attrition of love creates a rift between the "I" and the other. Political disillusionment destroys the hope of a possible harmony between the "I" and history:

> Non si poteva, e non si doveva più scrivere, era tutto un inganno [...] Del resto, di che e su che cosa bisognava scrivere? Questa società non voleva che specchi deformanti; gli altri, li spezzava. (R1 207)
>
> (One could not, and should not write any longer, it was all a deception [...] After all, about what and on what should we write? This society did not want anything more than fun house mirrors; any other it shattered.)

These three wounds, simultaneous and inseparable, almost cancel out the distance between author, narrator, and character. And it is through such solidarity that Ortese is able to entrust to her alter ego the explicit and extended formulation, regardless of how a-systematic, of her thinking. We could call it Bettina's utopia – hinted at and continuously repeated over the course of the narration, but stated unequivocally in two of the most crucial and explicitly essayistic chapters of the book, "Qualcosa non va, nell'universo" ("Something Isn't Right in the Universe") and "Un freddo terribile" ("A Terrible Cold"). In the first, Bettina's reflections on the "irrealtà fondamentale della realtà tutta" (R1 264; "fundamental unreality of all reality") are coupled with the appearance of the first fissures in her relationship with Gilliat ("In quel momento, di lui più non m'importava," R1 263; "In that moment, I didn't care about him anymore") and with a profound questioning of her motivations for writing ("Il mio lavoro subì una crisi," R1 264; "My work underwent a crisis"), only to culminate in a violent confrontation with her companion:

> In un fiato, temendo di sbagliare, di spaventarlo, ma anche di tradire quella nuova immagine che mi ero fatta delle cose e del nostro dovere [...] gli dissi ciò che pensavo: la verità, intesa come l'infinito essere delle cose, e susseguirsi eterno dei fatti, non era buona, non aveva luce, era anzi terribile; perciò l'Universo andava riesaminato, occorreva una grande unione di tutti, e la creazione di una nuova appassionata filosofia, che stringesse tutte le creature viventi in una lotta sola contro il non senso e la morte ch'erano il distintivo dell'Universo. (R1 266)
>
> (In one breath, afraid of making a mistake, of frightening him, but also of betraying that new image that I had made of things and of our duty [...] I told him what I thought: the truth, understood as the infinite being of things, and the eternal succession of events, was not good, was not positive, it was indeed terrible, so the Universe demanded to be examined again, a great union of all things was necessary, and the creation of a new passionate philosophy, that would embrace all living creatures in a single fight against the meaninglessness and death that were the insignia of the Universe.)

In the second chapter, the bond and interdependence of private anguish, creative paralysis, social discomfort, and "cosmic" utopia stand out even more:

> Ma che cosa doveva accadere, se io non scrivevo, e che cosa dovevo scrivere, se ero sempre più spaventata? [...] L'italiano, da anni era scaduto, invecchiato dall'assenza di carattere, di pensiero; nella città, poco alla volta, anche quelle tracce di linguaggio s'erano perdute, e si parlava un gergo tecnico-mondano, che di appartenente all'uomo non aveva più niente. Senza lingua, né cose per questa lingua, in che modo, e perché scrivere? Ero costretta a farmi una domanda, in quel tempo: accettavo o non accettavo la vita in questa società? E dovevo rispondermi che non l'accettavo. Essa mi pareva orribilmente priva di finalità umane [...] Quel dare *cose*! Miriadi di cose! L'uomo è forse una cosa? Quel dirgli "qui"; stabilire il suo orizzonte: qui. Cosa poteva essere qui? Mi pareva, a me, l'uomo, tutto fatto di *altrove*. Così era l'uomo, almeno per me, un *altrove*. (R1 292–94)
>
> (But what would have happened if I didn't write, and what was I supposed to write, if I was ever more frightened? [...] Italian had expired years ago, aged from a lack of character, of thought; in the city, little by little, even those traces of language had gone missing, and one spoke a technical-worldly jargon, which was no longer even remotely human. With neither language, nor things that correspond to this language, how, and why write? I was forced at that time to ask myself: do I accept or do I not accept life in this society? And I had to answer that I did not accept it. It seemed to me horribly devoid of human purpose [...] That giving of *things*! Myriads of things! Is man perhaps a thing? That telling him "here," establishing his horizon: here. What could here be? Man seemed entirely made up of *elsewheres*. Thus man was, at least for me, an *elsewhere*.)

It is no wonder that the concepts and tone of the essays and conversations in *Corpo celeste* (1997, but the texts collected in the volume date to the period 1974–89) almost literally resound in these pages. *Il cappello piumato*, in fact, is in a sense its pre-text or, if you prefer, its preparatory sketch, in being essentially, rather than an autobiographical novel, a book "di meditazione e di memoria" ("of meditation and of memory").[34] With the exception that here the existential wound, which is the origin of Ortese's thought, is still open and openly exhibited; and still tangible is the link that unites her love for a man and her devotion to all living things, the trauma of abandonment and its sublimation to a sort of universal *pietas*. Abstract thinking arises from the burning concreteness of individual experience, and public discourse reveals its private roots, in a "scrittura di esperienza" ("writing experience") that resets the contrast "tra l'aspetto particolare, contingente del vissuto, e quello generale, che sembra appartenere solo alla teoria e al pensiero interpretative" ("between the particular, contingent on that which is experienced, and the general, that which seems to pertain only to theory and to interpretive thinking").[35]

More than "un libro bambino" (R1 164; "a baby book"), *Il cappello piumato* is a mature book, narrated by an adult voice, through which the autobiographical impulse is inseparable from a similar impulse to a critical reading of reality. It may be a coincidence, but it is precisely in this book that Ortese first experiments with a rhetorical device that will later enter into common usage, namely, the direct address "dear Reader." Certainly a trick borrowed from the "old realism," enlivened by a filter of irony and often used, from *L'Iguana* to *Il cardillo addolorato,* in homage to her eighteenth and nineteenth century literary models and as an amplification of the play of mirrors between reality and fiction, storytelling and commentary. Even for the narrative voice of *Il cappello piumato* the spontaneous eye contact she makes with the reader is in turn a way to open a metanarrative space ("Povero Lettore che mi hai seguita finora, come sono mortificata di averti imposto queste minute e meschine descrizioni di ansie e vicende per le quali anche tu, forse, sarai passato," R1 218; "Poor Reader, you who have followed me this far, how mortified I am to have imposed on you these minute and petty descriptions of anxiety and events through which, perhaps, you will have passed") or to solicit the complicity of the audience, orienting their reading strategies:

> Lettore, dimmi, in realtà, se ti sembra che vi sia qualcosa di più "rassicurante" della "normalità e bontà" dell'Universo, della sua salute, della sua integrità, della sua buona disposizione verso di noi (per cui talvolta, nel nostro segreto, eleviamo preghiere). Tu dovrai rispondere di no. (R1 311)
>
> ["Reader, tell me, if it really seems like there is anything more "reassuring" of the "normality and goodness" of the Universe, of its health, its integrity, of its good disposition towards us (through which sometimes, in secret, we lift up our prayers). You should say no"].

But who knows whether Bettina, after having taken control of her author, so that she can recount what she wants, does not rather want to reaffirm, by means of the expedient of such exclusive "authorial" pertinence, her own power over the story.

I have already mentioned the role external circumstances played in impeding Ortese from developing both parts of the original manuscript into a single book. Despite the desire to assign all the weight and importance that they are likely to have had, the suspicion remains that the peculiarities of *Il cappello piumato* (an adult protagonist, a mature viewpoint, an accentuated essayistic dimension) might have played a role in the failure or abandonment of the project. They were an "unmanageable" subject matter for the representational strategy that the writer adopted six years later in *Poveri e semplici* and that aligns itself along two axes: the infantilization of the protagonist and the fairy-tale transfiguration of experience.

In the 1967 novel the most blatant violation of autobiographical referentiality involves the protagonist's birth certificate. The Bettina of *Poveri e semplici* is not only a few years younger than the character of the same name in *Il cappello piumato*, whose age is otherwise never specified: she is an adolescent who is going on "eighteen" (R1 7) at the beginning of the story, in autumn 1952, when the author is instead already thirty-eight years old.

In this falsification there is some truth. A truth that Ortese would later call "realtà (o verità) immaginaria" ["imaginary reality (or truth)"] in opposition "alla approssimativa verità storica" ("to an approximate historical truth").[36] The poet Alfonso Gatto intuited this with great subtlety: "Dopo la guerra, a Milano, la Ortese sembrò correre quasi da adolescente – e non lo era più – alle speranze, al nuovo senso di convivenza, di fiducia e di educazione ch'erano nell'aria" ("After the war, in Milan, Ortese seemed to run as if she were a teenager – which she no longer was – to the hopes, to the new sense of coexistence, of faith and of education that were in the air").[37] But the modification of the protagonist's age, extended not coincidentally to her virtual double "Volpicina" (R1 7), also serves other purposes. First, it amplifies the sense of orphanhood that permeates the entire novel. The main characters of *Poveri e semplici* are orphans – as the protagonists of fairy tales almost always are – and this characteristic acquires importance and significance because they are presented as adolescents. Bettina is an orphan twice over: her mother is already dead at the beginning of the novel, and in the third chapter, "La primavera" ("Spring"), she loses her father too; Gilliat is an orphan, as we learn in the chapter "La separazione" ("The Separation"); and Sonia is an orphan, who after the death of her father was abandoned by her mentally ill mother – all of them are children without families, deprived of the kind of shelter provided by adults, survivors of a disaster whose private dimension is only the external sign of a more profound significance, historical if not metaphysical.

The emphasis on Bettina's youthfulness also stresses – especially in comparison with *Il cappello piumato* – the distance that separates the narrating "I" from the narrated "I." Thus in *Poveri e semplici* two opposing ideas of time clash: an anxious expectation of the future in which the remembered Bettina is immersed and the melancholic amazement over the dissipation of the past that emerges in the voice of the Bettina who remembers. On the one hand, one encounters the sense of a beginning: "la vita, vera estasi, incominciava" (R1 64; "life, true ecstasy, was beginning"); on the other, the awareness of the end:

> I più bei giorni della mia vita cominciarono in questa città i primi di novembre.
>
> Sono trascorsi da quella data vari anni, e con essi è trascorsa la mia breve giovinezza e la sua felicità.
>
> [...] Così, per un momento [...] io mi volto ancora a guardarle, e vorrei capirne il perché, strappare ad esse un semplice significato, ma esse continuano a splendere, a sorridere, con un che di strano, di buono. Se ne vanno! I monti, i mari del tempo, cioè gli anni, il progresso della vita, aumentano ad ogni attimo la distanza che cominciò un giorno tra noi. (R1 5–6)

> (The best days of my life began in this city in early November.
>
> Several years have passed since then, and with them my brief youth passed, and its happiness. [...] So, for a moment [...] I still turn to look at them, and I want to understand why, wring from them a simple meaning, but they continue to shine, to smile, with something strange, something good. They flee! The mountains, the seas of time, the years, life's progress, widens from one moment to the next the chasm that opened one day between us.)

The present is evoked as an ecstatic enchantment; memory as a dream: "quei primi giorni della piena estate furono tali, che il loro ricordo rassomiglia a un sogno" (R1 56; "those first days of full-blown summer were such, that their memory is like a dream"). From the encounter of these two forms, different but complementary, to the transfiguration of reality, a fantastic vapour is unleashed, a vapour that "blurs" the events and characters of the novel and projects them into an almost fairy-tale dimension.[38] To reiterate the point, Ortese minimizes the moment of reflection, discussion, and self-analysis, which is so central in *Il cappello piumato.* And she entrusts it to an infantile linguistic register that in some of the most intense emotional passages is on the verge of stuttering. It flares up and collapses under the weight of the ineffable:

così ci si staccava gli uni dagli altri; e mi parve che fosse tutto un dividersi, uno staccarsi, questa vita, un non senso, un correre lontano gli uni dagli altri [...] Mi parve che non altro... risvegliare la bellezza e pietà dell'uomo... Ecco cosa urge [...]

Una notte [...] feci un sogno straordinario.

[...]

Avevo la sensazione che questo mondo, con le sue guerre, fosse superato... che fossimo insieme tutti, che scendesse o salisse nell'aria bianca una musica... che si alzava, che diveniva sottile, che poi copriva il cielo, copriva tutto. (R1 105–6)

(so we separated from each other, and I thought it was all a parting of ways, a breaking off, this life, a lot of nonsense, a running far away from each other [...] It seemed that nothing else... stirring the beauty and devotion of man... This is what is pressing [...]

One night [...] I had an extraordinary dream.

[...]

I had the sensation that this world, with its wars, had been overcome... that we were all together, that music sank or rose in the clear light... that it became tenuous, that it then covered the sky, covered everything.)

In such a language, which so disturbed the first reviewers of the book with its "eccesso di grazia stucchevole" ("excess of cloying grace") and its "caramelloso gusto 'diminutivo'" ("sugary 'diminutive' flavour"),[39] the critic Monica Farnetti correctly intuited an experiment that anticipates "quel talento espressivo dalle mosse associative inattese, quella pazzia stilistica" ("her expressive talent for unexpected free association, her stylistic madness")[40] that will find its complete realization in *Il porto di Toledo.* But perhaps there's something else to it.

In Milan, as we have seen, between 1952 and 1957, Ortese relived a sort of replica of her childhood and adolescence, a similar parable that touches on the canonical stages of her formation (the discovery of love, friendship, her literary vocation, the dream of a harmonious integration into the world) and that is shattered by the violence of history. *Il cappello piumato* treats this parable for what it actually was: the undoing of an adult woman, who while describing herself engages in self-analysis at the same time, reflects on herself, on her writing, and on that which surrounds her. In *Poveri e semplici,* however, it almost seems that the Naples of the thirties, the city of her adolescence, emerges out from under the Milan of the early fifties. It is as if the lengthy immersion into the past that she undertook in winter 1960–61 and continued for more than six years had gradually lead Ortese back to where it had all began: the original wound, the first and final encounter "con la doppia natura umana, con l'ebbrezza e la perdita" (R1 354; "with humanity's dual nature, with elation and loss").

The entire novel of 1967 is punctuated by small signs that attest to the ambiguity, or to the duplicity, of its actual autobiographical referent: they are representational strategies, stylistic choices, and thematic nuclei that return in a more radically subversive way in her autobiography *Il porto di Toledo* (1975). How these strategies change in the transition from *Il cappello piumato* and *Poveri e semplici* can be illustrated by a comparison between two versions of an episode narrated in both novels: Bettina and Gilliat's encounter at the restaurant after the night of the party and the journalist's declaration of love. In *Il cappello piumato* the scene spans more than four pages. The dialogue between the two is exhaustively recounted, along with a detailed description of the environment, clothing, and physical traits of both characters (Gilliat's beauty, Bettina's dignified poverty). The conflicting feelings aroused by love's ecstasy, the simultaneity of exaltation and terror, reckless abandon and shame, alternate with discussions on the nature and future of the bond the young couple shares, in a controlled linguistic register that intercepts and records the emotions without being influenced by them, yet into which irony can unexpectedly creep:

> L'effetto più importante che tutto questo faceva su di me, era una specie di freddo, di spavento silenzioso, a cui si mescolavano dei coraggi improvvisi, e allora lo fissavo, ma senza però vederlo distintamente, come se fissassi il sole, tentando di sorridere [...]
>
> Era buffo dover mangiare i ravioli in mezzo a questi discorsi. E infatti non li mangiammo. Furono presto freddi [...]
>
> Tuttavia la tristezza cresceva con la stessa rapidità della gioia, quasi fosse l'ombra di quella festa. Sì, potevo considerarmi sposata, ma per quanto? Le nozze di carta non sono come le nozze vere [...]
>
> Gli dissi ciò che pensavo; non discussi la validità delle nostre nozze con le collane, perché anch'io vi credevo, solo la loro solidità. Un giorno, lui se ne sarebbe andato.
>
> "Questo non si può dire" fece turbandosi. "Questa storia, invece, può durare tanti anni, credi!" (R1 188–90)

(The most important effect that all of this had on me was a sort of chill, a silent terror, which was mixed with sudden bursts of courage, and then I

> fixed my gaze on him, but without seeing him clearly, as if I were looking into the sun, trying to smile [...]
>
> It was funny to have to eat ravioli in the midst of this conversation. And, in fact, we didn't eat. They were soon cold [...] Nevertheless sadness grew at the same rate as my joy, as though it were the shadow of that party. Yes, I could consider myself married, but for how long? Paper weddings are not like real weddings [...] I told him what I thought; I didn't bring up the validity of our marriage through the necklaces, because I too believed in it, only its strength. One day, he would leave.
>
> "Don't talk like that," he said getting all worked up. "Our story can last a long time, trust me!")

Poveri e semplici condenses the scene into a page, where the same state of mind is expressed by the flash of an image and by the inexplicable violence of a gesture:

> Sembrava che il sole gli battesse sopra, e ora era bianco come la luce, ora gli occhi gli ardevano, ora su quella fronte passavano nuvole, e quel debole sorriso si spegneva [...]
>
> Appena fummo di fronte – io lo guardavo – egli mi prese un braccio, poi due, scotendoli, con parole che non afferravo; indi, piegò di colpo la testa sulla mia spalla, e mi abbracciò in modo che mai aveva fatto alcuno, come se io stessi per fuggire con qualcosa che rappresentava la sua salvezza, la sua vita stessa, ed egli si raccomandasse a me, perché non voleva morire. (R1 132)

> (It seemed as though the sun beat down on him, now he was as white as light, now his eyes set him ablaze, now clouds passed across his forehead, and that faint smile faded away [...]
>
> As soon as we were face to face – I studied him – he took me by the arm, then the other, shaking them, with words that I didn't understand; then, he suddenly rested his head on my shoulder, and he embraced me in a way that I had never been embraced before, as if I was about to escape with something that represented his salvation, his very life, and he entrusted himself to me, because he didn't want to die.)[41]

The desire of the protagonist "di tornare bambina nella casa di mio padre, risentire la dolce voce di mia madre" ("to be a little girl again in my father's house, to hear the sweet voice of my mother") – an unattainable desire "perché la mia casa era finita, e i miei genitori morti" (R1 104; "because my house was no longer, and my parents dead") – is not very far from the secret, and perhaps unconscious, goal to which the author of *Poveri e semplici* herself aims. But to achieve it she must go farther and "scendere risolutamente a patti con l'inconscio" ("come resolutely to terms with the unconscious").[42] She must travel the road that the Baron takes in a scene in *Il cappello piumato,* after a violent quarrel with Sonia and her flight from home:

> Era accaduto che tanto lui che l'Augusta [...] avevano preferito iniziare le ricerche separatamente, movendosi l'una in direzione del Naviglio [...] ed era stata la traccia fortunata, l'altro per Corso Italia, cioè verso San Celso, che poteva far pensare a un repentino delirio, e un confondersi nella mente delle cose passate e presenti: in altri termini, per ritrovare Soniuccia, il Barone si sarebbe addirittura diretto verso *il Passato*! (R1 253–54).

> (It happened that both he and Augusta [...] preferred to begin their search separately. One moving in the direction of the Naviglio [...] and that was the lucky path. The other down Corso Italia, toward San Celso, a decision which could be thought of as a sudden delirium, and as a confusion in the mind of things past and present: in other words, to find Soniuccia, the Baron would even have to go toward *the Past*!)

Thus the young Bettina of *Poveri e semplici* is abruptly dismissed. Instead of uniting her to the adult Bettina, or rather to the successive two hundred pages of the old manuscript, Ortese has her turn her attention to the past and sends her back to the gates of the port of Toledo, the Hispanic onomastic behind which hides Naples, the sumptuous and ragged city of her youth.

The protagonist of *Il porto di Toledo* is certainly indebted to the "cold" and "mute" Bettina of *Poveri e semplici,* always suspended between grief and stupor, between introversion and excruciating amazement. But she could not have come into existence without the Bettina of *Il cappello piumato* and her incessant speculative tenacity. It is as if the discursive strategies of both these experiments, taken to their extreme consequences, intersect one another in the great autobiographical novel that occupies the writer from 1969 to 1975: enchantment and reflection, the fantastic transfiguration of reality, and a metanarrative framework.

The Third Life of Bettina

Ortese's repeated attempts during the early seventies to publish the old Milanese manuscript also attest to how difficult it was for her to free herself from the "fascicoletto" (R1 168, "little booklet). And so in 1978, when she is finally able to find a publisher, Bettina makes her third and final appearance "in quel primo capitolo del *Cappello piumato* che, con esplicita funzione di prologo, costituisce probabilmente il solo intervento sulle, o intorno alle, famose duecento pagine in vista della loro pubblicazione" ("the first chapter of *Il cappello piumato* that, serving the explicit function of a prologue, is probably the only intervention on, or about, the famous two hundred pages in view of their impending publication").[43] Like a ghost from the past, the protagonist emerges from the unearthed pages of the manuscript. And because she is literally dealing with a spectre, Ortese prepares a perfect Gothic setting for her: an abandoned house, the same "casa tetra e imponente dove avevo già battuto su una macchinetta, ora allo stato di ferraglia, il mio vecchio *Racconto*" ("bleak and imposing house in which I had already typed on an old typewriter, now reduced to scrap metal, my old *Racconto*"), and "una sera di gennaio" ("a January evening"), the very day she kissed Gilliat, "il primo del nuovo anno" ("the first of the new year"), swept by the "vento delle Alpi, vero vento polare" (R1 157; "wind of the Alps, the true polar wind").

Introducing her readers to a text that was by then distant, and at the same time in order to connect it to the events narrated in *Poveri e semplici*, Ortese utilizes the self-commentary approach that she had already employed in *Il porto di Toledo*: that is, she outlines the history of the manuscript:

> a due livelli, come cronaca di una scrittura e insieme cronaca di una rilettura, procedendo nel secondo livello ad articolare testo (il testo riletto) e commento ed esplicitamente indicando nelle ormai mitiche quaranta cartelle originarie la sezione di raccordo tra un romanzo e l'altro. Quelle cartelle, già responsabili [...] della stesura di *Poveri e semplici*, si ritrovano infatti qui, selettivamente citate [...] e stanno ad attestare la continuità del progetto.[44]

> (on two levels, as the chronicle of a writing process and at the same time a chronicle of a re-reading, proceeding, on the second level, to the articulation of a text (the re-read text) and a commentary, and explicitly indicating in the by-now legendary original forty pages the section that connects one novel to the other. Those pages, already responsible [...] for the draft of *Poveri e semplici*, are, indeed, found here, selectively quoted [...] and they are meant to attest to the continuity of the project.)

To the doubly instrumental function of this stratagem – of summarizing and of distancing it from a text perceived to be foreign – Ortese adds a novelistic trick, a stroke of apparently gratuitous theatre: the appearance of the most tenacious of the "Ombre, [dei] piccoli Spiriti del Passato, [delle] Forme Incompiute, [delle] Irene morte, da strapazzo" (R1 165; "Shadows, [of the] little Spirits of the Past, [of the] Unfinished Forms; [of] worthless, dead Irenes"). What is Bettina's ghost doing in these cold and deserted rooms? First, she is defending her story. She presses the author of today, advocating for her version of the facts and the dignity of the "prosaccia" ("bad prose") in which they are recounted. And then she duplicates, as in a hall of mirrors, the metanarrative nature of the chapter, grafting onto the writing and re-reading dialectic the confrontation between the author and her character, or rather between the two different authors, that of yesterday (Bettina herself) and that of today (Anna Maria Ortese).

The re-reading process is divided and multiplies itself. The reader is introduced to the old manuscript through Ortese's contemptuous eyes as the author:

> Rimasi francamente sconvolta, pensierosa.
>
> Aggettivazione... punteggiatura: tutto era incredibilmente bambino!
>
> Questa non crebbe – dissi tra me – e scrisse un libro-bambino.
>
> Oh, come avrei voluto metterle sotto gli occhi il suo vecchio straccetto. (R1 164)

> (I was frankly shocked, pensive.
>
> Adjectives... punctuation: everything was incredibly childish!
>
> She never grew up – I said to myself – and she wrote a baby-book.
>
> Oh, how I would have liked to bring that little old rag to her attention.)

But at the same time, and quite unexpectedly, the reader is compelled to reconsider even the old manuscript of *Poveri e semplici* from Bettina-the-author's point of view:

> Insomma, c'era stata una festa! Motivo del lamento era che tale festa fosse stata da me snobisticamente tagliata, e ridotta a niente.
>
> Altro motivo – a sentire quella tempesta di vento – è che io mi fossi permessa di portare le Quaranta e successive pagine a un discorso compìto, come se il mondo non fosse stato quello che era: un gran vento, una notte buia, una solitudine, un inferno.
>
> Incredibilmente (vorrei dire stupidamente) ribattevo che sta bene, ma la vita non può passare nell'arte (dicevo così: *arte*!) così com'è. Bisogna mondarla! Come un pisello! Risposta:

> AILLALLILLIII!
> E dentro, come un filo:
> "Oh, non fare così! Non fare così!"
> [...]
> Ammetto! C'era stata veramente una festa [...] e non che Bettina non l'avesse registrata puntualmente, solo che io non l'avevo voluta vedere! (R1 159–68)

> (In short, there was a party! It was cause for lament that I had so snobbishly cut such a party and reduced it to nothing.
> Another reason – to listen to that wind storm – is that I allowed myself to bring those Forty and following pages to completion, as if the world were not what it was: a great wind, a dark night, a loneliness, an inferno.
> Surprisingly (I would say stupidly) I replied that it was all right, but life cannot pass directly into art (I said it like this: *art!*). It must be polished! Like a pea! Answer:
> AILLALLILLIII!
> And inside, like a thread:
> "Oh, don't act like that! Just don't!"
> [...]
> I admit! There really was a party [...] and it wasn't that Bettina hadn't registered it punctually, it was just that I didn't want to see it!)

For this reason Ortese summons her old character back to the page. To allow her to reassert her own truth: a "verità di cose incompiute, degradate – o Umanità, o Realtà, o triste Bellezza! – dove più o meno tutto confluisce" (R1 169; "truth of unfinished, degraded things – either Humanity, or Reality, or sad Beauty! – where more or less everything converges"). But also so that she might be able to replicate before the eyes of her reader the same gesture that almost twenty years earlier had caused the rift between the initial forty pages of the manuscript and the following two hundred: the anguished and imperious gesture, timid and determined, of finding a voice and authorial agency.

According to Paul De Man, autobiographical discourse is comparable to *prosopopea*, which he intends as the bestowing of the gift of speech to an absent or deceased one,[45] but that "in the case of texts attributed to a female subject" is also to be interpreted "in the other sense of the rhetorical figure that gives a voice to inanimate beings, incapable of language."[46] This is exactly what happens in the first chapter of *Il cappello piumato*, whose metanarrative nature is manifested also in a third sense: that of an autobiographical text that expresses the discursive strategy of the autobiography metaphorically, a *mise en abîme.* Or rather, it is *almost* exactly what happens in the first chapter of *Il cappello piumato.* Because Bettina is absent and dead, and even, inasmuch as she is a female writer, an inanimate being, or without an *anima,* she is thus deprived of language: "uno scrittore-donna, una bestia che parla" (CC 51; "a woman writer, a speaking beast"). However, no one gives her a voice: she bestows it upon herself, irrupting into an empty house with the east wind. Although she is nothing more than a product of the fiction, she is the one in the text who replicates the author's own act of self-expression.

An act of rebellion and authority; an act so unprecedented, and yet so fundamental, that the text is not enough to suggest it, but that it must be stated outright, expressed concretely in the representation. Since 1975, the year *Il porto di Toledo* was published, Ortese was almost obsessive about this necessity. On the back cover of this novel she presents the protagonist Damasa (her alter ego) as "a character that I had not foreseen at the beginning" and who

> si era sostituito al mio *io* reale – quello che ora scrive questa nota – portando il racconto, in modo neppure questo previsto, fino alla fine [...] Se mi si chiedesse cosa ne penso: ricordo solo la fatica, forse vana, che m'è costata: per sistemare passabilmente linguaggio e struttura che non avevo pensato così; per capire chi fosse questo personaggio tanto fuori di sé e malinconico (che a volte temevo poter essere stata io).
>
> [had replaced my actual "I" – the one who is presently composing this note – carrying the story, unexpected even in this respect, up to the end [...] If you were to ask me what I think: I remember only the toil, perhaps in vain, that it cost me: in arranging adequately the language and structure that I had not intended to turn out like this; in becoming acquainted with this character who was so crazy and melancholic (who I feared at times could have been me).][47]

Ten years later, in a note for the BUR edition of *Il porto di Toledo,* the shadow of Damasa comes even more clearly into focus, her self-narrating voice bursts even more dramatically onto the stage:

> M'impegnai dunque a scrivere un libro di memoria. E come lo pensai, venne fuori questa Damasa, a me sconosciuta [...]
>
> Prese il mio posto nella casa del Pilar, e descrisse tutto come a me non sarebbe mai potuto accadere. La guardavo allibita. Parlava di me (scrittore)

come un detenuto avrebbe parlato della Legge. Il mio essere, di oggi, nella convenzione dello scrivere, non la riguardava [...]

Con questo spirito, con questa cattiva e desolata ombra alle spalle, sotto il dominio, o fascino malato, di quest'ombra [...] "ricordai" Toledo, ne descrissi il silenzio, l'angoscia, i passi giovani (oggi perduti) per le sue strade contorte e ventose, in mezzo a ignote colline. (R1 998–99)

[I undertook to write a book of memory. And in the process, this Damasa, completely unknown to me, emerged [...]

She took my place at Pilar's house, and she described everything, as I would never have been able to. I watched her, speechless. She spoke about me (the writer) as a prisoner would speak of the Law. My being, in the present, according to the conventions of writing, did not concern her [...]

With this spirit, this poor and desolate shadow at my back, under the dominion, or sick charm, of this shade [...] "I remembered" Toledo, I described the silence, the anguish, the youthful steps (now lost) down its twisted and windy streets, through unknown hills.]

Between these two moments lies the metanarrative chapter of *Il cappello piumato,* which leads this gesture back to its origin and reveals its true "political" nature: a revolt against authority, represented in this case by the author; a self-conscious deviance from literary norms: "Nella vita non c'è soltanto la Letteratura, andiamo, né il Successo, né la Fortunata Carriera, la Giusta Previdenza, il Savio Ammiccare!" (R1 169; "In life there is not only Literature, come on, not Success, or a Charmed Career, the Proper Prudence, the Knowing Wink"); a claim to the right to speak for herself rather than to have someone speak on her behalf.[48]

"Da quando in qua le bestioline parlano?" (R1 267; "Since when do the little beasts speak?"), Gilliat asks his companion interrupting a discussion in which he is led to question all of his certainties. Since they learned to speak for themselves, respond Bettina and her ghost.

Translated by Steve Baker

NOTES

1 So Anna Maria Ortese defines *Il cappello piumato* in an interview given shortly after the book's release: see D'Ambra, "... Tutti i grandi romanzi non sono che storie di bambini," 41.

2 Philippe Lejeune speaks of this particular function of autobiography in the context of Gide: Lejeune, *Le pacte autobiografique,* 176–77. Something like this also happens for Ortese: after thirty years of literary activity focused until then exclusively on short works (short stories, inquiries, reportages), the writer begins to grapple with the novel, precisely in the early sixties.

3 Ortese, *Corpo celeste* (Milano: Adelphi, 1997). All citations from *Corpo celeste* are from this edition, which henceforth will be indicated in the text by the abbreviation CC followed by the page number.

4 Ortese, *Romanzi,* ed. Monica Farnetti, vol. 1 (Milan: Adelphi, 2002). All quotations from the novels of Anna Maria Ortese are from this edition, which henceforth will be indicated in the text by the letters R1 followed by the page number.

5 For a detailed reconstruction of Ortese's Milan, please refer to Luca Clerici's fundamental biography *Apparizione e visione,* 279–348.

6 Ortese's letter to the publishing house Einaudi, Editorial Director, Rome, 20 November 1963, Archivio Einaudi, Correspondence with authors and collaborators in Italy, folder 147, file 2243, Ortese (henceforth simply "AE"). I would like to thank Roberto Cerati for granting me permission to consult the file.

7 Geno Pampaloni's letter to Anna Maria Ortese, Florence, 16 January 1964, cited by Monica Farnetti in the notes to the text of *Poveri e semplici,* in Ortese, R1 1007.

8 Clerici presents the letter Ortese sent with the manuscript to Rizzoli, as well as Domenico Porzio's response, in *Apparizione e visione,* 380–81.

9 Ortese's letter to Italo Calvino, Rome, 14 November 1964, AE.

10 Ortese's letter to Italo Calvino, Rome, 12 February 1965, AE.

11 Ortese's letter to Italo Calvino, Rome, 14 September 1965, AE. Emphasis mine.

12 Ortese's letter to Italo Calvino, Roma, 22 November 1965, AE.

13 Barberis, "È così difficile trovare a Milano il silenzio," 9.

14 Geno Pampaloni's letter to Anna Maria Ortese, 28 July 1966, in Clerici, *Apparizione e visione,* 410.

15 Ibid., 410–11.

16 Pampaloni, "Incantesimo dell'innocenza," 4.

17 Pampaloni, "Ecologia sublime," 1.

18 Ortese's letter to Andrea Guano, 10 February 1979, in Clerici, *Apparizione e visione,* 517.

19 The reply, in which the writer expresses his doubts, is dated 26 September 1972 and is found in Calvino, *Lettere 1940–1985,* 1173.

20 Ortese's letter to Sergio Pautasso, 18 June 1977, in Clerici, *Apparizione e visione*, 516.

21 Sergio Pautasso's letter to Ortese, 15 September 1977, in Clerici, *Apparizione e visione*, 516.

22 See, for example, Paccagnini, "I dolori dell'angelica Ortese," 120: "Un romanzo, *Poveri e semplici*, che si offre con un pudore e un candore che si bagnano nello stile semplice, in una dimessa quanto avvincente colloquialità da *Fioretti*; caratteristica che non avrà invece *Il cappello piumato*, in cui il ricorso all'arma dell'autoironia non riesce a far velo al senso della definitiva perdita di un mondo e a un tono di mesta amarezza per gli inaridimenti umani" ("One novel, *Poveri e semplici*, which presents itself with a modesty and candour that bathes its reader in the simple style, in a conversational tone of a *fioretto* as modest as it is thrilling; a characteristic that *Il cappello piumato* does not possess, in which her recourse to the weapon of self-irony fails to veil the sense of the definitive loss of a world and to a tone of mournful bitterness over the disillusionment of mankind.")

23 On 18 August 1961, Ortese announces to Paolo Lecaldano: "in October I would like to get back to my dear work, of which only the first part is in place, and to finish it in its entirety this winter" (Anna Maria Ortese's letter to Paolo Lecaldano, 18 August 1961, in Clerici, *Apparizione e visione*, 371). But a year later: "the [...] book is not yet ready. Having *completely* finished the first part, I have to finish (that is, develop it further, *in certain places*) the second" (Anna Maria Ortese's letter to Paolo Lecaldano, 18 August 1961 in Clerici, *Apparizione e visione*, 378). And on 24 September 1962, responding to Lecaldano's insistent inquiry, the writer assures him that she has already begun "to recopy the first one hundred and fifty pages" and that "by the beginning of October I could send them to you" (Anna Maria Ortese's letter to Paolo Lecaldano, in Clerici, *Apparizione e visione*, 378).

24 This corresponds, to be precise, to Bettina's return from the Soviet Union; to the death of Sonia's uncle, which in *Poveri e semplici* occurs on the very same night that Bettina and Gilliat exchange necklaces, while in *Il cappello piumato* it happens in the autumn of the following year; and to the arrival in Milan of Sonia's mother and her move into a new home, along with her daughter and the Baron. All this is complicated by an unexplained chronological shift, so the night of the party, which in *Il cappello piumato* coincides with New Year's Eve 1953–54, is deferred for a year in *Poveri e semplici* (on this point see Clerici, *Apparizione e visione*, 345, n. 152).

25 *Il porto di Toledo* is divided into two main sections, *Mura apase o marine. Il primo mondo* and *Secondi ricordi di Toledo spezzati dal rumore del mare-tempo che si*

avvicina, whose titles eloquently sum up the trajectory of ascent and fall narrated in the novel.

26 See Pizzorusso, *Ai margini dell'autobiografia*, 189.

27 Starobinski, *The Living Eye*, 176.

28 Clerici, *Apparizione e visione*, 413.

29 Ibid., 379.

30 See Arriaga, *Mio amore, mio giudice*, 68.

31 After the introductory chapter, "Bettina's story" begins with a summary of her trip to Russia, that recycles, with some revisions, the episodes and impressions published in "L'Europeo" in 1954; Ortese's journalistic writing leaves further traces of itself in the evocation of her investigation of Salvatore Giuliano's Sicily and of the protagonist's enthusiastic participation in the Giro d'Italia in 1955, both recounted in the "Monti e mari" (Mountains and Seas) chapter. Two poems dedicated to Gilliat are also included in the novel, "Io sono così contenta, quando mi trovo con te" (I am so happy, when I'm with you) and "Quando io morirò nessuno saprà dire" (When I die no one will know), the second of which will be republished in the collection of poems *Il mio paese è la notte* (My Country is the Night) (Rome: Empiria, 1996), 122.

32 On diaristic writing, see Maurice Blanchot's reflections in *The Book To Come* and Jean Rousset's *Le lecteur intime*. On the relationship between the diary and the self-portrait, see Didier, "Autoportrait et journal intime," 167–82.

33 Gramigna, "Un matrimonio di carta," 10.

34 Thus reads the back cover of *Corpo celeste*.

35 Melandri, "Quel raccontare femminile," 19–20.

36 So the author says in a letter to her French translator Claude Schmitt, in which she clarifies certain obscure expressions in *Il cappello piumato*. The letter appears in an appendix of the notes to the text of *Il cappello piumato*, in Ortese, R1 1025.

37 Gatto, "Introduzione," xi.

38 Cesare Garboli calls the novel "a little fairy tale" in his review ("Il giglio di quell'amore," 20). More recently, Elisabetta Rasy has read, beneath the surface "of the screwy vicissitudes of the intellectual dreamers in the promising but also difficult Milan of the fifties," "the tale of the beast that speaks, namely, Bettina," with an intuition that I will develop further, except in the context of *Il cappello piumato* (Rasy, *Senza orologio né carta geografica*, xx).

39 Garboli, "Il giglio di quell'amore," 19.

40 Farnetti, *I romanzi di Anna Maria Ortese*, R1 xlv.

41 See, by analogy, the meeting between Dasa and Lemano at the end of the first part of *Il porto di Toledo*: "Come l'ebbe, la mia mano destra, ecco egli la

torce, quasi rapisce sotto il suo braccio all'altezza del petto ardente. Come era dall'altra parte della persona, anche il braccio rapito intorno al suo corpo stringe. Egli mi sembra, come al mattino di dolore, nemico. 'Stringa, no? Che fa?' grida. Come avesse detto: 'vira a babordo!', un semplice violento ordine. 'Ha capito? Ha capito?' 'Non so.' 'Io muoio, e lei *non sa*, lei *non sa*!' disse diventando abbagliante," (R1 667, "As he held my right hand he pulled it, as if abducting it under his arm at the height of his burning chest. As my left was already on the other side of his body, so the abducted arm was held around his shaking body. Like the morning of pain, he seemed to be an enemy. 'Hug me, no? What are you doing?' he cries. As if he had shouted a simple, violent order: 'Veer left!' 'Understand? Understand?' 'I don't know.' 'I'm dying, and you *don't* know, you don't know!' he said shining brightly").

42 Clerici, *Apparizione e visione*, 415.

43 Farnetti, note to the text of *Il cappello piumato*, in Ortese, R1 1013.

44 Ibid., 1013–14.

45 See De Man, "Autobiography as De-Facement," 67–81: "[...] it is the figure of *prosopopea*, the fiction of an apostrophe to an absent, deceased, or voiceless entity, which posits the possibility of the latter's reply and confers upon it the power of speech [...] Prosopopea is the trope of autobiography, by which one's name [...] is made intelligible and memorable as a face" (the citation is found on pages 75–76).

46 Arriaga, *Mio amore, mio giudice*, 45.

47 Ortese, backcover of *Il porto di Toledo* (Milan: Rizzoli, 1975).

48 For this idea of women's autobiography, recurrent in feminist theory and scholarship on this literary genre, see in particular Stanton, "Autogynography: Is the Subject Different?," 13 and Gilmore, *Autobiographics: A Feminist Theory of Women's Self-Representation*, 40.

WORKS CITED

Arriaga, Flórez Mercedes. *Mio amore, mio giudice: Alterità autobiografica femminile.* Lecce: Piero Manni, 1997.

Barberis, Alfredo. "È così difficile trovare a Milano il silenzio." *Il Giorno*, 6 April 1966.

Blanchot, Maurice. *The Book to Come.* Redwood City, CA: Stanford University Press, 2002.

Calvino, Italo. *Lettere 1940–1985.* Ed. Luca Baranelli. Milan: Mondadori, 2000.

Clerici, Luca. *Apparizione e visione: Vita e opere di Anna Maria Ortese.* Milan: Mondadori, 2002.

D'Ambra, Raffaella. "…Tutti i grandi romanzi non sono che storie di labirinti … La loro forza è che rispecchiano la condizione umana…" *Uomini e libri* 15, no. 75 (1979): 41–42.

De Man, Paul. "Autobiography as De-Facement." In *The Rhetoric of Romanticism*, 67–81. New York: Columbia University Press, 1984.

Didier, Béatrice. "Autoportrait et journal intime." *Corps écrit* (*L'autoportrait*) 5 (1983): 167–82.

Farnetti, Monica. "I romanzi di Anna Maria Ortese," in *Romanzi*, Vol. 1, by Anna Maria Ortese, ix–lxvi. Milan: Adelphi, 2002.

Garboli, Cesare. "Il giglio di quell'amore." *La Fiera letteraria*, 7 September (1967): 19–20 .

Gatto, Alfonso. "Introduzione" to *Poveri e semplici*, by Anna Maria Ortese, i–xiv. Milan: Rizzoli, 1974.

Gilmore, Leigh. *Autobiographics: A Feminist Theory of Women's Self-Representation.* Ithaca-London: Cornell University Press, 1994.

Gramigna, Giuliano. "Un matrimonio di carta." *Corriere della Sera*, 11 February 1979.

Lejeune, Philippe. *Le pacte autobiografique.* Paris: Éditions du Seuil, 1975.

Melandri, Lea. "Quel raccontare femminile." In *Lapis: Sezione aurea di una rivista*, ed. Laura Kreyder, Lea Melandri, Maria Nadotti, Rosella Prezzo,and Paola Redaelli, 17–23. Rome: manifestolibri, 1998.

Ortese, Anna Maria. *Il porto di Toledo.* In *Romanzi*, Vol 1. Milan: Adelphi, 2002

– Letter to Einaudi, Editorial Director, 20 November 1963. In Archivio Einaudi, Correspondence with authors and collaborators in Italy, folder 147, file 2243, Ortese.

– Letter to Italo Calvino, 14 November 1964. In Archivio Einaudi. Correspondence with authors and collaborators in Italy, folder 147, file 2243, Ortese.

– Letter to Italo Calvino, 12 February 1965. In I Archivio Einaudi. Correspondence with authors and collaborators in Italy, folder 147, file 2243, Ortese.

– Letter to Italo Calvino, 14 September 1965. In Archivio Einaudi. Correspondence with authors and collaborators in Italy, folder 147, file 2243, Ortese.

– Letter to Italo Calvino, 22 November 1965, In Archivio Einaudi. Correspondence with authors and collaborators in Italy, folder 147, file 2243, Ortese.

Paccagnini, Ermanno. "I dolori dell'angelica Ortese." *Letture* 536 (1997): 115–22.

Pampaloni, Geno. "Ecologia sublime." *Il Giornale*, 1 February 1988.

– "Incantesimo dell'innocenza." *Il Giornale*, 28 January 1979.
Pizzorusso, Arnaldo. *Ai margini dell'autobiografia.* Bologna: Il Mulino, 1986.
Rasy, Elisabetta. "Senza orologio né carta geografica," in *Poveri e semplici*, by Anna Maria Ortese, ix–xxi. Turin: Utet, 2006.
Rousset, Jean. *Le lecteur intime.* Paris: Librairie José Corti, 1986.
Stanton, Domna C. "Autogynography: Is the Subject Different?" In *The Female Autograph: Theory and Practice of Autobiography from the Tenth to the Twentieth Century*, ed. Domna C. Stanton, 3–20. Chicago and London: University of Chicago Press, 1984.
Starobinski, Jean. *The Living Eye.* Trans. Arthur Goldhammer. Cambridge, MA: Harvard University Press, 1989.

7 On the Ruins of Time: *Toledo* and the (Auto)fiction of the Ephemeral

FLORA GHEZZO

Toutes les biographies comme toutes les autobiographies comme tous les récits racontent une historie à la place d'une autre historie.

(All biographies like all autobiographies like all narratives tell one story in place of another.)

Hélène Cixous, *Hélène Cixous, Photos de Racines*

When, in March 1969, in the midst of a Milan rife with political violence and protests, Anna Maria Ortese sat down to write a commentary on her early writing – and then, almost involuntarily, the metanarration shifted towards the more complex framework of an actual narration – she hardly imagined the extraordinary feat she was undertaking. Anomalous and hybrid, enigmatic and cryptic, fascinating and repulsive, the text born out of this compositional undertaking was destined to leave a mark on the Italian literary *Novecento.*[1]

The exemplary status of *Il porto di Toledo* (Rizzoli, 1975; The Port of Toledo) – this is the definitive title given to the work – touches upon many planes. As a great metanovel, like few others, it poses questions to and about literature, interrogating the significance of literary creation, the relationship between poetic discourse, time, and memory. It fully exposes the mechanism of narration, complicating the dialectic between truth and fiction and exploring the interrelation between reality, irreality, dream, and everything that comes in-between. The exemplary status of the novel, however, relates as well to the neither avoidable nor disputable fact of its female authorship (fated, to say the least): and we are made to reflect more than a little on the undeniable relationship between the feminine and language, between body and logos, between gender and literary genre.

The first great *Künstlerroman* of a woman writer in Italian literature (those that preceded it being few, forgotten, or of little note),[2] *Il porto di Toledo* follows the authoritative literary model of Dante's *Vita Nuova*, as it has been said,[3] framing and providing commentary for the central nine of the thirteen autobiographical tales from the debut compilation (*Angelici dolori*, 1937) as well as for numerous hitherto unpublished early poems and verses. A story of poetics and eros, the novel also charts for the first time the groundwork for a semantics of feminine and adolescent desire, bringing out fragments of a stunning erotic and emotive discourse that somehow recalls the anguish and the ecstasy of the Dantean and *stilnovo* physiology of love, readapted to the culture of the twentieth century through the lens of psychoanalysis. *Il porto di Toledo*, finally, is also a splendid quasi-autobiography, albeit one that has been transferred to a fictional and vaguely fantastical world. Conspicuously transgressing certain traditional hallmarks of the genre, the novel demonstrates beyond the shadow of a doubt (to the joy of postmodern theorists) that every autobiography is always a fictitious as well as a performative effort.[4] Questioning the vacillating and unreliable nature of memory, the novel also forgoes the recuperation of the past and thus dismisses the modernist and Proustian *temps retrouvé*, which brought so much to bear on Western literature of the twentieth century.

Yet, about this complex novel there is still a lot (if not everything) to be said. If one excludes a few fundamental inquiries on the part of Monica Farnetti and Luca Clerici, the most authoritative Ortese critics to date, few scholars have ventured into the labyrinthine structure of the text and the coded nature of its language.[5] In this essay, choosing from the many interpretive paths, I set out to examine the novel through the lens of temporality. First, I seek to show how the impulse towards autobiographical writing (and re-writing) is directly correlated to the themes of impermanence, flux, and transience – the true and only protagonists of an enchanted novel and, at the same time, personal, psychological, and poetic obsessions of the author. Then, I direct my attention to the way Ortese's fixation on *fuga temporis* (and her concomitant desire to stop it) determines not just the novel's narrative strategies and structures, modes of emplotment, and tropological movements, but ultimately shapes Ortese's peculiar "technologies" and metaphors of the self and the very unfolding of the self-formation process. The first section of this analysis whisks us to the shore of Libya and the Mediterranean Sea, to the time of Ortese's adolescence, and then, subsequently, to the multiple "scenes of writing," where the actual writing of the novel *Il porto di Toledo* took place.

1. Oceanic and Celestial Epiphanies

As William Wordsworth writes in his "Prelude," there are fleeting moments that have a lasting quality and keep resonating within us: moments of revelation, of emotional intensity, of sudden awareness, functioning as a source of imaginative power and nourishment.[6] Nothing is better suited than this Wordsworthian notion of "spots of time" to capture the significance of two epiphanic moments that have marked Ortese's intellectual and poetic experience. The two instances are both recounted by Ortese in her collection of essays and prose meditations, *Corpo celeste* (1997). The first "spot of time" took place in 1928 upon her return from Libya – at the time a colonial territory which had just fallen under the control of Mussolini's fascist regime, following the defeat of the Senussis – where the Ortese family had moved three years prior to cultivate a "concession" of land, granted by the Italian government. The family's colonial enterprise was a failure: the land intended for cultivation was virtually barren, and the family returned to Italy few years later. While crossing the Mediterranean from Tripoli to Naples, the adolescent Anna Maria was struck by a sudden intuition as she sat entranced, as children often do, observing the white and foamy tread that the ship left on the blue water of the sea.

> Varcando il mare per rientrare in Italia, durante un viaggio di due giorni, mi colpì in modo intenso il duplice moto risultante dalla nave che solca l'acqua azzurra, e dall'acqua azzurra che, pur non essendo più la medesima di un attimo prima, si presenta come la medesima. Il medesimo luogo, pensavo, non vuol dire dunque l'identico tempo e situazione [...] Così c'era questo problema del tempo – delle dimensioni e i luoghi dove le cose passavano. Così le cose passavano! E irrevocabilmente, sembrava. Perciò tutto quanto accadeva, se la sua parte seconda era il non esistere più, era cosa illusoria. (CC 64)

> (Crossing the sea to return to Italy, during a two-day voyage, I was entranced by the dual current flowing out behind the ship as it skimmed along the blue water, which, while no longer the same blue water from the preceding instance, still appeared as such. A single place, I thought, does not equate

to an identical time and situation. And so there was this problem of time – of the dimensions and of the places where things were passing by. Thus things were passing by! And irrecoverably, it seemed. So everything that was happening, since its complementary part did no longer exist, was illusory.)

Ortese, here, on board the ship, seems to be playing "little Deleuze." With the precociousness of her intelligence, she intuits and puts together some of the same fundamental elements out of which the French philosopher would go on to build his theories: repetition, difference, perception, sameness, and time. The space and the mechanical action (the water, the ship that ploughs) could be one and the same – ponders the young girl – but the instance that produces a new event is always different. The only true repetition – Deleuze instead reflects – is the repetition of difference, eternally reaffirming the creative difference of life; while time is a process of differential becoming that constantly produces new events.[7] For the moment, however, on the bridge of the ship skidding across the Mediterranean Sea, Ortese is far from philosophical abstractions: what instead strikes her acute adolescent sensibilities is the painful perception of the ephemeral nature of time. Water, sea, fluidity, *fuga temporis*, but also becoming, repetition, circularity, eternal return are bound to nourish the author's profoundly Petrarchan imagination in the years to come, influencing her narrative strategies and determining her intellectual and poetic affinities: from the Spanish baroque poets of the *sueño* and the *disengaño* (Calderon de la Barca, Gongora, De Quevedo) to the "salt-encrusted pages" of English and American authors (Stevenson, Defoe, Melville, Conrad) – all writers united under the common thread of either a maritime, "watery" setting or an obsession for impermanence.

In a perfect parallel to the "oceanic epiphany" that took place on the ship, a second "spot of time" occupies the opposite and complementary pole, which proves just as essential to the development of Ortese's poetics. Enraptured by the memory of a Raphael's painting she viewed as a child, during a school trip at the Museo Capodimonte in Naples,[8] the author intuits the possibility of a flight from the illusory nature of time's phenomena and from its destructive force through artistic representation. There is a blueprint or matrix of reality – very much like the ancient Platonic eidola – that pre-exists the ephemeral, and therefore unreal, material world of change perceived by the senses. For the young Ortese this realization is a true "celestial epiphany," which counters the effects of the preceding "oceanic epiphany":

> Vidi un *Raffaello* di piccole proporzioni [...] Rappresentava un cielo. E quel cielo – in qualche modo che devo ritenere straordinario – capovolgeva ogni idea che avevo sulla realtà, era più vero, più reale di ogni cielo del mondo reale. Sulla sua consistenza non potevano esserci dubbi. E la sua straordinarietà era in questo: che *sostituiva* dunque *la prima* creazione con *una seconda,* che si poneva però *come la prima,* perchè preesistente a questa, essendo l'idea di questa. Diceva [...] al cielo *naturale:* "*Tu vai e vieni. Non resti. Ed ecco, io – Cielo di Raffaello – resto, perchè non sono il cielo naturale, sono l'idea di qualsiasi cielo. Così, resto.*" (CC 97)

> ("I saw a Raphael of small proportions [...] it depicted the sky. And that sky – in such a manner that left me awestruck – overturned every idea that I held about reality, it was truer, more real than any real-world sky. There could be no doubt as to its consistency. And the extraordinary quality was this: that it *substituted* thus *the first* creation with a *second,* which nonetheless posed *as the first,* by virtue of preexisting it, being its idea. It told [...] the *natural sky:* '*You come and you go. You do not remain. And here, I – the sky of Raphael – remain, for I am not the natural sky, I am the idea of any sky. Thus, I remain eternal.*'")

Thus, for Ortese, only *representation* (instead of being a replica of a shadow, as it is in Plato's philosophy) is able to transcend the flux of things and time, "to capture and fix [...] the marvellous phenomenon of living and feeling" ("cogliere e fissare [...] il meraviglioso fenomeno del vivere e del sentire," CC 61). The quasi-Platonic notion of writing as a "technology of transcendence" constitutes one of the foundations of the "*poetica dell'Espressività*" ("poetics of Expressiveness") formulated in the pages of *Il porto di Toledo*: a poetics rooted in the idea of an "aesthetics of opposites" and symbolically captured by the image of a mirror. The mirror's still and cold surface, in fact, just like Raphael's painting, has a quality opposite and contrary to the impermanent objects reflected in it. Only by virtue of this contraposition can it offer itself as a means of representation:

> Questo fenomeno apocalittico e incantatore del vivere, essendo tanto intenso, e sfuggente [...] essendo l'insondabile o inafferrabile stesso [...] non si può rendere che in uno stato d'animo contrario che indicherò come: l'ammirazione o contemplazione della sua immensità e (per noi) ferocia. Solo una superfice gelida ed elegante – assolutamente immobile – potrà ripendere il moto scompligliato di un albero scosso dal vento, o il levarsi fresco di belva di un'onda verde del mare [...] Questo è ciò che si

> dice qualità estetica. È la qualità dello specchio che si oppone – e perciò la cattura – alla cosa specchiata. (CC 66)
>
> (This apocalyptic and enchanting phenomenon of living, being so intense, and fleeting [...] being the unfathomable or the ungraspable itself [...] cannot be rendered unless in an opposite state of being that I will so describe: the admiration or the contemplation of its immensity and (for us) ferocity. Only a gelid and elegant surface – absolutely immobile – could recapture the motion of a windswept tree or the fresh beast-like heave of a wave from the sea [...] this is that which one calls aesthetic quality. It is the quality of the mirror that positions itself opposite – and thereby captures – the reflected object.)

Ortese's poetic "tools," however, will ultimately prove inadequate. Mirror-theory, aesthetics of opposites, writing-as-technology-of-transcendence are destined to falter, falling apart *during the very process* of writing. In a perfect Ortesian move, Ortese contradicts herself, disseminating false leads. In fact, not only does her writing never resolve the dialectical tension between ephemerality and permanence – which is continually flung back into a perpetual game of deferral and counterbalance – but, likewise, the metaphor of an "absolutely immobile" mirror is scarcely suited to represent *her* writing style. The fact of the matter is that Ortese, finely tuned to the sensibilities of the (post)modern era, has lost faith in the transparency of words and of simulacra: mimesis, the Platonic and Aristotelic idea of the world's reflection in art and language, which had been the great illusion of Western realism (and of Italian neorealism, to which the writer contributed in part), is no longer possible. Thus, *per speculum in aenigmate*, mirrors reflect blurred visions. And for that matter, Ortese's writing more closely resembles those baroque mirrors – anamorphic, parabolic, bent, and multiplied – commendably described by Jurgis Baltrusaitis[9] in his catoptric science: mirrors that reflect "infinite transformations and distortions of forms and figures, of spaces and perspectives";[10] mirrors that reveal fantastic and oneiric worlds, where unreal, dream, and shadow become metaphors for the illusory and fleeting nature of the real world. Like Alice in Wonderland, Ortese too has her *looking glass* to pass through.

2. The Scene(s) of Writing: Death, Time, and *Toledo*

Ortese began to lay out the first pages of a new creative project in Milan in 1969. Living in poverty, marginalized by both the literary establishment and the "leftist" cultural environment, Ortese, in her mid-fifties, had a vertiginous series of failures and unexpected successes (*Angelici dolori*, 1937; *Il mare non bagna Napoli*, 1953) under her belt, as well as an ample repertory of writings, genres, and styles: from magical-realist tales to travelogues, from journalistic prose to fantastic novels (*L'Iguana*, 1965). For some years, however, she had turned inward and towards the recovery of past memories: she had recently published a quasi-autobiographical novel (*Poveri e semplici*, 1967), which, by virtue of its extreme legibility and transparency, had garnered the *Premio Strega*, the most prestigious Italian literary award. In this work, Ortese dissolves in one fell swoop both the neorealistic faith in mimetic representation and the widespread hope that a utopian communism might revitalize post-war Italian society: both bold and radical decisions, given that neo-realism had been the most successful cultural trend of post-war Italy and that Marxism seemed to be the only possible ideological affiliation for an entire generation of post-fascist Italian intellectuals. The novel's archaeology and the genealogy are well noted: what started as a simple introduction to a few writings from her youth burgeoned out of all proportion, combining the writings of the past with those of today and becoming a new "fantastic and creative" enterprise of approximately five hundred pages: "Venne un lungo libro: remoto, disperso, qua e là di scrittura incomprensibile" ("Out came a long book: remote, scattered with incomprehensible writing here and there").[11] If the history of the novel's genesis was tormented, so too were the historical moment and the very biography of the author in those years: a historical and personal turmoil that disturbingly affected the "scene of writing," the material and psychological site where the novel was created.

The first of these "scenes of writing" – situated in two different Milanese apartments, between 1969 and 1975 – was haunted by the spectres of dissolution and death, at the same time intimate and collective, personal and historical, real and symbolic. Outside, in the external world, history and politics reared their violent head: Milan was at the centre of the protest movement; it was the stage of processions of workers and students, of the occupation of factories and universities, of strikes, of police charges and barricades. The Italian *Sessantotto* movement was demolishing in part the cornerstones of the bourgeois, clerical, and capitalist culture – bringing about renovations in culture and custom, women's and feminist liberty – but it slipped, unlike in other Western countries, into the whirlpool of ideological extremism and terrorism. On 12 December 1969, the Piazza Fontana Bombing, one of the darkest and most mysterious episodes in Italian history, unveiled the so-called "strategy of tension": between 1969 and 1975 – exactly the same years of the composition of the novel – Italy was bloodied by over 4,000 terrorist attacks at the hands of different political factions: Marxists, neo-fascists, and, presumably, the state secret service.[12] Rebuking ideological violence and hatred, Ortese – who already in 1954 dissociated herself from the Communist Party to which she had registered after the war, following the publication of a provocative "out of line" reportage about Russia – retreated into the private regions of her memory: "Il rumore, la violenza eterna della grande città, dalla quale non potevo mai fuggire, si accrescevano di questo riverbero 'politico.' Odiavo il 'politico' di tutti i tempi e in ogni sua espressione" ("The noise, the eternal violence of the great city, from which I could never escape, amplified with this 'political' agitation. I hated the 'politics' of all times and all its expressions thereof," R1 997). These affirmations notwithstanding, *Il porto di Toledo* is not an entirely apolitical novel, detached from history, as critics tend to believe: on the contrary, Ortese, with her intensely experimental writing, with her "rule-breaking" autobiography, unhinges the "laws" that govern literary genres, destabilizing the readers' horizon of expectation, thus challenging the Italian literary system. As a disenfranchised subject – an intellectual southern woman, with neither financial means nor affluent companionship nor political affiliation – she empowers herself as a self-representational subject, placing the importance of intellectuality and feminine creativity at the centre of her reflection. In her own way, then, Ortese demonstrates how "the personal can become political," as the feminist slogan of the time would have had it.

Just like the external world of history, Ortese's personal world was also marked by crisis and economic instability, so much so that the writer felt "svenuta a forza di vivere nell'inferno-convoglio delle emozioni reazioni immagini – e nella necessità di sopravvivere" (CC 83, "faint by dint of living in the hell-channel of emotions reactions images and in the necessity to survive"). Her writing room was thus haunted by personal nightmares, sentiments of malaise, and bursts of obsessive-compulsive mania that dictated to Ortese the rhythms and tempos of her work. Her creative process, moreover, took place as though amidst the piazza's barricades. "The room of one's own" was actually a tent or a makeshift shed, consisting of rags, cartons, and iron plates that Ortese constructed in the middle of her apartment space in order to seal herself off from the clamour outside.[13] Here she set to writing, shielded by earphones and wax plugs. Literally speaking, the writer was protecting herself from the racket caused by the remodelling in her building (ironically, the second apartment to which she moved out of desperation was also undergoing repairs). On the symbolic level, however, the writer was protecting herself from the violent clamour of history and its unwanted intrusions in her psycho-emotional field.

The novel *Il porto di Toledo* was thus born out of a *double* detachment from the world: the enclosed yet precarious space of a womb / tomb-like room within another room. In this space, risking both a symbolic death and a creative block, Ortese turned therapeutically to her past, to the very conditions from which her creativity first surged. To chart the unknown and slippery territory of memory, she employed as mapping tools her first autobiographical narrations (the 1937 short stories of *Angelici Dolori*) and an old, long-forgotten childhood diary.[14] The psychological mechanism that binds a situation of severe emotional malaise to autobiographical writing as a means of rebirth was destined to obsessively repeat itself over and over again, in a true Deleuzian fashion, unequivocally characterizing *all the scenes of writing* linked to *Il porto di Toledo.* The autobiographical thrust is thus the only antidote for loss, anxiety, pain, neurosis, a powerful deferring and deferral of the threat of dissolution and death – all aspects of the destructive force of time and transience.

Rather than being actual, the second set of writing scenes I want to discuss is merely fictional and takes place in an imaginary Naples-Toledo of the thirties.

> Sono figlia di nessuno. Nel senso che la società, quando io nacqui non c'era, o non c'era per tutti i figli dell'uomo. E nascendo senza società o bontà io stessa, in certo senso non nacqui nemmeno, tutto ciò che vidi e seppi fu illusorio, come i sogni che all'alba svaniscono. Non importa, così, dove nacqui, e come vissi fino agli anni tredici, età a cui risalgono questi scritti e confuse composizioni. So che un certo giorno mi guardai intorno, e vidi che anche il mondo nasceva; nascevano montagne, acque, nuvole, livide figure. (R1 363)

> (I am the daughter of no one. In the sense that society, when I was born, was not there, or was not there for all the sons of man. And being born without society or goodness myself, in a certain sense, I was not even born. All that I saw and knew was illusory, like dreams that dissipate at dawn, and thus it was for those who surrounded me. It does not matter so much where I was born, and how I lived up to the age of thirteen, the age to which these writings and vague compositions date back. I only know that, one day, I looked

around me and saw that even the world was being born; the mountains, the waters, the clouds, the livid figures were being born.)

In quel tempo, come dissi, la speranza dell'espressività mi dominava e io credevo veramente che fosse nella compostezza e valore formale la salvezza dal nulla delle cose e del tempo. (R1 377)

(At that time the hope for expressiveness dominated me. I truly believed that in the grace and the value of form dwelt the salvation from the nothingness of things and of time.)

These two citations, drawn from the novel, form a veritable "primal scene" of writing. In the first passage – the magnificent *incipit* of the text, a true stage for a Lacanian mirror phase – Ortese begets herself in the world by means of parthenogenesis ("I am the daughter of no one"), eschewing any biological or literary genealogy, and mirroring herself in "these writings and vague compositions." The second passage, for its part, explores and delves into the purposes behind her writing, which establishes itself as an instrument for the recovery of that which has been lost (the past, the dead). What do these fictional and metaliterary scenes have to do, one might argue, with the Milanese "shed of her own" of the 1960s? Although the two sets of writing scenes are profoundly different, a single psychological and symbolic strain courses through them both. The dialectical and figural oscillation is in fact the same: on the one hand, symbolic death ("I am not born"), real death (the brother Rassa), pain, dissolution of things ("all that I saw and knew was illusory"); on the other hand, the creation of the self and the crystallization of forms through the process of autobiographical writing, understood as a "technology of transcendence." Moreover, in both the real Milanese and the fictional Toledan writing scenes, the autobiographical material is *exactly* the same: the short surreal stories from the 1930s (published as *Angelici dolori*), originating from the death of her sailor brother Emanuele off the coast of Martinique, and successively reclaimed in 1968 Milan.

Thirty years later, in 1998, a third actual "scene of writing" took place: at the Milanese retirement home Anni Azzurri, the final writing scene gives way to the scene of Ortese's death. As Deleuze would say, repetition occurs only in order to reaffirm difference. The writer, by now old, frail, and gravely ill, returned for the third time to her *Il porto di Toledo*, in a frenzy of rewriting and attention to variants that proved as obstinate as it was incomprehensible: "senza voce quasi sempre, molto debole [...] e tuttavia sommersa dal lavoro di rilettura di *Toledo*" ("nearly always voiceless, very weak [...] and nonetheless overwhelmed by the re-reading of *Toledo*"), she writes in a letter to Franz Haas.[15] Sensing her impending death, this time a real and not a symbolic one, Ortese entrusted in the autobiographical pages a final and immortal image of herself as well as her literary legacy. The circle came to a close. Yet, as always in the case of Ortese, things are never the way they appear. Rather than establish themselves as an instrument of permanence and crystallization, the "prudent and gilded words" of her writing did nothing more than reassert fleetingness and transience, shadows and dreams, reaffirming obsessively all that which she wished to transcend. Truth be told, as critical theory maintains, looking in the mirror of an autobiography is always a duplicitous and contradictory affair. If, on the one hand, the mirror represents the birth of the self and the development of one's identity (even as "the other" professed by Lacan in his mirror stage theory), on the other hand the frigidity of the crystal recalls a rigor mortis, being the harbinger of an imminent end, as Ovid illustrates with the myth of Narcissus. Caught in the prison of ink and in the trap of words, the dynamism of life comes to be crystallized in a definitive and immobile form. As Andrea Battistini reminds us in his study on autobiography, the autobiographer purports to recapture the life that time had erased and instead consigns himself (or herself) to death.[16] *To crystallize, just like flowing, means to die. Il porto di Toledo* remains entrapped in this paradox.

3.Touring *Toledo* with a Map

Having thus far investigated Ortese's puzzling poetics, torn between time and death, transcendence and fleetingness, fluidity and crystallization, let us now turn to a close reading of the text. Just as the writer herself needs a topographic (and mental) map to plot her bearings in the slippery terrain of memory,[17] it is likewise necessary to furnish a map to any reader who undertakes the arduous reading of this novel, be it a mere schematic framework. In the following sections (3.1–3.5), I therefore chart the coordinates of the text, describing facts and details: the iconic hypotexts whence this text draws inspiration, the strategies of self-writing, the narrative structure and textual shape, the story's plot and its language. While some of this information is already known to Ortese readers and scholars, I look at these elements, whenever possible, through the lens of the dual theme of permanence and transience. Building on my previous observations, it is my thesis that Ortese responds to the temporal obsession using a complex narrative strategy that enables her, at the same time, to confront and defuse the passage of time. A paradoxical ambition lies at the heart of the novel, thus rendering its narrative fabric and tropological texture extremely complex and elusive. The paradox of wanting to fix and crystallize the self and the past (to counteract the flowing of time) and the fear of doing it (because to crystallize, like flowing, means to die); the paradox of wanting to transcend transience and flux and of doing it through a writing saturated with literal and symbolic "water." A fluid, wavering, circular writing, replete with maritime metaphors and figures of fluxing and refluxing – which are none other than the visual translation of the obsession with the *fuga temporis.*[18] Born out of the flux of a "water-time," in the blue vastness of the Mediterranean Sea, the writing of *Il porto di Toledo* ultimately returns whence it came.

3.1 Hypotexts of an Unreal City

It is not surprising that at the heart of an autobiographical project aimed at the recuperation of the past, of permanence and stability lies the influence of some works of art, which function as veritable hypotexts of the novel: yearning to recapture the celestial epiphany, the striking experience with the Raphael's painting she viewed as a child, Ortese attempts to transfix in writing the Platonic moment of duration and the eternal fixity of form. As she herself writes in a passage considered to be her metaliterary "manifesto," writing (she terms it "Expressivity")[19] is in fact "un secondo mondo o seconda irreale realtà [...] non tanto irreale poi se vedevamo la realtà vera disfarsi continuamente, al pari di un vapore acqueo (R1 470, "a second world or a second unreal reality [...] not so unreal then if we saw true reality continually undone, like water vapour").

This time, though, the "epiphany" is not in response to Raphael, but rather to El Greco, a painter Ortese admired since viewing his work in Geneva in 1939, at an exhibit on Renaissance and Baroque Spanish painters. Paradoxically, the great mannerist master, with his destabilizing poeticism and his bedazzling forms, is far better suited to the "neobaroque" sensibilities of Ortese, compared to Raphael's compositional harmony. El Greco – writes a much younger Ortese for the *Gazzettino di Venezia* – "si serve della pittura come di un velo bruno dietro cui palpita la luce di un altro mondo" ("uses painting as though it were a brown veil from behind which pulsates the light of another world").[20] As already noted by critics, El Greco's canvas *Entierro del Conte D'Orgaz*, explicitly cited in the novel, provides not only the model for one of the most outstanding scenes (the apotheosis of Aurora Belman) but also determines the physiognomy of the male characters (tall, subtle, the pallid elongated face with sidelong eyes), as well as the novel's chiaroscuro and overall chromatic qualities: yellowish-gold, red, azure tones with dreamily unreal skies, "tempests of purple and seas of violet hue" flecked with pale light of blue tinted-green and soft pink.[21] However, it is, most of all, the small canvas *Vista de Toledo* (painted between 1596 and 1600 and permanently on display at the Metropolitan Museum in New York) that operates in the most subtle and pervasive manner, as the hypotextual "filter" that mediates, determines, and regulates the visual representation of Naples. Ortese, in other words, "sees" and depicts the city (which is appropriately rechristened Toledo) exactly like El Greco depicts his Toledo: as Farnetti puts it, Ortese's fictional Toledo is born as the ekphrasis of an ekphrasis, a representation of a representation.[22] In El Greco's painting, the profile of an enigmatic, stone-coloured city emerges out of an almost nocturnal backdrop, painted with livid grey-blue tonalities and illuminated by the cold brightness of lightning bolts, which filter out of the clouds' jagged contours. Relegated to the background, at the right, the city of Toledo (one can recognize the royal palace of the Alcazars and the bell tower of the cathedral) is strongly stylized, radically distorted, and altered in its topography and proportions, while at an anterior position, a little stream spanned by a bridge divides the representation in half. In this enigmatic and mysterious atmosphere, at the boundaries of a Freudian uncanny, the city emerges as a veritable figuration of alterity. Just as El Greco edits and radically alters "his" city, so Ortese redesigns the urban topography of "her" city, transforming it into a space of memory and visions – highly subjective, psychological, and sentimental – and adorns the city's toponomastics with a Moresque Hispanic flavour. From the beloved *via del Piliero*, in the port neighbourhood, which becomes "rua Pilar" (where Toledana lives), to the compact network of "rue e ruelle" that surrounds it (Ahorcados, Azar, Compostela) up to the Spanish Vicolo which opens on the Guzmano plaza,[23] where stands the radiant Quiosco (the kiosk where the girl buys the *Literaria Gazeta*, containing her writings), and so forth, proceeding towards the hilly part of Toledo, with the Porta delle Cento Albe, la Certosa, the churches, the monasteries, the towers. The profile of "Mount Acklyns," the volcano Vesuvius, towers in the background.[24] In this Moresque city of phantasms, various quite incorporeal characters move about, shades and apparitions more than "flesh and blood" characters. Not unlike the urban topography, all of them are subjected to a peculiar process of *rinominatio*, which oftentimes affords them multiple names: the parents (Apo and Apa), the brothers (Rassa, Frisco, Albe Garcia-Capitano-Conte di Luna), the friends and lovers (Lemano-Finlandese-Espartero, Belman, Jorge-Bel Figlio, Ciprysso).[25] Even the protagonist herself hides behind various nominal "masks": Dasa, Toledana, Figueira, Misa, Infantilina, and Damasa (a name present in the Latin-American tradition dear to Ortese, but which in Arabic, the language brought into the Ortese house by her young Arab sister-in-law, aptly means "to hide, conceal, disguise"). All of these masks, travesties, multiple names, and characters in code function in the novel as tropes of the dissolution of the subject and of its identity. They are moreover figures of the instability of language and of the unknowability of a world eroded by the wings of wind and time, which, in a postmodern fashion, has lost any and all affinity to a metaphysics of certainty and of stability.

Like that of El Greco, Ortese's vision, four centuries later, is strongly subjective and psychologized, liberated from the plane of objective referentiality. The gaze of the author is visionary; it refutes mimesis, the direct representation both of the contemporary and of the past reality and favours imaginary reinvention and fantastical transfiguration. This hardly comes as a surprise: Ortese, who is *congenitally* predisposed to collapsing categories, accordingly founds her poetics and her writing on the lack of distinction between real life and visions, visible and the invisible, fantasies and dreams. In the particular case of the novel, moreover, her fantastical reinvention – onomastic, toponomastic, topographic, historic, and linguistic – is necessary, since the real city of her youth has been irrevocably barred to her by the *fuga temporis*: "Che ne è di queste strade, di questo vento, di quelle domeniche silenziose, piovose? Che ne è di questo quartiere di porto, barrio delicato, gloria della desolazione e dell'estasi marine?" (R1 397; "What became of these streets, of this wind, of those quiet, rainy Sundays? What became of this port neighbourhood, delicate barrio, glory of desolation and maritime ecstasy?")

There is no "madeleine" for Ortese, nor an unconscious *souvenir involontaire* as there is for Marcel Proust, allowing her to recuperate lost time in its original intensity, in the magnificence of its colours and of its sensations. For Ortese, as with Freud, memory is fallible and unreliable just as the past is illegible, irretrievable, *already* a figure of alterity. How is she then to go about retrieving the Naples of her adolescence except by relying on the mediation of a visual representation – El Greco's canvas – that serves as a trigger for a total fantastical reinvention of the past? Yet, what is more Ortesian than the paradoxical gesture of calling to mind a visual image that is unreal and visionary in the very moment of reprising the Platonic and Raffaelesque crystallization of forms and of fixing through writing "le sopraggiungenti visioni" (R1 388; "approaching visions")?

3.2 Technologies of Autofiction: Defacements and False Traces

Ortese makes direct reference to her desire to detach herself from phenomenal reality and historical becoming in the preface to the first edition of *Il porto di Toledo* (1975): here autobiographical writing, tension towards a noumenal permanence, and refutation of the real are explicitly codified in a coherent system: "C'era in me una grande negazione del reale. Lo vedevo come inganno e fuga e oggi questo reale era tutto. Inganno e fuga erano tutto. E pensai: dove sarà qualcosa di reale-reale? Un continuo come dicono i filosofi? E vidi che era la memoria. Mi impegnai dunque a scrivere un libro di memoria" (R1 998; "There was in me a major negation of the real. I viewed it as a ruse and escape and today this real was everything. Ruse and escape were everything. And I thought: where would there be something actually real? A 'continuum' as philosophers say? And I saw that it was memory. I thus engaged myself in writing a book of memory.")

These quasi-philosophical authorial declarations figure in the novel's opening pages, in that "metatextual space" commonly featured at the outset of many classical autobiographies, from at least Montaigne onwards (one of the *auctores* she considered among her most beloved): a liminal space that frames the autobiographical writing, a prefatory section intended to establish the "autobiographical pact" between author and reader, linking the world of fiction with that of the author's experiences and referential reality. Ortese, however, as we know, loves to complicate rather than to clarify and thus, in the novel, this traditional metatextual space holds more than a few surprises and twists, written as it is with the same allusive and encoded language of the text itself: it not only blurs the lines between fiction and reality, but also categorically contradicts the notion that memoir-writing can be a tool for accessing the noumenal substratum of things, thereby undermining the very premises on which the text bases itself. If in fact memory (as we have witnessed) is untenable and untrustworthy, then writing, by its nature, is also unable to represent reality in a transparent way. Memory and writing, in other words, are capable of generating only chimeras, metaphors, tropes, and fictions: "venne fuori *questa Damasa*" – Ortese continues in her preface, referring to her fictional alter ego – "a me sconosciuta [...] Prese il mio posto, nella casa del Pilar, e descrisse tutto come a me non sarebbe mai potuto accadere" (R1 998–99, "out came *this Damasa* – unbeknownst to me. She took my place in the house of the Pilar, and described everything as I never could have done").[26]

Ortese, thus, deliberately undercuts her original agenda, that is, the desire to access the space-time continuum, the noumenal dimension through memory. If autobiographical writing entails crystallization and therefore the death of the self, as we have previously seen, this is where Ortese bypasses the obstacle, tricking historical time and the tyranny of autobiographical discourse by devising a declaredly false autobiography and putting into play a series of figures and counter-figures under which to hide and preserve her "real" self. Thus, as I argue, the creation of Toledana-Damasa is certainly one of the most significant rhetorical twists of twentieth-century Italian literature. Is "this Damasa" a literalization of Paul de Man's claim – in *Autobiography as Defacement* – that self-writing is always impossible and always distorted? Is "this Damasa" a literal instance of that "deprived and disfigured representation" of the "I," which has taken up speaking, replacing "the voiceless one," "the one who speaks from beyond the grave" (which is the inevitable condition of the autobiographical subject, according to De Man)?[27] Is this novel, then, a real autobiography? If in fact Ortese openly breaks the contract that regulates the reading of an autobiography – a pact based on the triangulation between the name-signature of the author (which figures on the heading of the text), the narratorial voice (whose name corresponds to that of the author), and the reader who becomes judge of the pact's reliability – how should we read *Il porto di Toledo*? At a closer look, the autobiography that we have before us is a triumph of autobiographical deceits and denied expectations: from the title (*Port of Toledo* is clearly a "false geographic," since the city of Toledo does not have a port)[28] to the subheading – *Memories of an Unreal Life* – an oxymoron that, from the novel's outset, undermines the veracity of the facts, all the way through the above-mentioned metatextual spaces, where Ortese, with extreme lucidity, sets the scene for the unbelievable representation of an autobiographical artifice, of an *autofiction*[29] that overrides the autobiographical project: "Toledo non è una vera città, anche se immagini del vero ne emergono, né è reale la sua gente. Apa, Damasa, Aurora, gli studentucci che passano con il loro linguaggio astratto in queste false memorie, non sono più veri delle strade, i vichi, le rue della città lunatica di cui parlo.

Quelle tempeste di luna e questi lamenti di vento sono false tracce" (R1 355, "Toledo is not a true city, even if true images come out of it, nor is its people real. Apa, Damasa, Aurora, the little students speaking their abstract language as they pass by in these false memories, they are not more true than the streets, the alleyways, the side streets of this lunatic city. Those moon storms and these wind cries are false traces").

To complicate this magnificent theatre of programmatic fiction and of masked subjects, the text introduces the seemingly unrelated figure of Anne Hurdle, another spectral and ghost-like presence, who is the dedicatee of the novel and the protagonist of the third edition's preface (1998). With Anne, historical, political, social and gender perspectives burst into the autobiographic scene. Cited fleetingly by Benjamin Constant in his *Cahier Rouge*, Anne Hurdle is a poor young English woman prosecuted in eighteenth-century London for forgery. Constant recounts his astonishment at the woman's silence, as she refuses to speak in her own defence during the trial, letting out a solitary cry on the gallows, at the moment of her death. Ortese's feigned autobiographical discourse (is its falsity perhaps a reflection of Anne's act of forgery?) takes its start from *this* silence, from the death of a disenfranchised subject accused of having created fiction and falsity, and in so doing, had challenged the economic and sociopolitical systems of class, gender, and property. Ortese's autofictional discourse, thus, like a catachresis, takes the place of a speechless void, of a missing defence. As the author writes, hers is a discourse-turned-revolt against injustice, a restitution towards a marginal female subject crushed under the weight of history – at the machinations of patriarchal social and economic agendas.[30] The novel is thus a "ventriloquial" discourse voicing political matters.

What is ultimately at stake in these false memories, in this autobiographical discourse-turned-revolt? Let us summarize for the sake of clarity the different rhetorical and discursive strategies that Ortese employs to construct the novel's autobiographical mechanism: 1) the disavowal of the veracity of facts that are ascribed to the realm of fiction and "unreality"; 2) the de-authorization of the author, who renounces her own authorial agency, remaining faceless and voiceless, in favour of "this Damasa" who, in turn, also speaks in the place of an another missing voice, that of Anne Hurdle; 3) alienation and estrangement between the "I" and its disfigured alter ego; 4) blurring of the lines between fact and fiction. Through the employment of these "technologies of autofiction," Ortese aligns herself, albeit unwittingly, with many writers of autobiographies from marginalized groups, both past and present, who negotiate, destabilize, and reshape the confines and laws of a genre that has traditionally failed to authorize the voice of the disenfranchised. As Leigh Gilmore has suggested in her study on "autobiographics," these are widely used strategies of resistance to the textual restrictions of a discourse supposedly based on "telling the truth"; coping mechanisms against the discursive and societal constrains placed on the construction of subjectivity, class, and gender. Thus, Anne Hurdle's challenge to the economic and social systems, through her forgery, is mirrored in the challenge posed by Ortese to the cultural, literary, and political discursive systems via her false memories. For Ortese, as for many other writers, the author's name becomes ambivalent and unstable, a site of experimentation, of contradictions and interruptions, of multiple and experimental constructions rather than a confident contract of identity.[31] By unsettling the "laws of the genre," as Derrida would say,[32] by profoundly renegotiating the terms and the forms of self-writing and self-knowledge, Ortese forces the reader to come to terms with what constitutes an autobiography. Ultimately, then, *Il porto di Toledo* is an autobiography under the guise of a false memory that paradoxically interrogates itself on the very nature of an autobiography.

3.3 Topography of a Text

Ortese's playing with time, her search for a balance between permanence and transience, directly affects the novel's narrative structure and the ways the author manipulates the textual shape and the properties of narrativity. The fact that narrativity is profoundly enmeshed in temporality (i.e., there is a fundamental telos in the act of narration) is not a new observation. The reflection upon the link between narrative and time in fact spans the course of Western thought from Saint Augustine to Paul Ricoeur: narrativity along with its textual markers and constraints (plot, forward progression, beginnings, middles, endings) is nothing other than "time in its textual dress."[33] Thus, Ortese's project is twofold: on the one hand, in her quest for permanence, unity, and coherence, she wants to bind the tales from her early years (narrative fragments of her authorial past) together with a narrative framework, a plot, a story intended to elucidate, gloss the tales, and give them their narrative context. To this end, as we know, the novel insets thirty-four lyric compositions written in the thirties and heretofore unpublished (only recently published in separate collections) and nine of the thirteen stories published in 1937 in *Angelici dolori*. On the other hand, though, since accepting the rules and constraints of narrative structure implies a symbolic subjection of her text to the flux and passage of time, the author undermines the narrative thrust with a loose plot, with fragmentation, repetition, circularity, narrative stasis, enigmatic information, proliferation of endings, and games of mirrorings: strategies that, ultimately, halt the forward progression of the story, escaping time. Thus, in a true Petrarchan fashion, Ortese juxtaposes a "mode of binding" and a "mode of loosing."[34] The paradoxical nature of Ortese's "game with time" is evident from the inception of her project: by collecting the old tales, she undertakes an archaeological experiment, excavating fragments from the past. However, she immediately re-actualizes her fragments, bringing them to life in the present. The embedded tales, as it happens, have undergone a rewriting process, as in a palimpsest: from the basic level of revising titles, lexicon, and style to a more complex creative reworking and resemanticizing of the stories. As Beatrice Manetti claims from careful analysis, the total reworking is especially concentrated upon the tales' final sections: many of the embedded stories, as a matter of fact, not only end in a completely different way from the 1937 text, but also introduce procrastinations, proliferations of the "endings,"[35] and hesitations ("Forse il rendiconto era terminato; ma questo non sapevo, e ancora, per qualche rigo, incertamente, continuai" ["Perhaps the tale was finished; but this I did not know, and I even continued, for some lines, without certainty"]), all bearing testimony to Ortese's subconscious refusal (as opposed to her conscious desire) to subject her writing to the constrains of time, narrativity, and to anything definite and stable.

Ortese's "confrontation" with time also influences the relation between the frame story and the inserted writings, a relation that, as Manetti notes, gradually mutates: while at first the embedded narratives have a direct link to the framing narrative, which serves to explicate the events and circumstances out of which they were born, the gradient of correlation grows in complexity to the point of complete reversal – the later tales, in fact, allude proleptically and "prophetically" to events that "will" occur in the framing story.[36] In so breaking the structural and temporal logic that subtends the novel, Ortese confuses the past of the tales with the present of the frame narrative. Likewise, she destabilizes the layers of fiction as she is accustomed to do. Are the tales born out of their frame, or is the frame engendered by the tales themselves? Through this continual and disordered mirroring, the novel thus takes the form of a veritable hall of mirrors (and not merely of a labyrinth, as it has been previously suggested by critics):[37] once again, the mirror image, it seems to me, perfectly emblematizes both the dizzying myse-en-abîme that the text generates and, *at the same time,* the self-reflective nature of autobiographical writing.

The novel's palimpsestic and specular fabric is also cross-stitched with a dense metatextual and intertextual component: in fact, the author's reflections on the reasons behind her own writing are as numerous as Toledana's comments, for the most part negative or dismissive, on her literary works. In addition to this thick metatextual component, the text proves a trove of intertextual richness: while some references are explicit (Manrique, Gongora, Heine, Leopardi), twenty-five citations from both popular and literary sources (all men authors, from the Franco-German and Hispanic traditions) are deftly submerged and dissimulated throughout the text, having only been recently unearthed by criticism. These hidden voices – all of which underscore the themes of loss, struggle, and caducity – span from Paul Valéry to Fernardo Villalón, from Gongora and Heine to the *Songs of Roncisvalle* and *El Cid.*[38] This dense intertextual rubric is a narrative and stylistic strategy that Ortese often employs in her novels. Is it a means of giving in to the anxiety of authorial agency, de-authorizing oneself by making the literary fathers speak? Or rather, on the contrary, is it a clever strategy of appropriation and resemantization of a patrilinear literary tradition that finds itself refitted for the narrative agenda of a woman's story about art and eros? The question remains open. What we can say with certainty is that, in the text, the literary fragments of others (the genetic textual "other") operate in the same manner as the embedded early writings (the genetic intertextual "self"). They represent the sole anchor or stable pylon which, resisting the eddies of time and the dissipation into oblivion, allow for the working of memory: "[le storie], per me, costituiscono, col loro malinconico vuoto, ciò che pochi diruti piloni sono per un ponte, su acque abbandonate. E su quel ponte di nulla io devo passare, se voglio tornare indietro, in quel tempo dove giace la mia Toledo" (R1 370, "To me [these stories], with their melancholic void, constitute that which a few dilapidated pylons are for a bridge, on abandoned waters. And over the bridge of nothing I need to cross, if I desire to go back to the time wherein my Toledo resided.")

Like crumbling piers on abandoned waters, literary writing (one's own and that of others) stands against the fluid nature of life, as a relict of time.

3.4 An Ineffable Story

In 1980, writing to the editor Fisher regarding a possible German translation of the novel, Ortese describes it with these words: "un senso di solitudine e rovina umana, oltre che delle cose, se ne diparte, e forse gli dà il tono freddo di una stampa il cui soggetto sia stato già cancellato dalla storia, e confuso con i relitti del tempo" (R1 1058, "a sense of solitude and human ruin, as well as of things, comes from it, and perhaps lend it the cold tone of a print whose subject has already been erased from history, and mingled with the relicts of time.")

This citation, an illuminating insight into a self-exegized Ortese, introduces us to the heart of this novel where everything involves "solitude and human ruin." The plot is very fleeting, almost impalpable, orbiting around certain narrative nuclei: the long strolls taken through the city of Toledo by the young Dasa-Damasa-Toledana, who has just moved from an unspecified Iberian motherland to live in the squalid port-side barrio; the tragic death of her brother Rassa off the coast of Martinique, followed by the demise of Albe Garcia; her first poetic and literary compositions, from the age of thirteen onward; her first encounter with her mentor d'Orgaz, "Master of Arms," and the publication of her tales in the *Literaria Gazeta*; the arrival of her brother's young Arab wife in her home; the loss of her beloved "corner room" and her move to the *despacho*; her passionate feelings for the mysterious Lemano, her jealous friendship with the rich and beautiful Aurora Belman (Lemano's lover) and Belman's premature death; her contentious family dynamics (with Apo, Apa, Frisco, Juana, Albe Garcia) and the intense relations with her friends (Samana, Misa, Ciprisso, Jorge). These loose narrative nuclei foreground a coming-of-age story, a quest towards adulthood, in which the discovery of creativity becomes a catalyst for self-actualization. In the background, the historical framework – from the fascist era to the Allied bombardments during the Second World War – remains elusive, deftly obscured by means of a systematized symbolic code (the Biblical Fathers are the Americans, El Rey is Vittorio Emanuele III, Don Pedro is Mussolini). Toledana's story concludes under the bombings of the Uccelli Turchi (the Allied bombardiers). The destruction of the port and, with it, of the protagonist's house marks the symbolic end of an age and of a world: the ancient city of Toledo along with the childhood years with its hopes and dreams. Nothing remains but to leave. The text comes to a close, ten years having passed, in the Nordic city of the Mille Torri, with a tone of defeat and inward-focused melancholy.

3.5 The Maternal Language of "Durée"

If perhaps it is not within everyone's grasp to return to the freedom of an infantile language, once having entered into the constrictive structure of the logocentric language of adults, Ortese at least attempted it ("chi dei fanciulli che giacciono nella tomba di una carne adulta, di una lingua maturata, è mai veramente tornato indietro? Chi ha potuto? Chi?" R1 397, "who among the youths inhabiting the tomb of adult flesh, of a matured language, has ever really returned to the past? Who has been able to? Who?"). The text's language – a language that secures for Ortese a place at the vanguard of *Novecento* linguistic experimentation, alongside Gadda and Pasolini – is intensely poetic and metaphorical, luminous and airy, but at the same time obscure, difficult, and syncopated. It contributes to the novel's intriguing allure, however it sets limits, on account of its incomprehensibility. Ortese herself attributes "questo anagrammato, sigillato, incatenato, ribaltato discorso, veramente senza logica alcuna – vera conversazione della notte" (RI 760, "all this anagrammed, sealed, chain-linked, overturned discourse, truly lacking in logic – truly ramblings of the night") to the impossibility of representing that which is not representable (i.e., the intensity of the infant-adolescent linguistic inventions) simply because "quella lingua [...] non esiste" ("that language does not exist.")[39] Critics, however, namely Clerici and Farnetti, have provided psychological interpretations: Ortese's is a language that originates from the adolescent perspective to which the narratorial voice tunes itself; or, rather (but hardly different), it is a "toledano parlar materno," a truly matrilinear language in which "inversioni, anacoluti, reticenze e preterizioni, allusioni ed ellissi, chiasmi inconclusi, interpunzione squilibrata, elisione di passaggi logici, amnesie e smarrimenti, lapsus, troncamenti" ("inversions, anacoluthons, reticences and preteritions, allusions and elisions, unclosed chiasmus, unstable punctuation, elision of logical passages, amnesias and confusion, lapsus, truncations")[40] are none other than indications of a symbolic belonging: a belonging to the chaotic mix of feelings, perceptions, and drives of a maternal "chora," well before acquiring a logocentric and androcentric adult language. Whatever may be the definitions or interpretations that one wishes to posit, the Toledan maternal language could be also interpreted through the lens of time as a language of "*durée réele.*" A language linked to the ineffable "duration," as Henry Bergson, the French modernist philosopher of time and consciousness, would say. A language that springs forth from that interior and subjective psychological domain, governed by imagination and memory, from that subconscious dimension of circularity in which past, present, and future coexist so that time ceases to be an irredeemable destructive force.

* * *

With the help of the textual map I have sketched thus far, the readers can find their way into this enigmatic and elusive novel. It is interesting to note that even Ortese herself, for entirely different reasons, was thinking of placing a map on the novel's front cover as a key for the textual interpretation; a map like those "carte nautiche di secoli scorsi, libri di tempi remoti, in relazioni a viaggi, e indicazioni di coste, di acque imprecisate, di territori di cui si sapeva poco" ("nautical charts of times past, books of yore, charting voyages, with indications of coasts, of uncharted waters, of territories about which little was known," R1 1070); a map as a metaphor either of Toledana's coming-of-age story and of the narrative rhythm of the text, with its figurative open seas (the frame narrative) and its doldrums (the poetry and the embedded tales that necessarily slow the reader's pace). Ortese's idea about a nautical chart – doubtlessly inspired by Defoe's *Robinson Crusoe,* one of the novel's averred sources of influence[41] – strikes me as essential for the sake of illuminating the nexus of some of the novel's themes and motifs. It serves not merely to "spatialize" time, thereby foregrounding the solid connection between space, time, identity, and narrative, but also to introduce the more extensive tropological index of the novel, relating to water, sea, and navigation. Significantly, Ortese declares in a 1997 letter to her publisher Roberto Calasso: "rileggendo *Toledo,* mi colpisce la natura [...] di questa storia, che stabilisce un continuo raffronto della vita con la sua navigazione. La vita come scoperta di luoghi e temi sconosciuti" ("re-reading *Toledo,* I was struck by the nature [...] of this story, which sets up a continual comparison between life and its navigation. Life as discovery of unknown places and times. The discovery of time, of becoming").[42] With this new nautical map, we will now move across metaphorical seascapes and landscapes, charting a process of self-formation deeply affected by the perception not only of time but also of space.

4. The Space of the Subject: The Disavowed *Bildung* of a Young Woman Artist

As French historian Michel De Certeau claims, in a striking parallel to Ortese's own words, "every story is a travel story –a spatial practice."[43] Thus, it is not paradoxical that, in a novel obsessed with time and impermanence, the protagonist's process of self-formation and self-representation be expressed by means of spatial tropes, rather than by temporal-chronological patterns. In point of fact, if time is a dissipating and disjunctive force, only space can be an anchor for the subject and her story. Toledana-Damasa is then intimately connected to location and space both as material sites and metaphorical tropes (the city, the square, the churches, the port, the house, the room, the sea, the land), thus negotiating the complex relationship between self and spatiality. If identity, as Susan Stanford puts it, is "a historically embedded site, a positionality, a location, a standpoint, a terrain, an intersection, a network, a crossroads of multiple situated knowledges,"[44] *Il porto di Toledo* can be seen as charting a spatial practice, a true "geographics" of narrative subjectivity.

The novel opens against a dystopian psychosocial landscape, marked by disavowed genealogies (R1 363; "Sono figlia di nessuno," "I'm nobody's daughter"), exilic and expatriate subjectivities, refuted bodies, gender confusion and material and social destitution. Amidst shacks, slums, and fishmongers dwells the teenaged protagonist, in a squalid hovel in the barrio of the port. Her description conjures the image of a wretched creature, ambiguous with regard to gender (boy-girl): unkempt hair, ashen face, with black and ragged stockings, joined together by a thread.[45] Also the young protagonist's own sense of belonging and identity proves all the less stable and nomadic-like, denoted as it is by a whirlwind of given names, Dasa-Damasa-Toledana-Figueroa-Misa, as we have already noted. At the outset of the novel, the girl has just disembarked at Nuova Toledo together with her dysfunctional family, hailing from an undetermined "Madre Iberica": a mythical West, symbolic of an Edenic origin, removed from the flux of time. Thus, the blueprints of exile, fall, and displacement are encoded in Toledana's own's identity and sense of self: from an Edenic condition of plenitude – an undivided self, located in a utopian homeland – to a state of loss, mourning, alienation, and struggle, in a mysterious and enigmatic Nuova Toledo: "Ecco in lutto appare il mondo, e in lutto sono il mare e il cielo" (R1 622, "The whole world appears to mourn as well as the sea and the sky").

The girl's exilic and fragmented identity reflects (and is reflected in) the urban topography of the city. A gate separates the port neighbourhood, where the girl lives alongside sailors and rascals, from the rest of the city. It is a *limen* that is first and foremost physical, but also psychological, social, and meteorological: on *this* side of the barrier, it is the realm of anguish, poverty, struggle, and lack of material means necessary to come into a life. The rain beats heavily, nonstop. Up beyond the gate – in *that* "Toledo of light" where sprawl the facades of seventeenth century palaces and the lavish homes of nobles and princes – the urban and social space is associated, through metaphors of light and splendour, with the joy of living, from which the girl is exiled. The physical and social geography of Toledo is, then, that of a secluded and fragmented space (the windy port, the Regal city, the gloomy city of steeples and cloisters), impermeable to human fluctuations, exchanges, and to social mobility, notwithstanding the numerous gaps and openings (staircases and passageways).[46] In a way, Ortese's fractured and hierarchized city seems to contradict the famous metaphor of Naples' urban porosity and transience elaborated by Walter Benjamin with Asja Acis in the 1924 essay *Neapel* (Naples): allowing for the continual interpenetration of architectonic structures with human activity ("[b]uilding and action interpenetrate in the courtyards, arcades, and stairways"; "[b]alcony, courtyard, window, gateway, staircase, roof are at the same time stage and boxes"), Benjamin's porous city is marked by the commingling and intermixing of every form and phenomenon, of social bodies and classes, of public and private, of sacred and profane in a perpetual theatrical "improvisation" of life, where "the stamp of the definite is avoided."[47] Unlike Benjamin's porous city, the fragmented, hierarchized and unporous Ortesian urban space – where Toledana's formative experiences occur[48] – becomes also a medium for a covert critique of ideology: history and politics, even though Bourbon and Fascist power are disguised under coded terms, directly impacts the material condition of the common people that swarm the infernal Toledan underbelly. In *Il porto di Toledo,* thus, the discourse on history, urban space, and self-formation are strictly intertwined. Identity is always a historically embedded site.

Toledana's condition of alienation, exile, and estrangement is heightened furthermore by her acute perception of the passage of time. She experiences temporality as loss. "Sentivo il tempo come un'emorragia. Le ore battevano pesanti nel mio petto, e ogni istante qualcosa, come le acque di un fiume, staccavano e trascinavano via. E dove, dove via da questa terra?" (R1 378; "I experienced time like blood loss. The hours thumped away heavily in my chest, like the waters of a stream, pulsing out and flowing freely. Where to now, where forth from this land?"). The girl's acute perception of loss and impermanence is tragically realized in the sudden and untimely death of her brother Rassa: a catalyzing event that launches her into a frenzy of writing-as-recuperation, in an attempt not only to recapture what has been lost but to discover the self through creativity. Her childhood playmate and companion on adventures, Rassa, is soon replaced by her mentor Conte D'Orgaz, "Master of Arms," a mediator whose role is to initiate her into a more formal practice of writing. Entrenched in this dystopian psychosocial landscape, where fragmentation and loss threaten the integrity of the subject, Toledana then embarks – mainly through writing – on a quest for a different psychological territory removed both from the difficulties of her social and material condition and from the painful flux of time itself.

Il porto di Toledo can be seen, in this sense, as a novel of self-formation and self-discovery, a peculiar *Bildungsroman* (in the form of a *Künstlerroman*), under the deceptive guise of an impossible and unreliable autobiography. The trajectories that constitute the underlying thrust of the narrative are twofold – one functions at the superficial plot level while the other courses through the textual depths, contradicting the first one. In fact, like every classic autobiography – which tends towards a "*recherche du centre*," a pivotal moment of "conversion" or self-realization – *Il porto di Toledo* presents a teleological and euphoric thrust: that is to say, the character is projected towards the development of an adult identity, towards the integration into a real world, governed by the laws of logic and praxis, a world in which writing could become a means of economic emancipation and social affirmation. The Ortesian "*recherche du centre*" is encapsulated in an enigmatic cry that resounds obsessively throughout the course of the novel: "Ere successive" ("Successive Eras"). This cry comes from Lemano, the male character with the mediatory role of inducting the girl into adulthood through eros, desire, and betrayal. Contrary to this forward movement, a centripetal and / or circular movement of dysphoric nature operates simultaneously in the text, tending towards stagnation and the non-growing: the character thus gravitates towards the closure of an imaginary world of infancy, a maternal pre-oedipal dimension of reveries and dreams. In other words, the teleogical process of self-formation, which corresponds to the linear, forward unfolding of the narrative, is constantly uprooted and undercut by a circular tropological movement (a *circulata melodia* as Dante would say), engendering a tension between opposing meanings. This dialectic of binaries unfurls in a choreographed interplay of contrasting tropes: metaphors of the land and metaphors of the sea. At the crossroads of this dizzying network of spatial tropes and multiple locations stands Toledana, pursuing a quest for self-formation. Hers is a nonlinear journey, a perpetual *voyage en zigzag*[49] between seascapes and landscapes. Let us take a closer look at these intricate tropological movements.

a) *Seascape → Landscape.* In an initial instance, the material site upon which the spatial tropological configuration of sea and land hinges is Toledana's own room, "la stanza d'angolo" facing the waters of the port: a prized haven, a refuge, maternal in its uterine quality, where the girl immerses herself in her own delirious fantasizing,[50] where she draws enormous figures of Comanche Indians or else first tries her hand at poetic and narrative exercise ("righe ritmiche," "rendiconti"). From the estranged vantage point of her top floor room – through the opening of a little window, askew, ("finestruccia sbilenca") that overlooks the dynamic bustle of the port – Toledana takes on her first "scopic" enterprise, engaging through her subjective and twisted gaze a process of knowledge.[51] Thus, after observing the multicoloured sails of the ships, the young Dasa dreams of embarking, with her brother Rassa, on one of the mythical vessels, the *Katrina* or the *Maria Morales.* This desire to escape is projected onto her first writings.

> Ed io pregando le reali cose ed il lavoro che aspettino un poco, mi trovo a bordo della nave [...] invocando le Terre d'Heroes: "Aspettateci Terre grandiose! Luminose [...] raccoglieteci e sia per sempre, nella vostra luce rossa, Terre Beate, e voi Popoli dell'eterno, Appalchi, Comanche. E la nave corre, vola sulle acque montuose e in un istante è là." (R1 427)

> (And praying the real things and my work to wait for a little while, I find myself on the ship [...], invoking Heroes' Lands: "Wait for us, great Lands! Bright Lands [...] receive us now and forever, in your red light, Blessed Lands, and you, eternal People, Appalachians, Comanche. And the ship runs, flies on the montainous water and in a blink is there.")

In this passage, the sea spreads out into an epic, masculine space of scented gales, rife with adventures, and bottomless abysses. This seascape becomes an intermediary space between real life and blossoming Edenic paradises, figurations of a mythic original West uncontaminated by civilization, a metatemporal dimension removed from historical becoming and from the undoing of time.[52] However, in the dizzying interplay of contrapuntal metaphors, the epic and mythic sea can also invoke an opposite meaning: herein, Toledana perceives the grey waters of the port as stagnant, as the negation of vitality and growth. The girl's "condizione marine" ("seafaring stage") – that is, her adolescence spent in the port neighbourhood – is perceived as "unreal" life, a life dissipated into dream, daydreaming, and material insecurity: "Mi venne un' onda di disperazione a causa di tanto Irreale, e questo mio eterno stare davanti alla grigia linea dell'acqua [...] mi parve esatta condizione di orrore" (R1 509; "There washed over me a wave of desperation on account of this Unreality, and this tendency of mine to stand endlessly before the grey line of the water [...] seemed to me a true state of horror").

Even from within this feeling of horror comes the prospect of a voyage and a subsequent landfall: yet upon a land no longer mythical and removed from the erosion of historical time, but instead upon a real and metaphoric "land" understood as a Lacanian Symbolic Order, an adult world governed by rational logic and laws of praxis, language, and historical becoming (in opposition to the world of the Unreal and the Imaginary). This pervasive terrestrial trope thereby becomes the fulfilment of a teleological progression, of Toledana's "recherche du centre," the landfall upon the "Successive Eras" of adultlhood.

> Mi pareva a volte che tutto fosse da me inventato, dalla mia mente che mai toccava *terra,* mai sentiva, se non in rare occasioni, il rumore preciso e violento della reale vita, il passo delle reali cose, i duri suoni.
>
> Oh realtà, o realtà, torna *terra mia*! (R1 491)

> (It seemed to me at times as though everything were invented by me, by my mind that never touched *the land,* that never felt, if only on rare occasions, the precise and violent sound of the real life, the passing of real things, hard sounds.
>
> Oh reality, oh reality, come back *land of mine*!)[53]

b) *Landscape → Seascape.* In its constant contrapuntal tropological movement, Ortese's discourse configures an unstable semantic equilibrium as though it refuses to ossify language and its meanings. And indeed, as it is easy to foresee, the centrifugal trajectory of Toledana from the sea *towards a metaphorical land* can be transformed into an opposite dynamic, a centripetal motion *towards the sea* that, superimposed upon the preceding tropological movement, creates a very ambiguous inlay of meanings. At times, in fact, such a desire to embrace an adult identity (land, or "Successive Eras") is perceived as the negation of the subject's profoundest aspirations, configuring itself as a true and proper realm of *Thanatos.* Growing, in fact, implies the acceptance of the laws of history, temporality, and becoming and, consequently, of death: "Levarsi, grida brutalmente, follemente. Era successiva, Damasina mia. Era questo, avvertii di colpo, *il morire.* No, Lemano, là non portarmi, gridai. Lasciami ai miei anni marine!" (R1 452; "Get up, he yells harshly, in a fury. Successive era, my Damasina. This, I realized all of a sudden, was *dying.* No Lemano, do not take me there, I yelled. Leave me to my seafaring years!")

This passage can be read also from a gendered perspective, which superimposes itself upon the preceding layers of meaning. The induction into the adult territory of the Symbolic Order in fact implies not only the participation in the process of becoming, but also the acceptance of the Lacanian Law of the Father *(Nom du père)*, of patriarchal social and cultural confines, of roles and gendered identities, of logocentric rules that govern language and creative expression. Moreover, to enter the Symbolic realm of adulthood means for Toledana to face the social/cultural construction of femininity and to confront her own disavowed bodily desires.

> Mai e poi mai avrei voluto sposarmi! Talvolta l'inferno e i relativi strazi che mi aspettavano, per i quali ero spesso malinconica, quasi mi rassicuravano [...] Unica alternativa a tale destino vedevo il mare (e perciò lo amavo dolorosamente). Là su quelle acque azzurre non vi è più crescere, non vi sono né sponsali né supplizi: esse, da sole, quelle acque sempre varie, sono paradiso e inferno. (R1 400)

> (Never, ever had I desired to marry! Sometimes, the hell and the related pains that awaited me, that brought me such melancholy, almost reassured me [...] I saw the only alternative to such a fate in the sea (and for that I painfully loved it). Out on those blue waters there is no longer any growing, there are neither weddings nor torments: those ever changing waters, by themselves, are heaven and hell.)

What does this refusal of traditional womanhood and the consequent desire to cling to her "seafaring years" have to do with the awareness that, as Suskin Ostriker writes, "to be a creative woman in a gender-polarized culture is to be a divided self"?[54] What does the continuous shifting of perspectives expressed through the morphing metaphors of land and sea have to do with Toledana's contending with not only prescriptive social and cultural definitions of her role as a woman, but also with the very concept of herself as an artist? Facing both the prospect of death (what is to come; the becoming; the hereafter) and the rigid socio-cultural definition of adult female subjects which negate women's intellectual and creative selves, the only alternative seems to be a *journey back* into stasis and immobility, soaking in an "oceanic" dimension which blocks the linear and progressive impetus towards the land-locked and logocentric dimension of adulthood: "Viaggiare / io voglio, e molto: e immergermi nei rivi / turchini e lisci che fremendo al mare / tornano; al Mare / solo voglio dormire, o mia diletta ... Desideravo essere reale!" (R1 509; "To travel / I would like, and much: and to soak into the banks /

turquoise and smooth that trembling to the sea / they return; to the Sea / I want only to sleep, o my delight ... I wanted to be real!").

The journey towards the turquoise waters therefore reconfigures the vectors of the protagonist's Bildung as a *regressive, backward movement* ("lasciami ai mie anni marine," "leave me to my seafaring years") and thus *works against* the teleological trajectory towards maturity. The spatial trope of the sea hereby comes to incorporate temporal implications, thus becoming a space-time device, a chronotope. The desire for regression into liquidity corresponds to the sinking into the amniotic fluid of a pre-oedipal "oceanic feeling," in Freudian terminology: a state of amorous symbiosis, of deep connection with the other, with the maternal and the *chôra*, an infinite state preceding any differentiation between the I and the you, the self and the other, the male and the female.[55] The sea therefore represents a return to the mother (in Italian *ma(d)re* contains the word *mare*); the sea is the space of the absolute, an infinite *distentio* of water that reflects eternity ("Il tempo cadrà stanotte, l'ho visto: ma il mare non cadrà mai. Resta dunque fedele al mare, da dove si alzano scale al cielo, bimba mia," R1 515; "Time will fall tonight, I've seen it; but the sea will never fall. Therefore stay faithful to the sea, out of which rises the ladder to heaven, my child"). The sea, moreover, in its eternal ebb and flow, evokes a circular notion of time in which "the future assimilates the past": a notion that, ensconced in the metaphorical subtext, contradicts the textual and narrative logic of a historical, linear becoming.[56]

The analysis of the text's tropological and figural movements, and of their temporal implications, leads me back to the initial considerations about the relationship between self-formation and space. If identity, always embedded in space and place, is "a positionality, a location, a standpoint, a terrain, an intersection, a network,"[57] what does the map of the spatial constellations we have just analysed speak of? What does this map say about the sense of selfhood and the quest towards self-actualization?

The contrapuntal figural logic of *Il porto di Toledo*, mirroring the unconscious drives of the subject, first of all evokes a Lacanian scenario, as we have seen: in the process of self-development, Toledana is problematically blocked off at the crossroads between the Symbolic Order and the Imaginary Order (characterized by paradisiacal maternal plenitude and longing for an undivided self and, at the same time, by estrangement, alienation, narcissism, and multiple *étades du mirroir*). Toledana's self is fragmented, divided, eccentric – as Farnetti's analysis already indicates;[58] she is an unstable subject who constructs herself through progression and regression, challenging temporal and chronological categories, questioning the very unfolding of the self-formation process; she is a subject that does not conform to the limits of predetermined social and cultural roles (as represented by the solidity of land metaphors), but rather, *en travesti*, disguising herself under nominal masks (Damasa-Dasa-Toledana-Infantilina-Figueria), operates as free and prismatic, beyond cultural boundaries.

The postmodern notion of the "nomad" – reconceptualized in a feminist key by Rosi Braidotti, expanding upon Deleuze and Guattari[59] – already evoked by Farnetti in regard to Toledana, strikes me as particularly appropriate in order to close the discourse on Toledana's process of self-formation.[60] In the exact same way that Toledana refutes all form of authority (she quits school, abandons religion, and, free of familial constraints, grows through reading, drawing, daydreaming, writing, and walking around the city), the nomad resists and subverts structures, paradigms, institutions, conventional thought, hegemonic and codified behaviour; like Toledana, the nomad develops or constructs herself / himself not through a teleologically determined process but by virtue of multiple stages of transformation, transition, and change. Unlike Toledana however – who still longs for a mythical motherland and an undivided, totalizing self, and thus is vacillating between a modern and a postmodern condition – the nomad has abandoned every nostalgia for an identity that is coherent and fixed, in favour of an unstable physiognomy in a perennial state of construction and deconstruction. The condition of fluidity, then, is what Toledana and the nomadic subject of critical theory have in common.

Though the road to self-development and self-definition may prove complex and tortuous, torn between a teleological thrust and a circular disruption, the novel's narrative trajectory comes finally to a close, with Toledana's passage into adulthood or, to be precise, into the Symbolic Order. "Per i marine non più tempo, spazio, visioni, dilazioni, sogni, ma un ordine muto: affrettarsi. Divenire adulti. Partire" (R1 688; "For her sea mates no longer time, space, visions, dilations, dreams, but an unspoken command: to hurry up. To become adults. To leave"). Toledana's *bildung* is complete, just as the autobiographical writing has fulfilled its *recherche du centre*. In fact, in the final section of the novel, the "Successive Eras" come at last, marking an end to the Era of Desolation (adolescence) and to the longing for the sea. And they have arrived through the mediation of a rite of passage *par excellence*, which constitutes the novel's poignant climax: under the Uccelli Turchi aerial attack (the winter 1943 bombardment of Naples by Allied forces), Lemano and Toledana consummate their love, having sought refuge underneath a bridge ("e io stetti in questo deserto, sotto un ponte, con lui. E fu cosa delicatissima, buonissima, come il pane alla fame, l'acqua alla sete del povero" (R1 969; "and I stayed in this wasteland, under a bridge, with him. And it was delicate and wonderful, like bread for peaking hunger, water for the thirst of the poor"). Framed by this "abandoned bridge," a powerful symbol of transitions and crossings, the novel's passionate and tragic climax marks both a pivotal oedipal passage, an initiation into womanhood through *Eros* and desire *and* also, at the same time, an entry into the world of historical violence and therefore of *Thanatos*. The dust, the rubble, the bombs, the crumbling houses evoked in the scene do not merely represent the ruins of history and time, but they are also a powerful symbol of the adult subject's condition of loss, dissolution, and demediation. Not only the city crumbles ("Toledo, come un vecchio teatro, come se le sue case e strade fossero quinte, senza rumore cadeva," R1 696; "Toledo, like an old theatre, as though its homes and streets were the backstage, was falling apart without a sound"), but so does the totalizing, all-encompassing self of a pre-oedipal world of childhood, with its hopes and dreams.

> Toledo [..] era morta col silenzio del porto e tutte le meraviglie che sono nei porti, allorquando si attendono le Ere Successive. Allorquando si è fanciulli e si aspettano, con fiducia grande, o ingenuo tormento, le Ere successive.
>
> Verranno, poi? Questa la domanda. (R1 973)

> (Toledo [...] was dead with the silence of the port and all the marvels that are found in ports, whilst awaiting the Successive Eras. Whilst being young and awaiting, with great faith, or with naive dread, the Successive Eras.
>
> Will they come then? That is the question.)

This is the ending of Toledana's story. However, in its last pages, the text reserves a surprise, in a metaliterary gesture worthy of Cervantes (an author certainly present to Ortese): turning the page, the readers are confronted with a proliferation of epilogues (there are three of them, to be precise). And the last epilogue, in turn, reveals an unexpected narrative twist: the preceding five hundred plus pages we have just read (what we thought to be an autobiographical narrative framework), are nothing more than a macro-tale, the tale of the "Porto Silenzioso," which encompasses the nine short tales written by the young Toledana, but which is, effectively, a tale in itself, exactly like the others.[61] The many narrative layers and the many narratorial voices that are emerging from the novel trigger, at this point, a forceful destabilizing effect. Paradoxically, however, the narrative coup de theatre strengthens (instead of diminishing) the reality effect. Only now, having "pealed" back several fictional layers, the narratorial "I" – which now expresses herself in the present tense "per dare il senso della cosa che accade, mentre accade" (R1 975; "in order to give a sense of what is happening while it happens") – is what we expect from the narratorial voice in an autobiographical fiction.

Entering this "real" dimension painfully undermines the optimistic and teleological momentum of the protagonist's coming of age and reveals, on the contrary, a circular, repetitive pattern: the end of the story in fact mirrors the beginning. The process of self-development, the *recherche du centre* has lead in reality only to a *katabasis*, to a movement towards the kingdom of the dead and the shades, in the same way the ancient epic heroes descended into Hades. In the Nordic city of the *Mille Torri* (which we might infer to be Milano), ten years later, alone with one surviving sister, "Damasa Figuera, figlia di Apa e Apo, nella realtà anagrafica del tempo rispettivamente altri nomi" (R1 975; "Damasa Figuera, the daughter of Apo and Apa, in the anagraphic reality of time respectively other names") lives suspended between dreams and memories: her daily reality is made up either of letters sent to her from the past, bearing only notices of death or of bodily remains that literally or symbolically come back to her (her brother Albe, her mother and father). Friends, lovers, dear ones: all are shades.

> Sento piangere, gente che se ne va, figure care che se ne vanno, se ne vanno nel tramonto ispanico, dopo che il vicereame finì e giunse l'era successiva: D'Orgaz, Papasa, Thornton, Albe, Lee, Apo, Apa, gli Uccelli, Lemano mio, non verranno mai più; per l'eternità su questi vascelli del Tempo, s'imbarcano, emigrano ... Dio solo sa dove e quando giungeranno. Ma è un'ombra o una luce tale Dio? (R1 985)

> (I hear crying, people that are passing, dear figures that are passing, passing into the hispanic sunset, after the viceroyalty ended and the successive eras arrived: D'Orgaz, Papasa, Thornton, Albe, Lee, Apo, Apa, the Uccelli, my Lemano, they will not ever return: towards eternity they embark, they emigrate on these vessels of Time ... God only knows where and when they will land. Well, is such a God as this a light or a shade?)

And for that matter Damasa Figuera is a shade herself, in a certain sense, since the traces of her writing and of her creativity have been erased in the novel's epilogue: "Sul tavolo giace la *Literaria Gazeta* (R1 994; "upon the table lays the *Literaria Gazeta*"). Thus, in the very end, *Il porto di Toledo* is an inverted and negated *Künstlerroman* that openly questions the notion of creativity as a catalyst for self-actualization. Is the creative process of the woman artist hindered by social and cultural forces from without or rather by psychological impediments from within? Does entering adulthood for a woman mean unlearning, undoing, un-processing the self? Entering silence? Is the silent Damasa Figuera a dramatization of Ortese's self-fragmentation, a projection of her sense of guilt and transgression since she – unlike her fictional character – has found a voice of her own and does not want to acquiesce to silence?

The circular logic that has undercut and undermined the unfolding of the novel now comes fully to the foreground. Once again, exactly like in the Toledo of her childhood, reality is annihilated by the inexorable flux of time. "Nocturnal" and "subterranean," reality dissipates in smoke or fades into the inconsistency of a chimeric material: "Mah! Così se ne fugge tutto. E quello che sembrò vero è sogno [...] solo un po' di fumo, dunque, nostra orgogliosa realtà!" (R1 976; "And how, thus it all passes on. And that which seemed real is a dream [...] only a bit of smoke, our proud reality!")

In a frightful progression, the novel's figural logic, at the end, evokes a "petrification" of forms and figures. And the petrification stiffens into a rigor mortis the ancient city of her memory, the port of Toledo, once "mutable" and now only occupied by "vessels of stone":

> E ora mi ricordo cosa vedevo nel mio cuore, mentre definitivamente ci allontaniamo dalla nuova Toledo e le sue *rovine*, passando davanti alla città dei marine dormienti, tra vascelli di *pietra*. (R1 984)

> (And now I remember what I saw in my heart, while we distance ourselves definitively from the new Toledo and its *ruins*, passing in front of the city of the sleeping sailors, between vessels of *stone*.)

> Come adulta lavoravo, prendendo pochi denari [...] Solo che non vi era più quell'azzurro e freschezza; ma il mondo si avanzava come *pietra*. (R1 791)

> (As an adult I worked, making little money [...] Only that there was no longer that blue color and freshness: rather, the world advanced like a *stone*.)
>
> Mai più mare, mai più libero mare solo *pietra*, intendi? (R1 619)
>
> (Never again the sea, never again the free waters, only *stone* you understand?)[62]

And even the sea, which was complicit in Toledana's quest towards self-development and creative self-assertion with the motion of its waves, with its rhythms, melodies, brackish roars, and contrapuntal figural meanings, now envelops itself in silence: "Solo il mare, ai cancelli, non mormora più" (R1 993; "Only the sea at the gates murmurs no more"). The silence-petrification of the sea, which seals the closure of the text, resonates with another silence, that of the beloved Lemano:

> Solo Lemano non vidi mai. Egli non tornò mai, neppure nei sogni. Come quel mare del porto giovane disparve; e ora come lui – sempre muto e torvo, nella realtà – è quell'amato mare dei miei anni in Toledo, sotto le nubi che circondano, come vedette dell'eterno, la spenta Collina. (R1 995)
>
> (It was only Lemano I never saw again. He never returned, not even in my dreams. He disappeared much like that sea of the young port; now like him – always silent and grim, in reality – is that beloved sea from my years in Toledo, under the clouds that circle above, as eternal sentinels, the dormant Collina.)

Il porto di Toledo concludes with a whirlwind of loss and silence, both echoing Toledana's creative aphasia. In the end, time, flux, transience have taken their tolls.[63] Having eroded the stability of the (post)modern subject and her forward quest for self-actualization and creative expression, having turned space and history into a repository of ruins, memories, and phantoms, Ortese's splendid autofictional writing can only be a melancholic recollection of the ephemeral.[64]

NOTES

1 For an accurate analysis of the novel's structure, see the impressive study by Clerici, *Apparizione e visione*, 442–81; while, for an interpretive model, to

which these pages are greatly indebted, see Farnetti, *Anna Maria Ortese,* 111–13; and, especially, 79–89, where Farnetti outlines the importance of the "maritime" theme in relation to feminine writing and identity.

2 Among them, Sibilla Aleramo, *Una Donna,* 1906; Clarice Tartufari, *Il gomitolo d'oro,* 1924; Ada Negri, *Stella mattutina,* 1921; Grazia Deledda, *Cosima,* 1937; and, though in the transposed form of a historical novel, Anna Banti, *Artemisia,* 1947.

3 Farnetti, *Anna Maria Ortese,* 113.

4 On the relationship between Ortese's novel and the autobiographical genre, see Farnetti, *Il centro della cattedrale,* 89–101; in addition to her entry "Autobiografia (*Je est une autre*)" in the volume *Anna Maria Ortese,* 28–37, where the scholar outlines some fundamental theoretical frameworks for understanding the novel. From the massive English-language bibliography on autobiography and women writers, certain scholars (Shari Benstock, Celeste Schenk, Bella Brodzki, Carolyn Heilbrun, Estelle Jelinek) and certain significant texts have shaped my way of understanding this particular mode of writing and the relation between gender and genres. Among them, particularly inspiring were the texts by Sidonie Smith and Julia Watson, Martine Watson Brownley and Allison B. Kimmich, Estelle C. Jelinek, Linda Anderson, Rita Felski, and Elisabeth Youngh-Bruehl.

5 Among them, the most significant studies are by Beatrice Manetti, Paolo Giovanetti, Cosetta Seno Reed, Vilma De Gasperin, Siriana Sgravicchia, Alessandra Riccio, and Monica Farnetti, "Toledo o cara," 159–71.

6 Wordsworth, 12.208–18.

7 Deleuze, 1–35. For a critical introduction to Deleuze's idea see also Williams, *Gilles Deleuze's Difference and Repetition.*

8 The author does not provide accurate information about this painting. In my opinion, she is presumably referring to the small tableau *Madonna col bambino* (today in the Farnese Galleries of the Capodimonte Museum), which exhibits the two sacred figures beneath a blue sky. Erroneously attributed to Raphael until the beginning of the twentieth century, today the painting is ascribed to the work of the Perugino school.

9 Jurgis Baltrusaitis, *Anamorfosi,* 16ff.

10 Maddalena Mazzocut-Mis, *Deformazioni fantastiche,* 120.

11 Ortese describes the genetic mutation of the composition in these words: "[*Il porto di Toledo*] era all'inizo la presentazione del mio primo libro – *Angelici dolori* – che intendevo proporre all'editore Vallecchi. Non avevo altre idee e non potevo fare altri programmi. Perciò pensai liberamente a questa introduzione ai miei primi racconti (surreali), che poco alla volta si fece libro essa stessa, coinvolgendo questi primi scritti, e mutando quegli

stessi scritti fino a renderli irriconoscibili da ciò che erano" [(*Il porto di Toledo*) was in the beginning a presentation of my first book – *Angelici dolori* – which I intended to furnish to the publisher Vallecchi. I did not have any other ideas and I was not able to make other plans. For that I thought freely of this introduction to my first (surreal) tales, which little by little became a book in itself, incorporating these early writings and altering these same writings to the point of rendering them unrecognizable from what they were], Farnetti, "Nota al testo," R1 1027.

12 For an assessment on the "Years of Lead," cfr. Calvi et al., *Le date del terrore*; Galli, *Il partito armato*; and Scialò, *Le stragi dimenticate*.

13 Clerici, *Apparizione e visione*, 449–50.

14 The twenty-two typewritten pages of the fascinating diary (divided into two cahiers, *La Carbonera* and *Il mare morto*) have been published by Farnetti in the Appendix I of the Adelphi volume. The possibility that these pages are from Ortese's original diary and not from a later (at least partial) reworking, as certain textual occurrences might have one believe, nonetheless seems to me to be still open to debate.

15 Clerici, *Apparizione e visione*, 640.

16 Battistini, *Lo specchio di Dedalo*, 7–9.

17 "Nella carta da me pazientemente, eppure insanamente, elaborata della nuova Toledo, e che Tu, Spirito del Tempo, osservi certo con lacrime di gioia" (R1 398; "In the map that I patiently yet insanely drafted of the new Toledo, and that You, Spirit of Time, certainly look upon with tears of joy").

18 I must acknowledge here my intellectual debts. If, on the one hand, certain pages of Farnetti on Ortese's wavering style of writing have inspired my analysis (see, especially, Farnetti, *Anna Maria Ortese*, 79–89), on the other, it is an essay on Petrarch, by medievalist scholar Teodolinda Barolini, who strongly influenced the way I view and analyse the novel in its complexity. Ortese in fact shares with the poet of the *Canzoniere* not only the obsession for the *fuga temporis* (which comes to Ortese via the Spanish Baroque poets of her predilection) but also, and especially, the paradoxical and indispensable tension between stasis and fluidity, narrativity and non-narrativity, backward movement and forward thrust, just as Barolini evinces in her brilliant interpretation of Petrarch's *Rerum Vulgarium Fragmenta*. See Barolini, "The Making of a Lyric Sequence," 1–38.

19 On the *poetica dell'Espressività*, it is still interesting to read Di Biase, "*Il porto di Toledo*," 121–30.

20 Ortese, "Maestri spagnoli alla Mostra di Ginevra," 3 and "I capolavori del Prado nel Museo di Ginevra," 3.

21 Clerici, *Apparizione e visione*, 473.

22 Farnetti, "Toledo o cara," 162. On the influence of El Greco's *View of Toledo* cfr., also Farnetti, "Guida di Toledo," 1133–36. In my article "Chiaroscuro napoletano," published concurrently to the Adelphi volume edited by Farnetti, I likewise made note of the importance of El Greco's canvas for the writer, and I proposed, like Farnetti, the idea of a direct influence of the painting on Ortese's view of the city.

23 The fantastical, surreal topography of the city is reconstructed by Cajati and Tungbang, "Indice dei luoghi di Toledo," 1136–51. Even though it falls outside the scope of this article, I would nevertheless like to underline certain serious errors in the identification of the Neapolitan locations, such that could compromise the entire Ortesian geography. Among these errors, the identification of "Plaza del Quiosco" or "Plaza Guzmano," a central geographical and emotional location in the novel (very close to Ortese's home near the port), is one of the most evident. According to my personal reconstruction, this "plaza" does not refer to Piazza Municipio (a central and elegant piazza, the political and administrative center of the city, near the port, yet separated from it by a "psychological" class barrier), but instead to Piazza Giovanni Bovio (to this day still referred to by locals as Piazza Borsa, its traditional name), a small and monumental piazza onto which even today opens one of the main alleyways of the port neighbourhood, Via Marchese Campodisola (in the novel rechristened Vicolo Spagnolo, and erroneously identified by the two scholars as Via S. Giacomo degli Spagnoli). Following the logic of my reconstruction, then, the central Piazza Municipio becomes in the novel Piazza Theotokopulos, "on the corner of the Pilar." The same error also appears in Clerici, *Apparizione e visione*, 472. Regarding the location of Ortese's home, an important detail must be rectified: her modest building was located where the luxury Hotel Romeo stands today, on the corner of Via Cristoforo Colombo (Via Pilar in the fiction) and the narrow Vico Leone (which, in the novel, bears the intriguing name of Rua Ahorcados, erroneously identified by scholars as the Vico Sospira Bisi, located in an entirely different area). Another important misidentification to rectify is that of the Chiesa Spagnola, a small, dark, Spanish church situated in a narrow and dusty alley, very close both to Vicolo Spagnolo (Via Marchese Campodisola), Plaza Guzmano (Piazza Bovio) and the writer's home – where the young Ortese remains enchanted by the icon of a black Madonna: both the church and the sacred image will prove very important for her literary inspiration and thus occupy a central place in the writer's imaginary. The church is not to be identified with the church of Santa Maria di Monserrato (as the architects Cajati and Tungbang write), demolished during the renewal projects at the end of the

nineteenth century, but with a small church, destroyed by the bombardments of World War II: now in disuse, it is situated in the obscure Vico Monserrato, near the corner of Via Marchese Campodisola. The oral tradition of the residents I interviewed still recall the presence, before the war, of the sacred icon of a black Madonna, which was a copy of *la moreneta,* a twelfth-century dark-skinned statuette venerated in the Catalonian monastery of Santa Maria de Montserrat. Overall, Ortese's fantastical geography is not so fantastical, but is born entirely in the perimeter around her home in Via del Piliero.

24 In addition to these iconic models, another "screen," or intermediary mechanism operates within the novel. The name "Toledo" – a name profoundly rooted in Neapolitan culture and history – recalls not only the Spanish and Bourbon history of Naples but also evokes an ancient and central Neapolitan road, *via Toledo* (thus serving as a metonym for the city itself). It divides the city in half all the way down to the outlet of the sea – in the vicinity of the port – the very neighbourhood where the Ortese family landed, in 1928. They inhabited a "type of hovel," "miserable yellow house," on *via del Piliero* 29, facing the quays of the port (Clerici, *Apparizione e visione,* 473).

25 Ibid., 473–74.

26 Italics are my own.

27 "Our topic deals with the giving and taking away faces, with face and deface, *figure,* figuration and disfiguration," De Man, "Autobiography as Defacement," 75–76.

28 Seno Reed, "Partire da sé e non farsi trovare," 156. Seno Reed comments also on the author's unreliability and the betrayal of the referential pact. As she writes: "[Ortese's] autobiographical discourse sets itself in open resistance to the autobiography of literary tradition, eroding from the inside the three constitutive moments in favor of a dialogic and fluid writing and of a *sui generis* language that inserts itself naturally into the tradition of feminine writing" (Ibid., 155).

29 Originally coined by Serge Doubrovsky to indicate that his work belonged to the new genre of fictional autobiography, "autofiction" can be described as a postmodern take on autobiography, calling into question its central criterion, its veracity and autobiographical contracts. The most specific definition is that of a genre of its own, characterized by a double author-reader contract: the autobiographical contract demanding the author to tell the truth about his or her life, and the fictional contract allowing fabulations and inventions. The specificity of autofiction lies in the unresolvable paradox of these contradicting reading instructions (see Zipfel, "Autofiction," 36).

30 "Toledo non è dunque una storia vera, non è una autobiografia, è rivolta e 'reato' davanti alla pianificazione umana" (R1 355; "Toledo is not a true story, nor an autobiography, it is revolt and 'crime' against the human planning").

31 Leigh Gilmore, *Autobiographics,* 16–39. Also interesting are her insights on naming, 86–106.

32 Derrida and Ronell, "The Law of Genre," 55–81.

33 Barolini, "The Making of a Lyric Sequence," 6.

34 Ibid., 4.

35 Manetti, "*Toledo* nell'abisso," 185, 189–95.

36 Ibid.

37 On Ortese's claim that her writing is "come l'eterno Labirinto" (as the eternal Labirint), see Manetti, "*Toledo* nell'abisso," 198.

38 De Gasperin, "Appunti sulla citazione nel *Porto di Toledo,*" 57–74.

39 Clerici, *Apparizione e visione,* 475.

40 Farnetti, *Il centro della cattedrale,* 96. On the language of Toledo, seen as an expression of a *parlar materno,* and of a "logic" which is relational, emotive, and sensorial, Cosetta Seno Reed, building on the feminist insights of Cavarero and Cixous, offers interesting points with which I agree. See Seno Reed, "Partire da sé e non farsi trovare," 158–64. It is worth noting, however, that Ortese's relationship with the maternal is more complex and problematic than it first appears, encompassing also a pronounced matrophobia, a denial of the maternal, and a subtle misogyny that pervade many of her works.

41 In her letters to friends and publishers, Ortese herself reveals the literary models of her novel: Dumas' *The Three Musketeers,* Defoe's *Robinson Crusoe,* and De Quevedo's moral and love sonnets. See Clerici, *Apparizione e visione,* 460. Even though it is beyond the scope of this study, I would like to establish a connection with Virginia Woolf's *To the Lighthouse,* a text which can certainly be considered another implicit model for *Il porto di Toledo,* yet it has been overlooked by critics. The two texts share surprising thematic similarities: an obsession with temporal flux and instability, the subjective nature of reality, the search for permanence, cohesion, and meaning, the subversion of gender roles, the symbolic presence of a lighthouse, the complex symbolism of water, suggesting both permanence and erosion, and the role of art as a means of transcendence and endurance. Moreover, the artistic quest of one of Woolf's characters, Lily Briscoe, mirrors that of Toledana, though with some fundamental differences: while in fact the painter Lily, in applying her final stroke to the canvas, achieves through art the sense of unity, permanence, and cohesion she had been longing for,

Toledana is, on the contrary, silenced and swept away by the eternal ephemerality of time. Significantly, in a letter to Sergio Pautasso, Ortese writes that the only consolation from the difficult years during which she composed the novel were a few memorable readings: Virginia Woolf, James Joyce, and "the marvelous Lucretius." See Clerici, *Apparizione e visione*, 452.

42 Ortese, letter to Calasso, 1997 (R1 1070).

43 De Certeau, *The Practice of Everyday Life*, 115.

44 Stanford Friedman, *Mappings*, 19.

45 The interrelationship between body, sexuality, and desire remains a nexus of conflict and disavowal even as an adult, after her erotic liaison with Lemano.

46 For a more detailed treatment of Toledo's urban topography, see Ghezzo, "Tra Fantasticheria e scrittura" and "Chiaroscuro napoletano," 85–104, especially 89–93 and 94–99.

47 Walter Benjamin, "Naples," 165–66.

48 As I have argued in an article on Toledana's *flanerie*, only by walking innumerable kilometres by foot, through passageways and staircases, does Toledana succeed in "territorializing" the city, transforming it into a porous, traversable, and subjectivized space. Her "light and swift" pace, a sort of *refrain* as Deleuze and Guattari would have it, marks the fragmented urban space, turning it into a niche, a personal, fluid, ethereal territory she can resemanticize according to her desires (cfr. Deleuze and Guattari, "Of the refrain," 310–50). The city, ultimately, transforms into a hypnotic, spectral, and nocturnal image, completely dematerialized, reduced to a liquid and ethereal substance. Moreover, in this highly subjectivized space, Toledana becomes an invisible spectator, able to look without being looked at. And, as feminist critics on *flanerie* have pointed out, "the privilege of invisibility, of being relatively unnoticed, accompanies the control of space" (Meskimmon, *Engendering the City*, 16).

49 For a more detailed account of the interplay of contrasting metaphors, see Ghezzo, "Paesaggi del desiderio."

50 The relationship between certain spatial configurations, such as home / window / room and land / sea, is analysed from a perspective of gender by Horner and Zlosnick. The observations on the narratives by Perkins Gilman, Chopin, Wharton, Woolf, and Rhys prove to be extremely stimulating even for an interpretation of Ortese's novel.

51 On Toledana's scopic drive, see Farnetti, *Anna Maria Ortese*, 138–45.

52 These dimensions conflate at times with the precolonial land of Native Americans or the Pilgrim Fathers' America, or even the Iberian motherland, the ancient land of a lost childhood. It is worth noting that the novel's

epic and adventurous moments can be intertextually linked to other passages from Ortese's work (from the short story *Jane e il mare* to the novel *L'Iguana*), hearkening back to the "salt-encrusted" pages of the beloved sea-enchanted *auctores*: Stevenson, Defoe, Conrad, and Dickens.

53 All italics are mine.

54 Suskin Ostriker, *Stealing the Language*, 60.

55 For this particular experience, see Freud's pages on the "feeling of the oceanic" intended as an ecstatic or mystical moment, an infinite opening, characterized by the erosion of the bounds of individuality and by a state of fusion with the external world (see Freud, *Civilization and its Discontent*, 12). The oceanic feeling can be read in consonance with certain psychoanalytic notions, from the Freudian pre-oedipal to the Lacanian Imaginary, up through the kristevan semiotic *chora* understood as the maternal receptacle, an undifferentiated corporeal space, non-expressive and pre-linguistic totality, site of impulses, chaotic and uncontrollable desires. See Kristeva, *Revolution in Poetic Language*, 23–25.

56 With regard to the circularity of time, the text is explicit: "Solo in ciò credo [...] in uno scarnificato indietreggiare (essendo del resto la vita e l'universo cosmico cosa circolare, ciò non troppo avventurosa ipotesi)" [R1 911; "I believe in this alone [...] in an emaciated regression (the rest of life and the cosmos being cyclical in nature, this is hardly a radical hypothesis)"].

57 Stanford Friedan, *Mappings*, 19.

58 Farnetti, *Anna Maria Ortese*, 34.

59 For an in-depth analysis of the concept of nomadic subjectivity, see Braidotti, *Nomadic Subjects*.

60 Farnetti, *Anna Maria Ortese*, 30–31 and 79.

61 For this insight, see Manetti, "*Toledo* nell'abisso," 195.

62 All italics are mine.

63 Apparently muted and silenced at the end of the novel, the vast, open space of the sea acquires meaning and significance in the symbolic depths of the text. As I have argued elsewhere, the triumph of the liquid dimension and of the water metaphors, related to *fuga temporis*, should be interpreted also from a different perspective, not merely through the lens of temporality: water and the vast maritime expanses, in fact, at the symbolic level, as feminist criticism suggests, hearkens back to the liberty of a feminine writing that wants to corrode the solidity of the *logos* and of androcentric discourse. As in the writings of Virginia Woolf, the liquid element in Ortese (with all of the symbolic allusions that it carries with it: femininity, infancy, reverie, pre-oedipal plenitude, dream, circularity, memory, but also ephemerality and temporality) pervades the novel at every level: it breaks down the

syntax and grammar, it permeates the language and its metaphorical systems, it infiltrates the text's narrative structures, it dematerializes the substance of characters and places. For a more in-depth analysis, see Ghezzo, "Paesaggi del desiderio," 265–78, and "Chiaroscuro Napoletano," 94. On the maritime imaginary in Ortese and on the equation of the sea with feminine writing, see the fundamental pages of Farnetti, *Anna Maria Ortese,* 79–89. Among the numerous theoretical texts that treat the subject, it suffices here to cite Cixous, "The Laugh of Medusa," 875–93.

64 As the Arab poet Abdelfatth Kilito claims, the autobiographer is like a melancholy archaeologist, a patient decipherer of vanished or hardly visible traces, who has taken to speaking of the vestiges that the wind and rain efface little by little. See Battistini, *Lo specchio di Dedalo,* 13.

WORKS CITED

Anderson, Linda. *Autobiography.* London and New York: Routledge, 2001.

Baltrusaitis, Jurgis. *Anamorfosi o Thaumaturgus opticus.* Trans. P. Bertolucci and A. Bassan Levi. Milan: Adelphi, 1990.

Barolini, Teodolinda. "The Making of a Lyric Sequence: Time and Narrative in Petrarch's *Rerum vulgarium fragmenta.*" *MLN* 104 (1989): 1–38.

Battistini, Andrea. *Lo specchio di Dedalo.* Milan: Il Mulino, 2007.

Benjamin, Walter, and Lacis Asja. "Naples." In *Reflections: Essays, Aphorisms, Autobiographical Writings,* 163–66. Trans. Edmund Jephcott. Ed. Peter Demetz. New York and London: Harcourt Brace Jovanovich, 1978.

Braidotti, Rosi. *Nomadic Subjects: Embodiment and Sexual Difference in Contemporary Feminist Theory.* New York: Columbia University Press, 1994.

Cajati, Claudio, and Yolanda Tungbang. "Indice dei luogi di Toledo," in *Romanzi,* Vol. 1, by Anna Maria Ortese, 1136–51. Milan: Adelphi, 2002.

Calvi, Maurizio, Alessandro Ceci, Angelo Sessa, and Guilio Vasaturo. *Le date del terrore: La genesi del terrorismo italiano e il microclima dell'eversione dal 1945 al 2003.* Rome: Luca Sossella Editore, 2003.

Cixous, Hélène. "The Laugh of Medusa." *Signs: Journal of Women in Culture and Society* 1, no. 4 (1976): 875–93.

Cixous, Hélène, and Mireille Calle-Gruber. *Hélène Cixous, Photos de Racines.* Paris: Des Femmes, 1994.

Clerici, Luca. *Apparizione e visione: Vita e opere di Anna Maria Ortese.* Milan: Mondadori, 2002.

– ed. "Per Anna Maria Ortese." *Il Giannone* 4, no. 7–8 (January-December 2006).

De Certeau, Michel. *The Practice of Everyday Life.* Berkley and Los Angeles: University of California Press, 1984.

De Gasperin, Vilma. "Appunti sulla citazione nel *Porto di Toledo.*" *Esperienze letterarie* 34, no. 1 (2009): 57–74.
Deleuze, Gilles. *Difference and Repetition.* Trans. Paul Patterson. London: Athlone Press, 1994.
Deleuze, Gilles, and Felix Guattari. "Of the refrain." In *A Thousand Plateaus: Capitalism and Schizophrenia,* 310–50. Trans. Brian Massumi. London: Athlone Press, 1992.
De Man, Paul. "Autobiography as Defacement." *MLN* 94, no. 5 (Dec 1979): 919–30.
Derrida Jacques, and Avital Ronell. "The Law of Genre." *Critical Inquiry* 7, no. 1 (1980): 55–81.
Di Biase, Carmine. "*Il Porto di Toledo* (La poetica dell'Espressività)." In *L'altra Napoli: Scrittori napoletani d'oggi,* 121–30. Naples: Società Editrice Napoletana, 1978.
Farnetti, Monica. *Anna Maria Ortese.* Milan: Bruno Mondadori, 1998.
– *Il centro della cattedrale: I ricordi d'infanzia nella scrittura femminile.* Mantova: Tre Lune Edizioni, 2002.
– "I romanzi di Anna Maria Ortese." In *Romanzi,* Vol. 1, by Anna Maria Ortese, ix–lxvi. Milan: Adelphi, 2002.
– "Toledo o cara." In *Tutte signore di mio gusto: profili di scrittrici contemporanee,* 159–71. Milan: La Tartaruga, 2008.
Felski, Rita. "On Confession." In *Beyond Feminist Aesthetics,* 89–121. Cambridge, MA: Harvard University Press, 1989.
Freud, Sigmund. *Civilization and its Discontent.* New York: Norton, 1962.
Galli, Giorgio. *Il partito armato – Gli "anni di piombo" in Italia, 1968–1986.* Milan: Rizzoli, 1986.
Ghezzo, Flora. "Chiaroscuro napoletano: trasfigurazioni fantastiche di una città." *Narrativa* 24 (January 2003): 85–104.
– "Paesaggi del desiderio, ovvero *devenir femme* tra terra e acqua." In *E c'è di mezzo il mare: lingua, letteratura e civiltà marina,* 265–78. Firenze: Franco Cesati Editore, 2002.
– "Tra Fantasticheria e scrittura: la ricerca dell'Eden perduto nel *Porto di Toledo di Anna Maria Ortese.*" *Nemla Italian Studies* 12 (1997): 65–86.
Gilmore, Leigh. *Autobiographics: A Feminist Theory of Women's Self-Representation.* Ithaca, NY: Cornell University Press, 1994.
Giovanetti, Paolo. "Poesia in cerca di libro: sulla scrittura in versi di Anna Maria Ortese." In *Per Anna Maria Ortese,* ed. Luca Clerici. *Il Giannone* 4, no. 7–8 (January-December 2006): 165–81.
Horner, Avril, and Sue Zlosnick. *Landscapes of Desires.* Hertfordshire, UK: Harvester Wheatsheaf, 1990.

Jelinek, Estelle C. *Women's Autobiography: Essays in Criticism.* Bloomington and London: University of Indiana Press, 1980.

Kristeva, Julia. *Revolution in Poetic Language.* Trans. Margaret Waller. New York: Columbia University Press, 1984.

Manetti, Beatrice. "*Toledo* nell'abisso: nascita e metamorfosi di un romanzo labirinto." In *Per Anna Maria Ortese,* ed. Luca Clerici. *Il Giannone* 4, no. 7–8 (January–December 2006): 183–200.

Mazzocut-Mis, Maddalena. *Deformazioni fantastiche: introduzione all'estetica di Jurgis Baltrusaitis.* Milan: Mimesis, 1999.

Meskimmon, Marsha. *Engendering the City: Women Artists and Urban Space.* London: Scarlet Press, 1997.

Ortese, Anna Maria. "I capolavori del Prado nel Museo di Ginevra," *Il Gazzettino,* 27 July 1939, 3.

– "Maestri spagnoli alla Mostra di Ginevra." *Il Gazzettino,* 22 July 1939, 3.

Riccio, Alessandra. "*Toledo* ovvero l'indicibile." In *Paesaggio e memoria: Giornata di studi su Anna Maria Ortese,* ed. Caterina di Caprio and Laura Donadio, 21–32. Naples: Libreria Dante e Descartes, 2003.

Scialò, Luca. *Le stragi dimenticate: La strategia della tensione secondo la Commissione parlamentare d'inchiesta sul terrorismo in Italia.* Milan: Boopen, 2008.

Seno Reed, Cosetta. "Partire da sé e non farsi trovare: *Il Porto di Toledo*: storia di un'autobiografia fantastica." *MLN* 122, no. 1 (2007): 148–66.

Sgravicchia, Siriana. "Spazio reale e testuale nel *Porto di Toledo.*" *Avanguardia* 21 (2002): 89–99.

Smith, Sidonie, and Julia Watson, eds. *Reading Autobiography: A Guide for Interpreting Life Narratives.* Minneapolis: University of Minnesota Press, 2001.

– *Women, Autobiography, Theory: A Reader.* Madison: University of Wiscosin Press, 1998.

Stanford Friedman, Susan. *Mappings: Feminism and the Cultural Geographies of Encounter.* Princeton, NJ: Princeton University Press, 1988.

Suskin Ostriker, Alicia. *Stealing the Language: The Emergence of Women's Poetry in America.* Boston, MA: Beacon Press, 1986.

Watson Brownley, Martine, and Allison B. Kimmich. *Women and Autobiography.* Wilmington, DE: Scholarly Resources, 1999.

Williams, James. *Gilles Deleuze's Difference and Repetition: A Critical Introduction and a Guide.* Edinburgh: Edinburgh University Press, 2003.

Wordsworth, William. *The Prelude: The Four Texts (1798, 1799, 1805, 1850).* New York: Penguin Books, 2004.

Willan, Philip. *Puppetmasters: The Political Use of Terrorism in Italy.* London: Constable and Company, 1991.

Youngh-Bruehl, Elisabeth. *Subject to Biography: Psychoanalysis, Feminism, and Writing Women's Lives.* Cambridge, MA: Harvard University Press, 1998.
Zipfel, Frank. "Autofiction." In *The Routledge Encyclopedia of Narrative Theory*, ed. David Herman, Manfred Jahn, and Marie-Laure Ryan. Abingdon and New York: Routledge, 2005.

PART THREE

On Becoming Beast: Iguanas, Linnets, Lions, and the Geography of Otherness

8 Beasts, Goblins, and Other Chameleonic Creatures: Anna Maria Ortese's "Real Children of the Universe"

INGE LANSLOTS

Di nuovo odo il vento sotto la porta, e stento a credere che il Folletto sia realmente esistito. Suppongo (tra le lacrime) che solo nel cielo dei fanciulli – superbo cielo al disopra di tutte le Genova – egli abbia avuto vita: ma poi avverto non so che pianto [...] di altri Stellini, e ne deduco che i Folletti sulla Terra sono ancora tanti [...] sono infiniti.

(Once again I hear the wind beneath the door, and I cannot believe, without some special effort, that the pixie ever truly existed. I suppose (in the midst of tears) that the only life he ever knew was lived in the heavens of children – that splendid sky which lies over every Genoa. But then I discern an indescribable lament [...] the plaint of other Stellinos; and I conclude that the Follettos now on the earth are still quite numerous [...] or numberless.)

Anna Maria Ortese, *"Folletto a Genova,"* SV 70

Only recently literary criticism has assigned to the trilogy by Anna Maria Ortese, *L'Iguana* (1965), *Il cardillo addolorato* (1993), and *Alonso e i visionari* (1996), a key position within the author's work, and particularly within her non-realistic prose. Although Ortese's non-realistic prose is, as we shall see, quite unique, it relates to the rich tradition of the fantastic novel that started with the Scapigliatura production in the late nineteenth century, namely with *I racconti fantastici* (1869) by Ugo Tarchetti. Since then, the fantastic novel had many diversified outcomes, but it always reflected existential doubts and an anxiety towards the new socioeconomic reality. Two major representatives of the fantastic novel at the beginning of the twentieth century, Tommaso Landolfi and Alberto Savinio, for example, presented surreal events and monstrous characters in order to stress their questioning of reality. Later on, well-known writers such as Italo Calvino, Pier Paolo Pasolini, and Elsa Morante combined some fantastic elements within their work. However, labelling Ortese's work as a mere expression of the fantastic does not suffice to render Ortese's non-mimetic and iconoclast approach to reality, whose aim is to unveil its own inconsistency.[1] By adding a symbolic charge to her literary worlds, Ortese shows that the nature of the characters populating her stories is elusive and ungraspable.

In this essay, I will argue that in relation to Ortese's peculiar approach to reality, the nature of her trilogy's characters is marked by a strong dualism, or juxtaposition of opposites which strives to transcend itself and, in the end, give way to an ontological multiplicity that challenges our common, rational assumptions and the philosophical binarism upon which they are based. In order to do that, I will refer to the tables at the end of my essay: they visualize the multiformity of Ortese's "mostruoso cameleontismo" ("monstrous shape-shifting")[2], as Neria De Giovanni put it, and summarize the major outcomes of my analysis that will mainly focus on *L'Iguana*, the first novel of the trilogy.

Intertexture

L'Iguana, first published in 1965 and awarded the Premio Maria Cristina[3] the following year, was soon afterwards to be forgotten.[4] It was then republished in 1978 by Rizzoli and later in 1986 by the leading publishing house Adelphi, which, by means of its director, Roberto Calasso, revived the interest in Ortese's writing.[5]

At first sight, *L'Iguana* seems an example of "il rischioso gioco dell'ibridazione dei generi" ("the edgy game of hybridization of genres"):[6] adventure sea story (based on the premise of Stevenson's *Treasure Island* and Defoe's *Robinson Crusoe*), gothic and fantastic novel, combined with elements of mythology, legends, and fairy tales: these are just some of the subgenres to which Ortese's novel can be ascribed. Moreover, *L'Iguana* is also connected to the symbolism of the novel of ideas, and to the Enlightenment tradition of allegorism.[7]

L'Iguana tells the story of the overseas journey of a young nobleman from Milan, Carlo Ludovico di Grees, called Daddo, who, in search for new estate, lands on the unknown island of Ocaña, takes an interest in the house of the solitary family Guzman and gets enchanted by Estrellita (Spanish for "little star"), the young maid of the family. Surprisingly, Estrellita alternates between a human and a more animal appearance, assuming mainly the guise of an iguana, which explains the title of the novel. For this reason, what could initially appear as an idyllic love story (Daddo wants to take Estrellita with him to Milan and turn her into an educated young lady) ends tragically. Rising conflicts among the Guzman family members and the revelation of Estrellita's presumed true identity – the inhabitants of Ocaña see her as a selfish and monster-like creature – make Daddo lose himself in a fantasy world. He ultimately dies on Ocaña, leaving intact the mystery of the island and its inhabitants.

The Iguana's "doppia natura"

The linnet, she thought, might stand for love, that whimsical thing that was banished from that house. (LL 140)

After this initial presentation of the novel one could already sketch a first profile of the Iguana: the maiden is alternately portrayed as enchanting and fatal, devoted and envious, innocent and corrupt. Her nature is highly ambiguous, duplicitous (see Table 1, *Dualism*), and it relies on the subjective vision of the other characters. At his arrival on the island, Daddo is struck by the creature's look:

> Grande, a questo punto, fu la sorpresa del Daddo, nell'accorgersi che quella che egli aveva preso per una vecchia, altri non era che una bestiola verdissima e alta quanto un bambino, dall'apparente aspetto di una lucertola gigante, ma vestita da donna, con una sottanina scura, un corsetto bianco, palesemente lacero e antico, e un grembialetto fatto di vari colori, giacché era la somma evidente di tutti i cenci della famiglia. In testa, a nascondere l'ingenuo muso verdebianco, quella servente portava una pezzuola anche scura. Era scalza. E sembrava, benché quelle vesti, dovute a uno spirito puritano dei padroni, la impacciassero non poco, adatta a svolgere tutti i mestieri con una certa sveltezza.
>
> In quel momento, però, sembrava proprio non farcela. Una delle sue verdi zampette era fasciata, e con l'altra, sospirando intensamente, essa si sforzava invano di tirare su dal pozzo un grosso secchio. (R2 23)

("Daddo's surprise was tremendous. He had taken her for a shrunken old woman, but he was looking at an animal! In front of him was a bright green beast, about the height of a child – an enormous lizard from the look of her, but dressed in woman's clothes with dark skirt, a white corset, old and shabby, and a multicolored apron clearly patchworked from the family's stock of

> rags. To hide her ingenuous little snout, which was a sort of whitish green, she wore yet another dark cloth on her head. She was barefoot. These clothes reflected her masters' puritanical spirit and were considerably in her way, yet she seemed quite capable of everything a housekeeper has to do and of doing it with certain speed.
>
> Now however she was having trouble. One of her small green claws was bandaged, and she breathed laboriously while attempting with the other, in vain, to draw a large bucket up from the well." [TIG 17])

Estrellita's morphology is that of an at first indefinable old and small wounded green animal – almost a grotesque gnome – covered in rags. Immediately afterwards Daddo labels her as a female Iguana (R2 25), and this label becomes her name, a procedure the narrator of *L'Iguana*, like Ortese's other narrators, repeatedly resorts to. Often, Iguana becomes "Iguanuccia" ("cute little Iguana"), which carries a positive connotation sometimes used with an ironic intent.

For her portrayal of her Iguana, Ortese might have found inspiration also in Diego Velázquez's paintings ("Las Meninas" and the numerous Infanta Margarita portraits).[8] The Iguana is as small as the young princess Margarita, who – in spite of her dwarf-like size – is standing in an adult pose at the centre of some traditional portraits of Spanish court members, as the Iguana is at the very centre of Ortese's novel. Moreover, the baroque garments on the Infanta's clothing and hair, particularly the butterfly-like hair-ribbons, that we can see as a symbol of *vanitas*, could also be likened to the behaviour of the Iguana, who is disposed to dress up like an aristocratic young lady. In fact, despite her actual condition, the Iguana occasionally shows princess-like manners and acts as though she were wearing royal capes and fine clothing ("bei vestitini rosa e azzurri," R2 128; "the pretty blue and pink dresses," TIG 130). In the presence of others, the Iguana literally poses as though a painter were about to portray her. The Iguana's vanity explains her frequent use of mirrors, something that recalls the mirroring effect of Velázquez's baroque paintings, as in "Las Meninas" ("The Maids of Honor," 1656–57), which portrays the young princess at the centre of a room filled with paintings, surrounded by dogs and dwarves. Similarly to Ortese's novel, the representation in "Las Meninas" questions the boundaries between reality and illusion because it includes the portrayal of the painter himself (Velázquez), who looks from the pictorial space into that of the viewer. By analogy, the mirroring effect in *L'Iguana* also relates to the self-referential nature of the texts of Ortese's trilogy, narrowing the distance between the writer-narrator and the reader, and introducing the dizzying device of multiple perspectives.

Under Daddo's tender gaze, the vain Iguana slowly humanizes and loses her animal characteristics, turning into an enchanting young lady whom the Count considers alternately as his lover and daughter-to-be. If accepted and loved, the resemblance of Estrellita to humans prevails. Conversely, the more the creature gets rejected – from the father figures such as Ilario and Daddo, the stronger her animal look, the older her age, the more fragile and decrepit her body becomes.[9] In addition, the relationship between Daddo and the Iguana mirrors the relationship between the Iguana and the young marquis Ilario, Daddo's host and the Iguana's master.

In the past, before the beginning of the story, Ilario himself had fallen in love with Estrellita and had attempted to save her soul from evil by marrying her. When Estrellita fell into disgrace and the once-caring Ilario became harsh with her, Estrellita began to be perceived as a beast. At Daddo's arrival on the island the previous transformation reverts itself. In Daddo's eyes, the Iguana turns into a beautiful girl. So Daddo becomes Ilario's alter ego, and the story of the *Beauty and the Beast* by Madame Leprince de Beaumont, one of the sure sources of the novel, as Shirley A. Smith upholds, ends where it began, overturning the fairy-tale archetype: the beauty turns into a beast.[10]

One should notice that in the Iguana's continuous shifting between the extremes of human and animal there is no gradual progress. This same paradigm of duality, in a slightly modified form, especially as for the morphologic aspects, could be applied to some of the characters of *Il cardillo addolorato* and *Alonso e i visionari*, the other two novels of the trilogy.

In *Il cardillo addolorato* (1993), the changing morphology applies to the young boy that during the story is alternately referred to as goblin ("folletto"), Geronte, Gerontino, Berrettino, Lillot, or Hieronymus Käppchen.[11] His fate, analysed thoroughly in this collection by Margherita Pieracci-Harwell and Gala Rebane, is linked to Elmina, the oldest and extremely beautiful daughter of a Neapolitan glove maker, don Mariano. At the beginning of the novel, set in 1793, in the full glare of the Enlightenment, Elmina becomes the object of desire for three Belgian friends who venture to Naples: Ingmar de Neville, prince and magician; the impoverished sculptor Albert Dupré; and merchant Alphonse Nodier, who wants to do business with don Mariano, Elmina's father. Their friendship will degenerate into rivalry and dissent, since they all fall in love with

Elmina, who will eventually marry Dupré. The woman, however, cannot renounce her bond with the goblin. Through a series of mysterious appearances, which bear witness to the rather complex structure of the novel with its various subplots, the goblin is, in turn, tied to the *cardillo*, the little goldfinch that once belonged to Elmina and her younger sister and that they let die. Many stories, songs, and poems about the goldfinch keep popping up in the novel so that the bird becomes a haunting presence for the inhabitants of the glove maker's house and his guests. But the house is haunted also by other secrets.

In the epistolary novel, *Alonso e i visionari* (1996), the main narrator, Stella Winter, is an American woman living on the border between France and Italy, who attempts to reconstruct a family tragedy, started thirty years before, in the seventies. The harrowing story Stella is trying to reconstruct centres on the death of her Italian friend, Professor Decimo, and his two sons, Julio and Decio. Decio died at an early age in a car accident and Julio a few years later in mysterious circumstances. Some imagine that Decimo's second wife Lea, Decio's mother, was involved in a conspiracy against Julio. After these tragic losses, the professor's brilliant career comes to an end. His youngest son, however, seems to live on in the puma Alonso, which the Decimo family found during a trip in Arizona when Decio and Julio were kids. When the puma eventually dies, it keeps appearing as a ghost, a lingering presence. Also, the American Jimmy Op, professor at "H. University" and main addressee of Stella Winter's letters, believes to have spotted Alonso at Winter's home. Ultimately, since the information she collects is conflicting and contradictory, Mrs Winter will not be able to establish the truth about Alonso's identity or the story. The creature's double nature, similar to the one of the goldfinch or the iguana, enhances metamorphous appearances that haunt relatives and friends.

Mutants

The Iguana, the "cardillo," and Alonso, the three cluster characters of the trilogy, as well as Käppchen, all belong to disrupted families. The nature of the relationships between the family members is unclear to outsiders; the relationships themselves are dichotomous. The family members are cold or, on the contrary, warm and caring, closed or open, selfish or kind, dishonest or honest, guilty of some obscure crime or innocent. Their attitudes change over time and vary in the course of the narration. At the beginning of each story, the characters' perception of the "creatures" is extremely positive. At that stage they are anthropomorphized animals. With Decio, for example, Alonso the puma becomes like a brother. Such a strong relationship is deeply envied by the other family members, and it explains Julio's cruel behaviour towards Alonso. In *Il cardillo addolorato,* instead, the goldfinch's attention is exclusively claimed by Elmina and her possessiveness causes others to suffer.

Almost immediately in the stories though, all the creatures are labelled in a negative, opposing way, becoming the scapegoat of the family. Consequently, they are rejected and excluded as much as possible from the family life. The puma Alonso gets literally eliminated, but it will keep on reappearing, each time in a less tangible, more evanescent form. It becomes a kind of ghost that scares – or at least upsets – the characters who spot him; often they get to know of these appearances in an indirect way, through someone else's story. The goblin Käppchen, for his part, is the reason why Nodier breaks off his engagement with Elmina to marry her younger sister.

It is interesting to note that the metamorphism of the characters has a transcendental quality: whereas the Iguana remains a sea-like creature and the *folletto* Käppchen is earth-bound, tied to the underground world, the *cardillo* and the puma Alonso become embodiments of angelic creatures:

> è una creatura fatta di aria, e nel vasto Universo suppongo non possa darsi un altro cuore di una purezza simile! ... te ne prego, riguarda questo piccino come un angelo, o un messaggero del Cielo. (AV 108)
>
> (It's an ethereal creature, and in the vast universe I cannot imagine there being another heart so pure! ... I pray you, treat this little one like an angel, or a messenger from above.)
>
> un cucciolo speciale – diciamo la parola, siamo coraggiosi –, di razza angelica, soprannaturale? (AV 243)
>
> (a special cub – let's be brave and speak the word – , Angelic in nature, supernatural?)

Alonso will in fact be identified as Christ after his resurrection. As Farnetti argued, each creature of the trilogy has an ambiguous and amphibious nature and is suspended between sky and earth.[12] In my opinion, however, it is necessary to consider the different instances of metamorphosis of the protagonist creatures in each of the three novels, not only individually, but as parts of a cohesive metamorphic design. The metamorphism in Ortese's trilogy is progressive and teleological: its upward direction goes from earth to heaven. From the demonic Iguana, to the angelic and Christ-like qualities of Alonso, the metamorphic cycle of ascension reaches its completion. In general, in the novels of the trilogy, metamorphosis is in fact always accompanied by some measure of corporeal sublimation: the less the creature is physically present, the more volatile it becomes, as in the case of Käppchen the goblin-boy, who during Elmina's childhood lived in her house and became her soul mate.

After having been confined to live in a small box, Käppchen undergoes several metamorphoses before disappearing at the age of 300, as we learn from the inscription on his tombstone. Like his counterparts, the Iguana and the puma Alonso, Käppchen's identity is elusive: on several occasions, to complicate things even further, he is identified with the Cardillo, the mysterious bird.[13]

Even when Käppchen is physically absent, there is a strong, uncanny sense of his presence. The marks of his pervasiveness, his *presentia in absentia,* are acoustic elements: disembodied voices, sounds and, most importantly, the unintelligible cardillo's song. All these signs, some mere echoes of sounds, refer to the past, to the happier times of Käppchen and its fellow-like creatures. In *Alonso e i visionari,* instead, the signs of the puma's ghostly presence are visual metonymies: his yellowish fur, or his untouched bowl: "chi cercasse il Cucciolo, scruti, la notte, nel silenzio del mondo; non lo chiami, se non sottovoce, ma sempre abbia cura di rinnovare l'acqua della sua ciotola triste. Non visto, verrà" (R2 888; "if you are looking for the Cub, scan the night, in the silence of the world; don't call it, just whisper, but make sure to fill with fresh water its sad little bowl. When no one is looking, the Cub will come"). This passage recalls the description of the Iguana's bowl filled with roasted seeds to demonstrate the intricate genealogy and affinity between Ortese's creatures.

Although Alonso, the Iguana, and the Cardillo take many forms, their plural identity is nevertheless based upon a dualistic paradigm: they have a human side and an animal side referring to a specific animal group (feline, bird, reptile). On the human side, the Iguana covers all ages (from childhood to adulthood) and, at each stage / age of her life, the creature occupies a condition of subalternity, mainly as a servant.[14] The Iguana's nature is much more complex with respect to its counterparts in the novels of the trilogy, to the extent that her animal nature (monkey, bird, iguana) corresponds to three different species: mammal, bird, and reptile. The reptile is definitely the most frequent and dominant one.[15] Estrellita is alternately an iguana, a lizard, and a snake, but she also evokes the image of a dragon, like the one referred to by Ortese in her fictional interview "Piccolo drago" ("Little Dragon") that concludes the collection of short stories *In sonno e in veglia* and in which she comments on her own work and ideas about mankind and history.[16] In "Piccolo drago," Ortese claims that in order to express her criticism of the abuse of power and of the modern rationalist approach to life she had to create a world of estrangement. An unreal creature, therefore the dragon, belonging to the realm of the fantastic and to the bestiary tradition, becomes part of the rather long series of alter egos of the "animale umanoide" ("humanoid animal")[17] represented by the Iguana. For that reason, the Iguana may at first sight be seen as the less "plausible" creature of the trilogy but, together with Cardillo, it is the most anthropomorphic and hence gifted with speech and thought, enabling thus a major exchange and communication with other characters.

Out of Time

During her metamorphic process, the Iguana subtracts herself from the opposition of the binary system: her human and animal sides, her split self, unite. The Iguana is no longer young nor is she old, but ageless[18] – time no longer has a grip on her, and the age of the characters that are the closest to her will be as variable. Generally, the indeterminacy in time affects also the novel's temporal framework, often puzzling and conflicting:

> Il conte si sentiva stanco, ormai, parendogli questa una tormentata storia del Seicento spagnolo, pazzesca nella nostra epoca tanto chiara. (R2 100)
>
> ("The Count felt tired, finding this whole affair to resemble some tormented story out of Seventeenth-Century Spain, and utter madness within the clarity of the present age." [TIG 97])

Other signs of this atemporality can be detected: clocks stop ticking and dates are incomplete or even incongruous: "*Ocaña, addì 37 ottobre/Secolo Attuale*" (R2 41; "*Ocaña, the 37th day of October/Present Century,*" TIG 36). The creatures themselves transcend the paradigm of their double nature, blurring all boundaries and giving way to a mythological-legendary dimension, in which our conception of time does not work anymore. Exemplary is the incredible longevity of Käppchen, something that undermines our common conception of temporality.[19] Also, when the characters fall under the spell of one of these peculiar creatures they drift into oblivion.

It is also important to remember that the chameleonic transformations of the Iguana are based, in part, upon mythological or legendary monsters, like the mermaid, the half-woman, half-fish creature, symbol par excellence of hybridism, femininity, and deadly attraction. This explains the archetypal lunar images that recur in the novel and are often associated with the Iguana, who incarnates femininity. For instance, the moon turns green, exactly like Estrellita's snout ("il verde riflesso della luna che cadeva dalla botola," R2 105; "a green reflection moonlight falling through the hatchway," TIG 105), while in another remarkable scene the moon becomes red and doubles in size, thus underlining the ambiguity and duplicity of the Iguana's world:

> parve che il colore della notte mutasse [...] un più forte chiarore che vedeva nell'aria [...] chiarore che era, palesemente rosso (senza, per questo, perdere certe bianche e opaline trasparenze), come per una seconda levata della luna. (R2 69)[20]
>
> ("he seemed to see a change in the color of the night [...] a more powerful brightness [...] A clarity clearly red. The whole sky above Ocaña was turning red – but without any loss of its whitish, opalescent transparencies – as if due to a second moonrise." [TIG 64–65])

In addition, the island of Ocaña itself – realm of the mermaid-like creature – is shaped like a half moon: "la conformazione dell'isola [...] una mezzaluna col dorso ad oriente" (R2 81; "the island's conformation in a half-moon shape with its hump towards the cost of Portugal," TIG 78). And when asleep, the *genius loci* assumes a similar position, almost as to recall its profound connection with the astral body.

Although enchanted by her elusive nature and estranging environment, Daddo desires to free the Iguana from her ambiguous nature and therefore attempts to humanize her modelling her into a bright young lady. In his mind, he will bring her to Milan and give her a proper education and nice little dresses. Yet, he is as unsuccessful as Pygmalion. As a matter of fact, subtle and treacherous remarks on the Iguana's account and the discovery of her apparent greediness make Daddo abandon his plan. Due to these disruptive elements the animal aspects in the Iguana begin to predominate again. Her uncertain nature of "fanciulla bestia" ("maiden-beast") is crystallized on the onomastic level, in her multiple names: she is, at the same time, Perdita ("loss"), Iguana, Menina, and Estrellita ("little star"). Her name thus encapsulates the literary tropes of earth-hell (Perdita) and heaven-paradise (Estrellita), alluding also to the elevation to angelic status of all cluster characters.

The Iguana's sinuous, serpentine form must be interpreted not only within a mythological frame but also in ethical terms, as suggested by Paola Azzolini: "nella mitologia greca il serpente è male soltanto se tende a riportare natura e ragione nel caos originario. Il suo corpo sinuoso è il luogo dell'origine, e esso è perciò attributo delle dee madri, Iside, Cibele, Demetra" ("in Greek mythology the serpent is evil only when it tries to bring nature and reason to the original chaos. Its sinuous body is the place of the origin, and for this reason it is linked to the mother goddesses Iside, Cibeles, Demeter").[21] Thus, the presence of monstrous creatures in Ortese's novels seems to imply a ritual return to the beginning of times in which there was only a disturbing or uncanny Chaos, no principles, and a time "out of time":

> Il *perturbante*, fonte di attrazione e di timore, che sono le due pulsioni che troviamo nelle favole antiche, emana da questa identità migrante e instabile, vicina all'indistinto dell'origine. Nell'emblema del male, nel corpo femminile e mutante, tra bestia e creatura sta unito in un nesso inscindibile, il bene e il male e solo rispettando l'unione, il caos originario in esso riflesso, la compassione (da *con-patire*, patire insieme) ridà un senso complesso e totale al mondo. Ecco da dove nascono le creature umanissime e fantastiche come l'Iguana o il Folletto o il Puma.
>
> ("The uncanny, both attracting and scary, something that we find in the ancient tales, comes from this migrant and instable identity, close to confusion of the origin ... In the emblem of evil, that is in the feminine and mutant body, halfway between beast and creature, Evil and Good unite in a indissoluble knot. It is only by respecting this union, its original chaos, its compassion (from cum-patio, to suffer together) that the world regains its complex and whole meaning. Here is where such very human and fantastic creatures like the Iguana or the goblin of the Puma come from.")[22]

I would like to argue, at this point, that the time "out of time" ought to be connected to the aim of Daddo's voyage, which is in fact, to a certain extent, a search for Utopia, the fictional island society in the Atlantic Ocean described by Thomas More. At the beginning of the novel, Daddo stands for the perversion of modern society, symbolizing global capitalism and the unscrupulous loss of contact between mankind and nature. According to Ortese's conception, that contact can only be re-established by sacrificing the animals, which are what reminds us of Creation: "le bestie sono residui della cosiddetta Creazione, solo residui" (AV 62; "beasts are tailings of the so-called Creation, only scraps"). Since they represent irrationality, animals are seen by mankind as a threat or an imminent danger to the established order. For the sake of that rational order animals need to be sacrificed, as in a ritual offering. This lack of respect for nature stems from human beings' belief in culture, in knowledge, and progress – a petrified version of reason.[23] This is symbolized, in Ortese's opinion, by the myth of the fall of Adam and his expulsion from the Garden of Eden. One should then remember that one of the names of the Iguana is Perdita ("loss"): if "un tempo, Ocaña era l'Eden" ("once Ocaña was Eden"),[24] any possibility of redemption seems now to be lost.[25] The biblical reference is not casual, insomuch as some critics have read Daddo and his death as a symbolic representation of the figure of Christ. Also in *Alonso e i visionari*, the behaviour of the puma cub echoes Christ's attitude towards suffering (see AV 205ff): he passively undergoes the pain inflicted by others while maintaining his kind and forgiving nature.

The suffering described by Ortese recalls the great nineteenth-century poet Leopardi's conception of inevitable sorrow. Ortese represents again the classic antithesis of Pathos versus Logos, and in doing so she does not only show her affinity with Leopardi, but also with Chekhov and Victor Hugo, whose *Les Misérables* belongs to Ortese's first and irrefutably significant readings.[26] To paraphrase Monica Farnetti, nature is the place of exile for creatures in pain.[27]

In addition, Gottfried Leibniz's metaphysical optimism can help to identify Daddo's quest since he strives for a harmonic or monadic universe that excludes suffering.[28] Ortese's metamorphous creatures then act as the "monad" that forms the basis of Leibnitz's philosophy, which rejects Cartesian dualism: mechanical principles cannot determine existence, and, even though body and mind are not autonomous units, God will synchronize them in the present world. Compared to all the other worlds (their number is infinite), our world should be – according to Leibniz's philosophic conception – the most harmonic one. The universe's smallest components are atoms, but monads are responsible for the highest compatibility between things: they group our complex perceptions (such as joy, sadness...), they connect them, and thus can make the invisible visible, which brings us back to Ortese's objective to show the hidden dimension of reality. The striving for unity as exemplified by Daddo's quest, the potential dissolution, the overcoming of duality – that is, the becoming Other of what is usually considered the One – represents the positive counterpart of the return to the primary chaos, to an original undifferentiated condition normally perceived as negative. However, as the synopsis of the trilogy has already revealed, Ortese's characters in the end will fail to construct a harmonic universe.

Metamorphosis

To return to the Iguana, her hybridism and correlate ability to change, to metamorphose – proleptically announced by the significant comparisons with butterflies and the patchwork clothing she is wearing at the start of the novel – are also represented by her oblique eyes and the colour green.[29] This colour, dominant in the Iguana's morphology – green are her skin and her heart – symbolizes indeed her nature: "la sua personcina verdastra [...] le verdi spallucce" (R2 95; "her little green body [...] her thin green shoulders," TIG 92); "i battiti del suo verde cuore" (R2 133; "all the beats of her little green heart," TIG 134). In order to understand the importance of this colour, I would like to draw a parallel with "Vita di Dea," a short story in the collection *L'Infanta sepolta* (1950). In "Vita di Dea," a divine-looking green-eyed young creature predicts to a poor friend (the narrator of the story) that they will meet again after having become frogs. This transformation is proleptically represented by the scene depicted in a book in which the colour green is once again dominant:

> Una volta, mentre appunto eravamo sedute in quella stanza, sfogliando libri, e il nostro sguardo indugiava su una seducente immagine della Cina, dove la luna e una fanciulla verdastra, unici personaggi, si guardavano attratte, improvvisamente Dea si fece assorta, e fissando la propria immagine luminosa nello specchio d'argento, come parlando a se stessa: "Vedi," mi disse con grande semplicità "io sono stata quella fanciulla dal volto camuso, che guarda ansiosa la luna. Essa fu una delle mie espressioni, finché, a un tratto, non divenni bionda e bella." (IS 84)

> (Once, while we were sitting in that room, leafing through books, and our gaze lingered on a seductive image of China, where the moon and a greenish girl, only figures, attracted to one another's gaze, all of a sudden Dea

became preoccupied, and staring at her own luminous reflection in the silver mirror, as if talking to herself: "Look," she said quite simply, "I had been that snub-nosed girl, who anxiously eyes the moon. She was one of my manifestations, until suddenly I became blond and beautiful.")

The Iguana's eyes, instead, are often sweet and tender, and they become the mirror for both the hybrid creature's own soul and for those who look into them. Mostly, her eyes reflect sadness, sorrow, and grief caused by the pain afflicted upon her by others. Whereas both Dea and the Iguana are clearly related to the sea, Alonso is connected to the earth, and the Cardillo to the air. The dominance of their featured colours, respectively green, grey, yellow-red ... derives from this connection to one particular element of nature. Thus, at some level, the green colour of the Iguana's skin acts as a symbolic reminder of nature, which has been rejected and abused. Those who cherish the Iguana (in casu the narrator and the writer) also believe that she has a soul, a "animuccia bestiale" (R2 27; "little bestial soul," TIG 21) so that their fondness seems similar to the love of Saint Francis towards animals and nature in general.[30] For Ortese, from the very moment human beings started adapting nature to their needs they lost themselves in spite of their achievements: nature, particularly its irrational side, should not be tamed.[31] Just like beauty, mutability seems to lie in the eye of the beholder.

The Iguana's changing perception of herself depends largely on other people's perception: she is regarded as inferior and as the incarnation of good or evil, according to the different feelings which people project onto her. The Iguana, like all the other hybrid and metamorphic creatures of the trilogy, assumes a high symbolic value and an exemplary status. For this reason, all of them are often invoked with the generic name of their respective species (iguana, puma, linnet) alongside their proper names:

"Il Puma, prima di tutto [...] cioè il dolore del mondo, e la bontà e maestà della Natura [...] americana o di altri luoghi che possano essere." (AV 239)

("The puma, more than anything [...] that is the suffering of the world, and the goodness and majesty of Nature [...] American or other places they could be from.")

"Iguana," disse il conte (non voleva chiamarla col suo nome), sentendone non so che vergogna. (R2 152)

> ["'Iguana,' said the Count (and he didn't want to address her by name since her name somehow embarrassed him)." (TIG 152)]

As a result of their exemplarity, the metamorphic creatures in Ortese's novels can become scapegoats for mankind and, like the Iguana, are denied a soul ("nulla sostanziale," R2 130; "essential nothingness," R2 129), just as *Undine* (1811), the sea creature at the centre of a fairy tale by Friedrich de La Motte-Fouqué based upon the seventeenth-century zoological dictionary by Paracelsus.[32] As a scapegoat, the Iguana is forced to endure practices of exorcism (see R2 88–94). Evil needs to be expelled, and the repeated prayer "*Libera nos domine*" (R2 93) that Daddo witnesses is supposed to relegate Evil for good:

> E tutto ciò perché, una volta giunto nei pressi della casa, capì che sia i Guzman che gli altri erano già arrivati, e questo lo si vedeva chiaramente dalle finestre ch'erano spalancate nella notte, e mandavano fuori una uniforme luce rossastra, mista a volute di fumo denso, dove nardo e incenso si equilibravano; e lo si sentiva, anche più che vedere, a un suono alto e inebriato di inni religiosi, accompagnanti da basse litanie e dal rombo di un harmonium, che quando il giovane fu a pochi passi dall'abitazione, come casualmente si smorzarono e finirono. (R2 84)

> ("Nearing the house he realized that the Guzmans as well as the others had managed to arrive before him, as was really quite obvious from how the windows, thrown wide open to the night, emanated a uniform reddish light mixed with dense billows of smoke smelling of nard and incense; and even more than visible, it was audible from a high, impassioned sound of religious hymns, accompanied by low litanies and the rumble of an harmonium, all of which waned and came to a finish, a though by chance, when the Count was only a few steps away from the house." [TIG 81])

Metamorphoses undeniably imply a questioning of identity and integrity while they are a fundamental component of the Iguana's subjectivity. Changes undermine consistency – and according to some of the characters of the novel, changes can only lead to Evil.

Space

The fall of the Iguana, namely her personal failure to emancipate herself from the social scale, is spatially represented by the architecture of the

Guzmans' house, in which the Iguana occupies the lower level. From the beginning of the story, the Iguana is associated with the underground (see Table 2a, *Space/Habitat*). Her den is in the basement, the cellar of the house, which is a restricted, miniaturized space, as though she has to be kept secret. The underground is represented also by the well, where Daddo spots the Iguana for the very first time. The well is the ultimate element in the confusing system of communicating rooms and spaces described in the novel, and it is eventually equated to infernal depths:

> Da una botola di fianco al focolare, [l'Iguana] era scivolata rapida nella sua "stanza," un locale, forse la legnaia, sotto la cucina; e la botola si era richiusa. Ma non tanto che una fessura, ancora tremante fra la tavola e l'ammattonato, non indicasse una tenebra tanto assoluta, da chiedersi se quella era invero una stanza, e non il più segregato dei pozzi. (R2 26–27)

> ("She had disappeared rapidly through a trap door at the side of the stove and down into her 'room,' which must have been a cellar or a woodshed just beneath the kitchen. The door slammed shut, but a crack along its fitting with the floor tiles revealed the hole to be so completely dark as hardly to be a room at all and more like a dark and secret dungeon." [TIG 20])

If also in *Alonso e i visionari* the underground is represented by the basements of the houses where the puma Alonso is spotted, in *Il cardillo addolorato,* instead, the underground takes the size of the entire subterranean city of Naples, populated by other unfortunate creatures looking for shelter, as one of the characters explains:[33] "Non è gente di oggi, ma di tempi remoti assai ... Sofferse molto" (R2 468; "They are not people of today, but of long since. They suffered much," LL 203). (see Tables 2b, 2c, *Space/Habitat*)

Space can also become a prison. The Iguana's den is accessible only through a narrow "botola" or closet to keep others at a distance, and its interior is scarcely lighted: the play of light and shadow recalls the already mentioned lunar symbolism and the *chiaro-scuro* of Baroque painting. The Iguana's world is a micro-space within another closed space, the island of Ocaña. The only intruders, who in fact are always outsiders to the community, daring to come in without being invited, are those captivated by the hybrid beings. Significantly, the island's only house is compared to empty theatre stages, whereas, once inside, the house seems to be packed, a perfect depository for secrecy, pain, and suffering. Only terraces and balconies offer a remote escape opportunity and the possibility of a different view. The optical effects, the zooming in and out, and the distortion of spatial dimensions are drawn from a constant re-figuration of perspective.

In this spatial setting the characters' inner and outer world merge, making reality opaque.[34] The boundaries between reality, dream, and fantasy are blurred: the reader finds herself in a liminal territory that is between mental and spatial geography, a very uncanny construction:

> "Sì, vi è del vero in quanto asserivi tu, poco prima, Daddo, sulla inesistenza di un vero tratto di demarcazione tra reale e irreale. Ogni cosa, anche appena pensata, subito è reale. Ciò che si abbisogna, ecco ciò che è reale; e per ciò possiamo anche morire, o permettere ad altri di morire. La morte nostra, o altrui, più non importa." (R2 68)
>
> ("Yes, Daddo, there's a truth in what you said, not far back, about the lack of any real division between the real and the unreal. Anything we even barely conceive of is immediately real. What we need: that's what's real! And we're ready to die for that, or sacrifice others. Neither our own death nor the death of others any longer makes a difference." [TIG 64])

Ocaña materializes the unreal world of Daddo and the Iguana. Also in *Il cardillo addolorato* and *Alonso e i visionari* the real geography of Naples and Liguria-Arizona, respectively, is reshaped in a labyrinthine mental construct that in its turn mingles with a cosmic reality, all within the compactness of the narration.[35] Or, to put in other words: characters can switch from reality to imagination; they seem to be dreaming with their eyes wide open:[36]

> Dieci minuti più tardi, e cioè il tempo necessario a sdraiarsi nuovamente, nell'illusione di riposare, e poi a tirarsi su di nuovo, avvedendosi ch'era impossibile, il conte era convinto di aver sognato. (R2 70)
>
> ("Ten minutes later – the time it took to stretch out once again, with the illusion of finding repose, and then to get up again, having seen that all such hopes were vain – the Count was convinced he must have dreamed." [TIG 66])

This double, disturbing view constitutes another link to the poet of Recanati, Leopardi, and it unveils the metaphysical dimension of the text. In Ortese's novel, in fact, we do indeed recognize Leopardi's conception of space: looking at the nature that surrounds us automatically gives free space to one's imagination, brings to light existential depths, and gives an insight to one's soul.

Changing Perspectives: A Subjective-Imaginary Vision

In contrast to the visionary, complex, and ultimately unreliable narration of *Il cardillo addolorato* and *Alonso e i visionari*, the *L'Iguana* presents a bipartite and symmetrical structure. The beginning and the end of the plot are in fact narrated in an ostensibly objective and realistic manner, while at the centre of the novel we find the dream-like visionary narration of the sections titled "La tempesta" ("The Tempest") – a metaphorical storm which corresponds to an actual lapse in the reason of Daddo and to the moment of maximum narrative confusion. The "tempest" having passed, an apparently more objective and realistic writing prevails, a more plausible version of the events is presented and the characters seem to lose their duplicity. Surprisingly, the mystery about the Iguana's identity seems to be uncovered: at the very end of the novel, in some letters written by Mrs Rubens – a French guest in the tourist resort on the island –the Iguana is described simply as an unpleasant young girl, a hotel maid.

> ... e c'è anche una ragazzettta che non mi piace punto: l'età può essere molto, o nulla. Non si vede a causa di come si pettina. Uno sgarbo istintivo, e qualche trasognatezza, annullano tutte le qualità (improbabili) della sua personcina. Quanto ti guarda – e gli occhi per la verità, sono un lago di luce nera, sono fissi e dolci – può sembrare anche buona, ma poi capisci che non guarda te, guarda qualcosa, dietro di te, che non ritornerà, e ciò fa una cattiva impressione. (R2 189)

> ("and there is also a servant girl I don't like a bit. She could be any age at all, a hag or an infant. You just can't tell because of how she does her hair. An instinctive discourtesy combined with a little forgetfulness is quite enough to cancel out any of the qualities (quite unlikely) that this little person may possess. You look at her – and her eyes, really, are just a pool of black light, they're just that fixed and sweet – and you could even think she's nice, but then you catch on that she never looks at you at all. She's always looking, sort of behind you, at something missing that's never coming back. A thing like that gives you a funny, unpleasant feeling." [TI 191–92])

Thus, the enfolding narrative structure offers different perspectives and enables a non-chronologic storytelling (with frequent repetitions and prolepses). Within this ever-changing framework, the role of the narrator becomes very significant.

In *L'Iguana*, the perspective of the narratorial voice is strategic, because it focuses on Daddo's inner world and at the same time it presumes to provide a more objective perspective on the various incidents. Instead, the epistolary novel *Alonso e i visionari* is characterized from the beginning by multiple narrations and its narrators, having different perspectives, profile themselves to some degree as each others' interpreters: each narrator is corrected, contradicted, or criticized by the others. In *Alonso e i visionari*, there is also a constant self-censorship, compensated by unexpected moments in which the narrators express themselves freely, so that subjective and objective points of view, emotionality and absolute detachment, interact.[37] Often, the author addresses the reader directly in order to draw attention to seemingly insignificant details, remarks, or observations that are part of the strong metatextual component of the novel. In *Il cardillo addolorato*, the status of the third-person narrator is even more ambiguous because of the multiple shifts between different perspectives and the interlacing of various subplots. In *L'Iguana*, the dialogic exchange and the complementarily created by these narrator voices have a counterpart in the diversity of languages and registers: an intertwining of Italian, used in its high and sometimes archaic register, Portuguese, fragments of poetry, and a rich tapestry of intertextual and subtextual citations. One could say that the narration in Ortese's trilogy is as polymorph as the creatures depicted in the stories. Thus, morphology, ontology, ethics, and aesthetics closely reflect one another (see Table 1, *Dualism*).

Like the strategic role of the narratorial voice(s), the devices of narrative closure are extremely significant in Ortese's trilogy as well: an open ending often characterizes her fictional works. Such is the case with *L'Iguana*. At the end of the book, after Daddo's death, it is very unclear what happened to the mysterious creature. Did the Iguana become the servant of the hotel built on the island? Was she a girl since the beginning of the narration? Did she attempt to commit suicide? Or does she believe Daddo is still alive and will come back to marry her? Is she cruel or gentle, evil or innocent, beastly or human? What is the meaning of the poem that seals the novel's closure? The same thick layer of obscurity surrounds both the Cardillo, the goblin Kappchën, and the puma

Alonso. What's at the core of their puzzling identity? Will their spectral presence still haunt us? There is no easy and stable answer. In the three novels, in fact, the narrators question the reliability of their own perception so that the reader finds herself in front of infinite interpretations of the different, conflicting stories. In conclusion, given its narrative structure and the hybrid ontological status of its characters, Ortese's *L'Iguana* is characterized by a high degree of multiplicity: objects, places, characters, meaning, textual layers, and dense intertextual references (to models and genres like allegory, mystic texts, parables, mythological tales) all conjure up to create a multilayered, rhizomatic, dizzying tapestry.

The initially hybrid ontological status belonging to a fantastic-mythological intertext turns *L'Iguana* into a polyvalent cluster. A cluster that multiplies its doubles and includes the other into a labyrinthine space-time.[38] A cluster that privileges liminality, giving access to open or closed spaces and immersing the characters – and by extension the reader – into the uncanny. It is in this versatility that lies the true magic and the true nature of Ortese's creatures, "real children of the universe."

As Italo Calvino argued in his *Lezioni americane* (*Memos for the next Millennium*, 1988), the interweaving of genres, styles, models, and languages – skillfully deployed by Ortese – ultimately represents an epistemological search: "romanzo contemporaneo come enciclopedia, come metodo di conoscenza, rete di connessione tra i fatti, tra le persone, tra le cose del mondo" ("modern novel as encyclopedia, as system of knowledge, network of facts, people and things of the world").[39] In order to textualize this "mondo o ... golfo, mai saturabile di forme e d'immagini" ("world or ... ever saturable gulf of forms and images"),[40] the *spiritus fantasticus* of Ortese unveils the inconsistency and secrecy of reality ("una verità, come la luce della luna, del tutto presente eppure nascosta," R2 87 "some truth similar in every way to the light of that moon: an absolute presence, yet perfectly concealed," TIG 84) and the dreamy dimension of her writing combines lightness and multiplicity. In so doing, the writer profoundly destabilizes the conceptual framework of the Western tradition, leaving the reader eternally suspended in a state of disorientation and stupor.

(1) Dualism

Form	Human	Animal
Morphology	Beautiful when loved	Ugly when hated
	Young	Old / ageless
	Perfect	Wounded
	Normal size	Small
Identity	Plural	
Ethics	Evil	Good
	Sin	Grace
	Guilt	Messenger of God / Past
	Fatal attraction	Sweetness
	Envious	Willing / Devoted
	Corrupt	Pure
	Usefulness ("progress")	Uselessness
Ontology	Visible	Invisible
	Present	Absent
Aesthetics	Real	Unreal/Fantasy
		Visionary

(2) Space / Habitat
(2a)

Creature	Morphology / Aspect		Names	Role	Space / Habitat
L'Iguana	Animal				
	Dragon	Green			TrapdoorWell
	Lizard				
	Iguana		Iguana / Perdita	Maiden	
	Snake			Incarnation of the Devil	
	Monkey				
	Bird				
	Human				
	Child		Estrellita / Stellina	Daughter, Sister	
	Young woman			Lover	House
	Old woman			Maiden	Trapdoor

(2b)

Creature	Morpholoy/Aspect	Names	Role	Space/Habitat
Cardillo	Animal			
	Bird	Dodò, "il cardillo del cuore" (C: 83)	Company for sick people	Cage (or closed room); Box
	Toy (singing bird in cage)		Entertaining kids	
	Human → Angelic			
	Child Boy	Hieronymus Käp-pchen (il Piccolo)	Brother	BoxSubterra-nean city
	Adult	Ingmar/Other male characters	Scapegoat	Houses
	Identification owner bird – bird itself			

(2c)

Creature	Morphology/ Aspect		Names	Role	Space/Habitat
Alonso	Animal				
	Puma	Yellow (skin)	Alonso Lonsino	Pet	Desert Street
	Dog	Red (Arizona: soil + sunset)			Box Basement
	Bag of stones (label)			Messenger of Heaven	
	Human → Angelic/divine				
	Child				
	Alonso, the Spanish servant			Servant, or allegory/ fantasy	House
	Jimmy Op			Feeling of guilt	Upstairs, but attracted by the underground
	Ghost appearances			Resurrection	

NOTES

1 Also according to Daniela La Penna it is impossible to fit the novel into a single theoretical paradigm. See La Penna, "An Inquiry into Modality and Genre."
2 De Giovanni, "*L'Iguana* di Anna Maria Ortese," 425.
3 *L'Iguana* was co-winner with *La gloria che passò* by Umberto Cavasso. Mario Manzini, Nicola Lisi, Mario Pomilo, Michele Prisco, Edoardo Fenu, and Bonaventura Tecchi were the selected jury members of the Maria Cristina Award. The award, created in 1963 in honour of Maria Cristina di Savoia, recognized unpublished narratives excelling in morality and creativity.
4 Cf. Giacinto Spagnoletti's review in which he wrote about Ortese's "meraviglioso espressionismo": "De *L'Iguana* di Anna Ortese, (edizione Vallecchi), uno dei cinque romanzi finalisti del Premio Viareggio, si è parlato poco e in sordina, né è da sperare che le cose cambino, a estate inoltrata. A che si deve attribuire questo scarso interesse? Ai modesti meriti del romanzo oppure al fatto che esso non corrisponde ad alcuna formula corrente? Come accade spesso, la critica ha preferito liquidarlo con dubbiosi elogi e reticenze non del tutto plausibili, collocandolo fra le opere meno facili della stagione. In questi casi il giuoco è fatto. Il pubblico si spaventa di fronte ad aggettivi quali 'filosofico,' 'esoterico,' 'allegorico'; né tutti gli autori sentono il bisogno di spiegare i propri libri, mettendosi in piazza e fomentando discussioni. Meno che mai ciò rientra nello stile della Ortese." ("All mention regarding *L'Iguana* by Anna Ortese, (Vallecchi), one of the five finalist novels in the Viareggio competition, scant to begin with, has gone unnoticed and there is little hope that things will change through the course of the summer. To what does it owe this scarcity of interest? Is it due to the inferior merit of the novel, or rather to the fact that it does not conform to any current formula? As is often the case, critics have opted to pass it off with sceptical praise and a reticence that is not in the slightest bit plausible, classifying it amongst the less approachable works of the season. In such cases minds have been made up. The public is put off by adjectives such as 'philosophical,' 'esoteric,' 'allegorical'; at the same time, none of the authors feel the need to explain their own books, setting up in the square and engaging discussion. More often than not this is the case for Ortese"), Spagnoletti, "Realismo del "Meraviglioso" in *Scrittori di un secolo*, 7672–74.
5 Each edition presents no negligible variations analysed by Monica Farnetti, Andrea Baldi, and Filippo Secchieri in their 2002 Adelphi edition of Ortese's novels.
6 Amigoni, "I rottami del niente," 218.

7 In line with the eighteenth-century's large use of paratext, the titles of the chapters in Ortese's exemplary novel are charged with a synthetic and programmed value. Gérard Genette defined paratext as all textual elements that are not part of the text itself: titles, subtitles or chapter headings, epigraphs, notes ... Paratexts mediate between the world of the reader and the world of the text. (See Genette, *Paratexts.*)

8 Among the iconographic models, the Spanish baroque painting is the most prominent one. The pictorial hypotext infiltrates also the onomastics, as in the case of Mrs Rubens, the French tourist whose letters will reveal the real nature of the Iguana at the end of the novel.

9 See Professor Decimo's theory in *Alonso e i visionari*: "In breve [...] suppongo che nella vita universale nulla si faccia mai diverso *da ciò che era*, ma solo *si travesta* da altro. Ciò perché il dolore, a volte, è insostenibile, eppure *non può cessare*! Solo il suo travestimento in *altra forma* – quindi la tregua – lo rende accettabile. O la vita finirebbe." (AV 94–95, "In short [...] I presume that as far as universal life is concerned, nothing is ever done differently than *the way it had been*, there is only the illusion of alterity. This is because pain is, at times, unbearable, and yet *it cannot cease!* Only by disguising itself in a *different form* can it be tolerated – therein lies the compromise. Otherwise life would end").

10 Smith, "La Bella e la bestia," 29–35.

11 See Gala Rebane's essay in this collection and Flora Ghezzo, "Voci dall'oltrestoria: *Il cardillo addolorato* di Anna Maria Ortese e la crisi della modernità," in Clerici, ed., "Per Anna Maria Ortese," 221–43.

12 "Ciascuna [creatura], ha a suo modo, una natura ambigua e anfibia, sospesa fra cielo e terra," ("Every [creature], in its own way, has an ambiguous and amphibious nature, suspended between the sky and the earth"), Farnetti, "Appunti per una storia del bestiario femminile," 275. The title of this section ("Mutants") refers to a definition by Monica Farnetti: "essere mutanti" (see Farnetti, "Appunti per una storia del bestiario femminile," 275).

13 He also recalls Stellino, the protagonist of "Folletto a Genova," a short story included in the collection *In sonno e in veglia* ("La morte del folletto" is the title of the first draft of *Il cardillo addolorato.* It was published separately in 1987): "[il dubbio] sussisteva, forse, sulla sua realtà: chi era veramente questa creatura? Gnomo, fato, elfo, angelo del cielo? [...] Apparentemente, una bestiola, un gatto, ma forse anche una lepre ottobrina, uno scoiattolo di luna; ma la testa – benché di gatto o lepre o scoiattolo di luna – quel sublime espressione di bambino disamato e amante conservava: nel musetto" (66, "[The doubt] depended, perhaps, on its own reality: who really was this

creature? A gnome, a fate, and elf, and angel descended from the sky? [...] Apparently, a little beast, a cat, but also perhaps an October hare, a moon squirrel; but the head – though of a cat or of a hare or of a moon squirrel – it preserved that sublime expression of a helpless child and lover: through the muzzle"). This type kind of intra-textuality within Ortese's writings illustrates her tendency to engage in never-ending rewriting. I am not only thinking of the continuous rewriting and polishing of her texts, but also of the migration of characters and narrative nuclei from a text to another, after lengthy re-elaborations and revisions. Looking into that genetic process, one discovers thus a dense and multilayered intertext within Ortese's oeuvre. Therefore, the reader cannot underestimate the importance of Ortese's short stories that can be considered as an experimental laboratory for the longer texts in prose. In "Folletto a Genova," the narrator discovers – quite unexpectedly – an extraordinary, small, animal-like, sick creature in the house of friends who treat it most cruelly, while in the past they adored it. By its first name, Hiëronymus (spirit of the world), Käppchen also evokes "il monaciello di Napoli" ("the little monk from Naples"), protagonist of Ortese's *Il Monaciello di Napoli* (2001), the story of an unhappy servant in a Neapolitan household (Clerici, *Apparizione e visione*, 646–47).

14 Farnetti, exploring the possible intertextual references, argues that the combination of the animal aspect and its inferior role imply a double negativity (See, Farnetti, "Appunti per una storia del bestiario femminile," 277–83).

15 "Le serpent est un des archétypes les plus importants de l'âme humaine. Il est le plus *terrestre* des animaux. C'est vraiment la racine animalisée et, dans l'ordre des images, il est le trait d'union entre le règne végétal et le règne animal. Nous donnerons dans le chapitre sur la racine des exemples qui prouveront cette *évolution imaginaire*, cette évolution vivante encore dans toute imagination. Le serpent dort sous terre, dans l'ombre, dans le monde noir. Il sort de terre par la moindre fissure, entre deux pierres. Il rentre dans la terre avec une rapidité qui stupéfie" (Bachelard, *La terre et les rêveries du repos*, 192; "The serpent is one of the most important archetypes of the human soul. It is the most *earthly* of the animals. It is truly the animalistic root and, in the order of images, bridges the gap between the vegetal and animal realms. We will provide in the chapter on the root examples which support this *imaginary evolution*, this evolution that lives on in every imagination. The serpent sleeps under the earth, in the shadows, in the world of darkness. It breaches the surface through the smallest crack, between two rocks. It returns underground with an astounding swiftness").

16 Cf. "Piccolo drago (conversazione)," in Ortese SV, 163–81; 167–69.

17 There is another exception, namely the stuffed Cardillo, a mechanic singing bird in a cage whose only purpose consists in entertaining children (See Farnetti, "Appunti per una storia del bestiario femminile," 274.) It is also worth mentioning the persistency of the idea of captivity in the Cardillo's other forms: its habitat always remains a cage (or box).

18 Cf. "credere all'età della gente! In genere, è una convenzione. C'è gente che non è nata mai" (R2 577; "You still believe in people's ages! They are usually a complete convention. There are people who were never born," LL 282).

19 In Bontempelli's narrative, only myths unveil the fantastic, the unusual side of reality.

20 Afterwards, Daddo will discover that the second moon might have been the light of a ship (cf. R2 87).

21 Azzolini, "La donna iguana," in *Il cielo vuoto dell'eroina,* 214.

22 Ibid., 215–16.

23 See "Piccolo drago (conversazione)," SV 175.

24 Pietro Citati, "La principessa sull'isola," in Ortese, IG, 203.

25 The request for redemption is verbalized indirectly in the poem by the Guzmans. The name Perdita includes three meanings: being lost, loss, and perdition. See Frizzi, "Performance, or Getting a Piece of the Other," 386.

26 Clerici, *Apparizione e visione,* 43–44.

27 Farnetti, *Anna Maria Ortese,* 44.

28 Leibniz expressed this conception in his *Monadology* (1714).

29 Ortese, "Gli Ombra," in *L'Infanta sepolta,* portraits a family with a double, abnormal constitution, defined by the contrasting colours black and white and the green eyes.

30 Farnetti, *Anna Maria Ortese,* 17.

31 See "Piccolo drago (conversazione)," SV 181–91. It ought to be mentioned also that in a 1977 interview with Dario Bellezza, Ortese already discussed Nature as opposed to Reason (see IG 185–95). Nature stands for "l'uomo senza la difesa dell'intelligenza razionale, *sono* l'uomo *senza tempo, l'uomo che sogna*" (IG 191; "mankind without the defense of reason, men without time, men who dream").

32 This is just a sample of the intertextual density in *L'Iguana.* As Luca Clerici wrote, the figure of the Iguana also relates to the stories of nymphs, Lorelei, Melusine, the little mermaid, and to the maiden of the novella of Eça de Queiros (see Clerici, *Apparizione e visione,* 394*ff*).

33 In *Alonso e i visionari,* the last "home" of Alonso is down the stairs leading to the lower parts of a house.

34 See "il luogo era quello; e se esistente nel reale o nell'irreale, e fino a che punto nell'uno o nell'altro emisfero del nostro vivere, non osiamo indagare" (CA 173; "that place and no other; and whether it existed in reality or unreality and to what extent it entered the one or the other hemisphere of our being, we dare not enquire," LL 129). Both Sharon Wood and Adria Frizzi point out the parallels with the Elizabethan playhouse that is also characterized by the presence of many liminal spaces. These spaces facilitate abrupt and unstable changes on a vertical and horizontal level.

35 Clerici, *Apparizione e visione,* 398–99.

36 Ortese's short stories are often the description of a state of *rêverie.*

37 See the theory on detachment formulated by Professor Decimo in *Alonso e i visionari.*

38 See Azzolini, "La donna Iguana," 229.

39 Calvino, *Lezioni americane,* 103.

40 Ibid., 91.

WORKS CITED

Amigoni, Ferdinando. "I rottami del niente: il fantastico nell'opera di Anna Maria Ortese." *Strumenti critici* 17, no. 2 (2002).

Azzolini, Paola. "La donna Iguana." In *Il cielo vuoto dell'eroina: scrittura e identità femminile nel Novecento Italiano,* 209–36. Rome: Bulzoni, 2001.

Bachelard, Gaston. *La terre et les rêveries du repos.* Paris: Librairie José Corti, 1948.

Baldi, Andrea. "Infelicità senza desideri: *Il mare non bagna Napoli* di Anna Maria Ortese." *Italica* 77, no. 3 (2000): 81–104.

Bertone, Giorgio. "La lente di Anna Maria Ortese." In *Letteratura e paesaggio: Liguri e no. Montale, Caproni, Calvino, Ortese, Biamonti, Primo Levi, Yehoshua.* Lecce: Manni, 2001.

Calvino, Italo. *Lezioni americane: Sei proposte per il prossimo millennio.* Milan: Garzanti, 1988.

Clerici, Luca. "Anna Maria Ortese." *Belfagor* 46 (1991): 401–17.

– *Apparizione e visione: Vita e opere di Anna Maria Ortese.* Milan: Mondadori, 2002.

– ed. "Per Anna Maria Ortese." *Il Giannone* 4, no. 7–8 (January–December 2006).

De Caprio, Caterina, and Laura Donadio, eds. *Paesaggio e Memoria: Giornata di studio su Anna Maria Ortese. 26 maggio 2000. Università degli Studi di Napoli "L'Orientale" Cappella Pappacoda.* Napoli: Edizioni Dante & Descartes, 2003.

De Giovanni, Neria. "*L'Iguana* di Anna Maria Ortese: L'ambiguità di una metamorfosi incompiuta." *Italianistica: Rivista di letteratura italiana* 18, no. 2–3 (1989): 421–30.

Della Coletta, Cristina. "La lente scura *di Anna Maria Ortese*." *Italica* 76 (1999): 371–88.

Farnetti, Monica. *Anna Maria Ortese*. Milan: Mondadori, 1998.

– "Appunti per una storia del bestiario femminile: Il caso di Anna Maria Ortese." In *Bestiari del Novecento*, ed. Enza Biagini and Anna Nozzoli. Rome: Bulzoni, 2001.

Fortini, Franco. "Dieci domande a Anna Maria Ortese." *Nuovi argomenti* 51–52 (1976): 5–11.

Freud, Sigmund. "The Uncanny." In *The Standard Edition of the Complete Psychological Works of Sigmund Freud*. Vol. 17. Trans. James Strachey. London: Hogarth, 1919.

Frizzi, Adria. "Performance, or Getting a Piece of the Other, or In the Name of the Father, or The Dark Continent of Femininity, or Just Like a Woman: Anna Maria Ortese's *L'Iguana*." *Italica* 79 (2002): 379–90.

Genette, Gérard. *Paratexts: Thresholds of Interpretation*. Trans. Jane E. Lewin. New York: Cambridge University Press, 1997.

Gramone, Antonella. "Travelling through the I: Anna Maria Ortese's Melancholic Cities." *Romance Studies* 19 (2001): 95–108.

Lanslots, Inge. "Creature zoppicanti di Anna Maria Ortese." *Narrativa* 24 (2003): 105–21.

– "*L'Iguana* di Anna Maria Ortese: La molteplicità nel viaggio immobile di Daddo." In *Piccole finzioni con importanza: Valori della narrativa italiana contemporanea*, ed. Roelens Nathalie and Inge Lanslots. Ravenna: Longo Editore, 1993.

La Penna, Daniela. "An Inquiry into Modality and Genre: Re-Considering *L'Iguana* by Anna Maria Ortese." In *The Italian Gothic and Fantastic: Encounters and Rewritings of Narrative Traditions*, ed. F. Billiani and G. Sulis, 160–87. Madison, NJ: Fairleigh Dickinson University Press, 2007.

Smith, Shirley Ann. "'La Bella e la Bestia': Inversione di genere nell'Iguana di Anna Maria Ortese." *Cristallo: Rassegna di Varia Umanità* 3, no. 1 (December 1996): 29–35.

Spagnoletti, Giacinto. *Scrittori di un secolo: Volume secondo*. Milan: Marzorati editore, 1974.

Vigorelli, Giancarlo. "Anna Maria Ortese: Angelici dolori." *Letteratura* 4 (October 1937): 176.

Wood, Sharon. "Fantasy and Narrative in Anna Maria Ortese." *Italica* 71 (1994): 354–68.

9 "Call Me My Name": The Iguana, the Witch, and the Discovery of America

GIAN MARIA ANNOVI

Detestavo la storia, fino al 1492. Amavo solo la geografia, l'antica America.

(I detested history, up to 1492. I only loved geography, ancient America.)
Anna Maria Ortese, *E tu chi eri?*

How can Friday know what freedom means when he barely knows his name?
J.M. Coetzee, *Foe*

Among the over 1,300 pages of notes and sketches for *L'Iguana*, the most resistant to any genre-based definition of all Ortese's novels,[1] there is a draft of the episode in which the protagonist, Don Carlo Ludovico Aleardo di Grees, descendant of the Dukes of Estremadura-Aleardi and Count of Milan, who also goes by the nickname Daddo, takes a walk in modern-day Milan with his friend Adelchi. He is about to embark on a journey overseas, in search of a new estate. Daddo will eventually land on a tiny, desolate island inhabited by three lost Portuguese noblemen and their ill-treated servant, an iguana. In this draft, Daddo stops in front of the window of a bizarre gun shop:

> Lì lo ritrovò Adelchi, fermo davanti alla vetrina di un armaiolo. Sorrideva. "Guarda," gli disse. Lì, tra poche antiche e curiose armi (le moderne ed efficienti erano dentro) figurava un oggetto singolare, e diciamo oggetto in quanto inanimato, benché in origine non lo fosse stato. Era un iguanoide mummificato, piccolissimo se si voleva tener conto della grande natura che raggiungono questi animali, ma non meno vero e come, nel suo sonno,

> tragicamente assorto. Si sarebbe detto che camminasse, ed era fermo. Volgeva appena la misera testa e, fitta nel collo, aveva una bandiera. (R2 903)

> (Adelchi found him standing there in front of a gun shop window. He was smiling. "Look," he said. There, among a small array of antique and unusual arms (the modern, working ones were inside) a peculiar object was on display, and I say object because it was lifeless, although it was once alive. It was a mummified iguanid, a very small one if you consider the huge size these animals can reach in nature, but it was no less real as though it were tragically absorbed in sleep. It looked like it was walking, but it was still. Its poor head was slightly bent and its neck was transfixed by a flag.)

When Daddo asks about the origin of such a flag, the gun shop owner responds that the flag is from Portugal, but he adds that "l'esemplare [di iguana] che il signore ammira non alligna all'Europa; viene dai Caraibi" (R2 904; "the iguana specimen you are looking at does not come from Europe; it comes from the Caribbean"). Also the protagonist of Ortese's novel, the iguana-servant, Estrellita, or simply Iguana, happens to come from the Caribbean, a place that for Ortese does not represents something simply exotic.[2] On the contrary, in her mind the Caribbean stands for the location of a trauma, which is both personal and historical. On the one hand there is the trauma provoked by colonization from 1492, when Columbus landed in San Salvador and the violence of European imperialism entered the once Eden-like and peaceful world of Native Indians, which fascinated and peopled Ortese's imagination since her early childhood.[3] On the other hand, we find the trauma surrounding the death of one of Ortese's brothers, Manuele, a sailor who passed away in 1933 in Martinique. In her biblio-biographic transfiguration of *Il porto di Toledo,* this painful event coincides with the origin of her writing.[4] Ortese's writing indeed begins when something gets lost forever – be it freedom or life– on a far Caribbean island.[5]

The fact that the little iguanid is mummified (like the Islander in one of the famous *Operette* by Leopardi)[6] and displayed among antique arms, makes it seems some sort of souvenir of an ancient colonial enterprise, an atrocious reminder of the havoc that characterized the euphoric colonization of America and the end of its Eden. Even if the gun shop episode was never included in the published version of the novel, I believe that Ortese originally conceived the "mummified iguanid" as a proleptic element, as it shows in advance the destiny of the titular protagonist and the destiny of the island, which are deeply related. Just as the island at the centre of the novel will be described by Daddo as moving "per quanto impercettibilmente" (R2 19; "almost imperceptibly," TIG 13), the mummified iguanid in the gun shop "looked like it was walking, but it was still."

In my essay I will consider the island, and in particular the body of the Iguana, as a space where colonial power is painfully inscribed, and I will show that the possibility of a postcolonial reading of *L'Iguana* is confirmed by textual and extra-textual elements. In particular, I will discuss Ortese's postcolonial geography in the novel, and I will argue that the animalization of the green protagonist follows the different early stages of the colonization of America.

"A Spot of Green and Brown": The Island

In 1986, Ortese told journalist Giulia Massari that she first started conceiving the story of *L'Iguana* after having read an article in a local newspaper about a woman who lost, in Rome, her beloved exotic pet.[7] Nevertheless, we already find some traces of the island and of its little green inhabitant in the opening short story of *Angelici dolori* (1937), Ortese's very first book. The nameless island of her 1936 *L'isola* (*The Island*), is not a real geographical space, but the result of a solitary dream-like state of reverie, in which the subject gets in touch with the imaginary space of origin of her own writing:

> Durante tutto il corso soffocante delle 12 ore, nella mia casa del settimo piano, in Via dei Mercanti, io, distesa a bocconi sul mio letto, avevo finto (o piuttosto avevo tentato) di dormire ... [volevo] raggiungere non so che rive, navigare non so che mari (e ridevo), conoscere e adorare non so che impetuosa, sanguigna, demoniaca gente. (AD 14)

> (Over the course of those twelve suffocating hours, in my house on the seventh floor, in via dei Mercanti, lying facedown on my bed, I ended up (or rather I tried) falling asleep ... [I wanted] to reach I don't know which shores, to navigate I don't know which seas (and I laughed), to know and adore I don't know which violent, full-blooded, demonic people.)

The reader of *L'Iguana* will be certainly surprised by this early reference to "demonic people," since the eponymous character of that novel, "la fanciulla bestia" (R2 90; "the girl-beast," TIG 73), is considered "la figlia e madre del Male" (103; "the daughter and mother of Evil," 100), a real demon, by the other few inhabitants of the island where the story takes place.[8]

If the origin of *L'Iguana* seems close to a state of dream or hallucination, we know exactly where Ortese found Ocaña, the name of the island that lies at the centre of her novel. Taken from Spanish poet Jorge Manrique's *Coplas a la muerte de su padre* (Stanzas on his Father's Death),[9] one of the many intertexts of the novel, Ocaña is an actual toponym, a town of central Spain, in the province of Toledo. Nevertheless, like the island of Ortese's early story, Ocaña is above all a mental space, a solitary dream. "Dreaming of islands" – wrote Gilles Deleuze at the beginning of his philosophical career – "whether with joy or in fear, it doesn't matter – is dreaming of pulling away, of being already separate, far from any continent, of being lost and alone – or it is dreaming of starting from scratch, recreating, beginning anew."[10] In his essay, Deleuze unwittingly describes Ortese's double conception of writing and its link to imaginary islands. On the one hand, for Ortese to write is "come sognare" (CC 155; "like dreaming"), and it is to look for another world,[11] a New World; on the other hand, it is also an act of separation, solitude, and inner shipwreck.

This oneiric component of Ortese's geography explains only partially the reason why, from the very beginning of the novel, the island appears to be an actual cartographic anomaly, described as "un punto verde bruno, a forma di cono, o ciambella spezzata, che non risultava sulla carta" (R2 16; "a spot of green and brown in the shape of a horn, or a broken ring. It was nowhere on the map," TIG 10). A similar island, not to be found on any map, was imagined by a writer that Ortese highly admired: Herman Melville.[12] In *Moby-Dick* (1851), the island home of the "savage" cannibal Queequeg is indeed very similar to Ocaña: "It is not down in any map" – we are told at the beginning of Chapter 12 – "true places never are."[13] What Melville meant with his deceptively obscure statement is partially clarified by Ortese in her novel.

The description of the world, mapping as "geo-graphy (writing the world),"[14] is first of all a discourse marked by power and exclusion. Since they textualize the unknown spatial reality of the Other, maps have often been a falsification of the world, corresponding to the vision of a subject with representational power (such a subject is usually, as in our case, white, male, European, and Christian). The cartographic blank experienced by Daddo and his ship's boy when confronting Ocaña is a typical experience for the first explorers, who used to represent "graficamente i territori ignoti e non ancora 'conquistati' con spaziature bianche, spesso ornate da fantastiche figure teriomomofe – mostri, sirene, cannibali – a segnalare il *limine* oltre il quale il soggetto occidentale si confronta con la 'perturbante' alterità dell'ignoto" ("undiscovered and unknown lands with blank spaces, often decorated with monstrous figures – monsters, mermaids, cannibals – which mark the limit beyond which the Western subject has to face the 'uncanny' otherness of the unknown").[15]

To go back to Melville's definition of "true places," both Ortese and the American writer seem to acknowledge that maps do not represent a real world, a true place, but a world that often excludes the unknown, the other, something that in the case of *L'Iguana* one also might call the demonic.[16] Such a space is proleptically evoked by the hellish appearance of the island itself and its few imagined inhabitants: "uno squallido corno di roccia affiorante dal mare, e semibruciato. Là, probabilmente, solo radici e serpenti esistevano" (R2 17–18; "a desolate outcrop of reef, semi-arid and barely above sea level. Nothing would be alive there except roots and snakes," TIG 11). If Ocaña's truth is embodied in its otherness to Daddo's and Salvato's discursive order, the task of Ortese's writing is then to represent the unrepresented, to give shape to the complexity of the real, so that the blank spaces of colonial mapping become a white page waiting to be written.

It is possible that Ortese encountered an example of how cartographic whiteness generates the process of literary imagination and writing in *Heart of Darkness* (1902) by Joseph Conrad, an author who is at the core of her literary pantheon:

> Now, when I was a little chap I had a passion for maps. I would look for hours at South America, or Africa, or Australia, and lose myself in all the glories of exploration. At that time there were many blank spaces on the earth, and when I saw one that looked particularly inviting on a map (but they all look that) I would put my finger on it and say, "When I grow up I will go there."[17]

For Conrad-the-child, "there" is the blank space that Conrad-the-writer can fill with his writing.[18] In a more intriguing way, Ortese did not only make the island of Ocaña visible through writing, but she literally drew an imaginary map of it (R2 81; TIG 78), turning herself into a "honorary geographer" and thus regendering the otherwise typically masculine act of mapping.[19]

If mapping is usually an act of inclusion in the space of one's own discourse (the discourse of the explorer / colonizer), a rigid space closed to other visions, for Ortese it becomes a sort of opening. By filling in the blank space of Daddo's map, Ortese does not create a rigid space. On the contrary, she opens an interstice through which other discourses can filter: discourses of (or on) peripheral subjects. In this sense, Ortese's geography is to be conceived as an anti-colonial geography, and the map of Ocaña reveals itself as unreliable as the narrator of her story: not merely inaccurate, but ever-changing, open, opposed to the supposed realism of the colonial cartographic accuracy and discourse of (imperial) power.

According to art historian Svetlana Alpers, an expert on the origins of modern cartography in Dutch painting, mapping allows "one to see something that was otherwise invisible."[20] This is true also in Ortese's case, but in a very unique way, because for this Italian writer only the invisible is real, true, and thus worthy of representation, as Daddo explains in a very important passage of the novel:

> "Sentii parlare di realismo. Che cos'è questo?"
>
> "Dovrebbe essere" rispose il conte un po' impacciato "un'arte di illuminare il reale. Purtroppo, non si tiene conto che il reale è a più strati, e l'intero Creato, quando si è giunti ad analizzare fin l'ultimo strato, non risulta affatto reale, ma pure e profonda immaginazione." (R2 56)
>
> ("I've heard talk of realism. Maybe you can tell me what that means."
>
> "What it ought to be," replied the Count, feeling slightly clumsy, "is an art of illuminating the real. But people, unfortunately, don't always affirm the awareness that reality exists on many levels, and that the whole of creation, once you analyze the deepest level of reality, isn't real at all, and simply the purest and profoundest imagination." [TIG 52])

In *L'Iguana,* the island is the "otherwise invisible" which literally emerges on the page thanks to writing, like a volcanic atoll miraculously reemerging from the depths of the ocean where it remained for ages after the eruption that created it. Referring to the expression coined by Homi Bhabha, one could conceive Ocaña as a "third space," a space of hybridity that "gives rise to something different, something new and unrecognizable, a new area of negotiation of meaning and representation."[21] Such a third space, I would add, is also an "intensity zone," a site in which representation and control reach a maximum of intensity and thus become visible, a space of transparency – corresponding to and somehow overlapping with the Iguana's "corpicino verde" (R2 131; "little green body," TIG 130).

"A Bright Green Beast": The Iguana

When Daddo asks his ship's boy the reason why Ocaña is not on his map, Salvato's explanation, distinguishing between a Christian cartography and an unchartable devil's land, backdates for the reader Daddo's journey by a few centuries:

> "No, non è segnata," rispose asciutto il Salvato "perché," e cercava di guardare in qualche punto dove l'occhio non incontrasse la miseria di Ocaña "perché, grazie a Dio, quelli che fanno le carte sono cristiani, e le cose del diavolo non le degnano." (R2 17)
>
> ("No, it's not on the map," replied Salvato, dryly and seemingly attempting to look in a direction where this miserable scrap of land would remain out of view. "It's not on the map because the people who make maps, thank God, are all Christians and don't much bother about things that belong to the devil." [TIG 11])

Salvato's reference to the devil reminds us of the early examples of colonial literature, of the diaries of the first European explorers and conquistadores, who exterminated millions of indigenous people in a few decades, often in the name of religion. The Catholic Church, in fact, came to perceive the natives as nothing more than evil, soulless beings. In this regard, I direct the reader to the theological dispute between Spanish Dominican Priest Bartolomé de Las Casas and theologian Juan Ginés de Sepúlveda about the nature of the Native Americans being human or bestial. Sepúlveda, who never visited the New World, considered the natives as nothing more than the embodiment of evil, brutes with no soul, two elements that – according to the Aristotelian principles – would not make it morally wrong to turn the natives into slaves. De Las Casas, on the contrary, who has been called the father of anti-imperialism and anti-racism, was an advocate for the rights of native peoples. Needless to say, Sepúlveda's conception prevailed, for the real aim of the Christian Europe was to exploit as much and fast as possible the colonial subject.[22]

Our unfortunate Iguana, like a Native American, is immediately described as soulless, pagan, and evil, so that she cannot but be considered as "vittima deputata di poteri coloniali" ("an appointed victim of colonial power"),[23] something that the episode of the mummified iguanid, which I discussed at the beginning, already suggested. The two are very deeply connected, and in a sort of voodoo doll effect, in Chapter 18, Ortese persistently refers to a pain in the neck of the Iguana, which has no apparent other cause than the flag transfixing the mummified iguanid's neck:

> "il conte vide che il collo della creatura (un collo, per la verità, esile e grigio) presentava dei brutti segni (R2 152) [...] altro silenzio, in cui l'Iguana mosse lievemente il collo, come se là avesse male [...] ci fu, da parte della creatura, un altro lieve movimento del collo, come se proprio là qualcosa dolesse [...] e girando sempre il collo, come se il male le desse veramente fastidio, uscì tutta strana." (154)

> (the Count saw several ugly marks on her thin dirty neck [TIG 154] [...] Another silence, with the Iguana slightly turning her neck, wary of a returning pain [...] here again, the creature slightly stretched her neck, wanting to focus it as the site of all her hurts [...] still twisting her neck, and seeming to find the pain truly troublesome, she slipped into total estrangement. [155])

As there is no doubt that the embalmed iguana represents the souvenir/victim of a colonial conquest, the superinscription of colonial power, in the novel the reptilian metaphor itself "is intended as the result of the shaping power of the imperialist and colonial discourses."[24] Power and epistemic violence become visible on the servant's tiny body, a crucial site for colonial inscription, with the result that they literally make it green, turning a servant girl into an animal, a monster.[25] Power and violence are the forces at work behind the animalization of the Other, a process that in our case can be described as *iguanification*. The green and wrinkled skin of the iguana is then just a disguise, because – as Daddo realizes on his deathbed – "non ci sono iguane, ma solo travestimenti, ideati dall'uomo allo scopo d'opprimere il suo simile e mantenuti da una terribile società" (R2 178; "there are no iguanas, but only disguises, disguises thought up by human beings for the oppression of their neighbors and then held in place by a cruel and terrifying society," TIG 180). This is why, from the very beginning of the novel, the female protagonist's identity and physical features are ambiguous and shifting, like the morphology of Ocaña. When still on his lifeboat, Daddo believes she is "una vecchia" (R2 23; "an old woman," TIG 17) and calls her "nonnina" (24; "little grandmother," 17), but at the end of the story she appears to be a "creaturina bellissima, tutta vestita di merletto bianco" (164–65; "creature of exceptional beauty, dressed in a white lace dress," 165) a "fatata figurina" (165; "magic little figure," 165) and finally "una servetta come ce ne sono tante nelle isole" (181; "a servant girl like so many to be found in the islands," 184). Since in colonial discourse the subjectivity of the colonized is located in the gaze of the Imperial Other, the Iguana is also continually described through the gaze of the other characters, and the reader is left to deal alone with her metamorphic physiognomy (old woman, iguana, bird, monkey, little girl), her conflicting definitions (*menina*, demon, beast, beast-girl, creature, little whore, little thief, wretched filth of a woman, idiot) and interchangeable proper names (Iguana, Estrellita, Perdita).

"A Poor Thin Youth, Tall and Green": A Colonizer

If the entire body of the Iguana is metaphorically pierced by a flagstaff, Ocaña instead "non può sventolare bandiera alcuna" (R2 21; "has no right to fly any nation's flag," TIG 15). The space that Ocaña represents is neutral, a metaphor for any postcolonial space. Although the island refuses nationality, its inhabitants feel an attachment to a homeland: Portugal, a once immense colonial Empire, which in the 1960s, when Ortese was writing her novel, was still trying to resist the emerging nationalist guerrilla movements in some of its African territories.[26] Don Ilario, the decayed Portuguese nobleman who lives on Ocaña with his two brothers and Estrellita, embodies the old colonizer, a relic of the seventeenth century, the great era of Portuguese colonial expansion.[27] When Ilario puts on his antique noble clothes, reminiscent of Velasquez and Van Dyke's portraits, his whole body and face are transfigured as if his real nature were still to be found in his long-lost illustrious past:

> Le rughe, e gli affanni che le avevano causate, completamente cancellate, sparite. Liscio come un cammeo, ma acceso di rosa sulle guance sfilate, quel volto raccontava soltanto la gioventù, la forza, la gloria dei diciott'anni. Svaniti anche i cenciosi abiti, il marchese portava sulla testa un cappello di velluto azzurro, ornato di una vera cascata di piume scarlatte, che gli venivano fin sul collo, mentre sulle spalle, una corta cappa di raso nero non nascondeva un radioso giubbotto millecolori, disegnando le spalle

erette, eleganti nel gran vigore [...] Più nessuna traccia della sua tremenda vecchiezza. (R2 67)

("The lines and worries that had caused them had been entirely cancelled out. Had simply vanished. Smooth as a cameo, but with accents of pink on its finely smoothed cheeks, that face spoke solely of the youth, the strength, and the glory of living in an eighteen-year-old body. The raggedy clothing had likewise disappeared, and the Marquis wore a hat of blue velvet, adorned with a cascade of scarlet feathers down to the side of his neck; a short, black satin cape covered his back but offered no hiding to a gloriously pied blouse: a thousand radiant colors over finely outlined shoulders, erect, elegant, and full of vigor [...] There was no longer so much as a trace of the devastations of aging." [TIG 63])

Moreover, Ilario's two long and "assolutamente incomprensibili" (IG 53; "perfectly incomprehensible," TIG 44) poems – "Portugal" and "Penosa" – which he wrote over the course of many years, are certainly inspired by *Os Lusìadas* (The Lusiads), an epic work by Luís de Camões, the greatest poet of Portuguese colonialism and the creator of the Lusitanian mythology of conquest.[28]

Also in the case of Daddo, described as "il compratore di isole" ("the men who buys islands"), past and present merge. He embodies at once a new and old European colonizer, since the cartographic blank he experienced is the same one that Columbus himself had to face during his first voyage. Both the young Milanese and the famous explorer from Genoa are in fact associated in the novel through the repeated toponymic reference to Palos, a place which has strangely never intrigued critics: "Al tramonto era di nuovo a Palos, e la navigazione riprese" (R2 15; "By sunset he was back in Palos, and the Luisa returned off-shore," TIG 9); "E improvvisamente, egli sentì che la sua vita era finita, che mai più tornerebbe a Milano, nè a bordo, nè vedrebbe l'azzurro mare, e Palos, e altri porti" (R2 164; "He suddenly knew his life was over: that he would never return to Milan on board his boat or contemplate the blue of the sea; never again see Palos or other ports of call," TIG 165).[29]

Palos de la Frontera, a small town located in the southwestern Spanish province of Huelva, is now considered to be the "cuna de descubrimiento de America" ("cradle of the discovery of America") because on 3 August 1492 Columbus sailed from there with his three caravels. Nevertheless, Daddo is not simply to be conceived as a "European post-Colombian explorer,"[30] but as a modern Columbus, a man prone to doubt and error, surrounded by the vast unknown, similar to the protagonist of another of Leopardi's *Operette*, "The Dialogue of Christopher Columbus and Pedro Gutierrez."[31] As Columbus travelled to an unknown world, during his journey Daddo travels into the unknown within himself: he is "egli stesso di sè poco sicuro" (R2 115; "a person of little self-assurance," TIG 113). That is why, at the end of the novel, his journey appears to have been only stasis: "sentì che il suo viaggiare era stato immobilità" (R2 177–78; "he felt his voyaging had all amounted to immobility," TIG 180). In a dizzy entanglement of literary references, Ortese's Leopardian Columbus meets here with Eugenio Montale's famous antihero "Arsenio" and with his "immoto andare" ("stalled motion")[32], a metaphor for a not fully achieved existence. After Daddo goes insane, in a final splitting before his death, he projects himself in "un ragazzo alto e verde, con indosso una tunica verde grondante di alghe" (R2 176; "a poor thin youth, tall and green, wearing a green tunic, dripping with streamers of algae," TIG 178). This image is a very clear reference to "il viluppo dell'alghe" ("the tangled seaweed") which trips Arsenio in Montale's oneiric poem and to the "delirio [...] d'immobilità" ("frenzy [...] of immobility") of its character, swallowed – like Daddo – in a literary tempest at sea.

"The World Was Green": The Tempest

"Arsenio" is just one of the many hypotexts floating like seaweed on the literary surface of Ocaña,[33] but Montale's sea storm is not as relevant for a postcolonial reading of the novel as William Shakespeare's *The Tempest*, which provides the title of the second part of *L'Iguana*. As Daddo is the Count of Milan, Prospero, the protagonist of Shakespeare's play, is a duke from the very same city, and he stands for the English writer as a (positive) model of the European colonizer. Moreover, the Shakespearian drama takes place on an island, which – like Ocaña – is apparently enchanted, "a liminal place, a staging-post [...] where things pass from one form to another."[34] Still, the most striking similarity between *L'Iguana* and *The Tempest* concerns the role of the two bestial servants of the islands, the Iguana and Caliban, both standing for the Other, the demonic, the subdued colonial subject.[35]

In her essay "The Monster as a Refugee," Ginevra Bompiani argues that the Iguana and Caliban embody different political beings: "Caliban is a native on a foreign island. He is the natural victim of travelers, invaders, colonizers. The Iguana is a foreigner, an expatriate, a refugee, and the natural victim of dwellers, farmers, and landlord."[36] By refusing to consider her as native, Bompiani seems to subtract the Iguana from a possible postcolonial reading. And yet, as many scholars have pointed out, Caliban is not technically a native himself.[37] Caliban was born on *The Tempest*'s island only because his mother, the witch Sycorax, who was Algerian, was brought and abandoned there by some sailors while she was already pregnant with Caliban (his father is said to be the devil himself). The Iguana, on the contrary, is not completely a refugee, as Bompiani argues, because she did not have to flee her native country, the Caribbean, but was brought to the other side of the ocean by Don Ilario, at least if one identifies the Iguana also with Perdita, the little mysterious creature (possibly a monkey or a bird) seen by Daddo in a portrait of don Ilario's mother.[38]

Although Spivak proposed that we not consider Caliban as the "inescapable model"[39] of colonialized subjectivity, he really offers an interesting platform on which to study the colonial interaction between the Iguana and the other characters of Ortese's novel.[40] First of all, Caliban's master, Prospero, seems to be a model for Ilario's character. Prospero, despite his noble origins, describes himself as the "master of a full poor cell" (Act I, Scene II), but also as an intellectual and a bibliophile: "me, poor men, my library / was dukedom large enough" (Act I, Scene II). Also Ilario's house is described as very small, "una grigia e squallida costruzione a un sol piano" (R2 21; "a one-storey construction, ugly and grey," TIG 15) and the narrator underlines its theatrical quality: "più l'indicazione di una casa, come usa nel moderno teatro, che una vera abitazione" (R2 21; "the building struck the Count less as a house than as a stage prop," TIG 15). Finally, Ilario is said to be "un letterato, un bibliofilo, forse; comunque un uomo immerso in eterna fantasticheria" (R2 29; "a poet, perhaps a bibliophile, at any rate a spirit immersed in eternal fantasy," TIG 23). The similarities between these two characters make even stronger the parallelism with the master / servant relationship they have with Caliban and the Iguana. Before becoming a servant, Iguana-Estrellita was dearly loved by her master. And so was Caliban by his: "When thou camest first, / Thou strokedst me and madest much of me" (Act 1, Scene II). Once loved, both characters are later on degraded to simple exploitable "servant-monsters" (Act 3, Scene II) because of their discovered evil nature.

The exploitability of the servant-native is something to be considered very carefully. In *The Tempest*, the ship's boy Trinculo makes it clear in plain economical terms when he first sees Caliban. Strange beasts or monsters, two categories which in his mind include Native Americans, are good for making a profit: "Were I in England now, / as once I was, and had but this fish painted, / not a holiday fool there but would give a piece / of silver: there would this monster make a / man; any strange beast there makes a man: / when they will not give a doit to relieve a lame / beggar, they will lazy out ten to see a dead / Indian" (Act, 1 Scene, 2). Trinculo is here referring to the practice of showing Native Americans as wonders, something also very common in the great courts of Europe starting from the end of the sixteenth century, when chambers of marvels and cabinets of curiosities were extremely popular. Ortese's readers should not be surprised to find out that the Iguana was about to be sold by don Ilario to Mr Cole, owner of a circus and "agente teatrale, o qualcosa di simile [...] che compra e vende di tutto" (R2 144; "theater agent, or something like that [...] but he buys and sells just about everything," TIG 144). In Ortese's mind, Mr Cole's circus is probably a modern freak show, a genre brought to perfection by famous American businessman P.T. Barnum, who also took inspiration for his circus of wonders from the kind of early commercialization of colonial otherness described by Trinculo. Barnum's circus was in fact the capitalist model for what was later on called "human zoo," a show where natives from Africa, Asia, and the Americas were displayed alongside animals.[41] Interestingly enough, in 1842, Barnum's show included also "the Siren, or Mud Iguana, a connecting link between the reptiles and fish,"[42] along with other hoaxes, human curiosities like albinos and midgets, but also "exotic women," "savages," and Native Americans: all subjects made exploitable by their presumed *otherness.* For Ortese, Mr Cole and Daddo, who want to buy the Iguana and the island respectively, both represent the capitalist sacrilege over nature: "Comprare la realtà (territori, uomini, le dolci Bestie), per trasformarla in merce, è come trafficare in arcobaleni, canti di usignoli, gemiti d'erba che cresce" [SV 178; "to buy reality (land, men, sweet Beasts) in order to turn it into commodities, is like to trade in rainbows, nightingale's songs, wailing of growing grass"].[43]

Caliban and the Iguana are not only to be connected because someone wants to sell and buy them, or for their hybrid shape and their colonial subalternity, or because of their common Caribbean origin (the name Caliban may in fact derive from the ancient expression "cariban"). What makes them interesting is that they are both associated with the devil: Caliban is defined as "demi-devil" and "born devil" (Act 5, Scene 1 and Act 1, Scene 1) while the Iguana, as we have previously seen, is often referred to as a "demon." More interestingly, both characters have something to do with witches. Caliban is the son of a witch, Sycorax, and Estrellita seems to be identified with one, at least according to Adelchi's ideas about the title of the novel that Daddo should have written after his travels: "Voleva darle un titolo sensazionale, come ad esempio: 'Le notti di un pazzo,' oppure: 'La Strega,' o, meglio ancora: 'Bruciateli tutti!'" (R2 11; "He'd give it a sensational title, like 'The Nights of a Madman,' or 'The Witch,' or better still, 'Burn Them Alive!,'" TIG 5). But why this reference to a witch? The reason for such a title is not immediately clear, and the attempt to understand it could cast more light on Ortese's critique of colonialism.

Burning Passion: The Witch

When Christopher Columbus landed on an island in the Caribbean on 12 October 1492, he wrote in his journal about the mild character of the Taíno Indians: "they are very gentle and without knowledge of what is evil; nor do they murder or steal. Your highness may believe that in all the world there can be no better people."[44] Among the first explorers, it was common knowledge that the natives, for their mildness and natural communism, were the embodiment of the Good Savage of the Golden Age and that America was a real paradise. As Amerigo Vespucci wrote in a letter, when he first met the Brazilian Indians he thought "esser presso al Paradiso terrestre" ("to be by the Earthly Paradise").[45]

In his essay *La traversata delle streghe nei nomi e nei luoghi* (The Crossing of the Witches through Names and Places), controversial Italian philosopher Luciano Parinetto (an unfortunately obscure figure to the mainstream academy)[46] establishes a relationship between colonialism, witch-hunts, and the rise of capitalism, arguing that "eurocentristi e conquistatori non sanno che farsene dell'ideologia del buon selvaggio e loro stessi, o gli intellettuali al loro servizio, ben presto cominciano a propalare annotazioni inquietanti che trasformeranno gli indios, prima angelicati, in diavoli" ("Eurocentrists and conquerors do not know what to do with the Good Savage's ideology, and they – or the intellectuals at their service – start spreading disturbing information about the Indians, turning them from angel-like creatures into devils").[47] According to Parinetto, there are deep connections between the two crudest massacres of early modernity: the witch-hunt and the genocide of the Indians. The conquerors, in order to justify the exploitation and enslavement of the Indians, began to consider them *external witches* – in other words, external to the Old World. As Parinetto argues: "i conquistatori, i cui intellettuali organici (preti, frati, teologi e non solo) si portavano probabilmente in tasca il *Malleus Maleficarum*, da poco divulgato, scorsero nelle Americhe, invece dell'*Eden ritrovato* o del *Paradiso terrestre* (di cui vociferavano invece i primissimi scopritori, presto fatti ammutolire dall'interesse imperialistico), il Regno del diavolo" ["the conquerors, whose organic intellectuals (priests, friars, theologians and others) carried with them the recently released *Malleus Maleficarum*, saw in the Americas the reign of the devil, where instead the very first discoverers, silenced by the imperialist interest, saw the regained *Eden* or *Earthly Paradise*"].[48] According to the Franciscan missioner Motolinìa, one of the first twelve missionaries sent to the New World, that land was "a copy of hell," and "it was pitiable to see men created in the image of God become worse than brute beasts."[49]

It comes as no surprise that in Ortese's novel we also find an organic intellectual of this sort in the figure of Don Fidenzio Aureliano Bosio, Archbishop of Merida, who performs an exorcism or rite of purification in the den of the "diabolica Iguanuccia" (133; "diabolical little Iguana," 133). In a striking parallel between the story of Ortese's novel and the conquest of America, both the Iguana and the Indians are turned into witches by aligning them with the devil, as if the old European witches had crossed the ocean and landed in the New World, giving one more moral justification for the enslavement and eventual extermination of the natives. Such a process is evident in the parallel outbreak of a new epidemic of witch trials all over Europe after 1492. In the inquisitors' eyes, the appearance of the devil on the other side of the ocean – the phenomenon that Parinetto calls the "crossing of the witches" – was the clearest evidence of the ontological reality of evil.

Keeping this in mind, let us see for a moment how the apparition of the devil was represented among the Indians of Brazil in one of the extraordinary illustrations of Théodore de Bry's *Grands Voyages*, first published in Frankfurt in 1592, one hundred year after the discovery of America. The illustration, which shows Indians pursued by demons and flying creatures, is described as *L'Enfer américain*.[50] Still, as Frank Lestringant observed, this image does not represent America as the threshold of hell. It shows the more interesting dramatic action of hell taking possession of the New World. Here is a brief description of the image in Lestringant's words:

> Another devil hoists Satyr horns, angular vampire wings and breasts of a woman. His sex is replaced by fur and his hairy legs end in talons [...]

> Another devil, a sort of winged Melusine, gives a longing look to a reclining Indian [...] he has a twisted horn on his forehead. His sagging breasts and serpentine tail make him a succubus.[51]

The uncommon term "succubus" is used here to define a demon that assumes female form in order to have sexual intercourse with men in their sleep. It is in fact clear that demonic power is not only associated with animalization but also, and in a more interesting way, with feminization, for in the Western tradition, from Aristotle on, the evil and the monstrous is essentially feminine.[52] One need only think of the figure of Melusine, evoked by Lestringant, but often associated by critics with Ortese's Iguana. Melusine is, in fact, a snake-woman.[53]

The snake is of course one of the most common representations of the devil. The Peruvian-born historian Garcilaso de la Vega reported that Indians "worship the devil, when he presents himself in the form of any beast or serpent, and speaks to them."[54] When Estrellita sees her own image in a mirror for the very first time, she perceives herself to be "tutta verde e brutta, un vero serpente" (R2 127; "all green and ugly, nothing but a serpent," TIG 130), internalizing others' negative perception of her. It is interesting to notice how Columbus, in his *Journal of the First Voyage to America*, refers to the iguana, a species never seen before in Europe, as "sierpe" ("snake").[55] The snake is in fact one of the many metamorphoses that our green protagonist seems to have undergone, at least according to the story told by Hipolito, one of don Ilario's two brothers: "Non più di sei anni fa, *o demonio* apparve su questa terra in forma di uccelletto, poi si fece serpente, e subì molte altre trasformazioni" (R2 41; "No more than six years ago, *o demonio* appeared right here on this island – first in the form of a little bird, but then he changed himself into a snake, and later all sorts of other transformations. And he's still here now," TIG 30).

With great surprise, one can find the image of the winged iguana, a sort of drake or bird so similar to the demonic representation exemplified by De Bry's illustration and Hipolito's story, in one of Ortese's many drafts for her novel. In that version, Daddo returns to the island and sees "uno 'stormo di Iguane', che, in un'ennesima metamorfosi, figurano come uccelli, – trascurati dalla scienza ornitologica – 'di carattere assai strambo e selvatico'" (R2 923; "a 'flock of Iguanas,' which, in yet another in a long line of metamorphoses, are turned into 'really odd and wild' birds – unknown to ornithologists"). The flight of this flock of Iguanas crossing the novel somehow literalizes the history of the crossing – from Europe to America – of the witches.

Our Iguana, born in the Caribbean, is an Indian once regarded by Don Ilario as a heavenly creature, who seems to have undergone a similar *witchfication* process. One should not forget that the Iguana is also a gendered creature and that the witch-hunt was the first great movement of coercion, exclusion, and extermination of women by the patriarchal power embodied by the Church. Over the course of history, many women were literally burned alive just because they were women. And when burning women was not considered appropriate anymore, they were interned. Witchcraft and madness are in fact corresponding discourses in the case of women.

To find a link between madness, witchcraft, and colonialism one should briefly take a look at another female literary character who was born in the Caribbean and who died in a fire (like a witch), because the colonialist mindset of the British Empire considered her a mad woman. This character is Bertha Mason, the Creole first wife of Edward Rochester in Charlotte Brontë's *Jane Eyre,* one of Ortese's favourite authors. *Jane Eyre* was certainly present in Ortese's mind when she was writing *L'Iguana.*[56] Bertha's monstrous subjectivity as a defiant Caribbean-Creole was more than likely Ortese's inspiration in constructing Estrellita's character, a similar colonial Other.[57] As Spivak wrote in a masterly reading of Brontë's novel, "Bertha's function in *Jane Eyre* is to render indeterminate the boundary between human and animal."[58] Like the Iguana, Bertha is thus an image of "the in-between hybridity of the history of sexuality and race."[59] And yet the indeterminacy between human and animal was also one of the demonic signs that the inquisitor associated with the witch: "it is the devil who shape-shifts, and is bestial, pied, asymmetrical and otherwise jumbled and jangled."[60] For the Western, white, Christian gaze, both Bertha and the Iguana, like the real women burned alive, act as if they were possessed by the devil: "why must you act like such a little devil?" (152) is the question to Estrellita that Daddo repeats in his mind. Bertha and the Iguana live indeed in a space very close to the island of *The Tempest,* where "pagan notions of physical identity as multiple and shapeshifting clash [...] with a Christian idea of fixed, stable and seemly bodily identity."[61]

Call Me My Name

Just as "witch" is a polyvalent label to give to a subject, in Ortese's novel the label "iguana" is a multilayered one: shifting from identity to identity and thus refusing ontological stability.[62] "Witch," in fact, is a nomadic name. As Parinetto wrote, "solo bruciandola *per stregoneria* [la strega] viene tenuta ferma in un nome, che, d'altra parte, è sempre pronunciato dall'inquisitore (e a lei estorto con la tortura): è l'inquisitore nella *sua proiezione*, il portatore di quel nome" ["it is only by burning her *for sorcery*, that a witch is held still by a single name, which is always pronounced by the inquisitor (and wrung out of her through torture). The bearer of that name is the inquisitor himself in his own *projection*"].[63] Following this logic, the inquisitor's discourse – anxiously in need of fixing the other to a name – is the same as the colonizer's discourse, at least in Bhabha's reading of it:

> An important feature of colonial discourse is its dependence on the concept of "fixity" in the ideological construction of otherness. Fixity as the sign of cultural / historical / racial difference in the discourse of colonialism, is a paradoxical mode of representation: it connotes rigidity and an unchanging order as well as disorder, degeneracy and daemonic repetition.[64]

The Iguana, the epitome of the subaltern subject, refuses to be fixed to a single identity in order to reject the violence of colonial discourse. Like "witch," in Ortese's novel "Iguana" "è nome che trascina dentro di sé molti nomi, che è traversato da molti nomi" ("is a name that drags within itself many names, that is crossed by many names").[65] That is why our Iguana seems to possess infinite identities: Estrellita, Perdita, devil or maid, woman or animal, but also native. Women, for instance, are not the only ones who have been forced to undergo the process of being turned into witches over the centuries. They are in good company with the entire category of the "Other," namely, the kind of people that Ortese calls "the oppressed,"[66] from native peoples to gypsies, from homosexuals to wanderers, but above all the poor: "l'iguana [...] rappresenta gli esseri dei Paesi non industrializzati" ("the iguana represents the people of the developing countries").[67] As French sociologist Jean Palou argues in his study on the relationship between the great historical witch-hunts and poverty,[68] anyone who is not useful to the primary social and economic system – that is, the subalterns – is comparable to witches.[69] In this regard, *L'Iguana* appears to be not only a critique of colonial power, but also a critique of the cold-bloodedness of the capitalist system. What comes to mind is the excruciating image of the lonely green protagonist counting the stones she gets as her pay. Her worthless stones represent the unbalanced (and unjust) economy that fueled colonization: the exchange of glass beads for work and gold.

Following this interpretative path, it is easy to understand that "Iguana" is only one of the many symbolic representations of the term "witch," a subject that is intrinsically nomadic and itinerant. The nature of the Iguana, who represents the entire spectrum of the subaltern, is *endlessly* shape-shifting. This is why Daddo's death does not modify the *reality* of the Iguana's condition, but only the *perception* of her external reality: it does not fix her inner ambiguity. At the end of the novel, when the Iguana makes an appearance as nothing more than a little servant, "una servetta come ce ne sono tante nelle isole, con due occhi fissi e grandi, in un volto non più grande di un chicco di riso" (R2 181; "a servant girl like so many to be found in the islands, with two large staring eyes in a face no larger than a grain of rice," TIG 184), she still refuses a stable identity. Her identity resists the idea of fixity, she remains "mutevole come il mare" (189; "as changeable as the ocean," 192) and somehow deprived of a definite proper name: she is referred to as "persona" (188; "person," 191), "personcina" (194; "little person," 198), "servetta" (188; "servant," 191), "ragazzetta" (188; "servant girl," 191), and ultimately as Iguana. Her proper name, whatever it was (if she ever had one), has disappeared. The Iguana, then, stands for the condition of identity-void described by Ortese in *Corpo celeste,* a void in which "precipita tutto ciò che strazia la Terra: violenza, corruzione, menzogna, arbitrio" (CC 115; "everything tormenting the Hearth collapses: violence, corruption, falsehood, abuse"). However, one could argue, the Iguana's resistance to stable identity is not definitive, for in the poem at the end of the novel, the reader finds her apparent request for a unique name of her own:

Aiutami.
Riconoscimi.
Salutami.
Col mio nome chiamami,
non con quello del serpe. (R2 191–92)

(Help me.
Know me.
Greet me.
Call me by my name,
not by the serpent's. [TIG 195])

But what does this request for a name stand for? Does it really come from the Iguana? To understand it, let us consider that such a straightforward expression of a desire for an identity seems to parallel that of a very famous literary woman, who refuses her condition of oppressed. I am thinking of the ghost protagonist of Toni Morrison's masterpiece, *Beloved* (1987), which follows the story of Sethe and her daughter Denver as they try to build a normal life after escaping from slavery. They live in a house haunted by the ghost of Sethe's murdered daughter, whose tombstone reads only "Beloved." At some point in the story, Beloved expresses her desire for an identity: "I want you to touch me on the inside part and call me my name."[70] The astonishing similarity between Ortese's and Morrison's statements might induce us to think that the two situations are equally similar, inasmuch as they both seem to be dealing with a woman's affirmation through writing. On the contrary, in Ortese's case, the crude poem is a carefully set trap for anyone susceptible to a naïve feminist reading of the novel.

The servant girl can, in fact, neither write nor read. She is not the author of the poem. Nor she can be an author of any sort. She has no access to writing, and thus she is incapable of self-expression. As we learn from the narrator in the last few pages of *L'Iguana*, after the transformation of Ocaña into a tourist resort, to kill a little time the Guzman brothers and the girl "imparavano a leggere e scrivere, molto faticosamente, ma aiutandosi" (R2 190; "were learning, Reader, to read and write, with a great deal of difficulty, but mutually assisting each other," TIG 194). Nevertheless, "la ragazzetta, che non stava mai molto bene, ed era sempre disattenta, non primeggiava, pur desiderando con tutta l'umile forza del suo cuore" (R2 191; "the girl, whose health was never good and who was always inattentive, never excelled in her studies, even though she desired to do so with all the humble force of her heart," TIG 194). Her request for recognition, expressed in the first person, is actually written by one of the Guzman brothers. The Iguana's voice is still overwritten by a man's writing; she is once again deprived of her own voice. Like an animal, she is unqualified to produce real, meaningful words. She can only express herself through something inarticulate and thus very close to a cry (the poem's verses, for her, are really just animal "versi"):

> versi, questi, *se versi si possono chiamare*, che fecero scoppiare a ridere una certa personcina, la quale altro che in questo modo, o in altri più strambi, riusciva mai ad esprimere la forza del suo patire, della [...] inumana profondità del suo cuore. (R2 198; emphasis added)

> (These verses, *if we can call them verses*, made a certain little person break into laughter, since that was the only way, if not for others that were even stranger, in which she could ever express the force of her feelings, the force [...] of her heart's inhuman depth. [TIG 198])

The desire for recognition is thus not the key to humanizing the inhuman animal-woman, since that desire is based – once again – on the request formulated by a male gaze.

We should also remember that the already very unreliable narrator, at the end of the story, refuses to "speak of her directly" (TIG 191) and through an authorial proxy, uses the voice of the only tourist on the island, "Mrs. Rubens, the wife of a jeweler in Lyle" (TIG 191), who describes her experience on Ocaña in her letters to her husband. After Daddo's death, Ilario marries and moves to Caracas, Ocaña becomes a resort and the Guzmans' house a small hotel. Mrs Rubens' letters are an important conceptual device because, for the very first time, we as readers see through female eyes the creature that Daddo and the narrator first described as having the body of an old woman and later "un triste corpicino verde" (R2 128; "a sad, thin green body," TIG 127). The reader is of course expecting to discover the truth about the mysterious Iguana, but even Mrs Rubens has troubles in determining the girl's age ("l'età può essere molta, o nulla," R2 188; "she could be of any age at all, a hag or an infant," TIG 191), though she has little difficulty in discerning her inhuman nature ("ho capito quanto il suo cuore sia in realtà disumano e insensibile a tutto," 189; "I finally saw just how inhuman her heart really is, and thoroughly insensitive to everything" 192). Reinforcing a sort of parallel with Bertha Mason, Mrs Rubens even suggests she might be mad, a typical way to react to otherness, especially when the other is a woman ("più che deficiente, come assicura il prete, a me sembra matta," 188–89; "the priest says she's retarded, but I'd call her mad," 192). In short, even when removed from the male, white, privileged, Western gaze, the Iguana's subalternity with respect to power does not seem to have changed. The female gaze does not give us access to the Iguana's mystery because – like Parinetto's witches – she does not only represent the feminine condition but the condition of all the oppressed. The Iguana is "[il] vivente che piange da ogni parte: nei boschi, all'alba, prima del massacro; nelle città perdute ad ogni ora del giorno; nei continenti desertificati (e derubati di quel che resta) eternamente" ["the living being crying everywhere: in the woods, at dawn, before the massacre; at all hours in lost towns; in the continents eternally made desert (and deprived of what they have left)"].[71]

Since the Iguana fully belongs to that category of oppressed creatures – and is not even considered to be human – at the end of the story she still has neither name, nor voice. The Guzman brothers keep calling her Iguana, so that even the name pronounced by Daddo before dying, Perdita, turns – literally – into loss.[72] The poem, therefore, was but one final, ineffective attempt to anchor the subject to a fixed identity. As Adria Frizzi wrote in a brilliant essay:

> [the Iguana's] resistance to being named, and particularly to the proper name, which is the name received from the father-author, creator and master of the code, is directly linked to the Iguana's condition of repressed, other, female, and the logic underlying such a condition – unable to transform or entirely appropriate the dominant discourse that speaks for her and to which she has no access, but resisting it by transgressing it, undercutting it and making trouble.[73]

Frizzi is here referring to the Iguana's broken speech, "filled with interruptions, hesitations [...] and expressions of subordination."[74] I believe that one does not need to look only to the language of the Iguana for a system of resistance but – on the contrary – to her silence, the same obstinate silence that the "witch" assumes when confronted by the inquisitor.[75] According to my reading, in spite of the frequent critical references to the mermaid, the Iguana shares very little with this ancient myth, which is primarily a vocal myth.[76]

In postcolonial terms, the Iguana is closer to the kind of peculiar native that Spivak defines as "the curious guardian at the margin who will not inform."[77] She is like Friday, whose tongue has been cut off, in white South African author J.M. Coeetze's *Foe*, a postmodern and postcolonial rewriting of Daniel Defoe's *Robinson Crusoe* (1719). In *Foe*, Defoe's novel is reinscribed from the perspective of an English woman, Susan Barton, a castaway who lands on the same island once inhabited by Crusoe. Susan wants to know Friday and give him speech. Her project is to give a voice to the black servant, in order to know the "true story" buried within him. Like the Guzman brothers, she tries, unsuccessfully, to teach Friday how to write.

It is interesting that both Friday and the Iguana are presented in a ruinous attempt to learn how to write. What is truly relevant, however, is not that it is impossible for them to become narrators, or subjects of speech. What is important is that they both *refuse* to become narrators and to speak. They resist speech and in doing so they refuse to collaborate with the postcolonial discourse always charged with epistemic violence. They are a "figuration of the wholly other as margin,"[78] a margin that we – supposed white, Western readers – cannot penetrate. What they refuse is perfectly described by American social activist, feminist, and author bell hooks:

> No need to hear your voice when I can talk about you better than you can speak about yourself. No need to hear your voice. Only tell me about your pain. I want to know your story. And then I will tell it back to you in a new way. Tell it back to you in such a way that it has become mine, my own. Re-writing you I write myself anew. I am still author, authority. I am still colonizer the speaking subject and you are now at the centre of my talk.[79]

In this regard, Ortese is very far from Susan Barton. She does not fight to give voice to the subaltern, because she fully accepts and thus represents the Iguana's marginality, preserving her unique otherness.

NOTES

1 "Romanzo saggio" ("essayistic novel") and "fiaba critica" ("critical fairy tale") [Farnetti, *Anna Maria Ortese*, 123–24]; "antifiaba critica" ("critical anti-fairy tale") [Clerici, *Apparizione e visione*, 398]; "favola politica" ("political fairy tale") [Bellezza, "Fra incanto e furore," vi]. For a detailed discussion about the genre of *L'Iguana*, see La Penna, "An Inquiry into Modality and Genre," 160–87.

2 One of her names is "Estrellita dei Caraibi" (R2 123; "Estrellita of the Caribes," TIG 126).

3 In *Il porto di Toledo*, this is Ortese-Dasa's description of one of the rooms of her family home in Naples: "al di sopra di ceste e casse abbandonate [...] erano raccolti tutti i vari popoli d'America, Comanche, Appalachi, Piedi Neri ecc. [...] tutti da me dipinti. Vi era anche un tavolaccio [...] e qui io scrivevo" (PT 25; "above some abandoned baskets and boxes [...] there were all the various people of America, Comanche, Apalachee, Blackfeet etc. [...] all painted by me. There was also a bad table [...] where I used to write"). The fact that this room dedicated to the depiction of the "people of America" is also the space of writing is even more meaningful if one thinks that the title of Ortese's very first short story is "Pellirossa" ("American Indian"), published in *L'Italia letteraria* 10, no. 52, 29 December 1934, 3). It is in this short story that Ortese introduces for the first time one of the recurrent themes in her later work: the spread of civilization and so-called progress that often brings destruction, and consumes nature as well as human innocence. One can find a Native American also at the end of Ortese's life and career: Scotty Moore, a forty-year-old drug addict of Cherokee descent, who was sentenced to death on 9 November 1984 in the United States. After having read about his story in *Il Corriere della Sera*, Ortese took

to Mr Moore's defence in the same newspaper and started a long epistolary relationship with the Native American inmate, who eventually asked that his ashes be scattered in Rapallo, in the city of his Italian friend. See Anna Maria Ortese, "Il sentiero delle lacrime."

4 After the death of Manuele, who was sailing on a boat named "Colombo," Ortese experienced for the first time the impulse to write. The result was a long poem dedicated to her brother ("Manuele," *L'Italia letteraria* 9, no. 36, 3 September 1933, 3). To Manuele's death is dedicated the second chapter of *Il porto di Toledo*, where the first composition of the protagonist, Dasa, happens to be published in "Journal de l'Île" ("The Journal of the Island"), so that death and beginning of writing merge on the soil of a far Caribbean island. See Clerici, *Apparizione e visione*, 26–27.

5 See De Gasperin, "The Ship and the Sea in the Writing of Anna Maria Ortese."

6 "...a mighty wind arose while the Icelander was speaking, and bowled him over, and covered him with a most superb mausoleum of sand: beneath which, perfectly dried out, and turned into a fine mummy, he was later found by certain travelers, and installed in the museum of some town in Europe," Leopardi, "The Dialogue of Nature and an Icelander," in *The Moral Essays*, 104. A few years after the publication of *L'Iguana*, in 1969, another Leopardian body – extremely important for Ortese's poetics – was pierced by an American flag: the celestial body of the moon. Already in 1967, Ortese declared that she was very annoyed by all of the artificial satellites being sent for the conquest of space: "Ora, questo spazio, non importa da chi, forse da tutti i paesi progrediti, è sottratto al desiderio di riposo, di ordine, di beltà, allo straziante desiderio di riposo di gente che mi somiglia. Diventerà, fra breve, probabilmente, spazio edilizio. O nuovo territorio di caccia, di meccanico progresso, di corsa alla supremazia, al terrore" ("It's not important who is doing it, maybe it's all civilized countries, but space is now being taken away from the desire for repose, for order, for beauty, from the heartrending desire for repose of people like me. Very likely, it will shortly become a space for construction. Or a new hunting preserve, a space for mechanical progress, the next pawn in the race for supremacy, for terror"), Ortese, "Occhi al cielo" (orig. in *Corriere della Sera*, 24 December 1967), repr. in Calvino, *Una pietra sopra*, 220.

7 See Massari, "Ortese: la mia è la voce di un gatto," 3. "Nella piazza San Silvestro di Roma era stato trovato, infreddolito e spaventato, l'animale esotico che ha questo nome. Lo aveva smarrito una signora, o forse la bestiola si era allontanata da casa, come fanno talvolta gli animali, che si assuefanno e amano la comodità, certo, ma mai del tutto smarriscono la memoria del loro antichissimo passato. Che cosa fosse accaduto Anna Maria

Ortese non seppe, come non seppero i lettori del giornale" ("In San Silvestro square in Rome, was found a specimen of this exotic animal, cold and scared. A woman had lost it, or maybe the little animal had moved away from home, as animals sometimes do, for they get used to living in comfort, but never fully forget their very ancient past. Anna Maria Ortese never found out what really happened, like the readers of the newspaper.")

8 Moreover, in "L'isola," the woman wearing "uno scialle *verde*" (AD 14; "a *green* shawl") that the protagonist meets on her way to a mysterious house, seems to direct our attention to another insular short story, "Uomo nell'isola" ("Man on the Island"), published in 1950 in the collection *L'infanta sepolta*. According to Monica Farnetti, "Uomo nell'isola" is the first nucleus of *L'Iguana*. In "Uomo nell'isola," the little woman ("donnina"), who turns out to be the ape-servant of the protagonist's uncle, has "il viso grinzoso coperto da un velo *verde*" (IS 93; "a wrinkled face covered by a *green* veil"). Being associated with insularity and the colour green, this servant-beast, like the woman in the previous story, indeed seems to anticipate the heart-rending figure of the Iguana, described as "una bestiola verdissima e alta quanto un bambino, dall'apparente aspetto di una lucertola gigante, ma vestita da donna, con una sottanina scura" (R2 23; "a bright green beast, about the height of a child – an enormous lizard from the look of her, but dressed in woman's clothes with a dark skirt," TIG 7). The iguana is in fact a beast and a woman at the same time. Or, as someone has argued, she is a beast *because* she is a woman. [See De Giovanni, "*L'Iguana* di Anna Maria Ortese," 424 and Azzolini, "La donna iguana," 216.]

9 Jorge's father, Rodrigo Manrique, died in Ocaña in 1476. For Ortese's relationship with Spanish literature see Mazzocchi, "Anna Maria Ortese e l'ispanità," 90–104 and Cirillo, "Depistaggi e sdoppiamenti nell'*Iguana* di Anna Maria Ortese," 163–170. Tonia Fiornino states, without giving any actual textual reference, that Ocaña is "non a caso la terra favolosa de *L'isola del Tesoro* di Robert Louis Stevenson" ("not by chance the imaginary land of Robert Louis Stevenson's *Treasure Island*"). See Fiornino, "Spunti per una lettura de *L'Iguana*," 143. Also Cosetta Seno Reed runs into the same mistake in her entry for The Italian Women Writers Database of Chicago University: www.lib.uchicago.edu/efts/IWW/BIOS/A0225.html. The origin of this misreading is probably to be found in Citati's afterward, included in the 1986 Adelphi edition of *L'Iguana*: "Aleardo giunge alla sconosciuta isola di Ocaña – che è l'isola della *Tempesta*, l'isola di Stevenson, il luogo dove approdiamo quando balziamo fuori dalla curva della realtà" ("Aleardo arrives to the unknown Ocaña Island – which is the island of *The Tempest*, the island of Stevenson, the place in which we land when we jump outside the curve of reality"). Citati, 202.

10 Deleuze, *Desert Islands and Other Texts*, 10.

11 "scrivere...è proprio cercare un altro mondo. Cercarlo disperatamente" ("to write...is to look for another world. To look for it desperately"), in Ortese, "Interview with Dario Bellezza," (orig. *Paese Sera*, 31 January 1983), repr. in Clerici, *Per Anna Maria Ortese*, 66. According to Nadia De Giovanni, Ortese's is "un progetto di rifondazione su basi soggettive" ("a project of subjective reconstitution"). See De Giovanni, "L'Iguana di Anna Maria Ortese," 421.

12 Silvio Perrella identified in the novel "la presenza sotterranea e vivificante di *Benito Cereno*" ("the *concealed* and invigorating presence of *Benito Cereno*"). See Perrella, "Anna Maria Ortese o le metamorfosi addolorate," 115. For further references to Melville see also De Gasparin, *Loss and the Other in the Visionary Work of Anna Maria Ortese*, 232–33.

13 Melville, *Moby-Dick*, Chapter 12.

14 Spivak, *A Critique of Postcolonial Reason*, 30.

15 Ghezzo, "Mappe per una rilettura," 115.

16 *Autre* ("Other") was the name used by Montaigne (1533–92) to refer to the devil in his *Essays*. In his essay about cruelty, he proved to be a harsh critic of European colonialism, which he considered cruel and barbaric. Ortese was a great admirer of Montaigne, and she mentioned his essay on cruelty in an interview with Dario Bellezza: "La Francia è grande per Pascal, ma prima ancora per Montaigne. Leggi il suo saggio sulla crudeltà!" (R2 191; "France is great because of Pascal, but before that because of Montaigne, Read his essay on cruelty!").

17 Conrad, *Heart of Darkness*, 71.

18 Conrad's *Typhoon* (1902) is one of the models for the metaphorical tempest that takes place in the second part of *L'Iguana*. See R2 192.

19 Bruno, "*Viaggio in Italia*," 31.

20 Alpers, *The Art of Describing*, 133.

21 Bhabha, "The Third Space," 211.

22 See Losada, "The Controversy between Sepúlveda and Las Casas in the Junta of Valladolid."

23 Andrea Baldi, "Note ai testi," in R2 903.

24 La Penna, "An Inquiry into Modality and Genre," 169.

25 Significantly, Don Ilario's epic poems about the Portuguese empire are written with *green* ink.

26 In 1961, the African Party for the Independence of Guinea and Cape Verde began an armed rebellion against Portugal. Also in the early 1960s, other independence movements in the Portuguese overseas provinces of Angola and Mozambique resulted in the Portuguese Colonial War (1961–74). The rebellion in Cape Verde, whose name in Italian sounds like "Green Cape"

or "Green Head," might have influenced the Italian writer in the creation of her green character.

27 Don Ilario's description reminds of Don Benito Cereno, the eponymous protagonist of Herman Melville's novella. See Perrella, "Anna Maria Ortese o le metamorfosi addolorate."

28 Camões is openly mentioned in the novel and evoked by the name of Daddo's boat, *La Luisa.* In a very interesting way, Ortese depicts Portuguese language, when used by the Iguana, as a language of negations: "'*Nâo… Nâo… Nâo…*' e altre confuse interiezioni della lingua di Camões, nel balbettio di quell'essere avevano un che di miagolante, e ora, di atterrito" (R2 26; "'*Nâo… Nâo… Nâo…*' and a confusion of other phrases in the language of di Camões became a babble in the mouth of the creature, something whining and afraid," TIG 20).

29 It is worth mentioning that the name of the founder of Palos is Álvar Pérez de Guzmán and that Guzman is also Don Ilario's last name.

30 La Penna, "An Inquiry into Modality and Genre," 170.

31 See Leopardi, "The Dialogue of Christopher Columbus and Pedro Gutierrez," *Moral Essays,* 158–62.

32 Eugenio Montale, "Arsenio," in *Collected Poems 1920–1954,* 111–13.

33 See Ghezzo, "Mappe per una rilettura," 118–21.

34 Warner, "'The Foul Witch' and Her 'Freckled Whelp'," 105.

35 I disagree with Vilma De Gasperin when she suggests, without comparative textual analysis, that the Iguana shares *more* features with Ariel than Caliban, "as both appear as an intermediary between indigenous forces of nature and enslaving human beings" (see De Gasperin, *Loss and the Other in the Visionary Work of Anna Maria Ortese,* 227). In fact, Ariel's magical powers make him an active agent in the story: he is the one who causes the tempest and control the fate of the other characters following Prospero's instructions. The Iguana, on the contrary, is the epitome of the colonial subject's powerless passivity.

36 Bompiani, "The Monster as a Refugee," 269.

37 Skura, "Discourse and the Individual," 286–322.

38 See Chapter V: "un alto dipinto ovale, di due metri almeno, dove una signora dall'apparente età di trent'anni, … reggeva sulle spalle una minuscola e oscura creatura, che con una manina (il suo muso non si vedeva), andava aggiustandole sulla fronte un pallido ricciolo" (R2 39; "a high oval painting, some two meters tall, where a woman about thirty years old … carried some obscure, miniscule creature on her shoulder: it reached across a paw (its face couldn't be seen) to straighten a pale curl on her forehead," TIG 34). At first, Daddo doesn't know whether the creature is a bird or a monkey.

It is very hard, if not impossible, to find a precise iconographic reference to the painting described by Ortese. But there are at least four different portraits of a lady with a monkey that might have inspired the writer. The oldest one, and frankly the least likely, is a portrait by an unknown artist of Katherine of Aragon, one of Henry VIII's wives. On the contrary, Marcus Gheeraerts the Younger's astonishing *Portrait of Lady Arabella Stuart* (1575–1615) seems to have a lot in common with Ortese's description. In this painting, Lady Arabella is surrounded by a number of exotic pets: a parrot, a macaw, a monkey, a little dog, and two small parrots that are nestled in her right hand. Still, Gheeraerts the Younger's exoticism is not as disturbing as the one in Anthony Van Dyck's *Henrietta Maria and the Dwarf Sir Jeffrey Hudson* (1633), where Henrietta Maria is accompanied by her dwarf, who is holding a monkey that playfully grabs his hair. Exactly because of this detail, this masterpiece of the Flemish Baroque painter is the most probable source of Ortese's imagination. Still, it is worth mentioning also the *Portrait of a Young Lady with a Monkey* by Venetian Rococo painter Rosalba Carriera.

There is also another Baroque painting that seems to have influenced the idea of an indefinable creature, halfway between monkey and bird. It is the *Portrait of Antonietta Gonsalus* by Lavinia Fontana (Bologna 1552–Rome 1614). Antonietta was a woman who suffered from hepatoerythropoietic porphyria, a disease characterized by severe facial hypertrichosis. She inherited the disease from her father, Petrus Gonsalus, a man born in the Canary Islands, who toured the European courts like an exotic marvel. In Lavinia Fontana's painting, Antonietta looks like an indefinable small creature dressed like a little girl. Her hairy face makes her look like a little monkey, while her hook-bill nose resembles the beak of a bird.

39 Spivak, *A Critique of Postcolonial Reason,* 117.

40 See Wood, "Anna Maria Ortese and the Art of the Real," 177; La Penna "An Inquiry into Modality and Genre," 170.

41 See Blanchard et al., eds., *Human Zoo.*

42 Werner, *Barnum,* 59.

43 Ortese, "Piccolo Drago," SV 178.

44 Columbus, *The Diary of Christopher Columbus,* 55.

45 Bertolozzi, *Ricerche istorico-critiche,* 171.

46 See Poidimani, ed., *Luciano Parinetto.*

47 Parinetto, *Streghe e potere,* 327.

48 Ibid., 271. The *Malleus Maleficarum* ("The Hammer of Witches") is a famous treatise on witches, written in 1486 by Heinrich Kramer, an inquisitor of the Catholic Church. It was first published in Germany in 1487.

49 de Motolinia, *History of the Indians of New Spain,* 45. Fray Toribio de Benavente (1482, Benavente, Spain – 1568, Mexico City), also known as Motolinia, was a Franciscan missionary and among the first twelve clerics to arrive in New Spain in May 1524.
50 A similar infernal image, drawn from the same medieval imaginary, is evoked in Chapter XIX: "Vi fu un lungo minuto di silenzio, in cui, in luogo del tuono, si udì il vento, ed era come una folla di morti che attraversasse spaventata l'isola, inseguita da un esercito di demoni che li pungolavano, come fa il mandriano di buoi" (153; "There was a long moment of silence in which the thudding thunder of the surf was replaced by the wind. A flock of the dead was in flight from one side of the island to the other, pursued by a legion of demons who pushed and prodded them with sharpened sticks, as herdsmen handle cattle" [161]).
51 Lestringant, *Le huguenot et le sauvage,* 6.
52 Strangely enough, one of the most common accusations against witches was sodomy. Since they represented the paradigm of otherness, they also came to represent homosexuality.
53 See De Giovanni, "*L'Iguana* di Anna Maria Ortese," 427; Azzolini, "La donna iguana," 222. For Monica Farnetti as well, the Iguana is inscribed within the "tradizione delle Ondine e Morgane, Sirenette, Lorelei e belle Melusine" ("tradition of all sorts of Undine and Morgane, little Mermaids, Lorelei and beautiful Melusinas"), in *Anna Maria Ortese,* 62.
54 de la Vega, *Royal Commentaries of the Ynca,* 51.
55 Columbus, *Journal of the First Voyage,* 51.
56 See Ghezzo, "Mappe per una rilettura," 118–19.
57 As Flora Ghezzo already suggested, to some extent, *L'Iguana* is closer to *Wide Sargasso Sea,* the postcolonial rewriting of *Jane Eyre* by Caribbean writer Jean Rhys, from the point of view of Bertha. Like *L'Iguana, Wide Sargasso Sea* was also published in 1965, but it wasn't translated into Italian until 1971.
58 Spivak, *A Critique of Postcolonial Reason,* 125. "What it was, whether beast or human being, one could not … tell: it groveled, seemingly, on all fours; it snatched and growled like some strange wild animal," in Charlotte Brontë, *Jane Eyre,* 295.
59 Bhabha, *The Location of Culture,* 20.
60 Warner, "'The Foul Witch' and Her 'Freckled Whelp'," 99.
61 Ibid., 98.
62 To avoid any possible misunderstanding, allow me to be a little more precise: by drawing parallels between the Iguana and the history of witches I do not mean to attribute any kind of magic powers to her nor do I intend to

reduce her complex symbolism to a unilateral reading. Nor does it suppose a belief in the existence of sorcery. It means instead to accept her full overdetermination, her continuously moving subjectivity.

63 Parinetto, *Streghe e potere*, 269.
64 Bhabha, *The Location of Culture*, 66.
65 Parinetto, *Streghe e potere*, 269.
66 "Le creature oppresse, gli zingari, i vecchi, i bambini, gli animali" ("The oppressed creatures, gypsies, old people, kids and animals"), Ortese, CC, 30–31.
67 Barberis, "È così difficile trovare a Milano il silenzio," 6.
68 See Palou, *La sorcellerie*.
69 Sorcery is a Foucauldian discourse similar to madness: see Foucault, *History of Madness*.
70 Morrison, *Beloved*, 116.
71 Ortese, "Amica, ma delle vittime," 17.
72 Perdita is both the name of one of the heroines of Shakespeare's *The Winter's Tale* and the protagonist of d'Annunzio's *Il Fuoco*.
73 Frizzi, "Performance, or Getting a Piece of the Other," 386.
74 Ibid.
75 Ortese, "Autointervista," 5: "Ma io, dalla donna, proprio perché l'uomo manca, – o è sperduto – mi aspetto una resistenza, un coraggio" ("But I expect from the woman, just because man is missing – or lost – resistance and courage"), now in *Per Anna Maria Ortese*, 63. As Daniela La Penna argued, also in the case of *L'Iguana* one feels like "the sense that control of the language is a means of ensuring that the subjected can articulate their subjection only in a language which already defines their subordinate relationship to the powerful is one which speaks directly to the condition of the colonized," see La Penna, "An Inquiry into Modality and Genre," 175.
76 See Cavarero, "The Fate of the Sirens," in *For More Than One Voice*, 103:116.
77 Spivak, *A Critique of Postcolonial Reason*, 190.
78 Ibid., 174.
79 bell hooks, "marginality as site of resistance," 242.

WORKS CITED

Alpers, Svetlana. *The Art of Describing: Dutch Art in the Seventeenth Century*. Chicago, IL: University of Chicago Press, 1983.

Azzolini, Paola. "La donna iguana." In *Il cielo vuoto dell'eroina: Scrittura e identità femminile nel Novecento italiano*. Rome: Bulzoni, 2001.

Barberis, Alfredo. "È così difficile trovare a Milano il silenzio." Interview with A.M. Ortese. *Il Giorno,* 6 April 1966.
Bellezza, Dario. "Fra incanto e furore," in *L'Iguana,* by Anna Maria Ortese. Milan: Rizzoli, 1978.
Bertolozzi, Francesco. *Ricerche istorico-critiche circa alle scoperte d'Amerigo Vespucci con l'aggiunta di una relazione del medesimo fin ora inedita, compilate da Francesco Bartolozzi.* Florence: G. Cambiagi, 1789.
Bhabha, Homi. *The Location of Culture.* New York: Routledge, 2004.
– "The Third Space: Interview with Homi Bhabha." In *Identity: Community, Culture, Difference,* ed. J. Rutherford. London: Lawrence & Wishart, 1990.
Blanchard, Pascal, Nicolas Bancel, Eric Deroo, Sandrine Lemaire, and Charles Forsdick, eds. *Human Zoo: Science and Spectacle in the Age of Colonial Empire.* Liverpool, UK: Liverpool University Press, 2008.
Bompiani, Ginevra. "The Monster as a Refugee." In *Monsters in the Italian Literary Imagination,* ed. Keala Jewell. Detroit, MI: Wayne State University Press, 2001.
Bruno, Giuliana. "*Viaggio in Italia*: vedute da casa." In *Cartografie dell'immaginario: Cinema, corpo, memoria,* ed. Patrizia Calefato. Rome: Sossella, 2000.
Buffoni, Franco. "La fenomenologia della governante," in *Jane Eyre,* by Charlotte Brontë, v–xv. Milan: Mondadori, 1996.
Calvino, Italo. *Una pietra sopra.* Milan: Mondadori, 1995.
Cavarero, Adriana. *For More Than One Voice: Toward a Philosophy of Vocal Expression.* Trans. Paul A. Kottman. Redwood City, CA: Stanford University Press, 2005.
Cirillo, Silvana. "Depistages e sdoppiamenti nell'Iguana di Anna Maria Ortese." In *Nei dintorni del surrealismo: Da Alvaro a Zavattini umoristi balordi e sognatori nella letteratura italiana del Novecento,* 163–70. Rome: Editori Riuniti, 2006.
Citati, Piero. "La principessa dell'isola." In *L'iguana,* by Anna Maria Ortese, 197–204. Milan: Adelphi, 1997.
Clerici, Luca. *Apparizione e visione: Vita e opere di Anna Maria Ortese.* Milan: Mondadori, 2002.
– ed. "Per Anna Maria Ortese." *Il Giannone* 4, no. 7–8 (January–December 2006).
Columbus, Christopher. *The Diary of Christopher Columbus.* New York: NTC Contemporary Publishing Company, 1997.
– *Journal of the First Voyage.* Ed. and trans. B.W. Ife. Warminster, UK: Aris & Phillips, 1990.
Conrad, Joseph. *Heart of Darkness.* New York: Penguin, 1997.
De Gasperin, Vilma. *Loss and the Other in the Visionary Work of Anna Maria Ortese.* Oxford, UK: Oxford University Press, 2014.

– The Ship and the Sea in the Writing of Anna Maria Ortese: Autobiographical Experience and Literary Metaphor." *The Italianist 30* (2010): 81–98.

De Giovanni, Neria. "*L'Iguana* di Anna Maria Ortese: l'ambiguità di una metamorfosi incompiuta." *Italianistica* 18 (1989): 421–30.

de la Vega, Garcilaso. *Royal Commentaries of the Ynca.* Trans. and ed. Clements R. Markham. London: Burt Franklin, 1859.

Deleuze, Gilles. *Desert Islands and Other Texts.* Ed. David Lapoujade. Trans. Michael Taormina. Los Angeles- New York: Semiotext(e), 2004.

de Motolinia, Toribio. *History of the Indians of New Spain.* Trans. Elizabeth Andros Foster. Westport CT: Greenwood Press, 1977.

Farnetti, Monica. *Anna Maria Ortese.* Milan: Bruno Mondadori, 1998.

Fiornino, Tonia. "Spunti per una lettura de *L'Iguana.*" In *Paesaggio e Memoria: Giornata di studi su Anna Maria Ortese,* ed. Caterina De Caprio and Laura Donadio. Naples: Libreria Dante & Descartes, 2003.

Foucault, Michel. *History of Madness.* London and New York: Routledge, 2006.

Frizzi, Adria. "Performance, or Getting a Piece of the Other, or in the Name of the Father, or the Dark Continent of Femininity, or Just Like a Woman: Anna Maria Ortese's *L'Iguana.*" *Italica* 79, no. 3 (Autumn 2002): 379–90.

Ghezzo, Flora. "Mappe per una rilettura: orientalismo e intertestualità, ovvero il gioco dell'altro sull'isola dell' Iguana." In *Morfologie dell'* Iguana: *Anna Maria Ortese tra letteratura e cinema,* ed. Margherita Ganeri and Bruno Roberti. Lagonegro: LibrAre, 2011.

hooks, bell. "marginality as site of resistance." In *Out There: Marginalization and Contemporary Cultures,* ed. Russell Ferguson, Martha Gever, Trinh T. Minh-ha, and Cornel West. Cambridge, MA: MIT, 1990.

La Penna, Daniela. "An Inquiry into Modality and Genre: Reconsidering *L'Iguana* by Anna Maria Ortese." In *The Italian Gothic and Fantastic: Encounters and Rewritings of Narrative Traditions,* ed. Francesca Billiani and Gigliola Sulis, 160–87. Madison; Teaneck: Fairleigh Dickinson University Press, 2007.

Leopardi, Giacomo. *The Moral Essays: Operette morali.* Trans. Patrick Creagh. New York, NY: Columbia University Press, 1983.

Lestringant, Frank. *Le huguenot et le sauvage: l'Amérique et la controverse coloniale, en France, au temps des guerres de religion (1555–1589).* Genève: Droz, 2004.

Losada, Angel. "The Controversy between Sepúlveda and Las Casas in the Junta of Valladolid." In *Bartolomé de Las Casas in History: Toward an Understanding of the Man and His Work,* ed. and trans. Juan Friede and Benjamin Keen, 279–309. DeKalb: Northern Illinois University Press, 1971.

Massari, Giulia. "Ortese: la mia è la voce di un gatto." *Il Giornale,* 2 July 1986, 3.

Mazzocchi, Giuseppe. "Anna Maria Ortese e l'ispanità." *MLN* 112, no. 1 (1997): 90–104.

Melville, Herman. *Moby-Dick, or The Whale.* New York: Norton, 1970.
Montale, Eugenio. *Collected Poems 1920–1954.* Trans. Jonathan Galassi. New York: Farrar, Straus and Giroux, 1997.
Morrison, Toni. *Beloved.* New York: Penguin, 1987.
Ortese, Anna Maria. "Amica, ma delle vittime." *La Stampa,* 19 June 1990, 17.
– "Autointervista." *Paese sera,* 5 May 1976, 5.
– "Il sentiero delle lacrime." *Il Corriere della Sera,* 17 June 1996, 10.
Palou, Jean. *La sorcellerie.* Paris: PUF, 1957.
Parinetto, Luciano. *Streghe e potere: Il capitale e la persecuzione dei diversi.* Milan: Rusconi, 1998.
Perrella, Silvio. "Anna Maria Ortese o le metamorfosi addolorate." In *Il risveglio della ragione: Quarant'anni di narrativa a Napoli: 1953/93,* ed. G. Tortora. Naples: Avegliano, 1994.
Poidimani, Nicoletta, ed. *Luciano Parinetto: utopia di un eretico.* Milan: Mimesis, 2006.
Skura, Meredith Ann. "Discourse and the Individual: The Case of Colonialism in The Tempest." In *The Tempest: A Case Study in Critical Controversy,* ed. Gerald Graff and James Phelan, 286–322. Boston, MA: Bedford, 2000.
Spivak, Gayatri Chakravorty. *A Critique of Postcolonial Reason: Toward a History of the Vanishing Present.* Cambridge, MA: Harvard University Press, 1999.
Warner, Marina. "'The Foul Witch' and Her 'Freckled Whelp': Circean Mutations in the New World." In *"The Tempest" and Its Travels,* ed. Peter Hulme and William H. Sherman. London: Reaktion Books, 2000.
Werner, Morris Robert. *Barnum.* New York: Brace, 1923.
Wood, Sharon. "Anna Maria Ortese and the Art of the Real." In *Italian Women's Writing 1860–1994.* London; Atlantic Highlands, NJ: Athlone Press, 1995.

10 The Flickering Light of Reason: Anna Maria Ortese's *Il cardillo addolorato* and the Critique of European Modernity

GALA REBANE

Anna Maria Ortese is at once a grand and tragic figure in twentieth-century Italian literature. Anti-consumerist and bashful, a committed animal rights activist and ecologist animated by lay religiosity and an irrational vision of the world, a champion of anarchically libertarian political views, she resisted every attempt to inscribe herself and her art into a niche, to the point of renouncing her participation in prestigious literary competitions for the sake of her own inner peace. Ortese, quite simply, did not enter in syntony with the mainstream morale, ideology, and culture of her time.[1]

With the publication of *Il cardillo addolorato* in 1993, the aged writer was instantly retrieved from the ostentatious neglect of the Italian literary scene.[2] Yet, for many of its critics, *Il cardillo addolorato* and the vision of the world it sustains remained in many respects opaque. What largely accounts for this incomprehension is that *Il cardillo addolorato* represents the fullest compendium of Ortese's provocative political and cultural views, which often puzzled even the most benevolent reviewers. As Ortese herself proudly stated, "[I]o dò cose che non sono richieste. Non rispondo alle richieste degli altri. Per questo non ho avuto successo" ("I give things that are not asked of me. I don't respond to the demands of others. I have not been successful because of this").[3]

"By Necessity a Distortion": Approaching the Narrative

Critics have often noted that an attempt to briefly summarize the events narrated in this puzzling novel is an ungrateful task, leading by necessity to a distortion.[4] Starting as a romantic fairy tale, the story develops over 400 pages to the highest degree of philosophical and artistic complexity, which precludes an unequivocal definition of its genre and a straightforward interpretation.

At the end of the eighteenth century, three young Belgians – the Prince Ingmar Neville, the sculptor Dupré, and the merchant Nodier – travel to Naples. Nodier's aim is to meet with a famous glove maker, Don Mariano Civile, and to commission supplies for his fashion stores. Neville is attracted by the decadent fame and mythical atmosphere of the city, where he hopes to revive his long-lost poetic inspiration. As for their friend Dupré, the visit to Naples is a mere expression of his joyful enthusiasm for life itself.

At Don Mariano's house, the travellers make the acquaintance of two of his daughters, and Dupré immediately falls in love with the eldest of the two, Elmina. As early as the next morning the young sculptor proposes to her and, despite Neville's attempt to interfere and to thwart the betrothal, Dupré gets a favourable answer. In fact, Neville, who so openly displays his contempt towards haughty and impassive Elmina, has himself fallen in love with her. After the marriage, which Neville fails to prevent, the prince goes back to Belgium and returns to Naples only nine years later, to find that Don Mariano, Dupré, and his first-born child with Elmina, Alì Babà, are all dead.

Starting from the second part of the novel, the main plotline intertwines with other uncanny and contradictory subplots that bewilder the reader rather than provide her with insights into the characters' motivation and actions. Spectres of the dead, who dispute with their living relatives over financial matters, flying children, theriomorph creatures, revenants of the executed Jacobins fill the city of Naples and the novel's pages. Neville launches all his shrewdness into the unravelling of these mysteries, but finds himself ever more ensnared in the events which he can neither tackle nor logically grasp.

For Neville, Elmina remains a challenging riddle. She denies herself all joys of life, and favours poverty over all possible benefactions, working as a seamstress in order to preserve her emotional independence. As her sister Teresa states, she would prefer servitude to "l'obbligo del cuore verso altri" (R2 417; "placing her heart under an obligation to others," LL 165). Finally, the prince discovers Elmina's secret: she is bound by an oath given to her late father to protect the *folletto* Hieronymus Käppchen, a goblin of the wood whom Don Mariano had taken years before into his house. In order to avoid his imminent death, after reaching the age of 300 years, which is drawing ever nearer, Käppchen has to be legally adopted by a married couple. Love and concern for the goblin determine Elmina's behaviour, causing her to make self-destructive decisions in an attempt to save him.

In the final part of the novel, the merchant Nodier, who in the meantime had become unimaginably rich, proposes to the widowed Elmina; but as the merchant learns of the *folletto*, he withdraws his proposal, marrying her sister Teresa instead. Finally, Neville offers Elmina his hand and promises to adopt Käppchen, but Elmina turns down his proposal out of fear that her own love for the prince would stand between her and the magic creature. Powerless and despairing, the prince returns to Belgium, where he receives the news of Elmina's and Käppchen's deaths. The novel ends with Neville suddenly hearing the longing, sorrowful chant of a goldfinch, or *the* Goldfinch,[5] whose mysterious presence and enigmatic symbolism have haunted the novel. The *Cardillo*'s song reveals to him the sublime truth of existence: "Benedisse il Cardillo che arrivava, e finalmente gli avrebbe spiegato tutto. La follia e la separazione, il dolore e questa gioia che giungeva adesso con lui: tutta calma, fredda, infinita" (R2 630; "He blessed the Linnet even now arriving, who at last would explain it all. Folly, sorrow, separation, and this joy that he was bringing with him now: utterly calm, and cold, and infinite," LL 325).

An Imagined Community: France versus Naples

At a first glance, history seems to play no significant role in the novel. Although the first lines of the narration – "Verso la fine del Settecento, o Secolo dei Lumi..." (R2 199; "Towards the end of the eighteenth century, or Age of Enlightenment...," LL 3) – suggest the importance of the historical setting, the fairy-tale atmosphere of the first chapters subsequently submerges the historical connotation, making the opening phrase sound like the classical fairy-tale cliché "Once upon a time." The growing spectrality of the events invalidates all truth claims made from a cognitive viewpoint, and reality itself seems to disintegrate in a play of mirrors and shadows, the solutions of all secrets becoming accessible only as a result of "una tragica contrazione degli stati dell'animo" ("a tragic reduction of the state of minds and emotions") of the protagonists.[6]

This impression is, however, misleading. A retrospective calculation allows us to establish a more or less precise date of the travellers' first arrival to Naples. It is late April of 1795, the time when the still-young French Revolution had already made first steps "in fatto del culto dell'economia e della decenza (o dei limiti) del soccorso" [R2 316; "in terms of the cult of economy and decent moderation (or limitation) in questions of aid and comfort," LL 98]. Whereas the narration provides scarce clues to the coterminous events of history, the few directly mentioned dates and historical occurrences have major importance for an interpretation of the novel in endowing the seemingly fantastic plot with a poignant critical dimension. An insight into the complex and not immediately obvious interlacing of the protagonists' vicissitudes in the dreamlike Naples with the historical course of the European Age of Revolutions brings to light Ortese's troubled and polemical vision of modernity that underlies the metaphysics of *Il cardillo addolorato.*

The first part of the novel ends with the marriage of Elmina and Dupré, which takes place on 31 May 1795. This date coincides with the suppression of the Revolutionary Tribunal of Paris, which marked the virtual end of the Revolution and the beginning of Napoleon's ascendance to power. Although Napoleon is only cursorily mentioned in the novel as "il nuovo astro francese" (R2 238; "the rising star in France," LL 32), one of the main protagonists, the merchant Nodier, can be regarded, arguably, as his virtual doppelgänger. A parallel between them is established in the following passage, which aligns Nodier's burgeoning prosperity and influence with Napoleon's political rise:

> tale successo [di Nodier] testimoniava semplicemente dei tempi, e quasi li giustificava: propensione per l'opulenza, purché priva di stile e, naturalmente, ostilità per ogni forma di bellezza interiore e segreta (quindi realmente aristocratica) del vivere. La Rivoluzione c'era stata, ma Napoleone stava incendiando di un nuovo sole il cielo rosato del giovane secolo. La ricchezza non muore! La ricchezza è il reale Paradiso dell'uomo (e peggio per chi è rimasto fuori dai suoi cancelli, come la superba Elmina). (R2 449)

> (such success [of Nodier] was simply a sign of the times, if not indeed a justification of them: that is, a propensity for opulence, as long as deprived of *style,* and, naturally, a hostility towards any deep-felt, unspoken [and therefore truly aristocratic] mode of being. There had been the Revolution, but now Napoleon was lighting the rosy skies of the new century with a new sun. Wealth cannot die! Wealth is the only real Paradise of Mankind (and too bad for those who are stranded outside its gates, like the proud Elmina). [LL 190])

Both Nodier and Napoleon make their vertiginous careers between 1795 and 1804, the very time span in which the narration of *Il cardillo addolorato* unfolds. The political career of Napoleon culminates in 1804 when he is proclaimed emperor of France. In the same year, Neville returns back to Naples only to witness fantastic and tragic events, culminating in the disappearance of both Elmina and Käppchen and the triumph of the merchant.

Furthermore, in order to buttress his legitimacy, Napoleon changes his name from Nabolione di Buonaparte to the French-sounding variant. Similarly, in the novel, Nodier flanks with the historical victors and effectively adopts a new image, becoming known as "il *mercante francese*" ("the French merchant"), or "*il francese di Liegi*" (R2 610; "the Frenchman from Liège," LL 309). Nodier is represented as a "self-made man," a pragmatic and business-minded nouveau-riche, who came to power on the crest of new times. His lack of nobleness and of artistic sense is accentuated in the copious description of "lusso sbalorditivo" (R2 446; "an opulence scarcely imaginable," LL 187) of his Neapolitan mansion, dominated by a heavy palette of colours (golden, blue, pink, and green) in contrast to the delicate hues of rose and azure typical of Naples's interior decoration.[7] Yet the gamut of colours in the merchant's abode connotes realities other than the faerie atmosphere of Parthenope. The occasional "slip" in the combination of green with rose vividly reminds of a famous scene from *Three Sisters* by Chekhov, an author well known to Ortese, with whose "mondo amaro" ("bitter world") she sometimes compared her Naples.[8] In the episode to which I refer, the plebeian parvenu Natalya Ivanovna sports a pink dress mismatched with a green girdle, which stands for her lack of taste and arrant provincialism.[9] Nodier's ostentatious display of his status, assets, and riches echoes the mannerisms of the materialistic and callous Chekhovian character; in much the same way, both Natalya Ivanovna and Nodier manage to seize the domestic power, betraying and ruining their former friends, whose nobleness of spirit they at once envy and despise. The nouveau-riches' assertion of their role and status in society has, perhaps, at all times been accompanied by a vehement rejection and disrespect of tradition perceived as a possible threat to the legitimation of a new order. Yet on a larger scale, it is again to Napoleon, a parvenu himself, that modern history owes some of the most striking episodes of the destruction of traditionally rooted culture.

The enormous mirrors encased in massive frames provide another significant detail of the interior of Nodier's apartment, which confer to it "l'incanto, la profondità di un salotto parigino, e qualcosa di più: la solennità e il prodigio decorativo di un vasto appartamento reale" (R2 447f; "all the enchantment, the expanse and brilliance of a Parisian drawing-room – and something more: the solemnity and prodigality of decoration to be found in some vast chamber in the palace of a king," LL 189). By establishing an illusory connection between Nodier's home and Parisian palaces of French nobility and royalty, the mirrors suggest a metaphoric reflection of Napoleon's vertiginous career in the spectacular progress of the merchant. At the same time, they also imply an absence of depth beneath dazzling surfaces: the only thing that endows Nodier's celestial mirrors with physical substance is their convoluted, heavy, golden and bronze framings, which flaunt the merchant's affluence.

Nodier's guiding principle is economic rationality. Persuading Elmina to get rid of the goblin Käppchen, he proclaims: "Chi non lavora e non guadagna, fa male. È un peso per l'umanità" (R2 623; "Anyone who does no work and earns no money does harm. He is a burden on humanity," LL 319). By secretly marooning the *folletto* in the countryside, as is done with undesired pets, Nodier degrades Käppchen to an animal deprived of any rights. In the same year in which Nodier puts an end to the 300 years' existence of the *folletto,* Napoleon chases the Bourbons from Naples, ending the 300 years of their political dominion.[10] With the triumph of Napoleon in history and Nodier in the novel, modernity with its ideals of rationality and pragmatism fully takes over the old order, giving way to the marginalization of the weak, the powerless, and the destitute.

The intrinsic connection between the coterminous political change in France and the uncanny events in *Il cardillo addolorato*'s Naples, which is mostly revealed through the covert parallels between Nodier and Napoleon, is also explicitly sustained in the last part of the novel, when Ortese describes the victims of her "storie sotterranee" ("subterranean tales") – "fanciulle impassibili" ("impassive girls"), "Folletti disperati" ("desperate Elves"), "Streghe sentimentali" ("sentimental Witches") and "Principi squilibrati" ("deranged Princes") – as "povera gente del bel mondo euro-napoletano, prima e dopo il '93" (R2 606; "poor inhabitants of Europe and of Naples both before and after '93," LL 305). The defeated protagonists of *Il cardillo addolorato* are shown as victims of history and casualties of the betrayed ideals of the Enlightenment, whose weak implorations are drowned out by "rumorosi tempi moderni" (R2 606; "noisy modern times," LL 305).

The Unredeemed Reason

The concept of modernity represents one of the most complex issues in European historical and cultural theory. Critical debates on its essence, definition, duration, and effects encompass contributions by prominent contemporary figures from Habermas to Adorno, from Arendt to Jameson. According to some of these historians and cultural critics, the beginning of modern history dates back to the eighteenth, rather than the sixteenth, century. In their view, the scientific and cultural changes that took place during the Renaissance and the Reformation were merely programmatic, and did not lead to any significant social, cultural, and political changes until the late eighteenth century.[11] In *Il cardillo addolorato,* Ortese espouses a similar vision of the historical transition to European modernity in the decades between the French Revolution and the Restoration. The protagonists' vicissitudes follow upon the major political transformations that swept across Europe, and the dramatic twists of their destinies are much influenced by the changes in the ideology of the dominant order. Yet, whereas official historiography positively views the achievements of the Age of Reason as the formative basis for liberal and democratic aspirations of modern society, Ortese's personal vision of the Enlightenment legacy, expounded in her last book, *Corpo celeste* (*Celestial Body,* 1997), a collection of critical essays and meditations, runs counter to the established opinion.

As Ortese asserts, the Enlightenment gave rise to a new dehumanized culture based on economic rationality: "Una nuova cultura era nata, in vitro, intorno al Settecento, e nei duecento e più anni successivi divenne immensa, spodestò del tutto la prima cultura e oscurò lentamente la sovranità della *dea ragione.* Era la *cultura economica,* figlia primogenita della intelligenza" (CC 145; "A new culture was born in vitro around the eighteenth century that in the course of over two hundred years grew immense, fully supplanting the original culture and slowly eclipsing the sovereignty of the *goddess Reason.* It was the *economic culture,* the firstborn daughter of intelligence").[12] The writer regards both the French Revolution as the ultimate failure of hope for a better social order and future professed by the Enlightenment, and the storming of the Bastille as the very point at which the eighteenth-century ideals were irredeemably thwarted. In her view, at this particular historical juncture, Reason was substituted by Intelligence, which paved the way to the processes of oppression and marginalization disguised as a struggle for freedom and democracy:

Secondo le riflessioni di qualche storico o sociologo o studioso delle cose umane [...], questo ebbe inizio dal momento del suo massimo (della intelligenza) splendore. Dal suo luglio, diciamo. Che coincise con un luglio effettivo: il 14 Luglio francese. La presa della Bastiglia. Allora fu dichiarata la

> sovranità divina dell'Intelligenza, usando però la parola Ragione. Ma non era – nessuno allora poteva saperlo – la Ragione, perché la Ragione non agisce, *vede*, solo l'Intelligenza agisce. E l'Intelligenza, paludata di Ragione, aveva giurato di agire, e fondare la libertà democratica: che non è la libertà del Respiro. È semplicemente la libertà di tutti, la libertà senza limite, che alla fine toglie il Respiro a tutti. (CC 141f)

> (According to the reflections of some historian, sociologist or humanities scholar [...], this change started at the moment of the maximal splendor of Intelligence. Let's say, of its July. That coincided with a specific July: the French 14th of July. The storming of the Bastille. It was then that the divine supremacy of Intelligence was announced under the name of Reason. But it was not – and nobody back then could know it – Reason, because Reason does not act, it *sees*, only Intelligence acts. And Intelligence under the guise of Reason swore to act and to found democratic liberty: which is not the liberty of Breath. It is merely liberty of all, liberty without limits, which in the end takes away the Breath from all.)

The opposition between the apparently synonymous Reason and Intelligence plays an important role in *Il cardillo addolorato* and in Ortese's oeuvre. For Ortese, "la mite e umiliata Ragione" (CC 153; "the meek and humbled Reason") embodies the very spirit of nature, respect for all living things, and the ability to bestow selfless love and compassion on others. Intelligence, on the contrary, represents dehumanizing rationalism and uniformity, pragmatic erasure of differences between various life forms, and the constraint of altruistic impulses.

Finding its fullest expression in the character of Ingmar Neville, this antinomy is reflected and negotiated in the development he undergoes in the course of the novel. Neville has for too long refused to believe in the simple truth of Elmina's sufferance and devotion to the *folletto*. Striving instead to explain and solve her secret in a "rational" way, he irreparably misses the chance to redeem Käppchen and his "sister." In a conversation with the old Duke Benjamin Ruskaja, concerning the identity of the *folletto*, Neville presumes that Elmina's mysterious protégé is another, perhaps illegitimate son of the late Albert Dupré. Upon this erroneous conclusion, his perception of Käppchen instantly shifts from the vision of an "ossesso, col suo mal caduco e gli occhi ciechi, con la sua ripugnante penna di gallina in testa, quell'orrore vivente" ("half-witted child with his falling sickness and his blind eyes and that repugnant hen's feather on his head, that living horror") to the image of a "ragazzetto

[...] piuttosto maleducato [...] ma né insano né deforme" (R2 486; "somewhat ill-mannered [...] but at least not sick or deformed [boy]," LL 217) which fills the prince with joyous relief:

> "Dunque...aborri tanto la bruttezza...la miseria fisica...la malattia?" chiese, appena malinconico, in un mormorio, il Duca.
>
> "Oh, sì! È più forte di me...Le detesto!" ridendo, anche se un po' vergognoso, Ingmar.
>
> "Eppure, il mondo è proprio questo: decadenza, orrore, piccolo strazio o deformità quotidiana, e non vi è molta verità in tutto il resto." (R2 487)

> ("Do you have such an abhorrence of ugliness, sickness, bodily wretchedness?" asked the Duke in a faintly melancholy murmur.
>
> "Oh, yes! It is something stronger than I am...I detest them," replied Ingmar, laughing but a little shamefaced.
>
> "Yet this is what the world really is: horror and decay, small everyday torments and deformities; and there is not much truth in all the rest of it." [LL 217])

Convinced, at the beginning of the novel, of his ability as well as his right to fathom human minds and hearts, Neville believes himself authorized to interfere in, and to judge, others' lives, criminalizing those manifestations of autonomous will that do not comply with his wishful thinking. But as the narration unfolds, the prince's judgments and deeds are disclosed as being dictated by his egoism, arrogance, jealousy, and possessiveness. His "reason," which has to be understood in this context as an ability to comprehend and accept the *otherness* in its humblest forms, remains, for a long time, occluded by his personal psychological inhibitions and repressed desires. Only in the second half of the novel does the prince experience a painful transformation, learning to perceive deeper truths beneath the glossy veneer of "reality."

The ultimate defeat of Neville also appears to be a result of his self-justification with regard to the narrative of "reason," which serves to screen his egoistic drives and ambition for power, and has also contributed to the ruin of the *folletto,* by having denied Käppchen a place of recognition in the cognitive structures of "reality" and thereby abolishing his very right to exist. As the notary Scribblerus remarks with regard to the tragic end of Elmina and Käppchen, the devastation of small but dear liberties of humankind and of last secretive affections concealed in people's hearts is "la normale occupazione di tutti i forti, anche se mascherati da maestri e liberatori" (R2 626; "the normal occupation of all the potentates of the earth, even when disguised as teachers or as liberators," LL 321). Although Scribblerus apparently refers to the ignominious Nodier, his statement also bears covert judgment on Neville's former attitudes and behaviour.

At the end of the novel, Neville finally acknowledges his own connivance with the forces that ruined Käppchen and Elmina: "capì di essere anche lui parte di quella *infamia* di cui accusava sempre, con giovanile vivacità e ingiustizia, il mondo. Per prendere il posto del Portapacchi nel cuore dell'antica bambina, egli aveva già acconsentito, nel suo cuore di razza umana, alla totale rovina e scomparsa di H. Käppchen" (R2 587; "It came home to him that he too was part of that *iniquity* of which, with the vehemence and injustice of youth, he ceaselessly accused the world. To take the place of the Porter-Boy in Elmina's heart he had already consented, in his own all-too-human heart, to the total ruin and obliteration of H. Käppchen," LL 289). At the end of the novel, the sudden manifestation of the "cardillo," "*Padre degli orfani e delle stesse animucce infernali, come il piccolo vecchio Käppchen, che vagano smarrite sulla terra*" (R2 619; "*Father of orphans and even of the little souls from the lower regions, like poor agèd Käppchen, who wander bewildered over the face of the earth,*" LL 315)[13] to the dying Neville signals his final conversion to merciful and compassionate Reason, which for too long remained occluded by his yearning for power and control.

The Ideology of the Enlightenment: *La Joie*

While Neville's personal failure exemplifies the defeat of the political utopia of the Enlightenment, the short story of Albert Dupré provides an insight into the tragic fiasco of its ideology. Dupré, the epitome of the artist, pursues a sole project, *La Joie*, a bust of a child which should embody "una cosa superiore alla comprensione umana, di cui non c'è spiegazione, e perciò rassomigliante a un gemito in un cielo di bellezza altrettanto azzurra, totale, festosa, inesplicabile" (R2 344; "a thing transcending human comprehension, a thing for which there is no explanation, and therefore akin to a lamenting cry in a beauteous heaven as blue as it is total, gladsome, inexplicable," LL 110).

The model for the sculptures is his own son Alí Babá, born in April of 1800, a date that Albert renders in the terms of the French post-revolutionary calendar: for him, indeed, it is "18 germinale" (R2 343; "the 18th of germinal," LL 108). The importance placed on the revolutionary calendar pinpoints Dupré's enthusiasm for the Revolution, alluding with the word "germinal" to the germs of new artistic ideas that should burgeon. At the same time, the title of the novel's second part, "Breve storia di Babà (*La Joie*)" ("Brief Tale of Baba [*La Joie*]") suggests the brevity of the period of hope for a possible fundamental change professed by the Enlightenment enthusiasts, and pre-announces the imminent fiasco of their project curbed by "la infame galoppata della Rivoluzione francese" (R2 537; "the infamous onslaught of the French Revolution," LL 254).

Dupré chisels over 200 variants of *La Joie*, and yet remains dissatisfied with the results. The last sculpture, which stuns everyone by its superhuman expressivity, represents the child sleeping and smiling in his dream. Joy in the dream cannot, however, supersede the hostility of the real world. Baba dies and his posthumous bust becomes an object of art trade, acquired by the king of Naples for his antechamber. Later, Sasà Dupré, the second child of Albert and Elmina, calls the busts in the old atelier of her father "le uova del Cardillo" (R2 389; "the [Goldfinch's] eggs," LL 143). The unaccomplished project of *La Joie* reflects the actual defeat of the Enlightenment ideas: the germs that never burgeoned and the eggs that never hatched to free the progeny of the Goldfinch, the protector of all the oppressed and disempowered.

The failure of the great Enlightenment philosophers to make their dream of universal joy come true is later acknowledged by Neville, who finally understands the incompatibility of grand theoretical projects and the compassionate involvement with the marginal, the weak, and the powerless:

> anche lui, interrogato circa la propria devozione al Cardillo, non avrebbe saputo rispondere senza peccare di presunzione, o infilare sciocchezze – né avrebbe potuto appellarsi coerentemente a Rousseau o Voltaire e altri eminenti Maestri del Mutamento, in quanto vero Mutamento il loro pensiero non aveva portato [...]. E avvertiva che questo, appunto, era mancato, nel nuovo e antico farsi del mondo: il rispetto dell'alba, del pianto del Cardillo; e del suo ordine di restare fedeli – come i fanciulli dei boschi e le loro sorelle – al Nulla, al Poco, e alla pietà per il Nulla, alla compassione per l'Abbandonato, al riguardo sommo per ogni Hieronymus Käppchen e la sua penna di gallina. (R2 607)

> (even he, if questioned about his devotion to the Goldfinch, would not have been able to answer without erring on the side of presumptuousness, or coming out with a lot of nonsense. Nor would he have been able to make

> any coherent appeal to Rousseau, Voltaire or other eminent Masters of Change, since their thought had not brought about real Change (they held it was enough to understand the order of the stars). And he realized that what was lacking in both the old and the new ways of the world was precisely this: respect for the dawn and the weeping of the (Goldfinch), and his command to remain faithful – like the children of the woods and their sisters – to that which is Nothing, or Little, to have pity for Nothingness, compassion for those cast out and abandoned, and supreme regard for every Hieronymus Käppchen and his hen's feather. [LL 307])

Ortese's critique of the political programs that claim to benefit humankind in its totality but in reality lead to marginalization and exclusion is expressed in Elmina's refusal of *enjoyment,* in her "*No* sempiterno a tutti i programmi della *Joie*" (R2 540; "eternal *No* to any of the propositions of *la Joie,*" LL 256). It is only at the end of the novel that the prince Neville reappraises the ultimate reasons of Elmina' behaviour as having been caused not by the woman's "rusticity" but by her husband's betrayal, and he is finally able to see her silent resistance to the sculptor's ethically misplaced purports in a true light.

"La felicità in terra": The Declaration of the Rights of Man

Even the apparently most humanistic endeavours to create a better future in *Il cardillo addolorato* reveal their dark underside. One such master narrative, which directly contributes to the tragic end of Käppchen, is the French Declaration of the Rights of Man, whose first version, implemented in 1789, had in its turn been inspired by the United States' Declaration of Independence (1776).

1776 is another historical date that interrelates in a crucial manner to the destinies of the protagonists. In this year, Don Mariano's late wife, Brigitta Helm, "donated" him the family house Casarella (Little House). At the end of the novel, she returns as a spectre to claim the money for it from Elmina and enters into an alliance with Nodier. The connection between "grand" history and the characters' fates is underpinned in the scene of the negotiations between the dead and the living, when the old servant Ferrantina mockingly questions Neville and his friend, the Duke of Ruskaja, who try to interfere and help Elmina: "E questo ve l'ha detto l'America, con la sua Costituzione, che la felicità in terra esiste, e anzi è il primo dovere?" (R2 598; "Have you learned this from America and its blessed Constitution, this idea that happiness exists on earth, and is in fact our first duty?" LL 298). Indeed, in its first lines, the American Declaration of Independence stipulates: "We hold these truths to be self-evident, that all men are created equal, that they are endowed by their Creator with certain unalienable Rights, that among these are Life, Liberty and the pursuit of Happiness."[14]

The second, longer version of the French Declaration of the Rights of Man was adopted in 1793. Based on the philosophical tenets of the Enlightenment, the Declaration was devised as a set of universally valid laws that guaranteed the rights of all human beings. Yet, by placing "Man" at the centre of the universe, the Enlightenment thinkers also tacitly sustained his supremacy over Nature and all forms of Otherness, eschewing every mention of rights for those who did not comply with the concept of (hu)man.[15] In the novel, the Declaration plays an indeed fated role, being the very document which condemns Käppchen, "un'anima persa in questo mondo dopo la dichiarazione dei Diritti dell'Uomo e quindi della sua sovranità" (R2 536; "a lost soul in this world ever since the declaration of the Rights of Man and of his consequent sovereignty," LL 253), to an imminent death. Affirming, in a conversation with Neville, that Käppchen dreads Christianity, all of humankind, but especially human rights and the declaration, Nodier defines both Elmina and the *folletto* as "morti alla giustizia" (R2 537; "dead to Justice," LL 254).

Käppchen and all the other earthly creatures of the novel (the *piccerilli*, the little ones) are silenced by the means of proscriptive texts and narratives that legalized the compliant, and outlawed the nonconformist. As Neville retorts to the defenders of progress at the end of the novel, this leads to the justification of an infinite cruelty of the self-proclaimed masters of nature towards the hapless and marginalized "piccini della terra" ("the little ones of the Earth"): "Parlo dei potenti della terra, Signori, e della loro certezza – democratici o meno, buoni sovrani o cattivi dittatori – di essere 'i primi,' di essere in diritto di disporre dei boschi e dei loro fanciulli" (R2 607; "I am speaking of the potentates of the earth, gentlemen – democratic or otherwise, worthy sovereigns or wicked dictators – and their certainty that they are 'the First,' that they have a right to dispose at will of the woodlands and the children of the woodlands," LL 306f).

The Silence of Chimera: Discursive Marginalization and Narrative Resistance

Whereas the *folletto* is outlawed and doomed to death by the Declaration of the Rights of Man, which bestowed upon man the power over life and death of his "inferiors," Elmina, who unflaggingly follows her moral duty of protecting Käppchen, is subjected to discursive marginalization, inflicted on her by male-dominated narrative norms and conventions that deny her personal will and agency. Throughout the novel, she is seen mainly through Neville's perspective. Secretly craving Elmina but screening his desire even from himself, the prince attempts to appropriate and dominate her discursively through the incessantly changing and contradictory narratives, in which he sublimates his erotic drive.

Neville often refers to Elmina as "Chimera," or even, contemptuously, as "Capra" ("Goat"). In her interpretation of the semantics of this epithet, Flora Ghezzo observes that the theriomorphism of Elmina as Chimera connotes the woman's affinity with the *folletto*, and stands for the profound alterity of the feminine. The critic shows that the nexus between the female and the animal, which originated in the Aristotelian definition of the feminine as monstrous, anomalous, and incomplete, is deeply ingrained in the male imaginary.[16] Thus Neville's imputation reveals a phallogocentric bias determining his vision of Elmina.

Another male character, who also purports to objectify Elmina and inscribe her into his male fantasies, is Dupré. His first encounter with Don Mariano's two beautiful daughters, described as "insopportabilmente *mute*" (R2 200; "insufferably *silent,*" LL 3), takes place in a suggestive fairy-tale setting. The "fastoso palazzo a colonne doriche" ("splendid Doric-columned palace"), where Don Mariano resides, rises above the sea like a castle; a place full of roses, it is immersed in an atmosphere of "una stranezza o un sogno" (R2 202; "a dream or an incongruity," LL 5) – all of which is strongly reminiscent of *Sleeping Beauty*. The young sculptor eagerly takes upon himself the role of a prince who is to wake the enchanted princess. His wishful ideas are laid bare in the description of the dream Dupré has the following night, in which he envisages a miraculous resurrection of Elmina's and Teresa's goldfinch, whose death was discussed during the visit to the Civile family. The central elements of Dupré's vision – the *kiss* Teresa gives the bird, the *rose* light of the sunrise, the feeling that the wickedness of life is only a *dream* – likewise evoke the imagery of *Sleeping Beauty*. Waking up, Dupré exclaims: "È vivo! La malvagità non è vera! La morte mente, ed Elmina mi ama!" (R2 219; "It's alive! The cruelty isn't true! Death is a liar and Elmina loves me!," LL 18). The enthusiastic conclusion of the sculptor does not rely on any logic other than that of the fairy-tale scenario, from which Elmina's personality, will, and intentions are excluded.

In fact, Elmina's presumed *mutismo* is disclaimed already in the beginning of the novel. She speaks for herself and makes straightforward assertions, which, however, are dismissed as irrelevant by Dupré in his conversation with Neville:

> "Mi par strano che don Mariano ti abbia scelto come sposo – e sposo senza un soldo – della sua bella e ambitissima figlia; inoltre, dopo averti visto appena una seconda volta, e in una così brutta circostanza. La cosa mi sembra curiosa ... a te, no?"
>
> "No ... Perché?" ma subito il volto di Albert si fece pensoso [...] "Ma lasciami ritornare, ti prego, a quel momento meraviglioso, in cui l'ho vista venirmi incontro [...] e dirmi con bontà, guardandomi in fronte: 'Accetto la mia sorte per l'obbedienza che devo a mio padre, *mon cher Albert.* Non desideravo alcun matrimonio, ma vivere con lui sempre. Così non può essere. Sia come non detto.'" [...]
>
> "Forse ne ama un altro, ma ... sarà cosa da non poterci dire."
>
> "Possibile" annuì Albert senza veramente comprendere. "Ha un'anima così profonda, così meravigliosa ..." e, ciò dicendo, parve piombare in un sogno. (R2 243)
>
> ("To me it seems strange that Don Mariano has chosen you as a husband – and a penniless husband at that – for his beautiful and much sought-after daughter; and that when seeing you for only the second time, and in such distressing circumstances. It seems to me curious ... Does it not seem so to you?"
>
> "No... Why should it?" But Albert's face at once grew pensive. [...] "But please let me go back to that wonderful moment, when I saw her approaching me [...] to tell me graciously, looking me in the face: 'I accept my destiny on account of the obedience I owe my father, *mon cher Albert.* I did not desire any marriage, but rather to live with him for ever. That cannot be. Let it be forgotten.'" [...]
>
> "Perhaps she loves another, but...one can scarcely know."
>
> "Perhaps," agreed Albert without fully understanding. "She has such a profound, such a wonderful soul ..." And, so saying, he appeared to fall into a reverie. [LL 36])

Dupré falls prey to his blind belief in master narratives – the master narratives of fairy tales, to which he strives to reduce the complexity of life, eluding the unwanted truths. The first presage of both Dupré's imminent defeat and his inglorious part in Elmina's destiny appears already in the opening chapter where the sculptor is compared to the Greek hero Bellerophon. According to the myth, Bellerophon killed the monstrous

Chimera and tamed Pegasus; yet his feats led him to arrogance, for which the gods punished him with insanity. The tragic fate of Dupré uncannily parallels the myth. Disillusioned by the reality of his marriage, Dupré slights and ignores Elmina, the Chimera of the story, crushing her initial hopes of rescuing Käppchen through an adoption. He also fails in his pursuit of *La Joie*, both as an artistic project and as the happiness of fatherhood, losing his reason after Baba's death. Thinking of the misfortunes of the spouses, Neville refers again to the Greek myth: "'Povera Elmina,' pensò, 'tenera Chimera, e tu, mio sfortunato Bellerofonte!'" (R2 363; "'Poor Elmina,' he thought, 'tender Chimera! And you, luckless Bellerophon!,'" LL 125).[17]

Dupré is punished for his presumptuousness, which makes him forget his moral obligations and snub Elmina for her silent refusal to comply with the fairy-tale logic he has superimposed on her. The doom of the sculptor is an inevitable consequence of his attempt to master reality with narrative constructs. At this point, the Bellerophon parallel may also, supposedly, be read as an intertextual polemics with *Chimera* (1972) by John Barth, whose third novella, bearing the title "Bellerophoniad," retells the story of the Greek hero.[18] In Barth's novella, Bellerophon is an experimental novelist, an exemplification of the artist, who exhausts himself in the futile attempts to write a revolutionary novel, suffering an imminent fiasco. Striving to truly immortalize himself in the form of a permanent myth, the hero resolves to set off to slay "the Chimera of his life."

While Barth's is a playful elaboration on the postmodernist idea that "fictions" can be "truer than fact" (or even, as Jacques Derrida famously put it, "il n'y a rien hors du texte" – "there is nothing outside the text"), Ortese critically questions this proposition. In *Il cardillo addolorato*, she remarks that fiction and fairy tales only mask and hide away deeper truths of existence:

> Sono, retorica e letteratura da strapazzo, porte dorate e cesellate, opera dei gioiellieri del sogno. Ma, una volta aperte, solo la scura e fredda vita geme, come un'acqua, al piede degli scalini. E vedrai anche tu, curioso Lettore, seguendo questa storia, come là dietro, non c'è nulla. Udrai solo, là in fondo, un povero *glu-glu*. (R2 203)

> (Rhetoric and Grub Street literature are but carved and gilded doors wrought by the artificers of dreams. But, once they are opened, nothing stirs but life, dark and cold, like a trickle of water at the foot of the

doorsteps. You too, curious reader, as you follow this story, will see that they open onto nothing. And nothing will you hear, there below, but a pathetic *gurgle-gurgle.* [LL 6])

Whereas Barth's "chimera" – also ludically transformed through a play on words into "kamara," a hermetic sequence of Chinese boxes – metaphorically stands for fiction, which relentlessly coils upon itself absorbing into its endless spiral progression ever more layers of "reality," the Chimera of Ortese's novel represents the very opposite of it: the sublime truth that cannot be put into words and thus withstands its narrative profanation and distortion. The resistance of Elmina to all the attempts to inscribe her into the male-centred narratives assumes the form of silence. Yet it is not the passive *mutismo* attributed to her by Nodier and Dupré but, rather, silence as an active rejection of the male imputation, and, along with that, as a pledge of her autonomous will: "Il Cardillo, per salvare Käppchen, aveva fissato un prezzo: la giovinezza, e il silenzio eterno … di Elmina sul suo segreto" (R2 614; "To save Käppchen the cardillo had fixed a price: Elmina's youth and her eternal silence about her secret," LL 311). The mute rebellion of the protagonist is directed against the manipulative use of discourse by the potent and dominant order.

Reality beyond the Visible: Art and Language

Yet not only silence, but "parole" too, can become an instrument of resistance. In *Il cardillo,* language attains an important role, creating cognitive oscillation, which helps to accommodate both the "realistic" version of events and their oneiric transformation within the narration. As Mavina Papini states:

La parola acquista una portata dissacrante: si slega infatti dai vincoli per fluttuare nel mondo del forse, il luogo dove coesistono il vero e il suo contrario, e nel quale l'abisso – la soglia – si apre tra opposizioni antitetiche e viene colmato dalla magia e dal sogno. Si assiste al ribaltamento della struttura normativa, intesa quale strumento capace di arginare la libertà anche sul piano dell'espressione. L'ordine fondato sulla razionalità viene sovvertito e si afferma la "pervasività" del sogno e dell'irreale, che si impongono quali strumenti di trasgressione: una scelta per mezzo della quale la Ortese accorda la propria adesione poetica a una visione *mobile* del mondo, sul quale poggia il proprio sguardo per raccontare l'intrinseca ambiguità che lo contrassegna.

(Language acquires the ability to debunk. It unleashes itself from its own binds to float in the world of the maybe, the place of coexistence of the true and its opposite, and in that abyss – the threshold – it opens between antithetical oppositions and is filled by magic and dreams. We witness the overturning of the normative structure, understood as an instrument capable of limiting freedom, even of the level of expression. The order founded on rationality becomes subverted, affirming the "pervasiveness" of dreams and the unreal, both of which present themselves as instruments of transgression: a choice that allows Ortese to harmonize her own personal poetics with a *mobile* vision of the world, onto which she rests her gaze to tell the intrinsic ambiguity that characterizes it.)[19]

Still, Sharon Wood remarks that "Ortese may deal in metaphysics, but she has precise ideas about the need for a social order based on civil rights and obligations."[20] Ortese's insight into the malleable and inscrutable nature of reality is not an alternative mode of cognition but an exacting criticism on realism as the "literary outpost of an economic and social order, rooted in the distorted and corrupted ideals of the Enlightenment."[21]

At the same time, the relationship between the real and the fantastic in the novel is not that of a sheer antinomy. Rather, both are shown as inalienable and mutually complementary aspects of human existence: "[L]a 'realtà' e 'l'irrealtà' non sono in Anna Maria Ortese due entità distinte, due concetti separati e di norma incomunicabili; ma non sono neppure le facce speculari e contrapposte di una stessa dimensione, per cui il fatto o l'accadimento può essere visto e interpretato in almeno due modi del tutto diversi" ("'Reality' and 'unreality' are not two distinct entities in Anna Maria Ortese, two separate concepts of incommunicable norms; but they are neither the specular and opposing faces of one sole dimension, so that the fact or event can be seen and interpreted in at least two ways which are wholly different").[22]

The interrelation and the duplicitous co-presence of the "real" and the "fantastic" are prominently thematized in the novel with regard to the subject of art. Art as a non-cognitive, visionary experience transcends the boundaries of objective reality in an act of oneiric transformation. Ortese says that, while for an adult, or a highly civilized person, reality is "il mondo dell'ovvio, del luogo comune" (CC 58f; "the world of the obvious, of the common place"), for children and for a certain kind of artists the encounter with the world is an experience of sublime ecstasy.

In *Il cardillo addolorato,* children are represented as mediators between the domains of the real and the fantastic, and have an especially important role in two significant episodes dealing with art. Ortese observes that adult narratives deny proper recognition to children, replacing it with conventional structures of objectified inscription. Yet children invisibly partake in the events that they witness, and see things that are suppressed in the "realistic" accounts. The accessibility of the invisible to the child's gaze is reflected in the description of Baba's bust, which Dupré creates before his last masterpiece:

> L'artista era riuscito, si diceva, a rendere finalmente, forse per il gran male che aveva patito, tutta la dolcezza di quel visino, e lo sguardo spaurito degli occhi che sembrava seguissero una *palummella* invisibile agli altri, mentre si spostava nell'aria. E anzi Albert aveva chiamato quell'opera proprio *La paloma* (mentre solo una colombina, non una farfalla, accucciata sulla spalla del bambino, sembrava aver originato quella bontà e quella pace). (R2 166)

> (The artist had at last succeeded, it was said, owing perhaps to his great sufferings, in gendering all the sweetness of that face, and the startled look in the eyes that appeared to be following the aerial flutterings of a butterfly[23] invisible to others. Indeed Albert had entitled the work *La paloma* (while nothing less than a dove, by no means a butterfly, sitting on the child's shoulder, appeared to have created all that peace and heartsease). (LL 123f))

Just as a butterfly is invisibly present in this sculpture, the whole episode encompasses one more invisible character, Baba's younger sister, Alessandrina (Sasà) Dupré. The part of the novel assigned to her "*brutta storia*" is subtitled "*La Paummella*" – a name, meaning "butterfly" in the Neapolitan dialect ("*palummella*"), which Sasà mispronounces, even though it is her nickname.

The girl is never mentioned in the chapters dedicated to her father and elder brother, and appears in the narration only after their deaths. Sasà is described as the opposite of Baba's "splendore di mattino" (R2 373; "early-morning splendor," LL 132): she is tiny, unintelligent, and even a little ugly, which makes her unfit for the grand project of *La Joie*. Yet while Dupré, tragically torn between his ideological ambition and his creative talent, screens Sasà's existence in the last and the only marketable bust of a peacefully sleeping Baba, in his second to last sculpture, *La paloma*, which never finds a buyer, he nevertheless succumbs to his visionary artistic impulse, introducing Palummella-Sasà as an invisible and disquieting part of the composition that precludes it from lapsing into a bland self-acquiescence.

In the description of this sculpture Ortese plays with the consonance of the bust's title *Paloma* with both the Neapolitan dialectal word "*palomma*" (butterfly), synonymous with "*palummella*" and the Spanish word "*paloma*," meaning "dove." This paronomasia creates a moment of onto-epistemic uncertainty, connoting at once the visible and the concealed, the voiced and the unsaid. Sasà as a butterfly is a disturbing entity expelled from the tangible inventory of *La Joie* and replaced in the bust by a peaceful dove; yet the relation of an irresolvable indeterminacy between the sign, the signified, and the signifier, inscribes Sasà into the artistic composition as its inalienable, invisible element.

Simultaneous co-presence of the visible and the invisible, reflected in the duality of her identity, characterizes Sasà throughout the rest of the narration. The girl belongs, at once, to the adult-like realm of the "real" and the child-like realm of the "unreal." On the one hand, she already schemes in an adult manner her marriage with the rich Neapolitan heir Gerontino Durante, and in the end of the novel moves in with Nodier and Teresa, whose protection secures her a more advantageous future than a life with Elmina. At the same time, Sasà embodies a magic dimension: when no one can see her, she magically loses her gravity and flies. Catching a glimpse of the girl rising in the air, Prince Neville thinks that Sasà has two souls: "una piena di paura, e l'altra gioiosa" (R2 422; "the one full of fear and the other of joy," LL 169). Sasà's flights are acts of creative self-expression and assertion of her alter ego as *Paummella*, acts which liberate her from, and protect her against, the harsh reality of the grown-ups' world.

One further example of such "duality" of children's nature can be found in the story of Florì, the mysterious dead sister of Elmina. The girl figures in the novel under two names: that of the beautiful Floridia Helm and that of the humble Nadina Civile, or *Soricinella*. The narrative leaves this uncertainty largely unresolved, neither validating any version of the Civiles' family past that would give credit to the existence of either, nor ruling out the possibility of the existence of *two* children with non-autonomous, interrelated identities, some kind of ontological "Siamese twins." To make the mystery even more dense, Florì's image appears and disappears in a medallion; likewise, Nadina's name manifests and then fades before a bewildered prince Neville on a tombstone in the burial chapel of the Civiles, which also bears the names of Hieronymus Käppchen and the yet-unborn Babà. The deceitful miniature and the vanishing text suggest malleability and unreliability of the apparent, at the same time hinting at the presence of the invisible within the "real."

The issue of the "tangible" and the "illusory" aspects of reality, and of the role of art in their representation, is addressed with the juxtaposition of two homonymous characters: the spoilt young boy Gerontino Durante-Watteau, for whose aunt Elmina works as seamstress, and the *folletto*, one of whose many names is, effectively, Geronte. Contrary to the case of Floridia / Nadina, Durante-Watteau and Käppchen are two unambiguously different personae; yet they too, at some point appear to fuse into one character both for Neville, who is speculating on their respective identities and roles in Elmina's life, and for the puzzled reader of the novel.

While investigating Elmina's secret, Neville hears an enigmatic voice telling him to search for "*le Vieux Poussin*." This phrase is, arguably, another intelligent wordplay. First, it is a reference to Käppchen, who sometimes transforms into a little chick (*pulcino* in Italian, *poussin* in French), so that the denomination "*Vieux Poussin*" can be interpreted as "old chick," or "Geronte il Pulcino" (in Greek γέρος means old). Along with that, "the old Poussin" connotes the renowned classicist painter Nicolas Poussin (1594–1665). The double onomastic association of the *folletto* with Nicolas Poussin on the one hand and Gerontino Durante-Watteau on the other seems to serve the sole purpose of emphasizing the otherwise inconspicuous reference to another figure of art history: namely, Jean-Antoine Watteau (1684–1721), a famous late Baroque French painter.

Watteau's masterpiece, *L'Enseigne de Gersaint* (1720), which is often compared to Velázquez's *Las Meninas*, represents an art gallery with a magically vanished front wall. The picture creates a vision of multilayered reality(-ies), where the objects and their representations are inseparable, and merge into one theatrical event. There are no clues for the actual reasons that led Ortese to encode Jean-Antoine Watteau's name in the name of her lateral character Gerontino. At the same time, the hypothesis about a hidden reference to *L'Enseigne de Gersaint* readily evokes a wide range of associations that connect Watteau's painting to some of the central issues raised in *Il cardillo addolorato*: the arbitrariness of the spectator's gaze, the fluidity of the boundary between the phenomenal world and its artistic reflections, and the onto-epistemic value of the apparent. Just as the *mise en abyme* effected in *L'Enseigne de Gersaint* makes a viewer ponder the hierarchy of its different diegetic levels and her / his own position with relation to these, the multiple narrative leads of the novel raise the problem of the unresolved dialectical tension between reality and its representations, in whose Chinese-box convolutions Neville finds himself irremediably trapped. Paradoxically, the revelation at which Neville arrives may be related with the final words of the aforementioned novella by John Barth: "It is no *Bellerophoniad.* It is a." Yet while here the missing part of the last sentence is supplied by the novel's title – "It is no *Bellerophoniad.* It is a *Chimera,*" thus closing the mise-en-abyme sequence upon itself, in *Il cardillo addolorato* the self-referential and self-reproducing narratives of the "viaggio istruttivo di Bellerofonte" ("instructive excursion of Bellerophon") finally collapse, giving way to the "'silenzio' glaciale dell'Universo" (R2 605; "glacial 'silence' of the Universe," LL 306), the inaudible, invisible, and unspeakable truth of existence. This truth is exposed by the omission between the dying *folletto*'s "Nein ... Nein ... Nein..." and "Ja ... Ja ... Ja ...," the two opposite poles of a missing referent; it surfaces in the maddening moment of the realization that no signifier can be relied on as Florì's image is vanishing in the medallion and the name of her alter ego Nadina is fading from her tombstone (R2 600; LL 299).

And yet Albert Dupré's masterpiece *La paloma* manages to capture the very ineffable essence of truth. Although its disquieting presence is effaced from the name and forms of the sculpture, it nevertheless can be retraced in the child's awe in the face of the ensuing lacuna. In *Corpo Celeste,* Ortese says:

> La tragedia della mia vita [...] fu dunque nello scoprire quasi subito che tutte le cose – anche persone, volti, libri – erano vuoto e apparenza, erano *immagini,* la cui materialità e libertà erano tutte illusorie. Una sola cosa viveva veramente, era quasi altro dal vivere della materia: il dolore e l'emozione dolorosa (metto fra queste emozioni anche l'amore e la gioia). (CC 82)
>
> (The tragedy of my life [...] thus consisted in the nearly immediate discovery that everything – even people, faces, books – were void and appearance, they were *images,* whose substance and liberty were but just an illusion. Only one thing lived really, and was practically the reverse of a material being: pain and a painful emotion (and I also include in these emotions love and joy).)

For Ortese, visionary artists and children – those standing closest to nature, which itself is "l'uomo senza tempo, l'uomo che sogna" ("a man outside time, a dreaming man"), access the sublime truth of existence through their awed emotion – pain and joy at once – upon witnessing the universe: "il vero Irreale, il luogo non pensabile" (CC 102; "the true Unreal, an inconceivable place").

Submerged Geographies and the Realm of the Goldfinch

Il cardillo addolorato abounds with references to other countries, languages, and arts, all united in a "melancholic palimpsest."[24] The great European culture, which used to be "luogo di memoria e di avvertimenti" ("the site of memory and of warnings") but with the advent of modernity became "dormitorio di sogni e ufficio distribuzione di promesse menzognere" (CC 144; "a dormitory of dreams and an office of distribution of mendacious promises") is integrated into the narrative fabric through a series of complex onomastic puns and references, typical for Ortese's writing.[25]

The "documented" name of the *folletto*, Hieronymus Käppchen, apparently contains one further reference to the history of art. In her insightful article on *Il cardillo addolorato*, Flora Ghezzo makes a conjecture on a possible relation between Hieronymus Käppchen and the fifteenth-century artist Hieronymus Bosch, whose famous triptych, *Last Judgment*, features in the central panel "una bizzarra creatura antropomorfa, una sorta di gnomo o folletto fortemente raccorciato – un volto umano avvolto in un ampio copricapo da cui svettano due penne e un paio di piedi" ("a bizarre anthropomorphic creature, a sort of gnome or forcefully truncated goblin – one human face wrapped in an ample head scarf from which jut out two horns and a pair of feet"), strikingly reminiscent of *Il cardillo addolorato*'s uncanny protagonist.[26] Although the critic remarks that there is no substantial evidence of Ortese's actual intention to establish a link between the Flemish painter and this literary character,[27] the validity of her hypothesis is corroborated by several details. First, both the painter and the *folletto* come from late medieval northern Europe. Furthermore, Bosch's posthumous fame is also connected to Bourbon Spain: after the painter's death, many of Bosch's works were acquired by the Spanish king Phillip II, and some of them still belong to El Prado Museum of Madrid. Finally, the Spanish rendition of the artist's name is "El Bosco," homonymic with the Italian word "il bosco," the forest,[28] and it is in the woods near Cologne that the *folletto* Käppchen is found.

Besides, Ortese's possible intertextual allusion to Bosch may also be regarded as a way to intensify the authorial vision of the unfathomable and irrational complexity of the world. Bosch's oneiric pictures, densely populated by the most phantasmagorical creatures, call into question the very notion of "human." Two great visionaries, Bosch and Ortese, reflect in their works the intrinsic therianthropy of the living nature, the simultaneous presence of the bestial in humans and of the human element in animals. Bosch's pictorial worlds, whose compositional structure is at first blended out by the amassment of separate fragments and details, all of them endowed with a certain visual autonomy, uncannily parallel the narrative universe of *Il cardillo addolorato*, whose structural complexity makes the reader's alter ego, Neville, take numerous wrong leads before he is finally able to abstract from the often contradictory particulars and perceive the gist of the whole.

Even if Ortese's reference to Hieronymus Bosch should remain, in the absence of documented evidence, only a hypothesis, the attempted juxtaposition of the Italian writer and the medieval Flemish painter also serves the purpose of highlighting, as Ghezzo states, "gli inaspettati percorsi sotteranei dell'immaginario folklorico e leggendario europeo" ("the unexpected subterranean travels of folkloric imaginary and European legend").[29] As I have already stated, different names of the *folletto* Käppchen readily evoke Hieronymus Bosch and Nicolas Poussin; Gerontino Durante-Watteau is a namesake of Jean-Antoine Watteau; and with regard to Albert Dupré, Ortese makes a tongue-in-cheek remark that he has "nulla in comune con lo scultore francese" (R2 201; "nothing to do with the French sculptor," LL 4) possibly referring through this ostentatious negation to Guillaume Dupré, another French Baroque artist.[30]

The novel contains onomastic allusions not only to the art history of Europe, but also to its literature and film. The first name of Ingmar Neville is a possible tribute to the renowned Swedish filmmaker Ingmar Bergman, with whose protagonists' "sogni e incubi" ("dreams and nightmares") Ortese compared her own mental state during the last phase of work at *Il cardillo addolorato*.[31] Conversely, Neville's surname is consonant with that of the American writer Herman Melville, and Melville's works are an important source for *L'Iguana*,[32] the first novel of Ortese's "trilogia delle bestie-angelo" ("trilogy of the angel-beasts"),[33] which includes *Il cardillo addolorato*. Besides, as Lorenz Manthey asserts, Neville's name may also contain an allusion to Lord Oswald Nelvil from Mme de Staël's *Corinne ou l'Italie*. Manthey bases his assumption on the topicality of the Neapolitan myth in the Romantic literary tradition, mentioning in this regard one further writer, Alphonse de Lamartine, a reference to whom Ortese might possibly have encoded in the name of the merchant

Alphonse Nodier.[34] On the other hand, Nodier's surname is homonymic with that of Charles Nodier, a prominent French Romanticist, with whose fantastic narratives critics sometimes compare Ortese's narrative worlds.[35]

Like great masters of European Romanticism, in *Il cardillo addolorato* Ortese nostalgically evokes the premodern past, dramatically juxtaposed with modernity:

> Ricordiamo inoltre, volentieri, che allora – Illuministi a parte – sogni e presagi per la debolezza del cuore umano, e timore e pianto per l'invadenza di un qualche ignoto e sciocco Cardillo, dominavano ancora i comportamenti comuni. Non solo *l'argent,* Lettore, passava come un raggio nei boschi fioriti del cuore, nella sua primavera che era, allora, prodigiosa: ma amori, amicizie, damigelle ... e sogni e scherzi ed eleganze di vita, erano ancora un traguardo nello stile dei Signori. (R2 316)
>
> (We are also pleased to point out that that at that time – exception made for the Illuminati – dreams and superstitions due to the frailty of the human heart, and fears and tears occasioned by the intrusiveness of some unknown and foolish Linnet, still dominated everyday modes of conduct. Not only *l'argent,* dear Reader, glittered like a sunbeam in the flowery woods of a springtime of the heart that was, in those days, most wonderful; but also loves and friendships and fair damsels...while dreams and *jeux d'esprit* and the refinements of life were still coveted aims in the lifestyle of the lordly. [LL 87])

Yet with the advent of the modern times, the splendor of this culture submerges into the dormant repository of collective memory. A figure of the old cosmological and cultural order, Naples, traditionally distinguished by heterotopy, heterochrony, and heteroglossy, finds itself drawn into the inexorable course of historical progress that profanes and destroys the ancient habitat of the fantastic and the hybrid by imposing on it the totalizing categories of the "rational" and the "real"[36] and expelling its original dwellers to the liminal domains of existence. In *Il cardillo addolorato,* the city turns to the reader its other face, that of "case buie, deserte d'amore" ("dark houses, loveless houses"), invisibly populated by marginalized and silenced creatures without hope of recognition and redemption: "I fanciulli, sapete, se non appartengono alla *bonne société* conoscono subito, nascendo, il deserto. Ed è là, a Napoli, come a Parigi, Londra o Colonia, che poi scompaiono – si dileguano, dissolvono, come fumo nell'aria – prima ancora di diventare adulti..." (R2 469; "children, unless they belong to the *bonne société*, confront this desert from the very day of their birth. And it is for this reason that here in Naples, as in Paris, London or Cologne, they disappear, they vanish, they dissolve like smoke in the air, before they have time to grow up," LL 205.)

The chasm between humankind achievements and civilization and the unredeemed sufferance of its underworld is filled with laments of the enigmatic Goldfinch. The vertiginous and happy song of the enigmatic bird, whose visible and invisible, audible and inaudible presence pervades the story – Oò! Oò! Oò! Oh! Oh! Oh! – lacks any verbal substance, and gives expression to the pain and despair of the victims of progress, modernity, and history, the *piccerilli* of Ortese's "sublime Ökologie" [sublime ecology]:[37]

> questo dolore (o gioia? o anelito? o semplice desiderio di gioia?) che il famigerato uccello esprime, non ha [...] molta attinenza col mondo degli adulti, sia intellettuali che nobili, ma solo col mondo dei piccerilli [...] Vi è un dolore [...] dei fanciulli, nel mondo napoletano e altrove (fino, forse, alla remota Germania), che supera in gravità e dimensioni il dolore degli intellettuali, degli innamorati delle riforme e perfino degli ansiosi della Costituzione – un dolore *non* degli adulti, di cui sempre si parla, e a cui ci si riferisce generalmente pronunciando la parola magica: dolore. (R2 469)
>
> (this sorrow (or rejoicing? or longing? or mere longing for joy?) as expressed by this wretched bird has precious little to do [...] with the world of grown-ups, be they intellectuals or noblemen, but solely with the world of children [...] There is a sorrowfulness in children [...] in our world of Naples and elsewhere, even as far as distant Germany, that is both graver and greater than that of the intellectuals, of the reformers, even of those who are clamouring for a Constitution – a sorrow that is not that of grown-ups, whom we usually refer to when we utter the magic word "sorrow." (LL 204))

Ignorant of art like Elmina and inarticulate in his laments like Käppchen, the Goldfinch rises above the modern world, reigned by the material rationale, to address the oppressed and the potent alike, to announce the invisible in grand projects and the silenced in master narratives, to lend his voice and to give hope to all the desperate *piccerilli* and their faithful sisters.

NOTES

1 Clerici, *Apparizione e visione*, 598f.
2 Haas, "La Ortese nel porto di Adelphi," 233.
3 Pivetta, "Ortese e le occasioni di Alonso."
4 Wood, *Italian Women's Writing*, 179.
5 In the English translation by Patrick Creagh, *Cardillo* is rendered for euphonic reasons as "linnet"; however, here I employ the denomination "goldfinch," which directly corresponds to the Italian word "cardillo."
6 Papini, "Luoghi della soglia, tra epifania e miraggio," 111.
7 Citati, "Lo sa il Folletto," 150.
8 Clerici, *Apparizione e visione*, 144.
9 Chekhov, *Complete Works in 8 Volumes*, 262.
10 In the novel, the *folletto* is born in 1505; in the same year, the Bourbons established their political rule over the Kingdom of Naples.
11 Wiener, ed., *The Dictionary of the History of Ideas*, 90.
12 All English translations are the author's, with the assistance of Savannah Cooper-Ramsey.
13 Italics in the original.
14 *The Declaration of Independence: A Transcription* (in Congress, 4 July 1776), http://www.archives.gov/exhibits/charters/declaration_transcript.html (17.02.09).
15 In 1791, Olympe de Gouge (born Marie Gouze), a feminist political activist, put forth her own *Déclaration des Droits de la Femme et de la Citoyenne*, in which she challenged the male authority and male-dominated political practice. Whereas the official *Déclaration* asserted the supremacy of the written law, Olympe de Gouge championed in her contestatory treatise the idea of Nature and more egalitarian natural laws.
16 Ghezzo, "Voci dall'oltrestoria," 230.
17 Modified translation.
18 There is one more clue in *The Lament of the Linnet* that speaks in favour of the suggested hidden connection to Barth's *Chimera*. Its first part, "Dunyazadiad," is a postmodernist re-telling of the story of the stories of Scheherezade, the fictitious narrator of the *Thousand and One Nights*. In Ortese's novel, the reference to the Arabian collection of stories is, in fact, encoded in the very name of Dupré's and Elmina's child, Alí Babá, which "non faceva pensare a nulla di familare o domestico, ma solo a qualche favola del Vicino Oriente" (R2 342; "brought to mind nothing remotely domestic or 'family,' but merely a Middle-Eastern fairy tale," LL 108). The reasons for the peculiar choice of the child's name that otherwise remain

utterly inexplicable, might, indeed, serve as an additional evidence of the aforementioned intertextual link.

19 Papini, "Luoghi della soglia, tra epifania e miraggio," 110.
20 Wood, *Italian Women's Writing*, 182.
21 Ibid., 183.
22 Borri, *Invito alla lettura di Anna Maria Ortese*, 84.
23 At this place, Patrick Creagh translates *palummella* with the word "dove"; yet it not only appears to be linguistically incorrect but also contradicts the second part of the same sentence.
24 Gramone, "Travelling through the I," 97.
25 Kleinhans, "Schlafende Seele, errin're dich…," 19.
26 Ghezzo, "Voci dall'oltrestoria," 221.
27 Ibid., 222.
28 The Spanish word for forest is, however, "bosque."
29 Ghezzo, "Voci dall'oltrestoria," 222.
30 Lorenz Manthey asserts that, in the case of Albert Dupré, Ortese actually makes a reference *ex negativo* to the Italian sculptor Giovanni Dupré (see "Das Geheimnis der schönen Neapolitanerin," 283.
31 Malatesta, "Vola Cardillo."
32 Clerici, *Apparizione e visione*, 395.
33 Farnetti, *Anna Maria Ortese*, 17.
34 Manthey, "Das Geheimnis der schönen Neapolitanerin," 283.
35 Ibid.
36 Ghezzo, "Voci dall'oltrestoria," 226.
37 Kleiner, "Zwischen natürlichem Stolz und himmlischer Demut," 1082.

WORKS CITED

Barth, John. *Chimera*. Boston and New York: Houghton Mifflin, [1972] 2001.

Borri, Giancarlo. *Invito alla lettura di Anna Maria Ortese*. Milan: Mursia, 1988.

Chekhov, Anton. *Complete Works in 8 Volumes*. Ed. Mikhail Eryomin. Moscow: Pravda, 1970.

Citati, Piero. "Lo sa il Folletto." In *Per Anna Maria Ortese*, ed. Luca Clerici. *Il Giannone* 4, no. 7–8 (January–December 2006).

Clerici, Luca. *Apparizione e visione: Vita e opere di Anna Maria Ortese*. Milan: Mondadori, 2002.

Farnetti, Monica. *Anna Maria Ortese*. Milan: Mondadori, 1998.

Ghezzo, Flora. "Voci dall'oltrestoria: *Il cardillo addolorato* di Anna Maria Ortese e la crisi della modernità." In *Per Anna Maria Ortese*, ed. Luca Clerici. *Il Giannone* 4, no. 7–8 (January–December 2006): 221–43.

Gramone, Antonella. "Travelling through the I: Anna Maria Ortese's Melancholic Cities." *Romance Studies* 19, no. 1 (2001): 95–108.

Haas, Franz. "La Ortese nel porto di Adelphi." *Belfagor* 58 (2003): 232–36.

Kleiner, Barbara. "Zwischen natürlichem Stolz und himmlischer Demut." *Universitas* 10 (1988): 1079–88.

Kleinhans, Martha. "'Schlafende Seele, errin're dich…' Zur Funktion spanischer Literatur in Anna Maria Ortese's Roman *L'Iguana*." *Italienisch* 32 (1994): 18–36.

Malatesta, Stefano. "Vola Cardillo." *La Repubblica*, 7 May 2005.

Manthey, Lorenz. "Das Geheimnis der schönen Neapolitanerin – Anna Maria Orteses Initiationsroman *Il cardillo addolorato*." In *Scrittura femminile: Italienische Autorinnen im 20. Jahrhundert zwischen Historie, Fiktion und Autobiographie*, ed. Irmgard Scharold, 281–304. Tübingen: Gunter Narr Verlag, 2002.

Papini, Mavina. "Luoghi della soglia, tra epifania e miraggio." In *Paesaggio e Memoria: Giornata di studi su Anna Maria Ortese, 26 maggio 2000*, ed. Caterina De Caprio and Laura Donadio, 109–23. Cappella Pappacoda: Libreria Dante and Descartes, 2000.

Pivetta, Oreste. "Ortese e le occasioni di Alonso." *L'unità*, 25 May 1996.

Wiener, Philip P., ed. *The Dictionary of the History of Ideas*. New York: Charles Scribner's Sons, 1973/1974.

Wood, Sharon. *Italian Women's Writing 1860–1994*. London: Athlone, 1995.

11 The Enigmatic Character of Elmina: A Thread in a Vertiginous Web

MARGHERITA PIERACCI HARWELL

In May 1993, the Italian publisher Adelphi published a novel by Anna Maria Ortese with the cryptic title *Il cardillo addolorato.*[1] It had an astonishing success: in its first two months, it was reprinted four times and sold 60,000 copies – in time that would become 90,000, with an additional 22,000 copies sold in mass-market format – impressive numbers for a work of fiction of this type in the Italian market. It is worth keeping in mind how these figures compared with the 4,000 copies of *L'Iguana* sold in one year by Rizzoli – they republished the book ten years after the failure of its first edition, which had been published by Vallecchi in 1965 (at that time only 1,990 copies were sold in four years) – or with the reception of *Il porto di Toledo,* which the publisher refused to sell after forty days of frustration.

Reception from both the public and critics improved in the late eighties, but it was only with *Il cardillo addolorato* that the real transformation took place. The list of enthusiastic reviewers of this book reads like a "Who's Who" of Italian critics and essayists. Ortese was awarded the Special Culture Prize for 1993 by the head of the Italian government, and was recognized abroad, with such praise as illustrated by the following statement which opened the entry on Italian literature in *Encyclopaedia Britannica*'s 1994 *Book of the Year*:

> Literature stood no chance against the competition of reality in 1993. No fiction could beat the appeal of daily newspapers and TV news bulletins with their relentless stories of financial empires tumbling down, well-known magnates biting the dust, powerful political parties crumbling [...] Meanwhile, new literature continued to be published [...] By far the most compelling was *Il cardillo addolorato* by Anna Maria Ortese, a well-established

> though still somewhat underrated writer. Set at the end of the 18th century, and written in a rich transparent style, this remarkable novel told the story of three young men from Northern Europe who go to Naples and remain trapped there by the bewitching coldness of a mysterious young woman; the real protagonist, however, was the goldfinch of the title, whose haunting, magical singing time and again announces the defeat of reason and love and the triumph of a dark inhuman power over all human calculations and projects. It was a measure of the author's artistic achievement that her pervasive use of irony in respect to characters and events only served to increase the tension and suspense of the fiction.[2]

Although the minimal space allotted to such a complex work forced this reviewer to confine himself to only one of the many possible facets of interpretation, this page is a sign of the attention the novel awakened abroad.[3] Surely, it was not the only sign – in 1998 for example, *Il cardillo addolorato* was awarded the "Prix du meilleur livre étranger" dedicated to foreign literature published in France.[4]

I have taken the time to revisit these already-known facts because it seems to me that *Il cardillo addolorato*'s success and the transformation of Ortese's literary fortune contributes to the "enigmatic" character of the book. Leaving aside the position of a few of the most sensitive critics such as Roberto Calasso and Pietro Citati, whose adherence to the world of our writer doesn't surprise us in the least, how can we explain the sudden conversion of so many to an interpretation of "reality" that is, on the one hand, magical, light, and transparent – it has been said that *Il cardillo addolorato* evokes Mozart and the Opera Buffa – and on the other, extraordinarily and rigorously demanding in moral terms? From her readers Ortese expects an absolute respect for life, not only in its humblest but even in its "debased" forms. She demands that the trees and the flowers, which are the most direct expressions of nature, be given a level of respect not inferior to that generally afforded to "good human beings." But Ortese also expects equal compassion for the "less honourable" – be they snakes, dictators, or killers:

> "Chi sono io. Amica, ma delle vittime," dichiara pubblicamente Anna Maria nel 1990. "Vittime animali … vittime umane …"
>
> ("Who am I. A friend, but a friend of the victims," Anna Maria states publicly in 1990. "Animal victims … human victims …")[5]

> Chi è caduto va aiutato. Sia esso un verme, un dittatore, una creatura qualsiasi ... Bisogna aiutare il prossimo *sempre.*
>
> (Whoever has fallen must be helped. Whether it be a worm, a dictator, a creature of any kind ... Our fellow being must be helped – *always.*)[6]

Apparently, even in our times, readers and critics respond very well to the proposal of perfection, provided it is not presented in moralizing terms but rather as it emerges from a complex, beautiful, and ironic story. As a fairy tale, *Il cardillo addolorato* immerses us in an atmosphere of noble beauty as it manifests a succession of lofty feelings centred around the theme of devotion – Elmina's to the goblin Hieronymus / Lillot, Neville's to Elmina. This weighty atmosphere is lightened by a brilliant irony, and those feelings are made real through their juxtaposition to human weakness – even of the basest of human weaknesses. We will see how, while envy and jealousy taint Neville's love for Elmina, they never prevail; and how, at the peak of his generosity, Neville fails to overcome the sense of shame he derives from his association with the ugly, wretched Lillot. It is this contrast between lofty feelings and petty instincts that makes Neville the most realistic character in the novel.

Thus far I have hinted at the tone of the novel. We must now consider its mystery and complexity. The real challenge does not lie, however, in grasping the truly elusive form of the narrative and of its heroes – the reader should be able to come to terms with this after heeding the warning of the narrator herself, who repeatedly confesses her own inability to take hold of something stable, a kind of "essence," underlying the continual flux of nature, history, and characters. We can deal with the problem of elusiveness by accepting – as Ortese does while representing the multiform, ever-changing appearance of things and beings – that their very essence lies in their constant transformation. For the reader, then, the real challenge lies in trying to get as close as possible to the magic of the fairy tale, which is just beyond our reach, and as delicate in its nature as the "*palummella*" (Neapolitan for "butterfly"), without destroying the impalpable powder of its wings.

Let us nevertheless try to "understand" what the narrative does disclose about Elmina without flattening her essence. To this end, we can consider two approaches – we can explore similarities between Elmina and other characters in *Il cardillo addolorato*; and we can trace her gestation through characters in Ortese's other novels or in previous drafts of

Il cardillo addolorato itself. In this essay I intend to use both approaches to explore the vertiginous web of characters and themes in Ortese's work.

In *Il cardillo addolorato,* there are at least two other characters as elusive as Elmina and so strictly entangled with her that we cannot proceed without exploring them: the *Cardillo* (goldfinch)[7] himself, a mysterious presence whose sorrowful song haunts the novel, and the goblin-boy "Lillot portapacchi" ("Lillot Porter-Boy"), who in the most striking way keeps changing name, form, and identity. The character who remains most puzzling to our "French reason" to the very end is *Cardillo.* As for Lillot – we may refer to him as the "goblin" boy in his humblest designation – the many pieces of the puzzle start to come together in the second half of Part V, when the mystery regarding his identity becomes clear: that he and the little boy Geronte are one and the same. Moreover, Lillot's identity gets conflated with the mysterious Hieronymus Käppchen, whose name Neville witnessed appear and disappear on a tombstone in connection with completely absurd past and future dates and whom he had almost managed to forget.[8] Two-thirds of the way into the book, his full name, age, and story are revealed as is his ambiguous relationship to Elmina. Hieronymus Käppchen (*Berrettino* or, in English, "Little Cap"), a boy from Cologne born in 1505, had been "adopted" by Elmina's father Don Mariano in 1779. The boy had then arrived in Naples in a shoebox with holes in it (from the earliest pages of Ortese's 1928–29 journal, shoeboxes are a gloomy symbol for the writer, and eventually they will become humiliating coffins for scorned felines – from Stellino of "Folletto a Genova," in the collection of short stories *In sogno e in veglia* to Alonso in the novel *Alonso e i visionari*).[9] Since boys obviously do not travel in shoeboxes, nor do they live to be 300 years old, the reader requires no further confirmation that Hieronymus is an imp, a goblin, or a *folletto,* a fact that will soon be reinforced. At the time of the story, he is close to his 300th birthday, on which day he is condemned to "sparir[e] da questo mondo (e da qualsiasi altro mondo) per sempre" (R2 497–98; "vanish from this world (and any other) forever and ever," LL 225), unless a married couple legally adopts him. Here it is useful to consider Duke Ruskaija's description of the poor creature and his effect on those around him. The duke is endowed with magical powers and is a longtime friend of the Belgian prince Ingmar de Neville. Describing the goblin, the duke says:

> Non gli attribuisco malvagità. Ma debolezza e confusione e disperato desiderio di salvarsi, costi quel che costi alla sua protettrice, e di vivere ancora,

> sì. Era lui, comprendi?, il dolore segreto di Don Mariano [...] una disperazione assoluta, che annientò le sue forze. Salvarlo [...] fargli superare il pericolo di quella scadenza, che ora sta per verificarsi [...] fu, questo, il gran problema del Guantaio, che egli trasmise alla figlia prediletta. Ed Elmina, come suo padre, non visse che per questo scopo: aiutare costui a superare il destino, vanificare la scadenza verso cui correva il disgraziato Folletto. (R2 499)
>
> (I attribute no malice to him. But weakness, confusion and a desperate desire to save himself and to go on living, cost what it may to his protectress [Elmina]; these, yes. He, you understand, was the secret sorrow of Don Mariano ... it was the blackest despair, which robbed him of all his life and strength. To rescue him [the Goblin or Elf] to enable this person to get past that fatal date, which is now imminent ... This and no other was Don Mariano's terrible problem which he passed on to his favourite daughter. And Elmina, like her father, lived for nothing other than this: to help him to survive the fatal day, and to frustrate the time-limit approaching that luckless Elf. [LL 226])

Since Lillot is a goblin or elf – that is, a little demon banished from the Christian community – he has no soul. He may live for 300 years, but he is in no way immortal – "he will vanish from this world (and any other) forever and ever." As Ortese scholars know, since the time of her early stories, the concern for death and ephemerality, the need for immortality – for the survival of the essence of every living being – is a central theme in the writer's thought. Early on, during her adolescence, the writer was keenly aware of the transitory nature of things, as when – during her long contemplation of the sea on the voyage from Libya to Italy – she noted how the waves the ship left in its wake would never be, as Heraclitus had warned, the same as those ahead: "so all things are in flux, passing away, never to return." Then, a few years later, the death of her brother Manuele, the "marine," made her directly experience loss and the passing of life, as she recounts in her fictional autobiography *Il porto di Toledo.* After despair had rendered her speechless for a time, and after having helplessly observed the stunned, inconsolable suffering of her mother, she, much like her fictional alter ego Dasa of *Il porto di Toledo,* discovered the transformative power of words – or rather of the music of words, their ability to soothe mortally wounded souls by, in some way, restoring to life those who had disappeared from the scene of this world: "Sì, il dolore aveva avuto una svolta: era stato indicato, e solo per questo modificato. Non era trascorso, ma era modificato" (R1 391; "Yes, the suffering had been turned around: it had been expressed and because of this alone, modified. It had not passed, but it was modified").

Thus, art, namely poetry, had helped Dasa / Anna Maria, and through her, her mother – and had saved something of the lost "marine." But it did not take long for Ortese to realize that this kind of victory over death was only afforded to the few, another form of privilege. What would become of the many people that art could not reach, and what of the animals, and trees, and flowers, and pink clouds? Ortese wanted all to be eternal. Her sorrow over the evils of the world – poverty, humiliation, ugliness, disease, every form of misery – was doubled by her sorrow over the way everything vanished. Her mother would eventually find comfort in her faith, but early on Anna Maria had renounced the religious faith that she had come to know in the darkness of Naples' beautiful baroque churches. There, those she called the "Spanish priests" seemed to declare that the price to be paid for the hope of eternal life was voluntary renunciation of this natural, human life she felt pulsing all around her. Her sweet, tender, but absent mother seemed to be in full agreement with those "Spanish priests" who represented the "Church of the Pope":

> La visione che ella aveva di questo Altissimo – vera esistencia, realidad, bontà – era, credo, giusta; ma, poiché questo Altissimo, tramite la Chiesa del Papa, si presentava a noi come terrore e castigo, unicamente terrore e castigo del vivere da Lui stesso ordinato, i miei sentimenti per Lui erano violenti e muti, e presto, aggruppandosi, generarono la sedizione. (R1 372–73)

> (The vision she had of the Most High – true existence, reality, goodness – was, I believe, right; but since this Most High, by way of the Church of the Pope, presented Himself to us as terror and punishment, solely terror and punishment of that life which He himself had ordered, my feelings towards Him were violent and mute, and soon, coming together, they led to sedition.)

In 1973, when interviewed by Dacia Maraini, Ortese was quoted as saying:

> La religione mi attraeva e mi respingeva insieme. Le chiese mi incantavano e mi incupivano. Dio per me si identificava con la speranza di vivere eternamente e liberamente, era il nome, l'identità, la stabilità. Mi pareva terribile invece la chiesa storica; incomprensibile l'inferno, incomprensibile

l'inquisizione, inaccessibile poi la sorveglianza sulle coscienze. Poco alla volta mi allontanai. Oggi però, anzi non da oggi, non vedo chiavi al segreto del mondo che siano all'altezza della Bibbia, del Vecchio e del Nuovo Testamento. I principi di non uccidere, non rubare, onora il padre e la madre e così via mi sembrano fondamentali nel più modesto discorso per una rinascita del mondo e un mutamento di rotta (se ancora è possibile). Aggiungo che in questo non uccidere io includo il rispetto e la compassione anche per il mondo animale, l'intero mondo della vita terrestre dal quale siamo usciti e verso il quale sicuramente abbiamo doveri di solidarietà e di affetto. Per me, del resto, ogni pietra, ogni cosa più umile e muta esistente in questo universo, è sacra e rispettabile quanto l'Universo tutto.

(Religion both attracted and repelled me. Churches enchanted and depressed me. I identified God with the desire to live eternal and free, He was the name, identity and stability. Yet, the historic Church seemed terrible to me; incomprehensible the inferno, incomprehensible the Inquisition, unacceptable therefore the surveillance of consciences. I slowly distanced myself. Today, however, in fact for quite some time now, I cannot think of any key to the secrets of the world as deep as those found in the Bible, in the Old and New Testaments. The commandments to not kill, not steal, to honour one's father and mother and so on seem to me to be the fundamental ingredients in the fashioning of any discourse, even modest, for the rebirth of the world and a change of course (if it is still possible). I add that, in this commandment to not kill, I include also respect and compassion for the animal world, the entire world of earthly life from which we originated and towards which we are certainly bound by the duties of solidarity and love. Besides, for me, every stone, even the most humble and silent object existing in this Universe, is sacred and respectable inasmuch as the Universe as a whole is.)[10]

With a clearer understanding of Ortese's religious outlook and of her criticism of the crueler aspects of the church, we can readdress the goblin Lillot and the possibility of his salvation. Traditionally, in Christian terms, nature as a whole is considered devilish, just as the "flesh" is: the great "sin" of animals is that they lack a soul, even though they are in no way responsible for their condition, thus bear no blame. What Ortese emphasizes in *Il cardillo addolorato*, much as in *L'Iguana*, is the fact that the "sin" for which animals, otherworldly creatures, and nature itself are condemned is contagious; it inevitably and irreparably attaches itself to those people who would dare become mixed up with the "devilish" creatures. This is the tragic paradox: for their compassion, the most sensitive souls pay with the loss of their own soul, with their own damnation. In the novel, this tragic paradox is embodied by the enigmatic Elmina, and represents the core of her mystery. Elmina, the compassionate soul, concentrating the whole power of her emotions on the miserable creature she is to protect, stiffens emotionally. In this inhuman tension, she becomes incapable of any tenderness for any beings other than the beloved yet damned goblin. This renders her incapable of loving, at least apparently, even her own children, unable to appreciate all the enjoyable aspects of life (and art in particular).

To reach deeper into this paradox, thus, we first have to come to terms with the nature of the goblin or *monaciello*, since it is Elmina's attachment to "it" that will determine her destiny, a destiny of perennial suffering because of "its" cursed nature (and I have opted for the neutral "it" to emphasize the *monaciello*'s non-human nature). In Ortese's work, the very first apparition of the strange creature dates from as early as 1940, when the short story "Il monaciello di Napoli" ("The Little Monk of Naples") was published in the magazine *Ateneo Veneto.*[11] As many readers have noticed, this *monaciello* prefigures essential aspects of the "little one" of *Il cardillo addolorato,* especially in its graceless appearance and behaviour (which, according to the sympathetic author, constitute the consequence rather than the cause of the curse that has befallen it) and in its similarity to the traditional figure of the Neapolitan poor: our *monaciello* seems in fact to look and act very much like a *scugnizzo* (street urchin). In the 1940 story, however, its curse does not fall too tragically upon the persons who pity it or, more properly, love it: only a social punishment falls upon them. Those who are compassionate pay by becoming ridiculous or even contemptible in the eyes of those around them. More importantly, the "monaciello di Napoli," unlike the goblin of *Il cardillo addolorato,* can be saved – and indeed it will be in the course of the story. Another essential difference is that the "creature" from the 1940 tale is never likened to an animal. Ortese reaches this next step – identification of the most accursed poor, of the "last ones," with beasts and animals – twenty-five years later in the novel *L'Iguana* (1965). This identification will also occur with *monacielli* in one of the most striking (and not quite so elusive) stories of *In sonno e in veglia* (1987) – "Folletto a Genova" ("Folletto in Genoa"). However, both in *L'Iguana* and in "Folletto a Genova," the happy ending disappears. These two features, which go together – explicit inclusion of "i popoli muti" ("the voiceless ones," including the animals) in the category of the poorest, and the disappearance of the happy ending – will reappear in *Alonso e i visionari* (1996). During the years 1940 to 1965, from the time of the Second World War and its aftermath to the economic boom, Ortese clarified her conviction that the very "last" in our world, those most humble or most lacking a voice, are not simply the poorest of human beings, but rather the animals. This conviction is demonstrated in two stories, later collected for the volume *In sonno e in veglia* (1982): the tale of the cruel, poor man who spat in the eyes of an old exhausted horse, laden with an enormous load, and the story of the "little dragon" cruelly killed by Saint George (a reworking of the traditional Christian myth), which concludes the collection. As suffering beings, both the humiliated horse and the little dragon evoke the same compassion that Ortese as a child had felt for Mamota, a character from an episode of her fictional autobiography *Il porto di Toledo:*

> In una piazzetta di questa città [...] in una piazzetta oscura e infame, soggiornava perennemente una giovane infelice chiamata Mamota. Era un mostro: col corpo tutto rattorto da non so quale malattia o origine malata, eternamente vestita di nero, il viso grande e cereo illuminato da immensi e dolorosi occhi neri, che scendevano spalancati verso le tempie [...] Come questa giovane, nella città, era tutta una moltitudine di aborti che, dotati di infinita miseria, tendevano la mano. La loro vista mi scaldava: nel senso che l'orrore della loro condizione [...] mi dava di questa vita o società vicereale l'immagine di un inferno, di cui qualcuno o qualcosa erano responsabili ... Perciò, in un sentimento misterioso e simile appunto a un gran caldo, che provavo vedendo questi infelici, io dico che mi pareva di salvarmi. Non so se li amassi. Ma qualcosa di simile. Avrei voluto aiutarli. Ritrovarmi una regina per spargere al mio passaggio, invece di pezzi di pane rubati in casa, autentiche pietre preziose, diamanti e rubini. Mi fermavo accanto a Mamota e la guardavo. Essa, solo coi suoi occhi pietosi mi parlava. I poveri, lo notai in appresso, non parlano, i veri poveri, dico, non conoscono alcuna espressione, essendo ridotti a una quiete animale. (R1 375–76)

(In one of this city's little squares [...] in a dark and infamous little square a young wretch named Mamota perpetually resided. She was a monster: her body all twisted by I don't know which illness or diseased background, perennially dressed in black, her large waxen face illuminated by immense and sorrowful black eyes which descended wide open toward her temples

[...] Like this young woman, in the city there was a multitude of those misshapen who, endowed with unending poverty, begged for alms. The sight of them made me burn, in the sense that the horror of their condition [...] created in me the image of this vice-regal life or society as a kind of hell, for which someone or something were responsible [...] Therefore, with a mysterious feeling which was indeed like a great heat I felt while seeing these wretches, I say I thought I was saving myself. I don't know if I loved them. But something like that. I would have wanted to help them. To turn out to be a queen so as to hand out when I passed, not pieces of bread stolen from home, but genuine precious stones, diamonds, and rubies. I would stop next to Mamota and look at her. She only talked to me with her pitiable eyes. The poor, I noticed later, don't talk – the real poor, I say, know no form of expression, being reduced to an animal quiet.)

Thus to Ortese, already as a very young girl, the evil of this world had shown itself to be so widespread and pervasive. Yet her 1940 "Monaciello" tale could still have a happy ending (maybe too much like Pinocchio's, who becomes a good, clean little boy). As an adult, however, Ortese sees no alternative to despair, except in the sacrifice of the self for the other – evoking the figure of Christ, although never mentioning him (as well as the writings of Simone Weil, although Ortese never refers to her).

Sacrifice, in *Il cardillo addolorato,* is embodied by Elmina, the one who offers herself up for love of the *folletto*: she preferred "il Malato, lo Sciocco, il Perduto per sempre" (R2 487; "the Invalid, the Mental Deficient, the Lost Soul," LL 217). At this point, the enigma of Elmina, her hidden core, alternately alluded to and concealed throughout the course of the book, finally begins to be revealed, along with Lillot's true nature. It is the magician / Duke Ruskajia, in the middle of Part V, who uncovers Elmina's secrets in a dramatic exchange with his old friend, the Belgian prince Ingmar de Neville, Elmina's unhappy lover. This key passage of the novel merits quoting at length:

"Sfortunatamente, ella non ama alcuno, ragazzo mio. Tranne un certo individuo – ecco il mio sospetto – da cui purtroppo è ingannata. E questo rende la sua sventura degna d'infinito e straziato rispetto!" (R2 494)

("sad to say, she does not love anyone ... Except for a certain individual ... here is my suspicion – by whom she has unfortunately been deceived. And this makes her misfortune worthy of infinite and heart-rending respect!" [LL 223])

And Ingmar responds, after a silent pause:

> "Ella, dunque, non ama nulla di ciò che è bene; nessuna legge morale le consente di distinguere tra il bene e il suo contrario; e inoltre, peggio di tutto, preferisce proprio quest'ultimo … Ed è in ciò, forse, il suo peccato, io temo …" (R2 495)
>
> ("She, therefore, does not love anything that is good, no moral law enables her to distinguish between the good and its opposite; moreover, and worst of all, she positively prefers the latter. It is in that, I fear, that her sin resides." [LL 223])

And then the duke:

> "Non che lo preferisca … lo sceglie" disse grave il Duca. "Ciò che le torna di mero svantaggio (secondo il mondo) è la categoria cui si uniforma. Nulla, quindi, di ciò che è propriamente suo, o piacevole, è da lei preferito, anzi … lo abborre; quindi, se vogliamo seguire tali deduzioni, unicamente ciò che danneggia, o rattrista, il suo cuore … la cosa più amara, che lede i suoi interessi terreni, può dirsi la più amata. Ma, intendi, proprio perché non lo è." (R2 495)
>
> ("It is not that she prefers it, she chooses it," said the Duke gravely. "Whatever redounds to her disadvantage (in the eyes of the world) is what she complies with. She has no liking for what is really hers, or what is pleasing – indeed she abhors it … only what hurts, or saddens, her heart, the bitterest things, injurious to her worldly interests, can be said to be loved by her. But this, you understand, precisely because they are not [loved by her]." [LL 223])

Then Ingmar:

> "Capisco sempre meno" balbettò Ingmar. (R2 495)
>
> ("I understand less and less," stammered Ingmar." [LL 223])

And then later the Duke returns to the subject of Lillot, the Goblin, the cause of Elmina's suffering:

> "conosco (non chiedermi come) la sua totale innocenza; del resto, con quell'aspetto, solo uno sventurato, di cui Elmina nasconde a malapena il

ribrezzo. (Ma essenziale, forse, alla comprensione della nostra storia è la pietà di Elmina)." (R2 497)

("I know ... that he is completely innocent; at the most, with that appearance, only an unfortunate for whom Elmina can scarcely conceal her disgust. (Though Elmina's compassion is perhaps essential to the understanding of our story)." [LL 224]).

The novel is about two-thirds of the way finished before we finally get a sense of what motivates Elmina's incomprehensible behaviour.

Having acquired insights into the secret nature of Elmina, we can begin to look elsewhere to trace the genealogy of this unusual character in Ortese's work. While there are many prefigurations and variations of Lillot, Elmina's entire character is, by contrast, unique. In the scene quoted above, the duke's magic glass has allowed us to catch a glimpse of something that before had puzzled the reader. How Elmina's tender beauty – wrapped at first in delicate rosy dress and later mortified by orderly and severe old clothes – could coexist with such an iron coldness, a cruel denial of the most natural feelings, a firm refusal of any of life's blessings. How subsequently all this could be overturned to make room for the most passionate devotion (referring not only to her dedication to Lillot, but also to her devotion to her father, or to Geronte the Big). Only fragments of this whole may be detected in Ortese's previous stories – even in the story that seems to have been conceived as a canvas for *Il cardillo addolorato*: the unfinished *Mistero doloroso*, which Monica Farnetti has found among Ortese's papers and has included in the second volume of Ortese's *Romanzi*. It is revealing to apply to *Mistero doloroso* what Farnetti writes about "Carbonera," the 1928–29 diary that prepares the way for *Il porto di Toledo*:

La narrazione giovanile del diario, meno cooptata dall'esperienza e dal gusto dell'enigma, si ritrova a svelare molto di ciò che il romanzo al contrario vela, restituisce concretezza e attualità a quanto nel romanzo, fra mascheramenti e allusioni, tende ad apparire favoloso, ed esplicita ciò che il romanzo più volentieri affida al misterioso governo della reticenza. (R1 1030)

(The youthful narrative of the diary, less constrained by experience and by the taste for enigma, ends up revealing much of what the novel by contrast obscures, gives back concreteness and reality to what, in the novel, between masking and allusion, tends to look imaginary, and makes explicit what the novel prefers to entrust to the mysterious realm of reticence.)

The diary is extremely useful in clarifying biographical references in *Il porto di Toledo, Mistero doloroso* sheds relatively little limited light on *Il cardillo addolorato.* However, it does make evident, by way of contrast, the essential role that the magical dance of masking, allusion, and reticence, together with irony – all components totally lacking in *Mistero doloroso* – plays in Ortese's "finished" work.

Nevertheless, *Mistero doloroso* offers important clues as to the genealogy of Elmina's character. From the very beginning of *Il cardillo addolorato,* "iron bars" bind Elmina's heart: according to Neville, the "gentle" sixteen-year-old girl "coldly" revealed how she had once let a *cardillo* or goldfinch die. In *Mistero doloroso,* we find a first rough cast of Elmina in the guise of the main character, Ferrantina. She is described as: "una ragazza dagli occhi verdi e indifferenti come il mare di Posillipo" (R2 1062; "a girl with eyes as green and indifferent as the sea of Posillipo"). Here we have the same contrast between gentleness and iron coldness hinted at in Elmina.

The description of Ferrantina as an adult: "che [dopo la morte del figlio] rimase, davanti a questo fatto, di pietra" (R2 1063; "who [after her son's death] remained, in the face of this event, like a stone"), also inevitably takes us back to Ortese's grandfather, a gentle and genial sculptor who lost his reason – remained stupefied, sealed within himself like a stone – because of a similar misfortune. Here is how Ortese tells her grandfather's story in the interview with Maraini, also included in the present volume:

> Prima che nascesse lei [mia madre], suo padre faceva lo scultore. Era un uomo sensibile e gentile. Aveva avuto un figlio, Alberto, che amava di un amore tenerissimo. Ma questo bambino a due anni era morto. E il nonno aveva perso la ragione. Aveva chiuso lo studio di scultura, e non lavorava più. Correva dietro alle carrozze gridando: "Alberto, Alberto!" Per dieci anni fu pazzo. Poi gli tornò la ragione. Allora nacque mia madre. Dopo due anni lui morì.

> (Before [my mother] was born, her father was a sculptor. He was a sensitive and kind man. He had had a son, Alberto, whom he loved tenderly. But he died at the age of two. And my grandfather lost his head. He closed his

> sculpture studio and refused to work any longer. He would chase down carriages shouting: "Alberto, Alberto!" He was crazy for ten years. Then he returned to his right mind. And then my mother was born. Two years later he died.)[12]

Ortese's grandfather is in turn mirrored in the character of Elmina's husband, who is also a sculptor. Thus, the grandfather and Ferrantina allow us to better understand Elmina's husband, the once joyous Bellerofonte, who is stunned, driven crazy, and finally driven to his death by the death of Alì Babà-la Joie, his two-year-old son. In *Mistero doloroso,* Ferrantina is stunned in an identical way when her young daughter vanishes into a well, much like the poor Iguana at the end of the novel named after her.

Returning to parallels between Ferrantina and Elmina, the "iron bars" that bind Elmina's heart describe the very essence of Ferrantina, whose name itself contains the word "iron" (in Italian, *ferro*): "Ferrantina, nome assai buffo, [...] e forse a causa degli influssi del nome su un carattere [...] qualcosa, nella sua natura e in tutta la sua persona, evocava una forza addirittura strana, poco femminile, bisogna dire" (R2 1062; "Ferrantina, funny name [...] and perhaps because of the influence of a name on a personality, something in her nature and in the whole of her self conjured a quite strange force, we should say scarcely feminine").

The similarity between the two women ends here. Ferrantina is monolithic while Elmina's greatest charm comes from the perception that the reader shares with Neville and his friends: that underneath the placid, still surface, her elusive secret trembles unceasingly. Indeed, after a thorough explanation of the story of the goblin and its devoted protector, almost a third of the novel still remains, filling us with anticipation – of what, we are not exactly sure. Such is the wonder of Ortese's style – this elusive combination of irony and magic. In the end, we must concede that – beyond the suspense and surprises – what we are reading, without knowing it, is in essence a love story.

In addition to those aspects found in the early sketches of *Mistero doloroso,* there are other precursors to Elmina's unnatural or "iron" coldness in Ortese's work, especially with regard to maternal detachment. In *Il cardillo addolorato,* Elmina's cold detachment from her daughter Sasà slowly transforms the little girl into a flying *soricinella* (Neapolitan for "little witch") – a new kind of *palummella.* But we first encounter the effects of this detachment in one of Ortese's earliest stories – "Indifferenza della madre" ("The mother's indifference"), published in the collection

Infanta sepolta (1950) – which describes a void in the child's soul caused by the mother's cold detachment:

> uno spirito sensibile [...] cui bisognava, per svilupparsi dell'altro calore, un ulteriore riposo accanto alla carne affettuosa della madre. (IS 14)

> (a sensitive soul [...] which, in order to develop, would have needed some more warmth, further repose next to his mother's affectionate flesh.)

If we turn our attention to *Il porto di Toledo* – the fictional autobiography of a mature Ortese – we find another distant mother figure. Apa, who in this case, however, is protected by her daughter Dasa's tender understanding. Apa, nevertheless, is always absorbed in her own world of loss (her own mother – whose name "No" symbolizes the sense of negation found in Ortese's maternal figures – was buried in Libya; her favourite son Rassa was lost on a Caribbean island). While not cruel, the version of Anna Maria's mother reflected in Apa is almost completely absent, detached from her living children, much as Elmina remains distant and detached from the lonely *Soricinella*: "these children were like toys to her, sometimes she obsessed over us with her care and concern, other times she completely neglected us. In short, my father was a gypsy and my mother was a child,"[13] Anna Maria, describing her own mother, told Maraini.

Among Ortese's fictional mother figures, however, Apa is the exception. She is often shown watering carnations, and in this way still able to nurture life. Elmina, much like Ferrantina, embodies detachment, which begins as detachment from the self and generates a total inability to nurture the so-called "superfluous," the "small" things that enrich life and give one happiness. In *Il cardillo addolorato*, the frozen atmosphere of Elmina's father's house – the absence of paintings, carpets, and most other decorations – mirrors her cold detachment. Likewise, her father Don Mariano, himself entirely absorbed by the task of saving the *monaciello*, comes to share Elmina's drab and gelid taste.

These reflections shed more light on another character, Elmina's husband, Albert Dupré, and help explain his otherwise inexplicable metamorphosis as an effect of her freezing power. Her indifference transforms him from an exuberantly joyous Bellerofonte into a silent, lonely, and obsessive sculptor, persistently seeking in some mysterious other dimension – to which art perhaps alludes – the joy that should also enlighten life on this earth.

Joy, for Ortese – we must not forget – has always been a basic "human right." The discovery of a founding document that declares the right of every human being to happiness is probably one of the main reasons for her love for "America" (except she would have extended this right to every living being, not only humans) – just as the denial of this right, or its postponement to another world, is one of the main reasons for her resentment of dogmatic religion. For Ortese, it is certain that there cannot be life without joy. Life comes back to Albert-Bellerofonte through his son Alì Babà-la Joie (this form of his name – la Joie – is essential), but the young fruit of that strange marriage cannot long resist the emotionally frozen atmosphere surrounding his mother. Only Albert's art – in the form of his wonderful *testine* ("little heads") – can thrive even in this climate. Thus, the sculptures

> a detta di tutti, ricordava[no] a ciascuno *qualche cosa* appena intravista o subito perduta e per sempre amata. Il volto era bello, molto bello, di grazia irreale, ma non era la bellezza, in quel volto (che l'artista voleva intitolare *La Joie*), ciò che più veramente colpiva, quanto una espressione di disperata attesa, o visione di un bene insopportabile per i sensi umani, che quegli occhi miravano; e però era invisibile all'osservatore, quasi un raggio ricevuto dall'alto, o un bacio materno, o chissà che altro. (R2 331–32)
>
> ("everyone said, reminded them of *something* barely glimpsed and lost at once, but loved forever. The face was beautiful, very beautiful, of dreamlike charm, but in that face (which the artist intended to entitle *La Joie*) the most striking quality was not the beauty, so much as an expression of desperate expectancy, or else a vision of some benison too great for human senses to bear, at which those eyes were gazing; but which none the less was invisible to the observer, as might be a beam of light received from on high, or a mother's kiss, or who can tell what else." [LL 100])

Could this mean that art could thrive on tears, much like the kind of love Ortese references in connection to Provençal troubadour Bernart de Ventadorn, for whom true love will be recognized by the tears it causes? (See R2 683.) These tears spring from a longing for something almost forgotten, a faint memory of some more perfect world, which, in our world, art and love can reawaken. Thus the mystical "imagination" that critic Monica Farnetti (in "Pavana per una Infanta," her afterword to *L'infanta sepolta*) detects in the seditious Ortese, reappears here – a form of imagination which exposes a "second reality" behind the surface of outward reality, another reality which it is the poet's purpose to uncover, as so many have said, from Leopardi to Hofmannsthal.

In the novel's Part V, as mentioned earlier, many mysteries (though not all) are clarified. The reason for the hasty consent of both Elmina and her father Don Mariano to her marriage with the sculptor Albert Dupré is that she must be officially married in order to legally adopt, and thus to save, the *folletto* Lillot. The narrative soon reveals that Albert had refused to take part in this "adoption scheme" – a significant piece of the puzzle that explains the coldness of the couple: "in quanto, era chiaro, il fine, lo scopo del vivere dell'uno come dell'altro, non era più, o non era mai stato, il vivere matrimoniale" (R2 332, "insomuch as, quite clearly, for both the one and the other the be-all and end-all of living was no longer, or perhaps never had been, married life." [LL 100])

Before leaving the subject of Elmina and Albert's relationship, there is another important aspect of Elmina's behaviour to consider: her immediate, aggravated dismissal of the Alì Babà-la Joie "little heads" sculpted by Dupré – a sort of symmetric counterpoint to her indifference towards the other child Sasà-*soricinella*. The absolute focus on that which for her is "the be-all and end-all of living," that is her moral "duty" as it pertains to Lillot, seals – maybe "freezes" is the appropriate word – her soul, closes it to everything else, especially to the loftier aspects of life. Once again we may consider the link with the perennial "absence" of the mother figure in the autobiographical *Il porto di Toledo*. Apa, like Elmina, continues attending conscientiously to every chore – menial or not (cooking cabbage or trying to convert Dasa from her heresies) – all the while remaining very far away, emotionally distant, entirely absorbed by her sorrow and her religion.

There is, however, another character in *Il porto di Toledo* who bears a closer resemblance to Elmina than Apa. She is the protagonist Dasa, the Toledana, who stands for Anna Maria Ortese herself, notwithstanding the writer's contention that everything in *Il porto di Toledo* is familiar to her except Dasa. The similarity lies in Dasa's intense compassion ("I felt myself burn"), in her urge to *give aid* (*portare soccorso* is her motto) to the most humble, the most forgotten, like wretched and disfigured Mamota lying in a dark, squalid square of Naples. The compassion that links Elmina to Lillot is, literally, compassion for the very creature hiding in the shoebox, but, symbolically, Lillot can also represent a demand for compassion for all of Naples' unlucky ones: the *scugnizzo napoletano* ("street urchin"), the poor and wretched, the "popoli muti," as voiceless as animals, incapable of telling us of their torment. These are the ones who fill the city of Naples in *Il cardillo addolorato* no less than in *Il porto di*

Toledo. In the end, the cry of a mysterious goldfinch heard throughout the novel can be seen as the weeping of the city and its inhabitants. The mysterious bird – the most elusive character in Ortese's most elusive novel – may therefore be identified with Naples itself or with the poor in the poorest of cities. But the goldfinch may even represent something more than this, if viewed through through the Christian principle that those most humble are identified with Christ himself: "just as you did it to one of the least of these who are members of my family, you did it to me."[14] In a revealing description of the diplomat Neville – old but still active at the end of the novel – who sees the goldfinch as a reflection of God bringing justice to the world of the "first" and the "last":

> Un diplomatico non è mai in pensione; egli seguitò quindi a occuparsi di amici, ma anche di Stati amici, solo che il suo atteggiamento verso gli eventi politici degli ultimi decenni di storia d'Europa – tale atteggiamento mutò, si fece, da mondano e divertito, vagamente pedante e colto, bizzarramente critico, e quindi più esigente, un po' severo [...] Egli teneva a dire di chiunque gli vantasse il famoso benché ancora neonato Progresso, e curiosamente anche di alcuni Stati che gli venivano esaltati come conservatori, ma altamente benefici e amici dell'umanità: 'Sì ... d'accordo ... Ma si è mai costui (o codesto Stato o Nazione) levato presto, al mattino? Ha sentito il silenzio assoluto del mondo, la gioia imperiale dell'alba? Non lo ha toccato – un minuto più tardi – il grido dell'uccella cui hanno rapito i piccoli, e dei piccoli cui hanno strappato la madre? Parlo dei potenti della terra, Signori, e della loro certezza – democratici o meno, buoni sovrani o cattivi dittatori – di essere "i primi," di essere in diritto di disporre dei boschi e dei loro fanciulli. Ha veramente conosciuto – questo signore dell'alba – la sua propria malvagia vanità, la sua infinita crudeltà che lo porta a disporre dei piccini della terra? Come farà quindi a ignorare la presenza (o riderne) del Cardillo giustiziere?' [...] E avvertiva che questo, appunto, era mancato, nell'antico e nuovo farsi del mondo: il rispetto dell'alba, del pianto del Cardillo; e del suo ordine di restare fedeli – come i fanciulli dei boschi e le loro sorelle – al Nulla, al Poco, e alla pietà per il Nulla, alla compassione per l'abbandonato, al riguardo sommo per ogni Hieronymus Käppchen e la sua penna di gallina.' (R2 607–8)

> (A diplomat never really retires, therefore he continued to busy himself not only with friends but with friendly States. It was only that his attitude towards the last few decades of European history had changed. It was no longer worldly and derisory, but learned and slightly pedantic, oddly critical, and therefore more demanding and even severe. Of anyone who sang

the praises of Progress – already famous though still in its infancy – and curiously enough even of certain States which were lauded as conservative but highly beneficial and friendly to humanity, he made a point of saying: "Yes, very well ... But has that man (or that State or nation) ever risen right early in the morning? Has he heard the absolute silence of the world, the imperial gladness of dawn? Has he been touched, but a moment later, by the cry of the mother bird whose young have been stolen, or of the chicks whose mother has been wrested from them? I am speaking of the potentates of the earth, gentlemen – democratic or otherwise, worthy sovereigns or wicked dictators – and their certainty that they are 'the First,' that they have a right to dispose at will of the woodlands and the children of the woodlands. Has he – this gentleman of the dawn – ever realized his iniquitous vanity, the infinite cruelty which induces him to do as he pleases with the little ones of the earth? How in that case can he ignore, or even deride, the justicer, the Linnet?" [...] And he realized that what was lacking in both the old and the new ways of the world was precisely this: respect for the dawn and the weeping of the Linnet, and his command to remain faithful – like the children of the woods and their sisters – to that which is Nothing, or Little, to have pity for Nothingness, compassion for those cast out and abandoned, and supreme regard for every Hieronymus Käppchen and his hen's feather." [LL 306–7])

The above quotation makes clear how limited the definition of the goldfinch in the Britannica review quoted at the beginning of this essay had been, however enthusiastic it seemed:

> the real protagonist, however, was the goldfinch of the title, whose haunting, magical singing time and again announces the defeat of reason and love and the triumph of a dark inhuman power over all human calculations and projects. It was a measure of the author's artistic achievement that her pervasive use of irony in respect to characters and events only served to increase the tension and suspense of the fiction.[15]

This review also illustrates one of Ortese's most common complaints – the way readers (and critics) often focus on her irony to avoid the pain of taking her demanding message seriously.

The novel ends as it starts, focusing on Neville, the true lover of Elmina.

> Il principe, così, tra impulsi non buoni e lento divenire della coscienza del cuore (purtroppo solo il suo cuore era cosciente) non si dava pace.

> Poco alla volta, sentiva di aver contribuito [...] alla rovina di Hieronymus e a quella di Elmina. E non sapeva, tra i due, chi gli fosse più caro [...] ma avrebbe dato la vita per riaverli con sé. Capiva inoltre di avere offeso Elmina, per dieci anni, con tutto il suo denaro, e la vuota gelosia – quando ciò che ella chiedeva non era che la salvezza di H. Käppchen. Capiva che ella aveva rinunciato, fin da piccina, a ogni bene, e quella mattina alla stessa proprietà della Casarella, e infine alla buona grazia di lui – solo per impietosire il Cardillo, che la voleva priva di tutto, e desolata, per salvare così il Folletto. Ma il Cardillo non aveva avuto pietà. (R2 613)
>
> ("The prince, therefore, amid questionable impulses and the slow dawning of awareness in his heart (alas, only his heart was aware at all), gave himself no rest. Little by little [...] he had, he felt contributed to the ruin of both Hieronymus and Elmina. Of the two of them he did not know which was the dearer to him [...] but he would have given his life to have them with him now. He furthermore understood that he had for ten years offended Elmina with all that money of his, and his pointless jealousy, when all she wanted was to save H. Käppchen. He realized that ever since girlhood she had forgone all possessions, and on that now distant morning even the ownership of the Little House, and lastly his own good graces, purely and simply to soften the heart of the Linnet, who wanted her to be stripped of everything, and desolate, if she was to save the Elf. But the Linnet had had no mercy." [LL 310–11])

Here again for Ortese, the goldfinch stands in for a kind of divine presence – something which can give hope, but also inspires fear – and we are reminded of Apa's "Church of the Pope" in *Il porto di Toledo.* Then:

> Ricordava le parole di Elmina quella sera, dopo la cena con fili d'erba, alla casarella: "Nel mio cuore c'è un nome solo." Ora capiva. Quel nome era il suo, di Ingmar, ma non si poteva fare, e non era stato fatto. Il Cardillo, per salvare Käppchen, aveva fissato un prezzo: la giovinezza e il silenzio eterno (sorvoliamo sulla contraddizione in termini) di Elmina sul suo segreto. Allora sarebbe stata "ricompensata." Così diceva, ma non aveva mantenuto la promessa.' Aveva incassato il premio, ma la promessa non l'aveva mantenuta [...] (O forse non aveva potuto?). Infame Cardillo! Ma col Cardillo, pure, talvolta, maledicendolo, Ingmar era entrato a poco a poco, a furia di lacrime e di silenzi, in una sorta di triste dimestichezza, e spesso, qualche volta al mattino, e certe sere dei lunghi inverni, perfino lo pregava: "Cardillo, non dimenticarti di Elmina e di Käppchen. Cardillo, Uccello

santo, ascolta, se puoi, tutti i poveri Folletti e le loro mute sorelle. Liberali dal male. Proteggili, Angelo o Demone che tu sia, nobile Cardillo – finché il sole riempie di gioia tutto il cielo, e quando la notte si accosta. Conducili, se puoi, Cardillo, da me." (R2 613–14)

("He [Neville] recalled Elmina'a words, that even[ing] after their frugal supper at the Little House: 'In my heart there is but a single name.' Now he understood. That name was his, Ingmar's, but [it could not be uttered, and it had not been]. To save Käppchen the Linnet had fixed a price: Elmina's youth and her eternal silence [(let's pass over the contradiction in terms)] about her secret. If she paid that price she would be 'rewarded.' So he said: but he had not kept his promise. He had collected the prize but not kept his promise [...] (Or maybe it was not in his power?). Oh, villainous Linnet! And yet, though cursing him at times, by dint of silences and tears Ingmar had gradually crept into a sort of rueful familiarity with the Linnet, and often – sometimes in the morning, sometimes in the long winter evenings – he even used to pray to him:

'O Linnet, forget not Elmina and Käppchen. O Linnet, sacred Bird, be mindful, if thou may'st, of all poor Elves and their voiceless sisters. Deliver them from evil. Protect them, Angel or Demon as thou boast, noble Linnet, while the Sun suffuses the whole sky with joy and when the night draws nigh. And if thou may'st, lead them, O Linnet, to me.'" [LL 311])

This time, in a surreal way, his prayer will be answered. In the final scene, the butler enters and announces:

"Signore, un certo Cardillo, da Napoli, chiede di esser ricevuto da Sua Altezza." "Fatelo passare!" gridò ancora il principe, e fu preso da un gelo meraviglioso." (R2 630)

("'A Monsieur Linnet, from Naples, is asking to be received by Your Highness.' 'Show him in!' cried the prince once more, seized by an icy, wondrous chill." [LL 324])

At that moment we hear the Cardillo's cry, the "familiar refrain," heard throughout the novel:

Oò! Oò! Oò!
e poi:
Oò! Oò! Oò

Più lieto e mite di così non c'era nulla. E il principe benedisse la luna che riappariva sulle pareti, e quella voce sovrumana che gli aveva reso tanto cara – mentre passava sul suo capo – la oscura vita. Benedisse il Cardillo che arrivava, e finalmente gli avrebbe spiegato tutto. La follia e la separazione, il dolore e questa gioia che giungeva adesso con lui: tutta calma, fredda, infinita. (R2 630)

("*O-hoh! O-hoh! O-hoh!*
and then:
Ohhh! Ohhh! Ohhh!

(Nothing more gentle, nothing more gladsome. And the prince blessed the moon that gleamed on the walls and that superhuman voice that, passing above his head, had made his darkened life so dear to him. He blessed the Linnet even now arriving, who at last would explain it all. Folly, sorrow, separation, and this joy that he was bringing with him now: utterly calm, and cold, and infinite." [LL 325])

So ends *Il Cardillo addolorato* – with peace – because Ortese, this lucid writer, who does not shrink from showing us the horrors of Naples and of the whole planet, is ultimately a poet of the light.

I would like to close by quoting a paragraph that Leone Traverso wrote half a century ago about *Fiaba e mistero*, a book by Cristina Campo, a writer so different from and yet in so many ways so similar to Ortese:

Il tema stesso (il mistero) non viene affrontato, spogliato, frugato ed esposto alla curiosità "dissacrante," ma – nelle vesti mutevoli della fiaba e d'altri simboli – circuito e interrogato, con un amore intriso di reverenza, quale intima sostanza del mondo apparente e senso e motore della nostra vita.

("The theme itself (mystery) is not confronted, stripped, searched and exposed to 'desecrating'; curiosity, but rather – in the mutable garments of fairytales and other symbols – encircled and questioned, with a love suffused with reverence, being as the intimate substance of the apparent world and the meaning and mover of our life").[16]

NOTES

1 A literal translation of the title could be *The Sorrowful Goldfinch.*
2 "Britannica Book of the Year," *Encyclopaedia Britannica*, 222.

3 According to Sharon Wood, "the Sorrowing Goldfinch is a dense, complex tale which reworks the structures and conventions of the traditional fairy story to such a point that even a brief summary is of necessity a distortion." See Wood, "Such stuff as dreams are made on," 179. Also Luca Clerici and Claudio Marabini believe that the novel cannot be summarized. See Clerici, *Apparizione e visione,* 602; Marabini, "Diario di lettura," 222.
4 Clerici, *Apparizione e visione,* 597.
5 Ortese, "Ortese: chi sono io? Amica, ma delle vittime," 17, quoted in Clerici, *Apparizione e visione,* 624.
6 Ortese, "Il male freddo," 13, quoted in Clerici, *Apparizione e visione,* 630.
7 See note 6 in Gala Rebane, "The Flickering Light of Reason: Anna Maria Ortese's *Il cardillo addolorato* and the Critique of European Modernity."
8 As Flora Ghezzo and Gala Rebane have noticed, the name Hieronymus brings to mind Hieronymus Bosch, whose world is not so distant from the world in which Lillot moves. See, in this volume, Rebane's essay, and Ghezzo, "Voci dall'oltrestoria."
9 For a detailed analysis of Käppchen, see Papini, "Luoghi della soglia tra epifania e miraggio."
10 Maraini, "E tu chi eri?", 24–25 [464 in this volume].
11 Ortese, "Il monaciello di Napoli," published in *Ateneo veneto* in 1940. Then reprinted by Adelphi in 2001, in the volume *Il monaciello di Napoli,* with another story, *Il fantasma.* See Iannaccone, "Nota ai testi" and "Anna Maria Ortese: il 'Monaciello' e la nostalgia del perduto."
12 Maraini, "E tu chi eri?", 25 [461].
13 Ibid.
14 Matthew 25:40. *The New Oxford Annotated Bible with the Apocrypha: New Revised Standard Version.*
15 "Britannica Book of the Year," 222.
16 Traverso, review of Cristina Campo, "Fiaba e mistero," 3.

WORKS CITED

Clerici, Luca. *Apparizione e visione: Vita e opere di Anna Maria Ortese.* Milan: Mondadori, 2002.

Encyclopaedia Britannica, 8th ed., s.v. "Britannica Book of the Year." Cambridge, UK; New York: University Press, 1994.

Farnetti, Monica. "Note ai testi: *Il cardillo addolorato,*" in *Romanzi,* Vol. 2, by Anna Maria Ortese. Milan: Adelphi, 2005.

Ghezzo, Flora. "Voci dall'oltrestoria: *Il cardillo addolorato* di Anna Maria Ortese e la crisi della modernità." In "Per Anna Maria Ortese," ed. Luca Clerici. *Il Giannone* 4, no. 7–8 (January–December 2006): 221–43.

Haas, Franz. "Anna Maria Ortese, *Il cardillo addolorato*." *Belfagor* 49 (1994): 111–15.
Iannaccone, Giuseppe. "Anna Maria Ortese: il 'Monaciello' e la nostalgia del perduto." *Critica letteraria* 114 (2002): 109–21.
– "Nota ai testi," in *Il Monaciello di Napoli*, by Anna Maria Ortese, 133–37. Milan: Adelphi, 2001.
Marabini, Claudio. "Diario di lettura." *Nuova Antologia* 128 (October–December 1993): 229–31.
Maraini, Dacia. *E tu chi eri? Ventisei interviste sull'infanzia.* Milan: Rizzoli, 1998.
Ortese, Anna Maria. "Il male freddo." *Lo Straniero* 2 (Spring 1998): 13.
– "Il monaciello di Napoli." *Ateneo veneto* 127, no. 3–4 (March–April 1940): 105–22.
– "Ortese: chi sono io? Amica, ma delle vittime." *La Stampa*, 19 June 1990, 17.
Papini, Mavina. "Luoghi della soglia tra epifania e miraggio: *Il cardillo addolorato*." In *Paesaggio e memoria: giornata di studi su Anna Maria Ortese*, ed. Caterina De Caprio and Laura Donadio, 109–23. Naples: Libreria Dante & Decartes, 2003.
Traverso, Leone. "Fiaba e mistero." *La Nazione*, 5 December 1962, 3.
Wood, Sharon. "'Such stuff as dreams are made on': Anna Maria Ortese and the Art of the Real." In *Italian Women's Writing, 1860–1994.* London; Atlantic Highland, NJ: Athlone, 1995.

12 Alonso, the Poet and the Killer: Ortese's Eco-logical Reading of Modern Western History

TATIANA CRIVELLI SPECIALE

Tal fra le vaste californie selve
Nasce beata prole, a cui non sugge
Pallida cura il petto, a cui le membra
Fera tabe non doma; e vitto il bosco,
Nidi l'intima rupe, onde ministra
L'irrigua valle, inopinato il giorno
Dell'atra morte incombe. Oh contra il nostro
Scellerato ardimento inermi regni
Della saggia natura!

(So lives, in California's forests vast,
A happy race, whose life-blood is not drained
By pallid care, whose limbs are not by fierce
Disease consumed: the woods their food, their homes
The hollow rock, the streamlet of the vale
Its waters furnishes, and, unforeseen,
Dark death upon them steals. Ah, how unarmed,
Wise Nature's happy votaries, are ye,
Against our impious audacity!)

Giacomo Leopardi, *Inno ai patriarchi*, vv. 104–12.

About Animal and Human

Striving for a suitable designation of the *quid* that distinguishes beings as human or animal, Heidegger proposes that the particular mark of humans is the possession of an ontological self-consciousness, a specific trait that animals undoubtedly lack. Thus, in the years 1929–30 during his famous academic lecture, *Die Grundbegriffe der Metaphysik* (The Fundamental Concept of Metaphysics), he asserts a kind of spectrum of worldly consciousness in claiming that "the stone is worldless, the animal poor in world and man world-forming."[1] Seventy years later, Derrida approaches Heidegger's conclusion, pointing out the specific disadvantage of Heideggerian thought. He suggests that while the German philosopher moves towards a new questioning of the world and aims to deconstruct the metaphysical tradition of rational Cartesian subjectivity, his approach to understanding the differences between animals and human beings is nevertheless consistently and dogmatically Cartesian.[2] Derrida implies, rather, that the urge for distinction and for meticulous differentiation hides the need for a specific characterization of the human being – a view that discloses the desire to assign to mankind a spiritual or rational ability liable to prevail in the fight for immortality despite the animal component of our physical bodies and their inevitable death. This need is so strongly rooted in Western humanistic tradition that our profound affinity to the animal has been removed from the (metaphysical) philosophical discourse on the human being; the animal is observed abstractedly, and thus becomes a mere naming construction: an *animot*, as Derrida ironizes, rather than an *animal*.[3] In a profoundly human and in all a profoundly revolutionary move, the contemporary philosopher thus observes the world of the living, causing to integrate that which traditionally it seemed fundamental to keep separate, and provoking an interpretative short-circuit that disrupts both logic, one would say, and ecology ("eco-logic," a play on words of which Derrida might not disapprove). "By means of the chimera of this singular word, the *animot*," writes Derrida, "I bring together three heterogeneous elements within a single verbal body":

> 1. I would like to have the plural of animals heard in the singular. There is no animal in the general singular, separated from man by a single indivisible limit. We have to envisage the existence of "living creatures" whose plurality cannot be assembled within the single figure of an animality that is simply opposed to humanity [...]
>
> 2. The suffix mot in *l'animot* should bring us back to the word, namely, to the word named a noun [*nommé nom*]. It opens [...] to the reference point by means of which one has always sought to draw the limit, the unique and indivisible limit held to separate man from animal, namely the word [...]

3. It would not be a matter of "giving speech back" to animals but perhaps of acceding to a thinking, however fabulous and chimerical it might be, that thinks the absence of the name and of the word otherwise, as something other than a privation.[4]

Derrida's deconstruction of the philosophical mechanism of abstraction puts forward the perfect, yet utterly problematic model of the current widespread interest in the bioethical inquiry of Western philosophy, according to which the correlation, and more precisely the distinction, between human beings and (their) animal life has become a crucial issue.[5]

The relation between human beings and animal life has historically been a central topic of debate, traceable through a wide variety of texts and discourses. From the Aristotelian distinctions of the *De Anima*, to the medieval inquiries about the existence of the *anima brutorum*, to the sensistic and the rationalist philosophy in the seventeenth and eighteenth centuries to its modern revisions, the connection between humans and animals has been persistently related to religious debates about the immortality of the soul. In the postmodern era, however, the breakdown of values sustaining the metaphysical systems, the rapid development of medical and genetic research, as well as the increased discourse about biopolitics have characterized a new standard of the inquiry. At present, its most productive results no longer lie in emphasizing differences – more precisely marks of superiority of the human being to the animal – but far more in the discovery and exertion of analogies among beings.[6]

Amid these new paths of research, one may easily include, in a perfect postmodernist puzzle, the ancient mode of reflecting upon the world, namely poetry. In fact, if regarded in relation to its Greek significance ποιέω [poieo] – as an act of literary creation – poetry may contribute to understanding the relationship that humankind has with the "creation" in itself, that is the world and its inhabiting creatures. The reason why the human creator, the poet, can experiment the deepest empathy with creatures might be tragically simple, since, as Derrida claims referring to Jeremy Bentham's defence of the animal's faculties, "the question of the animal is not whether it can think or speak but whether it can *suffer*."[7] On that note, and in order to understand Ortese's novel of the "puma," I would like to consider here suffering and poetry as two modes placed at the disposal of human beings to connect with the world and to be in close communion with it. Suffering will then be regarded as a key element necessary to understanding the human need to create.

To put it another way, and considering Anna Maria Ortese's description of the puma Alonso, protagonist of the novel *Alonso e i visionari*, "il dolore del mondo, e la bontà e maestà della Natura" (R2 880; "the pain of the world and the goodness and majesty of Nature") are one, and some human beings, the most visionary ones, can die of their "partecipazione, davvero profonda, al dolore del mondo" (R2 870; "real, profound participation in the pain of the world") just as Professor Jimmy Op does.[8] The poet is in fact, by far, the most fitting being that may assume the role of the visionary highlighted in the title of the book. So that it is not surprising that Anna Maria Ortese asserts her profound poetic affinity with the visionary figure in her novel claiming that "Jimmy Op sono io, perché Jimmy Op è il portavoce della giustizia e della pietà in questo mondo a una sola dimensione, abitato dal superfluo" ("Jimmy Op is me, because Jimmy Op is the spokesperson of justice and compassion in this one-dimensional world in which superfluity lives").[9]

What Kind of Vision?

Alonso e i visionari, the story of a wild baby puma that lives both in and beyond the real world – suspended in a third, timeless and spaceless, dimension of doubt and hope – is also the eternal story of the encounter between the visionary human being and the animal. Broadly speaking, given that the puma assumes in the novel the form of an absence (it is either remembered in the past, believed dead, vanished, or has perhaps never existed) all those who see it, the reader included, could be consigned to the category of "visionaries," already mentioned in the title. However, those who are fated to encounter the puma constitute an especially singular group of visionaries. They range from the little ones of pure heart – as in the case of baby Decio – to the corrupt-minded adults who hover around the figure of Professor Antonio Decimo, Decio's father. The plot has at its core a crime and a secret: the killing of Professor Decimo's oldest son, who, on the lam after committing terrorist acts, is taken down in an ambush at his father's house in Tuscany, and the mystery of Alonso, the "figurina stellare che sembrava aver provocato la morte del giovane" ("glistening figurine who seemed to have caused the death of the little one").[10] In the background of this scenario, established through the complex intersecting of temporal planes and narratorial voices, there is an Italy shifting from the post-war period to the so-called *Anni di piombo* ("years of lead"), and there are the economic, cultural, and political forces that have impacted the country's development. These forces are embodied emblematically in the characters, places, and times which constitute the American component of the novel: in particular in the primordial Arizona of the puma and in the "Americanized" Italy, a product of the post-war reconstruction, as well as in the figures of the narrator ("Mi chiamo Winter. Stella Winter Grotz. Nata in Pennsylvania cinquantasei anni fa," R2 633; "My name is Winter. Stella Winter Grotz. Born in Pennsylvania fifty-six years ago")[11] and of Professor Jimmy Opfering, called Op, from the "University of H." in Boston.

Founded on the mechanisms of the *detective story*, the novel nonetheless stands apart, more for its attention to the clues than for its plot, and finds itself articulated in an intentionally weak narrative structure. Subdivided into four long chapters, the story unfolds through the filter of retrospective narration between Jimmy Op and Stella Winter. After having established the theme of the unresolved crime, the first chapter, "La vacanza in Arizona" (R2 633–76; "The Vacation in Arizona"), narrates the preceding events: a trip in America shared by Decimo and Op, who are both colleagues and friends; the encounter with the puma; the death of Decimo's younger child; and Alonso's move to Italy. The second chapter, "Conversazione e lettere" (R2 677–807), recounts the ensuing events through the correspondence between Op and his Italian colleague, from the presumed death of the puma to the elaboration of Professor Decimo's political ideology, from the anarchic terrorism of his son Julius to the crime of Prato and the successive investigations and speculations. These events intersect those of the past with the current investigations. The reading of the correspondence, not unlike the reading of the rest of the novel, proceeds with revelations of new interpretive keys about the previously accepted truth. In a trajectory that every now and then takes on the textures of a crime novel and of a political crime thriller but is also reminiscent of mystical, philosophical meditations on the world, the chapter concludes with the arrest of Op, on his deathbed, "incriminato, purtroppo, *di tutto*" (R2 806; "incriminated, alas, *in everything*.") In the third chapter, "Ultime Lettere" (R2 808–66), Stella Winter reflects on the developments in the case, on the basis of other pieces of information that come to her via correspondence either with Commissioner Ingres, who is in charge of the investigation, or directly with Op, who is incarcerated in Genoa, and who, in a letter addressed to Abraham Lincoln, declares himself willing to pay and be charged as "come complice massimo nella disgrazia del mondo (che è la persecuzione e morte del Cucciolo)" [R2 850; "as fully complicit in the disgrace of the world (which is the persecution and the death of the Cub)"] and asks for justice for the puma, which according to him has been killed.

The novel closes with a brief appended note from the narrator, under the heading "Distanze" (R2 867–88), which provides the reader with updates on the case two years after the deaths of Op and Decimo. The plot seems to conclude with the posthumous rehabilitation of Op's reputation, as he is proven innocent by new evidence, and on the reaffirmation of the presence of the ungraspable but persistent cub Alonso. "Questa, in breve, la storia del Puma, che è anche storia satirica, di una morale che esclude, con una frettolosa e falsa giustizia, tutti i veri moventi del male [...] Quindi, i *Visionari* è solo superficialmente storia di 'terrorismo': è storia dell'eterna persecuzione, morte, e quindi ritorno, per dare pace, del Puma" ("This is, in short, the story of the Puma, which is also a satirical story, one containing a moral, which excludes, with a hasty and false justice, all of the true motives of evil. [...] Therefore, the *Visionaries* is only superficially a story about 'terrorism': it is a story of the puma's eternal persecution, death, and thereby of its return, to bring peace").[12]

The individual's visionary capacity corresponds to the visionary capacity of nations and of their intellectual plans of "progress," in a jarring contradiction between laws of culture and natural occurrences, between historical circumstance and the universality of life. Contrasting an armed revolutionary vision of history, embodied by his Italian colleague, to a sacrificial vision that led him to take the guilt of the world on himself, Op-Ortese adopts the visionary manner of the poet. Although attracted to the teleological ideology of the intellectual, he cannot close his eyes to the pain of life, because this links him to the very essence of being and presses him to scan the horizon in search of the apparition of the glistening eyes of the puma. In the way of a Derridian "autobiographical animal" *ante litteram,* the poet knows to look at the world through the gaze of the puma: but he or she knows also that poetry, innocence, and the helpless and primordial nature are by now at most invisible apparitions.

Furthermore, the novel is written exactly in the liminal spaces that it explores, in the perpetual movements of exchange and suspense between human and animal, physical and metaphysical, real and ideal. Even as it reveals differences, it mostly recalls the profound and vanished consonances that bind humans and animals in a unifying "Spirit of the World" (R2 886). With respect to its primary inspiration, the novel could be regarded as an experiment of magic realism, especially since it strives to unmask the magic that inhabits the real world.[13] Yet, as it will later be discussed, the symbolic value of the central character, the puma, adds further complexity. On one hand, the novel is strongly embedded within the realistic narrative structures of a criminal novel's plot and at the same time it can be interpreted, as various critics suggest, as a mystical hymn to some lost gods of ancient times, or alternatively as a song for the utopia of a perfectly natural, or even of a Christian and redeemed, human world.[14] De facto, however, the purity and innocence of the puma Alonso and his best friend Decio not only end up misunderstood, but prove ultimately incapable of altering the course of the unfurling events as they are narrated: so that, more – and more simply – than a utopia, *Alonso e i visionari*, as its title evokes, has to be considered a poetical vision. As the author implies, the novel, "si presenta quindi come una difficile, sottile storia di evasione, in un primo tempo dal 'reale,' o almeno dalla sua dimensione più accettata; e poi, in un secondo tempo, nell'approfondimento del 'reale', per effetto della forza misteriosa della 'visione'" ("presents itself, therefore, as a difficult, subtle story of evasion, firstly from the 'real,' or at least from its most accepted dimension; and then, secondly, as an in-depth examination of the 'real,' through the effect of the mysterious force of the 'vision'").[15] In this poetical journey through the sufferings of the world, the perfect identification between human being and animal is disclosed in its original and potential charm of affinity as well as in its utterly bitter impossibility. From the perspective of Giacomo Leopardi – a thinker and poet who undoubtedly inspired Ortese[16] – we view the novel as a keepsake of the vast knowledge that animals, children, and all "savage" humans share, as the reservoir of the grand knowledge that humankind generally neglects in its opting for a rational, cultivated, and "progressive" idea of modern civilization whose task is to eradicate errors rather than to disseminate truths.[17]

Alonso's Gaze on Modernity

As I have argued elsewhere, the puma Alonso – along with the iguana and the *Cardillo* in the other two novels of Ortese's so-called "trilogy of the angel-beasts"– should be read as a significant postmodern "teratological sign," intended, as Sharon Wood suggests, to superimpose "onto our narrow consciousness of the present the hidden desires and anxieties which we prefer to omit from our definition of the real" and, in the specific case of *Alonso e i visionari*, our definition of the human.[18] The prodigy and diversity of Ortese's fantastic creatures are expressed mainly through the fluidity of their characterization, which inhibits their classification. Namely, they are relentlessly capable of metamorphosis: the puma Alonso, as well as its counterpart "Cane bianco," an abandoned maculated white dog that appears towards the end of the novel, is mistaken for a servant of the Decimo family, after whom it was named; likewise, his innocent and dead friend Decio *is*, in a way, the child Mohammed, his brother's son, who will be renamed after him, and who carries the same maculated spots of the "Cane bianco." Furthermore, zoomorphic Ortesian characters keep pushing themselves out of the boundaries of rational knowledge, while eradicating every known distance between humans and animals and thus erasing for the reader the opportunity to assess space and time: none of the characters can say with certainty if Alonso ever existed, if it died and was resurrected (those who believe in its reappearance disagree on how many times the puma returns), or if it is still alive, as suggested by the puma's water bowl being mysteriously emptied after its death.[19]

The weakening of the rational and cognitive experience pursued by Ortese through her imaginary creatures generates a powerful effect of endless intersecting of truths and facts, and, simultaneously, it questions the validity of our cognitive distinctions.[20] Therefore, it accomplishes through poetry what Derrida aims at through philosophical speculation, relativizing the specificity of the human being, so that "we shall have to move continuously along this coming and going between the oldest and what is coming, in the exchange among the new, the 'again [*de nouveau*],' and the 'anew [*à nouveau*]' of repetition."[21] Staging an anti-anthropocentric way of looking at life, *Alonso e i visionari* leads us to the dimension that the philosopher Rosi Braidotti defines as the postmodern "*continuum* con il mondo animale, minerale, vegetale, extraterrestre e tecnologico" ("*continuum* with the worlds of the animal, mineral, vegetal, extraterrestrial and technological").[22] This manner of understanding life, however, radically contradicts the human desire of superiority and domination, which instead expresses itself through the programmatic severance of the links with the rest of the living. As Professor Op clearly explains to Stella Winter, "questa non è una storia di animali" ("this is not a story about animals") as it is also "la storia di un odio, che ha generato altro odio e rovina; e alla base di quest'odio ci fu sempre [...] una dolcezza [...] di cui disfarsi" (R2 673; "the story of a hate that generated more hatred and ruin: at its origins there always was [...] a sweetness [...] to be casted off"). The visionaries who cherish Alonso, as well as those who try to eliminate him (the inspired caring poet and the ideology-driven killer) are both facing the most vivid problem of Western humanity in late modernity, that is the complexity of controlling and / or removing diversities. Yet, they accomplish the task with radically different means that inevitably engender fundamentally different solutions.

In such a sophisticated *mise en scène,* the chronological setting of Alonso's story during the Italian "anni di piombo" – the decade in which Italy lived its most tragic contrast of left- and right-wing extremisms, that ranged from the Piazza Fontana bombing (Milan 1969) to the kidnapping and executing of Aldo Moro, leader of the Christian Democracy (Rome 1978); that totalled almost 8,000 attacks, 69 deaths, and many thousands of injured; and that left behind a politically ravaged land – might not seem to hold a primary importance; yet, it is far from insignificant.[23] The victim, Julius, as well as his father Professor Decimo, do in fact represent the perfect incarnation of rationality's drift and of the oxymoronic claim to establish and to rule freedom: Professor Decimo through his theoretical writings; Julius through his actions as a terrorist leader, who proves responsible for many attacks on the representatives of the established order.[24] As a counterpoint to these characters, the meek Professor Op – whose name, Opfering, recalls the German word for "sacrifice," *Opfer*[25] – embodies the questioning and caring mind of a sensitive being for whom the puma is something to believe in. The American professor, though, is far from representing a simple and innocent being, as it is confirmed by the fact that his role in the story, instead of being clarified as the narrative progresses, becomes increasingly more complicated, so that the suspicion directed towards him grows as his involvement and his responsibility in the crimes are disclosed. He is much more an intellectual, a man inevitably corrupted by the vice of reasoning. Paradoxically, he is also a man who did not close the door on the "sacred," perhaps thanks to his American heritage of natural simplicity and humanitarian sociability ("ma forse io vedo le cose da Americano […] noi non abbiamo un vero culto della mente, non vediamo differenze […] tra un teorema e un albero, tra natura e uomo," R2 642; "but maybe I see things as an American […] we don't have a true cult of the mind, we don't see differences […] between a theorem and a tree, nature and man"). Or, perhaps because of his deep affinity with the literature he loves and teaches as an "italianista appassionato" (R2 634; "passionate Italianist"), he is open to what he calls "l'*imponderabile,* il *senza spiegazione* che è nella natura della vita, perfino – anzi soprattutto – dove essa è più umile e muta" (R2 742; "the *imponderable,* the *without explication* that is in the nature of life, even there – or better said most of all there – where it is most humble and mute").

The alarming otherness that these men are confronting – symbolized by Alonso – recalls, in the same disconcerting way, the experience with another feline, Derrida's notorious cat: both are meant to trigger a profound *animalséance* (and please note that the cat's gaze is called "visionary"):[26]

> I often ask myself, just to see, *who I am* – and who I am (following) at the moment when, caught naked, in silence, by the gaze of an animal, for example the eyes of a cat, I have trouble, yes, a bad time overcoming my embarrassment.
>
> Whence this malaise?
>
> I have trouble repressing a reflex dictated by immodesty. Trouble keeping silent within me a protest against indecency. Against the impropriety that comes of finding oneself naked, one's sex exposed, stark naked before a cat that looks at you without moving, just to see. The impropriety [*malséance*] of a certain animal nude before the other animal, from that point on one might call it a knife of *animalséance*: the single, incomparable and original experience of the impropriety that would come from appearing in truth naked, in front of the insistent gaze of the animal, a benevolent or pitiless gaze, surprised or cognizant. The gaze of a seer, visionary, or extra-lucid blind person. It is as if I were ashamed, therefore, naked in front of this cat but ashamed of being ashamed.[27]

In Ortese's novel, Alonso and its many metamorphic counterparts – the homonymous servant, the maculated white dog, the children Decio and Mohammed – fulfil the provocative role of the Derridian animal: all embody the disturbing imponderable, removed from the world of rationality, and they make visible the suffering beast of our desiring souls. Far from being a mere mythical creature of nature or a deity, as some critics have suggested, Alonso is the sign of what has been forgotten, left carelessly behind in the historical pursuit of development and modernity, chasing what Leopardi ironically defined as the "magnifiche sorti, e progressive" ("the magnificent progressive fate") of the positivistic faith in our rationality.[28] The puma from Arizona, a territory that is believed to be "la prima parte del mondo emersa, con tutti i suoi colori, dal Caos" (R2 638–39; "the first part of the world that emerged, with all of its colors, from Chaos"), represents that missing part of our thinking, which in *L'Iguana* is called indifferently "bellezza o mostro, non importa" (R1 68; "beauty or monster, it doesn't matter"). When our minds glimpse it, this "missing part" can alter the essence of our life. In Ortese's trilogy, what rational, Western, male thought is missing is expressed (albeit disguised) in the exotic traits of the servant-iguana Estrellita, in the childish weakness of the claws of the *cardillo*-Hieronymus, as well as in the natural, fiery tenderness of Alonso's look, whose eyes seem to pray to be acknowledged.[29] This forgotten sweetness still visits us in the guise of a cub. We, as readers, must be ready to give credit to the visionaries who leave the door open at night and prepare the water bowl for quenching the baby puma's thirst, or we won't be able to recognize its value, and we'll confound its healthy and childish foolishness with sterile anarchism.[30]

> La vita – come le ombre televisive – non è mai nella nostre stanze, ma altrove. Così, chi cercasse il Cucciolo, scruti, la notte, nel silenzio del mondo; non lo chiami, se non sottovoce, ma sempre abbia cura di rinnovare l'acqua della sua ciotola triste.
>
> Non visto, verrà. (R2 888)

> (Life – like televised projections – is never in our rooms, but elsewhere. Thus, if you seek out the Cub, search, at night, in the silence of the world; do not call out to it, if not in a low voice, but always take care to refill its sad water bowl.
>
> Unseen, it will come.)

Is There a Difference between a Theorem and a Tree?

Alonso e i visionari is also a detective story, which revolves around a killer who cannot be found despite all intellectual efforts, the inquiries being averted by the puma's disturbing archaic soul, a soul that can't be caught nor definitely eliminated. As I argue, the detective storyline within the novel reinforces the historical critique to Western modernity.

From Ortese's eco-logical perspective, as I defined it – that is, a point of view that wants to bridge the gap between the human rationality and the imponderable, between "a theorem and a tree" – a pivotal historical juncture of Western modernity is certainly represented by the European post-war period. It is a time marked by a deep cultural shift, in which "l'Europa si svegliava alla religione della specie umana, che pure la guerra aveva sbranato. Si tendeva a elevare un monumento all'uomo nuovo che era – doveva essere – privo di reverenza, di pietà per il bruto. Il *bruto* veniva odiato, proprio perché l'uomo nuovo era già bruto" (R2 643;

"Europe awoke to the religion of the human species, though the war had devoured it. It aimed to raise a monument to the new man, who was, and ought to be, deprived of respect or pity for the brute. The *brute* became despised, precisely because the new man was already a brute"). The need for a rational elaboration of war's horrors – that posed, as Adorno poignantly claims, the question of the possibility of poetry – was transmuted, according to Ortese, in the double attempt to explain the past and to plan the future expelling from the Western society the non-rational (in its various forms of memory, nature, desire, faith, magic, poetry) as something unworthy. Yet, to no avail, for, "to put it simply," to humankind the world still has "something unclear, desperate" (R2 703; "Dunque per lei, caro amico, il mondo ha qualcosa di non chiaro, di 'disperato,' per esprimerci semplicemente?" "Direi di sì"), since no ideology can fill that void. "Humankind lost forever something invaluable," something which is not "a thing" but "a memory":

"Cara signora, la cosa di cui parlo non è una cosa. È una memoria, direi."

"Ciò conferma quanto dico. Ma, di grazia, memoria di che?"

"Lei ha toccato il punto dolente. Può darsi anzi che io mi sia espresso con difetto. La cosa perduta non c'è più. Il vuoto c'è."

"Dobbiamo dunque supporre che fosse una cosa molto ... molto ..." commentò commossa Flora.

"Parole non ce ne sono per dirla. Che cosa sia non si sa. Ma non è mancanza recente. L'oggetto, anzi, è tutt'altro che recente. La sua assenza, dai più, non è avvertita se non con qualche tiepida malinconia. Ciò che li spinge, ridicolmente, a contemplare i tramonti. Da pochi è avvertita dalla nascita, subito, per sempre."

"Costoro sono poeti, immagino arrischiai un po' timida."

("Dear madam, the thing of which I speak is not a thing. It is a memory, I would say."

"So much confirms what I say. But, please, the memory of what?"

"You touched upon a sore point. It could be given rather that I expressed myself poorly. The lost thing is no longer there. There is emptiness."

"We must therefore suppose that the thing was very ... very ..." commented Flora, moved.

"There are no words to express it. Nobody knows what it is. But it is not a recent shortcoming. The object, rather, is anything but recent. Its absence, for most people, is not noticeable if not with some tepid melancholy. It is what drives them, ridiculously, to contemplate the sunsets. A few perceive it at birth, immediately, forever."

"Those are poets, I imagine." I hazarded a bit shyly).[31]

All individuals have – more or less intensely – the memory of this profound ancestral loss. Precisely this awareness generates the "uomini del lutto" or "della perdita" ("men of grief," or "of loss"), the few (poets and avengers) who feel this void from their birth, with great intensity: poets may act on lost memories thanks to the power of illusions, whereas avengers express their impotence through gratuitous killing. This existential grief, so similar to Leopardi's *noia*, is firmly bound to the illusion that human beings are superior to all other living creatures. In a passage very close to Ortese's poetics, Leopardi expresses the same idea. In his memorable "Dialogue of an Imp and a Gnome," he argues that humans:

> non solamente si persuadevano che le cose del mondo non avessero altro uffizio che di stare al servigio loro, ma facevano conto che tutte insieme, allato al genere umano, fossero una bagattella. E però le loro proprie vicende le chiamavano rivoluzioni del mondo, e le storie delle loro genti, storie del mondo: benché si potevano numerare, anche dentro ai termini della terra, forse tante altre specie, non dico di creature, ma solamente di animali, quanti capi d'uomini vivi: i quali animali, che erano fatti espressamente per coloro uso, non si accorgevano però mai che il mondo si rivoltasse.
>
> (when they not only persuaded themselves that the things of the world had no purpose other than to serve them, but reckoned that everything else put together, compared with the human race, was a mere trifle. And therefore their own adventures they called world revolutions, and the histories of their peoples, histories of the world; although even within the confines of the earth one could count perhaps as many species, not simply of creatures in general but just of animals, as there were living men. And yet these animals, who were made expressly for their use, never realized that the world was in rebellion).[32]

Through her visionary writing and the melancholic sweetness of Alonso's gazing, Ortese specifically gives voice to the loss, to what post-war modern society, having reached the end of its parabola, no longer sees. She thereby encroaches emotions onto the desert landscape of rationality and (re)introduces forgotten memories of nature onto the bare architecture of political ideologies. Like the perfume and the brightness of the Leopardian *ginestra*, the flower on the Vesuvius, the yellowish fur of Ortese's puma starkly contrasts with the stony ground it inhabits. Similarly, it bookmarks a page of our collective cultural history so as to remind us – as a living contradiction of our contemporary selves – of what humanity has forgotten during its blind march towards success.[33] The puma is, therefore, the insignificant but also the eternal, the rejected and the revenant, the unheard and the unseen, the forgotten that keeps coming back to our memories, the colonized that lives with its persecutors, the prisoner of civilization that reveals nature, the unknown that knows us, the defeated *servant* and the *loving father* or "l'immagine di colui che sta in fondo alla società, a raccoglierne i rifiuti, e di colui, l'essere amante, che talvolta vi abita" (R2 817–18; "the image of the one that is at the bottom of society, collecting its waste, and of the one, the loving being, that sometimes inhabits them").

Alonso's continuous persecution is the precise crime for which Professor Jimmy Op is arrested, sharing his responsibility along with "l'intero corpo della cultura occidentale, di ogni Occidente, che restò, inerte, nell'ombra, in tutti questi secoli o giorni mentre tale delitto si consumava" (R2 842; "the entire corpus of Western culture, of every West, which stayed, motionless, in the shadow, during all those centuries or days, while this crime was perpetrated"). As a most logical consequence, the American professor, prisoner of his lucid folly, addresses his supposed last letter to the person who, better than any other in Western history, became a dominant symbol of freedom and of dignity in the eyes of the oppressed, Abraham Lincoln:

> Al Signor Abramo Lincoln / (*Primo* Presidente degli Stati d'America – circa *trecento* anni fa) / – o a chi per Lui – … / (*ultimo inverno di questo secolo*). (R2 841)
>
> [To Mister Abraham Lincoln / (*First* President of the States of America – about *three hundred* years ago) / –or to whom it may concern– … / (*in the last winter of this century*).]

In Op's long writings, some passages of which are omitted and summed up by the narrator Stella Winter, the professor asks for justice: a dreadful act has been accomplished, which "sarà senza perdono se, almeno in ultimo, i nomi dei responsabili non saranno fatti e indicati" (R2 842; "will remain unforgiven if, at least at the end, the names of those responsible won't be mentioned and displayed"). The crime is, as we know, "la continua persecuzione, e tentata uccisione [...] del cucciolo chiamato Alonso" (R2 842; "the constant persecution and the attempted murder [...] of the cub named Alonso"). This "j'accuse" is met by confusion, embarrassment, and boredom: its mystical tone (Alonso *is* a god, and humanity needs redemption), veils a sharp interpretation of the historical development of Western society in what we now refer to as the postmodern age.

Ecce Animot

In Op's final revelation, at the end of the novel, the puma came from America to Europe in the 1950s, following therefore the liberation troops and bringing hope of friendship and mutual discovery under the infantile signs of peacefulness, sweetness, and goodness. Not only wasn't it cherished as it should have been, but those who could have explained the importance of this new relationship withheld details, so that its persecution was permitted and legitimated by a culture "fondata sul diritto, per l'uomo, per ogni uomo, dunque anche i Decimo e gli Opfering (e ogni più modesto esponente universitario), di considerarsi e agire come il Primo e il Migliore, colui cui spetta ogni bene, non importa se ne riceva strazio e follia la verde Terra" [R2 844; "founded on the right of man, of each man, that is also of Decimo and Opfering (and every single university's representative), to consider himself – and act as – the First and the Best, as the one who deserves every good, does not matter if green Earth receives injury and folly."] The post-war encounter and mutual friendship between the puma of Arizona, symbol of uncorrupted nature, and the little Italian child Decio are narrated as the possibility of a reciprocal acknowledgment, a long-needed reunion of brothers who have previously ignored the existence of each another. But Decio dies, and the puma falls victim to the intellectual sadism of the culture of human primacy. Nor do things improve with the next generation, after the so-called Revolution against the Father (Ortese refers here, as said, to the *Anni di piombo*), when "la Delusione e il Saccheggio, la collera calunniosa contro il Passato e la Debolezza riempirono di voci il mondo" (R2 845; "Delusion and Robbery, the calumnious rage against the Past and the Weakness filled the World with their voices"). The idealistic inspiration of these revolutionary attempts, which draw on the rational desire of a so-called egalitarianism, do in fact blindly forget to include subalterns, so that – with the silent and accountable approval of the intellectuals

– they relentlessly implode in their excesses, celebrating slaughters and cruelty: "in nome della libertà dai propri limiti, si varcarono tutti i limiti altrui" (R2 846; "in the name of the liberation from our limits, the limits of all others were overstepped").

In his fully visionary attitude, Jimmy Op, the poet, confesses to sharing the responsibility of the killing through omission and reticence: insisting that the virtue of the human intellect, acknowledged by the Enlightenment, achieved its utmost expression in affirming freedom and equality; yet overlooking that modern Western society has forgotten to include within its idea of equality "the integrity and gentleness of the Earth" as well as "the Past and the Weak," symbolized by primordial Arizona, and has worshipped the "divinità dell'utile e del Visibile" (R2 846; "god of utility and of Visible"). Living under the banner of knowledge, humankind fails to identify pain, persistently experienced by the vast majority of living beings: our revolt, our rage against the past and the weak, took us no further than to the "luoghi disperati a cui portano i grandi Mutamenti Esteriori" (R2 848; "desperate places the big External Changes are directed to"). The new slaves, to whom Abraham Lincoln should have guaranteed freedom, are, therefore, once again, the forgotten, and among them we should also include the non-human creatures with whom we share the earth. The intellectuals defining the discourse of modernity, guilty for their idleness, should finally sign this act of accusation and recognize that the poet and the killer have been one. As Rainer Maria Rilke memorably wrote: "We know what's out there only from the animal's / face," but we turn our eyes away, trapping "our way to freedom."[34]

Thus, Ortese proposes a significant and almost predictive reading of postmodern Western culture, putting forward the horrifying results of a failed dialogue of ideologies with nature and its principles. The puma Alonso is more than a symbol or a sign, it is a kind of literary and visual anticipation of the Derridian deconstruction of the *animot,* a living creature that far from being "poor in world" challenges with its presence the "world-forming" claim of human beings. Alonso's gaze embodies the deep pain of nature for humankind's crimes as well as the intensity of the human longing for a relation with the world and its living creatures. Alonso doesn't speak words, but the vision it represents is readable: as long as we pursue our happiness with the presumption of our distinctive superiority, we are led to a non-recognition of our true selves. We need, on the contrary, to be poetically visionary rather than Cartesianly rational. The beast of this novel constitutes an appalling element for the philosophical questioning about the nature of the human being, and it suggests a question mark after the ontological affirmation of our identity. As Derrida will put it, twenty years later than Ortese's imaginary creature:

> *Ecce animot*, that is the announcement of which I am (following) something like a trace, assuming the title of an autobiographical animal, in the form of a risky, fabulous, or chimerical response to the question "But me, who am I?" and that I have bet on treating as that of the autobiographical animal. Assuming that title, which is itself somewhat chimerical, might surprise you. It brings together two times two alliances, as unexpected as they are irrefutable.[35]

The *monstruum* enlightens, against every time-space convention, the disturbing continuity of the living creatures, our proximity to those beings we believe we should control. It also reinstates us to the centre of our natural dimension, pointing out, with no mercy, the limits of the Western intellectual tradition rooted in the Enlightenment. The puma is, therefore, not a ghost (as Jimmy Op admits, "Anch'io vi credo. Ma mi sembra un errore introdurli nella nostra storia. La quale [...] riguarda appunto la natura segreta del mondo ..." (R2 637; "I believe in ghosts, but I think it would be an error to introduce them in our story, which [...] concerns the secret nature of the world"), but a critical in-motion vision of ourselves and of our complex historical time. Ortese's characters are capable – if not of bringing back the irremediably lost harmony, killed by the rise of ideologies, between humankind and (its) nature – at least to present us the powerful and creative illusion of it.

Thus, *Alonso e i visionari* is the unreliable but deeply necessary vision of a poet, since history, as one of the greatest postmodern authors confirmed one year after Ortese's novel had been published, "is too innocent, to be left within the reach of anyone in Power, – who need but touch her, and all her Credit is in the instant vanished, as if it had never been. She needs rather to be tended lovingly and honorably by fabulists and counterfeiters, Ballad-Mongers and Cranks of every Radius, Masters of Disguise to provide her the Costume, Toilette, and Bearing, and Speech ..."[36]

NOTES

1 Heidegger, *The Fundamental Concepts of Metaphysics*. See in particular Part II, Chapter Three, 186–200.

2 See Derrida, *The Animal That Therefore I Am*, 147: "at this very moment, when Heidegger's gesture is to move forward in the direction of a new question, a new questioning concerning the world and the animal, when he claims to deconstruct the whole metaphysical tradition, notably that of subjectivity, Cartesian subjectivity, etc., insofar as the animal is concerned he remains, in spite of everything, profoundly Cartesian."
3 Ibid, 65.
4 Ibid.
5 A very well articulated bibliography on this topic can be found in Bruns, "Derrida's cat (who am I?)," 404–23. Here the author discusses Derrida's work on the present subject. Interesting suggestions for further reading are in the book review by Calarco, "The Question of the Animal," retrieved from http://www.electronicbookreview.com. Retrieved 31 March 2003. See also the distinction between bios and zoe in Rosi Braidotti's last book, *The Posthuman*.
6 As Giorgio Agamben warns, it is, therefore, more urgent to investigate the practices and the policies of the separation between humankind and animalship, rather than the metaphysical mystery of their proximity. See Agamben, *The Open: Man and Animal*.
7 See page 50 of the French text and page 396 of the English translation. Bentham's hope was clearly stated in his 1780 work: *An Introduction to the Principles of Morals and Legislation*: "The French have already discovered that the blackness of the skin is no reason a human being should be abandoned without redress to the caprice of a tormentor. It may one day come to be recognised that the number of the legs, the villosity of the skin, or the termination of the os sacrum are reasons equally insufficient for abandoning a sensitive being to the same fate. What else is it that should trace the insuperable line? Is it the faculty of reason or perhaps the faculty of discourse? But a full-grown horse or dog, is beyond comparison a more rational, as well as a more conversable animal, than an infant of a day or a week or even a month, old. But suppose the case were otherwise, what would it avail? the question is not, Can they *reason*? nor, Can they *talk*? but, Can they *suffer*?" Bentham, *An Introduction to the Principles of Morals and Legislation*, note 122 to the § XVII.6, text from the 1907 edition.
8 If not otherwise specified, all English translations are the author's, completed with the aid of Samuel Fleck and Savannah Cooper-Ramsey.
9 From an interview with Groppali, "Metti un puma nel romanzo," 14.
10 The description can be found in a self-comment by Anna Maria Ortese, which is preserved among the autographed pages. A reference to the ms. initialed E4, cited in the *Nota al testo* by Filippo Secchieri in R2 1113–30 [1124–25].

11 According to Paola Loreto, *Alonso e i visionari* can, after all, without straining things too much, be understood against the utopian backdrop of American Puritanism and can also be read as "the account of the 'conversion' of the narrator, the fifty-something American Stella Winter Grotz, who, thanks to the sacrifice of another American, the professor James Opfering, experiences a radical change of heart (intended in the sense of Jonathan Edwards, as biblical metonymy of the interiority of man) toward an acceptance of all in creation that is helpless and suffering. In other words, toward the sentiment of empathy that Emerson brings to the light of awareness in the American 'imaginary.'" Loreto, "*Alonso e i visionari*: La vocazione americana di Anna Maria Ortese," 251–71.

12 Ortese, *Lettera* to Henry Martin (Rapallo, 5 July 1996), published in Ortese, R2, *Appendice III*, 1141–43 [1143].

13 The relationship between Bontempelli's "realismo magico" and Ortese's writing has been the object of various discussions, also in the present volume (see, for instance, the introduction by Flora Ghezzo and the essays by Amelia Moser and Luigi Fontanella). I side with Farnetti, *Anna Maria Ortese,* 40, and her regard for Ortese's originality: "Mista di sapienza e *naïveté,* 'ragionamenti' e 'illazioni,' etica e metafisica, sogno e denuncia, l'opera della Ortese ha infatti sviluppato in direzione del tutto autonoma le sollecitazioni che, almeno inizialmente, potevano essere derivate dalla poetica bontempelliana" ("A mixture of wisdom and *naïveté,* 'reasoning' and 'inferences,' ethics and metaphysics, dream and denunciation, Ortese's work developed in a completely autonomous direction the impetus for which, at least in the beginning, could have derived from the poetics of Bontempelli").

14 See, for instance, the critical notes by Gramigna, "In nome del dio Puma," 27, that have the significant subtitle: "La Ortese fa dell'animale il simbolo dell'innocenza perseguitata, ma è un po' predicatoria" ("Ortese makes of the animal the symbol of persecuted innocent, but is a bit patronizing"). See also Vaccari, "Alonso e i visionari, una favola religiosa e pagana," and De Gasperin, *Loss and the Other in the Visionary Work of Anna Maria Ortese,* 251–71. The complete list of the book's reviews and a brief account of the not always benevolent readings can be found in Clerici, *Apparizione e visione,* 617.

15 Ortese, "Il puma dal cuore umano," 17. For a reading that, on the contrary, underscores the historical and political component of the narration and its relevance to contemporary Italy, see Seno, *Anna Maria Ortese: Un avventuroso realismo,* 137–52.

16 Affinities between their poetics had already been noticed when Ortese's first book, *Angelici dolori,* was published (see, for instance, the review by Fallacara, *Il Frontespizio,* 535–37). See also the entry "Leopardi" in the

repertory of Farnetti, *Anna Maria Ortese*, 68–69 and also the more recent Anedda, "Il grido del vero: Ortese e Leopardi," 257–69. In this volume, see Lucia Re's and Gian Maria Annovi's essays.

17 Giacomo Leopardi, *Zibaldone*, 2711–12, dated 21 May 1823: "Così lo spirito umano fa progressi: e tutte le scoperte fondate sulla nuda osservazione delle cose, [2712] non fanno quasi altro che convincerci de' nostri errori, e delle false opinioni da noi prese e formate e create col nostro proprio raziocinio o naturale o coltivato e (come si dice) istruito. Più oltre di questo non si va. Ogni passo della sapienza moderna svelle un errore; non pianta niuna verità (se non che tali tuttogiorno si chiamano le proposizioni, i dogmi, i sistemi in sostanza negativi). Dunque se l'uomo non avesse errato, sarebbe già sapientissimo, e giunto a quella meta a cui la filosofia moderna cammina con tanto sudore e difficoltà. Ma chi non ragiona, non erra. Dunque chi non ragiona, o per dirlo alla francese, non pensa, è sapientissimo. Dunque sapientissimi furono gli uomini prima della nascita della sapienza, e del raziocinio sulle cose: e sapientissimo è il fanciullo, e il selvaggio della California, che non conosce il pensare" ("Thus the human spirit makes progress: and all of the discoveries founded upon the naked observation of things, [2712] do little more than convince us of our errors, and of the false opinions taken by us and molded and created with our own common sense be it natural or cultivated (as one they say) and educated. One does not go beyond this. Every exercise of modern thought uproots an error; it does not plant a single truth (other than such everyday ones called propositions, dogma, systems which are essentially negative). Thus, if man had not erred, he would already be supremely wise, and have attained that aim toward which modern philosophy trudges along with such difficulty and ardor. But he who does not reason does not err. Thus, he who does not reason, or, to put it as the French do, does not think, is supremely wise. Thus, the men who came before the birth of reason and knowledge were supremely wise: and supremely wise is the youth, and the wild of California, who knows not to think").

18 Crivelli, "L'iguana, il cardillo, il puma," 79–88. The article can be downloaded from the webpage of the *Open Repository Archive* of the University of Zurich: www.zora.uzh.ch; Wood, "Fantasy and Narrative in Anna Maria Ortese," 354–68, 357.

19 The plot is structured around the similar insistence on the indetermination of time: for example, most letters by Prof. Decimo carry the same unspecified date: "Roma, il 18 maggio…"

20 Such analogous conclusions coincide, in the case of *Il cardillo addolorato,* also with the study by Ghezzo, "Voci dall'oltrestoria": "the tale, in short,

creates a short-circuit between the two antinomian significations of the story (the factual truth of the past and fiction), causing them to interact with the register of the fantastic visionary and decreeing for them at the same time absolute coincidence and credibility. Story, fiction and vision: the terms interweave, charge with implications, also in the *Cardillo*."(Ghezzo, "Voci dell'oltrestoria," 229)

21 Derrida, *The Animal That Therefore I Am*, 24.

22 Braidotti, *Madri, mostri, macchine*, 35.

23 The writer tends to minimize the importance of the historical setting – I believe – in order to avoid an excess of interpretation that could lead to reading the novel as a strictly political one, which is obviously not the case. In response to Paolo Mauri's question "why the terrorism?," she explains: "solo perchè quelli erano gli anni del terrorismo, non c'è una ragione precisa" ("only because those were the years of the terrorism, there is no particular reason"), Mauri, "Anna Maria Ortese un puma, un drago e altri animali," 27.

24 The ideological movement that involves Julius and destroys the lives of both son and father is believed to find its inspiration in Prof. Decimo's thinking. For him, the human being, as a superior being, has the right to enact justice *on* life ("diritto dell'uomo 'superiore' a fare giustizia *sulla* vita," as written on page 25 of the original novel). Julius's terrorist groups, on the other hand, "uccidevano senza scrupoli, ma ammantandosi di purezza, come cacciatori in un bosco" ("killed without regrets, but under the mask of purity, like hunters in the wood").

25 A discussion on the meaning of this name can be read in Borrelli, "Ortese: Incontro ai confini del surreale," 21. The passage is extensively quoted in the fundamental study by Clerici, *Apparizione e visione*, 615, which unfortunately dedicates but a few pages to *Alonso*'s analysis.

26 Derrida, *The Animal That Therefore I Am*, 372. The compound arranges the French words *animal* and *malséance* (discomfort).

27 Ibid.

28 Leopardi, *La Ginestra*, v. 51, in *Canti*.

29 Cfr. R2 644.

30 Stella Winter thinks of it in the following terms: "La pazzia vi visita, signori, vi passa accanto, ma voi non le siete riconoscenti, la credete anarchia," (R2 828; "Insanity visits you, sirs, it passes next to you, but you do not acknowledge it, you believe it to be anarchy").

31 See the whole conversation between Edwin, the would-be criminologist and specialist of the psychology of the unconscious, Miss Winter, and her friends (R2 704–5).

32 Leopardi, *The Moral Essays*, 60–61. Leopardi, *Operette morali*, 71–81.

33 The oxymoronic solution of dualisms is a typical mark of Ortese's writing, cared of and expressed at various levels, interestingly also within the formal choice of rhetorical figures and adjectival series. For a quite schematic, but nevertheless interesting, approach to the formal construction of the novel about Alonso, it is now possible to refer to the article by Zangrandi, "Dare voce alle cose del mondo prive di voce," 143–49.

34 R.M. Rilke, *Eighth Elegy*, vv. 1–13. See the *Duino Elegies*: "The creature gazes into openness with all / its eyes. But our eyes are / as if they were reversed, and surround it, / everywhere, like barriers against its free passage. / We know what is outside us from the animal's / face alone: since we already turn / the young child round and make it look / backwards at what is settled, not that openness / that is so deep in the animal's vision. Free from death. / We alone see that: the free creature / has its progress always behind it, / and God before it, and when it moves, it moves / in eternity, as streams do."

35 Derrida, *The Animal That Therefore I Am*, 416.

36 Pynchon, *Mason & Dixon*, 350.

WORKS CITED

Agamben, Giorgio. *The Open: Man and Animal.* Redwood City, CA: Stanford University Press, 2004.

Anedda, Antonella. "Il grido del vero: Ortese e Leopardi." In *Quel libro senza uguali: Le "Operette morali" e il Novecento italiano,* ed. Novella Bellucci and Andrea Cortellessa, 257–69. Rome: Bulzoni, 2000.

Bentham, Jeremy. *An Introduction to the Principles of Morals and Legislation.* 1780, 1823. Repr. Oxford: Clarendon Press, 1907.

Borrelli, Francesca. "Ortese: Incontro ai confini del surreale." *il manifesto,* 26 May 1996, 21.

Braidotti, Rosi. *Madri, mostri, macchine.* Trans. Anna Maria Crispino. Rome: Manifestolibri, 2005.

Braidotti, Rosi. *The Posthuman.* Cambridge: Polity Press, 2013.

Bruns, L. Gerald. "Derrida's cat (who am I?)." *Research in Phenomenology* 38, no. 3 (2008): 404–23.

Calarco, Matthew. "The Question of the Animal." Retrieved from http://www.electronicbookreview.com.

Clerici, Luca. *Apparizione e visione: Vita e opere di Anna Maria Ortese.* Milan: Mondadori, 2002.

Clerici, Luca, ed. "Per Anna Maria Ortese." *Il Giannone* 4, no. 7–8 (January–December 2006).

De Gasperin, Wilma. *Loss and the Other in the Visionary Work of Anna Maria Ortese.* Oxford: Oxford University Press, 214.

Crivelli, Tatiana. "L'iguana, il cardillo, il puma: animali come dispositivi teratologici nella narrativa di Anna Maria Ortese." *Versants* 55, no. 2 (2008): 79–88.

Derrida, Jacques. *The Animal That Therefore I Am.* Ed. Marie-Louise Mallet. Trans. David Wills. New York: Fordham University Press, 2008.

Fallacara, Luigi. *Il Frontespizio* 15 (1937): 535–37.

Farnetti, Monica. *Anna Maria Ortese.* Milan: Bruno Mondadori, 1998.

Ghezzo, "Voci dall'oltrestoria: *Il cardillo addolorato* di Anna Maria Ortese e la crisi della modernità." In *Per Anna Maria Ortese,* ed. Luca Clerici, *Il Giannone* 4, no. 7–8 (January–December 2006): 221–43.

Gramigna, Giuliano. "In nome del dio Puma." *Corriere della Sera,* 10 June 1996, 27.

Groppali, Enrico. "Metti un puma nel romanzo." *Il Giornale,* 8 June 1996, 14.

Heidegger, Martin. *The Fundamental Concepts of Metaphysics: World, Finitude, Solitude.* Trans. William McNeill and Nicholas Walker. Bloomington: Indiana University Press, 2001.

Leopardi, Giacomo. *Canti.* Ed. Andrea Campana. Rome: Carocci, 2014.

Leopardi, Giacomo. *The Moral Essays.* Trans. Patrick Creagh. New York: Columbia University Press, 1983.

Leopardi, Giacomo. *Operette morali.* Ed. Ottavio Besoni. Milan: Fondazione Arnoldo e Alberto Mondadori: 1979.

Leopardi, Giacomo. *Zibaldone, edizione critica commentata* Ed. Rolando Damiani. Milan: Mondadori, 2014.

Leopardi, Giacomo. *Zibaldone.* Ed. Michael Caesar and Franco D'Intino. Trans. Kathleen Baldwin et al. New York: Farrar, Straus and Giroux, 2013.

Loreto, Paola. "*Alonso e i visionari*: La vocazione americana di Anna Maria Ortese." In *Per Anna Maria Ortese,* ed. Luca Clerici. *Il Giannone* 4, no. 7–8 (January–December 2006): 245–64.

Mauri, Paolo. "Anna Maria Ortese un puma, un drago e altri animali." *La Repubblica,* 26 May 1996, 27.

Ortese, Anna Maria. "Il puma dal cuore umano." *La Stampa,* 2 June 1996, 17.

Pynchon, Thomas. *Mason & Dixon.* New York: Henry Holt, 1997.

Rilke, Rainer Maria. *Duino Elegies.* Trans. A.S. Kline. Pomona, NY: Kelly-Winterton Press, 2006.

Secchieri, Filippo. "Alonso e i visionari: Nota al testo." In R2, 1113–30.

Seno, Cosetta. *Anna Maria Ortese: Un avventuroso realismo.* Ravenna: Longo, 2013.

Vaccari, Luigi. "Alonso e i visionari: Una favola religiosa e pagana." *La terra vista dalla luna,* no. 16 (1996): 39–41

Wood, Sharon. "Fantasy and Narrative in Anna Maria Ortese." *Italica* 71, no. 3 (1994): 354–68.

Zangrandi, Silvia. "Dare voce alle cose del mondo prive di voce: 'Alonso e i visionari' di Anna Maria Ortese." *Italianistica* 37, no. 2 (2008): 143–49.

PART FOUR

An Uncommon Reader

13 An "Uncommon Reader": The Critical Writings of Anna Maria Ortese

MONICA FARNETTI

Que lisonsnous? non pas n'importe quoi à notre gré. Non pas, non plus, quelque chose qui ne dépendrait en aucune manière de nous.

(What do we read? Not just anything at all, according to inclination. Nor, of course, something which does not depend in any way whatsoever on ourselves.)

Simone Weil, *Cahiers*[1]

A thematic or generic categorization of the writings that Anna Maria Ortese published in daily newspapers and other periodicals shows that the author's journalistic output consisted mainly of travel writings, combined with a smaller number of investigative and social reports, autobiographical prose pieces, and moral reflections, written especially during the writer's later years.[2] A very small number of literary critical writings, ranging from reviews to authors' profiles and brief reading notes, rounds out this bibliography. Though few and far between, these critical writings deserve careful evaluation, for they allow us to begin to reconstruct a profile of Ortese as a reader.[3] In addition, from a theoretical perspective, these pieces enable us to bring the author's understanding and experience of reading to light. Therefore, while acknowledging the meager and provisional nature of this *corpus* (which permits only an initial consideration of the broad topic at hand), I would like briefly to examine some of Ortese's critical writings, gleaning from them a general understanding of the different modalities and protocols of reading that the author endorsed over the course of her career. These endorsements should also be compared with the observations on authors and literature that Ortese scattered throughout her books and interviews, observations that allow for fruitful reflection on the author's literary predilections.

The *corpus* that I consider here comprises fourteen pieces, published between 1939 and 1977 in various Italian newspapers, and slightly concentrated in the early 1950s. These writings treat a wide range of authors, mainly of the nineteenth and twentieth centuries, the earliest being Ortese's beloved Leopardi. These authors are Italian, European, and even non-European (as in the cases of Hemingway and Lu Hsun), and were committed to various literary genres: diaries, letters, novels, stories, plays, and poetry. With the exception of Anne Frank, all of the writers whose works Ortese considers are male.[4] Also included in her series of literary critical writings is an unpublished (or presumably unpublished) review of Dario Bellezza's novel *L'amore felice* that was found among Ortese's papers in the writer's house in Rapallo and is now in the collection of the Archivio Storico di Napoli.[5]

It is a *corpus* as curious as it is incoherent, a scattered set of texts shaped by the unpredictable and unsystematic nature of Ortese's journalistic writing, in keeping with the regimes and rhythms of the press. Knowing how rarely Ortese failed to convert a fortuitous occasion into an opportunity, however, we have reason to posit the existence of a different and more profound coherence beneath such an apparently arbitrary choice of authors, a deeper coherence rooted in unorthodox critical assumptions and uncommon criteria of literary worth. Even a cursory glance at the titles of Ortese's texts and the names of the authors whose work she discusses reveals that Ortese was not, in fact, a reader guided by whims or ephemeral motives, linked to the dictates of the market, the academy, or recent events. Instead, Ortese's choices followed from a carefully defined and (in its own way) sound orientation, and from an understanding of reading as an integral part of being in the world.

Let us first consider Ortese's essay on Chekhov. Because of the incomparable human sympathy that he bestows on his creatures, and because of his capacity to bear, "senza troppe parole" ("without too many words"), the confluence of these creatures' "innumerevoli patimenti" ("innumerable sufferings"), Chekhov not only earned Ortese's admiration but also conquered the heart of another great woman writer of the twentieth century, namely Cristina Campo.[6] For Ortese, Chekhov is a doctor-poet gifted with an extraordinarily acute awareness of the order of things and the pain that disrupts it.

From its very beginning, Ortese's essay, significantly entitled "Silenzio di Cechov" [sic] ("Chekhov's Silence"), carefully outlines a method or *technique* of reading. This technique is inseparable from the "double vision" of which Ortese was so intensely proud,[7] and according to which her world view was structured. The double vision allowed her to see, even at the moment of reading, something other than what the common reader saw. Specifically, for Ortese, subjecting great literary texts to a double vision meant transcending the sphere of the signifier and looking beyond it, to gaze directly into the ethical and human depths of writing. By means of this "double vision," the reader became aware of writing's capacity to alter the order of things and its ability to be converted from an intellectual process into an experience that concerns life in its totality.

> Leggere una pagina di Cechov è come mettere l'occhio su un vetro nitidissimo e guardare sotto scorrere la vita. Di solito, ogni volta che uno scrittore fissa il suo sguardo sulla vita, questa cosa imponderabile e meravigliosa – ora un fiume, ora un animale, ora un uomo – si turba e perde la sua incantevole naturalezza. I fiumi, i mari smarriscono le loro proporzioni e il movimento delle loro acque non è più perfetto: gli animali si mettono a rassomigliare a uomini oppure s'irrigidiscono in sagome geometriche; in quanto agli uomini stessi, che formano sempre il soggetto preferito d'osservazione di uno scrittore, si trasformano facilmente quali in montagne, quali, all'opposto, in sassolini; o diventano piante di bell'aspetto, ma più generalmente animali domestici o feroci; e anche in quei casi in cui riescano a conservare per gran parte o del tutto le loro caratteristiche umane, il loro linguaggio, i loro movimenti, le occhiate che gettano qua e là, hanno un che di strano, di rigido, d'impacciato, come se si sentissero guardati, che un po' irrita, un po' commuove.
>
> Cechov mi sembra l'unico scrittore che, senza essere grandissimo, o forse soprattutto per questo, non si è imposto alla vita, non le ha dato alcuna soggezione, non ha influenzato per nulla la misteriosa e innocente libertà dei suoi movimenti. È un prodigio tale che, a trovarsi in possesso di un minimo di barbarie, si griderebbe subito ch'è opera del diavolo. Personalmente, ragionando su ciò che fa un vero uomo, e quindi uno scrittore: voglio dire quel gesto di disperazione e d'amore, di disgusto e insieme di tenerezza, d'irrisione e di pietà, di stanchezza e di speranza, capisco che Cechov, che questi beni li aveva tutti e mescolati perfettamente nel suo sangue, facilmente avrebbe potuto dar punti al diavolo delle fantasie popolari, in quanto a purezza e splendore, a misura e magia di prodigi, a un maligno e ineffabile rispetto della libertà dei viventi.[8]

> (Reading a page of Chekhov is like peering through a perfectly clean plate of glass at the spectacle of life passing by on the other side of it. Usually,

> when a writer fixes his gaze on life, that imponderable and marvellous thing – now a river, now an animal, now a person – grows uneasy and loses its enchanting naturalness. Rivers and seas spill over disproportionately and the water's ebb and flow is no longer perfect; animals begin to resemble people or they harden into geometrical shapes; inasmuch as people, the preferred subjects for observing writers everywhere, are easily transformed into mountains, which are just as easily reduced to pebbles; or else they turn into handsome plants, but more often than not they become either domestic or ferocious animals; and even in those rare occurrences when someone manages to preserve most if not all of their human traits, from their language to their movements and the glances they cast furtively about, there is still something strange about them, something rigid, ill at ease, as though they sensed they were being watched, which is slightly irritating, slightly touching.
>
> Chekhov seems to be the only writer who, without being the greatest, or perhaps for this very reason, does not impose himself on the natural spectacle of life. He has never impeded life; never influenced the mysterious and innocent freedom of its movements. Chekhov's work is so miraculous that, if we were not already thoroughly civilized, we would undeniably deem it the work of the devil. Personally, reflecting upon what makes a real man, and therefore a writer – by which I mean that gesture of desperation and of love, of disgust and at the same time of tenderness, of derision and of pity, of weariness and of hope – I see that Chekhov, whose blood possesses all of these qualities and in proper measure, could have easily given pointers to the devil of popular imagination, with regard to purity and splendour, the magnitude and magic of a marvel, and the malignant and ineffable respect shown for the freedom of the living.)

It is therefore the protection of the primal value of "life," in the naturalness and freedom of its becoming, that defines the great (or "true") writer. Such a writer is able to respect the continuity of what Maria Zambrano has called the "tremendous and miniscule variations" that compose life, the continuity "in which things are born, perish, and are burned out."[9] Such a writer is all the more great and true the more she is capable of rendering intact and not at all altered by the artifice of writing, the simple and incredible fact of being. This value, precociously articulated by Ortese in her first stories,[10] will be subjected to a prolonged meditation over the course of her intellectual and artistic development, becoming a sign of the depth of her knowledge, not to say a sign of the strength of her inspiration. Ortese continues:

> È questo rispetto, dietro cui fremono crudeltà e pietà insieme, questa discrezione magnifica, questo silenzio pieno di beffa e di sospiri, che permette alle creature dello scrittore russo di andare e venire tranquillamente, come insetti sotto una lastra di vetro, mostrandoci tutta la loro ferita e incantevole intimità: le loro fantastiche antenne, le zampine magre e pelose, le ali commoventi, i ventri palpitanti, certi occhi come spilli e pieni di una misteriosa tristezza.

> (Extremes of cruelty and pity throb with vitality under the tutelage of this kind of respect, this magnificent discretion, this silence full of mockery and sighs, that allows this Russian writer's creatures to come and go calmly, like insects under a plate of glass, showing us all their colourful and enchanting intimacy: their fantastic antennae, their thin and bushy little legs, their sympathetic wings, their palpitating bellies, their pin-like eyes full of mysterious sadness).[11]

Ortese's "double vision" carries out the essential task of deforming the contours of things and creatures. "Double vision" thus induces the alteration of the boundaries of the visible that lies at the basis of Ortese's thought and poetics, and it is, or seems to be, the Kafka of *The Metamorphosis* who guides her reflections here. Kafka's works were obviously not missing from Ortese's library, and perhaps he is more responsible than has hitherto been acknowledged for her resolute conversion to stories of metamorphosis, anticipated by *L'Iguana* and clearly perceptible beginning in the early 1980s.[12] In any case, in her essay on Chekhov, Ortese proceeds to make several sharp and almost scholarly observations on the Russian author's dramaturgy (observations that are so apt that even Peter Szondi would agree with them).[13] Among other things, Ortese notes the lack of action in and the inconsistency of Chekhov's dialogues,[14] but she does so in a series of remarks that serve to complement her other major interpretive insight into Chekhov's humanity:

> Si prova una specie di riposo nell'ascoltare il loro dolce e vano chiacchiericcio; un chiacchiericcio interminabile come certi giorni di vacanza o convalescenza, in cui si sente tutto, con orecchie straordinariamente avide e raffinate, si vede tutto; quello a cui prima non avevamo mai badato; anche le incrostazioni strane di un muro, il colore della pendola e un disegno che scarabocchiamo da bambini dietro una porta. Ed è appunto da questa fatuità e indeterminatezza dei dialoghi, che nasce quel senso di fisso, d'immobile, d'eterno, di grande nella sua piccolezza, di dolce nella sua

stupidità, di sconsolato nella sua gaiezza, di disperato nella sua allegria, di tetro e sorridente; non inferno nè paradiso, ma cieco limbo, che è il genio di Cechov.

Oggi un autore di teatro è quasi sempre sulla scena, dietro i suoi personaggi, a suggerire loro battuta per battuta, col respiro ansante, tremando che a un tratto il personaggio si liberi e gridi una parola sua, o sbadigli... Lui, Cechov, era fin troppo conscio dello straordinario interesse della vita, troppo innamorato della sua purità e comunque troppo schivo di inganni e artifici, per permettersi di sostituire coi suoi argomenti quelli di lei. La lasciava fare. Balbettare e sorridere, addormentarsi e svegliarsi senza perché, con una strana tenerezza, come un uomo che sta per morire guarderebbe il sole nella finestra o un uccello che s'è fermato su un ramo, ch'è già prodigio, e che non lo sa.

(One experiences a sort of divine repose in listening to their sweet yet vain idle chatter; an interminable chatter like that of certain days spent on vacation or in convalescence, in which we hear everything, with extremely eager and fine-tuned ears, see everything; that which we had never paid much attention to before; including the strange incrustations on the wall, the color of the pendulum clock and the design we drew as children and tacked to the back of the door. And it is precisely the fatuousness and indeterminacy of these dialogues that produce that sense of fixity, immobility, eternity, grandeur in smallness, sweetness in stupidity, discontent in joy, desperation in happiness, gloominess beneath the surface of a smile. Neither hell nor heaven, but blind limbo, this is the genius of Chekhov.

Today, a playwright is almost always on the stage, behind his characters, feeding them line after line, panting anxiously, out of the fear that at any moment one of them might break free and speak a line of their own, or yawn ... Chekhov was all too aware of his extraordinary interest in life, too in love with his purity, and in any case too averse to deceit and artifice, to allow himself to substitute life's interests with his own. He let life do what it wanted. Stammer and smile, nod off and wake up without rhyme or reason, with a strange tenderness, the way a man who is about to die might watch the sun shine on a window pane or a bird perched momentarily on a branch, a bird that is already a marvel, and doesn't know it).[15]

This discourse on the author's love of life, his humanity and his defence of spiritual freedom even in the midst of a corrupt and insidious literary world, also provides the key to Ortese's reading of another of Chekhov's texts, namely the Russian master's correspondence with his friend, the writer Maxim Gorky. For Ortese, this correspondence confirmed that great spirits converse and necessarily show their solidarity with one another, and it showed that the young Gorky was worthy of his older and more celebrated friend's moral stature:

> Esemplare espressione di un costume e anche di un Paese dove le lettere, nella loro generalità, non furono mai fini a se stesse, ma modo di esprimersi di quegli interessi e passioni che, soli, fanno umana la vita dell'uomo, e proprio per questo diventano a volte altissima letteratura, è il carteggio Maksim Gorki – Anton Cechov. Due personalità, per definire le quali non basta più il critico letterario e gli strumenti di cui dispone, ma occorrono i mezzi con cui si cerca di misurare le montagne o stabilire la violenza e la pienezza dei fiumi, si trovano di fronte. Esercitano tutt'e due il mestiere di scrivere, ma quale mestiere! Leggendoli, si ha l'impressione di assistere alla prodigiosa avanzata di due uomini attraverso l'infetta oscurità di una palude, in questo caso la stupidità, il luogo comune, la non-esistenza [...] Nessun dubbio, leggendo questa strana e tumultuosa corrispondenza, che sia l'uno che l'altro dei due scrittori amasse soprattutto, da vero artista, la propria arte, la realizzazione del sé più alto, quello che contempla, che fissa la vita, e, fissandola, continuamente la travolge, la supera.
>
> (The correspondence between Maxim Gorky and Anton Chekhov is an exemplary expression of a custom and also of a country in which letters, in general, were never ends in themselves, but rather means of expressing the interests and passions that alone make the life of man human; and precisely for this reason these letters at times become great literature. Two personalities confront one another – personalities that literary criticism and its tools cannot suffice to define, except using the methods with which one tries to measure mountains or determine the violence and the fullness of a river. They both practise the profession of writing, but what a profession! Reading them, one has the sense that one is witnessing the marvellous advance of two men through the infected darkness of a swamp, in this case stupidity, commonplace, non-existence [...] There can be no doubt, reading this strange and tumultuous correspondence, that each of the two writers, like a true artist, loved his art above all – as the highest realization of the self, that which contemplates and fixes life and, in fixing it, continually sweeps it away, transcends it).[16]

Ortese concludes that neither of the two authors lived to write, that both instead "scrivevano *per vivere normalmente*, per divenire, per realizzarsi come uomini veramente liberi, come spiriti in cui moltitudini di uomini si sarebbero ritrovati" ("wrote *to live normally*, to become, to realize themselves as truly free men, as spirits in whom multitudes of men would see themselves"). Thus, embodying an ideal of dignity and freedom, Chekhov and Gorky also represented a touching model of friendship that elicited Ortese's respect and emotion, allowing her to imagine the two men hand in hand, gazing at one another, advancing in "immense" solidarity: "e gli occhi splendono, le mani ardono" ("and their eyes shine, their hands burn").

Indeed, for Ortese, human sympathy came to serve as a principle of selection in matters of reading, as her portrait of Ernest Hemingway indicates. Written in the style of an epitaph several days after the American author's death, "Hemingway un uomo" ("Hemingway, a Man"), appeared in *La Nazione* on 20 July 1961. Ortese expressed herself in an exceptionally powerful *planctus*, at once elaborating the pain of the writer's loss and transforming the mournful circumstance into the occasion for a vital and joyous hymn of gratitude.

> Caro e potente e sorridente Hemingway! Certo, non era cresciuto, al modo nostro, non era invecchiato, voglio dire. Le sue immagini, e non solo i suoi libri, ci dicono ciò che era veramente: una forza della natura, ma non una forza sinistra, come tante forze europee, che di natura hanno l'aspetto, ma non l'imperituro candore. Era veramente, Hemingway, un pezzo di mare e di vento, un pezzo di cielo, e una fitta di sole. Non posso guardare la sua immagine senza ringraziarlo, e non solo per le giovani commozioni che ha dato alla mia generazione, per la violenza e la gioia della sua partecipazione a tutto, ma proprio per quella infanzia meravigliosa piantata nei suoi occhi, per quel suo sorriso contento, insensato, amoroso, il sorriso di anni non ancora macchiati da carneficine o tumefatti in ghiacci spaventosi. Un sorriso di quando la terra era verde, le acque lucenti, e tutto fioriva. Un sorriso più lontano nella sua certezza, e più vicino di ogni altro, strano sorriso dei nostri padri, ch'erano leoni, erano foreste, erano fiumi, erano il vento e il tuono e il tubare raggiante della colomba, ed erano molte altre cose ancora, e non avevano terrori, perché non avevano colpe, e non ci conoscevano, forse, non sapevano le nostre crisi ma ci consolavano. Stavamo seduti vicino ad essi, e il solo guardarli – nella loro insensatezza e soave potenza – ci consolava.
>
> (Dear and powerful and smiling Hemingway! He certainly didn't grow up, as we did, I mean to say he didn't age. His pictures, and not just his

books, tell us what he really was: a force of nature, but not a sinister force, like so many European forces, which bear the appearance of nature, but not its eternal purity. Hemingway truly was a piece of sea and wind, a piece of sky and a stroke of sun. I cannot look at his likeness without thanking him, and not only for the youthful emotions he injected into my generation, for the violence and the joy of his participation in everything, but also really for that marvellous infancy lodged in his eyes, for his happy, senseless, loving smile; the smile of years that had yet to be stained by senseless slaughter or swollen in frightening ice. A smile from when the earth was green, the waters shining, and everything was in bloom. A smile more distant, in its certainty, and yet closer than any other; the strange smile of our fathers, who were lions, forests, rivers, wind, and thunder, and the radiant cooing of a dove, and who were still many other things, not to mention unafraid, because they were free from blame, and they didn't know us. They didn't know our crises, but they consoled us. We were seated next to them, and just looking at them – with their foolish, soothing power – they consoled us.)[17]

The lexicon from which Ortese draws here – the language of the "fiume di vita" ("river of life"), "abbagliante […] uomo" ("dazzling […] man"), "sana, tranquilla, maestosa e seria Natura" ("healthy, quiet, majestic, and serious Nature"), and so on, is one that she generally reserved for authors who wrote in English, and Americans in particular. According to Ortese, Hawthorne, Poe, Masters, Melville, Crane, Wilder, James, Whitman, Emerson, and Thoreau, together with Shakespeare, Tennyson, Keats, Shelley, and all the other "figli della luce" ("sons of light") gifted with "virtù celesti" ("celestial virtues"), had the sublime task and the sublime merit of "pensa[re] la natura prima ancora di pensare l'uomo" ("thinking of nature even before thinking of man"). They gave voice to nature in a language, and in a literature "di azione e visione, insegnamento, gioia, profezia insieme" ("of action and vision, teaching, joy, and prophecy together").[18] Ortese continues, "infinita dunque è la gratitudine […] alla loro lingua, alla meravigliosa natura e alle proposte civili di quei paesi che di tale letteratura hanno il vanto" ("therefore my gratitude is infinite […] for their language, for the marvellous nature and the civic ideals of those countries that can boast of such literature"). She then delineates Hemingway's entire context with vivid precision. In doing so, she begins to reveal the proximity between her ethical orientation as a writer and reader and her ecological position. This proximity will allow her, a few years hence, to declare her love for the earth and for life as it unfolds, not to say for the entire universe, in a book, *Corpo Celeste* (*Celestial Body*), which represents at once her recognition of an internal disposition and a moral choice.[19]

Ortese's Hemingway is thus a "son of light," the bearer not only of an overpowering feeling for nature but also, and consequently, of a complex conception of literature. Such a conception is more capacious than the traditional one, according to which reading is merely a privileged form of thought and a pure occupation of the mind.[20] Ortese concludes by elaborating (on the basis of what she calls the American author's "living books" or "creature-books") a notion of reading with a strong ethical valence, inextricably linked to a total and complex interpretation of the real. It is this that makes Ortese an exceptional reader, possessed of a creative and penetrating gaze rather than an objectifying one, capable of interacting with the page she reads and making reading itself into a transformative exercise. Ortese's understanding of reading shares much with Simone Weil's "desire to read with justice" (notwithstanding the obvious disparities between the two authors' lives and works), and with the "probity," at once moral and intellectual, that orients Weil's reading method.[21]

It is thus not surprising that Ortese's ethically oriented reading practice came to focus on texts in which a project of writing and a project of civilization are mutually integrated. Anne Frank's *Diary*, to which Ortese dedicated a deeply felt article in *Notiziario Einaudi* in September 1954, is one such text, and perhaps the most exemplary. Ortese writes:

> Anna Frank compiva tredici anni quando iniziò il suo diario. Cioè, lo iniziò due giorni dopo, il 14 giugno 1942. Benché la Guerra tuonasse su tutti i paesi e i mari d'Europa, era primavera alta, e verdi le campagne, i monti, azzurri i mari, i fiumi, limpidi e azzurri i canali d'Olanda. Anna possiamo figurarcela guardando le sue fotografie e soprattutto pensando alle ragazzine di tutti i tempi e i Paesi, su quell'età: non più bambine nè ancora donne, esseri di mezzo, franchi, spiritosi, dispettosi, gentili, sensibili, pieni di energia e di disperazioni, di curiosità e di smanie, avidi di apprendere, di essere, di capire, perennemente disgustati e divertiti, disorientati ed incantati, attratti e respinti da mille cose: il cielo, la gente, i libri, papà e mamma, quei piccolo uomini che sono i compagni, quei grandi ragazzi che sono gli adulti. Insieme alla natura, alla gente, alle cose, stupore per la propria persona: il corpo che cresce come un albero, gli occhi, le mani, i pensieri.
>
> A tredici anni la ragazzina di Amsterdam è tutto questo ma anche di più. È l'adolescenza, e anche il genio dell'adolescenza. Dietro la piccola faccia

arguta, tenera, amabile, misteriosa come l'innocenza stessa, brilla, alimentata da un vento più forte della sciagura che imperversa sul mondo, la luce della coscienza, e questa coscienza si fa continuamente e perfettamente "espressione," si traduce in un diario esemplare.

(Anne Frank had barely turned thirteen when she began her diary. In fact, she started writing it two days later, on 14 June 1942. Although the war raged across all of the countries and seas of Europe, it was high springtime for Holland, with its green-covered countryside and mountains, its azure waters, rivers and its clear blue canals. We can conjure up a mental picture of Anne by looking at photographs and especially by contemplating girls from every place and time of that age: no longer little girls and not yet women, at an in-between stage, frank, spirited, mischievous, kind, full of energy and desperations, of curiosities and yearnings, eager to learn, to live, to understand, perennially disgusted and amused, disoriented and enchanted, attracted to and put off by a thousand things: the sky, people, books, dad and mom, the little men that are companions, the older boys that are adults. Astonished by people and by nature, things, one's own self: the body that grows like a tree, eyes, hands, thoughts.

At thirteen, the little girl from Amsterdam embodies all of this and more. She is adolescence, as well as the genius of adolescence. Behind her small face, shrewd, lovable, mysterious as innocence itself, there shines the light of awareness, nourished by a wind stronger than the disaster that rages in the world. And this awareness continuously and perfectly becomes "expression"; it is translated into an exemplary diary).[22]

Ortese's empathetic tendency here betrays a partial identification, and the memory of her analogous (though Mediterranean) youthful seclusion in a different wretched time, a seclusion within which Ortese pursued "expression" or "expressivity."[23] The specularity here is discreet but undeniable, not nullified even by the Nazi persecution. As a matter of fact, Ortese writes: "Non hanno nome né volto né sguardo i nazisti per Anna, sono il male anonimo, la natura inquieta, la condizione dell'oscurità mentale" ("The Nazis have neither a name nor a face nor a gaze for Anne; they are anonymous evil, unquiet nature, the condition of mental darkness.") The world of the young girl from Amsterdam is thus not so different from the world of the adolescent from Toledo, who, in anticipation of the same tragedy, significantly describes her world in the same terms.[24]

Following this empathic and autobiographical logic in reading Frank's *Diary*, Ortese identifies her interpretive key, a key that allows her to distil in a few lines what she undoubtedly considers the essence of Frank's text:

> Il meraviglioso di questo libro, il suo senso più alto, che non appare subito, ma è la ragione del suo fascino, sta in questo: che attraverso una distesa infinita di giorni, un andare e venire continuo di sentimenti, di affanni, di angosce, di improvvise allegrie; un ribollire di desideri, d'immaginazioni, di slanci, di rivelazioni, di smarrimenti e di felicità giovani si delinea sempre più chiara un'esigenza di verità, di resistenza al male, dovunque esso sia, fuori e dentro l' "alloggio segreto," fra i tedeschi o nel giovane cuore di Anna.
>
> (The wonderful thing about this book, its highest meaning, which does not appear right away but is the reason for its allure, is that across an infinite expanse of days and a continual coming and going of emotions, of worries, of anguishes, of sudden joys; a fermentation of desires, of fancies, of impulses, of revelations, of confusions and of youthful delights, a demand for truth is delineated with increasing clarity – a demand for resistance to evil, wherever it may be, outside or within the "secret annex," among the Germans or in Anne's young heart.)[25]

The text ends under the sign of an elective sisterhood between writer and reader, a sisterhood enlarged to include every other analogous woman's experience of life and writing (or of life and reading):

> Vi sono libri che si chiudono ed altri che rimangono aperti; libri dai quali, come da una finestra, non si scorge che un muro, la facciata livida di una casa, una povera piazza; e i libri che guardano l'orizzonte.
>
> Il *Diario* di Anna Frank appartiene a questi ultimi. È il libro privato di una ragazzina qualunque, e anche il libro di tutte le generazioni giovani del mondo. È un libro dove viene registrato il quotidiano, ma anche l'eterno ch'è nel quotidiano; dove passano, col loro fascino, la fanciullezza e l'adolescenza, ma anche tutta la purezza, la generosità che fanno grandi la fanciullezza e l'adolescenza. Anna Frank, morta, è viva definitivamente; è tutte le ragazze e le donne del mondo in quanto hanno di meglio, il desiderio di capire, amare, proteggere la cara realtà del mondo, vestendo di grazia la forza, di dolcezza il coraggio, di pietà l'indignazione, partecipando attivamente, continuamente, senza farlo pesare, alla lotta per la liberazione dell'uomo dai suoi mali più cupi. Lotta che non può cominciare se non partendo da se stessi.

Consolante e puro in tempi di paura e vergogna ci sembra questo libro: ed è per questo che non ci lascia un senso di pena, ma di speranza; che non rimane documento, ma si fa lezione, e vorremmo vederlo in mano ai ragazzi in tutte le case e le scuole del mondo.

Vorremmo per Anna Frank qualcosa che fosse tenero e luminoso quanto la sua breve vita terrestre, che la ripagasse della sua amara morte, del silenzio impostole: l'interesse, l'amore, la gratitudine, un rapporto ancora trepido e alto, invisibile e puro, con le giovani generazioni di oggi e di domani.

(There are books that close and others that remain open; books from which, as from a window, one can only see a wall, the livid façade of a house, a poor square; and books that look out upon the horizon.

Anne Frank's *Diary* belongs with the latter. It is the private notebook of any little girl, and also the book of all the young generations of the world. It is a book that keeps record of quotidian matters but also the eternity that resides within the quotidian; where youth and adolescence pass in all of their mystique, but also the purity, the generosity, the strength that makes youth and adolescence so great. Anne Frank, though dead, possesses an everlasting vitality; she is all the girls and women in the world in the best that they have to offer, the desire to understand, to love, to protect the precious reality of the world, dressing power in grace, courage in sweetness, indignation in piety; participating actively, continuously, free from the burden of guilt in the struggle for man's liberation from his darkest evils. It's a struggle that cannot begin except by starting with oneself.

This book seems to be consoling and pure in times of fear and shame; and it is for this reason that it does not leave us with a sense of pain, but one of hope. This book does not remain a document but becomes a lesson, and we would like to see it in the hands of the children in all the houses and schools in the world.

We would like, for Anne Frank, something as tender and luminous as her short life on earth that might repay her for her bitter death, the silence imposed on her: attention, love, gratitude, a relation still anxious and exalted, invisible and pure, with the young generations of today and tomorrow.)[26]

Ortese's empathy does not arise only from a situation of affinity or consonance with respect to the author whose work she reads. In fact, Ortese distinguishes herself in welcoming difference and opening her heart even to extreme forms of alterity.[27] Her texts abundantly document this openness. In keeping with her own status as an ethical writer and with the principle whereby ethics is essentially based "on the experience of the other,"[28] Ortese displays nothing less than a fundamental tendency to listen freely and lovingly to those who speak through books, even from positions far from her own. Baudelaire provides one example. For Ortese, Baudelaire, like every authentic dandy, reveals the nature of the "essere dolcissimo [...] non armato di altro [...] che di una mortale e ben nascosta tristezza" ("sweetest being [...] not armed with anything [...] but a mortal and well-hidden sadness"). However, he is prone, on account of a spiritual confusion, to a "certa atrocità di accostamento dello squisito e del puro col turpe e il malato" ("certain atrocity, drawing the exquisite and the pure near to the base and the diseased").[29] Ortese also listens to Thomas Mann, or rather, to Tonio Kröger, the character behind whom Mann painfully conceals himself, atoning for the misadventures of a life not lived in full but rather "divisa in due, come le acque del Mar Rosso al passaggio degli ebrei, vissuta e pensata" ("divided in two, like the waters of the Red Sea during the passage of the Jews, lived and thought").[30] Or she listens to Dino Buzzati, "scrittore delicato e sinistro, di una splendida acutezza, sempre in allarme, inquieto, oscuro" ("a delicate and sinister writer, of a splendid sharpness, always on alert, disturbed, dark"). For Ortese, Buzzati "porta scritti sul viso ripudio e rimpianto, curiosità e ira, attrazione ed estasi" ("wears repudiation and regret, curiosity and anger, attraction and ecstasy written on his face"). We owe to him unforgettable passages such as the ones about "il cortile della Fortezza Bastiani, le dune e i sassi eternamente inanimati oltre le mura decrepite della caserma" ("the courtyard of the Bastiani Fortress, the dunes and the eternally inanimate rocks beyond the decrepit walls of the barracks"), where "l'attesa di battaglie e di gioie che non verranno" ("the wait for battles and for joys that will not come") wears on.[31]

But Ortese's most impetuous discursive tendencies and her most intense readerly happiness burst forth in the presence of her most beloved authors. Leopardi first and foremost, the man who "intese, sofferse tutte le nostre disperazioni, e godé tutti i nostri malinconici piaceri" ("understood, suffered all our desperations, and enjoyed all our melancholy pleasures").[32] Or Eduardo De Filippo, to whom Ortese was linked by Naples, the city that she never ceased to associate with happiness.[33] Or, in another way, the Pratolini of *Metello,* Lu Hsun, or the De Amicis of *Cuore,* a work of art "vivente di vita propria" ("alive with its own life"), which introduced Ortese to the notion of the "living book," a notion to which she would return, as we have just seen, in describing the work of

Hemingway.[34] Or her dear friend Dario Bellezza, "narratore puro, inconsapevole, inumano, che ci ridà il reale [...] con fanciullesco nitore, e la disperazione di chi entra nella vita dalla porta rovesciata, la porta di una cultura occidentale perduta" ("a pure, unconscious, inhuman storyteller who gives us the real back [...] with childish lucidity, and the desperation of whoever enters life through a ruined door, the door of a lost Western culture"), not to say a man possessed of a "mente eccezionalmente vigorosa, padrona del suo dolore, e – nel senso più alto – ingenua" ("exceptionally vigorous mind, in control of its pain, and – in the highest sense – naïve").[35]

It is regrettable that Ortese did not write more extensively about the authors for whom she expressed profound gratitude, authors who marked important steps in her long and inexhaustible development, and who allowed her to recognize the ties of her "invisibile appartenenza" ("invisible belonging") to literary history. Among these authors there are, not coincidentally, many women, ranging from Elsa Morante ("una montagna, un genio," ["a mountain, a genius"])[36] to Katherine Mansfield ("Un'atmosfera dorata, un'incertezza di sogno, sembrava avvicinare questi due modi – di Mansfield e dell'oscura ragazza – di vedere le cose: il senso, appunto, della ineffabilità, la inspiegabilità tenera delle cose, a cui posso aggiungere: e perdersi e tremare continuo dell'animo," ["A golden atmosphere, a dreamlike uncertainty, seemed to link these two ways of seeing things, Mansfield's and the mysterious girl's: precisely the sense of ineffability, the tender inexplicability of things, to which I can add: losing oneself and the continual trembling of the soul"]). And again, ranging from Emily Dickinson ("Dickinson, Keats, Borges. Ecco, *questi* poeti [...] ci raccontano senza sosta l'*unità* del mondo, e ci raccontano il mondo come emozione e ragione di un ignoto al quale tutti apparteniamo, così come la goccia di acqua azzurra appartiene all'immortale mare azzurro, e la foglia di acero alla immortale estensione di foreste e di piante da fiore e da frutto, che copre la Terra," CC 69–70; "Dickinson, Keats, Borges. Here: *these* poets [...] tell us of the *unity* of the world, without stopping, and they tell us of the world as of the emotion and reason of an unknown thing to which we all belong, just as the droplet of blue water belongs to the immortal blue sea, and the maple leaf to the immortal expanse of forests and of flower and fruit plants, which cover the Earth") to the Brontë sisters and the "incantevole Austen" (CC 123; "enchanting Austen"). And finally to Sappho, whose poetry provided Ortese with the nourishment that she needed for her journey to Sicily ("c'era qualcosa, là dentro [...] che in termini così lievi mi pareva contenesse tutto il suono di una terra, la storia e lo spirito di una terra non più toccata dal tempo, rimasta sospesa ai limiti di una eterna aurora ... *Ho parlato in sogno con te, Afrodite*: non solo l'amore, ma la bellezza, il dono dell'immagine, la grazia della forma" [SV 117–18; "there was something, there inside ... which in such light terms, seemed to me to contain all the sounds of a land, the history and the spirit of a land no longer touched by time, left suspended at the limits of an eternal dawn ... *I spoke to you in a dream, Aphrodite*: not only love, but also beauty, the gift of the image, the grace of form"]).

With respect to Elsa Morante, we should present at least a page from Ortese's correspondence with Citati, to whom, on 14 January 1986, she explains, in a deeply felt and thoughtful passage, her reasons for admiring the author of *Menzogna e sortilegio*. The letter is worth citing in its entirety.

> Se leggerà *Menzogna e sortilegio* [...] capirà perché ne sono rimasta altamente soggiogata. Proporzioni mostruose. Ma non solo nella misura esterna del romanzo, quanto nel suo tempo interiore. Come un mondo intravisto al lume debole, oscillante e magico di una candela, tutte le sue ombre sono in moto, crescita e diminuzione continua. A volte si alzano fino a diventare montagne, o si abbassano quasi a sparire. C'è una perfezione – di certi particolari – assoluta. Sembra il libro – la storia – del povero e feroce mondo femminile, il mondo antico, che vive tuttora, dell'Italia che ha mille anni di tenebra [...] Se ne esce come da una grotta infinita. Capisco che possa destare grandi riluttanze [...] Dopo *Menzogna e sortilegio, L'isola di Arturo* è un luogo, e una struttura, dove l'aria aperta circola ampiamente. Però, è anche vero che c'è un congegno, una chiusura invisibile; l'architettura del libro è fredda. Mi colpì, e commosse, all'inizio, quell'accenno alla *stella Arturo*. Forse, pensavo, Elsa Morante deve aver ricordato (ricordando la stella Arturo) quel mio racconto di *Angelici dolori*, "Il capitano," dove una ragazzetta si accorge di questo astro, e lo sceglie come confidente. Pensiero orgoglioso e malinconico. Perché in quella novella io avevo appena suggerito l'idea di una complicità con l'ordine celeste, mentre nel suo romanzo la Morante aveva lei stessa creato un ordine superiore, dei celesti comportamenti. Tutto qui.
>
> Di Elsa Morante so bene – ho saputo a suo tempo, ho inteso – la vita come (quasi) negazione o rovesciamento di quell'ordine che le era apparso all'inizio. Ma proprio per questo avvertivo quella sua vita come tragica e penosa. Perché la vedevo (solo la vita, non le opere) inadeguata a quelle. E questo, poi, dev'essere stato il suo profondo patire. Di capire che l'ordine

le era impossibile. Io stessa, da anni, vado sperimentando la difficoltà della coerenza, di serbarsi fedeli a una specie di giuramento fatto all'Invisibile. Di più non saprei dire. Ma follia e rivolta le intendo, le vedo ammissibili, solo in questo senso: di quasi militare obbedienza a un fanciullesco mite giuramento fatto, in passato, alla stella [...] Elsa ha creduto nella inesistenza, nel miraggio, ha visto terra dove non era. Questa, per me, la sua tragedia. Un'anima perduta.

(If you read *Menzogna e sortilegio* [...] you will understand why I was totally overpowered by it. Monstrous proportions. But not only when it comes to external measurements of the novel, but also in its internal time. Like a world seen by the weak, oscillating, and magical light of a candle, all of its shadows are in motion, continual growth and diminution. At times they rise to the point of becoming mountains, or they shrink almost to the point of disappearing. There is an absolute perfection, in certain details. It seems to be the book – the story – of the poor and savage world of women, the ancient world that lives on today, of the Italy that has a thousand years of darkness [...] One leaves it as one leaves an infinite cave. I understand that it can awaken great reluctances [...] After *Menzogna e sortilegio, Arturo's Island* is a place, and a structure, where the open air circulates widely. But it is also true that there is a device, an invisible closure in it; the architecture of the book is cold. I was struck, and moved, by the beginning, that allusion to the star Arcturus. Perhaps, I thought, Elsa Morante (recalling the star Arcturus) thought of my story in *Angelici dolori*, "Il capitano," where a little girl becomes aware of the same star and chooses it as a confidant. A proud and melancholy thought. Because in that tale I scarcely suggested the idea of a complicity with the celestial order, while in her novel Morante created, on her own, a superior order, of celestial behaviours. It's all here.

I know well – I knew during her lifetime, I understood – Elsa Morante's life as (almost) a negation or a reversal of the order that appeared to her in the beginning. But for precisely this reason I spoke of her life as tragic and painful. Because I saw her (only her life, not her works) as inadequate to it. And this, then, must have been the source of her profound suffering. Understanding that the order was impossible for her. I myself, for years, have been experiencing the difficulty of coherence, of remaining faithful to a sort of oath made to the Invisible. I wouldn't know what else to say. I understand, I see folly and revolt as admissible, only in this sense: in the sense of an almost militant obedience to a meek childish oath made, in the past, to a star [...] Elsa believed in nonexistence, in the mirage; she saw land where there was none. This, for me, was her tragedy. A lost soul).[37]

Another letter helps us to understand Ortese's relationship with Poe. Among numerous other documents, it attests to the American writer's importance for Ortese, not only during her formative years but throughout the arc of her reflection and writing. Addressed to Guido Ceronetti and dated 8 February 1983, the letter is replete with precious passages (on the pain of animals, the theme of rescue, solidarity with small things and relationships with the immense, and more), finally culminating in a cosmic sigh, inspired precisely by Poe. Ortese writes:

> Ho riletto un racconto di Poe: "L'isola della fata," dove si parla di una sensazione che ad alcuni è nota: che la terra sia un vero essere sensibile – un corpo meraviglioso, vivente. Lo rilegga, caro Ceronetti. Allora si vedrà da dove viene questa povertà infinita – e dolore – dentro cui respiriamo – secolo ventesimo. Una volta provai questa emozione passando in treno – d'estate, e terra e paesaggio deserti – davanti all'Appennino. Mi parve un immenso essere umano, addormentato, dimenticato. Così è tutta la nostra cara terra, se appena la guardiamo *da soli* – senza remore – senza "nostre" idee o avidità. [...] Come si potrà rivalutare – anzi risvegliare – tutto questo – il sentimento della terra dell'aria dell'acqua – come corpi soprannaturali, viventi, risvegliare questa religione – delle vere madri e veri padri – e fratelli – dell'umano come figlio (modesto) di tutti questi Spiriti di pace e di gioia?
>
> (I reread a story by Poe, "Fairy-Land," which talks about a sensation that is familiar to some: the sensation that the earth is a veritable sensate being, a wondrous, living body. Reread it, dear Ceronetti. Then you will see where this infinite poverty – and pain – amidst which we live and breathe comes from – the twentieth century. One time I felt this emotion while riding on a train – in the summer, in a deserted land and landscape – facing the Apennines. It looked to me like an immense human being, asleep, forgotten. Such is our dear earth, if we only look at her *on our own* – without qualm – without "our" ideas or avidities. [...] How can one reassess – or rather reawaken – all of this – the earth's feeling, or the air's, or the water's – as supernatural bodies, living, how to reawaken this religion – of true mothers and true fathers – and brothers – of the human as the (modest) son of all these Spirits of peace and joy?)[38]

Before concluding this brief examination of Ortese's critical writings (albeit with the hope that the author's epistolary legacy and the archive of her unpublished papers might still offer up other, similar pages), we must address her reading of the Gospels. It appeared in the Rapallo magazine *Ipotesi* in 1978 under the title "Cristo e il tempo" ("Christ and Time"). The article is a rare performance, in which Ortese positions herself as both a reader and a hermeneut, and it marks a peculiar circumstance, which nonetheless returns us to the guiding theme of this essay. The Gospels here emerge as the ethical book *par excellence,* a rational theory of good and evil and at the same time a table of imperatives and entreaties meant to safeguard the "fragility of goodness" in the world.[39] Christianity, instead, is an "enigma chiaro" ("clear enigma"), a guide for leaving behind the "strettoie del tempo" ("constraints of time") and evading the ambushes of the "ragione-madre di domande che lasciano intatto l'infinito" ("reason-mother of questions, who leaves the infinite intact").[40] The name of God is finally pronounced (here I am aided by Luisa Muraro) "to signify the origin of the feminine experience" and "remove it from the objectifying gaze of the human sciences."[41] As one reads in Ortese, God's word is effectively to be understood "alla luce sempre radente e obliqua della storia universale, dei terrori e misteri [...] via via più complessi e frananti intorno a qualunque scienza o filosofia dell'essere" ("in the always indirect and oblique light of universal history, of terrors and mysteries [...] always more complex and eluding any science or philosophy of being"). His son reveals himself to be the "scopritore di nuove terre, fondatore di un nuovo universo, legislatore e divulgatore di leggi contrarie a quest'ordine conosciuto" ("discoverer of new lands, the founder of a new universe, the legislator and propagator of laws contrary to those familiar to this order").[42]

"Non so bene che cosa chiam[o] Dio, ma so che così può essere chiamato" ("I do not know very well what I call God, but I know that thus he can be called"), writes Clarice Lispector, as cited by Muraro. Something similar can be said to hold true for Anna Maria Ortese. Something that can be discovered in the pages of the Gospel – the book that "illumina questo mondo, e ci dimostra che questo mondo non è" ("illuminates this world, and shows us that this world is not").[43] Unwittingly, Ortese draws inspiration for her future character Elmina, in the novel *Il cardillo addolorato,* from this book: "Per Cristo, infatti, se la nascita non è all'eterno, ma al tempo, nascere è sicuramente un male. Anche amare [...] è cosa da perduti [...] Non il tempo, e ciò che fugge, non l'apparenza e l'istante, ma l'Io senza tempo, l'Eterno felice da cui tutto è costantemente pensato e irradiato [...] sono terra e approdo e reale fondamento dell'uomo" ("For Christ, in fact, if birth is not to the eternal, but birth to time, to be born is surely an evil. To love too [...] is for the lost ones [...] The land and landing place and real foundation of man [...] is not time and that which is fleeting, not appearance and instant, but the timeless 'I,' the happy Eternal from which everything is constantly thought and irradiated").[44] Here Ortese takes her leave, having taught us, too, to read, with her uncommon freedom.

Translated by Ramsey McGlazer

NOTES

1 Weil, *Œuvres Complètes*, Vol. 1, K3[ms 6], 294 and Weil, *The Notebooks of Simone Weil*, 23.
2 See Giuseppe Jannaccone and Luca Clerici's recent bibliographies, published in Anna Maria Ortese, R2, and Clerici, *Apparizione e visione.*
3 See Secchieri, "Credere al lupo," 21–42.
4 I am grateful to Giuseppe Jannaccone for having helped me to view this material.
5 The papers found after Ortese's death in her house at Rapallo – the remains of a widely dispersed patrimony – were deposited in the collection of the Archivio Storico di Napoli in March 2003 at the behest of the author's granddaughter, Rita Ortese.
6 Campo, "Un medico," *Gli imperdonabili*, 93–203; 197.
7 See the entry "Leopardi" in my *Anna Maria Ortese*, and Margherita Pieracci Harwell, "Anna Maria Ortese," 246–83, 260ff.
8 Ortese, "Silenzio di Cechov," in MOB, 32–33.
9 Zambrano, *Filosofia e poesia*, 49.
10 See, for example, "Solitario Lume," in AD, subsequently published in PT with the title "Fhela e il Lume doloroso," and "Occhi obliqui," in IS.
11 Ortese, "Silenzio di Cechov," in MOB, 33–34.
12 See my "Nota al testo" on *Il cardillo addolorato*, in Ortese, R2.
13 I am referring to Szondi, *Theory of Modern Drama*, 24–31.
14 In "Silenzio di Cechov," Ortese in fact speaks of the "fatuità e indeterminatezza dei dialoghi" ("fatuousness and indeterminacy of the dialogues"), the only form of action in which Chekhov's characters engage ("Essi parlano, parlano, parlano, ecco la loro specialità," "They talk, and talk, and talk, this is their specialty"). A persuasive argument follows this observation; in his study of Chekhov and modern drama, Szondi will take this same intuition as his point of departure.
15 Ortese, "Silenzio di Cechov," in MOB, 35–36.

16 Ortese, "Il piacere di scrivere," in MOB, 77–78.
17 Ortese, "Hemingway un uomo," in MOB, 93–94.
18 See Ortese, SV, 100 and 176–77, and CC, 26–27 (from which text the following citations are also drawn).
19 See Ortese, CC, cit. and *passim.*
20 Here again, I am referring to Zambrano. See *Filosofia e poesia,* 67, as well as Zambrano, *Le parole del ritorno,* 131.
21 See Fulco, *Corrispondere al limite: Simone Weil: il pensiero e la luce.*
22 Ortese, "Un libro che rimane aperto," in MOB, 55–56.
23 On the discovery and the power of "espressività," as a guarantee of survival and a practice with which to confront the darkness of life, see Ortese, *Il porto di Toledo.*
24 See especially the last chapters of the text, in which Ortese situates the outbreak of the Second World War between "alterazioni del Sole" ("alterations of the Sun") and other figures of evil.
25 Ortese, "Un libro che rimane aperto," in MOB, 58–59.
26 Ibid, 61–62.
27 This theme is amply developed, in general and in its particular relation to Ortese's work, in Chiti et al., eds., *La perturbante: "Das Unheimliche" nella scrittura delle donne.*
28 See also Russ, *L'etica contemporanea,* 25.
29 Ortese, "Ritrattino del 'dandy,'" in MOB, 41.
30 Ortese, "Pensieri di capodanno," in MOB, 84.
31 Ortese, "Il male senza nome di uno scrittore d'oggi," in MOB, 48.
32 Ortese, "Pellegrinaggio alla tomba di Leopardi," in MOB, 18.
33 See Ortese, "Eduardo De Filippo, nato a Napoli."
34 See Ortese, "La sacra famiglia di Pratolini," 63–68; "Il 'bravo soldato Svejk' della letteratura cinese," 69–73; and "Il 'Cuore' di De Amicis è oggi da raccomandare o da sconsigliare ai nostri figli?," 52–53, respectively.
35 Ortese, review of Dario Bellezza's *L'amore felice,* typescript with manuscript corrections, undated, [1–2]; [2].
36 See also my introductory essay, "I romanzi di Anna Maria Ortese," in Ortese, R1, ix–lxix; xix.
37 Letter to Piero Citati, dated 14 January 1986. Now in MOB, 149–50.
38 Letter to Guido Cernetti, dated 8 February 1983, preserved among the papers mentioned above. (See note 5.)
39 See Nussbaum, *The Fragility of Goodness.*
40 Ortese, "Cristo e il tempo," in MOB, 110–14.
41 Muraro, *Il dio delle donne,* 48.

42 Ortese, "Cristo e il tempo," 104.
43 Ibid., 111.
44 Ibid., 107–8. See also Elmina's speech in Ortese's *Il cardillo addolorato*, among other eloquent passages: "La felicità è male, Albert. Amare le creature è male. Solo Dio si deve amare … Il resto è peccato… Dio ha fatto le creature e il loro dolore. Le creature vivono nel dolore, e solo il dolore si deve amare, solo quelli perduti si devono servire" (CA 93; "Happiness is evil, Albert. To love creatures is evil. One should only love God … The rest is sin … God made all creatures and their pain. All creatures live in pain, and one should only love pain; one should only serve those lost souls").

WORKS CITED

Campo, Cristina. *Gli imperdonabili.* Milan: Adelphi, 1987.
Chiti, Eleonora, Monica Farnetti, and Uta Treder, eds. *La perturbante: "Das Unheimliche" nella scrittura delle donne.* Perugia: Morlacchi, 2003.
Clerici, Luca. *Apparizione e visione: Vita e opera di Anna Maria Ortese.* Milan: Mondadori, 2002.
Farnetti, Monica. *Anna Maria Ortese.* Milan: Bruno Mondadori, 1998.
Fulco, Rita. *Corrispondere al limite: Simone Weil: il pensiero e la luce.* Rome: Studium, 2002.
Muraro, Luisa. *Il dio delle donne.* Milan: Mondadori, 2003.
Nussbaum, Martha C. *The Fragility of Goodness: Luck and Ethics in Greek Tragedy and Philosophy.* New York: Cambridge University Press, 1986.
Ortese, Anna Maria. *Da Moby Dick all'Orsa Bianca.* Ed. Monica Farnetti. Milan: Adelphi, 2011.
– "Cristo e il tempo." *Ipotesi* 4, no. 6–9 (1978): 348–51. Now in *Da Moby Dick all'Orsa Bianca,* 103–17.
– "Eduardo De Filippo, nato a Napoli." *Eduardo legge se stesso.* Turin: Cetra, 1960.
– "Hemingway, un uomo." *La Nazione,* 20 July 1961, 3. Now in *Da Moby Dick all'Orsa Bianca,* 91–96.
– "Il 'bravo soldato Svejk' della letteratura cinese." *L'Indicatore EDA* 2 (December 1955): 6–7. Now in *Da Moby Dick all'Orsa Bianca,* 69–73.
– "Il 'Cuore' di De Amicis è oggi da raccomandare o da sconsigliare ai nostri figli?" *Epoca* 4, no. 144 (5 July 1953): 6. Now in *Da Moby Dick all'Orsa Bianca.* 52–54.
– "Il male senza nome di uno scrittore d'oggi." *La Stampa,* 30 May 1953, 3. Now in *Da Moby Dick all'Orsa Bianca,* 47–51.
– "Il piacere di scrivere." *L'Unità,* 13 November 1957, 3. Now in *Da Moby Dick all'Orsa Bianca,* 74–82.

– "La sacra famiglia di Pratolini." *L'Indicatore EDA* 2 (Spring 1955): 1–2. Now in *Da Moby Dick all'Orsa Bianca,* 63–68.
– "Pellegrinaggio alla tomba di Leopardi." *La Gazzetta di Venezia,* 14 February 1939, 3. Now in *Da Moby Dick all'Orsa Bianca,* 11–19.
– "Pensieri di capodanno." *Il Mondo,* 20 January 1959, 15. Now in *Da Moby Dick all'Orsa Bianca,* 83–87.
– "Ritrattino del 'dandy.'" *Milano-Sera,* 15–16 November 1949, 3. Now in *Da Moby Dick all'Orsa Bianca,* 37–42.
– Review of Dario Bellezza's *L'amore felice,* typescript with manuscript corrections, undated, [1–2]; [2].
– "Silenzio di Cechov." *Risorgimento,* 28 February 1949, 3. [The text also appeared with the title "Silenzio di Cecov" in *Milano-Sera,* 10–11 June 1949, 3.]. Now in *Da Moby Dick all'Orsa Bianca,* 32–35.
– "Un libro che rimane aperto." *Notiziario Einaudi* 3, no. 9 (September 1954): 7–8. Now in *Da Moby Dick all'Orsa Bianca,* 55–62.
Pieracci Harwell, Margherita. "Anna Maria Ortese." *Humanitas* 2 (March–April 2002): 246–83.
Russ, Jacqueline. *L'etica contemporanea.* Trans. Aldo Pasquali. Bologna: Il Mulino, 1997.
Secchieri, Filippo. "Credere al lupo: Sulla lettura letteraria." *Strumenti critici* 1 (January 2004): 21–42.
Szondi, Peter. *Theory of Modern Drama.* Trans. Michael Hays. Minneapolis: University of Minnesota Press, 1987.
Weil, Simone. *Œuvres Complètes.* Vol. 1. Paris: Gallimard, 1989.
Weil, Simone. *The Notebooks of Simone Weil.* Trans. Arthur Wills. New York: Routledge [1956] 2004.
Zambrano, María. *Filosofia e poesia.* Ed. Pina De Luca. Bologna: Pendragon, 2002.
– *Le parole del ritorno.* Ed. Elena Laurenzi. Troina, Enna: Città Aperta Edizioni, 2003.

Appendix
*Who Were You?**
Interview with Anna Maria Ortese (1973)

DACIA MARAINI

Could you tell me something about yourself, about your childhood and adolescence?

Do you think it would be of any interest? Everything I remember from that period seems so sad and distant.

It is of great interest to me. I remember reading Il mare non bagna Napoli *when I was no more than fifteen years old. It's a book that made an impression on me. Since then I've always been curious to know more about you, about your life. You can't imagine later how much I enjoyed your book* L'Iguana, *which in my opinion deserved much more attention than it received.*

My fear, you see, is that superficial truths (because confused) might end up becoming non-truths.

I don't think the truth is of the most importance in this case. What matters is that you tell us a little bit about yourself when you were growing up, how you see yourself now and how you saw yourself then. Memories are always distorted.

Let's give it a try. If it doesn't work out will you promise to destroy it?

I promise.

Go ahead and ask me what you want to know.

What was your family like?

Modest. Not rich, but not entirely poor either. My father earned a white-collar living, but I had a lot of siblings and we led a life of poverty. At the time I didn't even know there were rich people in the world.

---

* Originally published in Dacia Maraini, *E tu chi eri? Interviste sull'infanzia.* (Milan: Bompiani, 1973).

Why is that?

Because I lived in poverty without knowing what it was. I couldn't make comparisons because I didn't really know what poverty was; we didn't really have many friends. I didn't really know the world at all.

Where were you born?

In Rome. But by chance. My father had a job that took him all over Italy.

How many of you were there?

Father, mother and six children. I was the second youngest.

Did you get along with your siblings?

We were constantly fighting. Though we were very close. Antonio and Emanuele died young, far from home. And this signalled the end of adolescence for all the rest of us.

How did they die?

Emanuele died on a ship, during a manoeuvre. The ship was already an hour away from Martinique.

Was he a sailor?

Yes.

And the other one?

Antonio, also a sailor, died in the war, in Albania.

What was your father's line of work?

He worked for the government, in the Prefecture. But he didn't have the character of a bureaucrat. He was restless, a dreamer. He could never stay put in one place. My mother grew very attached to the houses, the places. However as soon as we got settled somewhere, we would have to move. And we would have to start from scratch every time.

And did you suffer from this constant uprooting?

Me, no. It gave me an intoxicating thrill.

What was your father like physically?

He was a handsome man. Unlike all of his children who had dark hair, he was almost blonde. He had Arabic features and extremely pale skin. He was blue-eyed with sheen, light bronze, curly hair.

And his character?

Fickle. And whimsical. He fancied himself authoritative, but in reality nobody paid any attention to him. We were all fascinated by our mother.

How did he manifest his whimsical side?

He had a sense of adventure. He believed in countless impossibilities. He was excited by abstractions. He would lose his head over grandiose, unfeasible projects. None of us gave much importance to him because we knew that everything he did eventually ended up going nowhere. He never did anything right. He was full of vitality and vigour. He was passionate about great books. In the evening he would round us all up and he would read aloud the story of Jean Valjean and Monsignor Myriel. When we got sick, he was the one who cared for us: lovingly looking after us, day and night.

What was it, on the other hand, that fascinated you about your mother?

Her eccentricity and good-heartedness. She was slightly mysterious, absurd and childish all at the same time. Capable of great happiness and profound melancholy. She loved people. She would stop to talk with everyone, but she would never visit anyone at their home. With us she was affectionate, but she also left us to our own devices. Both of them, mother and father, were distracted, absent. I think that we loved them for precisely this reason and because they were individuals imbued with great charm.

What was your mother like physically?

She was a brunette, but not in the southern Italian way. She came from a Tuscan family, from Carrara. Her mother was Roman. She had a beautiful, pale face, strikingly pallid. She had straight, black hair, and piercing eyes. I often thought that her infantile character came from the fact that she had endured a childhood rather desolate and sad.

Sad, in what way?

Before she was born, her father was a sculptor. He was a sensitive and kind man. He had had a son, Alberto, whom he loved tenderly. But he died at the age of two. And my grandfather lost his head. He closed his sculpture studio and refused to work any longer. He would chase down carriages shouting: "Alberto, Alberto!" He was crazy for ten years. Then he returned to his right mind. And then my mother was born. Two years later he died. My grandmother was a seamstress. She worked by the day, going from one house to the next. As a child, therefore, my mother was always alone.

And at what age was she married?

At twenty-six or twenty-seven. But by the time she got married she had already been working for several years. She worked at the Post Office and continued to work there even after her wedding. In reality, she would have preferred not to get married. As soon as she was married she started having one child after another. But these children were like toys to her, sometimes she obsessed over us with her care and concern, other times she completely neglected us. In short, my father was a gypsy and my mother was a child. Which is not what they were in their true nature, only what their lives were like.

How was your father able to reconcile his gypsy-like life with his work as a state employee?

I don't know. He managed to get himself sent to some of the most unexpected places. Once, in 1924, he decided he wanted to go to Tripoli. And so he requested a transfer to Libya.

What was your experience in Libya like?

Extremely important. I grew accustomed to space there. This is the lesson of Africa. To exist *in* nature rather than outside it.

What are your strongest memories of life in Africa?

When I arrived in Tripoli I remember being most shocked by the lack of sidewalks. There were houses but no sidewalks. From the window you could see these oil lamps that gave off a smoky, red light.

How old were you?

Eight.

Do you remember the house in which you lived?

At first we lived in Tripoli. Then we moved to a government-provided settlement, forty kilometres outside the city. The first house was very small. It smelled of stucco and new paint. The second one was enormous, made entirely of stone. My father wanted it built out of the stone quarried from a cave on the property he bought. But he never managed to finish it.

Why is that?

Because he suddenly ran out of stone. And the house that my father had begun to build for us remained half-finished. It seemed like a haunted house. Without any doors or windows, with the roof half-covered and half-exposed, the floor half-paved, half dirt. Scorpions, mice, cockroaches tunneled through the dirt floor. Jackals often came in through the open doorways. It was a nightmare.

Did you go to school there?

Yes, I went to an Italian school in Tripoli.

What sort of child were you then?

Skinny. Quiet. Or at least that's what they tell me. One of my classmates once sent me a postcard on which she had written: "I remember you in Tripoli, dull and sad." I hardly remember. But that's how I must have been. I think I was very stupid. I behaved like an idiot. I wasn't expressive. I just didn't get it. In school I was always last. I detested history, up to 1492. I only loved geography, ancient America.

Were you sociable or solitary?

I liked things more than people. Or rather, things inspired more faith and more charm than people. I liked people too, but I hardly ever had anything to say or to listen to. To be around people was like being in the midst of objects. More than anything I preferred to be alone.

What did you think of yourself at the time? How self-aware were you?

Morally and intellectually I didn't exist. I lived like a cat. I was a non-existent creature.

And did you perceive yourself to be non-existent or did you only pass this judgment later, a posteriori?

This judgment came later. At the time I only had dream sensations, vaguely ecstatic. I only loved, I don't know why (I think it was a question of colors), the two Americas. Otherwise I was absorbed in the contemplation of a world that seemed menacing and incomprehensible.

When did you begin to become more self-aware?

I came to life when I was about twelve. All of a sudden I began to have specific interests. I began to reflect. But we had already left Africa. We were in Naples.

So, Africa for you was a sort of long lethargy?

Yes. Only later, in Naples, I became aware of my name and surname. I didn't have a name when I was there. I lived like a plant.

And in Naples where did you live?

Near the port. In a hovel of sorts, directly across from the docks. On the top floor. We lived there for twelve or thirteen years, right up to the first American bombings one afternoon. I had left the house at two o'clock in the afternoon and never saw it again. My parents also were saved by chance. Nor did they ever return to the house again. It didn't collapse, but it was uninhabitable. And all around there was nothing but ruin and desolation.

What place did religion have in your family?

My mother was religious. She believed in the future of the soul. She loved God.

And your father?

Perhaps a little less, I couldn't say.

And you?

Religion both attracted and repelled me. Churches enchanted and depressed me. I identified God with the desire to live eternal and free, He was the name, identity and stability. Yet, the historic Church seemed terrible to me; incomprehensible the inferno, incomprehensible the Inquisition, unacceptable therefore the surveillance of consciences. I slowly distanced myself. Today, however, in fact for quite some time now, I cannot think of any key to the secrets of the world as deep as those found in the Bible, in the Old and New Testaments. The commandments to not kill, not steal, to honour one's father and mother and so on seem to me to be the fundamental ingredients in the fashioning of any discourse, even modest, for the rebirth of the world and a change of course (if it is still possible). I add that, in this commandment to not kill, I include also respect and compassion for the animal world, the entire world of earthly life from which we originated and towards which we are certainly bound by the duties of solidarity and love. Besides, for me, every stone, even the most humble and silent object existing in this Universe, is sacred and respectable inasmuch as the Universe as a whole is.

It seems that your life has been a continual denial of cruelty. Do you not somehow think that there can be no life without cruelty?

This is true. All my life I've been asking myself: why is there cruelty? The principle of cruelty lies, in fact, not so much in the necessity to survive, as in the belief that survival is everything, and thus the decision to render this flash (the life of the individual) as pleasant as possible. This entails a breach, an intensive tearing of the fabric of life that surrounds us. Cruelty begins here. But at the root of this cruelty, if you look closely, there is nothing more than a loss of destiny, a lowering of the horizon.

There is in your nature a tendency to systematize your thinking. Can you say that you have ever lived in line with even one of these thoughts?

I don't think it's possible. However, little by little, the practice of reflection changes our habits, it creates almost a second nature.

What was your relationship to school as a child?

I did only three grades, third, fourth and fifth in Tripoli. Then when we returned to Italy, they enrolled me in a school in Naples, a trade school, which I attended for only a few months. Then I left.

Why?

I didn't like it there. The schedule was intense, from eight in the morning until four in the evening. Not being able to move about freely was worst of all. They had us doing things all day that seemed entirely useless.

For example?

Sewing, bookkeeping. They told us to buy new notebooks, new pen nibs, new books. At home we didn't have any money. Then one day the teacher, a certain Scotti from Milan, told me to create nameplates for my notebooks. I carved them on rather than draw them. Out of spite, after I had been scolded, I insisted that all the nameplates had been drawn on. And I did so stubbornly in front of everyone. I'm still ashamed of my behaviour. I upset her and humiliated myself by lying. But perhaps it wasn't a lie: it was an obscure and decisive act of rebellion. I never went back to school.

And how did your parents react to your decision?

My mother never said anything. But she wanted me to keep taking piano lessons, which I hated. I kept at it for a little while. Then I gave up on that too.

How old were you when you dropped out of school?

Thirteen.

And what did you do with yourself with all that free time?

I would read and take walks. I would help my brothers with their homework. And in this way I ended up finishing school vicariously through them in the end. There was a period in which my father wanted to send me back to school. But I told him: "If you send me to school, I'll kill myself." I was so calm and sure of myself that from then on they never brought it up again.

What were your interests outside of your studies?

I read a lot. I imagined trips I would have taken. I wanted to get out of Italy.

What did you read?

Adventure stories. My brothers could leave. They were boys. I wasn't. I travelled in my head. I already mentioned that we lived in a small apartment on the top floor, overlooking the port. From the window I could see the ships coming and going. I lived fantasizing about those ships. Every once in a while I would go out and walk the city. My parents never even noticed. I would come back exhausted with my feet aching.

Where would you go?

I would go all over Naples. From the port to Piazza Dante, to the Arenella, down the Petraio steps, and I'd walk the length of via Caracciolo. I never took the bus or the tram. I never had any money.

You didn't have any money because your parents wouldn't give you any or because they didn't have any?

They didn't have any. We lived in poverty in our house. We didn't even have a bathtub. We bathed with cold water, in the sink. Heating: was an unthinkable dream. We kept warm with braziers. In all of my childhood I had only two outfits. Meat never found its way into our home.

What did you usually eat?

Cheese, eggs, soup. Meat was a luxury. We had it maybe once a month at most. Then again, in Naples very few people ate meat in that period.

In which period did you suffer most from this poverty?

After the war. I experienced real hunger. A hunger so full of anguish that I could have eaten a boiled shoe. How I managed to survive I don't know. Even in '47-'48 the sight of a potato enlivened me. There was food everywhere, good food, but we couldn't afford it. I didn't even have a house: with my parents, we wandered like gypsies from one place to the next. In '48 I began to travel on my own to Rome and Milan by train. I would ride in the corridors, next to the toilet, dead on my feet from exhaustion. I don't know how long I went on like that. Eventually I ended up in Milan.

How old were you the first time you fell in love? Were you precocious in matters of love?

I was twelve. Shortly before leaving Tripoli. I fell in love with an Arab boy. I watched him walk. I liked his delicate, lean body. It was the first time that I discovered the magic of another person.

Did you talk to him? Did you approach him?

No. It was a love that only I knew about. My ingenuousness was frightening at the time. Just think that I made it to eighteen without knowing the difference between boys and girls. I thought that it was a sort of fascination that attracted one to the other.

Did you have many friends?

Not at all. Up until the publication of my first book *Angelici dolori*, when I was twenty, I didn't frequent anyone who wasn't part of my family.

And how was your first book received?

Poorly. The first criticism to appear was that of Falqui who wrote a scathing review full of derision. I was devastated. I couldn't understand why he had been so ruthless. In the end I had only written a book. I remember that, as naïve as I was, I sent him a letter saying that his article had hurt me a great deal and that I hoped to one day write something that he might like.

Did he respond to you?

He responded with a letter saying: "Dear Ortese, rest assured that anything you write will never please me."

What do you think he had against you?

I came to discover what he had against me, by chance, a couple of years ago. One day I was introduced to this Falqui whom I had never met. I had just won the Premio Strega. I reminded him of his venomous little letter. And he excused himself saying that he didn't have anything against me only against Bontempelli who had supported me. And he also added that: "It was no way to behave!"

What was death for you as a little girl and earlier still as a child?

When I was seven I got very sick. Pulmonary edema. I was convinced I was going to die. I heard the grown-ups talking about me as if I were dying. I grew mute. I was waiting to die. But I got better instead. Since then I haven't stopped thinking about death.

Even as an adult?

Yes, all the time. The thought of death is always the first of all thoughts. Then there's the thought of justice and then the thought of love.

Did your parents have political ideas?

Come to think of it, I don't think they had ideas at all. Perhaps opinions. I, on the other hand, wasn't concern with what my parents thought. It wasn't a problem. I know that they argued from time to time. My father was crazy. He took offence at the slightest thing. Once he tried to catch the house on fire in anger. But he also knew how to be happy. In any case, the most severe problem for us was money.

And when did you begin to develop an interest in politics?

Towards the end of the war, when I was about twenty-eight years old. The war was an injustice, interrupting our growth. I hated it. In '45, returning to Naples, I saw how it had interrupted everybody's growth. Or rather, how it had deviated it. Now I see the war, all wars as universal embarrassments, times of plunder, crime, lies.

You lived with your parents until you were twenty-eight?

No. When I was twenty-two I went to Venice. I worked for the *Gazzettino.* I corrected proofs. I lived in a frigid little room, with water that dripped from the ceiling. I had next to nothing to eat. It was the first time that I lived alone. I was afraid of ghosts. When I came home at night, before opening the door I bent down to look through the keyhole.

How long did you stay in Venice?

Two years. Then I went back to my parents in Naples. Just in time to experience eviction, exodus, the bombings, famine. I was terrorized and indignant. I joined the PCI (Italian Communist Party) because it seemed like the only thing to do.

And then?

Then I moved to Milan. I worked for *l'Unità.* But I experienced no happiness in Milan. It is an Austrian city, difficult, cruel. I underwent the deepest, darkest misery. I was alone. Then I left the party because they didn't want me to think with my own head but with theirs.

Was there a specific moment in which your difference in opinion came about?

I had been in Russia. Upon my return I wrote several articles recounting the things I had seen. The world of the Milanese left turned a cold shoulder on me.

Why?

The fact is that politicians don't want interference. I wrote in an unorthodox way. Our disagreement began there.

Do you have an interest in politics today?

I understand the importance of a different administration of the business of the world. But when societies decline, they decline for one reason: that they no longer possess the life of the spirit and thus moral life. And so, what could an interest in politics mean? My political interests are but few: I'm interested in solidarity, in the reawakening of solidarity, I am attentive to conscience, yes, this interests me a great deal.

Do you think about your childhood and adolescence often?

Not really. I think about the future, about what will be, more than the past.

Do you regret your youth?

Yes. But perhaps the things we love are only invisible, not lost. This sensation, that the whole infinite past of everyone accumulates somewhere and there, like a film, it will come back and unroll itself, or that we will come into possession of it again one day for real, concretely, I think this sensation is common to many. It is comforting and not at all incompatible with intelligence. Intelligence sees in what is nothing more than a few lines, a series of ironic signs. The sudden and constantly forgotten identification of what lies behind the first threshold pertains in reality only to the intuition, at other times to simple instinct.

Translated by Steve Baker

Primary Works by Anna Maria Ortese

In Italian

Angelici dolori. Milan: Bompiani, 1937.
L'infanta sepolta. Milan: Edizioni Milano Sera, 1950.
Il mare non bagna Napoli. Turin: Einaudi, 1953.
Silenzio a Milano. Bari: Laterza, 1958.
I giorni del cielo. Milan: Mondadori, 1958.
L'Iguana. Florence: Vallecchi, 1965.
Poveri e semplici. Florence: Vallecchi, 1967.
La luna sul muro. Florence: Vallecchi, 1968.
L'alone grigio. Florence: Vallecchi, 1969.
Il porto di Toledo. Milan: Rizzoli, 1975.
Il cappello piumato. Milan: Mondadori, 1979.
Il treno russo. Catania: Pellicanolibri, 1983.
Il mormorio di Parigi. Rome-Naples: Theoria, 1986.
La morte del folletto. Rome: Empirìa, 1986.
Estivi terrori. Catania: Pellicanolibri, 1987.
In sonno e in veglia. Milan: Adelphi, 1987.
La lente scura. Milan: Marcos y Marcos, 1991.
Il cardillo addolorato. Milan: Adelphi, 1993.
Alonso e i visionari. Milano: Adelphi, 1996.
Il mio paese è la notte. Rome: Empirìa, 1996.
Corpo celeste. Milan: Adelphi, 1997.
La luna che trascorre. Rome: Empirìa, 1998.
Il monaciello di Napoli. Milan: Adelphi, 2001.
Romanzi. Vol. I. Milan: Adelphi, 2002.
Romanzi. Vol. II. Milan: Adelphi, 2005.

Mistero doloroso. Ed. Monica Farnetti. Milan: Adelphi, 2009.
Da Moby Dick all'Orsa Bianca: Scritti sulla letteratura e sull'arte. Ed. Monica Farnetti. Milan: Adelphi, 2011.

In English

Books

The Bay Is Not Naples. Trans. Frances Frenaye. London: Collins, 1955.
The Iguana. Trans. Henry Martin. Kingston, NY: McPherson, 1987.
A Music Behind the Wall: Selected Stories. Vol. I. Trans. Henry Martin. Kingston, NY: McPherson & Company, 1994.
The Lament of the Linnet. Trans. Patrick Creagh. London: Harvill Press, 1997.
A Music Behind the Wall: Selected Stories. Vol. II. Trans. Henry Martin. Kingston, NY: McPherson & Company, 1998.

Short Stories

"Family Scene." In *Italian Stories of Today.* Ed. John Lehmann. London: Faber and Faber, 1959.
"A Pair of Glasses." In *Stories of Modern Italy, from Verga, Svevo and Pirandello to the Present.* Ed. and Trans. Ben Johnson. New York, NY: Modern Library, 1960.
"A Pair of Glasses." In *Name and Tears & Other Stories: Forty Years of Italian Fiction.* Ed. and Trans. Kathrine Jason. Saint Paul, MN: Graywolf Press, 1990.
"On the Neverending Terrace." In *The Quality of Light: Modern Italian Short Stories.* Ed. Ann Caesar and Michael Caesar. London; New York, NY: Serpent's Tail, 1993.
"The Bay Is Not Naples." In *Streets of Desire: Women's Fictions of the Twentieth Century City.* Ed. Liz Heron. London: Virago, 1993.
"A Pair of Glasses." In *Mothers and Daughters: An Anthology.* Ed. Alberto Manguel. San Francisco, CA: Chronicle Books, 1998.
"On the Neverending Terrace." In *Italian Tales: An Anthology of Contemporary Italian Fiction.* Ed. Massimo Riva. New Haven, CT; London: Yale University Press, 2005.
"Montelepre." In *Mafia and Outlaw Stories from Italian Life and Literature.* Ed. Robin Pickering-Iazzi. Toronto, ON: University of Toronto Press, 2007.

Contributors

Gian Maria Annovi is Assistant Professor of French and Italian at University of Southern California. He is the author of *Altri corpi: poesia e corporalità negli anni Sessanta* (Gedit, 2008), and he has published several articles on experimental poetry and the neo-avant-garde. Annovi is the editor of Antonio Porta's *Piercing the Page: Selected Poems 1958–1989* (Seismicity, 2012), *Fratello selvaggio: Pier Paolo Pasolini fra gioventù e nuova gioventù* (Transeuropa, 2013), and a trilingual edition of Amelia Rosselli's *Impromptu* (Guernica Editions, 2014).

Andrea Baldi is Professor of Italian at Rutgers University. He has published articles on sixteenth-century conduct books, a monograph on Alessandro Piccolomini (2001), and is the coeditor of *Essays in Honour of Marga Cottino-Jones* (2003). He has also devoted his critical attention to contemporary Italian literature, publishing articles on the relationship between literature and cinema, and on women's writing. He has worked extensively on Anna Maria Ortese, editing and prefacing *The Iguana* (Adelphi, 2005) and publishing a monograph on her short fiction, entitled *La meraviglia e il disincanto* (Loffredo, 2010).

Tatiana Crivelli Speciale is Professor of Italian Literature at University of Zurich, Switzerland. Her research ranges from seventeenth-century to modern literature. She has worked extensively publishing articles on Giacomo Leopardi's philosophical writing, the novel, and women's writing. She is the author of several critical editions, the coeditor of *La littérature au féminin* (Slatkine, 2003), and the editor of Alice Ceresa's *Piccolo dizionario dell'inuguaglianza femminile* (Edizioni Nottetempo, 2007).

Cristina Della Coletta is Dean of the Division of Arts and Humanities and Professor of Italian at University of California, San Diego. Her most recent book-length publications include *When Stories Travel: Cross-Cultural Encounters between Fiction and Film* (Johns Hopkins University Press, 2013) and *World's Fairs, Italian-Style: The Great Expositions in Turin and Their Narratives, 1850–1915* (University of Toronto Press, 2006). She has authored several articles on film adaptation theories, intertextuality, feminism and utopianism, historical narratives, and the genre of the fantastic.

Monica Farnetti is Associate Professor of Italian Literature at University of Sassari. She is the author of several monographs on the Italian fantastic and on Italian women writers: *Geografia storia e poetiche del fantastico* (1995), *Cristina Campo* (1996), *Anna Maria Ortese* (1998), *Il centro della cattedrale* (2002), and *Il manoscritto ritrovato* (2006). She has edited various collections, among them C. Campo, *Sotto falso nome* (1998), A.M. Ortese, *L'infanta sepolta* (2000), *Mistero doloroso* (2010), and *Da Moby Dick all'Orsa Bianca* (2011). She is the editor of the two-volume edition of Ortese's complete novels published by Adelphi.

Luigi Fontanella is Professor of Italian and director of the Italian program at Stony Brook University. Poet, critic, translator, and novelist, Fontanella has published fifteen books of poetry, nine of literary criticism, and three of narrative. His most recent volumes are *Pasolini rilegge Pasolini* (Archinto-Rizzoli, 2005, translated into various languages) and *Migrating Words: Italian Writers in the United States* (Bordighera Press, 2012). He is the editor of *Gradiva* and president of Italian Poetry in America (IPA).

Flora Ghezzo, an independent scholar, has taught Italian literature at Columbia University as an assistant professor, after being a lecturer at Princeton University. She has written articles on Masino, Ortese, colonial women writers, and on feminist theory in America. Her interests include gender theory, postcolonialism and migrant writers, and the relationship between fiction, memory, and history. She has completed a manuscript on Ortese in Italian (*L'ultima visionaria: Anna Maria Ortese e le forme della narrazione*) and is working on a book-length study on gender and power during Fascism (*The Seduction of Modernity: Women Writing Fascist Myths*) For this research project, she was awarded the 2007 Rome Prize at the American Academy in Rome.

Inge Lanslots is Assistant Professor in Italian at KU Leuven, University of Leuven, at Antwerp, Belgium. She has published several articles on contemporary authors (and singer-songwriters), on intermediality, and on cultural memory. She coedited *Piccole finzioni con importanza: Valori della narrativa italiana contemporanea* (1994) and *Noir de noir* (2010). She is co-editor of the Peter Lang Series "Moving Texts."

Beatrice Manetti is Assistant Professor of Contemporary Italian Literature at the University of Turin, Italy. Her research focuses on twentieth-century literature of the fantastic, the relation between literary writing, journalism, and the world of publishing, and women's writing. She has written on authors such as Paola Masino, Anna Maria Ortese, Anna Banti, Cristina Campo, Natalia Ginzburg, and Annie Vivanti.

Dacia Maraini is one of the most influential contemporary Italian authors. She has been awarded Italy's top two literary prizes, the Premio Strega and the Premio Campiello. Her fiction, which has been published in twenty-two countries, includes *Woman at War, Isolina, Voices,* and the worldwide bestseller *The Silent Duchess.* Several of her books have been made into films, and Maraini has also written screenplays for directors such as Pier Paolo Pasolini, Carlo di Palma, and Margarethe Von Trotta.

Amelia Moser received her PhD from Harvard University and is currently managing editor of *Italian Poetry Review* (Columbia University and Fordham University). In addition to her work as a literary translator, she has taught Italian language and literature at Yale, Columbia, Bard, and Iona Colleges and has published on Anna Maria Ortese and Massimo Bontempelli, among others.

Margherita Pieracci Harwell is Professor Emeritus of Modern and Contemporary Italian Literature, University of Illinois at Chicago (UIC). She is the author of essays on Anna Banti, Anna Maria Ortese, Simone Weil, and Cristina Campo, with whose family she has long remained in close contact. In addition to her research on Giacomo Leopardi and on some of the protagonists of the Novecento Italiano (Ignazio Silone, Anna Maria Ortese), she has worked steadfastly to make the work of her friend Cristina Campo known to critics and the general public. She has edited the volumes *Gli imperdonabili* and *La tigre assenza,* as well as *Lettere a Mita,* an edition of the letters sent to her by Campo from 1952 to 1975.

Lucia Re is Professor of Modern Italian Literature and Culture at UCLA. Her translation into Italian of *Borges: A Literary Biography* by Emìr Rodriguez Monegal received the 1982 Comisso Prize, and her *Calvino and the Age of Neorealism: Fables of Estrangement* (Stanford, 1990) was awarded the MLA Marraro Prize. With Paul Vangelisti she coauthored a translation of Amelia Rosselli's *War Variations* (Green Integer, 2005), which was awarded the 2006 Premio Flaiano and the 2006 PEN USA prize for literary translation. Lucia Re is cofounder of the multidisciplinary, peer-reviewed scholarly journal *Italian Studies CISJ* (California Italian Studies Journal).

Gala Rebane works at the Department of Intercultural Communication at University of Chemnitz, Germany. She is the author of *Re-making the Italians: Collective Identities in the Contemporary Italian Historical Novel* (Peter Lang, 2012) and the coeditor of *Humanismus polyphon: Menschlichkeit im Zeitalter der Globalisierung* (Transcript, 2009). Her research interests include present-day Italian literature, popular film, and cultural studies.

Index